2003

# The Educational Consultant

# The Educational Consultant

*Helping Professionals, Parents, and Students in Inclusive Classrooms*

**Fourth Edition**

Timothy E. Heron
and
Kathleen C. Harris

pro·ed
An International Publisher

8700 Shoal Creek Boulevard
Austin, Texas 78757-6897
800/897-3202 Fax 800/397-7633
www.proedinc.com

© 2001, 1993, 1987, 1982 by Timothy E. Heron and Kathleen C. Harris
8700 Shoal Creek Boulevard
Austin, Texas 78757-6897
800/897-3202 Fax 800/397-7633
www.proedinc.com

Library of Congress Cataloging-in-Publication Data

Heron, Timothy E.
    The educational consultant : helping professional, parents, and students in inclusive
classrooms / Timothy E. Heron, Kathleen C. Harris.—4th ed.
        p.    cm.
    Includes bibliographical references and indexes.
    ISBN 0-89079-852-4
        1. Handicapped children—Education—United States.   2. Educational consultants—United
States.   3. Mainstreaming in education—United States.   I. Harris, Hathleen C.   I. Title.
LC4019.H47  2000
371.9—dc21                                                              00-027976
                                                                            CIP

This book is designed in Sabon.

Production Manager: Chris Anne Worsham
Production Coordinator: Karen Swain
Managing Editor: Chris Olson
Designer: Jason Crosier
Print Buyer: Alicia Woods
Preproduction Coordinator: Martin Wilson
Project Editor: Jill Mason
Staff Copyeditor: Becky Shore
Publishing Assistant: Jason Morris

Printed in the United States of America

1  2  3  4  5  6  7  8  9  10      04  03  02  01  00

To our parents,
Raymond, Bernice, Roland, and Mary,
who continue to be our consultants,
and to
Marge, Kathy, and Christine Heron,
and Blaine Harris,
who are the bedrock of love and support,
despite our curious inclination to write books

# Contents

# Section II
## Teaming, Communication, and Problem Solving:
### Essential Skills for the Consultant                85

# Section III
## Consulting with Teachers and Parents and Multicultural Considerations Affecting the Consultative Process   179

# Section IV
## *Effective Assessment, Instruction, and Management Strategies   329*

# *Preface*

Since the enactment of Public Laws 94-142 and 101-476 and IDEA 1997 (the Individuals with Disabilities Education Act Amendments of 1997), an increasing number of students with disabilities have been included in general education classrooms. The provision of appropriate education programs for students with disabilities has become even more the shared responsibility of special and general educators. Planning and implementing programs for these students within an inclusive school environment have presented several challenges to professionals, parents, and the students themselves.

One challenge that has surfaced has been how to help educators devise, implement, and evaluate programs that meet the unique learning needs of students. Another challenge is, of course, how to involve the parents of students with disabilities appropriately and successfully in the educational process.

The fourth edition of *The Educational Consultant* is designed to provide educational consultants (e.g., consultants, special and general educators, supervisors, counselors, school psychologists, coordinators, administrators, bilingual teachers, English as a Second Language teachers, and related-service specialists) with the information necessary to consult with educators and parents effectively regarding the design and implementation of educational programs within the least restrictive environment. The ideas, strategies, and suggestions for the fourth edition have come from several sources: feedback received from users of the third edition (which has been extremely helpful); our continuing experiences in consultation and clinical supervision; the research literature; practitioners; and our students. We have made every attempt in the fourth edition to integrate these sources, because it is our belief that advances occur when consultants blend empirically demonstrated research findings with their personal consulting, teaching, and parenting behavior.

## New Features

We have sought to maintain important concepts addressed in the previous edition while including several new features and sections that we believe enhance the readability and applicability of the content:

- The text is now divided into 12 chapters, arranged within four sections, to further enhance organization and comprehension. The Sections are: I—Consultation and Its Litigative and Legislative Contexts; II—Teaming, Communication, and Problem Solving: Essential Skills for the Consultant; III—Consulting with Teachers and Parents and Multicultural Considerations Affecting the Consultative Process; and IV—Effective Assessment, Instruction, and Management Strategies.

- Marginal notes have been added to each chapter to extend the narrative discussion and to provide additional resources for consultants, practitioners, and researchers.
- Each chapter contains up-to-date references—well over 1,000—that represent the current thinking in educational consultation. Of particular interest to readers will be content related to the rules and regulations associated with IDEA '97. Increased emphasis has been given to such concepts as functional assessment and functional analysis, transition, manifestation determination, multicultural education, secondary-level programming, parenting, and many more. Given the mandates contained in IDEA '97, readers will find the expanded discussion of functional assessment, parents and families, and multicultural issues particularly useful.
- Given recent well-publicized national episodes of violence, readers will find beneficial a new section on school-based violence and how consultants can respond to it.
- Our chapters on teaming and problem solving, critical areas for conducting field-based programs, have been strengthened in breadth and scope. These chapters provide current information on how consultants can design intervention and co-teaching teams to collaborate more effectively with colleagues and to better serve their students.
- World Wide Web references have been added so that a fuller array of Web-based resources can be accessed.
- A new section on assistive technology has been added for consultants who work with teachers using such technology.
- Though we have maintained separate chapters on elementary and secondary consultation to assist consultants working at those levels, a new chapter on instructional strategies that "cross-over" the kindergarten through grade 12 levels has been included so that consultants who work across many schools and levels will have field-tested strategies to recommend and use that span these grade and age levels.
- A master glossary of terms has been added to the end of the text.
- An instructor's manual that includes an overview section, test questions (with answer keys), extended activities, and additional resources is also available.

# Section Synopsis

## Section I: Consultation and Its Litigative and Legislative Contexts

The first two chapters present information on the consultation process, the goals of consultation, and consultation models. Also treated in this section are the ways litigation and legislation affect consultation. Emphasis is placed on assuring the right to a free and appropriate public education (FAPE) for all students with disabilities.

## Section II: Teaming, Communication, and Problem Solving: Essential Skills for the Consultant

This section includes two chapters on the consultant's role with school-based teams, including discussions of collaborative teaching, problem-solving teams, interagency models, technology, and teaming. Chapter 3 discusses how consultants can design, implement, and evaluate teaming relationships. Chapter 4 focuses on key interpersonal and communication skills, including managing conflict and solving problems, that are essential for maintaining a working relationship with colleagues.

## Section III: Consulting with Teachers and Parents and Multicultural Considerations Affecting the Consultative Process

Section III emphasizes consulting with teachers in inclusive settings and includes an updated treatment of ways to help with the Individualized Education Program (IEP) and Individualized Family Services Plan (IFSP). A full discussion of inclusion is also provided, distinguishing full inclusion from more selective inclusion options. Relevant treatment of programming for the generality and maintenance of behavior change is also addressed. Chapter 6 presents new information on working with parents, especially within the family context. In Chapter 7, the issues associated with working with multicultural and culturally diverse populations receive added treatment, including a discussion of professional competencies for working with students who have disabilities and who are also culturally and linguistically diverse.

## Section IV: Effective Assessment, Instruction, and Management Strategies

Chapter 8 discusses various assessment strategies that can be used throughout the consultation process. A totally new section on functional assessment and functional analysis underscores the importance of collecting reliable and validated assessment data, especially in situations where practitioners must decide whether observed inappropriate behavior stems from the disability itself. The examination of effective instructional strategies in Chapters 9, 10, and 11 has been streamlined and reorganized into elementary levels (Chapter 9), secondary levels (Chapter 10), and cross-over levels (Chapter 11). Within each of these chapters, we discuss specific strategies for individualizing instruction and address the skills the consultant needs to help teachers adapt instruction in general education classrooms. Finally, Chapter 12 presents strategies to select, implement, and evaluate appropriate behavior management techniques for individuals and groups, clearly a growing concern in our field.

# Acknowledgments

The completion of this fourth edition could not have been accomplished without the support of colleagues, students, friends, and especially our families. We would first like to acknowledge the reviewers who provided us with technical assistance. Drs. Marilyn Gonyo-Diehl, Jeanne Bauwens, and Ed Fiscus contributed critical and insightful comments during initial stages of conceptualization. Dr. Howard Margolis of Queens College in New York has been a steady influence on our writing. As the former editor of the *Journal of Educational and*

*Psychological Consultation* (JEPC), Howard reviewed the entire manuscript with a keen eye. His comments shaped how content should be addressed. Dr. Joe Zins, current editor of JEPC, provided substantive comments from a school psychologist's and practicing consultant's perspective and helped to frame the treatment of parent and management issues. Dr. Rich Wilson of Bowling Green State University was very helpful with suggesting ways to address strategy instruction. Finally, a special thank you goes to Dr. Yvonne Goddard, who served as a coauthor for Chapter 1, and whose exceptional editorial skills were employed in several additional chapters.

Also, we would like to acknowledge the assistance and contributions of our long-time colleagues and associates Saul Axelrod, Leonard Baca, Patricia Barbetta, Sam Chan, Philip C. Chinn, John O. Cooper, Daniel Coury, T. K. Daniel, Jill Dardig, Gregg Drevno, Ralph Gardner III, Judith Garrett, Barbara C. Goldstein, William L. Heward, Richard Iano, Walter Kimball, M. Diane Klein, Steve Larsen, Belinda Lazarus, Elaine MacLeod, Janice Haller Mancuso, Stacy Martz, Bruce Meyer, April Miller, Ann Nevin, Beatrice Okyere, Mary Peters, Diane Sainato, Mike Sherman, John Shields, Michael Skinner, Marcia Smith, Matt Tincani, Mike Thomasgard, Lee Tracy, Jane Williams, Laura Wolfe, and Andrea Zetlin for their continued support of our professional activities and for their assistance with our work. We would like to express our appreciation to all of the students at California State University Los Angeles—Project Support; Arizona State University West; and The Ohio State University, as well as the practitioners in Maricopa County, Arizona, and Children's Hospital, Columbus, Ohio, who provided us with the opportunity to develop several concepts and features of the text.

Dr. Donald D. Hammill and Mr. Steve Mathews, president and vice president of PRO-ED, Inc., respectively, deserve our special gratitude for having steadfast confidence in our work. Their long-time assistance with this text is very much appreciated.

Dr. James Patton, executive editor at PRO-ED, guided this work through each stage of development. His highly refined skills as editor, coupled with his expert knowledge of the field, eased our tasks considerably. Several enhancements of the text are a direct result of Jim's recommendations.

Also, we would like to acknowledge the assistance of Ms. Katie Goolsby of Saint Mary's College, Notre Dame, Indiana, who was helpful with checking references, proofing early drafts, and typing many sections of the manuscript. Richard Welsch, OSU friend and colleague, deserves personal recognition for coauthoring the instructor's manual.

Last, and most important, we would like to thank our parents (Raymond, Bernice, Roland, and Mary) and our spouses (Marge and Blaine) for their continued encouragement and patience. Though Roland is not here to witness the completion of this fourth edition, the second author continues to feel and appreciate his unconditional love and support every day. Marge, Kathleen, and Christine Heron deserve special thanks for devoting part of their summer vacations, fall breaks, and weekend afternoons to tabbing articles, researching journals, chasing references, and keeping the first author's sense of perspective in check during the production of this work. Without their unfailing and unwavering support, the fourth edition of this text would likely have remained an unfulfilled promise.

# Section *I*

## Consultation and Its Litigative and Legislative Contexts

# The Consultation Process

Consultation involves the voluntary, reciprocal, interactive, collaborative, and mutual interaction between two or more parties to prevent or solve problems. The consultation process can be initiated by a consultant (e.g., the principal, supervisor, or resource room teacher), who might observe that a school-related problem needs attention, or by a consultee (regular class teacher, parent, or student), who might seek additional assistance with problem resolution.[1]

It is important to note, and it is a major focus of this text, that any person can serve in the roles of consultant or consultee: teacher, principal, diagnostician, therapist, psychologist. These roles are not reserved exclusively for one professional agent or another (e.g., special education teacher or school psychologist). Consultation is reciprocal, dynamic, and interactive. Although the consultee typically initiates the process, the two parties share the responsibility for each stage of the consultation process. Throughout this text we will use the term *consultant* to refer to the full range of agents who can perform that function.

The purpose of this chapter is to define consultation, outline its goals, and provide a nine-step process that delineates its major components. Also, the chapter provides several perspectives on consultation and addresses four popular models of consultation, with corresponding examples from educational, home, and field-based applications. Finally, the chapter outlines significant barriers that affect consultation and provides strategies for overcoming those barriers.

## Objectives

After reading this chapter, the reader should be able to:

1. define the term consultation and distinguish it from other related terms that are used in the field (e.g., school-based consultation, collaboration, collaborative consultation, and cooperation);

2. identify the two global goals of consultation;

3. define the consultation process and the role of the consultee in that process;

4. identify five critical skills that a consultant should possess;

---

[1]This chapter was coauthored by Dr. Yvonne L. Goddard.

5. list and describe the nine steps of the consultation process proposed by Kurpius;

6. state the doctrine of the least restrictive alternative;

7. identify five perspectives on consultation and provide an analysis of those perspectives;

8. identify four major consultation models and describe the principal components of each;

9. describe the relationship between the consultant and the consultee in the collaborative consultation model;

10. identify three barriers to consultation and provide ways of overcoming them.

## Key Terms

consultation

school-based consultation

cooperative relationship

consultative relationship

collaborative consultation

collaborative relationship

doctrine of the least restrictive alternative

mental health consultation model

organizational and systems consultation model

behavior consultation

collaborative consultation model

mediator

target

internal consultant

external consultant

## Definitions of Consultation

*Consultation* has several definitions, varying in substance and context, depending upon the setting, target, or intervention (Curtis & Meyers, 1989; Friend, 1985; Robinson, Cameron, & Raethel, 1985; Rosenfield, 1987). West and Idol (1987), for example, state that the term has been used in a general context, and its true meaning can only be derived when the defining contextual variables are known (e.g., setting, purpose of consultation, and target). Idol-Maestas (1983) indicates that consultation can be considered as any support service provided to the classroom teacher for the purpose of improving academic and social behavior of all students. Curtis and Meyers (1988) indicate that almost any type of interaction between professionals and parents can be termed consultation. Conoley and Conoley (1982) refer to consultation as a voluntary, nonsupervisory arrangement between parties to improve professional behavior. Parsons and Meyers (1984) suggest that consultation can be viewed as any professional interchange between colleagues. In their broad view, consultation is a collaborative, although not necessarily voluntary, interaction between two people, each of whom has expertise in a particular area. Brown, Wyne, Blackburn, and Powell (1979) state that consultation is defined as:

a process based upon an equal relationship characterized by mutual trust and open communication, joint approaches to problem identification, the pooling of personal resources to identify and select strategies that will have some probability of solving the problem that has been identified, and shared responsibility in the implementation and evaluation of the program or strategy that has been initiated. (p. 8)

Sugai and Tindal (1993) emphasize that problem solving is an integral component of the consultation process: "Consultation [is the] structured series of interactions or problem-solving steps that occur between two or more individuals" (p. 7). Caplan (1995), speaking from a mental health perspective, defines consultation as an interaction between two professionals in which a consultee requests help from a consultant, who is perceived to possess a specialized competence. Friend and Cook (1992) suggest that consultation is characterized as being triadic (consultant, consultee, and client), indirect, and voluntary, suggesting an expert relationship. This relationship embodies a problem-solving process and requires that parties have shared, but different, roles. Kampwirth (1999) adds that consultation usually implies trained professionals interacting in an honest, open, and egalitarian (equal) manner to address task- and content-related variables using a systematic problem-solving approach.

Zins and Ponti (1990a) and Kampwirth (1999) make reference to *school-based consultation,* defined as "a method of providing preventively oriented psychological and educational services in which a consultant and consultee(s) form a collaborative partnership in a systems context to engage in a reciprocal and systematic problem-solving process to empower consultee systems, thereby enhancing students' well being and experience" (Zins & Ponti, 1990a, p. 674). Kampwirth (1999) stresses that school-based consultation can occur with individuals or within the context of a team.

> Readers are referred to Gutkin & Curtis (1999) to learn more about the "art and science" of school-based consultation.
>
> Readers are referred to Chapter 3 to learn more about how teams are designed and function.

We maintain that while all the definitional issues associated with the term consultation have not been resolved fully, consultants can nevertheless use a set of operational parameters in their effort to launch consultation programs. Specifically, we concur with the general tenets of definitions that embrace behavioral and collaborative consultation models, emphasizing that consultation should be voluntary, reciprocal, and mutual, and that it should lead to the prevention and/or resolution of identified problems.

The term consultation has been commingled—and often confused—with other related terms in the literature. West and Idol (1990), Hord (1986), Friend and Cook (1992), and Thomas, Correa, and Morsink (1995) distinguish among the terms consultation, collaboration, collaborative consultation, and cooperation. Beyond the definitions of consultation presented earlier, the following distinctions may be useful for conceptualizing differences (real or perceived) between terms.

In a *consultative relationship,* individuals share expertise. A consultant, therefore, can be anyone who has the necessary expertise for a given situation. For example, if a special educator is developing a unit on study skills and wishes to help students generalize the application of study skills to the content area of history, the social science general educator could serve as a consultant to the special educator. Table 1.1 provides examples of areas of technical expertise and possible providers. Consultants who share their expertise perform activities consistent with the definition of consultation presented in this text.

A *collaborative relationship* connotes parity, reciprocity, mutual problem solving and shared resources, responsibility, and accountability. For example,

**Table 1.1**

Meeting Diverse Needs Through Collaborative Consultation

| Technical Expertise | Providers |
| --- | --- |
| Alternative communication | Sign language instructors<br>Braille instructors |
| Assessment of learning style/achievement | School psychologists<br>Educational diagnosticians |
| Basic life skills | Elementary teachers<br>Occupational therapists |
| Behavior management | Behavior management specialists |
| Community living skills | Orientation and mobility specialists |
| Computer literacy | Computer educators |
| Corrective speech and language | Speech and language specialists |
| General education curriculum | Elementary teachers<br>Middle school teachers<br>High school teachers |
| Instructional grouping | Cooperative learning specialists<br>Peer tutoring specialists |
| Language instruction for non-native<br>English speakers | Bilingual educators<br>English as a second language (ESL)<br>instructors |
| Motor skills | Physical education teachers<br>Physical therapists |
| Remedial reading | Reading specialists |
| Student reinforcers | Parents<br>Teachers |
| Vocational skills | Vocational educators |

*Note.* From "Support Networks for Inclusive Schooling: Interdependent Integrated Education," by K. C. Harris, 1990, in W. Stainback and S. Stainback (Eds.), p. 141. Baltimore: Paul H. Brookes. Adapted with permission.

A collaborative relationship between two individuals within a school does not necessarily mean that a collaborative "culture" exists within the school. Collaborative relationships become part of the school culture when the personal and professional growth of all parties is central to the mission of the school (Pugach & Johnson, 1995).

a preschool teacher and a special education resource teacher may work together, recognizing the value of each person's unique knowledge and experience with respect to preventing or resolving problems. According to Pugach and Johnson (1995), the use of the term collaboration has evolved over the past 25 years, shifting from a primarily prescriptive connotation to one in which parity and mutual problem solving are paramount. In their view, "providing direct prescriptions to classroom teachers began to be seen increasingly as inappropriate because it did not seem to fit the basic tenets of collaboration— namely, that equals with different kinds of expertise come together to solve problems, and that their joint efforts are more powerful than the efforts of either one in isolation" (p. 32).

Idol, Paolucci-Whitcomb, and Nevin (1995) offer a definition of *collaborative consultation* that serves as the basis for field-based research:

> Collaborative consultation is an interactive process which enables people with diverse expertise to generate creative solutions to mutually defined problems. The outcome is enhanced, altered, and produces solutions that are different from those that the individual team members would produce independently. The major outcome of collaborative consultation is to

provide comprehensive and effective programs for students with special needs within the most appropriate context, thereby enabling them to achieve maximum constructive interaction with their nonhandicapped peers. (p. 329)

West and Idol (1990) indicate that the term consultation is *not* synonymous with the more popular collegial interventions, such as co-teaching, content mastery learning, cooperative learning, or the Regular Education Initiative, that have emerged in recent years. Taken as a whole, those interventions do not constitute collaborative consultation because they do not embrace all the requisite dimensions of consultation, namely its voluntary, interactive, mutual problem-solving aspects. Stated in other terms: Practitioners can engage in those methodologies without designing, implementing, or evaluating programs jointly. They could be parallel processes or merely one component of the process. However, in our view, effective co-teaching requires consultation and is, therefore, discussed as a viable consultant activity in Chapter 3.

A *cooperative relationship* is one in which independent agents (e.g., a preschool teacher and a special education teacher) work autonomously to improve their *separate* instructional methods for the benefit of a commonly shared student who is instructed in both the preschool program and the special education resource program.

Villa, Thousand, Paolucci-Whitcomb, and Nevin (1990) state that the effective schools movement in the United States demands that consultation be examined in a broader context. Their call for a paradigm shift—a revolution in how consultants and consultees interact—is conceptualized and operationalized based on six domains: (a) the purpose of collaborative consultation, (b) eligibility of services issues, (c) empowerment interest, (d) staff and organizational assumptions, (e) accountability, and (f) theory building concerns. In their view, careful research and examination of those domains will lead to empirical questions that, in turn, will produce a better understanding of the definition, methods, processes, and outcomes of consultation.

Witt (1990) asserts that the typical description of collaboration in the literature as a nonhierarchical, collaborative engagement is misleading because the database for such a claim is not well established. For instance, the answers are not known to such questions as How are problems defined? Who defines the problem? Who controls the course of intervention? Who evaluates the outcome? Consequently, what might be reported as a collaborative consultation approach—two parties working together—may in fact represent only a variation of the expert-subordinate approach (e.g., the so-called doctor-patient relationship model). De Mesquita and Zollman (1995) suggest guarding against consultees' "passive acceptance" of recommendations followed by their failure to implement an agreed upon strategy. In such cases, consultees may be viewing the consultant as an expert and forgoing their role as collaborator; future efforts at collaborative consultation may therefore result in a lack of persistence. Furthermore, Witt (1990) maintains that the term collaboration is meaningless until practitioners change their behavior. Witt favors addressing the constellation of verbal and performance behaviors that consultants and consultees perform that achieve important outcomes.

Pugach and Johnson (1995) indicate (correctly in our view) that the distinctions between the terms consultation, collaboration, and collaborative consultation might, in the end, be moot. Schools are dynamic settings, and collaboration is not a singular process. Indeed, it is composed of supportive, facilitative, informative, and prescriptive roles that mark the interactions between professionals, staff, and parents along a broader spectrum. "Collaboration . . . exists along a continuum spanning the range from teachers' developing solutions together to specialists' prescribing solutions in the infrequent instances when unique expertise is needed" (Pugach & Johnson, 1995, p. 34).

While all the definitional issues have not been resolved, practitioners could use a set of operational parameters in their effort to launch consultation programs. Our efforts, combined with those of others in the field (e.g., Idol et al., 1995; Kampwirth, 1999; Zins & Ponti, 1990a), reaffirm that consultation is best characterized as being voluntary, reciprocal, interactive, collaborative, and mutual, and as leading to the prevention and resolution of identified problems.

# Goals of Consultation

Readers interested in learning more about the need for and approaches to prevention are referred to Zins, Heron, and Goddard (1999).

Bramlett and Murphy (1998), Gutkin and Curtis (1999), and Robbins and Gutkin (1994) indicate that there exist two global goals of consultation. The first, and most commonly addressed, goal is to provide remediation or resolutions to problems presented by clients. The focus of remediation involves the consultant and consultee working together to develop and implement effective interventions. Research has shown that remedial efforts in consultation are effective (Medway & Updyke, 1985). The second goal involves prevention, by improving the skills of consultees. There is less emphasis on prevention in the consultation literature; however, this goal is an important one (Meyers, 1995a). Ideally, as consultees become more adept at remediating skill deficits, they are acquiring the competence to apply interventions in the future with other students or in other settings (i.e., developing skills in prevention). In fact, Chandler (1980) found that the number of referrals for formal psychological evaluations decreased markedly after teachers gained experience with consultation, presumably because their skill level with prevention or management had improved. This research has been corroborated by more recent studies (Gutkin & Curtis, 1999).

More specifically, the goals of consultation have also been delineated. Idol et al. (1995) state that the goal of collaborative consultation involves developing and maintaining the skills of all those who educate students with disabilities.

Readers are referred to Gutkin and Conoley's (1990) article for a description of the "paradox of school psychology," which, in part, portrays the school psychologist as conducting a superior assessment, diagnosing the child's problem accurately, generating well-designed treatments, and communicating the treatment in a well-articulated report, only to have the program lapse and the potential benefit to the child be thwarted because the consultative link between the psychologist and the teacher was missing.

Finally, Gutkin and Conoley (cited in Gutkin and Curtis, 1999) remind related-service professionals, especially school psychologists, of the critical need for these services: "While consultation services have always been valued highly by both school psychologists and the consumers of school psychological services . . . recent events have served to underscore even further the centrality of this approach" (p. 599).

# Consultation Processes and Perspectives

The consultation process describes the relationship among the consultant, the consultee, and the client. Tharp (1975), for example, states that consultation services are provided through an intermediary—the consultee—with the expectation that behavior change will be observed in both the consultee and the client. Success with the consultation process is determined by noting improvement in both of these agents. The consultation process, however, also describes the stages these change agents encounter from the onset of consultation to its termination. At each stage in the process, a high degree of collaborative consultation is essential. Unlike an "expert" approach in which the consultant presumably knows something the consultee does not and the focus of the consultation is to impart that knowledge, collaborative consultation assumes that each party brings different knowledge to each stage of the process. Further, collaborative consultation implies that each party in the consultation plays an active role in the design, implementation, and evaluation of the program.

## Facilitating the Consultation Process

Even though a key component of consultation is that it is voluntary, it does not always occur smoothly. Consultants should be prepared to handle challenges to the process. Meyers (1995a), for example, indicates that a consultee's initial unwillingness to work collaboratively might be overcome when consultants (a) share the responsibility for problem solving, (b) view the teacher as an expert in dealing with the student's problems, (c) de-emphasize their contribution in the consultative process, and (d) communicate to teachers that they are free to accept or reject any recommendations. Nelson and Stevens (1979) state that to overcome personal as well as institutional resistance, consultants must be capable of changing a variety of behaviors and, more important, have a formal role in the school. That is, their role with respect to the rest of the school staff must be clear. Idol-Maestas, Nevin, and Paolucci-Whitcomb (1984) state that resistance can be overcome when consultants treat others with respect, share information, give and receive feedback, use confrontation skills appropriately, and employ situational leadership skills effectively. Gutkin and Curtis (1999) suggest that important dimensions of the consultant-consultee relationship be stressed. These include shared responsibility in decision making, consultants' acceptance that consultees may accept or reject ideas, conceptualization of consultation as a voluntary activity, and encouragement of active participation by consultees.

Gutkin and Curtis (1999) also highlight the importance of maintaining confidentiality with consultees: "Consultees have to feel free to communicate with consultants in an open and honest manner. It is unlikely that they would do so . . . if they perceived that this information might be leaked . . ." (p. 606). However, consistent with ethical practice, district policy, and common sense, consultants must be prepared to make professional judgments when events such as abuse or violence occur. The rights of students, administrators, and parents must also be balanced against the confidentiality rights of the consultee. Therefore, consultants and consultees should discuss openly, and reach consensus on, which aspects of the relationship will be confidential and which may remain open.

The authors caution against using electronic transmission (e.g., e-mail or fax transmissions) where appropriate security and training safeguards are not in place. For a discussion of the use of technology in teaming, see Chapter 3.

Morse (1976) suggests that consultants who help teachers make their work more meaningful and productive are more likely to gain acceptance in the school and to obtain favorable changes in behavior. Alderman and Gimpel (1996) found that teachers were likely to choose professional assistance based on situational needs. For example, the most likely situations for which teachers might seek consultation involved aggressive behavior. The school psychologist was identified as the consultant of choice in such cases. Family problems more often resulted in requesting assistance from guidance counselors. Other

See Chapter 6 for additional content on the interaction between consultants and family members.

teachers (general education and special education) were more likely to be consulted regarding motivational problems and inattentiveness. These findings suggest that teachers may be likely to seek out consultants who possess expertise perceived as most relevant to their needs.

Bergan and Tombari (1976) state that the consultation process serves as a link between knowledge producers (e.g., researchers) and knowledge consumers (e.g., teachers and parents). Since teachers and parents may not have access to educationally relevant research, the consultant can help bridge the gap by informing them of new materials, methods, and technology. Teachers and parents, on the other hand, can provide specific information at each stage of the process that helps to determine the applicability of a given material, method, or technology.

Several investigators have examined the issue of essential skills for consultation (Friend, 1984; Harris, 1991; Idol-Maestas & Ritter, 1985; West & Cannon, 1988). With the exception of Harris (1991), who identified consultation competencies for educators serving culturally and linguistically diverse populations, all of the other authors used a questionnaire format and asked practitioners, graduates of consultation training programs, or experts in the field, respectively, to rate essential skills needed for consultation irrespective of cultural background. West and Cannon (1988), for example, conducted a national validation study with a sample of 100 "experts" from around the country, and asked them to rate critical collaborative consultation skills. The results of their Delphi study showed that 47 skills clustered into seven categories: Consultation Theory and Models, Research, Personal Characteristics, Interactive Communication, Collaborative Problem Solving, Systems Change, Equity Issues and Values (see Table 1.2).

Tindal and Taylor-Pendergast (1989) reported on the use of the Resource Consultant Observation System as a measure of how consultants gain process skills. Also, their study was designed to document the main areas in which consultants participate. Data were obtained on written communication; interpersonal communication; noninteractive observation; interactive testing; obtaining, preparing, and reviewing materials; and modeling and demonstrating programs. These categories were rated across problem identification, development, intervention, and evaluation using 13 consultants enrolled in a graduate training program. The results showed that consultants spend most of their time alone, and a large measure of this time is spent engaged in problem identification and program evaluation, with substantially less time spent in program implementation.

Several specific skills may improve the consultation process. These include the ability to distribute leadership among participants, to manage controversy positively, to communicate without the use of jargon, and to maintain an awareness of and use positive nonverbal language (Idol et al., 1995). Sensitivity to multicultural issues, an understanding of organizations, and the ability to summarize important information verbally and in writing are all critical skills (Dougherty, Tack, Fullam, & Hammer, 1996). Additionally, active listening is a key skill, involving being open to discussion, remaining quiet while listening to others, and using nonverbal acknowledgments such as eye contact and nodding. The use of appropriate interview skills is also important, facilitating the exchange of specific information, the expression of feelings, the planning of future courses of action, and an enhancement of problem solving (Idol et al., 1995). A solid knowledge base composed of assessment techniques, instructional and behavioral interventions, potential adaptations to curricular

See Chapter 4 for additional information on active listening and Chapter 7 for content on multicultural issues.

See Section IV for a discussion of these technical areas of expertise.

Alderman and Gimpel (1996) state, "If one wants to be an effective consultant, one must be available to teachers" (p. 311).

**Table 1.2**

Essential Skills for the Process of Consultation

---

*Consultation Theory and Models*

1. Practice reciprocity of roles between consultant and consultee in facilitating the consultation process.
2. Demonstrate knowledge of various stages/phases of the consultation process.
3. Assume joint responsibility for identifying each stage of the consultation process and adjusting behavior accordingly.
4. Match consultation approach(es) to specific consultation situation(s), setting(s), and need(s).

*Research on Consultation Theory, Training, and Practice*

5. Translate relevant consultation research findings into effective school-based consultation practice.

*Personal Characteristics*

6. Exhibit ability to be caring, respectful, empathic, congruent, and open in consultation interactions.
7. Establish and maintain rapport with all persons involved in the consultation process, in both formal and informal interactions.
8. Identify and implement appropriate responses to stage of professional development of all persons involved in the consultation process.
9. Maintain positive self-concept and enthusiastic attitude throughout the consultation process.
10. Demonstrate willingness to learn from others throughout the consultation process.
11. Facilitate progress in consultation situations by managing personal stress, maintaining calm in time of crisis, taking risks, and remaining flexible and resilient.
12. Respect divergent points of view, acknowledging the right to hold different views and to act in accordance with convictions.

*Interactive Communication*

13. Communicate clearly and effectively in oral and written form.
14. Utilize active ongoing listening and responding skills to facilitate the consultation process (e.g., acknowledging, paraphrasing, reflecting, clarifying, elaborating, summarizing).
15. Determine own and others' willingness to enter consultative relationship.
16. Adjust consultation approach to the learning stage of individuals involved in the consultation process.
17. Exhibit ability to grasp and validate overt/covert meaning and affect in communications (perceptive).
18. Interpret nonverbal communications of self and others (e.g., eye contact, body language, personal boundaries in space) in appropriate context.
19. Interview effectively to elicit information, share information, explore problems, set goals and objectives.
20. Pursue issues with appropriate persistence once they arise in the consultation process.
21. Give and solicit continuous feedback that is specific, immediate, and objective.
22. Give credit to others for their ideas and accomplishments.
23. Manage conflict and confrontation skillfully throughout the consultation process to maintain collaborative relationship.
24. Manage timing of consultation activities to facilitate mutual decision making at each stage of the consultation process.
25. Apply the principle of positive reinforcement of one another in the collaborative team situation.
26. Be willing and safe enough to say "I don't know . . . let's find out."

---

*(continues)*

**Table 1.2** (*Continued*)

### Collaborative Problem Solving

27. Recognize that successful and lasting solutions require commonality of goals and collaboration throughout all phases of the problem-solving process.
28. Develop a variety of data collection techniques for problem identification and clarification.
29. Generate viable alternatives through brainstorming techniques characterized by active listening, nonjudgmental responding, and appropriate reframing.
30. Evaluate alternatives to anticipate possible consequences, narrow and combine choices, and assign priorities.
31. Integrate solutions into a flexible, feasible and easily implemented plan of action relevant to all persons affected by the problem.
32. Adopt a "pilot problem-solving" attitude, recognizing that adjustments to the plan of action are to be expected.
33. Remain available throughout implementation for support, modeling, and/or assistance in modification.
34. Redesign, maintain, or discontinue interventions using data-based evaluation.
35. Utilize observation, feedback, and interviewing skills to increase objectivity and mutuality throughout the problem-solving process.

### Systems Change

36. Develop roles as a change agent (e.g., implementing strategies for gaining support, overcoming resistance).
37. Identify benefits and negative effects that could result from change efforts.

### Equity Issues and Values/Beliefs Systems

38. Facilitate equal learning opportunities by showing respect for individual differences in physical appearance, race, sex, handicap, ethnicity, religion, SES, or ability.
39. Advocate for services that accommodate the educational, social, and vocational needs of all students, handicapped and nonhandicapped.
40. Encourage implementation of laws and regulations designed to provide appropriate education for all students with handicaps.
41. Utilize principles of the least restrictive environment in all decisions regarding students with handicaps.
42. Modify myths, beliefs, and attitudes that impede successful social and educational integration of students with handicaps into the least restrictive environment.
43. Recognize, respect, and respond appropriately to the effects of personal values and belief systems of self and others in the consultation process.
44. Ensure that persons involved in planning and implementing the consultation process are also involved in its evaluation.
45. Establish criteria for evaluating input, process, and outcome variables affected by the consultation process.
46. Engage in self-evaluation of strengths and weaknesses to modify personal behaviors influencing the consultation process.
47. Utilize continuous evaluative feedback to maintain, revise, or terminate consultation activities.

*Note.* From "Essential Collaborative Consultation Competencies for Regular and Special Educators," by J. F. West and G. S. Cannon, 1988, *Journal of Learning Disabilities, 21*(1), pp. 56–63. Copyright 1998 by PRO-ED, Inc. Adapted with permission.

materials, and classroom management skills is essential. Further, a sense of humor, as well as the ability to take risks, respond with integrity, and adapt easily, is helpful (Idol, Nevin, & Paolucci-Whitcomb, 1995). Vargo (1998) suggests that consultants make the process a positive one for consultees via methods such as proactively approaching teachers to determine in what ways the consultants might help (rather than waiting for a problem to arise), providing frequent positive feedback, and being "flexible, caring, respectful, empathetic, and open" (p. 55). Through emphasis on positive feedback and achievement of success for consultees, consultants may increase consultees' beliefs in their ability to execute a course of action leading to a desired attainment. Efficacy beliefs have documented effects on effort expended and persistence when encountering difficulties (Bandura, 1997; Pajares, 1997). "Feelings of self-efficacy and empowerment might be expected as outcomes of a teacher's success in obtaining services from a third party that she or he is unable to provide for a given student" (Schulte, Osborne, & Kauffman, 1993, p. 24).

There is a perspective in the literature that documents the scientific and artistic nature of consultation. Idol (1990), for example, refers to the "Artful Base of Consultation" as "basically the way in which the consultant works with consultees in solving the problem." She goes on to say, "This base is often referred to as the process skills of consultation. It is a demonstrable knowledge of how to bring about effective decision making, how to solve problems with others, and how to interact and communicate effectively with others" (p. 5). Clearly, more research needs to be conducted to identify the major factors in successful process studies.

## A Nine-Step Procedure

Sandoval, Lambert, and Davis (1977) indicate that the consultation process is interactive. They suggest that the consultee learn to use the services of a consultant more efficiently. They believe that consultees who learn which tasks consultants are able to perform with them and who are able to state their problems and evaluation strategies succinctly will find the consultation process the most rewarding. Curtis and Meyers (1989) state that the consultation process can be conceptualized in three phases: entry, problem clarification, and problem resolution. Kurpius (1978) outlines nine functions that define the consultation process and underscore Curtis and Meyers's later structure.

### Preentry

During the preentry phase, the consultant clarifies his or her own orientation toward the consultation process and various issues in the field (e.g., the relationship between consultant and consultee, intervention alternatives, the role of related-service personnel and parents in treatment, identification criteria). This self-examination forms the basis of the orientation the consultant brings to any problem-solving situation. For instance, if prior to beginning consultation the consultant is predisposed to believe that the client should gain insight into his or her personality and that the consultant should reflect the consultee's feelings, be supportive, and improve the consultee's skill and objectivity, then a mental health orientation could be claimed. Conversely, if the consultant believes that the application of behavior analysis principles (e.g., reinforcement) will form the basis of the consultation, then a behavioral orientation would emerge from the self-assessment (Medway & Forman, 1980).

### Entry

At the entry phase, three things happen. First, the consultant establishes rapport with the consultee, an important step if later success is to be achieved. De Mesquita and Zollman (1995) indicate that, rather than focusing on their theoretical perspectives, consultants should consider the attitudes and values of the consultee, including the consultee's preference for various models of consultation and views about specific intervention techniques. Second, the consultant determines the conditions surrounding the problem. Finally, an agreement is reached between the consultant and the consultee on the steps for solving the problem (e.g., identifying informational needs and resources, setting terminal goals, and determining responsibility for task completion).

## Gathering Information

In addition to whatever information might be available at the time consultation begins, the consultant and the consultee usually need to gather more data. The purpose of acquiring these data is to clarify the type, frequency, magnitude, or duration of the problem. Without adequate data, it is difficult to define the problem and to formulate an acceptable and effective intervention.

## Defining the Problem

Once data have been collected from a variety of sources (cf. Heron & Heward, 1982), the consultation process shifts to defining the problem in measurable terms. According to Bergan and Tombari (1976), success with problem identification invariably leads to problem resolution. Given that an individual or system may have multiple problems, it is helpful to arrange these situations from the most to the least severe with respect to difficulty. Jointly planned interventions should be initiated for the most severe problem first.

## Determining Solutions

See Chapter 4's section on problem-solving strategies for additional information on how to determine solutions.

Several acceptable solutions might be proposed to solve any given problem. To facilitate collaboration, de Mesquita and Zollman (1995) suggest that consultants offer a general strategy and encourage consultees to provide specific details for implementation. The ultimate guide in deciding which approach to use initially should be the *doctrine of the least restrictive alternative*. Essentially, this doctrine states that the most powerful, but least intrusive, intervention should be attempted before more restrictive or time-consuming approaches are tried (Evans & Meyer, 1985; Gast & Wolery, 1987). Gaylord-Ross (1980) offers a hierarchical decision-making model for the treatment of aberrant behavior that can be applied by consultants in many field-based settings. Briefly, the model outlines a series of intervention approaches that should be used prior to initiating restrictive strategies. The Gaylord-Ross model is described in more detail in Chapter 12.

## Stating Objectives

According to Kurpius (1978), the purpose for stating objectives is to describe the conditions under which the behavior should occur, the parameters of the behavior, and the method for evaluating success.

## Implementing the Plan

Plan implementation means that the jointly agreed upon program is placed into effect. If a change is needed during implementation because the original plan was not successful, then both parties must agree to an alternative plan. The important task to accomplish at this stage is to implement the plan as intended.

No plan can be evaluated accurately if it is not carried out in the manner prescribed during the planning stage.

## Evaluating the Plan

The purpose of evaluation is to determine whether a change has occurred in the desired direction. More important, the evaluation phase allows the consultant and the consultee to determine what variables account for the change. A goal for every consultation project should be to determine the functional or clinical significance for the intervention employed.

## Concluding Consultation

The consultation process is concluded when both parties agree that the objective has been met or that additional work is not warranted. This stage of the process should be a positive experience, conducted with the understanding that the consultation process can be reestablished in the future. Each party should recognize areas of professional growth as well as improvement in the conditions that prompted the initial consultation. Dougherty, Tack, Fullam, and Hammer (1996) indicate that more attention needs to be focused on this important stage of consultation. They suggest viewing disengagement as a reversal of the entry process. "Thus, disengagement can be viewed as the process of assessing the degree to which individual consultee needs have been met and the contract fulfilled, followed by a gradual psychological and physical exiting of the relationship" (p. 261).

# Perspectives on Consultation

Regardless of the consultation model that is used by practitioners, more professionals and parents are interacting at the consultative level than ever before. The field is exploding with applications within family and early childhood contexts, state-level adoptions, preservice and inservice training programs, and research efforts. Following are five perspectives of the field's past and future directions.

## Historical Perspective

Friend (1988) indicates that the early history of consultation was influenced by professionals who worked in clinical or counseling settings. As mental health services expanded and became more formalized, the demand for service produced a shift toward consultation. In part, this may have been due to the large numbers of cases that required attention, taxing the individualized counseling formats of the day. The emergence of the behavioral model, specialized programming for students with disabilities, increased funding, alternative options, and efficacy research helped to shape the growth of consultation as a viable option. Consultation programs were also promoted as a way to reduce referrals and to provide indirect services to teachers in their own rooms (Bramlett & Murphy, 1998; Johnson, Pugach, & Hammitte, 1988).

West and Idol (1990) state that the need for consultation is inextricably bound to the more recent effective school movement, a claim supported by Cohen (1983) and Purkey and Smith (1985). Taken as a whole, these studies indicate that effective schools are characterized by collegial and collaborative relationships between general and special education teachers, related-services personnel, and parents. Hence, consultation has emerged from a reactive mode (need to serve students whose behavior calls attention to itself) to a proactive mode (need to become effective for a wide range of students and the school as a whole).

## Statewide Adoption Perspective

Comprehensive data on the range of consultation services that are used across all 50 states and the District of Columbia do not exist. West and Brown's (1987) national survey of policies and procedural options was completed for only 35 of those 51 entities (68%) and showed that approximately three quarters (75%) of the respondents included direct or indirect consultation as part of a continuum of services. Nine respondents did not include consultation as an option. The remaining states listed varying degrees of usage. Of the states where consultation was listed as an option, only half provided specific job descriptions for such personnel, although a few others indicated that the local education agency (LEA) had the descriptions on file. Job titles (e.g., educational consultant) varied markedly from state to state, and respondents in eight states did not report having titles for this position. To sum up the current situation, West and Brown (1987) state, "There is a critical need for improved policies and leadership by state departments of education to assist local education agencies in the development of service options to provide effective educational programs for handicapped students in mainstreamed classrooms . . . it would appear that state departments of education, teacher educators, researchers, and practitioners have the resources to successfully address this need" (p. 51).

## Training Perspective

Idol and West (1987) conducted an analysis and critique of six special education and two interdisciplinary training programs that focused on teaching consultation skills. Essentially they were trying to answer the questions: Is consultation process training provided, and is the consultation knowledge base embedded within the curriculum? The schools that were included for analysis were selected from those offering a nationally known pool of programs considered to provide "model" training, based on their reputation through the Teacher Consultation Network, an association of professionals of the Teacher Education Division of the Council for Exceptional Children. Their findings showed that whereas all eight programs offered training in consultation knowledge, only four provided systematic training in performance outcomes for consultants. Further, there was wide variability in how the institutions accomplished consultation training objectives. The point that Idol and West make is that preservice training needs to be improved. In their view, training programs that attempt to provide an eclectic range of consultation perspectives might better serve their students by focusing on one consultation model and ensuring that performance-based objectives are developed and mastered.

Yocum and Cossairt (1996) conducted a nationwide survey of teacher training programs in special education. They found that 63% of the programs offered a consultation course and that collaborative consultation was the most frequently used model. Their conclusion was that the majority of university special education programs are beginning to address inclusion of consultation coursework.

An even greater need for consultation training exists at the inservice level (Friend & Cook, 1988; Idol & West, 1987; Kurpius & Lewis, 1988; Lehner,

1988). However, practical and logistical considerations associated with scheduling or the multiple commitments of staff may preclude the use of local resources. Consequently, administrators may favor employing external agents to deliver the inservice training. Friend and Cook (1988) suggest that a comprehensive locally arranged program, which may have focused on the eight competency areas outlined by West and Cannon (1988), may need to be modified in favor of training a smaller set of specific collaborative skills relevant to the particular situation.

> Readers interested in learning more about site-based interdisciplinary training can refer to Welch and Sheridan (1995) and Welch, Sheridan, Wilson, Colton, and Mayhew (1996).

To sum up the issue of training, few preservice programs offer comprehensive training in all "essential" competencies identified by West and Cannon (1988). Further, inservice education on consultation is virtually nonexistent, and where it does exist, there is great variability in the skills, methods, and outcomes that are achieved. Still, suggestions for what to teach with respect to consultation, how to teach it, and ways to demonstrate effectiveness during and after training can be derived from Friend (1985), Friend and Cook (1988), Kurpius and Lewis (1988), Lehner (1988), McClellan and Wheatley (1985), McGill and Robinson (1989), and Paolucci-Whitcomb and Nevin (1985). Collectively, these authors discuss the purposes, procedures, and methodological issues to be considered when conducting rigorous training at the preservice and inservice levels.

## Early Childhood and Transition Perspective

Since the passage of P.L. 99-457, the Early Childhood Education Act, an increased emphasis has been placed on the needs of preschool students with developmental disabilities and their parents. Implicit in that legislation is the need for practitioners to collaborate on developing, implementing, and evaluating programs for these students. However, two key barriers to full implementation are the levels of training of preschool staff regarding young children with disabilities, and the lack of consultant skills in staff currently serving this population. Compounding the problems caused by the lack of training and consultation skills is the fact that the student population in the United States is undergoing dramatic changes as ethnic minority populations grow. An interdisciplinary and consultative strategy is needed for assessing and intervening with at-risk young children and their families. Consultative services must be family centered and must relate to prevention and solution of social, medical, and mental health problems.

> See Chapter 7 for a complete discussion of multicultural factors.

At the other end of the continuum, many secondary-level students emerge from special and regular education programs inadequately prepared for the world of work. The needs for these adults are complex and require that consultants plan effective transition programs early in a student's career. The passage of IDEA '97 (P.L. 105-17) mandates that transition planning begin when a student reaches age 14. Consultants from within and outside of local education agencies must be prepared to assist school personnel with transition planning for younger students.

## Research Perspective

The research base for using an educational consultation model can be divided into three subareas: competencies to train, training orientation and methodology, and consultation effectiveness.

*Competencies to Train.* As stated previously, West and Cannon (1988) conducted an exhaustive study with over 100 professionals nationwide to identify the essential competencies that trained consultants need to perform their duties effectively. The results showed that the skills clustered around eight areas, with specific behaviors embedded within each of these areas. That research base has provided a validated array of competencies that can be integrated within preservice or inservice training programs. Further investigation should examine the best ways to teach these validated competencies (Bradley, 1994).

***Training Orientation and Methodology.*** Several educators have indicated that a transdisciplinary approach is a prerequisite for effective preservice and inservice training (Golightly, 1987). In a transdisciplinary approach, an emphasis is placed on teaming, joint decision making, communication, and coordination. Support for a transdisciplinary approach is also found in leadership preparation literature, especially with early intervention programs (Siders, Riall, Bennett, & Judd, 1987).

Methodologically, many consultant-educators favor an instructional approach that provides for expert modeling, multiple opportunities to practice consultation skills during and after training, and independent practice under supervision (Bergan, 1977; Friend & Cook, 1988; Idol, 1988; McGimsey, Greene, & Lutzker, 1995). This approach maximizes the participant's opportunity to respond and receive feedback, and promotes generality and maintenance of skill development (Cooper, Heron, & Heward, 1987).

***Consultation Effectiveness.*** Consultation programs have existed in schools for many years, yet the research base demonstrating their effectiveness is only beginning to emerge (cf. Robbins & Gutkin, 1994; Mayer et al., 1993). According to West and Idol (1987), "Despite the dramatic increase in the emphasis on school consultation in school settings in recent years, there are few empirical research studies examining school consultation appearing in special education journals or those of other related professions such as school or community psychology, counseling, or organizational development" (p. 396). Still, several reviews of the literature indicate that a consultation model is an effective method to prevent and solve academic and social skill deficiencies in student populations (Friend, 1988; Heron & Harris, 1993; Heron & Kimball, 1988; Idol, Nevin, & Paolucci-Whitcomb, 1995; McGimsey, Greene, & Lutzker, 1995; Medway, 1982; Medway & Updyke, 1985; West & Idol, 1987). Overall, these studies show that when (a) accurate problem identification occurs; (b) consultants and consultees work collaboratively on mutually recognized goals; (c) credibility and trust are established; (d) feedback is provided; and (e) information is disseminated, successful outcomes are achieved (Bergan & Tombari, 1976; Heron & Harris, 1993; Idol, Paolucci-Whitcomb, & Nevin, 1986). Meyers (1995b) sums up current research efforts as having the following results:

> (a) improved professional and problem-solving skills for teachers, (b) modified teacher attitudes regarding children's problems, (c) greater understanding of children's problems by teachers, (d) generalization of consultation effects to other children in the same classroom, (e) reduced referral rates, and (f) gains in long-term academic performance. (p. 79)

## Consultation Models

The nine-step consultation process outlined by Kurpius (1978) has been formalized and condensed into several consultation models. For instance, Gallessich (1982) refers to six broad consultation models: behavioral, clinical, education and training, mental health, organizational, and program. Babcock and Pryzwansky (1983) differentiate among collaborative, expert, mental health, and medical models. Gutkin and Curtis (1999) and Shields, Heron, Rubenstein, and Katz (1995) discuss the ecobehavioral model. West and Idol (1987) state that at least 10 consultation models can be identified. To the models posited by Gallessich, they add advocacy, collaborative, organizational thinking, and process models. Each of these models differs with respect to underlying theoretical assumptions, knowledge base, goals, stages, and consultant-consultee responsibility (see Table 1.3).

It is beyond the scope of this chapter to discuss each of West and Idol's 10 models in depth. However, the mental health, organizational and systems, behavioral, and collaborative consultation models will be addressed since there is widespread consensus that they represent the four major models used in schools (Curtis & Meyers, 1989; Idol et al., 1986; Kratochwill, Elliott, & Rotto, 1990; Kratochwill, Sheridan, & Van Someren, 1988; Zins & Ponti, 1990a, 1990b). The behavioral and collaborative consultation models are employed frequently with individuals, small groups, or large populations to prevent and/or resolve school-related challenges.

## The Mental Health Consultation Model

Caplan (1970) is usually credited with introducing the *mental health consultation model*. In the mental health model, "efforts are made to change consultees' behavior by focusing on their understanding of client problems and on the consultee's underlying feelings, beliefs, and conflicts" (Zins, 1988, p. 27). Meyers (as cited in Bramlett & Murphy, 1998) described three types of mental health consultation: system-centered, teacher-centered, and child-centered. Of these, teacher-centered consultation has received the most attention. Lack of knowledge, skill, objectivity, and confidence are often believed to attribute to teachers' difficulties in dealing with students (Caplan, 1995). The consultant serves the role of facilitator, diagnostician, and/or relationship builder by practicing one-downsmanship (i.e., playing down his or her role in the process) (Conoley & Conoley, 1982). Thomas, Gatz, and Luczak (1997) indicate that there are two critical features of the consultant-consultee relationship in the mental health consultation model: First, consultants should communicate their confidence in the ability of consultees to solve their own problems. Second, consultees should be involved as active participants in the consultation process.

The focus of mental health consultation can be individuals or organizations, and the consultant-consultee relationship can be characterized as expert or collaborative (Brown, Wyne, Blackburn, & Powell, 1979; Caplan, Caplan, & Erchul, 1995). An ecological perspective is often assumed, meaning that dynamic interactions occur between persons and settings; therefore, the focus of consultation is on the "person-in-context" (Thomas, Gatz, & Luczak, 1997). Success is determined by the ever increasing ability of the consultee to effect self-change or change in a third party (West & Idol, 1987).

## The Organizational and Systems Consultation Model

Although *organizational and systems consultation models* were originally conceptualized separately, current thinking views them as conjoint due to their

Table 1.3

Analysis of 10 Consultation Models in Response to 5 Criterial Questions

| Consultation Model | Theory for the Consultation Relationship | Knowledge Base for Problem Solving | Goals | Stages/Steps | Responsibilities |
|---|---|---|---|---|---|
| Mental Health Caplan (1970); Meyers et al. (1979) | Assumes that consultees have the capacity to solve most of their work problems and that consultants can help them increase their range of effectiveness (Gallessich, 1982). Theories that have been applied to how the consultant treats the consultee include those of neo-client-centered psychology (Rogers, 1942, 1951, 1959) and Adlerian psychology (Adler, 1964; Dreikurs, 1948, 1967). No single theory of communication has been applied. | Psychodynamics; clinical skills; crisis concepts; specialized diagnostic and decision-making skills; theme interference reduction; one downmanship; avoidance of therapy; relationship building. | Consultant chooses one of four possibilities: client-centered, consultee-centered, program-centered, and administrative- or consultee-centered. Success is measured by the degree to which the consultation expands the consultee's capacity to diagnose, cope with, and solve emotional or technical problems of the consultee or the client. | Consultant chooses type of consultation for the problem and primary target of interventions. *Example* 1. Consultant seeks information on nature and scope of work problem, consultee's capacity for problem solving, and ways the consultation might be useful. 2. Consultant "treats" the consultee by offering *expert* opinion *or* shared, straight-forward problem solving is used. | Consultant is responsible for gathering information on the nature of the problem and for providing solutions to problems. The consultant-consultee relationship is egalitarian (Gallessich, 1985). |

*(continues)*

**Table 1.3** (*Continued*)

| Consultation Model | Theory for the Consultation Relationship | Knowledge Base for Problem Solving | Goals | Stages/Steps | Responsibilities |
|---|---|---|---|---|---|
| Behavioral<br>Bergan & Tombari (1975, 1976); Kratochwill & Bergan (1978); McNamara & Dienl (1974); Tombari & Bergan (1978) | Assumes that consultant's application of behavioral/social learning theory will help consultee solve problems. Behavioral learning theory has been more consistently applied to methods for problem solving than to how the consultant interacts with the consultee, although the latter would also be applicable. | Flexible knowledge of behavioral programming and principles of social learning theory and applied behavior analysis. | To reduce the frequency of an undesirable client/consultee behavior; to increase the frequency of desirable client/consultee behavior. | 1. Problem identification<br>2. Problem analysis<br>3. Plan implementation<br>4. Problem evaluation<br>(Bergan, 1977) | Consultant serves as an expert; consultee is the recipient, although sometimes mutuality of problem solving is emphasized. |
| Organizational<br>A. Human Relations Model (Argyris, 1964; Bennis, 1969, 1970; Homans, 1950; Lippitt, 1969) | Organizational theory: Problems of organizations must be solved in a manner that incorporates into the process all individuals in the organization because of the focus that they bring to bear upon one another (Lewin, 1951), the influence of environment upon personal growth (Rogers, 1942, 1951, 1959). | Communication skills; decision-making skills; force-field-analysis approved, data collection and feedback, social/psychological, cognitive, behaviorism, ecology; psychodynamic systems, statistical models and methods, humanistic values and assumptions (Gallessich, 1985). | To bring about planned change by focusing upon individuals and their attitudes and values and group processes in the organization (Brown et al., 1979); to increase organizational productivity and morale (Gallessich, 1982). | 1. Orientation<br>2. Contract setting<br>3. Reconnaissance<br>4. Problem and opportunity development<br>5. Aspirations<br>6. Analysis<br>7. Experimentation<br>8. Results analysis<br>9. Program design<br>10. Implementation<br>11. Evaluation and feedback<br>12. Recycling<br>(Gardner, 1974) | Consultant facilitates the group's progression through all stages. |

*(continues)*

Table 1.3 (*Continued*)

| Consultation Model | Theory for the Consultation Relationship | Knowledge Base for Problem Solving | Goals | Stages/Steps | Responsibilities |
|---|---|---|---|---|---|
| B. Organizational Thinking (Schmuck & Runkel, 1972) | Same as for the Human Relations Model. | Group conflict, inter- and intra-group communication, decision making, methods of goal setting, defining roles. | 1. Working with subsystems of the organization as groups<br>2. Developing communication skills<br>3. Working with subsystems to develop problem-solving skills<br>4. Developing a series of training exercises that start with simulation and evolve to a point where the real issues of the school are the focus (Schmuck & Runkel, 1972) | 1. Entry phase<br>2. Diagnosis of organization's functioning<br>3. Selection of a subsystem of the organization<br>4. Demonstration of the intervention (Brown et al., 1979)<br>5. Organizational training | Consultant facilitates process, demonstrates interventions, and provides training. |

(*continues*)

Table 1.3 (*Continued*)

| Consultation Model | Theory for the Consultation Relationship | Knowledge Base for Problem Solving | Goals | Stages/Steps | Responsibilities |
|---|---|---|---|---|---|
| C. Advocacy | Any practitioners of other models may use advocacy consultation, based on conflict theory (i.e., Chesler, Bryant, & Crowfoot, 1981). | Knowledge of law, organizing people, organizing events, media use, negotiation, and parent partnership, persuasive writing and speaking, building support networks, tolerance for ambiguity and conflict; known for what they believe in *not* by particular methodologies. Some advocacy consultants have both expert content knowledge and advocacy process knowledge (Conoley & Conoley, 1982). | To seek due process for various types of clients; to facilitate group process to help people work together; to organize events; to develop partnerships with parents of clients. | *None specified.* | Consultant facilitates effectiveness of others. |
| Process (Schein, 1969) | Systems change theory (von Bertalanffy, 1950). | Understanding of process phenomena; process observation, interaction analysis; decision-making rules; data gathering; role identification; use of empirical approaches; reference for the unique (Conoley & Conoley, 1982; Neel, 1981). | Consultants work to make consultees more aware of events or processes that affect work production and social emotional atmospheres of the system (Schein, 1969); to leave a consultee (organization) with new skills (Conoley & Conoley, 1982). | 1. Process observation<br>2. Analysis of group interactions | Consultant analyzes interactions of the group/organization; consultant and consultee work collaboratively to identify problems and to generate solutions; consultee provides information on organizational structure, climate, norms. |

(*continues*)

**Table 1.3** (*Continued*)

| Consultation Model | Theory for the Consultation Relationship | Knowledge Base for Problem Solving | Goals | Stages/Steps | Responsibilities |
|---|---|---|---|---|---|
| Clinical (Doctor-Patient) | The general characteristic is that it is patterned after psychiatry and adapted for use when consulting with colleagues about clients' problems. No specified theory. | Specialized expertise concerning the client's problem; expert power; referent power based on specialized expertise. | Expert diagnosis of a client's mental or emotional condition and an authoritative recommendation as to how staff (consultees) should treat the patient (Gallessich, 1982). Problems are conceived as patient's (or program's, team's, organization's) problems; generally, goals are limited to the particular case; to increase consultee's coping effectiveness. | 1. Diagnosis<br>2. Prescription<br>3. Treatment | Consultant assumes responsibility for the case, determines data to be gathered and how to gather them, directly examines client, treats or prescribes treatment; consultant-consultee relationship is hierarchical. |

(continues)

**Table 1.3** (*Continued*)

| Consultation Model | Theory for the Consultation Relationship | Knowledge Base for Problem Solving | Goals | Stages/Steps | Responsibilities |
|---|---|---|---|---|---|
| Program | No specified theory. | Methods are difficult to define because of the diversity in the nature of the consultation (Gallessich, 1982). | To help agencies design, develop, implement, and evaluate programs. | *Example*<br>1. Consultee clarifies goals and objectives.<br>2. Consultant proposes ideal, theoretical approaches to objectives.<br>3. Consultee explains organizational constraints and resources.<br>4. Both "brainstorm" to develop practical implementation strategies.<br>5. Together they develop a research and implementation plan.<br>6. Consultee implements the plan (Gallessich, 1982). | Consultants may assist in all aspects of the program *or* be limited to a highly specific task. |
| Education/Training | No specified theory. | Knowledge of open systems operations; task analysis; needs assessment; instructional design; evaluation of training (Gallessich, 1982). | To transmit needed knowledge, information, and skills to consultees to alleviate problems (usually client centered). | No specific stages/steps. | Consultant serves as an expert. |

*(continues)*

**Table 1.3** (*Continued*)

| Consultation Model | Theory for the Consultation Relationship | Knowledge Base for Problem Solving | Goals | Stages/Steps | Responsibilities |
|---|---|---|---|---|---|
| Collaborative<br><br>Idol et al. (1986);<br>Kurpius &<br>Robinson (1978);<br>Sarason (1982) | Generic principles of collaboration and consultation have been hypothesized (Idol et al., 1986); based on triadic model of consultation (Tharp & Wetzel, 1969); no formal testing for theory development has been done. | Consultants possess knowledge of social learning theory, classroom assessment, learning processes, child management, and applied behavior analysis; consultees possess knowledge of scope and sequence of curricular instruction, theories of child development, and techniques for large-group instruction. | To develop parity between special and classroom teachers resulting in shared ownership of learning and management problems of exceptional and nonachieving students participating in regular classroom instruction. | 1. Gaining mutual acceptance<br>2. Assessing causes of problems themselves, and outcomes of problems<br>3. Formulating goals and objectives matched to assessment outcomes<br>4. Implementing teaching/learning procedures<br>5. Evaluating program outcomes including clients, consultants, consultees, parents of clients, program administrators, and overall programs (Idol et al., 1986) | Consultant emphasizes mutuality and parity in the consulting relationship, with the consultant serving as a learning specialist and the consultee serving as a curriculum and child development specialist; consultee is primarily responsible for program implementation; all other stages reflect mutual responsibility. |

*Note.* From "School Consultation (Part I): An Interdisciplinary Perspective on Theory, Models, and Research," by J. F. West and L. Idol, 1987, *Journal of Learning Disabilities,* 20(7), pp. 388–408. Copyright 1987 by PRO-ED, Inc. Reprinted with permission.

focus on change at the group, or organizational, level (cf. Gutkin & Curtis, 1999). Consultants using an organizational and systems change model may work with groups at various levels within an educational system, including classrooms; grade levels; and building, district, county, and state levels (Gutkin & Curtis, 1999).

The organizational consultation model was derived from human relations and organization theory (Schmuck & Runkel, 1985) and was predicated on the notion that problems must be solved taking into account the symbiotic relationship of all individuals involved in the organization (West & Idol, 1987). Organizational development, the cornerstone of the model, is defined as:

> a planned and sustained effort at system self-study and improvement that focuses on change in system norms, structures, and procedures. OD [organizational development] engages the system members in the active assessment, diagnosis, and transformation of their own educational organization. (Schmuck, 1995, p. 207)

The goal of organizational development "is to build self-renewing schools, schools that are able to adapt to current changes within the student body, community, and world while continuing to maintain an effective educational program" (Schmuck, 1995, p. 200). Schmuck outlines seven goals of organizational consultation: clarifying communication, establishing collective goals, uncovering conflicts and interdependence, improving group procedures, solving problems, making decisions, and assessing changes.

Similarly, Stephens (1977) and Curtis and Meyers (1989) describe a systems model for consulting with school personnel that basically integrates the major components of the behavioral, mental health, and collaborative consultation models. A major tenet of the systems model is that changes in one part of the system affect other components within the system. Stephens outlines five independent but self-regulatory phases for a systems model: assessment, specification of objectives, planning, implementation of treatment, and evaluation. Of note is the cyclic nature of Stephens's model, indicating that systems change is an ongoing process, with evaluation of prior interventions driving assessment for future changes. Alternatively, if prior plans were ineffective, further assessment is warranted.

According to Curtis and Meyers (1989), knowledge of systems theory is valuable to consultants because "it helps the consultant understand the consultative process itself as affected by numerous interactive variables . . . and it offers a framework for examining child-related concerns and for developing strategies for addressing those concerns within the context of the child as one component in an environmental setting (system)" (p. 40). Goldberg (1995) points out that consultants' knowledge of and appeal to the system within which they are working will help make the experience a positive one. Further, a system that is open to change will be likely to offer necessary supports.

Group interactions are primary concerns for consultants engaged in organization and systems consultation, and the consultant's role is to guide the process. Whereas in the behavioral and mental health consultation models, emphasis is placed on solving the problems of individuals through specific, personalized interventions, the organization and systems model focuses on modifying policies, procedures, group structure, and role responsibilities as the method for improving program effectiveness. Gutkin and Curtis (1999) discuss four crucial elements of successful consultation for the model: mutual adaptation (referring to the ability of school personnel to configure innovations to

Schmuck (1995) stated that anytime a major curriculum, instructional, and/or management technique is broadly adopted within a school system, the "culture" of the school district is likely to change. Consultants who fail to recognize this point risk losing opportunities to maintain trust, lines of communication, and shared decision making (Sugai & Tindal, 1993).

make them fit within the particular ecology of the existing system), the "involvement of all primary stakeholders in all aspects of the change process," the support of change efforts by key administrators, and "a coherent system of collaborative problem solving" (p. 623). Further, Zins and Illback (1995) stress that:

> Strategic change programs must reflect the complexity of the organizations they are trying to change. Adequate effort must be devoted to gathering diagnostic data, to assessing organizational readiness, and to following up on the implementation process. . . . Many educational reforms fail because they are unidimensional and do not take into account the interactive elements of organizational structure, process, and behavior. . . . Furthermore, lasting, significant change takes time. . . . Attempts to rush the process may be met with resistance and failure. (p. 239)

Central to a successful organizational consultation program is knowledge of how each of the respective subsystems operates (Forman, 1995; Schmuck, 1995). Forman highlights four organizational structures that may potentially influence the behavior of consultant and consultee, as well as the results of consultation: the authority structure, the decision-making structure, the reward structure, and the communication structure.

One of the more popular applications of organizational and systems consultation in schools is the move toward consultation or intervention assistance teams (Zins & Illback, 1995; Zins & Ponti, 1990b). Data on the effectiveness of organizational and systems consultation models are mixed given the lack of available instrumentation to measure complex and ever changing interactions (West & Idol, 1987). However, evaluation of outcomes must be documented to assess the effectiveness of organizational and systems procedures, because such programs are becoming more prevalent (Zins & Illback, 1995).

For further discussion of consultation assistance teams, see Chapter 3.

## The Behavioral Model

The behavioral model, while commonly conceived as a means to bring about changes in classroom behavior, can also be used to target academic improvement (de Mesquita & Zollman, 1995).

Kratochwill et al. (1990) state that *behavior consultation* "is a model for delivering psychoeducational assessment and intervention services to children via teachers and parents through a series of interviews . . . observational assessments, treatment of the target behavior, and evaluation of the intervention" (p. 150). According to Bramlett and Murphy (1998), the emphases for change in the behavioral consultation model focus on the role of environmental factors (e.g., antecedents and consequences) and on functional relations between behavior and environment. Bergan (1977, 1995), one of the leading authorities in behavioral consultation, describes the model as occurring within four stages: problem identification, problem analysis, plan implementation, and plan evaluation.

### Problem Identification

Problem identification involves the consultant and consultee working together to ascertain the specific problem(s) to target. Consultants should ask questions that are specific enough to evoke "concrete, observable examples of behavior" (Bramlett & Murphy, 1998, p. 35). Sugai and Tindal (1993) suggest that consultants ask questions that focus on descriptions of (a) the target behavior, (b) other behaviors that occur concomitantly with the target behavior, (c) presumed factors that surround behavior onset and consequences, (d) reactions of individuals in the environment of the behavior, and (e) alternative behaviors and interventions to be considered.

Problem identification is completed when assessment data are collected, criterion levels for the target behavior are determined, a prioritized set of objectives is generated, and the discrepancy between the current level of performance and the desired level of performance is ascertained (Bergan, 1977; Cipani, 1985). Included in problem identification are the requisite behaviors of defining the problem in specific, observable terms, selecting the exact behavior to change, identifying conditions in the environment that affect the behavior, determining appropriate assessment protocols, and empowering the change agents to solve the problem (Kratochwill et al., 1990).

## Problem Analysis

During problem analysis, mutual planning occurs with respect to the goals and objectives of the program. Specifically, the consultant and the consultee delineate the intervention that will be introduced, the criterion for acceptable performance, the data collection procedures that will guide decision making during implementation, and the evaluation protocol. The ultimate goal of problem analysis is to forge a mutual plan (Kratochwill et al., 1990). "Some important factors that influence consultees' acceptability of interventions include the (a) severity of the problem [complex interventions are more likely to be implemented for severe problems] (b) time efficiency of the treatment, (c) strength of the treatment, and (d) language or jargon used by the consultant" (Bramlett & Murphy, 1998, p. 36). Bergan and Caldwell (1995) state that when communicating with consultees during this stage, consultants should avoid using highly technical language.

## Plan Implementation

Plan implementation occurs when the mutual strategy agreed upon by the consultant and the consultee is placed into effect. According to Kratochwill et al. (1990), three events transpire during plan implementation: skill development, monitoring, and plan revision. Skill development may be needed for the consultee who is actually implementing the plan. For example, if a parent agrees to initiate a contracting system with her son but does not know how to formalize the agreement, a training session might be conducted to show how to delineate tasks and rewards. Monitoring occurs in two stages. First, the target individual's performance is noted. Second, the plan is reviewed to determine if it is being implemented as intended. Monitoring fulfills the "quality assurance" function insofar as the consultant and the consultee are able to examine the data obtained during implementation to determine the efficacy of the approach (Bergan, 1977; Cipani, 1985). Plan revision occurs if the teacher is unable or unwilling to implement the plan as intended, or if the intervention is not bringing about the desired change.

## Plan Evaluation

The reason for plan evaluation is to ascertain whether the goal for the mutually established program was reached. It is important that evaluation be based on individual student data, rather than group data assessing mean differences (Bergan & Caldwell, 1995). Graphic records of individual students offer more immediate feedback to, and are more easily interpreted by, teachers. Further,

Witt, Gresham, and Noell (1996) caution against the use of a "talk only" approach between consultant and consultee to assess integrity and conduct evaluations of consultation outcomes. Instead, they advocate collecting objective, empirical evidence that the intervention a) has been implemented as designed and b) was responsible for any changes in target behavior. Stated another way, consultants should collect data beyond consultee self-reports to verify that the intervention was implemented as designed and produced the desired change. Generally, three levels of data examination can take place: The goal may have been reached, been partially accomplished, or not been achieved at all. Presumably, the last level would not occur given the formative and redirective aspects of plan implementation. Finally, in post-implementation planning the consultant and the consultee decide whether to terminate consultation or to attempt to solve another problem (Bergan, 1977; Cipani, 1985; Kratochwill et al., 1990; Zins & Ponti, 1990a).

Increasing evidence indicates that the behavioral consultation model is the most researched, is backed by empirical support, and is the model most likely to be chosen by school consultants (Bramlett & Murphy, 1998; Erchul & Schulte, 1996).

The Vermont Consulting Teacher Program (Knight, Meyers, Paolucci-Whitcomb, Hasazi, & Nevin, 1981) and the Regular Education Consultant Program (McGill & Robinson, 1989) serve as two successful behavioral models of consultation.

## The Collaborative Consultation Model

The *collaborative consultation model* (Figure 1.1) in its most basic form is a linear sequence that portrays the relationships of the consultant, the consultee or mediator, and the client or target. This model is a variation of the triadic model introduced by Tharp and Wetzel (1969) and Tharp (1975). The bracket that connects the consultant and the consultee represents the collaborative consultation process.

The collaborative consultation model describes a functional rather than an absolute sequence for consultation. That is, any practitioner—principal, resource room teacher, supervisor, psychologist—could serve as the consultant. The only requirement is that the individual possess the knowledge, skills, and abilities needed to work collaboratively with the mediator or the target. A regular education teacher, paraprofessional, or parent could serve as a mediator.

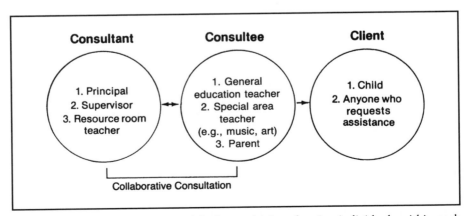

**Figure 1.1.** The collaborative model of consultation showing individuals within each role. From *Behavior Modification in the Natural Environment* (p. 47), by R. G. Tharp and R. J. Wetzel (1969), New York: Academic Press. Copyright 1969 by Academic Press. Adapted with permission of the publisher and authors.

The *mediator* has access to the target student and has some influence over him or her, while the consultant serves as a catalyst to activate the mediator. The *target* is the individual (or group) for whom the consultative service is intended, or any other person involved with the consultation (Tharp & Wetzel, 1969).

## Principles of Collaborative Consultation

According to Idol-Maestas et al. (1984) and Idol, Paolucci-Whitcomb, and Nevin (1995), four principles of collaborative consultation form the basis of the model: team ownership, recognition of individual differences, application of reinforcement, and data-based evaluation.

*Team Ownership.* The bi-directional arrow shown in Figure 1.1 indicates that equality and parity must exist between the consultant and the mediator for the triadic model to work effectively. According to Idol et al. (1995), "Equality can be demonstrated by listening, respecting and learning from each other. Parity is demonstrated as the mediator's skills and knowledge are blended with the different skills and knowledge of the consultant" (pp. 333–334). Further, Idol et al. indicate that both the consultant and the consultee "own" the targeted problem and share accountability for success or failure of the consultation effort.

It is important that each person's expertise be recognized and appreciated.

*Recognition of Individual Differences.* The collaborative consultation model focuses on the effect of change on the mediator and the target. That is, implicit in the implementation of the collaborative consultation model is that a change in procedure will occur, including planning, learning new behaviors and skills, and adapting to novel routines. For some people, making a change in a routine is uncomfortable. The consultant's role in the collaboration process is to be sensitive to the effects of change on the mediator and the target and to make transitions as nonthreatening as possible.

*Application of Reinforcement.* A distinguishing feature of the collaborative consultation model is its emphasis on the application of positive reinforcement. A basic tenet of this approach is that new behaviors are learned when their occurrence is followed by reinforcement. So, not only does the consultant use liberal amounts of reinforcement when teaching the mediator new behaviors, but the mediator also learns to use ample reinforcement with the target individual.

> When consultants and mediators learn to apply reinforcement principles to ameliorate and accelerate the academic and social progress of students, they typically begin to apply those same principles to their own interaction; as they "catch each other being good," they learn the new skills more effectively. (Idol et al., 1995, p. 335)

The emphasis on reinforcement does not mean that other behavior change principles or procedures are not used. Many educators have written extensively on how behaviors can be changed using a variety of acceleration and deceleration approaches (cf. Cooper, Heron, & Heward, 1987). The point is that positive reinforcement is a key principle in behavior development.

*Data-Based Evaluation.* The collaborative consultation model is evaluated by determining the extent to which improved performance in the consultant, consultee, or target is achieved. Success can be analyzed using a variety of qualitative and quantitative measures (cf. Heron & Catera, 1980; Idol et al., 1995; Kerr & Nelson, 1983; Tawney & Gast, 1984). Specifically, the consultant has two evaluative measures to index when using the collaborative consultation model. The first measure is the extent to which the consultant and the consultee acquire increased knowledge or skill subsequent to their interaction. The second measure is whether the application of this knowledge or skill affects student, parent, or system performance. It is possible for gains to be realized by a mediator when little or no improvement in student performance is obtained. As Heath and Nielson (1974) indicate, the relationship between the specific performance of the teacher and the achievement of the student is uncertain. But, as Idol et al. (1995) suggest, failure to achieve results should be interpreted as a procedural or system failure, not as a failure due to inherent deficits of the learner.

Evaluation also provides an opportunity for consultant and consultee to examine the social validity of the outcome(s) of the consultation process (Ehly & Macmann, 1994). Stated another way, the consultant and consultee should evaluate whether the plan as implemented was acceptable, or judged to be "likeable" to all parties involved (e.g., the consultee and the client). Thus, determination may be made regarding future acceptability or necessary changes for future consultation efforts.

## Barriers to Consultation

Institutional and personal barriers may exist that preclude the wholesale adoption of a consultation model (Gutkin & Hickman, 1990; Idol-Maestas & Ritter, 1985; Nevin, Thousand, Paolucci-Whitcomb, & Villa, 1990; West, 1988). Consultants must be aware of these barriers and be willing to continue their efforts despite them.

Johnson et al. (1988), for example, indicate that two types of barriers affect consultation programs: programmatic and conceptual. Programmatic barriers include lack of time, overextended case loads, and lack of administrative support. Conceptual barriers include lack of credibility of the consultant, a mismatch in thinking and problem-solving ability between the consultant and the consultee, a misguided hierarchical relationship, knowledge base differences between the consultant and the consultee, and attitude of the consultee (Johnson et al., 1988; Nevin, Thousand, & Villa, 1993; West, 1988). Gutkin and Hickman (1990) state that consultee resistance can be affected by consultant-consultee characteristics (e.g., negative attitude, prior consultation experience, problem-solving skills) and factors associated with the school itself (climate, time of consultation, principal's attitude). Further, lack of standardization of consultation, inadequate consultant or consultee training, inacceptability of consultation, or a counterproductive relationship between consultant and consultee may constitute a barrier to consultation (Kratochwill & Van Someren, 1995; Thomas, Gatz, & Luczak, 1997). Consultative incompatibility, described as occurring when a consultant and consultee disagree on the grounds of theoretical perspectives or instructional orientation, is a potential barrier (Lopez, Dalal, & Yoshida, 1993; de Mesquita & Zollman, 1995). Kratochwill, Sladeczek, and Plunge (1995) add that organizational characteristics, such as the building climate, the attitude and behavior of principals, classroom structures, and time allotted for consultation are all factors that affect the consultation process.

Fine (1990) suggests—based on his professional experience and his synthesis of the literature—that a constellation of school and home factors affects consultation. He points out that teachers may question parental competence or involvement, or they may not be prepared to individualize programs. Further, the ritualized processes of teacher conferences may impede parental compliance, or administrators may not encourage parental participation. Parents may be uncomfortable discussing their child's problem because of their own history with schools. The seemingly technical complexity of schools, cultural factors, and the day-to-day demands of parenting may restrict consultation.

Nevin et al. (1990) categorize potential barriers to effective consultation as lack of time, training, planning, common knowledge, ownership, and funding, as well as too large of a caseload for the consultant. Gutkin and Hickman (1990) conducted an empirical analysis of consultant, consultee, and organizational factors associated with impeding consultation. After delivering direct, indirect, and organizational consultation services for 14 weeks, 23 school psychologists were provided with two questionnaires for each of the cases they handled. A case description survey asked them to rate their perception of the cases, while an outcome questionnaire assessed their perception of consultation resistance. Results showed that their perception was influenced by the interactions of consultant, consultee, and organizational factors. Of these three, the consultee factors were considered the most influential in forming their perception. Gutkin and Hickman caution against overextending the results of this study due to the low experience level of the consultants and the subjective nature of the rating scales used in the data collection.

## Overcoming Barriers

It is beyond the scope of this chapter to be prescriptive with respect to overcoming every individual or institutional constraint that may affect consultation processes and outcomes. Reisberg and Wolf (1988), however, offer a guide for considering and selecting among potentially effective interventions. In their opinion, consultant and consultee selection should be based on four principles: (a) generalization (coordinated programming across settings), (b) generalized benefit (increased likelihood of the intervention affecting other students), (c) data-based decisions (use of objective data for decision making), and (d) parsimony (using the simplest, most powerful, but least intrusive method).

See Illback, Zins, & Maher (1999) for suggestions on how barriers and institutional resistance may be overcome.

Pedron and Evans (1990) hypothesize that consultee resistance can be overcome when interventions are directed at the consultee's appropriate "stage of concern." According to them, the stages of concern are hierarchical and include awareness, informational, personal, management, consequence, collaborative, and refocusing levels. Consultee resistance is diminished when the consultant directs interventions to the appropriate consultee stage. If the intervention is not stage appropriate, resistance will intensify. Pedron and Evans use a questionnaire format to determine the consultee's stage of concern. Perhaps Margolis (1991) sums up the situation regarding resistance to any educational change, including the use of consultation, when he states:

For further discussion of types of resistance and strategies to deal with resistance, see Chapter 4.

> It is true that change, even minor change, is difficult, and resistance is virtually inevitable. Resistance, however, is usually neither irrational nor the product of personal maliciousness. From the resistant teacher's perspective, maintaining the status quo makes perfect sense. . . . The key to overcoming resistance and securing cooperation is understanding and responding to both the structural and personal factors fueling resistance. Often,

this requires movement from a general to a specific perspective, and the up-front, influential participation in decision making of those responsible for implementation. (p. 7)

Based on the outcomes of consultation efforts at two contrasting sites, Thomas, Gatz, and Luczak (1997) outline three suggestions for overcoming barriers. First, consultants should conduct thorough assessments during the entry stage and consider their findings carefully. Difficulties at this step are likely to affect subsequent efforts. Second, consultants should become aware of ecological factors that may make implementation difficult or even impossible. At the same time, they need to realize that not all contextual demands can be met. Finally, university-based consultants should engage in school-based consultation efforts more frequently.

# Conclusion

Consultation is essentially a collaborative, interactive, mutual, reciprocal, and voluntary process that leads to the prevention and solution of problems. Each party brings to the consultation process particular expertise, and a skilled consultant capitalizes on the knowledge and experiences of those with whom she or he confers to ensure that the planned intervention is designed jointly and has the widest possible support.

While there are a number of consultation models available, the mental health, organizational and systems, behavioral, and collaborative models are used most frequently in school-based applications. Each of these models has applicability depending upon the type of problem to be addressed, the target of the intervention (individual or group), and the technical expertise of the consultant.

Clearly, there are individual and institutional constraints that reduce the probability of successful consultation programs. However, when consultants apply coordinated, systematic programs using data-based technology, their chances of achieving effective outcomes improve.

# Summary of Key Points

## Definitions of Consultation

1. Consultation has several definitions, varying in substance and context depending upon the setting, the target, and the intervention employed. At its core, consultation can be characterized as a voluntary, reciprocal, interactive, and mutual process that leads to the prevention and resolution of identified problems.

2. Collaborative consultation is characterized by voluntary, mutual, and interactive engagements between the consultant and the consultee. The outcome produced by joint planning is likely to be different from an outcome that might be produced by independent planning.

3. A collaborative relationship connotes parity, reciprocity, mutual problem solving, and shared resources, responsibility, and accountability.

4. A cooperative relationship is one in which independent agents (e.g., a preschool teacher and a special education teacher) work autonomously to improve their separate instructional methods for the benefit of a shared student.

5. School-based consultation occurs when psychological or educational services are shared between the consultant and the consultee using a collaborative, reciprocal, and systematic problem-solving process.

## Goals of Consultation

6. Consultation has basically two major goals: to provide remediation or resolutions for problems presented by clients, and to prevent future problems from occurring by improving the skills of consultees.

## Consultation Processes and Perspectives

7. The consultation process describes the relationship among the consultant, the consultee, and the client and the stages they encounter from the onset to the termination of consultation. Nine stages have been identified that represent this process: preentry, entry, gathering information, defining the problem, identifying and selecting alternative solutions, stating objectives, implementing the plan, evaluating the plan, and terminating consultation.

8. Resistance to the consultation process may be reduced when the consultant shares the responsibility for problem solving, encourages active participation by consultees, views the teacher as an expert, communicates that recommendations may be accepted or rejected, has a formal role in the school, and employs situational leadership skills effectively.

9. Critical skills that a consultant should possess include an ample knowledge base and the ability to: distribute leadership among participants, manage controversy positively, communicate without using technical jargon, maintain sensitivity to multicultural issues, communicate effectively orally and in writing, and provide positive feedback.

10. The process of consultation includes both scientific and artistic components.

11. At least five perspectives on consultation can be considered to gain a view of its past and future. These include perspectives on history, statewide adoption policies, training, early childhood and transition programs, and research.

## Consultation Models

12. Ten consultation models can be identified in the literature, but four are used most frequently: mental health, organizational, behavioral, and collaborative consultation.

13. The mental health model is designed to encourage the consultee to solve his or her own problems independently. The consultant plays down his or her contributions.

14. The organizational consultation model is derived from human relations, organization, and systems theory and assumes that symbiotic relationships between all individuals involved in the organization must be taken into account for problem resolution. The consultant's role is to guide the process for systemic change.

15. In the behavioral model, the emphasis for change evolves around functional relations occurring between behavior and the environment. Consultation occurs within four stages: problem identification, problem analysis, plan implementation, and plan evaluation.

16. The collaborative consultation model is a linear sequence that portrays the relationships among the consultant, the consultee or mediator, and the target. The relationship between the consultant and the mediator forms the basis for collaborative consultation. Any professional in the field can serve as the consultant.

17. The four principles that form the basis of the triadic model, a form of collaborative consultation, are: team ownership, recognition of individual differences, application of reinforcement, and data-based evaluation.

## Barriers to Consultation

18. Two types of barriers affect consultation programs: programmatic and conceptual. Programmatic barriers include lack of time, overextended case loads, and lack of administrative support. Conceptual barriers include lack of consultant credibility, different problem-solving skills and knowledge levels of consultant and consultee, and the receptivity of the consultee to the process.

19. A constellation of home and school factors can affect consultation processes and outcomes.

## Overcoming Barriers

20. Individual or institutional constraints that may affect consultation processes and outcomes can be overcome when consultants and consultees select interventions based on the (a) generalization principle, (b) generalized benefit principle, (c) data-based principle, and (d) principle of parsimony.

# Questions

1. Define the term consultation and state its key components.

2. What are the two global goals of consultation?

3. Name at least five skills that a consultant should possess.

4. The consultation process has at least nine stages. Outline these stages and indicate what is to be accomplished at each stage.

5. What factors have aided the movement of consultation from a reactive approach to a proactive approach?

6. Why do you believe states seem reluctant to provide policies and leadership with respect to establishing statewide consultation programs?

7. Differentiate between how consultation training might be conducted for preservice trainees and how it might be conducted for inservice professionals.

8. Why are consultation approaches important for students within early childhood or transition programs?

9. What do the data show with respect to the effectiveness of consultation?

10. Describe the three major consultation models outlined in the text. Compare and contrast them.

11. In what ways are the four principles of collaborative consultation implicit in other models?

12. Identify three barriers to effective consultation in schools and state an alternative for overcoming each.

13. What elements should be analyzed when choosing a consultation model?

14. What strategies should an external consultant use to establish entry?

# Discussion Points and Exercises

1. Conduct a meeting with teachers at the elementary, junior high, and senior high levels. Determine their views on the consultation process. Compare their perception of the consultation process with the stages presented in this chapter. Identify the "models" they use to prevent or solve problems.

2. Using any of the four major consultation models presented in the chapter, conduct a pilot study within your own district or region to determine the usefulness of the model. Evaluate your results.

3. Identify a classroom-related problem. Apply the behavioral model. Evaluate whether the model provides sufficient direction for school consultation and is effective at addressing the identified challenge.

4. Identify a "barrier to consultation" in your district. Apply Reisberg and Wolf's guidelines for selecting among potentially effective interventions with respect to overcoming the barrier.

5. Establish a consultation training program for the teachers or parents in your district. Identify the objectives, develop the training components, and evaluate the results. Share your data with administrators.

# Litigation and Legislation: Why and How They Affect Consultation

2

Educational services that children and youth with disabilities presently receive are, in part, a direct result of the reciprocal effect of litigative and legislative action. Decisions rendered by courts and federal laws enacted by Congress, recently and in the past, have greatly influenced the structure and operation of our nation's schools (Margolis, 1998; Yell, Rogers, & Rogers, 1998; Zins & Heron, 1996). For example, in the past, laws concerning the treatment of individuals with disabilities were permissive. That is, educational service for a school-aged child may or may not have been offered. The state department of education or the local school district had complete discretionary power. More often than not, services for students with special needs were not provided, or at best, were inadequate, unequal, and discriminatory (Yell et al., 1998).

For a review of the legal history of special education, refer to Yell, Rogers, and Rogers (1998).

With the enactment of recent legislation—especially P.L. 105-17, referred to as the Individuals with Disabilities Education Act (IDEA) Amendments of 1997—and judicial rulings, educational services and the requirements for those services for preschool and school-aged children have been mandated and expanded. Legislation, often spurred by litigation, has changed the way services are provided for children and youth with disabilities in this country.

Seeking recourse through the courts or Congress represents an important change in the way educational services are typically secured. No longer can local school districts or state departments of education arbitrarily exclude children with disabilities from receiving an appropriate education. To the contrary, local districts must follow specific procedures to identify and serve individuals with disabilities in the least restrictive environment, and those procedures are delineated in the federal statutes and regulations and within corresponding state codes. Margolis (1998), speaking about a consultant's role with respect to knowing relevant procedures and keeping up to date, correctly points out:

> It is essential to understand the concepts and directives . . . with the IDEA Amendments of 1997, case law, and related laws and ensure a high standard of professional practice. Because . . . new case law continues to be made, [consultants] are encouraged to study their state code; the IDEA Amendments of 1997 and related federal laws . . . ; the relevant federal codes . . . and Individuals with Disabilities Education Law Report . . . and other pertinent legal information. . . .Together with case law and state codes, this information defines and governs the nature of special education at the macro and micro levels. (p. 249)

The purpose of this chapter is to define *litigation* and *legislation* and to establish their importance in the consultation process. The implications that these court rulings and federal and state laws have for consultants are addressed, especially as they relate to thorny issues associated with eligibility, free and appropriate public education, least restrictive environment, least restrictive alternatives, and best practice. After reading the chapter, consultants working with special and general education teachers should be aware of key issues regarding the right to education and how that right affects their relationships with teachers, administrators, parents, students, and the family as a whole.

## Objectives

After reading this chapter, the reader will be able to:

1. define the term litigation;
2. cite the effects of litigation, especially class-action litigation, on future litigation;
3. define the term legislation;
4. cite three important lawsuits concerning the right to education and discuss why they are important;
5. discuss the meaning and trend of educational opportunity in the United States;
6. discuss the relevance of Section 504 of the Rehabilitation Act of 1973 to the right of education for individuals with disabilities;
7. define the major provisions of P.L. 94-142, P.L. 99-457, P.L. 101-476, and P.L. 105-17 (IDEA '97);
8. distinguish between the terms substantive due process and procedural due process;
9. discuss three components of a free appropriate educational program;
10. cite four lawsuits pertinent to the assurance of a free appropriate education for students with disabilities;
11. define the term appropriate in the context of educational programming;
12. indicate the components of a due process hearing;
13. compare the Daubert, portability, inclusion, and balancing standards as they apply to placement decisions;
14. discuss how guns, violence, drugs, and special health care cases have affected the scope of consultant activities;
15. define the terms manifestation determination and interim alternative education setting and state how they are used in the context of students with disciplinary challenges;
16. identify several methods of funding educational programs for students with disabilities;
17. list five implications for consultants with respect to litigation and legislation.

# Key Terms

litigation

case law

class action suit

litigative decisions

consent decrees

judicial opinions

legislation

rules and regulations

right to education

Section 504

IDEA '97

Individualized Education
    Program (IEP)

Individualized Family Services
    Plan (IFSP)

due process

substantive due process

procedural due process

appropriate education

nondiscriminatory evaluation

Daubert standard

impartial hearing process

portability standard

inclusion standard

balancing standard

positive behavioral support

manifestation determination
    evaluation

interim alternative educational
    setting

# Definition of Litigation

*Litigation,* or *case law,* refers to the act or process of bringing a court suit against another party for the purpose of redressing an alleged injustice. Suits bring a plaintiff and a defendant before a judge or a panel of judges. The judge, or panel, is empowered to decide upon the merits of a case based on present facts, past precedents, and legislative intent. Court rulings have influence based on the level at which the case is heard. The higher the level, the more impact. Prasse (1990) makes this point:

In the federal court system, three levels exist: U.S. District Court, U.S. Court of Appeals, and the U.S. Supreme Court. State court systems may use circuit courts, appellate courts, and the state supreme court (Prasse, 1990).

> The potential impact of case law is thus twofold. First, the jurisdiction of the court (where it is in the hierarchy) determines the influence of a decision. Second is the influence established through a series of decisions which when taken together establish a clear and unequivocal historical trend, pattern, or precedent. (p. 472)

According to Ysseldyke and Algozzine (1982), special education litigation has had two foci: (a) correcting the denial of opportunity for education and (b) correcting the failure to provide an appropriate educational experience.

Litigative suits can be filed by individual citizens on their own behalf, or by individuals on behalf of themselves and others in similar circumstances. The latter is referred to as a *class action suit.* Many court cases heard in the 1960s and 1970s were class action suits aimed at addressing the right to education for class members, the plaintiffs in the suit. More recent court cases, however, have focused on specific questions of that right (e.g., What constitutes an appropriate education? Can students with disabilities be expelled from school for longer than 10 days? Are school personnel required to catheterize students?). Brady, McDougall, and Dennis (1989) summarize right-to-treatment court rulings by stating:

> In many of the right-to-treatment cases of the 1970s, class action suits were common. Given the nature of the substantial issues involving integration,

courts seem increasingly reluctant to issue "group" decisions. We believe this tendency towards individual litigation reflects (a) a lessened need to effect substantial social change and (b) a heightened need to refine educational concepts and practice. (p. 54)

## Class Action Litigation

There have been many class action suits involving individuals with disabilities. For example, *Pennsylvania Association for Retarded Children v. Commonwealth of Pennsylvania* (1972); *Mills v. Board of Education* (1972); *Maryland Association for Retarded Children v. State of Maryland* (1974); and *José P. v. Ambach* (1979, 1983) were class action suits brought before the court by one or several individuals on behalf of themselves and other individuals with a similar situation. No specified number of plaintiffs is required to initiate a class action suit (*Stoner v. Miller,* 1974). The Federal Rules of Civil Procedure (28 USC.A.) lists the following requirements for filing class action suits: (a) there are too many members to have codefendants or co-plaintiffs in an individual suit; (b) there are questions of law or fact common to the class; (c) the claims of the defense of the representative parties are typical of the claims of the defenses of the class; and (d) the representative parties will fairly and adequately protect the interest of the class.

### Advantages of Class Action Suits

Compared to individual lawsuits, class action suits are economical. That is, if an individual or small group succeeds in persuading the court, a much larger group benefits from the action. Likewise, the court's calendar is not consumed with cases having essentially the same grievance. For example, suppose a class action suit is filed for an individual with mental retardation on behalf of all people with mental retardation, alleging that a free and appropriate public education has been denied. If the court agrees with the plaintiff, a decision would be rendered that would affect not only the plaintiff, but also the total population of individuals with mental retardation specified in the suit. Even if a class action suit is lost, future cases might not need to be filed if public policymakers and legislators take steps to correct the pertinent injustice through legislation. Precisely such a situation occurred when the U.S. Supreme Court ruled on *Smith v. Robinson* (1984), a decision, in part, that denied reimbursement of attorney fees to parents even though the parents' claim was upheld by the Court. In denying the payment of attorney fees, the Court stated that P.L. 94-142 did not specify that attorney fees should be paid. Congress disagreed with the Court's interpretation of its original legislative intent. Consequently, in 1986, Congress passed P.L. 99-352, The Handicapped Children's Protection Act, reversing by legislation a previous court ruling (Osborne, 1988). Congress's implied legislative plan for attorney fees to be paid, although not spelled out in detail in P.L. 94-142, ultimately was reaffirmed in P.L. 99-352, despite an opposite court ruling.

### A Disadvantage of Class Action Suits

A distinct disadvantage of the class action suit occurs when the individual or group fails to achieve a favorable court decision. The ability of other individuals or groups similarly situated to file suits, individually or collectively, might be compromised. As Abeson (1976) indicates, litigated cases are lost despite the presence of competent attorneys and "what seems the most noble of causes" (p. 241).

## Main Effects of Litigation

As Turnbull and Turnbull (1978) indicate, litigation has been the primary, but not exclusive, method used to establish and maintain the educational rights of exceptional children and youth. *Litigative decisions, consent decrees,* and *judicial opinions* are three major methods that courts use to provide interpretations of legislation. Litigative decisions are rulings that result from fully tried cases. Consent decrees are agreements between or among parties based on negotiations. Consent decrees do not represent judicial decisions resulting from a fully litigated case. Rather, a consent decree represents a compromise achieved outside of the court. It has the same effect as a fully litigated case, however, and can serve as a legal precedent for future cases. The PARC decision (*Pennsylvania Association for Retarded Children v. Commonwealth of Pennsylvania,* 1972), a class action suit representing school-age mentally retarded children of the Commonwealth of Pennsylvania, was resolved with a consent decree. A judicial opinion is rendered when the court interprets the meaning of a particular legislative issue (e.g., What constitutes an appropriate education?).

Whether the case is fully litigated, resolved by means of a consent decree, or ruled on through a judicial opinion, the net effect for the plaintiff is similar. If a favorable decision is rendered, the case is won. If an unfavorable decision is obtained, the plaintiff's grievance will probably continue. Further, precedent for future litigation or legislation often results from rulings issued under any of these options.

Reschly (1989) identifies the main types of legal influence that affect special needs students:

- reciprocal influence (litigation affects legislation and vice versa);

- dynamic and evolutionary (court rulings are not static; reinterpretations occur);

- relative and ambiguous (interpretations of the principles of law can be broad statements issued in the context of the sociopolitical time);

- different levels of implementation (practice varies from surface to full-scale compliance); and

- compliance through professional standards and best practice (professional organizations generate codes of conduct or best-practice procedures regarding professional and ethical behavior).

With respect to rulings at the school district level, litigation can also have the effect of changing identification, implementation, evaluation, and compliance procedures, as in *Diana v. the State of California* (1970); *Wyatt v. Stickney* (1972); *Armstrong v. Kline* (1979); and *José P. v. Ambach* (1979), respectively. Cases such as those fundamentally changed how teachers, administrators, and parents advance the instructional program for students with special needs. In *José P. v. Ambach,* the court showed that it sets a high standard for obedience and is not satisfied with programs that appear to meet the spirit, but not the letter, of the law. In *José P.* a suit was brought against the State Department of

Education of New York alleging that timely compliance with the full range of IEP procedures did not occur. The plaintiffs claimed that special education students were not being evaluated and that access to specialized instruction and related and mainstreamed services was being denied. Under a court order, Committees of the Handicapped (COH) and School-Based Support Teams (SBST) were formed to alleviate the delays in complying with IEP procedures. Also, annual census taking, regular meetings with personnel, and the designation of a placement officer were ordered by the court. After years of complying with these demands, and claiming that the number of students awaiting IEP evaluation and placement had been reduced substantially, the district sought relief from the court order. However, the judge denied a request to vacate (modify) his former judgment. Instead, he ordered still more areas to be addressed. Ultimately, the district agreed (a) to hire 600 new clerical staff and 600 new teachers, (b) to create a computerized system to track IEP programs, and (c) to complete 51,000 overdue evaluations (Fafard, Hanlon, & Bryson, 1986).

## Other Effects of Litigation

Although a court may render a decision in favor of students with disabilities, increased services are not automatically provided as a result. The defendants have the right to appeal, and even if their appeal is lost, they are not immediately compelled to comply with the court order. The implementation of several decisions has been delayed because defendants failed to comply with the court mandates (Turnbull & Turnbull, 1978). An important case in the field of special education that illustrates this point is *Mills v. Board of Education* (1972).

*Mills v. Board of Education* (1972) was a class action suit filed by the parents of seven students with developmental disabilities against the District of Columbia Board of Education, Department of Human Resources, and mayor for failure to provide all children with a public education. The court ruled in favor of the parents and issued a court order on December 20, 1971, stating that by January 3, 1972, all plaintiffs must be provided with a publicly supported education. The defendants failed to comply, and further action by the plaintiffs was required. The defendants claimed, in response to this later action, that they were unable to comply with the court order due to insufficient funds. The court did not find that to be an adequate defense. The following court response resulted:

> The District of Columbia's interest in educating the excluded children clearly must outweigh its interest in preserving its financial resources. If sufficient funds are not available to finance all of the services and programs that are needed and desirable in the system, then the available funds must be expended equitably in such a manner that no child is entirely excluded from a publicly supported education consistent with his needs and ability to benefit therefrom. The inadequacies of the District of Columbia public school system, whether occasioned by insufficient funding or administrative inefficiency, certainly cannot be permitted to bear more heavily on the "exceptional" or handicapped child than on the normal child (*Mills v. Board of Education,* 1972, p. 856).

Although the court ruled in favor of the parents in the first action, provision of services did not result until further litigative action had been sought by the plaintiffs. The reader is referred to Turnbull and Turnbull (1978) for a full discussion of options available to plaintiffs in cases in which court mandates have been ignored and noncompliance with critical elements of the court order has occurred.

# Definition of Legislation

*Legislation* refers to the act or process whereby elected representatives embody within a single document law that becomes applicable to the general public. The intent of a federal or state statute is to serve the common good: the greatest majority of the citizens. Whereas litigative action is an attempt to solve a specific problem through a court remedy, legislative action is designed to solve broader societal problems. Bersoff (1979) sums up the distinction between these two avenues of social change:

> Courts develop rules of conduct in piecemeal fashion and only after litigants have presented legally cognizable issues. Rulemaking bodies such as legislatures and government agencies, on the other hand, need not wait for complaining litigants. When, among other reasons, problems need a broader solution than courts can provide, or they affect many people, lawmakers enact statutes and administrators promulgate regulations that have comprehensive effects. (p. 77)

According to Prasse (1990), legislation can take one of two forms: program legislation or civil rights legislation. With program legislation—such as P.L. 94-142—Congress approves and/or appropriates money to fund the provisions of the statute. Also, the Department of Education becomes responsible for monitoring the implementation of educational legislation. Civil rights legislation, on the other hand, may not have funding levels prescribed, and its provisions address more fundamental rights. The Department of Justice monitors compliance with civil rights legislation. The Rehabilitation Act of 1973 and the Americans with Disabilities Act of 1990 are examples of civil rights legislation.

A legislative process has been devised that encourages public participation during the draft stages of the bill. One process that a bill—a draft of proposed legislation—might follow before it is enacted into law is shown in Figure 2.1.

Figure 2.1 illustrates that before a bill is enacted into law, its specific provisions are examined by subcommittees, committees, and finally the House of Representatives. At any of those stages, the bill is subject to amendments prompted by citizens' groups, lobbyists, congressional representatives, and the bill's sponsors. Conference committees are established to resolve discrepancies between House and Senate versions of a bill. At the federal level, the president can veto a bill, and the Congress can override the veto.

After any federal law is passed, proposed *rules and regulations* are published. These are statements proposing how that law will be implemented and interpreted. Definitions for key terms in the law are provided as well as regulations for implementing the law. The general public is informed of proposed rule changes through the *Federal Register,* a daily publication of the United States government, and public responses to proposed rules are solicited for several months. After reviewing and commenting upon oral and written testimony, the government office responsible for the legislation publishes the final rules and regulations relative to the statute.

Often when federal legislation is enacted, state law is also changed—via so-called companion legislation—to conform to the new federal law. However,

An opportunity for public participation also occurs during the rule-making process, the stage that takes place after a bill has been enacted into law. This opportunity is significant because the rules and regulations ultimately delineate the procedural steps for implementation.

Final rules for IDEA '97 were published in the *Federal Register* on March 12, 1999.

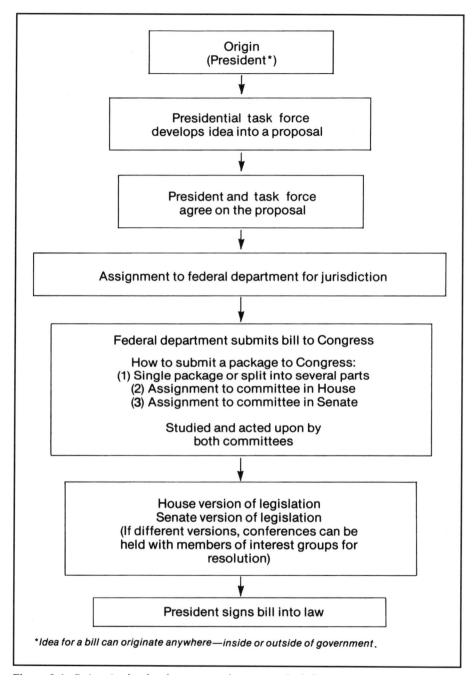

**Figure 2.1.** Points in the development and passage of a bill.

the enactment of legislation does not always guarantee that compliance will occur. Implementation is greatly dependent on the publication of clear regulations that specify the consequences for noncompliance.

From an educational perspective it is clear that litigative decisions and federal and state statutes have the potential to affect the population and nature of consultation services. For example, children with mental retardation, who prior to the PARC decision were excluded from attending school, currently receive a free appropriate public education. Teachers instructing those children gain and presumably will continue to benefit from direct or indirect consultation services.

Legislation pertinent to the right to education and, more broadly, to the equal protection of the disabled can be found in a number of federal statutes (see Table 2.1). As noted earlier, previous legislation regarding education was primarily permissive; that is, states could provide educational services if they so desired. Legislation between the 1970s and 1990s, especially P.L. 94-142, P.L. 99-457, and P.L. 101-476, have mandated the education of all children with disabilities, including preschoolers. The enactment of mandatory legislation could be viewed as a reflection of the changing societal approach to provide comprehensive services for exceptional individuals.

# The Right to Education

Many view the *right to education* movement for individuals with disabilities as part of the trend to increase the civil rights of all minority groups. A number of major court decisions have been rendered over the last 20 years that have greatly influenced the type, variety, and duration of services to students with disabilities.

The following section will briefly cite litigative and legislative actions pertinent to the right to education, the principle stating that all children are entitled to receive free appropriate public education. Some of the resulting benefits will be discussed. This discussion of specific laws or court decisions is not intended to be exhaustive. Landmark court cases and legislation relevant to the right to education for individuals with disabilities will be presented. In our opinion, these litigative and legislative actions have had a significant impact upon the quantity and quality of educational services provided to exceptional individuals. Consultants who are well grounded in these cases and laws will have an enhanced understanding of their roles and functions within the school and how those roles and functions were determined.

## *Brown v. Board of Education* (1954)

The classic case of separate but equal educational opportunity was tested in *Brown v. Board of Education* (1954). This litigation was a class action suit, representing all African American children of school age in Topeka, Kansas.

Essentially, the case focused on the legality of separate but equal educational opportunity. The plaintiffs contested that their rights under the equal protection clause of the Fourteenth Amendment, Section 1 (i.e., "nor deny to any person within its jurisdiction the equal protection of the laws") were violated. Equal protection, according to Weintraub and Abeson (1974), means that whatever action is taken with some individuals must be taken with all individuals on equal terms. Supreme Court Justice Earl Warren, ruling on the Brown case, stated that separate educational facilities are inherently unequal. In addition, Justice Warren stated, "It is doubtful that any child may reasonably be expected to succeed in life if he is denied the opportunity of an education" (*Brown v. Board of Education,* 1954, p. 493).

Justice Warren's statement had a great impact upon the education of exceptional persons, because in the past there had been legal precedent for excluding

**Table 2.1**

Federal Legislation Pertinent to the Education of Individuals with Disabilities

| Title | Comments |
|---|---|
| Title 1, Elementary and Secondary Education Act of 1965, P.L. 89-10. | In light of the special educational needs of children of low-income families, the act provides federal assistance to local education agencies for the improvement of educational programs in low-income areas. |
| National Technical Institute for the Deaf Act of 1965, P.L. 89-36. | This act provides for the construction and operation of a residential institution for post-secondary technical training and education for deaf individuals. The goal of education is to prepare deaf individuals for successful employment. |
| Vocational Education Amendments of 1968 (Title 1, Vocational Education), P.L. 90-576. | This act stipulates that 10% of vocational education funds are to be spent for individuals with disabilities. |
| Developmental Disabilities Services and Facilities Construction Amendments of 1970, P.L. 91-517. | This act amends the Mental Retardation Facilities and Community Health Centers Construction Act of 1963 (P.L. 88-164). It provides for assistance to states to furnish comprehensive services to people affected by mental retardation and other developmental disabilities originating in childhood. |
| Higher Education Amendments of 1972, P.L. 92-328. | This act provides for grants and contracts with institutions of higher education to assist youth with academic potential who are from low-income families and may lack adequate secondary school preparation or may be physically disabled. |
| The Economic Opportunity Act Amendments of 1972, P.L. 92-424. | This act affects preschool services (e.g., it makes enrollment in Head Start available to children with disabilities). |
| The Rehabilitation Act of 1973, P.L. 93-112. | This act replaces all Vocational Rehabilitation Act Amendments since P.L. 66-236. It provides for an individualized written rehabilitation program for each individual with disabilities (similar to the IEP required in P.L. 94-142). |
| The Education of the Handicapped Act of 1970, P.L. 91-230. | This act extends the powers of the Bureau for the Education of the Handicapped. It provides authorization to disburse funds for training and research. |
| Title III, Elementary and Secondary Education Act of 1965 (P.L. 89-10) as amended by P.L. 93-380 (1974), Educational Amendments of 1974. Education of the Gifted and Talented, P.L. 93-380, Title IV, Section 404. | This act provides funding for supplementary educational programs, including programs for children with disabilities. P.L. 93-380 provides for the establishment of an administrative unit with the Office of Education to coordinate programs and activities related to the gifted and talented as well as a national clearinghouse to collect and disseminate relevant data. |
| The Developmentally Disabled Assistance and Bill of Rights Act of 1974, P.L. 94-103. | This act amended P.L. 91-517. Changes made include the following: The definition of the term *developmental disability* was broadened |

*(continues)*

**Table 2.1**  (*Continued*)

| Title | Comments |
|-------|----------|
| | to include autism and dyslexia; however, people with the latter must also suffer from mental retardation, cerebral palsy, or autism; all developmental disabilities grantees must take affirmative action to employ and advance qualified persons with disabilities; a comprehensive performance-based system for evaluation of services must be provided. |
| The Education of All Handicapped Children Act of 1975, P.L. 94-142. | This act, now named the Individuals with Disabilities Act, contains the major financial support mechanism and represents the essential educational rights guarantees for individuals with disabilities. |
| Amendments to the Education of All Handicapped Children Act of 1983 (P.L. 98-199). | These amendments extended many of the provisions of P.L. 94-142, including permission for states to use incentive funds to serve preschool children less than 3 years of age; required census data on exceptional students exiting programs; and the development of transition programs. |
| Handicapped Children Protection Act (P.L. 99-372). | This act provided for the awarding of attorney fees to parents who prevail in court. |
| The Education of the Handicapped Amendments of 1986 (P.L. 99-467). | This legislation extended rights and protections of P.L. 94-142 to all students from birth to 5 and their families. Contains infant and preschool components with differential funding. An Individual Family Services Plan (IFSP) is prescribed by the law. |
| Americans with Disabilities Act of 1990 (P.L. 101-336). | This is civil rights legislation aimed at protecting the rights of people with disabilities in the private sector. |
| Education of the Handicapped Act Amendments of 1990 (P.L. 101-476). | Aside from renaming previous Education of the Handicapped Acts as the Individuals with Disabilities Act, this act adds two categories of disability (autism and brain injury). It also provides for the specification of transition services on the IEP and upgrades related services to include rehabilitation counseling and social work services. |
| The Individuals with Disabilities Education Act of 1997 (IDEA '97) | This act contains comprehensive reauthorization of P.L. 101-476. Among the many provisions cited in this reauthorization are statements that relate to students without disabilities, general education teacher involvement in the IEP process, and processes for addressing the discipline of students with disabilities. |

*Note.* The reader is referred to Ballard (1976), La Vor (1976), Ysseldyke and Algozzine (1982), and Turnbull (1986). The final rules for IDEA '97 can be accessed through several sources, including the *Federal Register* and the U.S. Department of Education Web site: www.ed.gov/offices/OSERS/IDEA/regs.html.

students with disabilities from educational instruction (Daniel, 1997; Yell et al., 1998). For example, the Wisconsin Supreme Court in the case of *State ex rel Beattie v. Board of Education of City of Antigo (Wis.)* (1919) upheld the decision that a child's cerebral palsied condition "was harmful to the best interests of the school" (p. 154). The major argument presented by the Board of Education was that such a condition produced "a depressing and nauseating effect on the teachers and school children and that he [the student] required an undue portion of the teacher's time" (p. 154).

The *Brown v. Board of Education* (1954) case served as the catalyst for providing equal educational opportunity for students with disabilities. It also laid the foundation for the eventual reduction of self-contained classrooms for placement of these students.

## Pennsylvania Association for Retarded Children v. Commonwealth of Pennsylvania (1972)

The exclusion of individuals with developmental disabilities from educational opportunity was challenged directly in the PARC case, a class action suit representing school-age children with mental retardation in the Commonwealth of Pennsylvania.

The right of this population to a free public education was argued on several grounds, including the equal protection clause of the Fourteenth Amendment. Essentially, Pennsylvania law at that time stated that a proper education should be provided for all children with disabilities. However, the law also stated that children who were uneducable and untrainable, and who had not yet attained a mental age of 5 years, could be excluded from the public schools (Gilhool, 1973). The plaintiffs used two primary arguments in their case. One argument was based on the legal decision rendered in *Brown v. Board of Education*. The second was based on the testimony of expert witnesses who stated that individuals with disabilities could benefit from an education.

Importantly, in the PARC case expert witnesses challenged the historical arguments for exclusion or segregation of children with disabilities from public education. Kubetz (1972) summarizes those historical arguments as follows: (a) individuals with retardation could not profit from instruction; (b) such students would cause harm to the welfare of other students; and (c) instruction of such individuals, if attempted, would be impractical.

Expert witnesses countered those arguments by testifying that systematic education programs for children with retardation would produce learning, and also that education could not be defined solely in terms of academic gains. Rather, they said, "Education must be seen as a continuous process by which individuals learn to cope and function within their environment. Thus, for children to learn to clothe and feed themselves is a legitimate outcome achievable through an educational program" (Weintraub & Abeson, 1974, p. 527). This statement of educational goals, developed by experts in the PARC case, should be considered in light of the meaning of equal educational opportunity (Yell et al., 1998).

Weintraub and Abeson (1974) trace the evolution of the meaning of equal educational opportunity in this country. Initially, as a populist concept, equal education opportunity meant equal access to resources and equal opportunity to meet common objectives. In other words, the resources were the same, the goals were the same, and everyone had equal access to goals. Each student went through the same educational program to achieve his or her educational goal—for example, to master the skills to achieve a high school diploma. In the 1960s the concept was changed to mean equal access to differing resources to meet common objectives. For everyone to master the skills necessary to achieve a high school diploma, students would not necessarily go through the same educational program. Rather, those who needed it would receive additional remedial assistance. Finally, in the 1970s and 1980s, the meaning changed once again. Now, educational opportunity means equal access to differing resources for the attainment of different objectives. In other words, not only educational services may differ depending on needs, but also the goals of education may not be the same for all students. One need not receive educational services only to achieve a high school diploma; it is also legitimate to receive educational services to learn to clothe and feed oneself.

Thus, the major impact of the PARC case on the education of children with disabilities is illustrated by noting the revised definitions of educational opportunity. As Reynolds and Rosen (1976) point out, in the PARC case the court clearly indicated that the enhancement of individual development, rather than the potential return to society, is the critical objective of education.

## Timothy W. v. Rochester School District (1988)

The right to education, codified in P.L. 94-142 and reaffirmed by P.L. 105-17 and several court cases, was challenged by a court ruling in the state of New Hampshire in 1988. In the *Timothy W.* case, a lower court judge ruled that a 13-year-old student was not eligible to receive services under P.L. 94-142 because he did not "benefit" from the educational experience. The lower court judge misapplied a previous Supreme Court ruling (*Board of Education v. Rowley,* 1982) and disregarded congressional intent (all children with disabilities are entitled to a free appropriate public education) in issuing that ruling. Fortunately, when the case was appealed to a higher court, that decision was overturned. The effect of overturning the lower court ruling was to reassert that students with disabilities have a fundamental right derived from constitutional and case law to receive educational services despite the severity of disability.

## The Rehabilitation Act of 1973, Section 504

*Section 504* of the Rehabilitation Act of 1973 (P.L. 93-112) was the first federal civil rights law to specifically protect the rights of people with disabilities against discrimination on the basis of physical or mental disability. The specific wording of Section 504 attests to its comprehensive civil rights mandate:

> No otherwise qualified handicapped individual in the United States . . . shall, solely by reason of his handicap be excluded from participation in, be denied the benefits of, or be subjected to discrimination under any program or activity receiving Federal financial assistance.

The nondiscriminatory provisions of this law are almost identical to the nondiscriminatory provisions related to race that are included in Title VI of the Civil Rights Act of 1964, and in Title IX of the Education Amendments of 1972, Public Law 92-318. Originally, Section 504 was restricted primarily to employment, but later it was amended to include educational services. It is important to note that all these laws, including Section 504, preclude

The Rehabilitation Act contains several sections that address protections for obtaining employment, using public transportation, and receiving federal contracts. The most notable part is Section 504, the nondiscrimination clause.

discrimination against individuals by recipients of federal funds (Daniel, personal communication, October 20, 1998).

In April 1975, four years after initial passage, the final regulations for Section 504 were issued for all recipients of funds from the Department of Health, Education and Welfare (HEW), including elementary and secondary schools, colleges, hospitals, social service agencies, and, in some instances, doctors. In a Section 504 fact sheet published in July 1975, the term *handicapped* was defined, and the rights of people with handicaps were outlined.

The term *handicapped* includes such diseases or conditions as speech, hearing, visual, and orthopedic impairments; cerebral palsy; epilepsy; muscular dystrophy; multiple sclerosis; cancer; diabetes; heart disease; mental retardation; emotional illness; and specific learning disabilities such as perceptual handicaps, dyslexia, minimal brain dysfunction, and developmental aphasia, as well as alcohol and drug addiction. Section 504 notes that physical and mental impairments do not constitute a disability unless they are severe enough to limit one or more of the major life functions, such as learning. It is possible for an individual who does not qualify for special education services under IDEA legislation to be eligible for accommodation under Section 504. Major accommodations that are typically considered include: curricular, scheduling, test-taking, environmental, organizational, behavioral, and grading (Conderman & Katsiyannis, 1995). Figure 2.2 provides a sample 504 Plan (General Education Accommodation Plan) showing the areas of curricular concern, the intervention or teaching strategy to be employed, and the person responsible for the accommodation.

The rights of people with disabilities included under Section 504 of the Rehabilitation Act will be examined briefly in the following paragraph.

## Program Accessibility

Programs as a whole must be accessible to people with disabilities. Structural changes are required to make a program accessible only if an alternative, such as reassignment of classes or home visits, is not possible. The deadline for making structural changes in existing facilities to achieve program accessibility was June 23, 1980.

## Free Appropriate Public Education

Every child with disabilities at the preschool, elementary, secondary, and adult educational levels is entitled to a free appropriate public education, regardless of the nature or severity of the disability. School systems have the responsibility of providing transportation for students with disabilities to and from educational programs. The compliance date for providing a free appropriate education for children ages 3 to 21 was September 1, 1978, for public elementary and secondary schools.

## Colleges and Other Postsecondary Institutions

Recruitment, admission, and treatment of students must be free of discrimination. Quotas for admission of students with disabilities are not permissible.

## Health, Welfare, and Social Services

The provisions for accessibility and reasonable accommodation also apply to health, welfare, and social services. Benefits and services may not be denied on the basis of disability.

# General Education Accommodation Plan

Name: _Josua Green_

Date: _6/5/01_

School/Grade: _Platta Valley Elementary, 3rd_

Teacher: _Myrna Mae (lead teacher)_

Participants in Development of Accommodation Plan

_Mr. and Mrs. Walter Green_    _Julie Hartson_    _Myrna Mae, Teacher_    _Arlo Wachal, Teacher_
parent(s)/guardian(s)                  principal                    teacher(s)

_Joel Schaeffer, Counselor_    _Violette Schelldorf, Nurse_

Building Person responsible for monitoring plan: _Joel Schaeffer, Counselor_    Follow-up Date: _6/5/04_

Currently on Medication  _X_ Yes ___ No    Physician _Eveard Ewing, M.D._    Type _Ritalin_    Dosage _15 mg. twice daily_

| Area of Concern | Intervention of Teaching Strategies | Person Responsible for Accommodation |
|---|---|---|
| 1. Assignment Completion | 1. Daily assignment sheet sent home with Josh<br>2. Contract system initiated for assignment completion in math and social studies | Myrna Mae<br>Parents will initial daily, and Josh will return the form.<br>Myrna Mae, Arlo Wachal |
| 2. Behavior/Distractibility | 1. Preferential seating—study carrel or near teacher, as needed<br>2. Daily behavior card sent home with Josh | Myrna Mae, Arlo Wachal<br>Parents will initial daily; and Josh will return the form. |
| 3. Consistency of Medication | 1. Medication to be administered in private by school nurse daily at noon | Violette Schelldorf |

Comments:

Josh will remain in the general education classroom with the accommodations noted above.

Parental Authorization for 504 Plan

_Mr. and Mrs. Walter Green_

I agree with the accommodations described in this 504 plan.

I do not agree with the accommodations described in this 504 plan. I understand I have the right to appeal.

**Figure 2.2.** General education accommodation plan—example. (Note: Information and names are fictional.) From "Section 504 Accommodation Plans," by G. Conderman and A. Katsiyannis, 1995, *Intervention in School and Clinic, 31*(1), 44. Copyright 1995 by PRO-ED, Inc. Reprinted with permission.

53

### General Employment Provisions

Employers may not refuse to hire or promote people with disabilities solely because of their disability. Also, accessibility to the employment location is required, and, therefore, reasonable accommodation may have to be made for the person's disability. The compliance date for those employers who receive federal funds and who employ 15 or more people was September 2, 1975.

### Failure To Comply with Section 504

Another major component of the Section 504 rules and regulations is the provision for failure to comply. The primary consequence for violating Section 504 is that federal funds can be withheld from the state agency, institution, or district until such time as full compliance with Section 504 is achieved.

## The Americans with Disabilities Act of 1990

The Americans with Disabilities Act of 1990 (ADA) was signed into law on July 26, 1990, as P.L. 101-336. The primary intent of this legislation was to extend civil rights protection to people with disabilities in the private sector, even to organizations that do not receive federal funding (Daniel, personal communication, October 20, 1998). This law, fashioned after the Rehabilitation Act of 1973, provides for pubic service and telecommunication accommodations and mandates that employers with 25 or more employees must make reasonable adjustments to the work environment to allow a person with a disability to perform his or her job. The law went into effect between 1992 and 1994, with increasing compliance requirements over that period.

Under the ADA, a person with disabilities is defined as:

> (1) a person with a physical or mental impairment that substantially limits that person in some major life activity (such as walking, talking, breathing, or working); (2) a person with a record of such a physical or mental impairment (such as a person with a history of mental illness or heart disease who no longer has the disease, but who is discriminated against because of their record of an impairment); or (3) a person who is regarded as having such an impairment (such as a person who has a significant burn on his/her face which does not limit him/her in any major life activity but who is discriminated against).

This legislation is especially important for consultants who work with secondary-level students or post-secondary adults who are making a transition to the world of work. Knowledge of the key provisions of ADA will enable the consultant to assist an employer with physical or telecommunications accommodations that might be needed to maintain a person with disabilities in the labor market. Daniel adds this point about ADA legislation:

> ADA legislation is also important because it corresponds with and supports legislation under Section 504 of the Rehabilitation Act of 1973 and relevant case law. For example, the term "reasonable accommodation" appears in ADA but nowhere in Section 504. The term, however, is used by various courts in cases brought under Section 504. (personal communication, October 20, 1998)

# The Education of All Handicapped Children Act of 1975

The right to education is embodied within the Education of All Handicapped Children's Act of 1975 (P.L. 94-142). This federal statute is a comprehensive law that states as one of its central provisions that all children with disabilities are entitled to a free appropriate public education designed to meet their unique needs. According to the statute:

> It is the purpose of this Act to assure that all handicapped children have available to them . . . a free appropriate public education that emphasizes special education and related services designed to meet their unique needs, to assure that the rights of handicapped children and their parents or guardians are protected, to assist States and localities to provide for the education of all handicapped children, and to assess and assure the effectiveness of efforts to educate handicapped children.

*This piece of legislation and its amendments were renamed the Individuals with Disabilities Education Act when amended in 1990.*

# The Education of the Handicapped Act Amendments of 1986

The Education of the Handicapped Act Amendments of 1986 (P.L. 99-457) was signed into law on October 8, 1986, and contains several key provisions that significantly extend earlier rights and protections granted under P.L. 94-142. Ballard, Ramirez, and Zantal-Wiener (1987) detail its major amendments:

- All the rights and protections of P.L. 94-142 (Part B) are extended to children with disabilities ages 3 through 5 years in school year 1990–91. To support the achievement of this objective, the prior Preschool Incentive Grant program (P.L. 94-142, Section 619) is revised to reflect authorization of a dramatic increase in federal fiscal contribution to this age group.

- A new state grant program for disabled infants and toddlers (ages birth through 2 years) is established for the purpose of providing early intervention services for all eligible children as defined by the legislation. This program appears as a new Part H of the existing Education of the Handicapped Act (EHA).

- The proven components of the EHA, Part C, early education authority, are retained and refined to maximize support toward achieving the objectives of the new early intervention and preschool initiatives. (p. 12)

P.L. 99-457 consists of two components: the preschool component, which is mandatory, and the infant component, which is discretionary. Essentially, the preschool component requires that all states provide services for children ages 3 to 5 beginning in the 1990–91 academic year. The infant component provides a mechanism for the states to compete for incentive grants to develop voluntary interagency arrangements so that a coordinated program in the birth to age 2 range is ensured (Patton, Beirne-Smith, & Payne, 1990). Differing federal rules apply to the implementation and federal funding reimbursement or grant schedule for each component.

A key element of P.L. 99-457 relates to the use of an Individual Family Services Plan (IFSP). This plan is the analog of the IEP prescribed by P.L. 94-142, but it contains additional features. For instance, the IFSP must contain statements of how the needs of the child and family will be met, including documentation of how the transition to preschool will be accomplished.

Rules regarding the transition of secondary and post-secondary students, support for teacher preparation, parent training, and dissemination are also contained in P.L. 99-457. Table 2.2 shows a three-way comparison of the required components of P.L. 94-142, IDEA '97, and P.L. 99-457.

## The Education of the Handicapped Act Amendments of 1990

The Education of the Handicapped Act Amendments of 1990 (P.L. 101-476) is the third revision to P.L. 94-142 since it was enacted originally in 1975. P.L. 101-476 officially changed the title of the Education of the Handicapped Act to the Individuals with Disabilities Education Act and made this change applicable to all prior EHA laws (P.L. 94-142, P.L. 99-457), reflecting Congress's preference to use the term *disabled* instead of the term *handicapped*.

For a comparison of the provisions of P.L. 101-476 with P.L. 94-142, the reader is referred to the *Education Daily* (Special Supplement), vol. 24, no. 42, Monday, March 4, 1991.

P.L. 101-476 contains several key provisions designed to improve services for a wider range of students with disabilities. First, autism and traumatic brain injury were added to the categorical list of disabilities that qualify for service. Second, rehabilitation counseling and social work now are fundable. Third, the IEP must include a statement of transition services for students by age 16. Fourth, the law reaffirms Congress's intent to provide services to underrepresented groups, including minorities, the poor, and people with limited English proficiency. Finally, the law codifies new language for the federal government's role in funding regional resource centers, services for deaf-blind children, early education, secondary and transition services, training, and research.

## Contrasting IDEA with Section 504

Katsiyannis and Conderman (1994) provide an analysis of the differences between IDEA legislation and Section 504 of the Rehabilitation Act of 1973. Their analysis is instructive for consultants as it helps to elucidate how services are provided, which government agencies hold jurisdiction over the services, and who potentially funds the program (see Table 2.3).

## The Individuals with Disabilities Education Act of 1997

For a synopsis of key provisions of IDEA '97, the reader is referred to the *National Information Center for Children and Youth with Disabilities Newsletter (NICHCY)*, vol. 26 (revised edition), June 1998.

The Individuals with Disabilities Education Act of 1997 (P.L. 105-17), referred to as *IDEA '97*, was signed by President Clinton on June 4, 1997. IDEA '97 mandates a number of changes related to the IEP, conflict resolution between the school district and parents, proactive behavioral management plans, and disciplinary procedures for students with disabilities (Yell et al., 1998). The *NICHCY* outlines seven changes the IDEA '97 amendments address:

- the participation of students with disabilities in state- or district-wide assessment (testing) programs;
- the manner in which evaluations are conducted;
- parent participation in eligibility and placement decisions;

**Table 2.2**

Comparison of IEP and IFSP Components Across P.L. 94-142, IDEA '97, & P.L. 99-457

| P.L. 94-142 | IDEA '97 | P.L. 99-457 |
|---|---|---|
| 1. Statement of the child's present levels of achievement. | 1. Statement of the child's present levels of educational performance, including: (a) how the child's disability affects the child's involvement and progress in general curriculum; and (b), for preschool children, as appropriate, how the disability affects the child's participation in appropriate activities. | 1. Statement of the child's present levels of development in cognitive, language, motor, psychosocial, and self-help areas. |
| 2. Annual goals. | 2. A statement of measurable annual goals, including benchmarks or short-term objectives, related to (a) meeting the child's needs that result from the child's disability to enable the child to be involved in and progress in the general curriculum; and (b) meeting each of the child's other educational needs that result from the child's disability. | 2. Statement of the family's present needs. |
| 3. Short-term objectives (intermediate steps toward achieving the annual goal). | 3. A statement of the special education, related services, and supplementary aids and services to be provided to the child, or on behalf of the child, and a statement of program modifications or supports for school personnel that will be provided for the child: (a) to advance appropriately toward attaining annual goals; (b) to be involved and progress in the general education curriculum in accordance with clause (i) and to participate in extracurricular and other nonacademic activities; and (c) to be educated and participate with other children with disabilities and nondisabled children in the activities described in this paragraph. | 3. Statement of the major child and family outcomes to be achieved. |
| 4. Special education and related services that will be provided. | 4. An explanation of the extent, if any, to which the child will not participate with nondisabled children in the regular class and in the activities described in clause (iii). | 4. Criteria, procedures, and timelines for measuring progress. |
| 5. Extent of participation in the general education curriculum. | 5. (a) A statement of any individual modifications in the administration of state or districtwide assessments of student achievement that are needed in order for the child to participate in such assessments; and (b) if the IEP team determines that the child will not participate in a particular state or districtwide assessment of student achievement (or part of such an assessment), a statement of why that assessment is not appropriate for the child; and how the child will be assessed. | 5. Description of the early intervention services that will be required to meet the family's and the child's unique needs. Services must be described in detail. |

*(continues)*

Table 2.2 (Continued)

| P.L. 94-142 | IDEA '97 | P.L. 99-457 |
|---|---|---|
| 6. Start dates and duration of services. | 6. The projected date for the beginning of the services and modifications described in clause (iii), and the anticipated frequency, location, and duration of those services and modifications. | 6. Projected start date and duration of service. |
| 7. Evaluation criteria for determining mastery of short-term objectives. | 7. (a) Beginning at age 14, and updated annually, a statement of the transition service needs of the child under the applicable components of the child's IEP that focuses on the child's courses of study (such as participation in advanced-placement courses or a vocational education program);<br>(b) beginning at age 16 (or younger, if determined appropriate by the IEP team), a statement of needed transition services for the child, including, when appropriate, a statement of the interagency responsibilities or any needed linkages; and (c) beginning at least 1 year before the child reaches the age of majority under state law, a statement that the child has been informed of his or her rights under this title, if any, that will transfer to the child on reaching the age of majority under Section 615(m). | 7. The name of the case manager. |
| | 8. A statement of (a) how the child's progress toward the annual goals described in clause (ii) will be measured; and (b) how the child's parents will be regularly informed (by such means as periodic report cards), at least as often as parents are informed of their nondisabled children's progress, of their progress toward the annual goals described in clause (ii); and the extent to which that progress is sufficient to enable the child to achieve the goals by the end of the year. | 8. Procedures for transition from early intervention to preschool. |

Note: The reader is referred to Turnbull, Strickland, and Brantley (1982), Turnbull (1993), the NICHCY newsletter, and the rules and regulations accompanying each of these pieces of legislation for more detail on the procedural requirements of the IEP and IFSP.
From "Section 504 Policies and Procedures: An Established Necessity," by A. Katsiyannis and G. Conderman, 1994, *Remedial and Special Education, 15*(5), 311–318. Copyright 1994 by PRO-ED, Inc. Adapted with permission.

**Table 2.3**

Matrix Comparing IDEA with Section 504

|  | Section 504 | IDEA |
|---|---|---|
| Application | ALL institutions receiving federal financial assistance. | Qualified individuals w/ a disability. |
| Funding | No funding provided. | Funding as prescribed by federal law and congressional appropriations. |
| Participation | Required | Voluntary |
| Monitored by . . . | Office of Special Education and Rehabilitation Services | Office of Civil Rights |
| Appropriate Education defined . . . | General education accommodations, usually without an IEP; 504 plans instead. | Special and related services as prescribed by the IEP. |
| Disability | Broadly defined; affecting life functions. | Defined narrowly and categorically. |

*Note.* From "Section 504 Policies and Procedures: An Established Necessity," by A. Katsiyannis and G. Conderman, 1994, *Remedial and Special Education, 15*(5), 311–318. Copyright 1994 by PRO-ED, Inc. Adapted with permission.

- development and review of IEPs, including increased emphasis on participation of children and youth with disabilities in the general education classroom and in the general curriculum, with appropriate learning aids and services;

- the addition of transition programming;

- voluntary mediation as a means of resolving parent-school controversies; and

- the discipline of children with disabilities. (p. 2)

Welch (1998) reviews the specific components of P.L. 105-17 that in his view relate to collaborative consultation. These include eligibility and labeling, Individualized Education Programs, and least restrictive environment (LRE).

## Eligibility and Labeling

Welch makes a distinction between the paradigm and the promise of IDEA '97 with respect to eligibility and labeling. The former paradigm essentially provided discretionary authority to the school psychologist and perhaps the special educator to determine a child's eligibility for services. Now, with IDEA '97, a collaborative approach is required, including conducting ecological and functional assessments (Heron & Heward, 1982; Witt, Elliott, Daly, Gresham, & Kramer, 1998). Despite the logistical or institutional difficulties to conduct such an assessment, IDEA '97 challenges professionals to work collaboratively with other teachers and parents to achieve this goal.

## Individualized Education Programs

All students receiving services under IDEA '97 must have an *Individualized Education Program* or *Individualized Family Services Plan* (Bauwens &

See Chapters 5 and 9–11 for further discussion of IEPs.

Korinek, 1993; Turnbull, 1993). Further, students must have transition plans from early childhood to school-age programs and from school-age programs to the world of work. Of necessity, these programs must include plans or statements for the purposeful interactions between and among relevant teachers, administrators, related services professionals, parents, and, to the extent appropriate, the student. Shared responsibilities, including any interagency cooperative services, are to be delineated in the IEP transition section (Welch, 1998).

### Least Restrictive Environment

Welch (1998) believes that the least restrictive environment component of IDEA '97 could be considered the most "provocative" of all its sections because it will place more emphasis on the student's program than on placement. LREs might very well be achieved by using a combination of team teaching and community-based education programs, as well as consultation services. The challenge is that "the predominant models are resource and self-contained settings, which continue to be emphasized despite the definition of least restrictive environment that clearly mandates removal from general education settings as a last resort" (Welch, 1998, pp. 135–136).

Public Law 105-17 also addresses the issue of suspension and expulsion of students with disabilities. The law seeks to ensure the due process rights of students with disabilities to receive a free appropriate public education while simultaneously ensuring the safety of the student and other students in the school (Zurkowski, Kelly, & Griswold, 1998). Policies and procedures for striking this balance will be addressed later in the chapter.

## Assuring the Right to Education

In our judgment, six federal statutes have been instrumental in assuring the right to an appropriate education for all individuals with disabilities. First, P.L. 93-380 established a national policy of equal educational opportunity by declaring that every citizen is entitled at public expense to an education that is designed to achieve the individual's full potential. Second, P.L. 94-142, an amendment to P.L. 93-380, extended equal educational opportunity specifically to populations with disabilities. P.L. 94-142 has been described as the Bill of Rights for the Handicapped because it is designed to correct inequities on behalf of students with disabilities. Third, P.L. 99-352, the Handicapped Child Protection Law, was enacted to overturn a Supreme Court decision that would have made it difficult—if not impossible—for parents to be awarded attorney's fees subsequent to a positive ruling in their favor. Fourth, P.L. 99-457 provided substantive changes in providing the right to an appropriate education for preschool children, ages 3 to 5. Fifth, P.L. 101-476 further specified Congress's intent to provide a full range of special education services—including services for transition programs and family intervention—for people ages birth through 21 and into adulthood. Finally, P.L. 105-17 (IDEA '97) reaffirms congressional intent to provide a free appropriate public education to students with disabilities in the least restrictive environment. Without these fundamental pieces of legislation, the right to an appropriate education would not be a national standard for children with disabilities.

Brimer and Barudin (1977) outline four basic principles designed to assure the rights of all students with disabilities: (a) due process; (b) a free appropriate public education for all children with disabilities; (c) financial assistance to states, and (d) federal training and technical assistance. A close examination of the first two principles follows, as they relate most directly to day-to-day issues faced by consultants.

## Due Process

*Due process* can be defined as a vehicle for judicial protection of liberty and property against unreasonable government action. This protection is embodied within the Fifth Amendment of the Constitution: ". . . nor shall any State deprive any person of life, liberty, or property, without due process of law." Essentially, due process consists of two components, substantive and procedural.

### Substantive Due Process

*Substantive due process* refers to the threatened or actual denial of life, liberty, or property. It weighs fundamental fairness against arbitrariness or unreasonableness. That is, a court decision cannot be based on whim but must follow a logical process. Also, a decision that is made must be enforced equally and fairly. Substantive due process can be viewed as the degree of protection under a given set of circumstances before a decision is rendered. The court determines the cutoff point for deciding to hear a case based on alleged violations of substantive due process by weighing the seriousness of the offense and the harm to the individual (Goldstein, 1975). As Brimer and Barudin (1977) point out, due process is not a dichotomous situation that is appropriate in some cases and inappropriate in others but rather a continuum of procedures that offers the appropriate protection of the rights of the individual. As Fischer (1970) emphasizes, due process helps to protect a person from an arbitrary or capricious judgment.

### Procedural Due Process

*Procedural due process* refers to the standards specifying how due process is to be applied. The procedural safeguards delineated in P.L. 94-142, and its subsequent revisions, provide an example of procedural due process. The Individuals with Disabilities Acts, alone and collectively, provides children with disabilities and their parents or guardians certain procedural safeguards with respect to the provision of free appropriate public education. A summary of selected procedural safeguards is found in Table 2.4.

Many of the plaintiffs' arguments in the PARC case were based on procedural due process infringements (Brimer & Barudin, 1977). The parents in the PARC case were not notified as to why their children were excluded from school; neither were they afforded a hearing to counter the school's action. In support of these two arguments, the plaintiffs in the PARC case quoted judicial decisions from prior litigation (i.e., Supreme Court Justice Felix Frankfurter, who stated, "The right to be heard before being condemned to suffer grievous loss of any kind . . . is a principle basic to our society" (*Joint Anti-Fascist Committee v. McGrath,* 1951, p. 168).

Another procedural due process argument used in the PARC case concerned the issue of labeling. The point was that the label "mentally retarded" stigmatized the child and should not have been attached without prior notice to the parents and without allowing the parents an opportunity to challenge the

**Table 2.4**

Summary of Selected Procedural Safeguards Specified in P.L. 94-142,
P.L. 99-457, and P.L. 101-476

1. The parents or guardian of a child with disabilities are to be provided with the opportunity to examine all records relevant to the educational programming of their child,* as well as the opportunity to obtain an independent educational evaluation of the child, if they desire.**
2. If there is no parent or guardian, an individual who is not involved in the education of the child will be appointed to act as the surrogate for the parents or guardian.
3. Written notice is to be provided to the parent or guardian when an educational agency proposes or refuses to initiate or change the child's educational program.
4. The parents or guardian must have the opportunity to present complaints with respect to any matter related to the educational programming of their child.
5. If the parents or guardian make a complaint regarding the educational programming of their child, they shall have the opportunity for an impartial due process hearing.
6. School records must be made available.
7. Statements related to transition services must appear on the IEP and IFSP.
8. Due process relates to individuals who are incarcerated as well as to school-aged populations attending public facilities.

* The Buckley Amendment of 1975 (Title V, Sec. 513, 514, P.L. 93-380) gave to parents of public school students under age 18 the right to see, correct, and control access to school records.

** A list of independent evaluators can be obtained from the superintendent of the school district or county program.

labeling. Justice William O. Douglas of the United States Supreme Court, in a previous case related to labeling (*Wisconsin v. Constantineau,* 1971), rendered the following decision: "Where a person's good name, reputation, honor or integrity are at stake because of what the government is doing to him, notice and opportunity to be heard are essential" (p. 435). Thus, the Supreme Court had made it clear that a label is a stigma and as such cannot be imposed without due process of law.

A fourth argument presented in PARC was that the educational process is a fundamental interest and should not be withheld without notice of the impending deprivation and a chance to be heard. This argument relates to both substantive due process (i.e., the notion of fair play) and procedural due process (i.e., the right to be heard before a fundamental interest, such as education, can be denied).

Margolis (1998) states that when occasions arise wherein school district personnel and parents do not see eye to eye on the best program for a student, these conflicts are sometimes resolved without litigation, meaning that all parties come to a resolution short of filing a lawsuit. However, some situations deteriorate to the point of confrontation and hostility, and legal recourse is initiated. Margolis (1998), Heron, Martz, and Margolis (1996), and Katsiyannis and Maag (1997) believe that consultants can help prevent costly litigation between parents and a school district without compromising services, ethics, or best practice by following a few basic guidelines. Included in these guidelines is the recommendation that if a student does not qualify for services under IDEA '97, the IEP team should be reconstituted as a 504 team to determine if eligibility for services within a full continuum of service provisions is possible under that legislation (Hakola, 1992; Katsiyannis & Maag, 1997). Table 2.5 summarizes further guidelines that will assist consultants with avoiding costly litigation.

## Table 2.5

Guidelines to Avoid Litigation

| Lessons or Guidelines | Implications for (Consultant) Practice |
|---|---|
| Listen to parents' concerns and fears. | • Have an IEP member meet w/ the parent regularly.<br>• Arrange for specialists to meet individually to discuss findings and progress.<br>• Encourage parents to express concerns.<br>• Collaborate w/ parents to prepare IEP agenda.<br>• Plan meeting times consistent w/ parent needs. |
| Develop realistic goals and objectives. | • Collaborate w/ parents on the analysis of present educational growth.<br>• Conduct joint task analysis w/ parents when instructional tasks are demanding.<br>• Collect data on progress and conduct formative evaluations.<br>• Establish differential mastery levels for different skills.<br>• Establish appropriate functioning levels depending on skills to be learned.<br>• Program for generalization of skills. |
| Develop explicit goals and objectives. | • Place statements of the student's current status before goals.<br>• Include specific performance standards w/ each goal.<br>• Write comprehensive short-term instructional objectives that delineate the behavior, criteria for success, and anticipated date of completion. |
| Frequently assess student progress and parent satisfaction with student progress and program; quickly respond to identified needs. | • State specifically how annual goals will be measured.<br>• Consider curriculum-based measures to assess progress more frequently.<br>• Generate weekly, but not labor-intensive, progress reports for parents.<br>• At the onset of difficulty w/ meeting a goal, contact the parents for a problem-solving session.<br>• Seek external consultation if local resources do not produce timely solutions.<br>• Conduct social validation surveys regularly to assess parental satisfaction. |
| Design meetings to help parents understand and remember what is discussed. | • Provide a written and easily readable agenda.<br>• Obtain consensus on a problem-solving approach (write it down on a flip chart for easy viewing).<br>• Record major comments on the flip chart.<br>• Avoid private note taking; it instills distrust.<br>• Provide a summary at the end of the meeting. |
| Know the federal special education laws, rules, and regulations and IDEA case law. | • Assess *all* areas of suspected disability.<br>• Recall the purpose of assessment.<br>• Employ multimodal assessment instruments and protocols.<br>• Use only validated assessments.<br>• Include nonacademic measures in the assessment.<br>• Determine if assessment and goals and objectives are consistent with the main thrust of IDEA '97 to prepare students for employment and independence.<br>• Match the child's need with the appropriate service, irrespective of cost.<br>• Base all decisions on need, not the child's label.<br>• Provide for the least restrictive environment, based on the child's need. |

*(continues)*

**Table 2.5**  (*Continued*)

| Lessons or Guidelines | Implications for (Consultant) Practice |
|---|---|
| | • Avoid expedient decisions and placements.<br>• Placement decisions should be based on need, not geography or location.<br>• Generate the IEP to ensure "educational benefit," not trivial, de minimis, or superficial gains.<br>• Ensure compliance w/ Section 504, if applicable. |
| Avoid positional bargaining. | • Engage in active "self-listening" and listen to parents.<br>• Challenge all inaccurate labels and characterizations of parents and children.<br>• Provide organized, relevant data in the form of charts, graphs, or tables.<br>• Define problems w/ parents so that systematic problem solving can occur.<br>• Conduct an analysis of problems and solutions that accounts for benefits, criteria for success, signs of difficulty, and need for further resources.<br>• Encourage mediation if parent-teacher discussions are derailed. |
| Continue to problem solve during litigation. | • Obtain consensus from school administrators and attorneys on respective roles.<br>• Remember that the IEP is designed to serve the student's needs.<br>• Listen carefully to the viewpoint expressed by parents, their attorney, etc. Their comments may provide the basis for new discussion.<br>• Remain optimistic. |

*Note.* From "Avoiding Special Education Due Process Hearings: Lessons from the Field," by H. Margolis, 1998, *Journal of Educational and Psychological Consultation, 9*(3), 233–260. Copyright 1998 by Lawrence Erlbaum Associates, Inc. Adapted with permission.

## A Free Appropriate Public Education for All Children with Disabilities

Taken as a whole, legislation has stated that educational programs for students with disabilities is to be commensurate with their needs and conducted in a least restrictive setting. Additionally, parents and guardians are to be involved to the maximum extent possible. P.L. 94-142, P.L. 99-457, and P.L. 105-17 further codify that an Individualized Educational Program or Individualized Family Services Plan is a required part of students' education. This educational program must also meet state educational agency standards and be provided at public expense.

But what constitutes an *appropriate education* for a student with disabilities? This essential question has been the focus of several major lawsuits: *Board of Education v. Rowley*, 1982; *Armstrong v. Kline*, 1979; (*Battle v. Commonwealth of Pennsylvania, 1980*); *Irving Independent School District v. Tatro*, 1984; and *Burlington v. Department of Education*, 1985.

### Board of Education v. Rowley

The main issue in the *Board of Education v. Rowley* (1982) case was whether Amy Rowley, a hearing-impaired student, was entitled to the services of a sign language interpreter as part of her Individualized Education Program. Briefly, Amy was an entering first-grade student, who because of the nature of her hearing loss (she had approximately 50% residual hearing) needed special education services in the general education classroom. The district provided her with a hearing aid, speech therapy, and a tutor. The district also provided her with a sign language interpreter but discontinued that service after the interpreter reported that Amy resisted her services. That is, Amy looked at the teacher to read her lips and asked the teacher to repeat instructions rather than looking at the interpreter. The parents' claimed that because Amy was not provided with a sign language interpreter, she missed 50% of her instruction and therefore was denied an appropriate public education, even though she was making satisfactory progress in school and passing from grade to grade.

The case reached the Supreme Court of the United States, where in a 6-3 decision it ruled that the school district was not required to provide a sign language interpreter to Amy. Justice William Rehnquist, writing for the majority and basing his decision on his interpretation of the congressional intent of the legislation, stated that P.L. 94-142 was written to provide an appropriate educational opportunity for students with disabilities, consisting of instructions and related services to provide "educational benefit" to the child (Yell, 1998). He stated:

> By passing the Act, Congress sought primarily to make public education available to handicapped children. But in seeking to provide such access to public education, Congress did not impose upon the States any greater substantive standard than would be necessary to make such access meaningful.

The Court essentially overturned the ruling of the U.S. District Court of Appeals that P.L. 94-142 was designed so that each child would achieve his or her maximum potential. In short, the U.S. Supreme Court ruled that P.L. 94-142 was designed to assist the student with a disability to achieve self-sufficiency commensurate with the opportunity provided to other children, not his or her full potential.

### *Armstrong v. Kline*

*Armstrong v. Kline* (1979) was a class action suit brought to the court on behalf of three children with severe disabilities and their parents. The purpose of the suit was to challenge the Pennsylvania Department of Education's policy, which stated that programs for students with disabilities would not be funded for a longer period of time than those for general education students (i.e., 180 school days). The plaintiff's position was that the "180-day rule" violated provisions of P.L. 94-142 regarding a free appropriate public education, because the policy prohibited formulating funded IEPs that extended beyond 180 days.

In June 1979, the U.S. District Court for Eastern Pennsylvania ruled that the 180-day rule was illegal because it made it extremely difficult for students to achieve self-sufficiency and independence. In essence, the court ruled that the 180-day rule denied these children a free appropriate public education (Stotland & Mancuso, 1981).

On July 17, 1980, the U.S. Third Circuit of Appeals in *Battle v. Commonwealth* upheld the lower court's ruling. In part, the court of appeals ruled that "inflexible application of a 180-day maximum prevents the proper formulation of appropriate educational goals for individual members of the plaintiff class" (p. 28).

More recently, Olmi, Walker, and Ruthven (1995) conducted a survey of local education agencies within two federal judiciary circuit court districts that had (the Fifth Federal Judicial Circuit) and did not have (the Tenth Federal Judicial Circuit) a history of extended school year (ESY) litigation. While the response rate for the survey was low and Olmi et al. concede the preliminary nature of the data, the results suggest that within the Fifth District, which had more litigation relative to ESY, districts provided more ESY services to students (86% reported providing services). In the Tenth District, without the litigative history, only 65% of districts reported provided services beyond 180 days. Olmi et al. conclude, based on their survey and an analysis of the extant literature on ESY, that great variability exists across state departments of education and local education agencies on policies and procedures with respect to ESY eligibility and services.

According to Stotland and Mancuso (1981), an "appropriate education" must "be based on an individualized assessment and an individual planning process that must result in an individualized program designed to meet each child's unique needs" (p. 270). In *Polk v. Central Susquehanna* (1988), a clarification of the benefit test was outlined. Briefly, the court ruled that the educational benefit derived from programming has to be more than trivial, de minimis, or token gestures of accommodation; otherwise, the district runs the risk of violating the FAPE (free appropriate public education) directive (*Oberti v. Clementon,* 1992). Heron et al. (1996) provide this summary of what constitutes a free appropriate public education: "FAPE requires adequate opportunity for the child to make meaningful progress commensurate with the nature and severity of the student's disability" (p. 380). Thomas and Rapport (1998) are even more specific:

> Under the IDEA, children with disabilities must be provided with a FAPE in the least restrictive environment. The FAPE mandate is first and foremost—it is the ultimate objective. Among numerous additional requirements that enable the school district to meet this objective is the mandate to select a placement along a continuum of alternative placements that is least restrictive. Determining the LRE is simply a means to an appropriate end—*for a placement to be "appropriate" it must be "least restrictive."* The former includes the latter. (p. 74, italics in original)

We shall consider three aspects of providing an individualized program: (a) nondiscriminatory evaluation and the placement decision, (b) the Individualized Education Program, and (c) educational placement in the least restrictive environment.

*Nondiscriminatory Evaluation and the Placement Decision.* There has been a long-standing concern with the nature of programs for children who are provided with special education services. According to Hoffman (1975), special classes during the early part of the 20th century were often considered a hodgepodge. Non-English–speaking students, for example, were grouped with mentally and behaviorally disordered children. Classes were disproportionately filled with minority children because of faulty diagnosis and poor administration of services.

In the 1990s there was a concern that special education programs were used indiscriminately. Many minority group children may be inappropriately placed. Advocates for these children are attempting to deal with the problem through the judicial process. Additionally, parents are demanding the right to question the appropriateness of a school's classification of their children, and they are demanding the right of due process. A brief discussion of three key lawsuits conducted in the 1970s pertinent to this aspect of educational programming are presented in the following paragraphs.

In *Diana v. State Board of Education of California* (1970), the plaintiffs argued that nine Mexican American public school students had been improperly placed in classes for the mentally retarded on the basis of inaccurate and discriminatory tests. That is, individualized intelligence tests were administered to these Spanish-speaking children by an English-speaking examiner. The plaintiffs argued that the tests relied primarily on verbal aptitude in English, thereby ignoring learning abilities in Spanish. In addition, they alleged that the intelligence tests were standardized on Americans and were therefore inappropriate for Spanish-speaking, Mexican American students. The court sustained those arguments.

Further, subsequent legislation passed in California disallowed IQ scores as a single measure to place students in special education classrooms. The decision rendered in *Diana* set the occasion for subsequent federal legislation that prohibited intelligence test scores from being used as only one measure of a multifactored evaluation and mandated that tests must be given in the student's native language.

In *Larry P. v. Riles* (1972), the plaintiffs sought an injunction restraining the San Francisco school district from administering intelligence tests for determining the placement of African American students in classes for the educable mentally retarded. The plaintiffs alleged that placement in classes for the mentally retarded carried a stigma and a life sentence of illiteracy. The injunction was upheld if the use of the intelligence tests resulted in racial imbalance in the composition of such classes.

In the *Diana* and *Larry P.* cases, the use of standardized tests, especially intelligence tests, for making placement decisions was at issue. According to Singletary, Collings, and Dennis (1978), two factors that expand on this issue are: (a) that no child can be placed in a special education program on the basis of an intelligence test if that placement results in racial imbalance, and (b) that those students already enrolled in special programs must be reevaluated periodically.

The *LeBanks v. Spears* (1973) case was a class action suit representing students ages 5 through 21 in the public school district of Orleans Parish, Louisiana, who were described as, identified as, or suspected of being retarded. The plaintiffs asserted that they were denied publicly supported educational programs. A preliminary consent agreement was ordered on May 3, 1973, that expanded the dimension of nondiscriminatory evaluation. The consent decree delineated the steps necessary to ensure that appropriate services were afforded to mentally retarded children.

Subsequent legislation, Section 504 of P.L. 93-112, was based on the rulings issued in *Lebanks v. Spears*. In Section 504, procedures for nondiscriminatory materials and evaluation were provided. A summary of these procedures is found in Table 2.6.

*Nondiscriminatory evaluation,* specified in Section 503 and EHA, means that the standardized tests used to evaluate children and youth should be normed or standardized for that child's particular age and ethnic or cultural group. Also, testing must be conducted using the child's primary language, and written permission must be obtained from the parents prior to testing.

There are several important considerations for educational consultants with respect to nondiscriminatory evaluation. First, the consultant may be

Readers are referred to Chapter 7 for a more extensive discussion of multicultural issues and to Chapter 8 for a discussion of assessment as it relates to non-English–speaking students.

**Table 2.6**

Nondiscriminatory Materials and Evaluation Procedures as
Specified in Section 504 of P.L. 93-112.

- Tests and evaluation materials are to be validated and administered by qualified evaluators.
- Texts and other evaluation materials are to assess specific areas of educational need.
- Tests are to be selected and administered so as not to reflect impairment but to accurately reflect aptitude and/or achievement.
- For educational placement, one must draw upon a variety of sources, carefully document and consider all information, and make group placement decisions.
- Educational programming must undergo periodic reevaluation.

responsible for administering standardized tests to students. Based on the outcome of previous litigation and recent legislation, it is imperative that measures be taken to ensure that the test is age and culture appropriate. In addition, the evaluation of the child must assure the careful assessment of all areas of weakness, not just overall general aptitude, using protocols and procedures that meet the *Daubert standard*. That is, consultants are bound to use protocols that are reliable and valid, not just popular and available (Heron et al., 1996). Further, if the child's primary language is not English, or if the child does not use expressive language, then provisions must be made to test the child through his or her primary language or mode of communication. Second, the consultant might be responsible for observing that the due process procedures established by the district are carried out. It is important that procedures be followed exactly, especially those procedures that specify the parents' rights. Third, educational placement must be based on a careful consideration of all data obtained through a multifactored evaluation. The placement decision should reflect the consensus of the placement team, and if there are dissenting opinions regarding the placement, those opinions must be documented. Finally, the consultant might be responsible for scheduling periodic reviews. The purpose of a review is to reexamine the student's need based on progress observed since the last review. Reviews are an integral part of a child's Individualized Education Program.

*Individualized Education Program.* As stated previously, an Individualized Education Program or an Individualized Family Services Plan must be developed for children who receive special education and related services at school-age or preschool levels, respectively. Both documents must be written, and they must specify the child's (or family's) educational program, based on assessed need, for a specified period of time, usually an academic year (refer to Table 2.2).

A considerable amount of literature describes suggested steps to generate an IEP or IFSP, as well as the guidelines to assure due process procedures (Meyen, 1978; Turnbull, Strickland, & Brantley, 1982). Basically, all parties involved in the process must come to an agreement on the content of the written document— that is, its development and implementation. If there is a disagreement, a hearing may be conducted according to due process safeguards. A hearing may be requested by any party in disagreement.

In the *impartial hearing process,* three hierarchical steps are available to the dissenting party. First, a hearing may be called at the local level to review all pertinent information (e.g., assessment results, placement, related-service needs). If the dissenting party is not satisfied, a state-level review may be called. If the dissenting party is still aggrieved, civil action through a state or federal district court may be taken. As noted by Abeson, Bolick, and Hass (1975), an impartial hearing includes the right of the dissenting party to receive timely and specific notice of the hearing, all pertinent records, an independent evaluation if desired, and representation by counsel. Also, the plaintiff is entitled to cross-examine witnesses and bring witnesses of his or her own.

Hearing officers—there are approximately 1,500 nationwide—are involved in the first two levels (Katsiyannis & Klare, 1991). The role of a hearing officer is not to place blame or determine right or wrong but to achieve resolution of the conflict with final determination of an appropriate program for the child. As Abeson et al. (1975) note, the specification of criteria to be used in selecting effective hearing officers in all settings is difficult because of changing circumstances. Nevertheless, the authors provide general guidelines in Table 2.7.

The IEP and impartial hearing processes have several implications for consultants. For example, if a consultant served as a representative from the local education agency during the IEP conference, he or she would share responsibility for seeing that the services prescribed were actually delivered. Also, the consultant might bear some responsibility for monitoring the instructional program of the child. The monitoring process might consist of brief contacts or more extensive discussions with the teacher (Bergan, 1977). Further, the consultant might be responsible for scheduling a periodic or annual review. If so, arrangements for assessment and data collection may have to be made so that current information is available for the team.

Finally, in the event that a due process proceeding (i.e., an impartial hearing) is initiated, the consultant might be required to document all the steps taken with the student and his or her parents. Importantly, a consultant must be able to communicate these data effectively to the hearing officer so that an impartial decision can be rendered (Turnbull et al., 1982).

### Table 2.7
#### Guidelines for Selecting Hearing Officers

1. The hearing officer should not have been involved in decisions already made about a child regarding identification, evaluation, placement, or review.
2. The hearing officer should possess special knowledge, acquired through training and/or experience, about the nature and needs of exceptional children. An awareness and understanding of the types and quality of programs that are available for exceptional children are essential.
3. The hearing officer should be sufficiently open-minded so that he or she will not be predisposed toward any decisions that he or she must make or review. However, the hearing officer must also be capable of making decisions.
4. The hearing officer should possess the ability to objectively, sensitively, and directly solicit and evaluate both oral and written information that needs to be considered in relation to decision making.
5. The hearing officer should have sufficient experience to effectively structure and operate hearings in conformity with standard requirements and limits, and to encourage the participation of the principal parties and their representatives.
6. The hearing officer should be free enough of other obligations to give sufficient priority to hearing officer responsibilities. He or she must be able to meet the required deadlines for conducting hearings and reporting written decisions.
7. The hearing officer should be aware that this role is unique. It will require constant evaluation of the hearing processes and the behavior of all the parties involved, including the hearing officer's.

*Note.* From "A Primer on Due Process: Education Decisions for Handicapped Children," by A. Abeson, N. Bolick, and J. A. Hass, 1975, *Exceptional Children, 42*, 72–73. Reprinted with permission.

*Educational Placement in the Least Restrictive Environment.* Ennis (1976) states that the notion of the least restrictive environment is the legal corollary of the social science principle of normalization, that is, existence as close as possible to normal. Wolfensberger (1972) reformulated the normalization principle for application to human management—specifically, the management of people with mental retardation. He defines normalization as the use of means to establish or maintain personal behaviors and characteristics that conform to the cultural norm.

There has been considerable litigation concerning the issue of the least restrictive environment, some that predates P.L. 94-142 (cf. *Warren v. Nussbaum,* 1974; *Panitch v. State of Wisconsin,* 1974). In *Lake v. Cameron* (1966), the conclusion was that the government may not elect a convenient alternative of service if another choice would be more appropriate. In this case, the plaintiff was confined to a hospital for the insane. She was described as senile, with a poor memory, and unable to care for herself but not insane. The plaintiff was in a hospital because her family was unable to provide care. The ruling in this case was that it is the obligation of the state to explore other possible alternatives to meet the individual's needs. This case demonstrated that the government cannot overextend protection of an individual to the point of deprivation of personal liberty. In other terms, the state was obliged to find the least restrictive placement for the plaintiff, that is, a setting less restrictive than a mental hospital, that would meet the plaintiff's needs.

Several cases have focused on the provision of the least restrictive environment. In *Mattie T. v. Holladay* (1981), for example, the court asserted that placement in a self-contained classroom effectively removed students with disabilities from the opportunity to interact with their general education peers, thus not meeting the educational and social needs of the students. The case was settled by consent decree in favor of the plaintiffs. Conversely, in *San Francisco v. State* (1982), *Victoria v. District* (1984), and *David v. Dartmouth* (1985), courts have ruled that segregated placements can constitute the least restrictive environment when there is evidence that the student's behavior will place him or her or other students at risk of harm in the integrated settings (Brady, McDougall, & Dennis, 1989).

See Thomas and Rapport (1998) for a comprehensive listing of Federal Circuit Court decisions (1981–97) regarding least restrictive environment.

Recent cases that examined least restrictive environments have also been precedent setting (cf. *Daniel R.R. v. State Board of Education,* 1989).

*Daniel R.R.* In *Daniel R.R. v. State Board of Education,* the Fifth Circuit Court of Appeals rejected an earlier *portability standard* outlined in the *Roncker v. Walter* case, where a more intrusive and restrictive educational program within a segregated county was recommended as an LRE by the school district rather than the self-contained classroom in a regular public school that the parents sought. In *Daniel R.R.,* and subsequently in several other cases, including *Greer v. Rome City School District* (1991) and *Oberti v. Board of Education of Clementon School District* (1992), the court proposed a two-prong test—which became known as the *inclusion standard*—to determine least restrictive environment (Heron et al., 1996; Osborne & DiMattia, 1994; Thomas & Rapport, 1998):

- Prong 1. Can the student be educated in the general education classroom satisfactorily if supplemental learning aids are provided?

- Prong 2. If education in the general education classroom cannot occur satisfactorily, is the student placed with nondisabled peers to the maximum extent possible?

In *Daniel R.R.,* Daniel was a student with Down's syndrome. The court ruled that his placement within a segregated setting did provide him with educational benefit, that his presence in the general education classroom was counterproductive for the rest of the class, and that the teacher spent an undue amount of time trying to accommodate him.

*Oberti v. Board of Education of Clementon.* In *Oberti v. Board of Education of Clementon,* however, the court required a general education placement for an 8-year-old student with Down's syndrome because, in the court's view, the school district failed to give "serious consideration to accommodating the plaintiff in the mainstream, in violation of the first test under *Daniel R.R.*" (p. 53). A similar ruling was pronounced in *Greer v. Rome City School District* insofar as the district failed to comply with the first prong of the *Daniel R.R.* test. One lesson for consultants when determining an LRE is that the district must consider placements within general education settings and provide supplemental learning aids and services, if appropriate, to enhance the educational experience of the student (Osborne & DiMattia, 1994). Moreover, these aids and services must be substantive and designed to meet the child's unique needs. They may not be limited to existing and available services within the district. Instead, services must be provided to meet the student's unique needs.

Consultants should be aware that in trying to meet the first prong of the *Daniel R.R.* test, the court did not intend that *every conceivable* supplemental aid must be used, nor does the program in a general education classroom have to be modified beyond recognition to meet the standard (Heron et al., 1996). Further, consultants should recognize that the *Daniel R.R.* two-prong test has been used to provide both more and less restrictive environments for students.

The key to determining least restrictive environment, affirmed by several cases and based on the fundamental value of the right of students to be educated with their peers in public settings, is whether the district is:

- acting in good faith to meet the individualized educational needs of students;

- maximizing the extent possible to provide an educational experience in environments as close as conceivable to the environments provided to general education students;

- ensuring that students are deriving educational benefit (academic and social) from a placement by providing supplemental learning aids as needed (Heron et al., 1996; Osborne & DiMattia, 1994; Yell, 1998).

*Rachel H.* The *Board of Education Sacramento City Unified School District v. Rachel Hollard* (1994) established the *balancing standard* for what constitutes the least restrictive environment. In that case, a district-proposed placement would have had Rachel, an 11-year-old student with moderate mental retardation, attend a special class for academics and a general education class for nonacademics. The parents wanted the total program in the general education class (full inclusion). The court applied a four-part *balancing standard* (i.e., educational benefit, nonacademic benefit, Rachel's potential detrimental presence in the general education room, and cost) in making its decision that the district had violated the intent of LRE.

Specifically, "this standard requires the court to weigh both the benefits and costs (both monetary and nonmonetary) of a given placement in determining the LRE" (Thomas & Rapport, 1998, p. 73). The Ninth Circuit Court of Appeals ruled in favor of Rachel, reaffirming the position that the district "carried the burden of demonstrating that its proposed placement provided mainstreaming to the maximum extent appropriate" (Yell, 1995, p. 399).

In sum, districts must balance providing wholesale general education placements for students with disabilities (full inclusion), believing (mistakenly) that they are providing a least restrictive environment, with unduly failing to consider a continuum of services, including mainstreaming (Thomas & Rapport, 1998; Yell, 1995). Yell (1995) outlines several principles that consultants would be well advised to recognize when determining LRE:

- Determining LRE must be based on the unique and individualized needs of *each* student.

- A continuum of services must be available through district or consortium arrangements to meet those needs.

- The peer group must be considered.

- If a more restrictive placement is decided upon, the student must still be integrated with general education students to the maximum extent possible.

- The burden of proof for placement decisions rests with the school district.

Table 2.8 provides a summary of the "test" questions used to establish the standards for portability, inclusion, and balance across three court cases: *Roncker, Daniel R.R.,* and *Rachel H.*

### Irving Independent School District v. Tatro

The first case was, of course, the *Rowley* case.

*Irving Independent School District v. Tatro* (1984) was the second case to come before the Supreme Court with respect to the legal standard for appropriate education. The main issue of the case was whether a clean intermittent catheterization (CIC) procedure for Amber Tatro was considered a related service to be provided by the school district so that she could "benefit" from the school experience, or a medical service not covered under the EHA. The school district's position was that the CIC was a medical procedure, and it refused to provide the service to the child.

In the U.S. District Court of Texas, the parents lost. The lower court ruled that CIC was a medical procedure and not required under the EHA. The parents won a reversal in the U.S. Court of Appeals, where the judge ruled that CIC was necessary for Amber to benefit from her education. The court also awarded compensatory damage and legal fees to the parents. The school district appealed the case to the U.S. Supreme Court.

The Supreme Court reaffirmed the court of appeals ruling with respect to Amber's right to CIC under EHA legislation as a supportive service but reversed the ruling on the awarding of attorney fees. According to Vitello (1986), the Tatro case is important for two reasons:

> First, it affirms judicial review of the appropriateness of a handicapped child's IEP, not merely review of adherence to procedural safeguards under the EHA. Second, the Court's decision broadens the related services construct to include not only services to enable a handicapped child to benefit from education, but obtain access to beneficial educational services. (p. 355)

In making its judgment, the Court was equating the CIC procedure with other services that are available for children to reach, enter, exit, and have full access to programs (Osborne, 1988).

**Table 2.8**

A Summary of the "Test" Questions Used To Establish the Standards for Portability, Inclusion, and Balance Across Three Court Cases: Roncker, Daniel R.R., and Rachel H.

| *Roncker* **Portability Standard** | *Daniel R. R.* **Inclusion Standard** | *Rachel H.* **Balancing Standard** |
|---|---|---|
| • Can the services that made a segregated facility superior be provided in the regular education environment? | • Can the student be educated in the general education classroom satisfactorily if supplemental learning aids are provided? | • What are the educational benefits available to the child in a general education classroom supplemented with appropriate aids and services, as compared with the educational benefits of a special education classroom? |
| • Can the child benefit from a general education environment? | • If education in the general education classroom cannot occur satisfactorily, is the student placed with nondisabled peers to the maximum extent possible? | • Are there nonacademic benefits of instruction with children who are not disabled? |
| • Are the benefits of a general education placement far outweighed by the benefits gained from services that could not feasibly be provided in general education placement? | | • What effect does the child's presence have on the teacher and other children in the classroom? |
| • Would the child significantly disrupt the general education environment? | | • What is the cost of educating the child in the general education environment? |
| • Is the cost so excessive as to deprive other children of an education? | | |

*Note.* From "Least Restrictive Environment: Understanding the Directions of the Courts," by S. B. Thomas and M. J. K. Rapport, 1998, *Journal of Special Education, 32*(2), 66–78. Adapted with permission.

## *Burlington v. Department of Education*

The question in *Burlington v. Department of Education* (1985) was whether parents could be reimbursed for expenses incurred when they placed their child in a private school unilaterally after disagreeing with the public school's placement option. This case arose out of difficulties with determining the placement for a student with specific learning disabilities in Burlington, Massachusetts. Both plaintiffs and defendants agreed that the student had learning disabilities. The parents believed that their son's problem was neurologically based, while the district believed that the child's learning was affected by emotional factors (Goldberg, 1986). After seeking consultation from outside the district, the parents enrolled the child in a private school, without the school district's approval. The district refused to pay the tuition or reimburse the parents for expenses, believing that the public school program was appropriate.

In a decision at the district level, the court initially ruled that the parents were not entitled to reimbursement for tuition, despite a state hearing officer's opinion that the placement was appropriate. On appeal, the court ruled that the parents were entitled to tuition because the final placement (i.e., in the private school) was judged to be appropriate.

The U.S. Supreme Court ruled that parents are entitled to reimbursement for tuition for private school placement in order to obtain a "free, appropriate" education. The Court warned parents, however, that unilateral actions must be undertaken at their risk.

Turnbull (1986) provides a synopsis of how the term "appropriate" has been defined in legislative language and litigative decisions. In the first instance, legislative rubric usually refers to appropriate in the context of an educational process (i.e., nondiscriminatory evaluation, multifactored decision making, comprehensive IEP, parent participation and access, and so forth). However, the language of the EHA also speaks of an appropriate education with respect to state-level standards and the IEP. Section 504 of the Rehabilitation Act views appropriateness in terms of equivalency with programs for general education students within least restrictive settings (i.e., programs must be comparable). Finally, rulings in *Rowley, Armstrong, Tatro,* and *Burlington* define the term appropriate squarely with respect to the child having access to and deriving benefit and self-sufficiency from an educational placement, not just mere engagement (Yell, 1995). "They keep the IEP as the focal point of appropriateness. . . . They recognize the appropriateness of related services. . . . And they emphasize the child's right to and need for an appropriate (beneficial) education" (Turnbull, 1986, p. 351). Lehr and Haubrich (1986) reiterate the point: "The courts view the IEP as a critical document in setting the standard for an appropriate program for a student" (p. 363).

Prasse (1986) sums up the implications of these legislative acts and court cases for educational consultants when he writes:

> The law is not fixed or static. Rather it is fluid and dynamic. To that end, we must continuously work to stay abreast of evolving changes, so our professional practice remains within legally established parameters—parameters which ideally ensure the foundations necessary for providing services to handicapped persons. It is equally important that we understand the issues involved with each major legal influence (statute and litigation) inasmuch as sound professional practice demands that we along with lawyers and courts be active participants in debating, reviewing, and shaping future legal influences on the profession. (p. 311)

# Guns, Violence, Drugs, Extreme Disruption, and Special Health Care Cases: New Frontiers for Educational Consultants

The tremendous influx of weapons, illegal substances, aggressive students, and chronic and extremely disruptive students is unprecedented in American schools. Innumerable reports (e.g., Gardner, 1983; United States Department of

Education, 1993), books (e.g., Bennett, 1994), and news media provide a seemingly endless chronicle portraying the decay of our educational system, especially as it relates to student performance, teachers, and cultural values. Recent massive and fatal shootings on or near school grounds (e.g., Jonesboro, Arizona, 1998; Littleton, Colorado, 1999) galvanize opinion and crystalize the public view that the educational system and schools in general are failing in their mission.

While these factors present challenges for the general education curriculum, they present even larger and thornier problems for consultants working with special needs populations. Ultimately, consultants must address this question: Are students' assault behaviors, aggressive tendencies, disruptive episodes, and substance abuse manifestations of disabilities, and, if so, to what extent?

Educational consultants must be able to navigate the full range of due process procedures to address the assessment, intervention, and evaluation implications that a student with an aggressive profile presents, while simultaneously protecting that student from him or herself, and protecting other students in the school as well. With growing numbers of these students to consider—especially in large urban settings—the task can be daunting to say the least.

At the same time, school faculty have been asked to accommodate a widening spectrum of children, including those who require special accommodations, supervision, or care. Among those populations are students on ventilators; catheters; and pharmacological medications for behavior, attention deficit, or seizures, and students who require other medical or behavioral treatments that were not considered the responsibility of the general educator a generation ago. The primary question for consultants with respect to those children is: Is the child's primary need medical or educational? The answer to that question will dictate the course of action that the consultant should recommend.

> Changes in IDEA '97 emphasize that state education agencies (SEAs) and local education agencies (LEAs) need to ensure that all school-related personnel have the requisite knowledge and skills to address academic and social behavior problems appropriately.

The next section will outline what the law says regarding the treatment of such students, provide suggestions for deciding whether a manifestation evaluation is needed, and provide recommendations for interim alternative educational placements.

## The Language of the Law

Public Law 105-17, IDEA '97, is clear in its mandate that students receive a free appropriate public education. However, given the tide of increasing violence in schools, coupled with IDEA '97 language that requires educational programming for students with special needs, the law attempts to provide new protections for students whose behavior is an issue and also provide teachers and administrators with new tactics to maintain safe schools. The language in the IDEA '97 final rules makes this point succinctly:

> These changes reflect very serious consideration of the concerns of school administrators and teachers regarding preserving school safety and order without unduly burdensome requirements, while helping schools respond appropriately to a child's behavior, promoting the use of appropriate behavioral interventions, and increasing the likelihood of success in school and school completion for some of our most at-risk students. (*Federal Register*, 1999, p. 12413)

### Protections

Central to IDEA '97 language for protecting students is the shift from long-term punishment approaches (expulsion) to what is termed positive behavioral

See Chapter 8 for more discussion of functional assessments.

IDEA '97 amendments address timelines and reporting requirements with respect to the IEP team developing a Behavioral Intervention Plan, or if the child has one, reviewing that plan.

support (Artesani & Mallar, 1998; Ruef, Higgins, Glaeser, & Patnode, 1998; Zurkowski et al., 1998). *Positive behavioral support* rests on the multifactored evaluation team conducting a functional behavioral assessment for any student with disabilities when there is a high probability that suspension of that student will occur at some point during the academic year for longer than 10 school days. Further, a Behavioral Intervention Plan (BIP) must be developed that outlines the methods to be used to address the student's challenging behavior. Specifically, BIPs are required only when the child has first been removed from the current placement for more than 10 school days in the year and the removal constitutes a change in placement.

## New Tools for Administrators

School administrators are permitted to remove students with special needs from educational programs under certain conditions. For instance, if a student with behavior disabilities brings a gun to school, or sells narcotics on the school grounds, administrators can remove that student on the grounds that he or she is dangerous to the school population. Short- and long-term (up to 10 days) suspension provisions (e.g., contacting the parents, determining if a functional behavioral assessment has been conducted, determining if IEP goals have been implemented as intended) are delineated in IDEA '97 and executed, depending on the nature of the offense. Figure 2.3 shows a schematic of behavioral and disciplinary options that are available under IDEA '97 (Zurkowski et al., 1998).

## Manifestation Determination Evaluations

A *manifestation determination evaluation* is warranted if three conditions are met (Zurkowski et al., 1998): (a) Are weapons or guns involved in an infraction? (b) Is the student's conduct dangerous? and (c) Were school rules of conduct violated? The purpose of the manifestation determination evaluation is to ascertain whether a student's violent, drug-related, or dangerous behavior is part of his or her disability. This determination must be made by the IEP team if the student is to be considered for suspension for longer than 10 days. Four questions constitute the evaluation: Were the student's IEP and placement appropriate? Was the IEP implemented as written? Does the disability impair the student's understanding of the impact of the consequences of the behavior? Does the disability impair the student's ability to control his or her misbehavior? Figure 2.4 shows a flow chart, hinged to these four questions, for determining whether the disability is related to the misconduct.

As Yell (1998) indicates, however, even if a student is suspended for social misconduct, special educational services must continue in the interim alternative education setting (IAES). Zurkowski et al. (1998) remind consultants that IDEA '97 language associated with IAES applies equally to students who at the time of the infraction were being considered, but not yet deemed eligible, for special education programming.

School officials cannot use their authority to remove a student from his or her current placement repeatedly. The final rules for IDEA '97 make it clear that a "series of removals" or removals for longer than 10 school days means a *de facto* change in placement has occurred. A placement change cannot occur without considering due process and rewriting the IEP.

## Interim Alternative Educational Setting

The *interim alternative educational setting* is that setting that allows the student to maintain his or her special education program during the period when he or she is not able to be maintained in the general education classroom. Zurkowski et al. specify the three conditions that constitute the IAES: (a) special

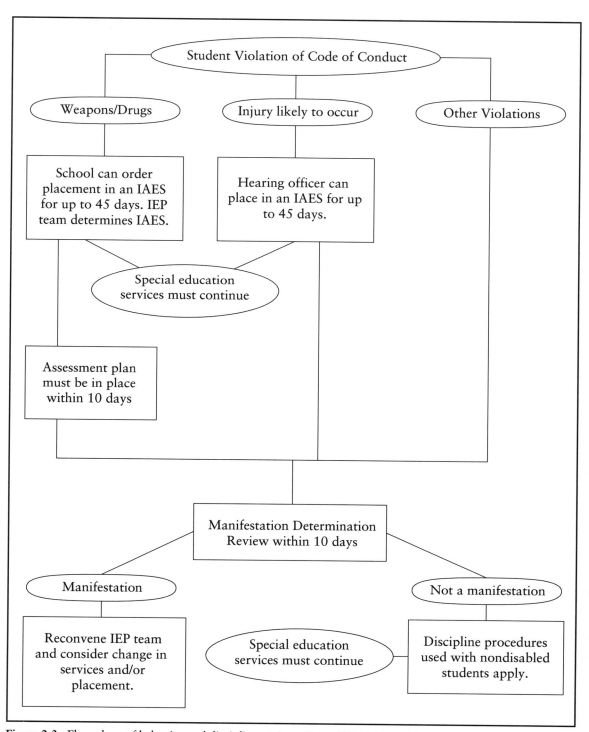

**Figure 2.3.** Flow chart of behavior and discipline options. From "Discipline and IDEA 1997: Instituting a New Balance," by J. K. Zurkowski, P. S. Kelly, and D. E. Griswold, 1998, *Intervention in School and Clinic,* 34(1), 9. Copyright 1997 by PRO-ED, Inc. Reprinted with permission.

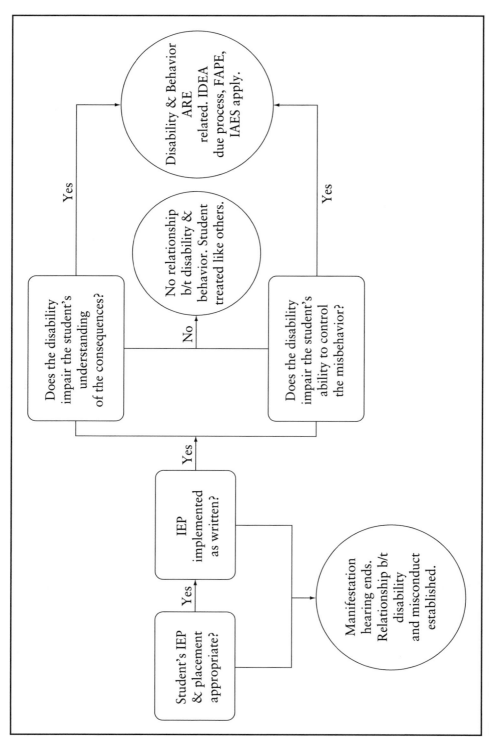

**Figure 2.4.** Decision tree for deciding if a student's conduct is related to a disability. From "Discipline and IDEA 1997: Instituting a New Balance," by J. K. Zurkowski, P. S. Kelly, and D. E. Griswold, 1998, *Intervention in School and Clinic, 34*(1), 3–9. Copyright 1997 by PRO-ED, Inc. Adapted with permission.

educational services must continue; (b) IEP goals must continue to be addressed; and (c) services and programs designed to address the behavior that led to the IAES determination must be initiated. In short, IDEA '97 mandates that services are to continue even when for disciplinary reasons the student is suspended from school. For egregious offenses, like bringing a weapon to school, the principal has the authority to remove a student from the school immediately (even over parental objection), and removal may last upwards to 45 days. However, within 45 days a manifestation hearing must be conducted to determine if the violation was a function of the student's disability (Yell, 1998). The student cannot be unilaterally expelled from school without due process.

# Impact of Litigation and Legislation for Consultants

The impact of right to education litigation and legislation for consultants is evident in several areas. First, those court rulings and federal and state laws have provided the opportunity to serve, directly and indirectly, populations of children from birth to age 21 with disabilities who were not receiving services previously (e.g., children with autism or traumatic brain injury).

Second, the structure and administrative procedures of many schools changed as a function of those rulings and laws. In some cases, referral teams or Committees on the Handicapped have been mandated by court order. In other cases, physical barriers for students with disabilities have been greatly reduced or eliminated, and administrative procedures for identification, placement, and the timely delivery of services have been modified.

Third, consultants should be aware of compliance requirements for Section 504, federal regulations (e.g., IDEA '97), and state standards. For instance, IDEA '97, although an amendment to existing legislation (IDEA), requires compliance with several procedures that did not exist in former legislation. Manifestation determination, individual alternative education placements, and the IEP itself are but a few examples that exemplify this point. Further, by noting inconsistencies or inadequacies in their districts' programs, and making recommendations to change those deficiencies, consultants may be able to avoid a federal or state citation for noncompliance and, therefore, prevent existing programs for the disabled from being jeopardized. Working through professional organizations and state associations can be an excellent way to keep abreast of requirements and make timely suggestions for improving services (Reschly, 1989).

Fourth, congressional intent that parents participate as equals with educational personnel has been reaffirmed. Consultants would be wise to continue their efforts to actively seek parental input with respect to identification and treatment within the least restrictive environment. As Margolis and Tewel (1990) state, "All children are entitled to treatment that offers the promise of effectively addressing their needs" (p. 286). The child's interests are probably best served when skilled consultants encourage active parental participation and negotiate with parents so that protracted and costly litigation is avoided. Cases that go through district due process procedures, appeals, and the Supreme Court are extremely expensive in terms of time, resources, and legal fees (cf. the *Board of Education v. Rowley* case), and the financial burden alone on parents can be enormous (Luckasson, 1986).

Finally, practitioners must be aware that compliance with state standards does not necessarily protect the district from litigation. Courts have mandated changes in deficient programs even when those programs met established guidelines. School districts must show that they are striving for "state-of-the-art" programming for their students and are continually searching for better methodologies to improve service. Brady, McDougall, and Dennis (1989) sum up the situation succinctly: "It is the responsibility of schools to keep abreast of current trends, research, and program development since such information is necessary for delivering appropriate services" (p. 53). Consultants, given their array of technical competencies, their communication skills, and their position of coordination, are ideally suited to fulfill this commitment.

# Conclusion

Special education litigation and legislation have significantly affected the delivery of services for students with disabilities. Due process, nondiscriminatory testing, free appropriate education, and funding issues are now viewed in a much different light than they were prior to IDEA '97 legislation or to landmark court rulings during the 1980s and 1990s. To meet their ethical and legal obligations to children, consultants must keep current with laws and court rulings that govern and, to a large extent, define special education and the consultant's role.

# Summary of Key Points

## Definition of Litigation

1. Litigation refers to the act or process of bringing a court suit against another party for the purpose of redressing an alleged injustice.

2. A class action suit refers to a suit brought by one or more individuals on behalf of themselves and others in similar circumstances.

3. Litigative decisions, consent decrees, and judicial opinions are three major methods that courts use to provide interpretations of legislation.

4. One of the main effects of litigated cases is that rights for individuals with disabilities have been obtained.

## Definition of Legislation

5. Legislation refers to the act or process whereby elected representatives embody within a single document law that becomes applicable to the general public. Legislation can take one of two forms: program or civil rights.

6. Once a federal law is enacted, state law is usually changed to be in compliance with it.

7. Rules and regulations that describe how a law will operate are written after the law is enacted.

# The Right to Education

8. The right to education is based on the principle that all children are entitled to a free appropriate public education, and on constitutional law, litigative rulings, and federal statutes.

9. Section 504 of the Rehabilitation Act of 1973 is termed the civil rights law for people with disabilities because of its comprehensive and far-reaching implications. It specifically prohibits discrimination in education and employment based on disability.

10. Several public laws have been enacted that are designed specifically to address the right of children with disabilities to a free appropriate public education.

11. The Americans with Disabilities Act of 1990 extended civil rights protection to people with disabilities in the private sector. This law, fashioned after the Rehabilitation Act of 1973, provides for public service and telecommunication accommodations and mandates that employers with 25 or more employees must make reasonable adjustments to the work environment to allow a person with disabilities to perform his or her job.

12. IDEA '97 mandates a number of changes related to the IEP, to conflict resolution between the school district and parents, to proactive behavioral management plans, and to disciplinary procedures for students with disabilities. Specific components that relate to collaborative consultation include: eligibility and labeling, Individualized Education Programs, and least restrictive environment (LRE).

# Assuring the Right to Education

13. The right to an educational experience is assured by the following provisions of law: due process, free appropriate public education, nondiscriminatory evaluation, the IEP, and the least restrictive environment.

# Guns, Violence, Drugs, Extreme Disruption, and Special Health Care Cases

14. The basic question with respect to violence in schools and disabilities is: Is the student's assault behavior, aggressive tendencies, disruptive episodes, or substance abuse a manifestation of the disability or not? Educational consultants must be prepared to address the assessment, intervention, and evaluation implications that a student with an aggressive profile presents, while simultaneously protecting that student from him or herself, and protecting other students in the school as well.

15. IDEA '97 includes provisions and procedures that address how teachers and administrators should manage disciplinary challenges.

16. A manifestation determination evaluation is warranted if three conditions are met (Zurkowski et al., 1998): (a) Are weapons or guns involved in an infraction? (b) Is the student's conduct dangerous? and (c) Were school rules of conduct violated?

17. The interim alternative educational setting (IAES) is that placement that allows the student to maintain his or her special education program during the period when he or she is not able to be maintained in the general education classroom.

## Impact of Litigation and Legislation for Consultants

18. Litigation and legislation affect consultants in several ways: (a) expanded services for students (e.g., brain injured students) who previously have not had access, (b) administrative structure (e.g., formation of referral terms), (c) compliance requirements (e.g., manifestation determination), (d) parent participation, and (e) best practice procedures.

## Questions

1. What are some advantages and disadvantages of class action suits?

2. Define the term litigation.

3. Distinguish between a fully litigated case, judicial opinion, and a case that has been resolved by a consent decree.

4. Define the term legislation and identify the key right to education laws that have been enacted since 1975, including IDEA '97.

5. Explain the meaning of the term educational opportunity over the past 30 years. Provide reasons for any change in meaning.

6. What litigative action had an impact on the current meaning of educational opportunity in this country?

7. Compare and contrast key provisions of IDEA with IDEA '97. Why has IDEA '97 placed greater emphasis on positive behavioral support?

8. Discuss how the Daubert, portability, inclusion, and balancing standards apply to students with disabilities.

9. How has the increased appearance of guns, violence, drugs, and special health care cases affected the role of the consultant?

10. Explain what is meant by a manifestation determination evaluation and an interim alternative educational setting.

11. What are two major components of the Section 504 rules and regulations?

12. Identify the federal laws and court rulings that are crucial to the assurance of an appropriate education for all children with disabilities? Contrast how the term appropriate is used across these instances.

13. What are the four basic principles embodied within federal special education legislative mandates?

14. What is a basic distinction between substantive and procedural due process?

15. What are two aspects of nondiscriminatory evaluation resulting from litigated cases?

16. What three hierarchical steps are available to the dissenting party in the impartial due process hearing procedures?

17. The notion of the least restrictive environment is the legal corollary of what social science principle?

# Discussion Points and Exercises

1. Compare the special education programming that existed in your school district in the 1980s with the program that exists today, especially with respect to provisions embedded within IDEA '97. What are some of the similarities? What are some of the differences? Can you foresee the need to amend recent legislation (e.g., IDEA '97)? What would be the nature of such amendments?

2. As a consultant in your school district, you are involved in the implementation of special education programming. You are requested to make a presentation at the next parent-teacher meeting outlining the service delivery system to your school district. State how all children, with and without disabilities, will receive a quality education under either IDEA '97 or Section 504. Points to consider: (a) factors essential for quality education, (b) factors unique to students with disabilities, and (c) service delivery procedures best suited to meet the needs of all children in the school district.

3. There has been a complaint regarding the educational program of a special education student who has been reintegrated into your general education program. You are requested to attend a local hearing. What would be the nature of the information you, as a consultant, supervisor, or local education agency representative, should be prepared to supply?

4. Provide your definition of the term *free appropriate public education* based on (a) your own experiences as a consultant, (b) your understanding of federal statutes, and (c) court rulings.

5. State implications that would exist for the consultant if court rulings permitted the segregation of exceptional students because of a perception that they could not benefit from an educational experience.

6. Identify a student in one of your classrooms who exhibits aggressive behavior. Apply the Daubert, inclusion, portability, or balancing standard to the case. Indicate the role of the manifestation determination evaluation if suspension or expulsion is being considered.

# Section *II*

## *Teaming, Communication, and Problem Solving: Essential Skills for the Consultant*

# Teaming and Co-Teaching 3

IDEA '97 and best practice require that consultants work effectively and efficiently in a variety of teaming relationships. As Friend and Cook (1997) state, "Teams have become a standard way of doing business in schools" (p. 3). In middle schools, for example, consultants may be part of an interdisciplinary team, working with teachers to develop an integrated curriculum, planning lessons, and delivering and evaluating instruction. Co-teaching also represents a team format, as two professionals share planning and teaching responsibility for a class of students. Problem-solving teams are often used in schools to help teachers deal with students who experience academic, social, or emotional difficulties in school (cf. Harris, 1995).

In this chapter, we discuss how consultants can design, implement, and evaluate teaming relationships. First, we provide a brief discussion of the distinction between direct service and indirect service. Then, we discuss co-teaching arrangements and problem-solving teams. Finally, we discuss interagency models and technology and teaming.

## Objectives

After reading this chapter, the reader should be able to:

1. distinguish between direct and indirect consultation services;

2. explain eight components that contribute to a co-teaching environment;

3. demonstrate schedules that co-teachers can use;

4. discuss strategies for establishing and maintaining professional relationships between co-teachers;

5. discuss different co-teaching structures;

6. identify strategies for evaluating co-teaching;

7. identify key issues to consider when planning for co-teaching;

8. distinguish among multidisciplinary, interdisciplinary, and transdisciplinary teams;

9. define consultation assistance team;

10. identify stages of team development;

11. describe team member roles;

12. compare the characteristics of effective and ineffective teams;

13. state several strategies for improving team effectiveness;

14. identify the key components of a "bottom up" model for initiating a consultation assistance team;

15. describe factors to address in interagency consultation;

16. discuss the role of technology in consultation.

## Key Terms

| | |
|---|---|
| direct service | consultation assistance teams |
| indirect service | teacher assistance teams |
| co-teaching | intervention assistance teams |
| curriculum-centered problem-solving approach | mainstream assistance teams |
| | team roles |
| co-teaching structures | reciprocity |
| co-planning | collaborative planning guide |
| multidisciplinary teams | consultation assistance team |
| interdisciplinary teams | structures |
| transdisciplinary teams | interagency collaborative teams |

# Direct Versus Indirect Service

Service to students will be discussed along a continuum of direct to indirect service. Figure 3.1 clarifies the distinction between direct and indirect service using the triadic model.

*Direct service* to students includes any task in which the consultant actually works with the student without a mediator. Instructing a student is the most common example of direct service to a student. As stated by Meyers, Parsons, and Martin (1979): "When direct service is applied appropriately, it invariably involves consultative aspects; thus to exclude direct service from consultation would be artificial" (p. 89).

*Indirect service* to students includes any task in which the consultant works with a mediator (e.g., a teacher or parent) who in turn works to change a student's behavior. Indirect services to students are accomplished by providing direct service to the mediator. Generating ideas for interventions as a member of a consultation assistance team is an example of an indirect service to a student because the student benefits indirectly from the consultant's intervention with the teacher.

For the purposes of discussion within this chapter, we will reserve our analysis to two key functions of consultants: being a member of a co-teaching team and participating within a consultation assistance team.

# Co-Teaching

Consultants can provide a form of direct service with mediators using co-teaching techniques. Co-teaching usually takes place in the general education environment and is defined as two or more teachers planning and instructing the same group of students at the same time and in the same place. Co-teaching

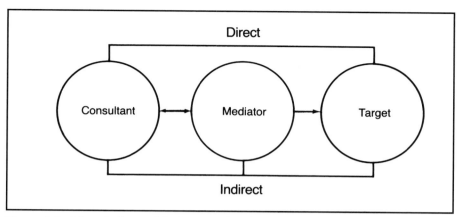

**Figure 3.1.** The triadic model showing the distinction between direct and indirect consultation (modification of Figure 2.1—3rd edition).

is a promising approach. Though much has been written in recent years about co-teaching among general and special educators (e.g., Bauwens & Hourcade, 1997, 1995; Cook & Friend, 1995; Dieker & Barnett, 1996; Dyke, Sundbye, & Pemberton, 1997; Harris, 1998a, b; Harris & Smith, 1998; Reeve & Hallahan, 1994; Salend, Johansen, Mumper, Chase, Pike, & Dorner, 1997; Schumm, Vaughn, & Harris, 1997; Vaughn, Schumm, & Arguelles, 1997; Walther-Thomas, Bryant, & Land, 1996), it can occur among a variety of individuals (e.g., fourth-grade teachers, special educators and speech and language therapists, and bilingual and special educators).

## Components

The literature suggests that eight components contribute to a co-teaching environment: interpersonal communication, physical arrangement of the classroom, familiarity with the curriculum, curriculum goals and modifications, behavior management, instructional presentation, grading and evaluation, and instructional planning (Bauwens & Hourcade, 1995, 1991; Cook & Friend, 1995; Gately & Gately, 1993; Vaughn, Schumm, & Arguelles, 1997; Warger & Pugach, 1996).

### Interpersonal Communication

Interpersonal communication is the cornerstone of a co-teaching relationship and at the beginning level is characterized by limited, respectful, and distant communication (Gately & Gately, 1993). Sometimes at this stage, there may be a clash of teaching styles. As the co-teaching relationship develops, however, communication increases, which is demonstrated by sharing ideas, respecting each other's teaching styles, and using more humor in communication. Co-teachers who have worked together for extended periods often use nonverbal communication within the classroom. The interpersonal and communication skills discussed in the following chapter help teachers to develop their co-teaching relationship.

It is important for co-teachers to recognize that they are establishing a working partnership as well as maintaining it once it has been developed. Tables 3.1 and 3.2 provide tips for establishing and maintaining such a working partnership.

**Table 3.1**

Tips for *Establishing* a Working Partnership

---

- Encourage and seek volunteers.
- Know it is a journey. There really isn't a roadmap.
- Realize that styles can blend and merge.
- It is more of a "shared" effort than an "equal" effort.
- Realize that it requires long-term staff development of relationship skills as well as "concept" information.
- Make a habit of using inclusive language, e.g., "we," "us," "our."
- Realize that it is not forever. When students' needs are being met, co-teachers move to a different collaborative structure.
- Be sure to schedule visits. Don't just "drop in."
- Build flexible and fluid schedules, aligning blocks of time based on student needs.
- Use a systematic format for planning and debriefing co-teaching experiences.
- In instruction, use numerous materials and varied approaches, focus on a few critical concepts, and use varied rates and pacing.
- Be willing to change teaching styles and preferences.
- Be willing to work closely with another adult.
- Be willing to share responsibility.
- Be willing to rely on another person to perform tasks previously done alone.
- Be flexible.
- Be committed to co-teaching and to the co-teaching relationship.
- Use effective interpersonal communication skills, particularly for problem solving and decision making.
- Assess the co-teaching situation through discussion of the following questions with your co-teaching partner(s):
  1. How willing am I to let a colleague observe me teaching content with which I am not particularly familiar?
  2. How willing am I to consider and experiment with different ways of teaching?
  3. Am I willing to let someone else take responsibility for tasks at which I am particularly skilled?
  4. What is my level of comfort about relying on someone else in a joint project?

---

*Note.* From *Collaborative Teaching Casebooks: Facilitator's Guide* (p. 13), by K. C. Harris, 1998b, Austin, TX: PRO-ED. Copyright 1998 by PRO-ED. Reprinted with permission.

## Physical Arrangement of the Classroom

Physical arrangement includes the use of space and the position of desks, tables, materials, students, and teachers within the classroom. According to Gately and Gately (1993), when co-teaching relationships begin, they are characterized by separate use of classroom space with little ownership by the special educator. Territoriality by the general educator becomes less evident as the relationship develops.

As a well-developed co-teaching partnership unfolds, students are often arranged in integrated, small groups for cooperative learning activities or receiving whole class instruction from both teachers. Further, co-teachers are comfortable in all areas of the classroom; they are aware of each other and reposition themselves as needed. Joint ownership of the classroom is evident in the use of space as well as materials. Often special and general education materials are housed together in the general education classroom.

## Table 3.2
### Tips for *Maintaining* a Working Partnership

- Remember that co-teaching is an evolving relationship. Don't expect perfection. Adopt the attitude that "problems are our friends."
- Build on the strengths of each partner.
- Think of co-teaching as a dialogue among two people, not a "you teach, then I'll teach" approach.
- Recognize that you are both responsible for ALL the students in your class.
- Be sure to talk about the roles each of you assumes in the class.
- Recognize that one teacher leads and the other anticipates what's needed and you alternate those roles.
- Keep teaching and learning active.
- Instead of a "well but" attitude, have a "how might, how can" attitude.
- Have high expectations for what you will do and how it will work.
- Realize that, as adults, you are learning too.
- Collect data and disseminate to others the effectiveness of your work.
- Avoid limiting words such as "can't." Use words such as "can," "will," "do."
- Explore the degree to which you agree on philosophies and beliefs. Establish a common ground from which to work.
- Discuss and develop classroom routines.
- Talk about the following throughout the co-teaching relationship:
  - how to designate your partnership (e.g., by putting both teachers' names on the board)
  - which organizational structures both of you can support (e.g., how students ask to leave the room)
  - which instructional routines both of you can support (e.g., how students organize their work and time)
  - which discipline routines both of you can support (e.g., what is unacceptable student behavior, what are agreed upon consequences for unacceptable student behavior)
  - your idiosyncratic pet peeves (e.g., failure to put away the stapler!) and what you can do about them.
  - when and how you will provide each other with feedback on your co-teaching. Be sure to talk about co-teaching periodically and choose a method to debrief that is comfortable for both of you. For example, some teachers may want to talk about co-teaching efforts right away. Others may want to wait a day and reflect on the co-teaching effort. Establish a process for talking that will enable you to be honest and maintain mutual respect and trust.

*Note.* From *Collaborative Teaching Casebooks: Facilitator's Guide* (p. 15), by K. C. Harris, 1998b, Austin, TX: PRO-ED. Copyright 1998 by PRO-ED. Reprinted with permission.

## Familiarity with the Curriculum

It is essential that co-teachers have an understanding of the scope and sequence of the curriculum. Though different co-teaching structures can accommodate different skill levels in curriculum and instruction, co-teachers should know the curriculum objectives. To establish credibility with their partners and the students, co-teachers need to take responsibility for learning the curriculum. As cooperative learning activities or small group instruction occurs, skill and confidence increase (Gately & Gately, 1993).

In subsequent chapters of this book, we provide an overview of curriculum areas, accounting for differences in abilities, grade levels, and language.

## Curriculum Goals and Modifications

When co-teachers initiate their partnership, there is usually little flexibility in goal setting and few, if any, curricular modifications. As the co-teaching partnership develops, co-teachers become aware of the need for student-centered goals and objectives and become more willing to implement modifications. Integrated, student-centered objectives are included in the curriculum by mutual agreement as the co-teaching relationship matures. The consultant can facilitate this integration by providing lists of objectives for students who may be able to achieve only some of the objectives. A discussion of this process of adaptation is discussed in chapters in Sections III and IV.

Warger and Pugach (1996) describe a *curriculum-centered problem-solving approach* that naturally fits with co-teaching. This approach incorporates the essence of the problem-solving process discussed in the following chapter. The four steps of this approach are: (1) establish rapport and set boundaries for collaboration, (2) identify the problem, (3) develop an intervention plan, and (4) evaluate the collaboration.

In the curriculum-centered problem-solving approach, the attention of the conversation of the co-teachers shifts from the student to the curriculum. Co-teachers are encouraged to visualize the classroom problem from a proactive perspective in which the target of the intervention is the curriculum and its relationship to the student.

## Behavior Management

Chapter 12 provides the reader with a full discussion of issues associated with behavior management.

When co-teachers begin to work together, either management of student behavior is the sole responsibility of the general educator, or the specialist assumes management duties for students with disabilities. As the co-teaching relationship develops, co-teachers mutually develop rules, routines, expectations, and consequences. Beliefs about the management of students are tied to the instructional beliefs of the teacher. When developing a classroom management plan, co-teachers must clarify their beliefs and agree to a plan. Discussing classroom management styles and roles allows both co-teachers to maintain an orderly learning environment. The suggestions offered in Tables 3.1 and 3.2 will provide co-teachers with a process for examining the co-teaching partnership. The following section on grading and evaluation also offers suggestions for evaluation of the co-teaching partnership.

## Instructional Presentation

For sources of descriptions of co-teaching programs, readers are referred to the following: National Education Association (1994), Nowacek (1992), Harris (1998a), and Harris & Smith (1998).

Instructional presentation refers to the *co-teaching structures* used to deliver instruction. Use of co-teaching structures changes as the co-teaching partnership matures. In the beginning, special educators often provide instruction to small groups or individual students, or they circulate around the class providing help to individual students as the need arises. However, although the general educator will usually remain the lead teacher even as the co-teaching team employs different co-teaching structures, it is inappropriate to remain at this level. A mature co-teaching relationship is reflected in co-teaching structures that involve both co-teachers presenting lessons and students perceiving the co-teachers as a team, both of whom are in charge. Specialists can facilitate this evolution by developing lessons useful to all students, not just students with special needs (Gately & Gately, 1993).

**Table 3.3**

Seven Co-Teaching Structures

*One Teaching, One Supporting.* One teacher designs and delivers instruction to the entire group. The second teacher supports the lead teacher, providing assistance as needed. This is a simple approach used by many new co-teaching partners. If used indiscriminately or exclusively, it can result in one teacher being only an assistant.

*Station Teaching.* The teachers divide responsibility for planning and delivering instruction. Students move among the stations set up by the teachers. It does reduce the teacher-student ratio but requires carefully monitoring noise and activity levels as well as transitions from station to station.

*Parallel Teaching.* The teachers jointly plan instruction but each delivers it to a heterogeneous group composed of half of the students in the class. This does lower the teacher-to-student ratio. It requires that teachers deliver the same instruction, so they must have comparable skills and carefully coordinate their efforts.

*Alternative Teaching.* This occurs when a small group of students receives preteaching or reteaching of the instructional content. This approach can provide an opportunity for students to receive small-group instruction but can be stigmatizing if only the same students (e.g., students with special needs) consistently receive small-group support.

*Team Teaching.* In this co-teaching structure, the initial presentation of some content is shared between two teachers who jointly plan and present academic content to all students. This is particularly effective when the two teachers possess similar areas of expertise—for example, if the special educator also possesses an elementary or secondary teaching certification.

*Complementary Teaching.* This co-teaching structure is especially useful to address specific school problems of students. The general educator might maintain primary responsibility for teaching the subject matter, and the special educator might assume responsibility for addressing students' specific problems such as the need for study skills.

*Supportive Learning Activities.* These are educator-developed student activities that supplement the primary instruction to enhance student learning. Typically, the general educator maintains responsibility for delivering the essential content, while the special educator identifies, develops, and leads student activities designed to reinforce, enrich, and augment student learning. For example, small-group team discussions may be an appropriate supplementary activity for a science lesson. Usually, both educators are present and monitor the primary instruction and the supportive learning activities.

*Note.* From *Collaborative Teaching Casebooks: Facilitator's Guide* (p. 27), by K. C. Harris, 1998b, Austin, TX: PRO-ED. Copyright 1998 by PRO-ED. Adapted with permission.

There are many possible co-teaching structures. It is important for general educators and specialists to realize that co-teaching is an instructional tool. They should choose the co-teaching structure that matches the needs of the students and the skills of the co-teachers. Table 3.3 provides a description of seven co-teaching structures and suggestions for their use.

Bauwens and Hourcade (1997), Cook and Friend (1995), and Vaughn, Schumm, and Arguelles (1997) explore a number of ways co-teaching can be implemented in the classroom.

## Grading and Evaluation

Grading and evaluation address the performance of students as well as assessing the effectiveness of co-teaching. Vaughn, Schumm, and Arguelles (1997) consider the issue of grading to be the foremost discussion point that must be resolved prior to launching a co-teaching relationship. Grades awarded by special educators, for example, often reflect effort, motivation, and abilities of students, whereas grades awarded by general educators often are based on a uniform set of expectations that are adjusted slightly, if at all, to reflect those dimensions. Joint decisions about how grades will be awarded for in-class assignments, homework, and tests reduce conflicts between parties.

*Student Evaluation.* Grading and evaluation procedures evolve as the co-teaching partnership develops. In the beginning of the co-teaching partnership, co-teachers usually have separate procedures and employ little variety in the evaluation measures. As the co-teachers engage in more discussion, they may increase the use of evaluation measures. Experienced co-teachers tend to use a multitude of grading measures, which include modifications to the curriculum made for students with special needs. It is important that specialists take responsibility for assuring the accountability of assignments, sharing IEPs with general educators, and encouraging their general education partners to incorporate all this information when developing grading policies.

Bauwens and Hourcade (1997) provide an example of how co-teaching can facilitate the evaluation of students. One educator can administer and monitor the larger group taking a test while the other teacher provides needed accommodations for students in a smaller group. When students complete a test, they can take it to either of the teachers for immediate feedback. Finally, when the quiz is completed, students can be paired and exchange their ungraded tests. One teacher can give the correct answers to the students orally, while the other circulates and monitors student grading of the quiz.

*Co-teaching Evaluation.* Evaluation of student achievement is not the only consideration. Bauwens and Hourcade (1991) indicate that it is crucial to evaluate the effectiveness of co-teaching arrangements. This may be done by using a variety of sources of information such as students' academic progress, parental satisfaction, teachers' attitudes, student attitudes, and referral or placement trends. Table 3.4 provides tips for evaluating co-teaching. These tips incorporate the sources of evaluative information identified by Bauwens and Hourcade (1991) within a suggested monitoring process.

It is important that co-teachers incorporate evaluation of the co-teaching process or arrangement as part of their ongoing activities just as they would incorporate evaluation of student progress as part of their ongoing activities. This will enable co-teachers to develop and refine a process that works for all participants in the co-teaching program. For instance, co-teachers might evaluate which of seven co-teaching structures produces optimal student learning. Co-teaching is not a specified instructional procedure. Rather, it is an instructional tool that educators can use to better meet the needs of all students. To decide how best to use this tool, educators need ongoing information.

## Instructional Planning

Co-teachers should cooperatively develop instructional planning so that both teachers can be actively involved in the classroom environment. Co-teachers cannot appropriately monitor and adjust if either is unfamiliar with curriculum goals or instructional strategies.

*Co-planning* is defined as two or more teachers determining the who, what, where, and how of co-taught instruction. Walther-Thomas et al. (1996) describe five themes of effective co-planning: First, co-teachers trust each other's professional skills, enabling them to work through problems that may emerge during the partnership. Second, learning environments should incorporate the active involvement of the students and the co-teachers. Third, effective co-planners create learning environments that value each person's contributions, allowing for equally shared roles and responsibilities. Fourth, routines are developed to facilitate effective co-planning. Finally, co-planners become more skilled over

**Table 3.4**

Tips for Evaluating Co-Teaching

*Evaluation should be conceptualized as part of an ongoing feedback loop in which program outcomes are judged against both process and product program goals.*

### Identify the Purpose—Possibilities

1. informing program participants
2. informing constituents
3. informing the profession

### Identify Needed Information—Possibilities

1. description of model and activities
2. comparison with other approaches
3. cost of implementing the model
4. training activities
5. reactions of participants
6. lessons learned

### Identify Sources of Information—Possibilities

1. students:
   - *subjective information*—e.g., surveys or interview data regarding usefulness or feelings as a participant in the program
   - *objective information*—e.g., standardized test scores, curriculum-based measures, grades

2. system:
   - *subjective information*—e.g., surveys or interview data regarding ability to service all students, efficiency of program, effectiveness of program
   - *objective information*—e.g., frequency of suspensions, rates of absenteeism, rates of grade retention, numbers of students identified as in need of special services

3. educators:
   - *subjective information*—e.g., surveys or interview data regarding usefulness or feelings as a participant in the program
   - *objective information*—e.g., educator burnout rates, rate of transfer requests, number of educators who sign up and attend training sessions or volunteer to participate as co-teachers, number of students continuing to be removed from the general education classroom for support services

4. parents and community:
   - *subjective information*—e.g., surveys or interview data regarding beliefs concerning instruction of students with special needs, beliefs about co-teaching program
   - *objective information*—e.g., attendance at parent-teacher meetings about program, voting patterns of school board members

### Guidelines

1. clearly identify program goals
2. clearly identify desired outcomes of the program as well as the process of program implementation; specify measurable objectives that will reflect desired program outcomes
3. evaluate the usefulness of monitoring activities
4. assure the propriety of monitoring activities
5. assure the accuracy of monitoring data collection activities
6. identify the resources available within or outside the school to conduct the monitoring activities
7. include consumers of the program as a source of information

*Note.* From *Collaborative Teaching Casebooks: Facilitator's Guide* (p. 19), by K. C. Harris, 1998b, Austin, TX: PRO-ED. Copyright 1998 by PRO-ED. Adapted with permission.

time, gradually improving the quality of the classroom instruction. Table 3.5 provides tips for co-teachers as they plan activities.

According to Walther-Thomas et al. (1996), co-teachers involved in regularly scheduled, weekly co-planning meetings typically address the three issues of content goals, learner needs, and effective instructional delivery. Bauwens and Hourcade (1995) also suggest that co-planners should reflect on the process of co-teaching and incorporate within their planning an identification of co-teaching strategies that have worked as well as strategies to try in subsequent lessons.

When content goals are discussed, a link should be made between the content goals specified by the district curriculum guides and the IEP goals of the identified students to determine the extent of the modifications needed. The instructional plans developed should weave together content, expected learning outcomes, and instructional strategies.

Co-planners must also consider the diverse learning needs of the students. A variety of sources provide information for effective instruction, such as IEPs, report cards, standardized test scores, pretest information, curriculum-based assessments, informal assessments, and teacher observations. As the school year progresses, co-teachers rely on their knowledge of students' needs, abilities, and interests to facilitate instructional planning.

An advantage to co-planning is that co-teachers can use their complementary professional skills, enabling them to employ a variety of instructional strategies, guided practice strategies, and monitoring procedures to create active, appropriate, and productive learning environments. Several planning tools have been designed to facilitate co-teaching. Vaughn, Schumm, and Arguelles (1997) provide the following questions for co-teachers to answer in developing their daily lesson plans:

1. What are you going to teach?
2. Which co-teaching technique will you use?
3. What are the specific tasks of both teachers?
4. What materials are needed?
5. How will you evaluate learning?
6. What student follow-up information is needed?

The planning pyramid (Schumm, Vaughn, & Harris, 1997) provides another planning strategy. The planning pyramid is a framework for planning instruction to enhance learning for all students in an inclusive classroom. There are three layers, or degrees of learning, to the pyramid, based on the premise that all students are capable of learning but not all students will learn all the curriculum material. The largest layer, on the bottom of the pyramid, represents what all students will learn. The middle layer represents what most students will learn. The smallest, top layer represents what some students will learn.

Dyke, Sundbye, and Pemberton (1997) provide an example of the use of the planning pyramid. Another example of the use of this lesson plan format can be found in Chapter 7.

Points of entry also guide the planning pyramid. Each axis, or point, of the pyramid represents one aspect of instruction: teacher, topic, content, student, or instructional practice. Questions focused on each point of entry are provided to help teachers plan lessons and courses, e.g., Is the material new or review? What prior knowledge do I have of this topic? Will the students with reading difficulties be able to function independently in learning the concepts from the text? How will the class size affect my teaching of this concept? What grouping pattern is most appropriate?

A second issue when planning for co-teaching is finding time to plan and discuss instruction and student progress. This may be especially difficult for the

## Table 3.5

Tips for Planning Effectively

1. Realize that planning in terms of general and special educators is a new experience for many teachers.
2. Be flexible with the amount and scheduling of planning time to be able to address problems as they arise.
3. Realize different co-teaching options require different amounts and types of planning.
4. The physical proximity of teachers enhances joint planning.
5. Schedule joint planning times as part of the master building schedule.
6. Be prepared to address the following issues when planning co-teaching sessions:
   - classroom design
   - academic content
   - process skills
   - learning strategies
   - social skills
   - IEP goals and student outcomes
   - behavior management
   - monitoring progress
7. During planning meetings address the following:
   a. Reflection:
      How did we do last week?
      - What were the best things that happened in our co-teaching this past week?
      - What did either of us make mental notes to talk about improving?
   b. Goal-setting:
      What could we do, and what should we do, this next week?
      - What are the possible things we might do?
      - Which of these things will best help us to effectively teach all students?
   c. Resources:
      What are the resources we'll need to achieve the goals we've set for the next week?
      - What are the physical resources (materials, equipment, and so forth) that will be required?
      - What are the personal resources that will be required?
   d. Responsibilities: Which of us will be responsible for goals and activities?
8. Set time limits
9. Control interruptions
10. Establish priorities, with 1 equaling the most important (and sometimes the toughest); address the number 1 priority first, but start the conversation with something positive using effective interpersonal and communication and conflict resolution strategies, if necessary.
11. Before leaving, write down the agenda for the next meeting.

*Note.* From *Collaborative Teaching Casebooks: Facilitator's Guide* (p. 21), by K. C. Harris, 1998b, Austin, TX: PRO-ED. Copyright 1998 by PRO-ED. Reprinted with permission.

special educator who is working with more than one general educator (e.g., at the middle or high school levels). Although many teachers find time before or after school, or in allotted preparation periods, some school districts or individual schools have developed innovative practices to allow their teachers the

**Table 3.6**

Some Ways To Schedule Time To Plan

- Fewer staff could supervise large group meetings of students for special types of school experiences (e.g., guest speakers, films, plays).
- Principal or other support staff or supervisor could teach a period a day on a regularly scheduled basis.
- When students are working on the same independent assignment or study activity, they could be clustered in large groups (e.g., in multipurpose room or library).
- A permanent "floating" substitute could be hired.
- Aides or volunteers could guide or supervise groups and classes of students at class-changing time, lunch, and recess.
- Specific time each week could be assigned by principal for staff collaboration.
- The school day could be altered to provide staff collaboration without students (e.g., the last Friday afternoon each month).
- One day per grading period could be established as "collaboration day" (no other activities could be substituted on that day).
- A common planning period could be scheduled.

*Note.* Adapted from "Collaborative Consultation in the Education of Mildly Handicapped and At-risk Students," by J. F. West and L. Idol, 1990, *Remedial and Special Education, 11*(1), 29–30. Copyright 1990 by PRO-ED, Inc. Adapted with permission.

time it takes to plan for successful co-teaching. Raywid (1993) describes the ways 15 schools met the challenge of providing collaborative planning time for teachers. The schools' administrator hired substitutes to allow teacher planning time, used two or three days of the intercessions between quarters in the year-round school calendar for planning, implemented a variety of grouping patterns, and assigned volunteers to assist teaching teams. Table 3.6 provides suggestions for ways to schedule time to plan.

Finding time for planning is only one of the coordinating issues teachers face when designing and implementing co-teaching programs. Scheduling issues are identified and discussed in the following section.

## Scheduling Co-Teaching

Bauwens and Hourcade (1995) discuss different schedules co-teachers can use. They indicate that educators who have been most successful in co-teaching began simply. It is important to determine how much time per day and how many days per week will be spent in co-teaching. Two schedules co-teachers can consider are presented in Table 3.7.

To help co-teachers decide on the type of schedule to implement, there are several questions that educators should ask themselves. These questions and some scheduling suggestions are listed in Table 3.8 By answering these questions, educators will be able to ascertain their commitment to co-teaching as well as the issues they need to consider when determining a schedule for co-teaching.

When scheduling activities, it is suggested that co-teachers incorporate the following: (a) collaborative planning and problem-solving time, (b) time for the activities of all program participants, and (c) flexibility. Collaborative planning

**Table 3.7**

Co-Teaching Schedules

*Dyadic Stable Schedule.* A schedule in which one support service provider works with one general educator in a fixed daily schedule. Such a schedule is usually easy for students and educators to remember, and carryover and follow-up are consistent. It also makes planning easier and facilitates the development of professional relationships. However, some burnout and/or boredom could occur, as the two educators are together every day. Also, it prevents the support services provider from working with many students and general educators. It is also possible that some students would become dependent on this intensive level of support.

*Rollover Schedule.* A schedule in which the support service provider works with more than one general educator and varies the schedule. For example, the special educator may come into classroom 1 on Monday, Wednesday, and Friday and classroom 2 on Tuesday and Thursday. This allows the special educator to work with a greater number of general educators and students. This could result in general educators acquiring some specialized skills, students being exposed to different teaching styles, and the monotony of a daily co-teaching schedule being broken up. However, this schedule is more demanding of the special educator and planning is more difficult, as there are more people with whom to plan. The special educator also has to accommodate to the teaching styles of more colleagues, and general educators receive the services of special educators on a more limited basis.

*Note.* From *Collaborative Teaching Casebooks: Facilitator's Guide* (p. 25), by K. C. Harris, 1998b, Austin, TX: PRO-ED. Copyright 1998 by PRO-ED. Adapted with permission.

and problem-solving time is essential for consultation activities to work. Figures 3.2, 3.3, 3.4, and 3.5 provide schedules for a high school paraprofessional, special day class teacher, and resource specialist and a student receiving inclusive special education services.

In this case, four special educators and their paraprofessionals served students in general education classrooms; they also maintained a resource room for students on an as-needed basis. These schedules reflect, for each educator, independent activities in self-contained special education settings, co-teaching activities in general education classrooms, and consultation time with general educators as well as special education department members. The sample student schedule provides the reader with an idea of the services a student might receive. That schedule indicates that the student receives instruction in general education classes that are co-taught with several members of the special education staff.

At the elementary level, scheduling activities is just as important and often more difficult since the school day is usually not organized into discrete blocks of time. Figures 3.6, 3.7, and 3.8 provide schedules for a real resource specialist, a paraprofessional, and a student receiving inclusive special education services.

The resource specialist and paraprofessional provided services in special education self-contained situations as well as in general education classrooms. It was important to the teacher that she instruct all the students in her caseload within each week, that she have time to consult with her paraprofessional, that she have time to consult with general educators, and that she have time to perform her IEP responsibilities.

These schedules are meant not to be models but, rather, examples of the kinds of schedules made by teachers who are attempting to incorporate co-teaching into their daily activities.

## Table 3.8
### Co-Teaching Scheduling Considerations

- Initially, how much do you wish to participate in co-teaching?
- How much time do you have available for co-teaching?
- How many other support service providers (e.g., special educators, English as a second language educators) are available and willing to participate in co-teaching?
- In which classrooms are the students who might benefit most from co-teaching?
- To what degree are the school's regular curriculum and materials appropriate for students with special needs?
- What are the wishes of the students, including those with special needs?
- How much support do the students need?
- What are your potential co-teaching partners' wishes and comfort levels with co-teaching?
- What are the wishes of parents?
- What are the unique strengths of the individual educators involved in co-teaching?
- When scheduling activities, attend to the following:
  1. Be sure there is a suitable split between teaching and planning time in your schedule.
  2. Rotate the days and times for planning.
  3. Manage time and coordinate activities efficiently.
  4. Assess your use of time. Use time logs or time questionnaires. You may find that:
     a. much time is spent on routine tasks and activities of low priority;
     b. little time is spent planning and working toward established goals;
     c. uncommitted time during the typical school day is limited to about 1 hour;
     d. time is wasted in roughly the same way each day and each week.
  5. Identify "time robbers":
     a. External sources (e.g., meetings, paperwork)
     b. Internal sources (e.g., inability to say no)
  6. Accommodate for the activities of all program participants in the co-teaching schedule.
  7. Involve administrators.
  8. Prioritize a common planning period among co-teaching partners.
  9. Be flexible.

*Note.* From *Collaborative Teaching Casebooks: Facilitator's Guide* (p. 25), by K. C. Harris, 1998b, Austin, TX: PRO-ED. Copyright 1998 by PRO-ED. Adapted with permission.

| Period | Monday | Tuesday | Wednesday | Thursday | Friday |
|--------|--------|---------|-----------|----------|--------|
| 2 | Introduction to Science | Basic English | Basic English | Basic English | Introduction to Science |
| 3 | RR* | RR | RR | RR | RR |
| 4 | Biology | Clerical | Biology | Clerical | Clerical |
| 5 | Clerical | Clerical | Clerical | Essentials of Arithmetic | Clerical |
| 6 | Clerical | Essentials of Arithmetic | Clerical | Essentials of Arithmetic | Clerical |

*RR = Special education resource room.

**Figure 3.2.** Sample schedule for a high school paraprofessional. From "Meeting the Needs of Special High School Students in Regular Education Classrooms," by K. C. Harris, P. Harvey, L. Garcia, D. Innes, P. Lynn, D. Muñoz, K. Sexton, and R. Stoica, 1987, *Teacher Education and Special Education, 10*(4), 147. Copyright 1987 by *Teacher Education and Special Education*. Reprinted with permission.

| Period | Monday | Tuesday | Wednesday | Thursday | Friday |
|---|---|---|---|---|---|
| 1 | Consultation | Consultation | Consultation | Department Consultation | Consultation |
| 2 | SDC* | SDC | SDC | Department Consultation | SDC |
| 3 | Basic Math | Basic Math | Basic Math | Basic Math | Basic Math |
| 4 | Freshman Studies | Consult | Freshman Studies | Consult | Freshman Studies |
| 5 | SDC | SDC | SDC | SDC | SDC |
| 6 | SDC | SDC | SDC | SDC | SDC |

*SDC = Special day class.

**Figure 3.3.** Sample schedule for a high school special day class teacher. From "Meeting the Needs of Special High School Students in Regular Education Classrooms," by K. C. Harris, P. Harvey, L. Garcia, D. Innes, P. Lynn, D. Muñoz, K. Sexton, and R. Stoica, 1987, *Teacher Education and Special Education, 10*(4), 147. Copyright 1987 by *Teacher Education and Special Education*. Reprinted with permission.

| Period | Monday | Tuesday | Wednesday | Thursday | Friday |
|---|---|---|---|---|---|
| 1 | IEP Meeting | Consultation | World Civilization | Department Consultation | World Civilization |
| 2 | IEP Meeting | Consultation | U.S. History | Department Consultation | U.S. History |
| 3 | RR* | U.S. History | RR | U.S. History | RR |
| 4 | Applied Math | Essentials of Arithmetic | Consultation | Essentials of Arithmetic | Consultation |
| 5 | Essentials of Arithmetic | RR | Consultation | RR | Consultation |
| 6 | Applied Math | U.S. History | Essentials of Arithmetic | U.S. History | Essentials of Arithmetic |

*RR = Special education resource room.

**Figure 3.4.** Sample schedule for a high school resource specialist. From "Meeting the Needs of Special High School Students in Regular Education Classrooms," by K. C. Harris, P. Harvey, L. Garcia, D. Innes, P. Lynn, D. Muñoz, K. Sexton, and R. Stoica, 1987, *Teacher Education and Special Education, 10*(4), 148. Copyright 1987 by *Teacher Education and Special Education*. Reprinted with permission.

# School-Based Teams

School-based teams have existed for decades (cf. Zins et al., 1988). In their review of the literature, Friend and Cook (1997) identify two types of student-based or student-centered teams in schools. First, there are teams that make decisions about students' referral to special education, as well as the special education assessment process, the determination of eligibility for special education, and the programs in special education (special education team). Second, there are teams that focus on helping teachers deal with the problems experienced by students in schools (consultation assistance teams).

| General Ed Course | Monday | Tuesday | Wednesday | Thursday | Friday |
|---|---|---|---|---|---|
| Applied Math | C1 | | C1 | | |
| Introduction to Biological Sciences | P1 | P1 | P1 | | C3 |
| Reading | | C1 | | C1 | |
| World Civics | | | C4 | | C4 |
| Physical Education | | | | | |

C = Special educator (collaborator).
P = Paraprofessional.

**Figure 3.5.** Sample schedule for a high school special education student. From "Meeting the Needs of Special High School Students in Regular Education Classrooms," by K. C. Harris, P. Harvey, L. Garcia, D. Innes, P. Lynn, D. Muñoz, K. Sexton, and R. Stoica, 1987, *Teacher Education and Special Education, 10*(4), 147. Copyright 1987 by *Teacher Education and Special Education*. Reprinted with permission.

| TIME | Monday | Tuesday | Wednesday | Thursday | Friday |
|---|---|---|---|---|---|
| 8:30–9:30 | LA-GEC | LA-SEC | LA-GEC | LA-SEC | LA-GEC |
| 9:30–10:00 | PP | PGE | PP | PGE | PP |
| 10:00–11:00 | MATH-GEC | MATH-SEC | MATH-GEC | MATH-SEC | MATH-GEC |
| 11:00–11:30 | MATH-SEC | PP | MATH-SEC | PP | MATH-SEC |
| 11:30–12:15 | LUNCH | LUNCH | LUNCH | LUNCH | LUNCH |
| 12:15–1:30 | PGE | LA-SEC | PGE | LA-SEC | PGE |
| 1:30–2:30 | IEP/SIT | IEP/SIT | IEP/SIT | IEP/SIT | IEP/SIT |

SEC = Direct service by resource specialist in special ed classroom.
GEC = Direct service by resource specialist in general ed classroom.
PP  = Planning with paraprofessional.
PGE = Planning with general educator.
IEP = Activities such as referral processing, assessment, meetings.
SIT = Student intervention team meetings.
LA  = Language arts.

**Figure 3.6.** Sample schedule for an elementary resource specialist.

## Special Education Teams

Special education teams are referenced by a variety of names, including multidisciplinary team, child study team, transdisciplinary team, and case conference team (Friend & Cook, 1997). With the legal requirement for involvement of general educators in the special education program planning process (IDEA '97), general educators as well as special educators, administrators, and parents find themselves members of special education teams.

Special education teams review information gathered about a referred student and make decisions about whether an individual assessment is needed. If

| TIME | Monday | Tuesday | Wednesday | Thursday | Friday |
|------|--------|---------|-----------|----------|--------|
| 8:30–9:30 | LA-SEC | LA-GEC | LA-SEC | LA-GEC | LA-SEC |
| 9:30–10:00 | PSE | PGE | PSE | PGE | PSE |
| 10:00–11:00 | MATH-SEC | MATH-GEC | MATH-SEC | MATH-GEC | MATH-SEC |
| 11:00–11:30 | SCST-GEC | PSE | SCST-GEC | PSE | SCST-GEC |
| 11:30–12:15 | LUNCH | LUNCH | LUNCH | LUNCH | LUNCH |
| 12:15–1:30 | LA-SEC | CLER | LA-SEC | CLER | LA-SEC |

CLER = Clerical work.
SEC  = Direct service by special ed paraprofessional in special ed classroom.
GEC  = Direct service by special ed paraprofessional in general ed classroom.
PSE  = Planning with special educator.
PGE  = Planning with general educator.
LA   = Language arts.
SCST = Social studies/science.

**Figure 3.7.** Sample schedule for an elementary paraprofessional.

| TIME | CLASS | Monday | Tuesday | Wednesday | Thursday | Friday |
|------|-------|--------|---------|-----------|----------|--------|
| 8:30–9:45 | LANGUAGE ARTS | PSEC | RSEC | PSEC | RSEC | PSEC |
| 9:45–10:00 | RECESS | GEC | GEC | GEC | GEC | GEC |
| 10:00–11:00 | MATH | RGEC | PGEC | RGEC | PGEC | RGEC |
| 11:00–11:30 | SCIENCE/SOC ST | PGEC | GEC | PGEC | GEC | PGEC |
| 11:30–12:15 | LUNCH | GEC | GEC | GEC | GEC | GEC |
| 12:15–1:30 | STORYTIME | GEC | RGEC | GEC | RGEC | GEC |
| 1:30–2:30 | PHYS ED/MUS/ART | GEC | GEC | GEC | GEC | GEC |

RSEC = Direct service by resource specialist in special ed classroom.
PSEC = Direct service by special ed paraprofessional in special ed classroom.
GEC  = Direct service by general education teacher in general education classroom.
RGEC = Direct service by resource specialist in general ed classroom.
PGEC = Direct service by special ed paraprofessional in general ed classroom.

**Figure 3.8.** Sample schedule for an elementary special education student.

an assessment is called for, the team determines the student's eligibility for special education services on the basis of the assessment results. If the student is deemed eligible for special education services, then the parents and special and general educators develop an educational program for the student (i.e., an IEP or IFSP).

The team process varies depending on how the special education teams are implemented in each school. McGonigel, Woodruff, and Roszmann-Millican (1994) distinguish between multidisciplinary teams, interdisciplinary teams, and transdisciplinary teams.

## Multidisciplinary Teams

Multidisciplinary teams consist of professionals from several different disciplines (e.g., school psychologists, speech and language therapists, physical therapists, educators) working independently of each other, "like parallel play in young children" (McGonigel, Woodruff, & Roszmann-Millican, 1994, p. 99).

Team members using this approach generally conduct separate assessments, write separate assessment reports, and develop interventions specific to their disciplines.

## Interdisciplinary Teams

Interdisciplinary teams usually include the family as part of the team, but the primary difference between interdisciplinary teams and multidisciplinary teams is in the nature of the team interaction. Though team members assess children separately, team meetings encourage members to share information, discuss their individual assessments jointly, and plan interventions collaboratively.

## Transdisciplinary Teams

Transdisciplinary teams differ from the two team models discussed above. First, parents are crucial team members. In the models discussed above, though parents often participate, they are not central to the team's functioning. Interdisciplinary and multidisciplinary teams have been known to function even if parents or family members decline to participate. However, in the transdisciplinary team, parents or other family members play a crucial role in all team activities, and the other team members facilitate parents' and family members' decisions. As discussed by McGonigel, Woodruff, and Roszmann-Millican (1994), a transdisciplinary team concept assumes that children must be served within the context of the family. The choices of the family predominate, and the family and the designated direct service provider (see below) implement the plan. Second, there is a high degree of collaboration and joint decision making among team members in conducting assessments as well as designing interventions. Team members plan what to assess and how to assess, and they conduct assessments as a team. This is very different from multidisciplinary teams, in which team members come to meetings with discipline-specific assessments already completed. Third, team members teach the skills traditionally associated with their own discipline to other team members. Since only one or two team members are responsible for providing direct service to the student, team members must not only share information but also help each other develop the skills necessary to implement the suggested interventions by those selected to be the direct service providers. Achieving this "role release" among team members is a foundation of transdisciplinary teaming, and it requires continuous attention to team building and team maintenance.

The challenges faced by transdisciplinary teams are discussed by several authors (e.g., Hanft & Place, 1996; McGonigel, Woodruff, & Roszmann-Millican, 1994; Orelove & Sobsey, 1996; Rainforth & York-Barr, 1997; York, Rainforth, & Giangreco, 1990). One professional challenge that might be faced by transdisciplinary team members is that of differences in philosophy and orientation among team members. Team members represent a variety of professions, depending on the needs of the student. For example, one team may include physical therapists, speech and language therapists, educators, physicians, and parents. Team members must deal with differences in training and orientation as well as their own professional language. Some of the personal and interpersonal challenges that may be faced by team members relate to the process of "role release." Team members must learn how to train one another without feeling threatened by training or being trained. Team members must clarify and release themselves from traditional service roles. There are also logistical challenges in finding time for all team members to meet.

# Consultation Assistance Teams

Consultation assistance teams (CATs) are known by many names (e.g., teacher assistance teams, intervention assistance teams, mainstream assistance teams, prereferral teams, and student support teams). Regardless of the name, the basic premise of these groups is that professionals in a building or district work cooperatively using a problem-solving approach to address the learning needs of students and/or the professional concerns of teachers. In addition to providing diagnostic and prescriptive services to students, the purpose of these teams is to address the larger issues of curriculum, management, technology, parent participation, and the like.

For a discussion of intervention assistance programs and prereferral teams, the reader is referred to Safran and Safran (1996).

## Purpose and Advantages of Consultation Assistance Teams

Consultation assistance teams (CATs) are designed to achieve several outcomes. First is to alleviate or reduce invalid special education referrals and placements (Fuchs, Fuchs, & Bahr, 1990; Graden, Casey, & Christenson, 1985), a particularly laudable goal since the data indicate that once students are referred formally for consideration for special education, such placement occurs (Algozzine & Ysseldyke, 1981). Second is to help classroom teachers solve academic or social problems, short of full-scale referral to special education (Friend & Cook, 1996; Pugach & Johnson, 1989; Fuchs, Fuchs, & Bahr, 1990). Likewise, CATs help to reduce the misleading perception that formal testing of students by a psychologist is required before programmatic changes can be introduced into the classroom. Third, a key purpose of the CAT concept is to prevent future problems in the classroom (Fuchs & Fuchs, 1989; Graden, Casey, & Christenson, 1985; Pugach & Johnson, 1989; Zins, Heron, & Goddard, 1999). By helping teachers develop problem-solving skills, CATs can prevent each new instance of academic or social behavior problems from immediately invoking a teacher referral. The CAT concept is supported by legislation (e.g., P.L.105-17) requiring that teams be used for decision making. There is an implicit assumption that the collective decision-making ability of the group supersedes the decision-making ability of an individual member and is less biased (Kabler & Genshaft, 1983; Moore, Fifield, Spira, & Scarlato, 1989). Graden, Casey, and Bonstrom (1985) assert that prereferral teams are based on an ecological model and that the efficacy research showing positive outcomes for consultation has fueled the growth of these teams (Medway, 1982; Medway & Updyke, 1985; Heron & Kimball, 1988). CATs are popular. Carter and Sugai (1989) report that the majority of states either require or strongly encourage school personnel to use CATs, apparently satisfying a field-based demand.

Readers are referred to Zins et al. (1999) for a complete discussion of secondary prevention through the application of intervention assistance programs.

## Consultation Assistance Team Options

Consultation assistance teams can comprise two members or more. However, any consultant can be engaged in a problem-solving team when working with others. For example, when a special education teacher plans a co-teaching session with a general education teacher, they are managing the day-to-day interactions as a dyadic team. School psychologists often consult with referring teachers regarding inappropriate behavior of students; this, too, is an example of a consultation assistance team.

***Teacher Assistance Teams.*** Chalfant, Pysh, and Moultrie (1979) developed teacher assistance teams (TAT). In this model, a teacher refers a student to a

TAT team through the team coordinator. The coordinator reviews the referral, arranges to have the student observed in the classroom, summarizes information about the student, distributes information to team members, and gathers the team, which consists primarily of general education teachers, for a meeting. The team, with the referring teacher, conducts a problem-solving session focused on the referring problem of the student. Follow-up meetings are scheduled to monitor progress related to the chosen interventions.

***Intervention Assistance Teams.*** Intervention assistance teams operate on the same premise as TATs, but they tend to extend membership to all the resources available at the school, including those of special education and related services. Intervention assistance teams have been found to be successful in meeting many student needs and in providing teachers with support (Whitten & Dieker, 1995), although research shows that the direct measures of student improvement are not clear (Safran & Safran, 1996).

***Mainstream Assistance Teams.*** Mainstream assistance teams have generally consisted of two professionals, e.g., consultant and consultee (Fuchs et al., 1990). Consultants generally use a behavioral consultation approach that has been shown to produce measurable improvement in student learning (Safran & Safran, 1996). Specific interventions are selected by consultees and implemented with the support of the consultant. Staff development and short- and long-term planning are critical to successful implementation of mainstream assistance teams (Fuchs et al., 1990; Safran & Safran, 1996).

# Team Development

Regardless of the nature of the team, the research on team development summarized by Ellis and Fisher (1994) indicates that teams develop as they strive to address their tasks. There are at least two ways to describe team development. Equilibrium models suggest that teams fluctuate between attempting to solve their task problems and trying to maintain group solidarity. Phase models suggest that teams go through a sequence of different kinds of interaction. Perhaps the most famous team development model is that proposed by Tuckman (cited in Ellis and Fisher, 1994). Tuckman synthesized the work of others and proposed the following four-phase model of team development:

- Phase 1—forming: Team members test their independence and attempt to identify the task.

- Phase 2—storming: Intragroup conflicts develop, and team members have an emotional response to task demands.

- Phase 3—norming: Group cohesion develops, and team members are able to express their opinions.

- Phase 4—performing: Team roles related to function are evident, and solutions emerge.

In summarizing the literature on team development, Ellis and Fisher (1994) have identified the following commonalties: All teams have at least three stages. The first stage is an orientation stage. During this stage, team members adjust their individualities to group membership and accustom themselves to the task at hand. All teams go through a conflict stage as a middle stage. During this middle stage, team members have differences of opinion on task ideas as well as on how the team should function. The final stage is a completion stage. During the final stage, group members achieve consensus and validate decisions made in previous stages.

To work effectively in a team, it is necessary to help the team develop. Being aware of stages of team development is important, as well as using the interpersonal and communication skills discussed in the following chapter. Friend and Cook (1997) suggest that members of school teams should regularly review the purposes for which the teams exist as a way to help teams move through developmental phases.

## Team Roles

As a member of a team, it is quite likely that you will assume one (or several) roles. *Team roles* are defined as perspectives team members take related to the team task, as well as team building and maintenance. Team roles vary depending on the team. According to Ellis and Fisher (1994), task roles include the following: information seeker (one who seeks information, clarification, and evidence for conclusions reached by the team), coordinator (one who shows the relationship between ideas and facts), and orienter (one who keeps the group focused and moving toward its goal). Group building and maintenance roles include: encourager (one who reinforces the ideas of other group members), compromiser (one who offers solutions that satisfy everyone), and group observer (one who makes comments about the group process such as "We're stuck"). However, as Ellis and Fisher caution, it's really not possible to identify a complete list of all the roles in a group. Highly effective teams are well balanced with respect to group roles and have excellent linking skills (Ellis & Fisher, 1994).

Regardless of the team roles, it's important to recognize that the team will develop norms for its successful functioning. Group norms develop because members establish expectations about what ought to occur. As a result of feedback and patterns of reinforcement, members establish an idea of suitable group behavior and identify patterns that fall below or above those expectations (Ellis & Fisher, 1994).

Membership on school-based teams is not always constant. This may represent a challenge to team functioning. Friend and Cook (1997) suggest that it might be advisable to directly discuss with transient team members (e.g., referring teachers) the nature of their roles and facilitate their active participation.

A useful norm that team members should consider adopting is the norm of *reciprocity,* meaning team members have a tendency to reciprocate similar behavior in response to the behavior of others. This norm is nearly universal among social systems (Ellis & Fisher, 1994). Reciprocity creates a snowball effect as each person's behavior reinforces the similar behavior of others. Therefore, to establish productive group norms, each team member should display the behavior he or she wishes all team members to display.

## Working Effectively with Teams

According to Friend and Cook (1996), there are at least four characteristics of effective teams: (a) team goals are clear, and members remain focused on the overall requirements of the task at hand; (b) the core group's professional and personal needs are met through the team's interactions; (c) members understand the reciprocal relationship between their behavior and the team's output; and (d) the group works within an organized system of leadership and participation, recognizing shared responsibility in a decentralized process.

Orelove and Sobsey (1996), in a discussion of Fisher's work, describe intrapersonal and interpersonal factors that influence team effectiveness. These factors are summarized in Table 3.9. Consultants should keep in mind that the personal characteristics they bring to team activities will greatly influence team effectiveness. Using the interpersonal and communication skills discussed in the following chapter will assist consultants in positively influencing team effectiveness.

## Characteristics of Effective Teams

Figure 3.9 shows a matrix of a team's output when high and low involvement by members is matched with effort, knowledge, and skill alone and combined. The chart shows that when a team is highly involved, with members who are knowledgeable and who use flexible strategies, the best solutions to achieving the common purpose of the team are likely. Conversely, when little effort is exerted—for whatever reason—and the members lack knowledge, or use strategies that are not adaptable, the team goal is not likely to be reached.

## Characteristics of Ineffective Teams

There are at least five factors that inhibit the team process. Moore, Fifield, Spira, and Scarlato (1989) indicate that one of the main reasons for team failure is that members lack the skill to work together. That is, the core group does not know how to arrange meetings, conduct business efficiently, move through the problem-solving stages, or follow up with recommendations. Second, the team does not know how to access the knowledge of multidisciplinary members. Because of lack of training, unfamiliarity with other disciplines, or some combination, team cohesion is not developed. A third reason for failure is that the team's goals are unclear and limiting. Fourth, team members lack interpersonal skills (e.g., active listening skills, interaction skills, and leadership skills) that make for a smoothly running committee. Finally, the team lacks knowledge of curriculum-based assessment, thereby reducing the usefulness of recommendations to teachers.

## Improving Team Effectiveness

To improve team effectiveness, Thousand and Villa (1990) suggest that the team might attempt any of the five recommendations they provide.

### Face-to-Face Interactions

Frequent face-to-face interactions help maintain a team's focus on the problem. Admittedly, time constraints and overcommitted work schedules might affect weekly meetings, but Thousand and Villa (1990) suggest that written communications through memoranda are not a sufficient substitute for actual encounters. Principals or other supervisory staff may be used on a short-term basis to "cover" a teacher's class to allow time for consultation (Whittaker, 1992), or the

**Table 3.9**

Factors Influencing Team Effectiveness

*Intrapersonal Factors*

- Individuals' attitudes toward the group reflect open-mindedness about possible outcomes and a sensitivity toward the feelings and beliefs of other group members. The individual is committed to the group and to the process. The individual also has a sense of responsibility to the group and is willing to expend time and energy for the benefit of the group.
- Individuals who are committed to a group participate actively, share responsibility for the group's decisions, and express ideas, even at the risk of being proved wrong.
- Individuals demonstrate creativity, proposing numerous ideas, especially during the group's early stages.
- Individuals take stands and defend their beliefs, even if they leave themselves open to criticism. In addition, they constructively criticize others and try to do so at appropriate moments in the group process.
- Individuals express themselves honestly. They say what they mean.

*Interpersonal Factors*

- All members must participate for group decision making to be effective; members who remain silent do not contribute.
- Groups in which members are more skilled at the art of communicating are more effective.
- Members engage in supportive, not defensive, communication. Supportive communications evaluate problems or issues, not other members, thus creating a climate of mutual trust.
- Members make sure that they understand one another; they do this by checking others' reactions, being specific in describing an idea, and being descriptive, rather than judgmental, in response to others' ideas.

*Group Identity Factors*

The identity of the group flows directly from intrapersonal and interpersonal factors such as the following:

- Members are sensitive to the group process; they sense when to communicate a particular idea.
- Members who fail to contribute and hence are uncommitted to the group or the task should consider quitting the group. Having uncommitted members reduces the group's effectiveness.
- Members who understand the group process exhibit patience at the slowness of change, particularly in the early stages. Allowing time to think through ideas is important to creative and effective decision making.
- Succesful groups avoid unrealistic formulas for difficult problems.

*Note.* Form *Educating Children with Multiple Disabilities: A Transdisciplinary Approach* (3rd ed., p. 23), by F. P. Orelove and D. Sobsey, 1996, Baltimore: Paul H. Brookes. Copyright 1996 by Paul H. Brookes, Inc. Adapted with permission.

teachers may use part of their preparation time for such meetings. As discussed previously, Raywid (1993) outlined several options that met this purpose.

## Interdependence

Group members must realize the interdependent nature of their configuration. As stated earlier, members must understand how their roles within the team affect other members of the team and the output of the team as a committee.

TEAM OUTPUT MATRIX

| | Level of Effort (alone) | Knowledge & Skill (alone) | Program Strategies (alone) | Effort, Knowledge & Strategies (combined) |
|---|---|---|---|---|
| High | Team works hard but is misdirected | Team is competent but not focused on efficient process | Team is flexible but lacks precision about when and how to implement | Best outcomes possible Common purpose likely to be achieved |
| Low | Team is not focused, is overcommitted, or does not understand personal involvement | Team has yet to tap collective knowledge of members | Team is fixated on single solutions, not adaptable | Worst outcomes possible Lacks common focus Goals not likely to be achieved |

Figure 3.9. A matrix depicting a team's level of effort, knowledge and skill, and problem-solving strategies with respect to the degree of their involvement.

## Consensus Building

Effective teams do not vote on most issues. Such a situation can lead to disenfranchisement; team members who vote in the minority may come to believe that their viewpoints are not considered. Consensus building occurs when general agreement on the key issues is achieved, often after a full discussion. For a discussion of consensus, see Chapter 4.

## Assessing Group Function

Periodically, teams should conduct a self-diagnostic to ascertain how effectively they function. Measures might be taken on the level of individual participation, output, or distribution of leadership roles. Questions to consider might be: What is the team doing that results in superior or inferior decisions? Are specific members being over- or underutilized? Are the strengths of individual team members tapped to their maximum potential? Is the team meeting self-determined goals for conducting its business (e.g., getting reports out on time, conducting observations, and so forth)?

## Accountability for Personal Responsibility

While the term accountability may have a negative connotation because of an association with "blame" or "fault," in this context it refers to responsibility for completing selective objectives that make up the larger task. In a collaborative planning mode, each member of a team assumes responsibility for completing a portion of the total task and reporting to the group on the accomplishment of that subtask.

Heron (1990) suggests that consultants use cooperative learning strategies when trying to establish personal responsibility for various components of a project. Specifically, Heron indicates that obtaining a "critical mass" (core group) of professionals, deciding on the group goal, sharing task responsibilities, and reinforcing effort and accomplishment assist with conveying the perception that individual contributions are valuable. Abbott et al. (1990) demonstrates how a team used a *collaborative planning guide,* a matrix of people, tasks, dates, and responsibilities, to design and implement a school-wide program to improve the social performance and decrease the inappropriate behaviors of middle school students (see Figure 3.10).

The guide was used in all stages of the process and was refined as tasks were completed and new ones were assigned. Each member of the team had a copy of it. With respect to individual accountability, a team member's initials next to particular tasks represented that member's willingness to assume responsibility for completing that assignment. Ideally, members should take on tasks that are within their skill and knowledge repertoires. For instance, BT agreed to assess student reinforcers, DS agreed to present the program to the faculty, and CC agreed to prepare the training scripts because of self-determined skills in those areas.

## Problem Solving with the Team

Given that a team is working collaboratively, and that its members have the knowledge to do so, the team's efforts center on problem solving and decision making. With respect to problem identification, teams often use questionnaires, surveys, or prereferral forms to obtain initial information on the type, level, or magnitude of the problem. Figures 3.11, 3.12, and 3.13 provide illustrations of Problem solving is extensively discussed in Chapter 4.

| Colleagues Involved | Basic Idea | Project Start Date | Tasks/Person Responsible | Resources Needed/Item |
|---|---|---|---|---|
| Barb, Mary Ann, Debbie, Hazel, Connie, Cindy, Karen, Sue, and Tim | Institute a school-wide "Ranger Bucks" program whereby students earn facsimile money contingent on appropriate behavior. Bucks are exchanged every week for small prizes or special school privileges. | January 15 | 1. Assess student reinforcement preference (BT). 2. Contact distributors for prizes (MA/KZ). 3. Prepare presentation for the total school staff (DS). 4. Generate advertising and fliers for the program (HA). 5. Prepare training script for students (CC). 6. Set up exchange booths (CR). 7. Generate tracking and evaluation forms (SA). 8. Generate correspondence (principal & parents) (TH). | 1. Assessment survey forms. 2. Office supplies for ads/fliers and correspondence 3. Samples of previous training scripts. 4. Cardboard boxes for exchange display. 5. Samples of daily and cumulative tracking sheets. |

**Figure 3.10.** A sample initial collaborative planning guide. From "Lessons from the Classroom: Using a Cooperative Learning Arrangement to Facilitate Consultation," by T. E. Heron, 1990, *Journal of Educational and Psychological Consultation, 1*(4), 359–363. Copyright 1990 by Lawrence Erlbaum Associates, Inc. Reprinted with permission.

## Consultation Assistance Team
## Team Invitation

Date _____

Dear _____,

　　Your participation has been requested to asist with the Consultation Assistance Team concerning (name of student). This student has been referred by (name of referring individual). The reason for referral is (state reason). Please let us know if you will be able to assist at the meeting planned for _____ in _____ at _____.

date　　　　　　place　　　　　　time

　　Attached you will find a Consultation Assistance Team Planner that provides background information on this student to help you reflect on possible strategies that may be shared at the meeting.

**Figure 3.11.** A prereferral cover letter to a teacher.

## Consultation Assistance Team Planner
## Student Background Information

Teacher Referral Date _____

**A. Identification Information**
Student's Name _____
Sex _____ DOB _____
Referring Teacher _____ Grade _____
Parent/Guardian _____
Phone _____
Address _____

**B. Reasons for Consultation**
Please indicate strengths (+) or weaknesses (–) or leave blank if neither applies

| Academic Areas | Academic Behaviors | Social/Emotional |
|---|---|---|
| ____ Reading | ____ Attention | ____ Motivation |
| ____ Comprehension | ____ Attendance | ____ Adult relations |
| ____ Word recognition | ____ Activity level | ____ Peer relations |
| ____ Math | ____ Rate of work | ____ Authority figures |
| ____ Language arts | ____ Quality of work | ____ Emotional |
| ____ Content areas | ____ Following directions | ____ Attitude |
| ____ Speech/Language | ____ Organization | ____ Family problems |
| ____ Receptive | ____ Material retention | ____ Withdrawn |
| ____ Expressive | ____ Study skills | ____ Physical/fights |
| ____ OTHER | | |

_____
_____

**C. Classroom Interventions/Strategies**
Check/list those already attempted (and if possible, the length of time tried).

Intervention　　　　　　　　　　Comments/Child's Reaction

☐ Moved seat　　　　　_____
☐ Positive reinforcement　_____
☐ Removed privileges　　_____
☐ Parent contact　　　　_____
☐ OTHER/Modified assignment　_____

**D. What progress has the student made this year?**
_____
_____

**Figure 3.12.** A prereferral survey and planner using a variety of written responses.

## Consultation Assistance Team
## Summary of CAT Meeting

Student _____

Meeting date _____

Previous meeting date(s)_____

Consulting team members

_____

_____

Review summary of meeting

_____

_____

Next consultation/intervention step for this student

_____

_____

**Figure 3.13.** A prereferral summary form that allows the consultant to aggregate data over consecutive meetings.

a prereferral cover letter, form survey and planner, and summary document, respectively, for a CAT. Efficient teams attempt to reduce the amount of paper-work and written responses required for respondents by using rating scales, short-answer templates, charts, and graphs.

# Building a Team from the Bottom Up

Even though teams are a popular configuration in schools (Fuchs & Fuchs, 1996), they are by no means universal. Consultants interested in initiating team arrangements in schools or districts might be overwhelmed by the prospect of how to begin. Heron and Swanson (1991) recognize that establishing a useful consultation assistance team is not easy. In their view, "It takes the commitment of several professionals, the support of administrators, and a vision of how school services for all students should be delivered" (p. 98). They offer a 4-step procedure for establishing a team using a "bottom-up" approach (see Figure 3.14). Fuchs and Fuchs (1996) add: "A bottom up perspective calls for a devo-lution of control, the decentralization of decision making" (p. 388). Essentially, the process involves an ad hoc committee, the principal (or superintendent), and the faculty. The CAT is launched after consensus is achieved during the first three phases.

## The Ad Hoc Committee

The Ad Hoc or steering committee is comprised of those practitioners within the building or district who are interested in initiating the team concept. Within the bottom-up model, this group generates a written proposal that outlines the purpose and objectives of the team. The proposal addresses team compo-sition, faculty commitments, benefits, institutional constraints, and logistical

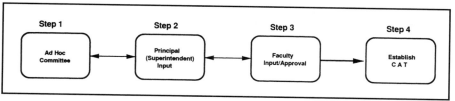

**Figure 3.14.** A bottom-up model for establishing a consultation assistance team. The bidirectional arrows indicate that input, feedback, and revision—collaborative consultation—occur between the agents. From "Establishing a Consultation Assistance Team: A 4-Step Practical Procedure," by T. E. Heron and P. Swanson, 1991, *Journal of Educational and Psychological Consultation, 2,* 96. Copyright 1991 by Lawrence Erlbaum Associates, Inc. Reprinted with permission.

considerations. Essentially, the committee prepares an internal document that initially will be submitted to the principal—and ultimately to the faculty—for comment and approval.

## Principal Input

The principal's input at an early stage is critical for several reasons. First, the principal should be aware of any procedural changes that might affect the referral process, faculty time commitments, or the overall program. Second, the principal can assist the committee by providing recommendations and suggestions with respect to resources and logistical problems unanticipated by the ad hoc committee. Finally, the principal might offer ways to present the proposal to the total faculty that would likely gain its support. Heron and Swanson (1991) suggest that the proposal to the principal should be written in nonthreatening language and identify the conditions under which the CAT will work.

## Faculty Input and Approval

Faculty must have the opportunity to provide comments on the proposal. The ad hoc committee should plan for at least two levels of input. First, oral discussion of the rationale, procedures, committee membership, resources, and logistics should be addressed openly at a faculty meeting. Second, a period of time—perhaps several weeks—should be reserved to receive additional oral and/or written comments from the faculty. At a future meeting, all other concerns and questions must be discussed. By either consensus or a vote, action should be taken on the proposal. If the outcome is to proceed, step 4 begins.

## Establishing the Consultation Assistance Team

Heron and Swanson (1991) state, "Probably one of the better ways to gain support for the concept of Consultation Assistance Team is to ensure all parties that it will be inaugurated on a trial basis" (p. 98). If the staff is aware that a 1-year trial is planned and that the process will be monitored regularly, they may be more likely to approve the concept initially. If staff are still reticent about establishing the team on a school-wide basis, perhaps the committee could suggest that the process be initiated on a pilot basis for selected students. Table 3.10 provides guidelines for implementing and facilitating the maintenance of the team.

## Table 3.10

### Considerations for Facilitating the Maintenance of a Consultation Assistance Team

1. Establish the program on a pilot basis. One school year, for example, would be a reasonable trial period.

2. Rotate membership on the CAT during the year to set the occasion for fuller involvement by staff. In subsequent years, a staggered approach can be used.

3. Adhere to all district procedures with respect to observations and recommendations that might be offered.

4. Ensure that due process procedures are followed, including notification to parents and provisions associated with section 104.36 of Section 504 regulations. Prereferral procedures have been interpreted as evaluation procedures subject to 504 regulations.

5. Build flexibility into the system. The procedures, atmosphere, methods of collecting information, and paperwork must be adaptable so that teachers can come to the team knowing their views will be respected.

6. Have a clear routing process for students who have been referred. Lost, misplaced, or delayed responses to teachers will impede efficient work.

7. Alert CAT members to the details of the cases that will be discussed at meetings.

8. Provide immediate acknowledgment and/or feedback to teachers who refer students or who have questions regarding procedures.

9. Keep records confidential. It is important for the children and for the team's professional integrity to maintain high ethical standards.

10. Evaluate the faculty, students, and parents at least twice during the year to determine if the team is operating effectively and meeting expectations.

*Note.* From "Establishing a Consultation Assistance Team: A 4-Step Practical Procedure," by T. E. Heron and P. Swanson, 1991, *Journal of Educational and Psychological Consultation, 2*(1), 95–98. Copyright 1991 by Lawrence Erlbaum Associates, Inc. Reprinted with permission.

**Figure 3.15.** A consultation assistance team reviewing the case of a student referred for special services.

# Consultation Assistance Team Structures

There are many possible consultation assistance team structures, defined as the organization used to deliver consultation assistance team services. The structure of consultation assistance teams should depend on school resources and the needs of students. Harris and Smith (1996) discuss four approaches to structuring consultation assistance teams.

## One Team for the Whole School

Having one team for the whole school is a traditional way to structure consultation assistance teams. There are at least three advantages to this approach. First, members are usually selected across grades and specialists, representing the skills and interests of the whole school. A team might include an administrator, two primary teachers (e.g., one bilingual and one general), two intermediate teachers (e.g., one bilingual and one general), and one special educator. Team members may be volunteers, selected by the principal, or chosen by the staff.

Second, due to the variety in team membership, team members often identify a wide variety of strategies that an elementary teacher can use in meeting the diverse needs of the students in her or his classroom. Third, members often volunteer to serve on such a team, and, therefore, the team's purpose is valued and promoted by team members.

Despite the advantages, there are also some clear disadvantages in having one team for the whole school. First, this team represents yet another add-on "committee," and teachers may be reluctant to volunteer for another "job." Second, scheduling team meetings for individuals on variable schedules has also presented a challenge. Often, team meetings are scheduled before or after school. This results in an added burden for the teachers serving on the team. Third, though team members represent the school, they may not always be the best group to generate ideas for every problem faced by a teacher trying to meet the diverse needs of students. Fourth, none of the team members may be knowledgeable about the student or the situation. Team members may need to do some research about the student or situation before they can actually problem-solve with the referring teacher. Finally, one team may find it difficult to handle all the teacher referrals. If the team meets only once a week, it may not be able to meet the needs of all the teachers in the school.

Despite the disadvantages, many schools provide a school-wide consultation assistance team. The process described in Table 3.11 is one that can be used by any consultation assistance team, regardless of the organizational structure.

## Ad Hoc Teams

In this structure, the referring teacher selects those she or he would like to be on the team at any one time, according to the needs of the student and the expertise of individuals in the school.

Ad hoc teams are able to meet some of the challenges faced by one team serving the whole school. First, since the referring teacher selects the team members, they are usually equipped to handle the referring problem. Second, if they agree to help the teacher, they are then willing to serve and interested in brainstorming solutions to a particular problem. Finally, because this type of consultation assistance team is formed "on demand" and any teacher can serve, there are usually fewer problems handling the number of referrals generated by teachers in the school.

## Table 3.11

### Example of a Process for Deciding on the Structure of a Consultation Assistance Team

The school staff realized the need for inclusion of all of the students and staff so that problem-solving strategies would be effective on all levels. The "buy-in" of the staff was paramount to the success of the program. The members of the team were then specifically selected to represent all aspects of education, i.e., early childhood, intermediate, special, bilingual, counseling, gifted, remedial, and administrative. The members were also trained in various team-building strategies. These brought the team closer together and added to the congeniality of the group. This created a warm atmosphere for the referring teacher and put him at ease. An extensive reference loose-leaf binder was prepared for each team member. It included many studies that support the need for intervention and an abundance of background information on how to improve the academic and emotional well-being of students.

Teachers refer students they feel need additional help in achieving success. Each team member plays a specific role in the assessment process. A nonjudgmental brainstorming session provides ideas. The referring teacher selects several strategies to implement. Team members give assistance in this phase if it is needed. A follow-up session provides an opportunity for feedback for both the classroom teacher and the team members.

There are disadvantages to this approach. First, the referring teacher, in addition to having a problem, has the added responsibility for forming a consultation assistance team. This may discourage some teachers from pursuing a consultation assistance team approach. Second, the time to meet may still represent a problem. Since the consultation assistance team in this structure is called "on demand," the team meeting will probably have to be conducted before or after school or at least at a time when teachers are not committed to other activities. This makes the team meeting an added challenge, not a part of the normal school day activities of a teacher. Third, since the team is formed on demand, any teacher should be able and willing to function as a team member. That means all teachers should be trained in the consultation assistance team process and be willing to serve when called upon.

### Grade-Level Teams

A grade-level team can serve as a consultation assistance team, and this structure allows for more than one team to be functioning in a school at one time. The advantages to this structure are several. First, the grade-level teachers usually know the students and the situations that may present a problem. Second, it is expected that grade-level teams will meet regularly as part of teachers' responsibilities. Therefore, scheduling a time to meet is generally not an issue. Most grade-level teams that function as consultation assistance teams allocate at least one time per month when they will meet as a consultation assistance team. Third, since each grade-level team functions as a consultation assistance team, there are several such teams operating in the school. With this structure, it is likely that the consultation assistance teams in the school will be able to handle the number of teacher referrals.

There are some disadvantages to this approach. First, since all teachers on a team are at the same grade level, there may be limitations in the variety of referring problems that can be handled effectively by each team. Second, teachers at every grade level must be willing and able to function as consultation assistance team members. Though worth it in the long run, it may require initial training for all school staff. Third, the role of specialists has to be considered. In many schools who have adopted this model, specialists are assigned to grade-level teams. Therefore, each grade-level team may also have a special education teacher or a remedial reading teacher or a counselor assigned to its consultation assistance team. This extends the expertise of the grade-level consultation assistance team.

## Mixed Grade-Level Teams

A compromise between grade-level teams and one team for the whole school is the mixed grade-level team. This structure establishes more than one team but allows for different knowledge and variety in each team, addressing some of the disadvantages of other structures. First, because teams are composed of teachers across grade levels (e.g., a team of kindergarten, first-, and second-grade teachers and a team of third-, fourth-, and fifth-grade teachers), the consultation assistance team members have some variety in expertise and are usually able to develop appropriate interventions for the referring problems. Second, having more than one team in the school enables the consultation assistance teams to handle the number of teacher referrals throughout the school. Third, not all teachers have to be willing and able to serve on the consultation assistance team since representatives are chosen from each grade level. Fourth, specialists can be assigned to consultation assistance teams as discussed previously, extending the expertise of the team. Fifth, because each grade level is represented, there is a likelihood that the team members will be familiar with the referring problems.

The primary disadvantage of this structure is providing time for the consultation assistance team to meet. Maintenance of consultation assistance teams seems to depend on their institutionalization as part of the regularly scheduled responsibilities of the team teachers. If team teachers need to meet outside of the normal school day, then their time should be reallocated (e.g., they could be freed from other after-school committee responsibilities).

Regardless of the structure adopted, we suggest that staff members consider the following suggestions offered by Chalfant (1994):

- Design the school plan according to the individual needs of each school.
- Identify the school organizational structure.
- Clarify the history of the CAT in the school.
- Develop the school plan with the school staff.
- Secure administrative support for the school plan.
- Have CAT activities as part of the normal school day.
- Minimize paperwork.
- Use the existing organizational structure to design the school plan.

## Effectiveness of Consultation Assistance Team Arrangements

The effectiveness of CAT configurations has been examined by several researchers (Chalfant & Van Dusen Pysh, 1989; Fuchs, Fuchs, & Bahr, 1990; Graden, Casey, & Bonstrom, 1985; Kruger, Struzziero, Watts, & Vacca, 1995; Meyers, Valentino, Meyers, Boretti, & Brent, 1996; Rankin & Aksamit, 1994). Results indicate that CATs have popular appeal, and teachers and staff believe that they are helpful. Evidence of improved student performance exists, but

For a discussion of consultation effectiveness, readers can refer to Sheridan, Welch, and Orme (1996).

questions abound about the methodological integrity of the data. Fuchs and Fuchs (1996) summarize the situation: "Whereas many have touted their potential as prereferral interventions and inclusionary strategies, there is virtually no direct evidence that they strengthen students' academic performance or improve their school behavior" (p. 390).

# Interagency Collaborative Teams

For a description of coordinating councils, see Baldwin, Jeffries, Jones, Thorp, and Walsh (1992); Gallagher, Trohanis, and Clifford (1989); Garrett (1998); Hepp (1991); Thiele and Hamilton (1991).

With the movement toward full-service schools (cf. Dryfoos, 1994) and other collaborative arrangements between schools and community organizations to provide integrated services, individuals from different agencies recognize the need to work together to identify and offer appropriate services. For example, health care providers and educators have become involved in providing services for children with HIV infection and their families (e.g., Woodruff & Sterzin, 1988). Social workers, rehabilitation counselors, and educators have become involved in facilitating transition plans for students with special needs (Aune & Johnson, 1992). Individuals who have multiple needs cannot usually be serviced by one agency; therefore, interagency collaborative teams are needed to develop and implement interventions for them. In fact, interagency collaborative teams can be found in the establishment of local interagency collaborative councils, mandated by P.L. 99-457, to serve young children with disabilities and their families.

As discussed by Welch and Sheridan (1995), school-community partnerships are varied and can occur in a variety of settings. A school-based model is an approach in which services are offered in schools. In the community-based model, students receive services in settings such as businesses. Interagency collaboration models do not dictate a specific setting; instead, a group of agencies may provide services in a number of different settings.

Garner and Orelove (1994) offer the following characteristics of interagency collaboration (developed by the Regional Resource Center Task Force of the U.S. Office of Special Education):

- encourages and facilitates an open and honest exchange of ideas, plans, approaches, and resources across disciplines, programs, and agencies;

- enables all participants to jointly define their separate interests by mutually identifying changes that may be needed to best achieve common purposes;

- utilizes formal procedures to help clarify issues, define problems, and make decisions relative to them.

Clark (1992) identifies the following components as common to successful school-community partnerships:

- a shared vision formally articulated in a written mission statement that includes specific goals;

- visible administrative commitment and support;

- a willingness among team members to cross traditional institutional boundaries;

- a willingness to subordinate traditional roles and adopt new ones;

- continually open communication.

**Table 3.12**

Suggestions for Interorganizational Collaboration

1. Explain your expectations for meeting a student's needs and your concerns about designing an appropriate educational environment with examples, sample schedules, and other specific information. Encourage others to do the same. Be clear and concrete with the messages you send.

2. Expect a getting-to-know-you period. Allow time for general conversations about expectations from everyone involved and move gradually into the partnership.

3. Use negotiation skills to clarify any agreements. For example, you may need to negotiate the use of facilities, materials and equipment, personnel time, funds, and any number of other resources.

4. Recognize that the nature and extent of your partnership may be determined partly by factors you do not control. You may be constrained in obtaining services or resources because of organizational agreements.

*Note.* From *Interactions: Collaboration Skills for School Professionals* (2nd ed., p. 243), by M. Friend and L. Cook, 1996, White Plains, NY: Longman. Copyright 1996 by Longman. Adapted with permission.

Interagency collaborative teams are like interdisciplinary teams in that they must recognize and appreciate individual differences of team members. However, members of interagency collaborative teams must understand and appreciate the differences not only of the individuals on the team but also of the agencies represented by those individuals. Therefore, it is important for all team members to understand the services, policies, and funding streams of the agencies represented on the team, as well as the orientation and skills of team members. It is also helpful if members of interagency collaborative teams develop their own uniform terminology, referral forms, referral processes, and transitions across agencies (Garner & Orelove, 1994). Team members may also need to reach agreement on the problem-solving style they will use. For example, public school teachers may be used to brainstorming ideas for intervention, while health care providers may be used to an expert model of consultation whereby an intervention is proposed by an expert and others assist only in determining how the intervention will be implemented.

Descriptions of interagency collaborative teams can be found in Klapstein (1994) and Morse (1994).

It is also likely that interagency collaborative teams will not always consist of the same individuals. Though agencies may have agreements to collaborate, the individuals representing those agencies may change. Teams should be aware of the regression in team development that may occur as a result of such changes and plan for them. Teams may revert temporarily to the beginning or middle stages of team development. A team facilitator should use the strategies mentioned under "Team Development," as well as the interpersonal and communication strategies discussed in the following chapter, to facilitate final-stage team development among interagency team members. Friend and Cook (1996) offer the suggestions in Table 3.12 to consultants who serve on interagency collaborative teams.

## Technology and Teaming

With the increased common use of technology, it is appropriate to consider how it might be used to facilitate consultation activities. Electronic meeting systems such as bulletin boards and electronic mail (email) can enable groups to overcome some of the barriers to effective group interaction and productive meetings (Pappas, 1994). When there are logistical problems getting the team together in one place, it may be possible to bring team members together at one time (though not one place) and have them talk through electronic bulletin boards. Further, equitable participation of all members, especially those representing people from different cultures, may be enhanced, as even a reserved person can participate electronically. Electronic meetings can also serve to document team activities, as they can maintain a record of team members' contributions and team decisions.

Kruger and Struzziero (1997) used computers to mediate peer support of school psychologists as they attempted to consult with teachers. Though only two psychologists received this support, they reported that the majority of the messages contributed to their becoming more knowledgeable about consultation. They also reported the computer-mediated group to be highly cohesive.

Nevin and Hood (1998) have also explored the use of computers to engage teams in learning and decision making. As part of a teacher-training program, individuals worked as a team via the computer on the task of raising and educating a hypothetical child with special needs. The authors questioned such a team's effectiveness as team members would not be interacting face to face and wondered whether the unavailability of body language and tone of voice would be an impediment. However, they found that participants accessed the bulletin board discussion rooms and adjusted for the electronic medium. Participants used additional signals to express their internal state or the emotional intent of a message via "emoticons" like the smiley face consisting of a colon followed by a dash followed by a closing paren :-). Other signals that were used included multiple question marks (???) to express confusion and multiple explanation marks to show enthusiasm or happiness (!!!).

An unexpected outcome was the introduction of personal disclosures, which are a byproduct of face-to-face teams but were not anticipated for electronic teams. However, it seems that several teams expressed warmth and support as well as compassion and friendship for individual team members who were facing particularly difficult life challenges ranging from temporary illnesses to the heart attack of a relative and the death of a relative. In one case, a team member agreed to take on extra tasks.

When analyzing the messages, the authors found that both task and relationship concerns emerged; the electronic communication, therefore, was reflective of the team development process.

The team roles of public and private recorder were combined into the role of electronic synthesizer (a person who took on the responsibility of summarizing the information previously posted by team members). Teams were also given private discussion rooms with user names and passwords so as to simulate private meetings.

In summary, it seems that electronic communication holds promise as a tool for team members. However, team members should exercise caution in sending electronic transmissions that might contain confidential information. Likewise, while email can be a beneficial and efficient way to communicate, it can also create problems if transmissions are sent too quickly, in anger, or to the wrong people.

Team members may need to alter their communication methods, but the interpersonal and communication skills discussed in the following chapter should provide the needed foundation for electronic teaming.

# Conclusion

Educational consultants will find themselves in a variety of teaming situations. Whether those teaming situations involve the provision of direct or indirect services to students, consultants need to be aware of ways to organize teams and maintain effective teams. Teams are only as effective as their members. When members expend the effort, are knowledgeable about strategies, and provide flexible options, effectiveness is enhanced.

# Summary of Key Points

## Direct Versus Indirect Service

1. *Direct service* includes any task in which the consultant works directly with the target individual (i.e., student, teacher, parent, and/or administrator).

2. *Indirect service* includes any task in which the consultant works with a mediator who works with the target individual (e.g., a consultant works with a teacher who works with a target student).

## Co-Teaching

3. Co-teaching usually takes place in general education settings and is a form of direct service in collaboration with mediators.

4. The eight components that contribute to a collaborative learning environment are: interpersonal communication, physical arrangement of the classroom, familiarity with the curriculum, curriculum goals and modifications, behavior management, instructional presentation, grading and evaluation, and instructional planning.

5. There are a variety of co-teaching structures including the following: one teaching, one supporting; station teaching; parallel teaching; alternative teaching; team teaching; complementary teaching; and supportive learning activities.

6. There are five themes of effective planning for co-teaching: (1) trust each other's professional skills, (2) incorporate active involvement of the students and the co-teachers, (3) create learning environments that allow for equally shared roles and responsibilities, (4) develop routines to facilitate effective co-planning, and (5) become skilled in improving the quality of the classroom instruction.

7. Two types of co-teaching schedules were discussed: the *dyadic stable schedule* (one support service provider works with one general educator in a fixed daily schedule), and the *rollover schedule* (one support service provider works with more than one general educator and varies the schedule).

## School-Based Teams

8. *Multidisciplinary teams* consist of professionals from several different disciplines who work independently of each other in assessing and intervening for a particular student.

9. *Interdisciplinary teams* consist of family members and professionals from several different disciplines who meet to jointly plan interventions.

10. *Transdisciplinary teams* center around the parent playing a crucial role in assessing and intervening with a group of professionals from different disciplines.

11. *Consultation assistance team* is a generic term that can be used to refer to a teacher assistance team, an intervention assistance team, or a mainstream assistance team.

12. A consultation assistance team helps to alleviate or reduce invalid special education referrals and placements, helps the classroom teacher solve academic or social problems, reduces the misleading perception that formal testing is a necessary prerequisite for service, and serves a preventative function by providing problem-solving skills to teachers.

## Team Development

13. Teams develop as they work on tasks, and most teams experience three stages: (1) orientation, when team members adjust to group membership; (2) conflict, when team members have differences of opinion regarding task ideas and team process; and (3) completion, when team members achieve consensus.

## Team Roles

14. Team members assume roles related to the task and to group building and maintenance.

## Working Effectively with Teams

15. Effective teams have clear goals, and their members remain focused on tasks throughout the process. The team ensures that the core group's professional and personal needs are met; members understand the reciprocal relationship between individual work and the team's output; and the team shares responsibility in a decentralized process.

16. Ineffective teams do not know how to arrange meetings, conduct business efficiently, move through the problem-solving stages, or follow up with recommendations. Such teams do not know how to access the knowledge of team members, and members may lack interpersonal skills.

17. Team effectiveness can improve when face-to-face interactions occur, interdependence is fostered, consensus among members is established, group function is assessed, and accountability for personal responsibility is clear.

## Building a Team from the Bottom Up

18. Establishing a consultation assistance team from the bottom up can be accomplished by using a 4-step procedure that includes an ad hoc committee, the principal (or superintendent), the faculty, and a trial basis for the team.

## Interagency Collaborative Teams

19. Interagency collaborative teams are needed to develop interventions for individuals with multiple needs.

20. To function effectively on an interagency collaborative team, team members must understand the agencies each team member represents as well as the orientation and skills of individual team members.

21. Team members should develop their own uniform terminology, referral forms, referral process, and transitions across agencies.

22. Team members must determine a team process that can account for changing team members since although agencies have agreements to collaborate, the individuals representing those agencies may change.

## Technology and Teaming

23. Electronic meeting systems such as bulletin boards and email can enable groups to overcome some of the barriers to group meetings.

24. When using electronic meeting systems, team members should adjust their communication accordingly (e.g., express the emotional intent of messages by using symbols such as a smiley face or multiple question marks) and realize that one team member will need to take responsibility for summarizing messages previously posted by team members.

# Questions

1. Explain how the following components contribute to a co-teaching environment: interpersonal communication, physical arrangement of the classroom, familiarity with the curriculum, curriculum goals and modifications, behavior management, instructional presentation, grading and evaluation, and instructional planning.

2. Explain how a consultant can use a curriculum-centered problem-solving approach for planning goals and objectives for students in co-taught inclusive classrooms.

3. Distinguish between team teaching and alternative teaching. Provide examples of the appropriate use of each of these co-teaching structures.

4. What should co-teachers be prepared to address when planning their lessons?

5. Describe two types of co-teaching schedules.

6. Distinguish between multidisciplinary, interdisciplinary, and transdisciplinary teams.

7. Define *consultation assistance team* and identify its purposes, advantages, and any potential shortcomings.

8. Describe at least two consultation assistance team structures and identify the advantages and disadvantages of each.

9. Why is it useful for teams to adopt the norm of reciprocity?

10. What characteristics seem to define effective teams? Ineffective teams?

11. What procedures might be followed to improve team effectiveness?

12. What are the major steps involved in establishing a consultation assistance team from the bottom up?

13. Provide three suggestions for consultants who serve as members of interagency collaborative teams.

14. What communication skills will enhance electronic teaming?

# Discussion Points and Exercises

1. Describe a co-teaching program. Develop an evaluation plan that addresses student achievement and the co-teaching process.

2. Launch a consultation assistance team in your school or district using the bottom-up model. Note the effects.

3. Observe and interview consultation assistance teams in different schools and districts. Note how they are organized and the forms and procedures they use. What seems to work best in each team? Why?

4. Interview individuals who participate as members of interagency collaborative teams. What challenges do they face? How do they recommend meeting those challenges?

5. Start an electronic teaming project. Note the activities team members must conduct to establish and maintain electronic communication.

6. Examine the case that follows these questions. If you have an opportunity to discuss the case with a group, you may want to follow the procedure outlined by Harris (1998b). Minimally, we encourage you to perform the following activities after you read the case.

Understand the dilemma from multiple points of view. After you read the story, identify the problem from Wanda's point of view. Then identify the problem from Sara's point of view.

Explore the issues raised in this case, define the problem, generate solutions, and develop an action plan. Consider the following: How do you think discussion between consultation assistance team and the child study team (special education referral team) could be coordinated in this case as well as other cases? How could the leader of this consultation assistance team assure that the needs of the teachers in her family would be met and morale would be maintained? What are some ways that consultation assistance team activities across the school could be shared with all school staff, including the child study team?

If possible, discuss your ideas with someone who has also read the case. Go back and review your analysis and your action plan. How would you modify your analysis and solutions based on this discussion? How were the points raised in the solutions reflective of the points raised in this chapter?

### Are We Helping Each Other or Just Adding a Step to the Special Education Referral Process?

### Background

This K–5 elementary school is located in a primarily Hispanic, low-socio-economic neighborhood. In addition to the general education program, the school offers bilingual education, special education, and a Title I reading program. The staff is ready to implement a consultation assistance team in the school, but they want to be involved in planning it and how it is introduced.

For years, the school staff has implemented a literature-based, whole language curriculum and has been organized into quads. Each quad is considered a family. As described in one of the district brochures:

> The faculty and staff have created an innovative, family-like climate where children of varying age groups work cooperatively in classes. A literature-based, whole language curriculum forms the foundation for instruction at this school. Teachers, on a daily basis, are involved in planning for school activities that address the needs of running a multi-age campus.

Given this school structure, the staff decided to conduct CAT activities at their bi-weekly family meetings. Each family has a Mama Bear who provides leadership for the teachers in the family or quad. It's the Mama Bear's responsibility to schedule students for CAT as needed.

### Story

My name is Wanda. I am the Mama Bear for a fifth-grade family. Fifth grade is new for our school. We used to have just kindergarten through grade 3 at this school, but we now have kindergarten through grade 5. We quickly organized ourselves into a working fifth-grade family. We've only been working together for a few months now. One of the first students who was referred to our CAT presented quite a challenge for us. The fifth-grade teacher who referred this student (Sara) has a lot of experience, and she really felt that this child should be in special education. Apparently, this child has had problems in school since the first grade. Recently, his mother died, and he has been impossible. Sara really felt that, given his history, he needed to go right to special education. We are all members of the same family, so, of course, we wanted to support her in any way we could. However, we knew that we had to meet and as a group come up with some interventions that Sara could implement for at least 4 weeks before we could determine if the child is just in crisis or should go for special education referral and placement.

So we met. We made copies of the attached referral form so that all the team members would have a copy. Sara presented her case, and her frustration level was really high. She felt that something had to be done. The child liked to play with matches. He was acting out and being defiant. He was now in a foster placement, and he was absent a lot. When he did come to school, he was dirty.

As the team went through the child's file, it was discovered that he did not have a lot of trouble when he was in third grade. His report card indicated that he performed satisfactorily and seemed to have a good rapport with his third-grade teacher. The team decided to see if we could come up with interventions that Sara could try to help build rapport and support this child through this time of crisis (see the attached recommendations by CAT). Sara wanted psychological testing as the first intervention to try, but the team felt that we couldn't do this until some interventions were tried in the classroom. By the end of the team meeting, Sara agreed to a set of interventions (see action plan), but she didn't really seem pleased. Many of us on the team felt uneasy. We felt as if we had alienated Sara, and we weren't sure if she would really implement the interventions as intended. Did we do the right thing? Should we talk with members of the child study team (CST) about this case? We knew the CST was only supposed to deal with students suspected of needing special education services. Did this student fit that category? Are other CAT teams in the school experiencing similar issues? We really weren't sure what to do.

## Consultation Assistance Teams

### Referral Form

Name of Student: _José_

Date of Meeting: _11-6-00_

Presenting Problem: _He is dangerous, as he likes to play with matches. He comes to school mainly to fight. You never know what will set this child off day to day. He will fight anyone, even the teacher._

Recommendations by CAT:

1. _rewards_

2. _picnic with principal_

3. _contracts_

4. _psychological testing_

5. _placement in another class when he fights_

6. _work in office_

7. _literature on self-esteem_

8. _cross-age tutoring_

9. interest survey

10. Big Brother program

11. family counseling

12. journal

13. individual projects

14. decorate a bulletin board—head committee

15. jobs around school, e.g., picking up trash, bathroom monitor

Action Plan:

Referring teacher has committed to try the following interventions with the student:

1. family counseling

2. work in office

3. Big Brother program

4. individual projects

5. literature on self-esteem

6. interest survey

The CAT will meet again on the following date: ASAP

TAT Members:

_____   _____   _____

_____   _____   _____

_____   _____   _____

# Interpersonal, Communication, and Problem-Solving Skills for Effective Consultation

*4*

As discussed in Chapter 3, consultants can work directly with students, educators, or parents or indirectly with mediators who, in turn, work with those agents. Whether providing direct or indirect services, consultants who use appropriate interpersonal, communication, and problem-solving skills are more likely to be successful than those who do not.

The purpose of this chapter is to discuss the skills needed to conduct the consultation activities described in the previous chapter. It presents a model for communication that addresses the consultant's primary reasons for communication, i.e., developing appropriate programs and disseminating information about those programs. It describes strategies for listening; questioning; providing feedback; gaining acceptance; managing conflict, resistance, and change; and solving problems. The chapter concludes with strategies for disseminating information about consultation activities.

## Objectives

After reading this chapter, the reader should be able to:

1. describe the components of a group decision-making process

2. describe a model for communication reflective of a group decision-making process

3. identify strategies for communicating

4. identify strategies for managing conflict

5. describe a collaborative problem-solving process

6. identify steps for facilitators of a problem-solving process

7. identify essential principles for disseminating information through staff development activities

## Key Terms

group decision-making process

consensus

defensive communication

supportive communication

active or critical listening

competency resistance

social resistance

security resistance

change process

conflict management techniques

| | |
|---|---|
| nonverbal communication | collaborative problem solving |
| vocal intonations | principled negotiation |
| passive listening | brainstorming |
| empathetic responding | sharewriting |
| critical questioning | nominal group technique |
| verbal feedback | pattern interruption |
| substantive conflict | positive climate |
| constructive conflict | staff development |
| affective conflict | orientation stage |
| destructive conflict | integration stage |
| path of least resistance | refinement stage |
| status resistance | structured feedback |
| emotional resistance | unstructured feedback |
| economic resistance | coaching |
| rational resistance | |

Many individuals have written extensively on the specific and necessary interpersonal and communication skills for effective consultation (e.g., Conoley & Conoley, 1982; DeBoer, 1986; Idol et al., 1994; Mostert, 1998; Pugach & Johnson, 1995; Rosenfield, 1987; Thomas, Correa, & Morsink, 1995; Welch & Sheridan, 1995). Further West, Idol, and Cannon (1989), extending research findings into practical areas, have developed a training curriculum specific to this purpose. Table 4.1 lists essential interpersonal and communication skills for educational consultants identified in the literature.

Since educational consultation often unfolds within a group context, we'll begin our discussion of group process as one mechanism for preventing or resolving problems.

Readers should know that the authors do not view "problems" from a deficit-driven perspective alone, that is, that a student is presenting disruptive behavior and it has to be "fixed." We also believe that many other issues (e.g., improving the curriculum, addressing sensitive multicultural issues within schools, improving proficiency scores) are important for consultants to address.

Readers are reminded that groups are defined as two or more people. The differences between working with a group of two (e.g., in co-teaching) and working with a larger group (e.g., school-based teams) are discussed in Chapter 3.

## Group Decision Making

Ellis and Fisher (1994) indicate that a *group decision-making process* is different from the decision-making process of an individual, in that group decision making involves not only the task but also the social dimension of effective group interaction. All groups, regardless of size, perform their functions in light of these two dimensions. Educational consultants have the responsibility to facilitate the completion of a task (e.g., the development of an appropriate behavior management program for a student who is disruptive in class). However, to develop a program that will be delivered effectively in the classroom, the consultant must collaborate with the classroom teacher, taking into account all the social interaction factors that surround interpersonal communication. This collaboration is reflective of the social dimension of the decision-making process. Table 4.2 depicts components of group and individual decision making.

Since the group decision-making process addresses task and social dimensions, it can be inefficient and slow when compared to individual decision making. Still, group decision making is the best strategy to use when (a) several alternatives are possible, (b) there is a need to have commitment from group members, and (c) group members may be involved at some level with

## Table 4.1
Interpersonal and Communication Skills

### Interpersonal Skills

- Be caring
- Be congruent
- Show positive self-concept
- Be calm
- Know & trust each other
- Be a risk taker
- Communicate with each other accurately and unambiguously
- Manage time
- Have a sense of humor
- Resolve conflicts and relationship problems constructively

- Be respectful
- Be open
- Show enthusiastic attitude
- Try to live stress free
- Be flexible
- Be resilient
- Tolerate ambiguity
- Accept and support each other
- Be prepared and willing to share information about yourself

- Be empathetic
- Make continued and sincere attempts to understand a situation from others' points of view
- Manage conflict and confrontation
- Move fluidly between the roles of giver and taker of information

### Communication Skills

- Listening
- Reflecting
- Summarizing
- Interpreting nonverbal communication
- Responding non-judgmentally
- Using communication to create systems of meaning
- Ensuring that problem identification does not conflict with beliefs

- Acknowledging
- Clarifying
- Grasping overt meaning
- Interviewing effectively
- Providing feedback
- Developing an action plan
- Identifying language practices that are disabling and changing them

- Paraphrasing
- Elaborating
- Grasping covert meaning
- Using nontechnical language
- Brainstorming
- Acknowledging differences in communication and relationship building
- Using information regarding socially hidden aspects of power that privilege individuals in problem solving

*Note.* From "Collaboration Within a Multicultural Society: Issues for Consideration," by K. C. Harris, 1996, *Remedial and Special Education, 17*(6), 355–362, 376. Copyright 1996 by PRO-ED. Reprinted with permission.

implementation. Without involvement of all group members, it's possible that the group's decision will not be implemented successfully. Therefore, even though group decision making may appear to be more time consuming at the beginning of problem solving, dealing with the task and social dimensions of the group make it well worth the effort in the long run.

# Model for Communication

Communication models abound in the educational literature. However, since Ellis and Fisher (1994) discuss the act of communication within a group

**Table 4.2**

Group and Individual Decision Making

| Group Decision Making | Individual Decision Making |
|---|---|
| Two dimensions: task and social | One dimension: task |
| Tendency to polarize decisions | Tendency not to polarize decisions |
| Inefficient and slow | Efficient |
| Best when no single answer is correct and group commitment is needed for successful performance | Best for high-quality technical expertise and questions for which there is one correct answer |

*Note.* From *Small Group Decision Making: Communication and the Group Process* (4th ed., p. 17–19), by D. G. Ellis and B. A. Fisher, 1994, NY: McGraw-Hill. Copyright 1994 by McGraw-Hill, Inc. Adapted with permission.

context—the context within which most educational consultants find themselves—we have elected to adapt their communication model to the consultation process. According to Ellis and Fisher, communication and interaction are interrelated since communication is conducted in a particular social situation. Therefore, "the speaker is both communicating and interacting; communicating because the language carries meaning and content, and interacting because the language functions to express social relationships" (p. 84). Hence, there are at least five components of communication (see Figure 4.1). The sender and receiver represent two components. The message itself is a third component. The delivery of the message contains the fourth and fifth components (i.e., the context or social situation in which the message is sent and the language or code in which the message is composed).

To communicate effectively in a group decision-making process, more than just an exchange of messages must occur. For group members to make decisions, the communication must be substantive, analytical, and cooperative. Cooperation alone, however, is often not sufficient. Since implementation of an educational program requires commitment from group members, it is essential for group members to reach *consensus,* i.e., to agree on substantive issues (Ellis & Fisher, 1994).

Briefly, cooperation results in an agreement on form—e.g., agreeing to disagree. Yet agreeing on form will not result in commitment to the action plan that results from a decision. To achieve commitment, it is necessary to reach agree-

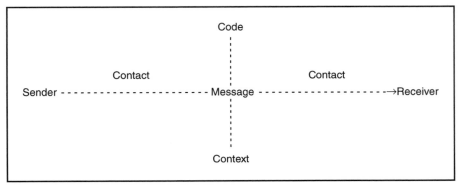

**Figure 4.1.** The components of communication. *Note:* From *Small group decision making: Communication and the group process* (4th ed., p. 85, Figure 4.1) by D. G. Ellis & B. Aubrey Fisher (1994), New York: McGraw-Hill. Reprinted with permission.

**Table 4.3**

Consensus Versus Cooperation

| Consensus | Cooperation |
|---|---|
| Internal agreement | No such assumption |
| Agreement on content (substantive ideas) | Agreement on form (agree to disagree) |
| Substantive differences abolished | Substantive differences tolerated |

*Note.* From *Small Group Decision Making: Communication and the Group Process* (4th ed., p. 226), by D. G. Ellis and B. A. Fisher, 1994, NY: McGraw-Hill. Copyright 1994 by McGraw-Hill, Inc. Adapted with permission.

ment on the content or substance of the plan. Groups should be careful to avoid false consensus (i.e., when group members agree to a decision but are not really committed to it). Table 4.3 distinguishes between consensus and cooperation.

# Strategies for Communicating

Communication behaviors in group decision making can be classified as defensive or supportive (Ellis & Fisher, 1994). That is, it is not only what is said but how it is said that communicates a message to group members. Those who attempt to manipulate group interaction by evaluating others, threatening others, or communicating a lack of interest engage in *defensive communication*. Those who focus on issues and solutions, minimize differences among group members, and communicate openness to others engage in *supportive communication*. Table 4.4 presents the most common defensive and supportive communication behaviors.

To provide supportive communication during a group decision-making process, it is important to use effective communication skills. As indicated by Ellis and Fisher (1994):

> Asking questions and listening to others helps increase involvement and builds a sense of mutuality; that is, everyone is working as a system and immersing themselves in the task at hand. Listening to other group members and asking questions that draw out the opinions and perspectives of others are the best ways to develop supportive and cooperative environments for group functioning. (p. 103)

## Listening Skills

Listening skills include verbal and nonverbal behaviors. As discussed by Ellis and Fisher (1994), there are different ways of listening. For example, we listen appreciatively when enjoying music; however, we may listen evaluatively when analyzing and making judgments about the platform of a political speaker. We discuss ways of listening that are essential for educational consultants below.

### Active or Critical Listening

In group decision making, it is important to engage in *active* or *critical listening*. That is, you engage the speaker actively, you analyze what the speaker says,

## Table 4.4

Defensive and Supportive Communication

| Defensive Communication | Supportive Communication |
| --- | --- |
| *Evaluation:* Judging others and making them feel judged. | *Description:* Describing your feelings without making the other person feel wrong. |
| *Control:* Threatening and dominating others. | *Problem oriented:* Focusing on issues and good solutions. |
| *Strategizing:* Trying to manipulate others for your own ends. | *Spontaneity:* Communicating openly and honestly. |
| *Neutrality:* Communicating disinterest and lack of caring. | *Empathy:* Showing your regard for the other person. |
| *Distancing:* Emphasizing differences in status and roles. | *Equality:* Minimizing differences, treating others equally. |
| *Certainty:* Implying that you are always right, never being unsure or open to suggestion. | *Provisionalism:* communicating tentativeness and openness to others. |

*Note.* From *Small Group Decision Making: Communication and the Group Process* (4th ed., p. 29), by D. G. Ellis and B. A. Fisher, 1994, NY: McGraw-Hill. Copyright 1994 by McGraw-Hill, Inc. Reprinted with permission.

and you analyze yourself as a listener. This three-part sequence is also referred to as active listening. Table 4.5 presents strategies for active or critical listening.

### Nonverbal Feedback

Table 4.5 shows that the suggested techniques, though nonverbal, require the listener to be actively engaged. We can provide *nonverbal communication* through our facial expressions, body postures, and use of space. As summarized by Miller (1986), we use nonverbal communication because: (a) words have limitations; (b) nonverbal signals are powerful; (c) nonverbal messages are likely to be more genuine as they cannot be controlled as easily as spoken words; (d) nonverbal signals can express feelings too disturbing to state; and (e) nonverbal communication assists in sending complex verbal messages. Clearly, nonverbal communication influences the meaning of messages (Ellis & Fisher, 1994). We elaborate below on three types of nonverbal communication.

*Facial Expressions.* The face can relay a multitude of information. Facial appearance tells about the age and sex of an individual as well as possible ethnic origins. The style of hair can indicate comfort or discomfort with certain mores. Fleeting facial expressions are often indicative of emotion (e.g., interest, expressed in raised eyebrows; disdain, expressed in eyes raised to the ceiling). Further, eye contact is a powerful sender as well as a receiver of information. People tend to look longer and more often at those they trust, respect, and care about than at those they doubt or dislike (Miller, 1986). In addition, eye contact can be used to encourage or discourage communication. In Western society, it is difficult to ignore someone who is establishing eye contact.

In other cultures (e.g., Eastern, African, Asian), eye contact, especially across gender or social class, carries different connotations.

*Body Postures and Movement.* Body postures and movements often communicate what we feel more clearly than words do. Because body postures are visual, they are unaffected by noise or interruptions to speech. One tends to be

**Table 4.5**

Strategies for Active or Critical Listening

| Strategy | Technique |
|---|---|
| Eliminate distractions. | Assume an open posture. |
| | Lean forward slightly. |
| | Maintain eye contact. |
| | Position yourself so that you face the speaker. |
| | Appear relaxed, interested, and available. |
| Listen for concepts and ideas. | Identify the speaker's main points. |
| | Don't be distracted by minor points or irrelevancies. |
| | Think about what the speaker is NOT saying. |
| | Ask yourself if there is additional information you need. |
| Organize what you hear. | Use the main idea as an organizational tool. |
| | Make logical connections among ideas. |
| Evaluate what you hear. | Is the information logical and appropriate? |
| | Withhold judgment until you have all the information you need and it has been thoroughly explained. |

*Note.* From *Small Group Decision Making: Communication and the Group Process* (4th ed., p. 104), by D. G. Ellis and B. A. Fisher, 1994, NY: McGraw-Hill. Copyright 1994 by McGraw-Hill, Inc. Adapted with permission.

more relaxed with friends or when conversing with an individual of lower status and less relaxed with strangers and individuals of higher status.

If the body is positioned in the direction of an individual, it suggests a positive attitude toward that individual (Miller, 1986). It is important for consultants to remember that postural differences vary from culture to culture. One should be aware of the significance of body postures and movements when interacting with people who have a strong identification with a culture different from one's own.

*Use of Space.* Most people use space to communicate. For example, informal conversations between friends occur in a .5- to 1-meter zone, whereas an extended distance of 1 to 4 meters is acceptable for interaction between strangers (Miller, 1986). The consultation literature discusses how rooms should be arranged to facilitate communication (cf. Nevin, 1989). It is important for the consultant to recognize that if communication is intended to express comfort and friendship, the spatial arrangement should also communicate this intent and occur within a .5-meter zone.

Placement of furniture is also influential in the communication process. A furniture arrangement that is conducive to conversation (e.g., comfortable chairs facing each other and without an obvious physical barrier between parties) is recommended.

*Vocal Intonations.* Vocal intonations are paralinguistic or vocal qualities that have no dictionary meaning but influence communication (Ellis & Fisher,

1994). If vocal intonation contradicts verbal expression, vocal intonation will dominate (Miller, 1986). If a consultant is trying to communicate interest in understanding a consultee's problem, the tone of the consultant's voice will also communicate that message. If the consultant's speech is characterized as moderately fast, with a tendency toward a high pitch and slightly upward inflection, then the message communicated to the consultee may be one of impatience or nervousness, even though the words used are intended to communicate just the opposite (see Table 4.6).

### Passive Listening

In addition to critical or active listening, there may be times when it is important for the consultant to engage in a different type of listening. For example, when a speaker needs to express something difficult, it may be more important for the consultant to establish a comfortable atmosphere for the speaker to express herself or himself than to critically analyze what is being said. In *passive listening*, the listener remains quiet but attends to the speaker. This is accomplished by giving encouraging nonverbal feedback to the speaker through the use of head nods, facial expressions, and body postures. Another type of passive listening, *empathetic responding*, does not involve judging, agreeing, or feeling sympathy for the other party. Rather, the listener's physical presence conveys understanding of another's feelings, thoughts, values, or beliefs (Briggs, 1993). The nonverbal techniques for eliminating distractions would be appropriate to use during empathetic responding (see Table 4.5).

## Questioning Skills

As indicated above, listening and questioning are essential skills for the group decision-making process. Questioning is effective in encouraging group members to share ideas and information as well as in critically examining ideas and information. *Critical questioning* occurs when group members are asked to elaborate upon, clarify, or justify the information they are sharing. This is different from criticizing people or their ideas. By asking questions, you move the group forward in the decision-making process (Ellis & Fisher, 1994). Table 4.7 provides strategies for effective critical questioning. It is important for consultants to use a variety of questions to elicit information from speakers as well as to analyze the information shared so that acceptable and effective decisions can be reached.

### Verbal Feedback

To maintain the group decision-making process, it is essential that group members provide feedback to each other so that information sharing and decision making are facilitated. In addition to the nonverbal feedback strategies discussed above, consultants should provide *verbal feedback* to group members by making statements that facilitate the problem-solving process (see Table 4.8). All these strategies should be used, as appropriate, during group decision making. Perhaps the most important strategy is "Use good timing." "What is said, how it is said, and even who says it, may not be nearly as significant to the group process and to effective decision-making as *when* it is said" (Ellis & Fisher,

## Table 4.6

### Characteristics of Vocal Expressions

| Feeling | Loudness | Pitch | Timbre | Rate | Inflection | Rhythm | Enunciation |
|---|---|---|---|---|---|---|---|
| Affection | Soft | Low | Resonant | Slow | Steady and slightly upward | Regular | Slurred |
| Anger | Loud | High | Blaring | Fast | Irregular up and down | Irregular | Clipped |
| Boredom | Moderate to low | Moderate to low | Moderately resonant | Moderately slow | Monotone or gradually falling | . . . | Somewhat slurred |
| Cheerfulness | Moderately high | Moderately high | Moderately blaring | Moderately fast | Up and down; overall upward | Regular | . . . |
| Impatience | Normal | Normal to moderately high | Moderately blaring | Moderately fast | Slightly upward | . . . | Somewhat clipped |
| Joy | Loud | High | Moderately blaring | Fast | Upward | Regular | . . . |
| Sadness | Soft | Low | Resonant | Slow | Downward | Irregular pauses | Slurred |
| Satisfaction | Normal | Normal | Somewhat resonant | Normal | Slightly upward | Regular | Somewhat slurred |

*Note.* From *The Communication of Emotional Meaning* (p. 63), by J. Davitz, 1964, NY: McGraw-Hill. Copyright 1964 by McGraw-Hill. Reprinted with permission.

## Table 4.7

### Critical Questioning Strategies

| Strategy | Examples |
|---|---|
| Request clarification—be sure you know what the speaker is saying before asking for justification. | Would you say that again please? |
| Ask analytical questions when it is necessary to determine causes and consequences. | What is the reason for this?<br><br>What are the implications of using this behavior management strategy? |
| Ask ethical questions by relating information to the decisions and not to individual ethical motives. | What values are we conveying to the parents by suggesting that their child should speak only English in school, though their home language is Farsi? |
| Ask speaker to elaborate. This may be necessary when group members don't want to take too much time to express themselves. | Would you say more about your child's schooling in the first grade?<br><br>Can you give us an example of what you mean by peer tutoring? |
| Use tactful strategies to obtain permission to ask questions. | I'm sorry, but can I ask a question? |

*Note.* From *Small Group Decision Making: Communication and the Group Process* (4th ed., p. 104–105), by D. G. Ellis and B. A. Fisher, 1994, NY: McGraw-Hill. Copyright 1994 by McGraw-Hill, Inc. Reprinted with permission.

1994, p. 62). This requires the consultant to monitor the communication of the group and the use of feedback. The consultant, as group facilitator, needs to help the group move through the phases of group decision making.

The communication process involves listening as well as speaking. It is necessary to listen to establish rapport as well as to identify information that is accurate and comprehensive. Verbal and nonverbal behaviors can show one's willingness to listen, one's intent to understand and encourage talking. When speaking, one should avoid double messages, use appropriate terminology (avoid jargon), establish a physical as well as a psychological climate for communication, and verify that the listener understands. Table 4.9 lists barriers to effective communication that all group members should avoid.

In Chapter 1, we discussed a consultation process, the essence of which was to use interpersonal and communication skills in a problem-solving sequence. Anecdote 4.1 provides a transcription of a communication process between a special education teacher and a fifth-grade teacher. In the first dialogue, a problem is identified. In the second dialogue, solutions are proposed. In the third dialogue, criteria for evaluating the progress of the student are proposed. In the last dialogue, participants discuss the results of the implemented program. This anecdote is provided not as a model, but as an example of what one should and shouldn't do during the consultation process. The reader is encouraged to read this anecdote and critique it from several different perspectives (e.g., evidence of appropriate interpersonal skills, evidence of shared problem solving, evidence of active listening, evidence of miscommunications, evidence of appropriate instructional strategies, evidence of minimization of resistance, etc.). Some of these aspects will be discussed in the next section.

## Table 4.8
### Verbal Feedback Strategies

| Strategy | Example |
|---|---|
| Say words of encouragement. | "I see." |
| Reflect content and feelings. | "You're concerned about Joe's lack of progress and the amount of time it takes for the special education referral process to be completed." |
| Be specific and clear. | "Today our task is to develop a co-teaching schedule for the month of February." |
| Support comments with evidence. | "Since Tim didn't start the math assignment until 10 minutes after you gave the assignment, it seems that we need to identify an intervention that will help him start math assignments quickly, i.e., within 3 minutes of receiving the assignment." |
| Separate the issues from the people. | "The issue is how to coordinate the schedules of occupational therapists and the preschool special education teachers so that occupational therapy can be delivered in the special education classroom in a co-teaching relationship with the preschool special education teacher." |
| Soften negative messages. | "We can develop a plan to use Blaine's excellent listening skills to help him compensate for lower than expected reading skills." |
| Pose the situation as a mutual problem. | "At a staff meeting, the principal announced that they have an increased enrollment of students but no money to hire new teachers. He said, 'What creative solutions can we develop to provide appropriate instruction with our existing personnel?'" |
| Check on agreements before proceeding to decisions. | "Are we in agreement that we should focus on developing a plan to increase Sara's reading vocabulary?" |
| Engage in neutral questioning to open discussion to an exploration of ideas and emotions. | "What would happen if Tony were placed in Mr. Jones's social studies class?" |
| Summarize ideas when checking on group commitment and to help a group achieve consensus. | "So let's review. We've agreed today to . . ." |
| Use good timing. | The consultant waited for group members to share their feelings about a decision they had reached before saying, "So let's review. We've agreed today to . . ." |

*Note.* From "Team Talk: Communication Skills for Early Intervention Teams," by M. H. Briggs, 1993, *Journal of Childhood Communication Disorders, 15*(1), p. 37–38. Copyright 1993 by the *Council for Exceptional Children*. And from "Feedback Process in Task Groups," by B. Haslett and J. R. Ogilvie, 1992, in *Small Group Communication*, 6th ed., by R. Cathcart and L. Samovar (Eds.), p. 352, Dubuque, IA: Brown. Copyright by Brown. Both adapted with permission.

## Table 4.9
Barriers to Effective Communication

| Barrier | Effect |
| --- | --- |
| Giving advice too quickly or too strongly. | May foster dependence. |
| Providing false reassurances. | Effectively dismisses the problem. |
| Asking misdirected questions. | Can confuse the situation. |
| Engaging in wandering interaction. | Shows not listening. |
| Allowing interruptions. | Interferes with the focus of communication. |
| Using cliches. | Effectively diminishes feelings. |
| Minimizing feelings. | Devalues the person and his or her concerns. |
| Using quick fixes. | Similar to giving advice; wastes time on symptoms, not real problem. |
| Praising. | False praise or flattery among equals is condescending. |
| Prying or interrogating. | Makes the speaker feel "on the spot." |

*Note.* From *Collaborative Practitioners, Collaborative Schools* (p. 89–105), by M. C. Pugach and L. J. Johnson, 1995, Denver: Love. Copyright 1995 by Love. And from "Team Talk: Communication Skills for Early Intervention Teams," by M. H. Briggs, 1993, *Journal of Childhood Communication Disorders, 15*(1), p. 38–39. Copyright 1993 by the *Council for Exceptional Children.* Both adapted with permission.

## Anecdote 4.1

*Dialogue 1.* First day of consultation between Jean, a special education teacher, and Ken, a fifth-grade teacher.

KEN:    Hi, Jean.

JEAN:    Hi, how are you?

KEN:    Fine, thanks. Well, I came here with a little problem. As you know, my class has been dedicated to all the new arrivals from Mexico and Central America, and a couple of weeks ago, I received a new kid, Arturo, who claimed that he graduated from the fourth grade in Nicaragua. Now, I have a few problems with this new kid. First, he can hardly decode anything in Spanish, so I can't even place his reading level at a first- or second-grade level.

JEAN:    That's a real problem.

KEN:    Apart from that, he has very little comprehension. Even when he's read to, he doesn't seem to comprehend what he's just heard, and . . .

JEAN:    How is his behavior?

KEN:    Well, that's another problem I have, but I'll come to that when I'm finished with his math skills.

JEAN:    Oh, Okay.

KEN:    His math skills are also quite a disaster. Although he claimed he's a fifth grader or rather that he graduated from the fourth grade, he can add only single-digit numbers. So these are the academic problems I have.

JEAN: He seems to be very low in all academic areas.

KEN: Yes, and on top of that, he has behavior problems. Ever since he arrived, he has been beating up on the other kids—fighting with everybody. He's been feeling very self-conscious and thinks people are making fun of him or something. He has difficulty sitting down and staying on task. He talks a lot and has been quite disruptive. So with twenty-eight other children in the class . . .

JEAN: You sure didn't need that to happen to you.

KEN: I didn't need another problem. So I came here to see you as the expert to help me design some kind of program that will hopefully help this kid to learn something before he graduates to the sixth grade in just a couple of semesters.

JEAN: Well, I'm glad you came to me because I would be glad to help you design a program. It seems like you feel very overwhelmed. This kid is coming from Nicaragua with basically no idea of how to behave. He doesn't seem to understand what is expected of him.

KEN: Yes, that's what it looks like.

JEAN: Okay, Ken, from what I see you have a new child who arrives new in the country, who doesn't seem to know what is expected of him, and what is going on. He's not following academically and is, from what you told me, very much lagging behind in reading and math skills. I would be glad to help you develop a program that would improve his math and reading skills. And I suppose when we take care of the reading and the math problem, his behavior will slowly fall into place. So, if you're willing to put up with him for a couple of months, we will see how it goes.

KEN: That's fine. I'm all for it so long as we have something to help this poor kid because, obviously, we are here to help him out; otherwise, he'd just fall through the cracks.

JEAN: Yes, and I think that he is very lucky to be in your class. You do have a lot of empathy, and I know you're a bilingual teacher so these are all pluses for him.

KEN: Thank you very much for the compliment.

JEAN: Okay, then, let's go for it. See you next week. We will discuss a plan, and I will support you with it.

KEN: Sure, and I'll keep you posted.

JEAN: Okay.

***Dialogue 2.*** Second meeting to establish a program in reading and math to accommodate Arturo's needs.

JEAN: Hello.

KEN: Hi again.

JEAN: Okay. At the last meeting, we talked about Arturo and came up with the suggestion that we should help him academically, help him with his reading and his math, and hopefully his behavior would come into place. So, what have you been doing in reading?

KEN :   Well, first of all, I'll tell you what my reading groups are. I have high, medium, and low reading groups.

JEAN:   Okay.

KEN :   And I also have a fourth group that comprises two other kids who have decoding problems, who have problems similar to Arturo's. So I have assigned my aide exclusively to these two kids, and there are now going to be three, to work on the basic skills that these kids need before they can successfully read. Other than that, there isn't any other program that I can think of that I have put in place to improve the situation.

JEAN:   Okay, so now it seems like Arturo fits into the fourth group.

KEN:   I have actually already put him in that group.

JEAN:   So, that's good because there will be two other kids who could benefit from the program also. Okay, what do they read? What do the medium and high groups read? Basically, what is their level?

KEN:   Well, we have a number of books that are literature based. I also use as a supplementary reader the textbooks, the basals, the basals for fifth graders—actually, it is for fourth graders and is called *Campeones*—because even though some of these kids are at a high reading group, they . . .

JEAN:   They are still below grade level.

KEN:   Yes, below grade level. So I use selections from the stories that I feel are relevant to their background, and we use those texts.

JEAN:   What about writing?

KEN:   We do quite a bit of writing, and in fact, I have a few very good writers who are naturals.

JEAN:   Have you thought of using cooperative learning groups? Have you ever tried it in your classroom?

KEN:   I think there would be too much chaos. I haven't tried it, although I think it would be difficult to manage because of the different levels of the kids that I have in the classroom and, more importantly, because of the discipline problems I have. But if you have any "tricks," let me know.

JEAN:   Well, this is just a suggestion, and I don't know how you would feel about it. How about starting a cooperative learning program with the high and medium groups, which might be more self-sufficient? Since you have a few good writers, maybe you could have a writing activity in which they'd all be involved and work as teams and that would free your hands for the group of three kids that includes Arturo.

KEN:   That sounds like a good idea. Okay.

JEAN:   I would be willing to help you . . .

KEN: Oh, you're welcome. You're welcome. That would be great. We could get started with the high and medium groups.

JEAN: Okay, and you'd have more time to work with the lowest group and Arturo's group.

KEN: Okay.

JEAN: I think that might work out. I also suggest that we control the content of the reading . . .

KEN: How?

JEAN: In a way that would include Arturo more. Since he comes from Nicaragua, we could have a unit about Nicaragua or let him write about his country and use his own writing as a basis for reading.

KEN: You mean . . . I should listen to his own dictation? In fact, the aide could write out the story he dictates and use that as the basis for reading. That's a good idea.

JEAN: Do you see it as a possible alternative?

KEN: Oh, yeah. Yeah, I think so.

JEAN: So, basically, the idea would be to free your hands a little bit by having the high and medium groups work independently and to spend more time with Arturo and integrate him. And work out a cooperative learning group, which might be better for them, too.

KEN: Okay, and I think that would also improve his social skills if he is able to stay within a group. Yes, and if he is monitored . . .

JEAN: Yes, okay. It might be easier for him. If he is involved in an activity, he may not feel so left out or laughed at, as you mentioned earlier.

KEN: Okay, I think it is a very good idea. Well, how about the math, then?

JEAN: Yeah, can you tell me about your math program, too? What do you do? What are the students learning currently?

KEN: Well, for the math, I have three groups, also: those who have mastered the basic skills, up to knowing their products up to 9; the medium group; and the low group, especially those who are still getting familiar with the basic facts. What I do is, I teach a concept to the whole class, and then I will let the high group work independently when I have ascertained that they understand, and then I spend some time with the lower groups.

JEAN: Would Arturo fit in your lowest group, or is he at a much lower level than the rest of your students?

KEN: Well, to tell you the truth, I don't know what to do with Arturo because by the time we have math, the aide would have left because she works for only 3 hours. Because of that, I have started Arturo with some manipulatives.

JEAN: Which is a good idea.

KEN: But, again, there isn't much time, and with 28 kids who . . .

JEAN:    All require a lot of attention . . .

KEN:    Yes, who need a lot of attention, and one kid who needs all the help for the whole day.

JEAN:    I noticed that you have a computer in the classroom.

KEN:    Yes, I have a computer in the classroom, but I don't use it for math that much . . .

JEAN:    Yes, because you have so many kids?

KEN:    Yes.

JEAN:    I know you're an expert in computers and that you know about different programs. How about creating a program for Arturo's level that would allow him to work independently?

KEN:    Yes, that's a good idea. I have thought about it. Actually, I have a program called "Math Blasters," a program published by Davidson and Associates. It is a drill program, and I guess I could begin him on drill practices in various math facts. But the problem is that sometimes it is distractive. If you let one child alone go to the computer, the other students are going to complain and say, "How come you are allowing only this kid to use the computer?"

JEAN:    Yes.

KEN:    So I have to deal with that kind of thing.

JEAN:    Yes, maybe you can assign a partner to work with him and to assist him. And that would help him become more popular. You could switch the partners, and you can also tell the kids that Arturo really needs to catch up with the rest of the class.

KEN:    Do you think that would raise his self-concept or what?

JEAN:    I think so, and I think that coming from Nicaragua, he may not have worked on the computer before, and it will certainly boost his motivation to learn.

KEN:    Okay.

JEAN:    And computers are nonthreatening, and I think that he will be able to progress a lot faster.

KEN:    Okay, it's a good idea.

JEAN:    So, in conclusion, it would be more one-on-one attention during reading and more independent work with the computer during math periods. He'll be able to work at his own pace, and we will be able to evaluate better how much he's been learning in 2 months.

KEN:    Okay, but I hope that you keep your promise of coming to set up the cooperative learning program.

JEAN:    Absolutely. How about tomorrow?

KEN:    That's wonderful. That's fast.

JEAN:    At what time is your reading?

KEN:    I start reading at 8:40 and end at 9:30.

JEAN: From 8:40 to 9:30. Okay, I will be there. I will work something out with my aide and Mrs. Scher. Okay. So, I'll see you tomorrow.

KEN: See you tomorrow. Bye.

*Dialogue 3.* To set criteria for evaluating Arturo's progress.

JEAN: Hi, Ken. I felt that yesterday you were really tired, and as you left, I realized that we did not discuss ways of evaluating Arturo's progress.

KEN: Oh, yes. I thought about it last night after talking about all these programs and so forth. I'm glad that you called me last night to go over the points. Can you go over them again, please?

JEAN: Yes. We decided that in reading, you would put the medium and high groups together so you could put more emphasis on teaching the lower group and Arturo's group, and they would be writing their own context-embedded text; he would feel in control of what he's reading and then decode what he has been writing. So, what criteria would we use for evaluating decoding? What would we expect Arturo to do? How many words would you expect him to read?

KEN: Well, I have a list of sight words, a list of 255 most commonly used words . . .

JEAN: 255 words a month, a year?

KEN: Oh, no! It is the total battery of words that the child should be able to know in order to read at a second-grade level. . . . So I figure that if we continue with the sight words, he should be able to read at least 20 words within the next couple of weeks.

JEAN: Okay. So your criterion will be 20 words at the end of the next 2 weeks. Yes, he will be able to decode 20 words from his own dictated story.

KEN: No, from the San Diego battery of words.

JEAN: Oh, okay.

KEN: And then in addition to that, he will be able to decode the things that he dictated to me. You know what I'm saying?

JEAN: Yes.

KEN: So that if the story that he dictated about Nicaragua were read to him, at the end of the 2 weeks, he should be able to read the same story back to me, in addition to being able to decode the 20 words that I select from the San Diego battery of words.

JEAN: Oh, how about selecting the 20 words from his own writing, such as the most common words that . . .

KEN: Yes. I think so. I will use those for dictation to see if apart from decoding those words, he will be able to write them correctly, from what he already knows as words.

JEAN: Okay, so you're having a spelling goal as well?

KEN: A spelling goal also, yes.

JEAN:   Okay.

KEN:   Do you think it's okay?

JEAN:   Yes, we can try it out.

KEN:   Of course, if you think it's too much, we can . . .

JEAN:   You are the one who works with Arturo, so . . .

KEN:   Well, I guess I'm trying to set high expectations for him because . . .

JEAN:   Well, you know the student, so you know what he can achieve.

KEN:   Yes, I think that he can achieve. He is good with his oral language except that he can't read.

JEAN:   Okay, so let's go for 20 words from the San Diego sight words list plus being able to decode his own story.

KEN:   Okay.

JEAN:   So that will be the goal in reading. And in math, what do you expect Arturo to do?

KEN:   Well, since he is already able to add single-digit numbers, I would say that the next step is that he would be able to regroup.

JEAN:   Okay, regrouping two digits?

KEN:   Yes, two digits in addition problems.

JEAN:   All right.

KEN:   And I think that at the end of the 2 weeks, I will give him 10 problems.

JEAN:   Okay.

KEN:   And I would expect him to achieve at 60% accuracy . . . Did I say 60% or 80%? 80%. Yes, 80%. 60% was too loose, okay?

JEAN:   Okay, so let these be our two goals.

KEN:   Okay.

JEAN:   All right, I'll see you during reading time today.

KEN:   Okay.

JEAN:   Bye.

*Dialogue 4.* Evaluation of the consultation and Arturo's progress after 2 weeks.

JEAN:   So, how did it go? How do you feel about Arturo's progress?

KEN:   Well, as your visits to the classroom have shown, I'm happy to announce that it's been going pretty well.

JEAN:   Wonderful. How is his behavior?

KEN:   I'm surprised to say that now Arturo is not really the problem. The other kids are more problematic than Arturo now. He seems to be working well with the group, and he looks forward to telling his own stories and seeing them written down. He is proud of those things. I think that it is a good arrangement.

JEAN:   He is building up his self-esteem.

KEN:    His self-image, yeah.

JEAN:   And how about our goals? Have they been met?

KEN:    Actually, yeah. The last time I gave him a dictation, he missed only a couple of words.

JEAN:   That's great. That was very high. So you were right in having high expectations for him.

KEN:    Yeah. It did pay off. He really looks forward to reading his own stories because he likes to hear himself talk.

JEAN:   Yeah.

KEN:    And he is able—I don't know whether it is pure memorization or not—but he is able to read without pausing the way he used to and stumbling on words.

JEAN:   Yes, he is definitely in control of the content.

KEN:    Yeah, he is in control of the content. Yes. So I would imagine that if we continued with this strategy and let the kids do more and more stories and become familiar with various words, then maybe we will be able to move him into reading textbook stories, beginning with very simple ones.

JEAN:   Wonderful. How about the math?

KEN:    Yeah. The math also has been quite a bit of success. I guess it is the mystery around the computer. Right now he is able to add single-digit numbers without counting his fingers because he has been doing it so often on the computer.

JEAN:   Because he is competing with himself.

KEN:    Yeah, and as for the regrouping goal that we set for him, he has been doing wonderfully well to the extent that when he had a quiz last time, he missed only one.

JEAN:   Yes.

KEN:    Yes, so I would imagine that we keep up this strategy until we add more and more complex problems.

JEAN:   Yes, then he'll build up more confidence.

KEN:    More confidence, yes.

JEAN:   So you think he will be catching up with the others?

KEN:    I think so. I hope that this is not a flash in the pan. I guess the idea is to keep him challenged all the time. Because he likes to hear himself talk, dictating his own stories seems to have solved his talking problem some.

JEAN:   Have you seen other changes in his behavior since his academics started improving?

KEN:    Well, for one thing, he's been able to stay on task, especially when it comes to the computer, and he can stay on the computer for longer than anything I would have imagined. And he also gets excited about telling his own stories because he has all these little stories that his abuelita told him . . .

JEAN: Oh!

KEN: That he wants to recount . . .

JEAN: Then maybe he could type them on the computer later on.

KEN: Oh, well, when he is able to decode enough.

JEAN: Okay, that would be great motivation.

KEN: Well, that's it. Thank you very much for the suggestions.

JEAN: Thank you. And shall we continue with the plan? Should we meet again in 2 weeks?

KEN: Yeah, I think . . .

JEAN: Would you like me to keep helping you in the classroom? If there's anything you'd like me to . . .

KEN: Well, you can drop by once in a while, but you don't have to. I think in the next couple of weeks, we should sit down and reevaluate all the progress so far and then re-plan some other strategies to challenge him some more.

JEAN: Okay. Then, let's see each other in 2 weeks.

KEN: Okay.

JEAN: Bye.

## Managing Conflict

Managing conflict is inevitable in group decision making. Conflict is an essential component in the group decision-making process (Fullen, 1982). As discussed by Ellis and Fisher (1994), the presence of conflict is one commonality across descriptive models of group decision making, as differences of opinion are expressed about task ideas and social norms.

## Gaining Acceptance

Gaining acceptance and establishing rapport are important components of effective consultation (Idol et al., 1994; Pedron & Evans, 1990; Rosenfield, 1987). Both are accomplished through effective interpersonal and communication skills. Three skills essential for establishing rapport and gaining acceptance are positive regard, empathy, and congruence. *Positive regard* refers to the need to treat others with respect. *Empathy* indicates an attempt to understand the other person's perspective. *Congruence* refers to establishing common ground to converse and honestly share thoughts and feelings about the topic under discussion (Rogers, 1965).

To gain acceptance and establish rapport, Idol et al. (1994) recommend treating others with respect, shifting credit for ideas and accomplishments to others, and willingly sharing information and learning with others. Acceptance can be achieved when individuals participate fully in school or agency functions (e.g., serving on committees, assisting with school activities). Full participation provides visibility and demonstrates a commitment to the overall educational process. It also helps the consultant better understand the culture of the school and the needs of the staff. Consultants can gain acceptance by clearly defining, or having superiors define, their role in the school. Letting colleagues know what you can and cannot do decreases the likelihood that misconstrued expectations will jeopardize acceptance. Consultants should realize that gaining acceptance and establishing rapport take time. This is why consulting often occurs among individuals who have established positive relationships.

## Types of Conflict

There are times when conflict is a normal part of the group decision-making process and times when it is inappropriate and needs to be managed. There are different types of conflict, as well. *Substantive conflict* is an intellectual opposition to the content of the ideas. It is the type of conflict one would expect to experience in the group decision-making process. The conflict is focused on the content of the task, and communication revolves around issues that are pertinent to the group task. Substantive conflict is also *constructive conflict* because it promotes an increased understanding of issues among group members and results in a quality decision. To obtain the benefits of constructive conflict, communication during this stage of the group decision-making process should be focused on an interaction that tests ideas. Problems during this stage of the process can result from the group's inability to deal with all the task-related information that has been uncovered. The consultant, as group facilitator, should move the group into a discussion of how the information can be reduced to its main points and those main points used as the basis for decision making (Ellis & Fisher, 1994).

Affective conflict refers to the ineffective interpersonal interactions of group members. It usually results from inappropriate interpersonal skills. Often the conflict revolves around emotional clashes between individuals or personal agendas that participants bring to a meeting. Affective conflict can also be *destructive conflict* since it can result in the group failing to make a decision or making one without consensus and commitment. Personality differences among group members need not clash if the facilitator can be sure that all group members have the necessary information about the task and can focus group communication on that information. However, if a substantive conflict escalates to emotional clashes between individuals, it is important to determine the source of that interpersonal conflict. One source of conflict is resistance to change.

## The Multiple Faces of Resistance

Resistance may be shown through reluctance to participate as well as by failing to follow through with an agreed upon plan (Polsgrove & McNeil, 1989). Margolis and McCabe (1988) and Margolis, Fish, and Wepner (1990) discuss some of the more common sources of resistance: (a) feared loss of instructional time; (b) misunderstanding change; (c) disagreement with the recommended change; (d) lack of participation in the change process; (e) fear of the new or unknown; and (f) preservation of the status quo. The work of Gutkin and

Hickman (1990) suggests that resistance to school-based consultation is complex. There are many possible reasons for consultee resistance, and resistance will directly affect the success of consultation activities.

## Types of Resistance

Project Vision (1993) presents eight categories of resistance that are known to occur when educators are attempting to change a school-based program. The first, *path of least resistance,* represents a reluctance to do anything different from the status quo. *Status resistance* involves a fear that the current situation might change for the worse, e.g., one's job might require more skill. *Emotional resistance* has its roots in the individual's fear of the situation, e.g., being afraid to touch a child with physical disabilities. When an individual experiences *economic resistance,* she or he is often afraid of losing her or his job. *Rational resistance* involves a lack of understanding about how a proposed change could occur. *Competency resistance* represents the fear of not being able to do what is required as a result of the proposed change. *Social resistance* reflects an individual's failure to see the need to change. Finally, *security resistance* reflects an understanding of the need for change but a level of discomfort in implementing the change. Resistance can be categorized many ways. An underlying feature of all resistance is fear.

## Strategies for Dealing with Resistance

Strategies for dealing with the eight types of resistance mentioned above are presented in Table 4.10. As can be seen from this table, many of the strategies for dealing with different types of resistance encourage using effective listening, sharing task-related information, involving participants in planning for change, and, most important, managing time. One of the key points made by Ellis and Fisher (1994) is that conflict management takes time. Rushing to resolve conflicts can be detrimental.

Hoskins (1996) suggests using the following strategy if resistance is encountered:

1. Identify the perspective of the resistor (e.g., busy, bully, victim).

2. Identify the fears or concerns of the resistor (e.g., fear of losing control or failing).

3. Identify what the resistor really wants (e.g., to be in control, to be successful).

4. Identify strategies to help the resistor achieve what she or he wants while addressing the needs of the resistor and all other members of the group (e.g., to help both the teacher and the student be successful).

If the resistor becomes angry, Margolis and Fiorelli (1987) suggest the following steps to manage anger in a cooperative problem-solving manner: (a) maintain your composure; (b) listen carefully and empathetically, showing that you care about the reasons for the anger; (c) encourage consultees to identify and share the reasons for their anger and fully release their anger; (d) resist attempts to invalidate the information that has been shared; (e) highlight areas of agreement; (f) move slowly from problem perception to problem definition; and (g) help the consultee to maintain self-respect.

**Table 4.10**

Types of Resistance and Strategies

| Types of Resistance | Expressed As | Strategies |
| --- | --- | --- |
| Path of Least Resistance | "If it ain't broke, don't fix it." | Share information about the benefits of change. Provide assurance that individual will be involved in planning. |
| Status Resistance | "Will my job responsibilities change?" | Give individual opportunity to describe and negotiate his/her role and provide support to develop a clear positive vision. |
| Emotional Resistance | "I'm afraid of this. This overwhelms me." | Carefully listen to his/her fears. Offer knowledge regarding his/her fears. Expose individual slowly to new situations and assure him/her that key people will provide assistance. |
| Economic Resistance | "Will I lose my job?" | Involve immediate supervisors in planning to assure job stability. Help individual to recognize his/her new role. Involve individual in planning for change. |
| Rational Resistance | "How will change occur in the current system?" | Provide extensive information about the proposed change. Provide individual with an opportunity to talk and problem-solve about the proposed change. |
| Competency Resistance | "Will I be competent in the new system?" | Provide training in the new system. Provide reinforcement for skills individual can use in the new system. Assist individual in seeing how he/she can carry out his/her new role. |
| Social Resistance | "I'm comfortable. I don't want anything to change." | Provide this person with time to adjust to the change. Provide individual with information about the change and the opportunity to work with others in planning the change. |
| Security Resistance | "This change is needed, but I'm not comfortable doing it." | Individual needs to feel like a contributor to the change. Provide time to think, give input, and plan the change. |

*Note.* From *Resistance to Change* (video), by Project Vision, 1993, University of Idaho. Copyright 1993 by Project Vision. Reprinted with permission.

To *manage conflict* resulting from resistance, it is important to be aware of the process of change and some assumptions about it.

## The Change Process

Many educators who incorporate consultation into their school role also are likely to attempt personal and institutional changes (Idol & West, 1987; Kurpius & Lewis, 1988; Reisberg, 1988; Reisberg & Wolf, 1986; West, Idol, & Cannon, 1989). The *change process* is highly personal and relational. Those involved are personally affected by changes in roles and relationships (Rainforth & York-Barr, 1997). The personal component of change is reflected in the research of Goldenberg and Gallimore (1991), who provide a compelling description of educational change and the factors that affect it. As they report, "Achieving change was partially dependent on local action and understanding of the local school culture. It could not be done exclusively through reference to research knowledge, no matter how compellingly documented in the national literature" (p. 2).

### Assumptions

According to Goldenberg and Gallimore (1991), one cannot make the assumption that educational change occurs as a function of researchers generating and disseminating knowledge and policymakers and practitioners accepting and implementing the results of scientifically valid research. To the contrary, one needs to understand the people involved in the change, their goals, and their overall cultural system.

Table 4.11 provides a summary of basic assumptions about the change process that is of distinct benefit to all consultants involved in change (University of Kansas Institute for Research in Learning Disabilities, 1987).

### Strategies for Dealing with Change

There are many strategies consultants can use to understand the personal dynamics and interpersonal conflicts involved in change. We can attempt to identify the sources of resistance by using appropriate communication skills. Rainforth and York-Barr (1997) suggest that, when implementing educational changes, there should be an emphasis on purpose as opposed to structure. For example, therapists may view collaborative teamwork as changing from a back-to-back schedule of direct therapy to long blocks of time in classrooms. Once the schedule is changed, they may not know what to do within the new structure.

The consultant also needs to be aware of the organizational dynamics that effect change. Table 4.12 provides organizational guidelines consultants should consider when implementing educational changes. The guidelines address the personal behaviors of key individuals, such as the principal, as well as key organizational features, such as scheduling and staff development.

Adams and Cessna (1991) also provide suggestions for changing school-wide programs. Their suggestions are provided to avoid two problems: (1) implementing educational changes without participants understanding the need for change or how to change, and (2) implementing educational change without organizational changes. Their suggestions are incorporated in Table 4.13. The questions posed by these authors address many of the sources of resistance identified above. Their implementation guidelines accommodate time—a necessary ingredient for change.

# Table 4.11

## Assumptions About the Change Process

1. Significant change in the beliefs and attitudes of teachers about instruction takes place after learning outcomes for students show clear change.
2. Experienced teachers seldom become committed to new programs until they have seen the new practices succeed with students in their classrooms.
3. When planning and implementing effective staff development programs, keep in mind that change is a slow, difficult, and gradual process for teachers; teachers need to receive regular feedback on student learning outcomes, and continued support and follow-up are necessary after initial training.
4. New practices that entail significant amounts of change live or die by the amount of personal assistance teachers receive (e.g., reassurance, support, problem solving).
5. Forceful leadership contributes most directly and surely to major, effective changes in classroom practice that become firmly incorporated into everyday routines.
6. Implementation is a necessary but not a sufficient step toward sustained improvement. Institutionalization should include writing practices into the school curricula, standard operating procedures and policies, yearly materials, and staffing cycles. Competing practices should be eliminated.
7. Researchers and educators tend to agree that an effective improvement strategy centers on involvement more than on content.
8. School-wide staff development programs are more likely to influence behavior changes and student achievement than small, isolated programs.
9. To effect change, practices must be used on a large enough scale to alter entire patterns of learning and teaching.
10. Lasting learning is most likely to occur within a supportive environment that encourages practice, idea sharing between teachers, and peer observation.
11. The two most common faults ignored in educational change are the underestimation of teacher training needs and the absence of attention to cultural norms and contexts in which change is attempted.
12. School improvement can work, and we know how and why: quality innovations are carefully implemented.
13. Adaptation of the innovation is to be expected; the critical skill is that of making innovation and organization adjustments while preserving the "core," the spirit of the innovation.
14. Consultants should not assume that their version of change should be the one that is implemented. Assume that successful implementation consists of some transformation of initial ideas.
15. Administrators and teachers live in different worlds. Effective school improvement requires bridging the gaps between administrative initiative, pressure, and support on the one hand, and teacher's effort, mastery, and commitment on the other.
16. Conflict and disagreement are inevitable but fundamental components of successful change. Attempts at collective change will necessarily involve conflict.
17. Most people or groups do not readily change. Progress occurs when steps are taken that increase the number of people affected.
18. Good implementation takes time, 18 months for small-scale change is usual.
19. Change takes considerable time. Unrealistic or undefined time lines fail to recognize that implementation occurs developmentally. Expect significant change to take a minimum of 2 to 3 years.
20. Attempting more often yields more. More demanding innovations, well implemented, induce change and growth in teachers and organizations.
21. There are four types of practices called the critical practices of adaptability that clearly distinguish the more successful from the less successful schools in their ability to change and improve. These are: (a) teachers engage in frequent, continual, and increasingly concrete and precise talk about teaching practice; (b) teachers and administrators frequently observe each other teaching and provide each other with useful (if potentially frightening) evaluations of their teaching; (c) teachers and administrators plan, design, research, evaluate, and prepare teaching materials together; and (d) teachers and administrators teach each other the practice of teaching.

# Table 4.12
## Organizational Guidelines for Educational Change

Have the "change facilitator" at your school (hopefully the principal) conduct the following activities:

1. Develop supportive organizational arrangements (e.g., assist in scheduling and planning)
2. Provide for appropriate staff development
3. Consult and reinforce (make provisions to address present and evolving needs of program participants)
4. Monitor (help develop and support functional and authentic evaluative procedures)
5. Communicate with others (elicit support from individuals and agencies external to the program)
6. Disseminate (provide information to help those just beginning similar programs)

Encourage the principal at your school to use an *initiator* style of change facilitation. The three styles of change facilitation are listed here in order of the greatest to the least likelihood of program success:

1. *Initiator:* holds decisive long-range goals; solicits input from professional staff; takes active steps based on that input; pushes self, staff, and students in desired direction; obtains necessary resources
2. *Manager:* is an efficient and supportive change agent in the school, protects staff from excessive demands, is sensitive to educator needs, questions changes in beginning stages, will support change when external pressure is applied
3. *Responder:* is concerned with how others perceive his or her decisions and the direction of the school, delegates decisions while soliciting as much feedback from all concerned as possible, is concerned with making professionals and students content, makes decisions based more on immediate circumstances than on long-range goals, maintains decisions once they are made

If the principal is not an initiator, solicit support based on the principal's style. The following chart shows characteristics of different change facilitator styles.

| Receptivity to externally imposed changes | | |
|---|---|---|
| Very Receptive | | Not Very Receptive |
| X ——————— | X ——————— | X |
| Responders | Managers | Initiators |
| Level of personal involvement in change | | |
| Very Involved | | Not Very Involved |
| X ——————— | X ——————— | X |
| Initiators | Managers | Responders |

Use the following guidelines for building a program from the bottom up.

1. Have an ad hoc committee or steering committee composed of those practitioners interested in initiating the program generate a written proposal. The written proposal is an internal document initially submitted to the principal and ultimately submitted to the faculty for comment and approval.
2. Obtain the principal's input at an early stage. Be sure the principal is aware of any possible changes in the schoolwide program. Solicit the principal's suggestions for modifications of the proposal, along with his or her support and suggestions before presenting the proposal to the total faculty.
3. Have the ad hoc committee arrange for two levels of faculty input and approval. First, the program should be discussed openly at a suitable type of faculty meeting. Second, a period of time—perhaps up to several weeks—should be reserved to receive additional oral and/or written comments from the faculty. At a future meeting, other concerns and all questions should be addressed. Either by consensus or a vote, action should be taken on the proposal.
4. Establish the program on a trial basis (e.g., for 1 year or 1 marking period) and monitor the program on an ongoing basis (at least twice if the trial period is 1 year).

*Note.* From *Collaborative Teaching Casebooks: Facilitator's Guide* (p. 7), by K. C. Harris, 1998b, Austin, TX: PRO-ED. Copyright 1998 by PRO-ED. Adapted with permission.

## Table 4.13

Suggested Process for Educational Changes

Strategy: Develop a common understanding that results in a mission statement for support specialists that interfaces with the overall school mission.

1. Ask the following questions:

   - What are we about? (goals of students, needs of students, relationship of support specialists' purpose and building mission)
   - What are we doing? (what is working, what do we need to change, who are team members, how do we function as a team?)
   - What do we need to do? (school structure changes, support service delivery system changes, curriculum changes, team changes)
   - What is our action plan? (roles of team members, focus for year 1, first steps in making changes)

2. Use the following guidelines:

   - Begin early—a year of planning is not too much. Use the following meeting schedule to enable participants to reflect on work but also tackle issues that may require extended discussion:

     a. several short meetings close together;

     b. one long session (full day, off school site, no students in building); and

     c. another series of short meetings.

   - Conduct all meetings with a sense of humor and food!
   - Provide participants with skills in: group dynamics, team building, interpersonal problem solving, running effective meetings, and leadership styles.
   - Give teams the opportunity to develop.

*Note.* From *Collaborative Teaching Casebooks: Facilitator's Guide* (p. 11), by K. C. Harris, 1998b, Austin, TX: PRO-ED. Copyright 1998 by PRO-ED. Adapted with permission.

## Strategies for Managing Conflict

We've identified types of conflict and sources of conflict as well as strategies for dealing with resistance and change However, to have an "awareness level of knowledge" related to the types and sources of conflict and/or strategies for dealing with them does not mean that the consultant will be able to manage conflict situations. We'll turn our attention now to this important area.

There are at least three standard *conflict management techniques:* majority vote, third-party arbitration, and authoritative rule. However, these standard strategies are ineffective for group decision making because they do not provide an opportunity for consensus and subsequent commitment. They are based on one party gaining and the other losing (Ellis & Fisher, 1994). Johnson and Johnson (1994) offer the following guidelines for making decisions by consensus: (a) avoid arguing blindly for your own opinions; (b) avoid changing your mind only to reach agreement and avoid conflict; (c) avoid procedures that will end the conflict prematurely; (d) seek out differences of opinion; (e) do not assume that someone must win and someone must lose; and (f) discuss underlying assumptions.

Much has been written about conflict management. Readers might find Fisher, Ury, and Patton's *Getting to Yes: Negotiating Agreement Without Giving In* (1998, 2nd ed.) useful.

When dealing with conflict, the group needs to address two major concerns: achieving a goal (task) and maintaining a relationship (the social aspect of group decision making) (Johnson & Johnson, 1995). The group orientation toward conflict will dictate how it deals with conflict. Johnson and Johnson

## Table 4.14
### Strategies for Establishing Trust

1. Provide your complete and unhurried attention.
2. Keep your word.
3. Listen to understand rather than to challenge.
4. Understand what matters to people. Work hard to protect that.
5. Use easily understood language.
6. Share yourself honestly.
7. Share your expertise without dominating the conversation. Solicit input from others to make their participation in the discussion as easy as possible (e.g., "I'm wondering what you think about my recommendations for Harry's new program.").
8. Employ empathetic listening. Frequently use short, fresh, tentative statements to rephrase your interpretation of the parent's or teacher's concerns and ideas (e.g., "Correct me if I'm wrong; you don't want to modify David's program because . . .").
9. Don't push others to trust you further than you trust them. Trust is mutual or shallow.
10. Try extending your trust of others a little further. Being trusting makes one more trustworthy.
11. Don't confuse being trustworthy with being a buddy. Being a buddy for a purpose is an untrustworthy act.
12. If resistance persists, employ systematic interactive problem-solving techniques.

*Note.* From *Managing Transitions: Making the Most of Change* (p. 78–79), by W. Bridges, 1991, Reading, MA: Addison-Wesley. Copyright 1991 by Addison-Wesley, Inc. And from "Overcoming Resistance to a New Remedial Program," by H. Margolis and P. P. McCabe, 1988, *The Clearing House, 62*(3), p. 132–133. Copyright 1988 by Heldref Publications. Adapted with permission.

(1995) and Ellis and Fisher (1994) both discuss individual styles of dealing with conflict: One could avoid the situation and refuse to become involved. One could propose a compromise in order to "keep the peace" among group members. One could try to persuade other group members to agree to a specific decision. Or one could relinquish one's group decision-making responsibility by just agreeing to any outcome (essentially false consensus). None of these approaches produces an effective resolution to a conflict situation.

Collaboration is the ideal method for conflict management because it requires everyone's participation. Such participation leads to commitment. Collaboration should emphasize stable long-term decisions, not solutions that offer immediate gratification, especially for only one group member (Ellis & Fisher, 1994).

## Establishing Trust

A key interpersonal skill is the establishment of trust. Without trust, it is unlikely that a positive climate for communication can be achieved. Table 4.14 presents some strategies for establishing trust. As can be seen in this table, keys to the establishment of trust are listening, being honest with oneself and others, and discussing needs rather than presenting solutions.

**Table 4.15**

A Process for Dealing with Conflict

1. Pause and take a breath.
2. Name the conflict or source of conflict.
3. Identify the part you play in the conflict.
4. Engage in problem-solving negotiations:
    a. Define the problem in terms of needs, not solutions or personalities.
    b. Brainstorm possible solutions.
    c. Select the solution (or solutions) that will best address the needs of all concerned.
    d. Plan who will do what, where, and by when.
    e. Implement the plan.
    f. Evaluate the plan.

*Note.* From *Collaborative Teaching Casebooks: Facilitator's Guide* (p. 23), by K. C. Harris, 1998b, Austin, TX: PRO-ED. Copyright 1998 by PRO-ED. Adapted with permission.

## A Process for Dealing with Conflict

We've identified types of conflict, sources of conflict, and strategies for managing conflict. In Table 4.15 we provide a process that all consultants can use for dealing with conflict. The first step, pause and take a breath, is essential because you want to *deal with* the conflict, not *react to* the conflict. You need to control your emotions skillfully and use your sense of humor when dealing with conflict. This step is very important for diffusing the emotions arising from conflict. Therefore, you should learn and use positive ways of handling stress (the body's automatic physiologic reaction to circumstances that require behavioral adjustments), decreasing levels of anxiety, and improving self-control and mood states. As stress and anxiety increase, so do performance and efficiency, but only to a point. Beyond a certain level, if stress continues to increase, performance and efficiency diminish. A negative stress cycle can develop—that is, an event perceived as stressful causes physical and psychological symptoms, and those, in turn, increase our stress (Harvard Medical School & Deaconess Hospital, 1997). By relaxing, focusing, and breathing it is possible to have effective personal interactions; therefore, one should stop, breathe, reflect, and then choose an action instead of a reaction.

Since conflict can result from many sources, the following questions may assist in assessing the source of a conflict:

- Do we all have the same information?
- Is the information we have complete?
- Are the goals we have compatible?
- Are the methods we are using effective?
- Is it comfortable for us to disagree openly with one another?

As a member of a group decision-making process, one needs to identify one's part in the conflict before resolutions to the conflict can be pursued. For example, it would be useful to know if the mother had one goal and the father, teacher, and consultant another. It would also be helpful to know if participants were choosing to avoid the conflict or dealing with it in a way that would preserve a suitable goal and the relationship of all parties (Pickett & Gerlach, 1997). Engaging in *collaborative problem solving* is suggested as an effective way for dealing with conflict.

# A Collaborative Problem-Solving Process

Another term often used to describe an approach similar to collaborative problem solving is *principled negotiation* (Carney & Gamel-McCormick, 1996). In this approach to decision making, efforts are made to separate the people from the problem, focus on interests or needs rather than positions or solutions, create options for mutual gain, and use objective criteria to evaluate outcomes.

Collaborative problem solving is the preferred strategy for conflict management because it preserves goals and relationships. Group members seek solutions that ensure that all participants fully achieve goals and resolve—or at least set aside—any tensions and negative feelings. Participants maintain their interests and try to find ways of reconciling their interests with the interests of other participants. The process requires participants to express their views of the conflict directly, and their feelings about them.

The following problem-solving sequence is provided to assist consultants in managing the group decision-making process and solving problems. Though a prescribed problem-solving sequence is efficient, it may not be the best process for all groups. According to Ellis and Fisher (1994), there are three criticisms of prescriptive approaches to decision making. First, practical, prescriptive problem-solving approaches may stifle creativity. Second, prescriptions typically assume that group members will act rationally and unemotionally. Third, there is conflicting evidence about whether prescriptive procedures improve the quality of a group's outcome. However, prescriptive procedures do help avoid inefficiency, redundancy, and delay.

The problem-solving sequence described below is offered as a *guideline* to consultants. Consultants are encouraged to develop and use the most effective problem-solving process for each group decision-making venture in which they engage.

The collaborative problem-solving sequence described below was developed with reference to the work of Ellis and Fisher (1994), Kurpius (1978), and Bauwens and Hourcade (1995). It incorporates the components of principled negotiation. The following stages need not be completed sequentially. Stages 1 and 2 could be addressed simultaneoulsy, for example, though one would expect them to be completed before stage 3. Consultants should attempt to address all stages in problem solving, however.

## Stage 1: Clarify Expectations Toward the Process and Issues

The first stage in this problem-solving sequence is similar to the preentry aspect of problem solving proposed by Kurpius (1978). Consultants should answer the following questions before engaging in a discussion about the problem: (a) What are participants' beliefs about the issue? and (b) Is the consultant expected to be a collaborator or an expert?

Answering the first question will help consultants to understand the perspective consultees are taking on the issue and to learn if there are differences in how the problem is viewed. Consultants may need to help consultees reach congruence about the problem before resolution can be found. Answers to the second question will help consultants determine the role consultees are expecting them to assume in the problem-solving process. The consultant should clarify role expectations before beginning, since the consultees may assume that the consultant will resolve the problem (the expert role) while the consultant expects to facilitate the problem-solving process among consultees (the collaborator role).

## Stage 2: Establish Rapport and Build Trust

This stage should also be completed before engaging in a discussion about the problem. The consultant should provide an opportunity for group members to visit with one another and come to appreciate the knowledge and experiences each can bring to resolving the issue.

## Stage 3: Determine Conditions Surrounding the Problem

The group discussion now focuses on the problem. The consultant should solicit from group members the conditions under which the problem exists (e.g., the child acts up only upon arrival at school). The group should also clarify the range of changes that are possible in the environment. For example, the group could clarify that school arrival times are fixed, but the parent's work schedule is flexible.

Recall that all issues that may be targeted for consultation are not deficit driven. Some issues, like improving the curriculum offerings across grade levels, are "positive" challenges to address.

## Stage 4: Agree on How to Approach the Problem

The consultant should engage group members in a discussion about who should be involved in resolving the problem (e.g., the teacher and the parent may be available to help when the child arrives at school, but the consultant is available only after 10:00 A.M.). The group members should also clarify the roles each of them will assume during the problem-solving process (e.g., who will facilitate the meetings, who will record the plan that is developed, and so forth).

## Stage 5: Define the Problem

The consultant should assist group members to define the problem in terms of needs, standards, behaviors, and contextual variables, not solutions or personalities. The group's goals should be discussed and the following questions and requests addressed by group members:

- Define the problem from the perspective of each group member in terms of frequency, intensity, duration, and context.
- Describe what each person wants to achieve.
- Describe what each person feels about the behavior that is occurring and how others in the environment are interpreting the behavior.
- Exchange reasons for positions.
- Understand each other's perspective.
- Use reframing to alter how the problem might be viewed. A new view of the situation may lead to different behavior or different responses. For example, a teacher may "frame" the following situation a number of ways: A group of children enter the classroom noisily and spend time talking with each

Imagination primers: What perspective will the other people involved (student, parents, and teachers) be likely to take? How do you think you might view the situation 5 years from now? How would you have viewed it 10 years ago? If someone had successfully resolved a similar problem, how would she or he see it?

other about their home life instead of coming in to class quietly, putting their possessions away, and sitting down. The teacher may frame this situation as deliberately disruptive behavior, which may lead to failed or frustrated attempts to take control of the children's behavior. However, the teacher could reframe the situation as one of good friends needing time to catch up with one another before starting the day. Instead of perceiving the students as being deliberately disruptive or trying to sabotage the teacher's program, the situation can then be viewed as appropriate behavior (good social interaction among friends), but poorly timed (students should be attending to their morning work). This is a key step for increasing change possibilities. Be creative and use brainstorming as a way to generate as many alternatives as possible.

See Peters and Heron (1993) for more information on best practice.

- Select one or more useful perspectives that offer a solution, consistent with best practice and least restrictive alternative principles.
- State the problem in measurable terms (e.g., "Eliminate Diane's tantrum behavior upon her arrival at school").

## Stage 6: Analyze the Problem and Gather Information

Analyzing the problem and gathering information are essential stages of the decision-making process. It is important to spend time on this combined stage before suggesting solutions. The purpose of this stage is to collect evidence and information that will help the group explore and clarify the problem. Conduct the following activities:

See Chapter 8 for further treatment on these protocols.

- Research and establish the history and possible causes of the problem.
- Discuss how the problem relates to other issues.
- Collect relevant information, especially using ecological and functional assessment protocols.
- Discuss this information in the group.
- Critically examine the facts and information. This means challenging the facts and assumptions to make sure that they stand the test of scrutiny. Use critical listening and questioning skills.
- Make sure that the group has comprehensive information.

## Stage 7: Establish Decision Criteria

It is important to determine what type of decision would be acceptable to the group. Therefore, the consultant should help group members to answer the following questions:

- What would an ideal decision look like? What would it include? What would it exclude?
- What would a reasonable, but less than ideal, solution look like? This is important because it is not always possible to reach an ideal decision.
- What standards should the group use to judge or evaluate the decision?

## Stage 8: Identify Possible Solutions

Proposed solutions should be identified and then discussed. Lack of adequate discussion can lead to poor decision making (Ellis & Fisher, 1994). The

## Table 4.16
### Three Common Strategies for Generating Ideas

| Brainstorming | Sharewriting | Nominal Group Technique |
|---|---|---|
| Ideas are presented verbally by group participants (individual members may or may not contribute). | Similar to brainstorming, except that team members write their ideas, comments, or solutions. | Group members write ideas individually. |
| Clarification queries on contributions are acceptable. | All members of the group participate (self-identification). | Participants offer one idea at a time in a "round robin" fashion until all ideas have been presented and recorded. |
| Comments and criticisms are reserved. | Ideas, comments, and solutions are exchanged with other members. | Each group member conducts an initial rank ordering of ideas, which are grouped by frequency counts into the most important ones. |
| Ideas are recorded verbatim (w/ friendly amendments). | Once ideas are exchanged, extended comments are written on each (self-identification continues). | Group members interact about this initial ranking. |
| Ideas are ranked and group decides on a course of action. | Process continues until all members' ideas, comments, and solutions have been circulated. | Participants reach a final resolution (Moore et al., 1989, p. 54). |
|  | Emphasize methodology whenever possible. |  |

*Note.* From *Interactions: Collaboration Skills for School Professionals* (2nd ed., p. 113–116), by M. Friend and L. Cook, 1996, NY: Longman. Copyright 1996 by Longman. And from *The Educational Consultant: Helping Professionals, Parents, and Mainstreamed Students* (3rd ed., p. 92–93), by T. E. Heron and K. C. Harris, 1993, Austin, TX: PRO-ED. Copyright by T. E. Heron and K. C. Harris. And from "Child Study Team Decision Making in Special Education: Improving the Process," by K. J. Moore, M. B. Fifield, D. A. Spira, and M. Scarlato, 1989, *Remedial and Special Education*, 10(4), 50–59. Copyright 1989 by PRO-ED. All adapted with permission.

consultant should ensure that the group has considered all possible solutions as well as the evidence in support of each proposed solution.

There are three techniques that are useful for identifying possible solutions (Friend & Cook, 1996). One is *brainstorming,* in which solutions are generated without judgments or discussion. Another is *sharewriting,* in which ideas are written down and shared with others. A third is the *nominal group technique,* in which group members generate ideas individually. Each of these techniques is discussed in the following section.

The goal of each of these approaches is to ensure that all team members have a fair and equal opportunity to participate in the process. Using written instead of oral participation methods might be especially helpful when the consultant suspects that one or more team members might dominate the conversation or where cultural background or gender issues may apply. Each of these idea generating approaches helps to ensure that idea production is separated from idea evaluation, ensuring the flow of potentially productive ideas (See Table 4.16).

### Brainstorming

Most educators have engaged in brainstorming. However, it's important to adhere to certain principles so that all possible solutions are generated using this technique. All participants should be encouraged to propose solutions. Solutions are named, not discussed, initially. No one in the group judges the ideas at this point. A recorder lists the ideas, preferably so that all participants can see them (e.g., in large print on poster paper).

Sometimes brainstorming gets bogged down, especially if it is not the first time a problem has been addressed. To move the process forward, consider the following solutions consistent with a "brief therapy approach" (Durrant, 1995).

- *Pattern interruption.* Altering the "doing" of the problem or introducing a small change into the habitual sequence of events that surrounds the problem may lead to bigger changes. A deliberate small change can bring an otherwise "unconscious" habit into conscious control. For example: Team members in one group talked excessively about an issue without moving toward the generation of possible solutions. This behavior was first seen by the consultant as essential to clearly identify the problem, but the group often ran out of time and insufficient attention was paid to generating solutions and developing an action plan. However, when the consultant started the meeting by reminding everyone of the agenda and the time limits for completing the agenda and asked one of the team members to keep track of time, team members monitored how long they were spending on each agenda item.

- *Observational tasks.* Look for those times when things go well. This will yield information about success that can be built on, and it orients the child, parent, or teacher toward success. The consultant could reinforce accomplishment of agenda items by checking off completed items on a prominently displayed poster. This demonstrates to all involved that the team can complete agenda items and do so in a way that does not jeopardize effective problem resolution.

- *Explore goals.* How will you know when things are better? That takes the focus away from the problem and onto solutions—descriptions of behavior that will be happening. For example, if a teacher comes to the group for suggestions to help a student stay on task, and we respond with a list of behaviors that she or he needs to change to maintain attention to task, it might easily seem unattainable to that teacher. But if the teacher is involved in generating and selecting the strategies to maintain attention to task in the classroom, then she or he is more likely to implement the behaviors listed.

- *Practicing (or continuing) success.* Do more of what works by building on exceptions to typical behavior and/or practice small steps that are part of the solution picture. Often, individuals have already begun to solve their own problems. The idea of practice includes the notion that it doesn't have to work all the time—the desired change can be broken into small steps and those steps practiced one at a time.

- *Pretend tasks.* Act "as if" the goal has been achieved. It allows participants in the problem to behave differently, others to look for difference, and adds an element of fun. The consultant may be working with a teacher who has sought help dealing with a girl who is constantly disruptive in the classroom. In a meeting with the teacher and the girl, the consultant asks the teacher, "How will you know when things are better?" The teacher first suggests more compliant behaviors. When questioned why those behaviors would make a difference, the teacher says, "She will seem happier." When asked, "How will you

## Table 4.17

### Sharewriting Example

This is an example of one participant's comments (TH), extended by three other participants on the sharewriting team (JC, WL, and DS). The initial target behavior was improving homework completion and submission in a middle school student with learning disabilities and attention deficit disorder. Note: JC, WL, and DS would each also have produced an independent primary idea for TH and the others to extend. Hence, in a four-member team, 16 possible ideas would be generated.

*Target Behavior: Homework Completion and Submission*

- Initiate homework log (assignments, dates, signatures). (TH)
- Establish FR 1 (FR 2, FR 3) schedules of reinforcement. (JC)
- Establish a "parental postcard system" to inform parents of assignments completed and missing. (WL)
- Combine a dependent group-oriented contingency (hero procedure) to boost performance. (DS)

---

know that she seems happier?" the teacher mentions things such as putting up her hand to answer questions and choosing a toy that she enjoys. The child could then begin to see what might be different "when things are better." The child suggests that the teacher would say something nice about her work and not yell at her when she speaks to her best friend. It could then be suggested that the student choose two sessions over the next few days and pretend that "things are better." That is, she is to pretend that she doesn't feel like throwing things at other students and that she is having fun. She only has to pretend, she doesn't really have to have fun. The student says she could manage this. The teacher is to try to guess which sessions the student chooses as her pretend sessions, but she is not to comment to the student about those sessions.

This strategy introduces a saving face element into any change that happens. The fact that the pretend sessions are secret allows the student to pretend or not to pretend. Even if she does not pretend, the teacher is looking for different behavior and so is more likely to respond to any examples, however small, of the student behaving differently.

## Sharewriting

In sharewriting, a process similar to brainstorming ensues, except that team members write their solutions and exchange them with other members. In turn, members write extensions on ideas generated by others, identifying the source of each extension with their initials. The process continues until all possible ideas are produced. Sharewriting offers several advantages for consultants. First, a permanent product is produced. Written responses generated during the process can be viewed at future times, adding to their utility. Second, unlike brainstorming, in which group members are encouraged to participate but may not, in sharewriting all members contribute by (a) generating an original idea to address the issue before the group, and (b) extending the comments of their fellow participants. In this way, multiple ideas are produced. Finally, because group members from different cultures may be reluctant to participate verbally within a group context, a written medium for participation offers them a functional way to contribute. An example of a sharewriting approach is shown in Table 4.17.

### Nominal Group Technique

Brainstorming and sharewriting are not the only strategies for generating ideas. If participants are reluctant to respond, consultants might consider a nominal group technique (NGT) (Ellis & Fisher, 1994). With this technique, group members work individually and use a process to share ideas with the group. NGT steps are listed below.

1. The group identifies the problem.
2. Individual idea generation—Each person individually and silently writes ideas that come to mind (individual brainstorming). This should take about 15 minutes. Individual and thoughtful ideas are the goal.
3. Recording ideas—The consultant, as group facilitator, asks each person to contribute one or more of their ideas. These ideas are recorded on a chart visible to all members. Ideas are recorded until everyone agrees that a sufficient number have been produced.
4. Clarification of ideas—Each item is discussed for clarification. The consultant should discourage arguing or criticizing until all members are satisfied that they understand all ideas. Ideas can be ranked in order of importance.
5. Discussion and decision—The consultant then facilitates an open and thorough discussion of the top-rated ideas. The originator of each idea should begin its discussion. The consultant should use listening, feedback, and questioning skills to draw ideas and opinions from others.

## Stage 9:  Select the Best Solution

Select the solution (or solutions) that will best address the previously identified target behavior, consistent with the perspectives expressed by the group. The consultant should help group members answer the following questions about the chosen solution:

- Does the solution minimize the problem?
- Is it workable?
- What are the limitations?
- Are there more advantages to the solution than disadvantages?
- How does the solution compare to the decision criteria?
- Are the facts and information gathered consistent with the proposed solution?

Federal laws and regulations strongly encourage the inclusion of students in the design, implementation, and evaluation of their own programs.

Where possible, consultants should give the opportunity to select solutions to those who will be implementing the solutions. For example, if a student needs to improve his or her social behavior, the student may assist with selecting from among various options to try. Including the student will likely promote ownership in the problem resolution as well as the solution implementation.

## Stage 10:  Develop a Plan

Plan who will do what, where, and by when. Consultants should help group members answer the following questions:

- Given the agreed upon resolution, which participant will do what activities in what locations at what times?
- Are additional resources necessary for this? Be sure all resources are provided.

- Are all aspects and dimensions of the agreed upon resolution adequately covered in these arrangements?

- How will the effectiveness of the proposed solution be measured? Using an unobtrusive way to determine effectiveness is important. If the measure is complicated or difficult to implement, it is unlikely to be accomplished.

## Stage 11: Implement the Plan

The consultant should help group members determine how they will monitor program implementation. Before the plan is implemented, the following questions should be answered: Is each step of the plan defined clearly enough to be implemented? and Is each step of the plan practical enough to be implemented? During implementation and at the conclusion of implementation the following question should be answered: Has each step been implemented as outlined and designed?

## Stage 12: Evaluate the Plan

Evaluation is useful. It shows all parties whether the desired change has been accomplished. It is also needed to determine if consultation on the problem can be terminated or needs to be continued. The following questions should be addressed before the plan is implemented:

- What are the individual processes of the plan that might be evaluated, and how will each be evaluated?

- What are the individual outcomes of the plan that might be evaluated, and how will each be evaluated?

## Stage 13: Continue the Consultation

If the implemented plan is successful, the group may no longer need to work on this problem. For example, if Diane stopped her tantrums upon arrival to school, then the problem has been resolved. However, it's also possible that Diane exhibits a number of problems, and that was the one the group decided to address first. The parents may have other issues that they would like the group to address (e.g., How can we stop Diane's tantrums at home?). In that case, the consultation is continued.

The consultation may also need to be continued if the plan was not successful. The group may want to revisit the ideas generated in stage 8. It's possible that one of the ideas not chosen might be a better alternative. The group would then proceed through stage 10, develop a plan; stage 11, implement the plan; and stage 12, evaluate the plan.

# Role of Facilitator

Usually, consultants facilitate consultees' problem resolution by helping them to complete the stages outlined above. However, as facilitators, consultants should consider the following principles when facilitating problem solving (Ellis & Fisher, 1994).

## Clarify the Issues

Identify, define, and sharpen the issues. This can be accomplished in several ways. First, discuss the historical roots of the problem. Such a discussion will promote a thorough understanding of the problem. Second, create a positive atmosphere for discussion so that all members are encouraged to express their needs. At this stage, it's important to discuss the range of issues before the group and not try to jump to solutions. Approaches to solutions will emerge as a result of the problem-solving process. If participants start the discussion by offering individual solutions to the problem, redirect discussion to member issues. Be sure group members can answer the following questions: What are the members' needs? How does each member view the needs of other members? Third, categorize the issues. Deal with each small category individually.

## Promote a Positive Climate

A *positive climate* enhances communication and relationships. The facilitator should encourage open discussion so that all group members can communicate without negative consequences. The facilitator should focus discussion on issues, not on personalized argument. Group members should also be encouraged to communicate their feelings as they relate to the central issue. The facilitator can reinforce open discussion by honestly expressing feelings and disagreements and reinforcing others with direct feedback (e.g., "I'm glad you said that. Now I understand.") The facilitator can also model group communication by referring to group agreements and discussions with "we" instead of "I."

## Allow Group Members to Save Face

The facilitator can accomplish this step through a number of activities. First, establishing a positive climate for communication is essential. Second, the facilitator can reduce defensiveness during conflict by having each party to a conflict state that he or she understands the other side of the issue and recognizes its validity (e.g., "I understand how you can feel that your job is threatened if I, as the classroom teacher, use your physical therapy techniques with Josh."). Such an acknowledgment is a step toward establishing a climate that is receptive to open discussion. Third, the facilitator should extinguish any accusatory or intimidating messages. Such messages can't be ignored because they will influence future interactions and could destroy the group. The facilitator should encourage members of the group who engage in intimidating behavior to explain their behavior. Once the reason for this behavior is understood, affective conflict will be revealed and the destructive effect of such behavior can be reduced.

## Develop Integration Skills

As indicated above, one of the group tasks is to manage the information shared by the group so that the decision reached reflects the data collected. The facilitator should help group members integrate information. Progress toward integration can be documented by keeping track of the points of agreement and clarifying the integrative process that group members are experiencing.

# Disseminating Information Through Staff Development

There are many reasons for disseminating information about consultation activities (e.g., as a professional courtesy to other team members; as part of an evaluative plan; or as a mechanism for sharing results with school personnel, parents, or other members of the educational community). Group members can disseminate information about the consultation process in several useful ways. Informally, one can talk about the consultation activities with educators, parent groups, or community members. Informal conversations that occur, for example, in the hallways, lounge areas, and parking lots of school buildings and at Parent-Teacher Association meetings provide a valuable medium through which information flows. Formal means of communication occur through established newsletters, staff development activities, conferences, journal articles, television, or print media. Table 4.18 provides tips for disseminating information. Minimally, consultants should keep all consultees and clients informed of the consultation activities. However, as with all communication, consultants should respect the confidentiality of information.

See Idol, 1998, for a suggested master plan for staff development that addresses school collaboration.

To implement many consultation activities effectively, it is likely that staff development may be needed. For example, to help consultees design and implement effective programs for students and families, it may be necessary to supervise staff development activities related to educational adaptations, understanding cultural perspectives, strategies for implementing co-teaching, and principles to follow as members of teams, among other topics. Consultants can find information that would be helpful to them in conducting staff development activities in each of these topic areas in the chapters of this text. Glickman, Gordon, and Ross-Gordon (1995), in a review of the literature, conclude that the characteristics of effective staff development programs are: (a) involving participants in planning and implementing; (b) long-range planning; (c) an integration of individual and school improvement goals; (d) procedures based on principles of adult development and learning; (e) release time for participants; (f) incentives for participating, such as support and rewards; (g) small-group learning activities; (h) using concrete and specific activities, demonstration, trial, and feedback during the staff development activities and classroom coaching following presentation of content if skill development is expected; (i) encouraging participants to experiment and take risks; (j) regular participant meetings for problem solving and program revisions; (k) instructional and school leaders participating in staff development activities; and (l) ongoing staff development as part of the school culture.

Consultants should be aware that staff development typically involves three stages of learning: orientation, integration, and refinement (Glickman et al., 1995). In the *orientation stage,* teachers become aware of the benefits, responsibilities, and actions necessary to use the content that is presented. Successful staff development programs take teachers beyond this stage. The *integration stage* is when teachers apply knowledge to their classrooms or schools. Teachers must develop competence and confidence to make new knowledge and skills part of their standard repertoire of instructional strategies. Finally, they must refine their skills to move from basic competence to expertness through continual experimentation and reflection. The final, *refinement stage* requires the synthesis of different types of previous learning into new learning.

## Table 4.18

### Tips for Disseminating Consultation Information

1. Identify essential elements in effective dissemination

   - Have the essential elements of the consultation been specified adequately?
   - Do consultees follow the essential elements of the action plan as specified?
   - Do the students served through the consultation respond as predicted?
   - What additional costs are involved in the development and implementation of the consultation plan (e.g., for initial and ongoing staff development, travel for visits to exemplary programs, release time, hiring of paraprofessionals)?

2. Identify the intended purpose of dissemination. Possibilities include:

   - informing others about the results of the program (e.g., reporting to an agency that supplied resources to implement the program);
   - training others so that they might develop and implement a similar program.

3. Identify the target audience for dissemination (e.g., parents, educators at your school, local school board members, educators at other schools, professors at teacher training institutions).

4. Conduct different types of dissemination activities:

   - Offering staff development activities for colleagues—consider the following features:
     a. staff development based in schools
     b. participation of attendees in staff development activities as helpers and planners of a staff development program
     c. participation of school professionals in constructing and generating ideas for the staff development program
     d. developers of staff development programs encourage educators to share ideas
     e. developers of staff development programs realize it is part of a long-term professional development plan
     f. developers of staff development program provide specific and practical hands-on experience
     g. developers of staff development program provide opportunity to observe exemplary practices

   - Presenting at professional meetings—consider the following features:
     a. single-page handout with skeletal outline of presentation and presenters' names, addresses, and phone numbers;
     b. presentation sequence—concise overview of theory underlying the consultation activity; explanation of basic procedures involved in implementing the consultation activity; and presentation of visuals to show procedures in operation.

   - Writing for professional publications—determine an outlet (e.g., school district or state department of education bulletin, state journal or newsletter in your discipline, journal published by a professional organization).

*Note.* From *Collaborative Teaching Casebooks: Facilitator's Guide* (p. 9), by K. C. Harris, 1998b, Austin, TX: PRO-ED. Copyright 1998 by PRO-ED. Adapted with permission.

Six strategies for staff development have been discussed by Joyce and Showers (1980) and Idol (1998). One is presentation of theory. This is "the rationale, theoretical base, and verbal description of an approach to teaching a skill or instructional technique" (Joyce & Showers, 1980, p. 382). Examples of presenting theory are readings, lectures, films, and discussions. It can raise awareness and increase conceptual control of an area, but few teachers will acquire skills they can transfer into the classroom setting if they receive only presentation of theory. When used in conjunction with other training components, it will increase conceptual control, skill development, and chances of transfer.

## Modeling

"*Modeling* involves enactment of the teaching skill or strategy either through a live demonstration with children or adults, or through television, film or other media" (Joyce & Showers, 1980, p. 382, italics added). Strategies or skills can be modeled numerous times within one training activity. This component has considerable effect on awareness and some effect on knowledge, and it increases the mastery of theory. Many teachers will be able to transfer skills demonstrated by modeling to the classroom, but many more teachers will need another component.

## Practice

*Practice* under simulated or actual conditions requires that the practitioner actually use the new skill or strategy with peers or small groups of students under supervised conditions. Practice is a very efficient way to acquire skills and strategies. The greater the amount of practice (with feedback and reinforcement), the more likely the behavior will generalize to the classroom.

## Structured Feedback

*Structured feedback* involves learning a system for observing teaching behavior and providing an opportunity to reflect on teaching by using that system. Structured feedback can be self-administered, provided by observers, or conducted by peers or coaches on a regular basis. It can also be combined with other components that are organized for the acquisition of specific skills and strategies (e.g., practice-feedback). Feedback alone results in ample awareness of teaching behaviors and knowledge about alternatives and the transfer of that knowledge to the classroom situation. It does not appear to provide permanent changes. Still, it is necessary if practitioners are to make changes in their behavior and maintain those changes.

## Unstructured Feedback

Open-ended or *unstructured feedback* refers to informal discussions following observation and has unpredictable impact. It best accomplishes an awareness of one's teaching style that may be useful in providing groundwork for more extensive, directed training activities.

## Coaching

*Coaching* for application can be used whether teachers are refining their skills or striving for mastery of new skills. It involves helping a teacher analyze the content to be taught, decide upon the approach to be taken, and make a specific plan to help the student adapt to the new teaching approach.

The best scenario for training is a combination of components. Fine tuning can be facilitated with modeling, practice under simulated conditions, and practice in the classroom that is reinforced and complemented with feedback (Idol, 1998). Mastery of new skills and strategies is best done with the addition of presentations and discussions of theory and coaching for application.

# Conclusion

Two important consultation issues were examined in this chapter: interpersonal and communication skills and collaborative problem-solving skills. A communication model reflective of the group decision-making process was presented. Listening and questioning strategies that will help consultants facilitate decision making were described. We explored and offered techniques to manage conflict resistance and change. Guidelines for collaborative problem solving were provided as well as an opportunity to apply the skills discussed in this chapter to an anecdote and a challenging consultation case. Finally, we presented ideas for disseminating information, especially through staff development.

# Summary of Key Points

## Group Decision Making

1. A group decision-making process is the best process to use when several alternative solutions are possible and there is a need for commitment from group members to implement the group decision.

## Model for Communication

2. Communication and interaction are interrelated since communication is conducted in a particular social situation.

3. The five components of communication are: sender, receiver, message, context of the situation, and language of the situation.

## Strategies for Communicating

4. Listening skills include verbal and nonverbal communication.

5. Critical or active listening—when one actively engages the speaker, analyzes what the speaker is saying, and analyzes oneself as a listener—is crucial for effective group decision making.

6. Nonverbal feedback is provided through one's facial expressions, body postures and movements, use of space, and vocal intonations.

7. The process of group decision making should occur in a space where individuals can face each other and sit about .5 meter apart.

8. When a consultant uses critical questioning techniques, group members are asked to elaborate upon, clarify, or justify the information they are sharing in a way that is critical of neither other group members nor their ideas.

9. The most important feedback strategy is the use of good timing.

## Managing Conflict

10. Gaining acceptance and establishing rapport are important components of effective consultation.

11. To gain acceptance and establish rapport, consultants should treat others with respect, shift credit for ideas and accomplishments to others, and willingly share information and learning with others.

12. Managing conflict is inevitable in group decision making since the middle stage of group decision making involves conflict.

13. Substantive, and constructive, conflict is the type of conflict one would expect to experience in the group decision-making process and involves an intellectual opposition to the content of the ideas that are pertinent to the group task.

14. Affective, and destructive, conflict must be handled, or the group process will fail.

15. Destructive conflict is evident in resistance to change.

16. Resistance can be categorized a number of different ways, but an underlying feature of all resistance is fear.

17. Strategies for dealing with resistance include using effective listening, sharing task-related information, involving participants in planning for change, and providing time to resolve issues.

18. Change is highly personal and relational.

19. To effectively deal with change, consultants should identify sources of resistance to change as well as organizational dynamics that could effect change.

20. Consultants should use strategies for implementing educational changes that avoid the following problems: lack of participant knowledge of the need or process for change and lack of organizational changes to support educational changes.

21. When dealing with conflict, educational consultants should address two major concerns: achieving a goal (the task) and maintaining a relationship (the social aspect of group decision making).

22. Collaboration is the ideal method for conflict management because it requires the participation of everyone, thereby leading to commitment among participants and consensus regarding the group decision.

23. Establishing trust is essential to group decision making.

24. Keys to the establishment of trust are listening, being honest with oneself and others, and discussing needs rather than presenting solutions.

25. Educational consultants are encouraged to use the following process for dealing with conflict: (a) pause and take a breath; (b) name the conflict or source of conflict; (c) identify the part you play in the conflict; and (d) engage in collaborative problem solving.

## A Collaborative Problem-Solving Process

26. The thirteen stages of a collaborative problem-solving approach are: (1) clarify expectations toward the process and issues; (2) establish rapport and build trust; (3) determine conditions surrounding the problem;

(4) agree on how to approach the problem; (5) define the problem; (6) analyze the problem and gather information; (7) establish decision criteria; (8) identify possible solutions; (9) select the best solution; (10) develop a plan; (11) implement the plan; (12) evaluate the plan; and (13) continue the consultation.

27. Reframing is a process that alters how a problem is viewed.

28. Nominal group technique (NGT) is a process for generating possible solutions among group members who are reluctant to participate.

## Role of Facilitator

29. The consultant, as facilitator of the group decision-making process, should: (a) clarify the issues; (b) promote a positive climate; (c) allow group members to save face; and (d) develop integration skills among group members.

## Disseminating Information Through Staff Development

30. Information about consultant activities can be disseminated for a variety of reasons and in a variety of ways, including informal conversations, newsletters, conferences, journal articles, television or print media, web pages, and staff development activities.

31. Staff development activities should include appropriate adult learning situations and progression through the following stages: orientation, integration, and application.

32. Staff development strategies include the following: presentation of theory, modeling, practice, structured and unstructured feedback, and coaching.

## Questions

1. Provide a definition of communication that you would use to guide your activities as an educational consultant.

2. Describe a communication model that incorporates a group decision-making process.

3. What are the main components of critical or active listening?

4. Describe three nonverbal communication strategies that an educational consultant could use.

5. Describe a process for using critical questioning skills.

6. What are some strategies for gaining acceptance and establishing rapport?

7. What are some strategies for establishing trust in a consultative relationship?

8. What are some key aspects known about the change process?

9. Discuss how one might manage a conflict situation.

10. List and explain the 13 stages of the problem-solving process presented in this chapter.

11. What four steps should a consultant take when facilitating a decision-making process?

12. When disseminating information through staff development, what strategies should the consultant use and in what situations?

# Discussion Points and Exercises

1. Why is it important for an individual functioning as a consultant to establish a role in the consultation process before service is delivered?

2. Conduct a meeting with elementary- and secondary-level teachers to obtain their views on staff development. Solicit from them alternatives to the traditional lecture format of staff development.

3. List myths and truths about dealing with resistance, change, and conflict management.

4. Conduct the following communication activity:

   Procedure: (1) Decide who will play each role (listed and defined below). (2) For 3 minutes have the speaker talk; then have the listener restate what was said before making comments or asking questions; the observer should watch for encouraging and discouraging communication actions the whole time. (3) Ask the observer to provide feedback to the group. (4) Ask the listener to summarize the main feeling and content of the speaker. (5) Ask the speaker to verify or negate the listener's summary. (6) Change roles.

   • Speaker: Describes one student in your class who is having problems learning.

   • Listener: Listens, using body and/or verbal encouragers, avoids talking about own problems, restates before asking questions, is sensitive to feeling and information of speech, summarizes what was said.

   • Observer: Says nothing during the session unless there is no restating or the listener is relaying information or interrupting; provides feedback on the behavior of the speaker and the listener.

5. The following case will provide you with an opportunity to apply the skills discussed above. If you have an opportunity to discuss the case with a group, you may want to follow the procedure outlined by Harris (1998b). Minimally, we encourage you to complete the following activities after you read Anne Marie's story:

   • Understand the dilemma from multiple points of view. First, identify the problem from Anne Marie's point of view. Then identify the problem from Kathy's point of view. Finally, pretend you are Mary, and identify the problem from her point of view.
   • Follow the procedures outlined above to explore the issues raised in this case, define the problem, generate solutions, and develop a plan.
   • If possible, discuss your ideas with someone else who has read the case. Then go back and review your analysis and your action plan. How would you modify your analysis and solutions based on that discussion? How were the points raised in the solutions reflective of best practice?

**Anne Marie's Story: What Do I Do for Michael?**

### Background

Anne Marie is an inclusion support consultant. This is her story about Michael. Michael was about 2½ years old and attended a day-care center that was not at all what she thought it would be. Anne Marie believed that it was very below standard. This center did not have adequate resources, and the staff did not engage in appropriate interactions with the children.

Michael had adequate fine- and gross-motor coordination but overall delays in language and socialization, with some behavior concerns. He would grab and scream a lot when he didn't get his way. He didn't have a diagnosis, but autism was being considered. He was a very engaging child. He had no problems with eye contact or with doing things for people. He had a gorgeous smile. Anne Marie saw him every other week. When she came into the room, his face would light up, and he would come over to greet her.

Michael grew up in a house where multiple languages were spoken. His mom came from Colombia and spoke English and Spanish. Michael and his mom lived with his father's parents, who spoke Italian. English was spoken at his day care. Michael seemed to respond to Spanish and Italian. Some of the words he spoke were Spanish, and some were English. He had severe language delays. He would repeat words and two- or three-word phrases, but he couldn't initiate many phrases at all. Behaviorally, he could be "like an angel," but he could not stand to share anything.

### Key Participants

Michael
Anne Marie
Kathy (teacher)
Mary (mother)

### Anne Marie's Perspective

Michael was in a day-care center that was new to me. When I visited, I was shocked at how poorly organized and academic it was. Children that were 2, 3, and 4 years old were expected to complete ditto sheets! There was no sign of any kind of free-form art work. The toys were either broken or filthy. There were no areas like a housekeeping area or a block area. The toys were all just junked onto shelves. It was a very small, one-room center. A large shelf was placed in the middle of the room to divide the younger and the older child groups.

There was an adequate outside yard, but there were no toys. The children used the paper cups they used for drinking water as toys. There were no shovels. There were no pails. There were no sand toys. The sandbox was littered with these crushed paper cups that obviously were useless in the sand anyway. Several times I visited when they were outside. I said to Kathy once: "It would be so great if Michael had a chance to use a little shovel and pail in the sand so that he could practice his fine-motor skills." She said: "We just haven't gotten around to buying more. The kids always throw them over the fence." Ugh! I thought to myself: "How long before you buy more stuff?" Occasionally, a toy that a kid brought from home would be fought over by several children. Unless the kid started to cry, Kathy did not interact with the child.

Kathy really didn't interact appropriately with the children whether they were inside or outside. Neither did the other teachers. Often, the teachers would interrupt the children while they were playing. For example, the teachers would have the children clean up, sit down for a 15-minute snack, and then go back to playing. I felt that the children were constantly on edge because they didn't know when their play was going to be interrupted. Then, when the children were playing, the teachers were talking with each other, but what they talked about had nothing to do with the children. They talked about what they did outside of this job that they had.

The activities in the center were academically focused. When they had their so-called work groups, it was all paper and pencil. Once they did a collage thing. I told them I was going to come at art time just to watch. We are talking about 2 and 3 year olds, and they had tiny pieces of collage stuff. None of the big kinds of things the kids could pick up easily. Then, five kids would share one bottle of glue, and Kathy wouldn't let them use the glue. Only Kathy used the glue.

Another example of inappropriate instruction and teacher interaction was during circle time. Actually, they were doing the calendar but called it circle time. I was shocked! It was all academic. They didn't even have a preschool-size calendar. They had a regular, wall-sized calendar. Kathy counted through and marked off each day. The kids were supposed to count. The kids had to sit in their chairs for this terrible, terrible circle time that lasted about 30 minutes. Michael cued in to what the other kids were doing and sat there. But when the other children would start kicking their feet because they were bored, Michael would smile and start kicking his feet. Obviously, he had learned that he had to stay sitting in his chair, and he did not try to get out. I was amazed and appalled that he had learned that. It stood out from the other stuff that he did. He obviously realized that this is what you had to do when you were at this kind of time. This was a kid who knew the routine and knew how to follow the routine very successfully in spite of the inappropriate atmosphere of the environment.

Michael had a hard time when I was there. He identified me as someone who came in to spend some time with him. However, since I was also working on his social skills, I gave attention to him but also to the other children around him. Also, Kathy didn't interact appropriately with Michael when I was there. One time, we were playing a bouncing game or a jumping game, and Michael let out this high-pitched shriek. It got Kathy's attention. She said: "No, no, no, Michael. You can't do that." I wanted to say: "Wouldn't it be better if you ignored that? If you focus on the screaming, he's going to scream more." But I didn't. Very few of my suggestions were used. She did ask me about some of the other kids, but her attitude seemed to be: "Oh, hi! Are you here to take care of Michael? Great."

I'm supposed to work with this child and the teachers in this setting? Impossible! I know you can't always choose your day-care setting, but this place was hopeless. I didn't feel that I could talk to Mary immediately about that because it was basically implying that she had made a lousy choice, and he'd been there for several months already. She had expressed to me that she was very pleased with the place. So, I was caught because I didn't want to come across as being very critical. The other constraints were that Mary needed a place that was a preschool day care because she worked and she needed child care for her son. She'd had difficulty finding a place for her son before. Here I was trying to support the child, the family, and the teachers, and I couldn't get beyond the immediate environment. How can I get around that?

# Section *III*

*Consulting with Teachers and Parents and Multicultural Considerations Affecting the Consultative Process*

# Consulting with Teachers in Inclusive Classrooms

5

Students with disabilities are being placed in general education classrooms, consistent with their Individualized Education Program (IEP) goals and consistent with a movement toward inclusion. General education teachers who previously believed that exceptional children and youth were the sole responsibility of special educators now face the challenge of providing instruction to those children within their own classrooms. Many general educators believe that they are unprepared to assume the responsibility for teaching such students. Nevertheless, IDEA '97 clearly states that students with disabilities are to be educated with their general education peers to the maximum extent possible.

Unfortunately, most general education teachers, and many special education teachers, have only a vague understanding of the intent of federal and state legislation. For example, many general education teachers contend erroneously that all students enrolled in self-contained classrooms must now be integrated into the general education classroom. Further, many general education teachers mistakenly maintain that they will be the sole person in charge of the students' education and, consequently, held accountable for any student's rate of progress—or lack of it.

This chapter begins by defining the term *inclusion*. Further, the chapter discriminates between related terms such as *mainstreaming* and *least restrictive environment*. Next, concerns that teachers, parents, and students have about this process are explored. Additionally, variables that affect students with disabilities and research conducted within inclusive classrooms will be presented. Given that the IEP is a critical component of a successful inclusion program, we'll discuss ways for teachers to design, plan, implement, and monitor effective IEPs. Finally, inclusion is likely to be facilitated when appropriate thought and consideration have been given to programming for generality and maintenance. Our discussion will focus on field-test methods for programming within these important areas.

Consultants interested in learning about the trends in the number (or percentage) of students with special needs being integrated into general education classrooms can read a series of analytic articles by McLeskey, Henry, and Hodges in *Teaching Exceptional Children* (1998, 1999).

Preservice general education teachers do not believe that they are adequately prepared to address the needs of students with special needs included within the classroom. They lack the basic information and skills with respect to concepts, practices, and consultation (Reed & Monda-Amaya, 1995).

Readers interested in a full range of topics on educating children in inclusive settings are referred to the anthology titled *Educating Exceptional Children* (eleventh edition, 1999), edited by Karen L. Freiberg. Also available through www.dushkin.com/annual editions/.

## Objectives

After reading this chapter, the reader will be able to:

1. define the term *inclusion* and distinguish among its various connotations;

2. differentiate among the terms *inclusion, mainstreaming,* and *least restrictive environment;*

3. compare and contrast teacher, parent, and student concerns about inclusion;

4. identify the three aspects of Heron and Skinner's definition of the least restrictive environment;

5. cite four variables that affect exceptional students within the inclusive classroom;

6. identify keys to successful inclusion programs;

7. summarize major research findings on inclusion effectiveness;

8. identify how a consultant could assist a teacher to develop and/or evaluate an IEP or IFSP;

9. specify several education areas in need of assessment (e.g., academic achievement, learning style, and preferred reinforcers);

10. distinguish between an annual goal and a short-term objective;

11. suggest a format for curriculum and materials monitoring and evaluating that could be used for individual students, small groups, or total programs;

12. contrast stimulus and response generality;

13. suggest a method for improving maintenance of skills subsequent to initial acquisition;

14. provide planning-and-implementing suggestions for promoting generality of behavior change across settings, students, and environments that also are sensitive to curriculum-based measures.

## Key Terms

| | |
|---|---|
| inclusion | teacher acceptability |
| full inclusion | mastery |
| selective inclusion | preferred reinforcers |
| mainstreaming | annual goal |
| temporal integration | benchmark |
| social integration | short-term objective |
| eligibility | stimulus generality |
| least restrictive environment | response generality |
| opportunity to respond | maintenance |
| proportional interaction | intermittent schedule of reinforcement |
| social relationships | |

See *Educational Leadership,* December 1994–January 1995, vol. 52, no. 4, for an array of special-issue articles related to inclusive schools. Also, the issue of the *Journal of Special Education,* Summer 1995, vol. 29, no. 2, contains 16 articles on how inclusion has worked in several states, as well as reaction statements by notable educators.

# Inclusion, Mainstreaming, and the Least Restrictive Environment

To discuss the concepts of inclusion, mainstreaming, and least restrictive environment, a definition of each must be provided. In our view, the terms have sometimes been used interchangeably; however, there are clear differences between them.

## Table 5.1
Definitions of Inclusion

| Authors | Definition: Inclusion means that . . . |
| --- | --- |
| Bassett et al. (1996) | the general education classroom is the origin for the educational experiences of all students (p. 356). |
| Phillips, Sapona, & Lubis (1995) | the general education classroom changes to meet all the needs of all the students. |
| Turnbull & Turnbull (1998) | consideration extends beyond mere placement in the general education classroom. It also includes extra-curricular activities and other nonacademic areas. |
| Winger & Mazurek (1998) | students with disabilities participate in the general education classroom, and it embraces a wider view of the integration of diverse groups representing different ethnicities, social classes, religious affiliations, and cultural backgrounds. The classroom is a community. |
| Giangreco, Baumgart, & Doyle (1995) | generic educational access, equity, and quality are provided. Inclusion is not solely an issue related to the integration of students with disabilities. |
| Rogers (1993) | "the commitment to educate each child, to the maximum extent possible, in the school and class-room he or she would have otherwise attended. . . . [Inclusion brings] the support services to the student and requires only that the student benefit from being in the [general education] classroom" (p. 1). |
| Banerji & Dailey (1995) | in a broader sense, a philosophy is advanced that advocates for complete participation of students with disabilities in all aspects of the school program; in a narrow sense, inclusion refers to strategies and models for service delivery. |
| Sage (1993) | one unified school approach is used to meet the needs of all students. |
| Vaughn & Schumm (1995) | a continuum of services, including professional development, curriculum modifications, and provision for adequate resources, must be in place. |

## Definition of Inclusion

Not since the term *mainstreaming* was introduced in the mid 1970s has a concept been as controversial as inclusion. It's been a lightning rod for educators, parents, students, and attorneys, pitting proponents (TASH, 1990; Sailor, 1991; Stainback & Stainback, 1984) against opponents (Council for Learning Disabilities, 1993; Kauffman & Hallahan, 1993; Fuchs & Fuchs, 1994), both sides mustering philosophical, social, instructional, behavioral, and legal arguments to buttress their view. *Inclusion,* like other related terms in the field (e.g., *mainstreaming, least restrictive environment, integration*), has multiple definitions, connotations, and meanings. Table 5.1 shows a representative list of the ways inclusion has been defined in the literature since 1993.

Simpson (1996), Heward (1996), and Heron and Harris (1993) have attempted to untangle the thorny definitional issues associated with *full inclusion,* meaning a classroom where all students with disabilities and a rich mixture of culturally diverse students are integrated. As Simpson states, the problem rests

Readers are referred to the *Journal of Learning Disabilities,* 1993, *26*(9), pp. 593–596, for position statements on full inclusion from the National Joint Committee on Learning Disabilities (NJCLD), the Learning Disabilities Association (LDA), and the Council for Learning Disabilities (CLD).

For a discussion of inclusion from multiple perspectives, see Kauffman and Hallahan (1993).

Simpson (1996) provides a series of recommendations to parents for making informed decisions with respect to inclusion.

squarely with the manner in which a variety of other terms (e.g., least restrictive environment, regular education initiative, mainstreaming, and normalization) have been used in the literature. A brief examination of three such terms—*inclusion, mainstreaming,* and *least restrictive environment*—is warranted so as to contextualize services for students within a general education setting.

The range of connotations spans *full inclusion* to *selective inclusion options,* and there is no clear consensus on any definition (Winger & Mazurek, 1998; Heward, 2000; Friend & Bursuck, 1996; Soodak & Erwin, 1995). Still, some definitions appear to be more broadly defined, embracing richer and more diverse populations within the general education classroom (e.g., Giangreco, Baumgart, & Doyle, 1995; Rogers, 1993; Sage, 1993). Other definitions address *selective inclusion* as one option whereby a continuum of services is provided (Kauffman & Hallahan, 1993). For example, Winger and Mazurek suggest that the term should include the full diversity of students who might be enrolled in a classroom, that is, students representing culturally and ethnically diverse populations as well as students with disabilities. Giangreco, Baumgart, and Doyle believe that *inclusion* represents a generic philosophy embracing access, equity, and quality. Banerji and Dailey (1995) expand the connotations even further by suggesting that inclusion refers to strategies and models for service delivery; and Vaughn and Schumm (1995) indicate that professional development, curricular modifications, and provisions for adequate resources to meet an expanding and challenging environment must be added to any conceptualization of inclusion. Winger and Mazurek (1998) perhaps sum up the diversity of meanings of the term when they state:

> Inclusive schools begin with a philosophy and vision that all children belong and can learn in the mainstream of school and community life. The classroom is seen as a community where diversity is valued and celebrated and all children work, talk, cooperate, and share. (p. 103)

For a discussion of the trends toward inclusion across states, especially between 1988 and 1995, the reader is referred to McLeskey et al. (1999).

In our view, whether a student receives instruction as part of a full-inclusion program (participates totally in the general education classroom) or is selectively included (receives instruction along a continuum of services, some of which of may occur in general education settings) rests with the student's Individualized Education Program. By keeping our educational focus on the student, we are less likely to adopt methods based on well-intended but misguided considerations of what's best for the student. Also, we are less likely to be convinced by well-sounding but hollow or politically motivated rhetoric. In short, despite the increase in the number of students who are being placed in "inclusive classrooms," we do not find that one size (inclusion) can possibly fit all of the students, with and without disabilities, who attend school.

## Definitions of Mainstreaming

See McLean and Hanline (1990) for a discussion of terms such as *educational mainstreaming, noneducational mainstreaming, reverse mainstreaming,* and *partial mainstreaming.* Also, see Salisbury (1991) for a distinction between *mainstreaming* and *inclusion.*

According to an early definition, *mainstreaming* is "the temporal, instructional, and social integration of eligible exceptional children with general education peers based on an on-going, individually determined, educational planning and programming process and requires clarification of responsibility among regular and special education administrative, instruction, and supportive personnel" (Kauffman, Gottleib, Agard, & Kukic, 1975, p. 4). Embedded in this definition are a number of conditions and concepts that many professionals have failed to understand fully. Let us examine briefly some of the key concepts of Kauffman et al.'s definition.

## Temporal Integration

*Temporal integration* is defined as the total amount of time a student with disabilities spends with general education peers, expressed in "periods per day" or "academic subject areas." For example, a student might be mainstreamed for mathematics but remain within a self-contained classroom or resource room for other academic or vocational subjects.

## Instructional and Social Integration

Kauffman et al. (1975) view *instructional integration* as teaching arranged so that children with disabilities partake in the same educational activities as their general education peers but do not share in areas that are too difficult for them. This may be achieved by presenting information at a suitable level, through various modalities, and modifying the expected response. For example, a high school student with physical disabilities may be able to participate in a class science lesson successfully if the teacher carefully structures the tasks. This student might have to describe the steps of an experiment and predict the outcome, while another student manipulates the apparatus and a third student takes notes on the process and writes up the results.

    *Social integration* means that the student is provided with the opportunity to establish relationships with peers and others. Consultants can recommend a number of strategies to teachers to foster social integration, even before a student's placement in a regular setting. For instance, consultants could suggest a peer group activity involving students with disabilities and general education partners. Games, athletic events, or playground activities could be arranged to maximize positive social exchanges between the two groups.

## Eligibility

Several authors have proposed eligibility criteria for placement (Hundert, 1982; Salend & Lutz, 1984). Overall, these criteria are based either on the student's readiness to perform academic and social competencies deemed necessary for successful functioning in the general education classroom, or on state or federal standards. According to Salend (1984), a competency-based approach allows a consultant to help determine who might be a successful candidate for mainstreaming and who might need additional remediation in special education programs prior to reentry.

    At the preschool or early childhood level, the argument for eligibility can be based on legal, moral, philosophical, or educational rationales (Odom & Karnes, 1988). Clearly, IDEA '97 legislation contains provisions for the legal basis. The guiding principles of normalization serve as the moral and philosophical standard, while the belief in the advantage of early stimulation and training programs serves as the grounds for educational programming with nondisabled peers (Guralnick, 1981; Odom & McEvoy, 1990). For example, there appears to be growing consensus that the social, communication, and language skills of preschool children are enhanced considerably when educational programming occurs in the presence of nondisabled peers (Jenkins, Odom, & Speltz, 1989; Odom & McEvoy, 1990; Strain, 1983).

    In the final analysis, eligibility for placement of a student with disabilities in a general education setting is determined by a multidisciplinary evaluation team, including the student's regular teacher, the special education teacher, the school psychologist, the parents, and others with knowledge in the area of suspected disability.

It is interesting to note that nowhere in P.L. 94-142, its subsequent revisions, or IDEA '97 is the term *mainstreaming* used. Rather, the law and the regulations speak to the issue of an educational experience within the context of the least restrictive environment. Many general educators continue to perceive mainstreaming or inclusion—erroneously in our view—to be a process whereby all exceptional children are integrated into their classrooms. Such misperceptions need to be clarified.

## Definition of Least Restrictive Environment

Readers interested in obtaining the full text of the regulations can access them through the U.S. Department of Education's Web site (http://ed.gov/offices/OSERS/IDEA/regs.html). Also, the *Federal Register* can be accessed through http://www.access.gpo.gov/su_docs/.

According to the rules and regulations of IDEA '97, published in the *Federal Register,* March 12, 1999, the least restrictive environment has essentially two components. First, to the maximum extent possible the student is to be educated with his or her general education peers; and second, the student should be removed from that setting only when the nature of his or her disability precludes an adequate educational experience even when supplementary learning aids are used.

### The Components of LRE

Heron and Skinner (1981) have proposed a definition of *least restrictive environment* that is consistent with research studies completed within the last two decades. The use of their definition facilitates data collection on the effectiveness of integration efforts. Heron and Skinner favor a movement toward programming options and social interactions with general education populations rather than thinking exclusively in terms of placement alternatives. Their definition reads:

> The least restrictive environment is defined as that educational setting that maximizes the learning-disabled student's opportunity to respond and achieve, permits the regular education teacher to interact proportionally with all the students in the classroom, and fosters acceptable social relationships between nonhandicapped and learning-disabled students. (p. 116)

The definition has three essential components: opportunity to respond and achieve, proportional interaction between teachers and students, and acceptable social relationships between general education and exceptional students. Each component, along with supporting documentation, is addressed in the next sections.

*Opportunity to Respond and Achieve.* According to Greenwood, Delquadri, and Hall (1984) and Greenwood, Hart, Walker, & Risley (1994), *opportunity to respond* is defined as "the interaction between: (a) teacher formulated instructional antecedent stimuli [e.g., the materials presented, prompts, questions asked, signals to respond] and (b) their success in establishing the academic responding desired or implied by the materials. . . . Opportunity to respond implies the use of instructional tactics that involve presenting, questioning, and correcting so that all students have, in fact, made the desired response" (Greenwood et al., 1984, pp. 64–65). Educational researchers have investigated variables that set the occasion for active student response (Barbetta, Heron, & Heward, 1993; Barbetta & Heward, 1993; Heward, 1994). Such variables as class-wide choral responding (Heward, Courson, & Narayan, 1989; Sterling, Barbetta, Heward, & Heron, 1997), response cards (Cavanaugh, Heward, & Donelson, 1996), guided notes (Courson, 1989; Kline, 1986; Rindfuss, 1997) have been used successfully. Each tactic is designed to increase student response opportunities. When opportunities for response increase, sizable changes in student performance occur independent of specific reinforcement procedures, a point that should not escape the attention of consultants who recognize the positive correlation between achievement and self-esteem (cf. Duncan & Biddle, 1974).

*Proportional Interaction. Proportional interaction* means that all students receive the teacher's attention for appropriate behavior on a consistent enough basis to maintain desired levels of performance. One way to determine how much interaction is sufficient for the student with disabilities is to assess the rate or percentage of teacher interactions in the special education class before placement occurs in the regular classroom. If the observations indicate that the student requires 15 direct initiations from the teacher each day to achieve desirable performance levels in the self-contained or resource room, ideally at least 15 initiations should be provided in the regular classroom. The essential contribution of this component of the definition is that the regular teacher is relieved of any psychological pressure to provide equal amounts of attention to all students. Rather, it provides a data-based context for determining if a student is likely to receive an appropriate amount of teacher attention. Also, it could serve to allay any fears parents might have that students with special needs would take the teacher's attention away from the task of educating the other children.

> Two points need to be underscored regarding the number of initiations expected from general education teachers. First, although it is difficult to deliver 15 direct initiatives to the student with disabilities in the general education classroom, where 35 other students may be competing for the teacher's attention, it is not impossible. Second, the initial level of interactions would decrease as soon as the performance of the student with disabilities could be maintained with fewer direct contacts.

*Social Relationships.* Anyone who has worked with students with disabilities and general education students together realizes that the *social relationships* (i.e., the complex mixture of verbal and nonverbal interactions) between these students (or adults) can be strained. Often these students can be rejected, ostracized, or actively ignored by students in the regular classroom (Gresham, 1981; Strain & Kerr, 1981). They are also less accurate perceivers of their social status than their peers (Bruininks, 1978a). For example, students with disabilities often rate their social status in the classroom higher than their classmates do.

Of course, all interactions between students will not be positive and supportive. Such situations do not usually exist in regular classrooms. Still, York et al. (1992) found that students with disabilities can be accepted by general education peers and that such acceptance is accompanied by the general education students' increased awareness of the characteristics they share with the students with disabilities. With respect to including students with severe disabilities in general education classrooms, Hunt and Goetz (1997), in their review of 19 studies on this subject, found that positive academic, social, and affective gains can be achieved for both the general education students and the students with severe disabilities. However, strong parent involvement, focused collaborative effort, and functional curricular adaptations were vital to achieving a successful inclusion program.

In practice, however, consultants often face situations where special education students are not accommodated easily in inclusive situations. To place a student with disabilities in a regular classroom is a decision requiring careful analysis and planning. The consultant's responsibility precludes placing students in environments where general education students do not accept and are not likely to work with them.

## The Dimensions of Measurement of LRE

Heron and Skinner's (1981) definition of the least restrictive environment offers consultants a number of advantages over previous definitions. Specifically, consultants are able to determine whether the environment is least restrictive by examining three dimensions: measurable outcomes, teacher benefits, and parent benefits. Heretofore such documentation was not possible.

*Measurable Outcomes.* The three components of LRE (response opportunities and achievement, proportional interaction, and appropriate social exchange) are measurable. If consultants help to provide data in these areas, placement team members can determine whether a general education setting is least restrictive. The placement decision can be made on the basis of an objective analysis rather than an intuitive notion about the efficacy of a particular classroom.

Further, once integration has been completed, consultants can use measurable data to monitor the process more closely and compare the effects of the special and regular environments (Cooper et al., 1987). By noting differences that may arise across the three areas, consultants are able to recommend specific interventions to the classroom teacher. For instance, suppose that prior to the inclusion of a student with disabilities, it was found that the general education teacher distributed her interactions equally to all students. After inclusion, however, she gave the student with disabilities more attention than was needed to maintain performance. In this case, the consultant might recommend to the teacher that she return to the attention distribution techniques she used prior to placement. These might include walking around the room regularly to monitor student seatwork, using prompting strategies more effectively during class discussion, and praising all the students, not just a select few, on a regular basis.

*Teacher Benefits.* As stated previously, the classroom teacher will not need to provide one-to-one instruction for the student with disabilities unless the data so indicate. If proportional attention is provided in sufficient amounts to maintain the performance of students at an acceptable level, teacher anxiety should be reduced.

Also, successful inclusion of a student with disabilities may set the occasion for the regular educator to use a wider variety of content and teaching materials, as well as instructional techniques, in both academic and nonacademic areas. As a result, the teacher may become more sensitive to the unique learning needs of the student with disabilities and, with guidance from the consultant, may begin to see how each student's demands can be addressed systematically.

Finally, by addressing the three areas in the definition of least restrictive environment, consultants will be able to focus on preventive measures the regular teacher can use to reduce possible classroom management problems as well as to enhance the learning atmosphere. Presently, consultants spend a disproportionate amount of time helping teachers solve problems that might have been prevented.

*Parent Benefits.* Parents of student with disabilities would likely view Heron and Skinner's (1981) definition in a positive light because of the multiple criteria used. In the past, their children have been placed in special classrooms usually on the basis of low achievement scores or poor social behavior. With multiple criteria the opportunity arises for children to participate in some aspects of the regular curriculum and for the parents to monitor their child's progress. For example, during parent-teacher conferences, the parents would be able to ask direct questions about the academic achievement of their child, the level of teacher-student contacts, and social acceptance (cf. Tawney & Gast, 1984). The conference would be more structured, and the parents would be able to establish whether the goals of their child's Individualized Education or Family Services Program were being addressed.

Procedurally, Margolis and Tewel (1990) emphasize that the building-level administrator must play a key role with teachers, staff, and parents with respect to determining the least restrictive environment. In their view, fostering the development of new instructional strategies, using paraprofessionals effectively, and establishing working groups with parents can facilitate this process.

In summary, the terms *inclusion, mainstreaming,* and *least restrictive environment* are *not* synonymous. There are considerable differences among these concepts and terms. While recognizing the benefits of full inclusion for some students, consultants should also recognize that a continuum of services is likely to be appropriate for many other students. Professionals and parents must collaborate to achieve functional outcomes for the student that are consistent with the Individualized Education or Individualized Family Services Program.

## Teacher Concerns About Inclusion

Although reasons for the lack of enthusiasm about inclusion are as varied as the teachers themselves, there are some common concerns. First, many regular educators believe that they lack the specialized training needed to teach academic, social, or adaptive behaviors to students with disabilities (Bender & Golden, 1988). Furthermore, according to Stainback and Stainback (1988), "The prevalent current attitude is that if some students' needs cannot be met in general education, a different or special education option is needed for them" (p. 19). Stainback and Stainback would argue that this attitude, although perhaps understandable from the perspective of regular educators, given their background, training, and experience, needs to be changed from a segregationist position to an inclusive point of view.

General educators' attitude about accepting students with disabilities into their classrooms is also related to their competence and willingness, and varies from teacher to teacher (Whinnery, Fuchs, & Fuchs, 1991). It seems that willingness is dependent on teacher knowledge, opportunity to provide input into decisions, and perceptions of the disability. Teachers may feel hostile toward or threatened by some disability labels. Soodak, Podell, and Lehman (1998) state: "Teachers are more hostile toward including students with mental retardation, learning disabilities, and behavior disorders than those with hearing impairments or physical handicaps" (pp. 491–492). Still, the more knowledgeable teachers are with respect to adapting instructional and behavioral strategies *and* the more highly developed their personal self-efficacy skills (i.e., their teaching makes a difference for all children), the more willing they are to participate in inclusion (Salvia & Munson, 1986; Soodak et al., 1998). Further, when general education teachers have a direct voice in selecting mainstreaming modifications, they are more apt to support integration (Myles & Simpson, 1989), although the exact nature of the accommodation affects its desirability (Schumm & Vaughn, 1991). Changes that do not require environmental modifications to the classroom are more desirable than changes that do, for example. Therefore, consultants who provide increased opportunities for general educators to gain proficiency in adapting curricular materials, managing behavior, and accommodating test taking, and who provide the latitude for

*See Learning Disability Quarterly* (Winter, 1998) for a special issue on teacher perception of students with learning disabilities in general education settings.

teachers to express opinions increase the probability of teacher participation in inclusion programs.

Second, though recommended support services can help regular educators teach exceptional learners, support services vary widely across schools and districts. Many regular educators are unfamiliar with such services or how to locate them. They are concerned that exceptional students will be "dumped" in their classrooms and they will have to sink or swim with the added challenges. Third, general education teachers are concerned about accountability. Before regular teachers accept students into their classroom, they want to know to what extent they will be held accountable for student gains.

Consultants need to impress upon regular educators that the rules and regulations of existing legislation (e.g., IDEA '97) specify that neither the teacher nor the school district will be held accountable if a student with disabilities fails to achieve the goals prescribed in his or her IEP or IFSP. However, educational personnel are required to show "good faith" in their efforts to accomplish IEP or IFSP goals and objectives.

York, Vandercock, MacDonald, Heise-Neff, and Caughey (1992) report the results of a survey with general educators who had middle school students with severe disabilities integrated into their rooms. The special education teachers reported that IEP goals were achieved by their students, but unfortunately those gains were not clearly recognized by the general education teachers. When asked to identify performance changes in students with disabilities who had been integrated for one year, the general education teachers remarked on their "limited" progress, whereas the special educators reported their accomplishments in terms of their IEP behavioral and mobility goals. The general education teachers were seemingly happy that the special educators saw progress, even if they did not. In essence, the general educators' frame of reference, attitude, or perception impeded them from seeing that their efforts were yielding tangible dividends. York et al. recommend that special educators (consultants) outline succinct expectations and accomplishments for general educators.

Scruggs and Mastropieri (1996) synthesized the results of 28 survey investigations conducted between 1958 and 1995. Their primary purpose was to assess changes in teacher perceptions over time, location, and responses from a collective pool of 10,560 teachers. Their data revealed that most teachers agreed with the philosophical purposes of inclusion, but only a slight majority were willing to implement inclusion in *their* classrooms, especially in cases where the perceived intensity of the inclusion effort would be high (i.e., where the severity of the disability would require more effort). Further, most teachers believed that they still did not have sufficient preservice or inservice training to manage students with special needs, especially when specialized services might be needed or when the level of schooling changed (i.e., elementary to secondary). In the researchers' analysis, even though two decades had passed since P.L. 94-142 was enacted, teachers continued to believe that they lacked the time, resources, or materials to meet the individual needs of students with disabilities adequately. Scruggs and Mastropieri's findings should serve as a signal for consultants that successful inclusion programs involve more than just placing students with disabilities in general education programs, a lesson that O'Shea and O'Shea (1998) claim must be recognized early and revisited often in the process.

Finally, many general education teachers argue that they should share the instructional responsibility for exceptional students with support personnel. Instructional responsibilities include planning, teaching, and evaluation. Many authors advocate shared or cross-over instructional responsibility between general educators at schools and parents at home (Barbetta & Heron, 1991; Turnbull & Schulz, 1979; Wang & Birch, 1984).

Consultants can play an active role in the instructional process by recommending appropriate teaching strategies, materials, and evaluation techniques. At the secondary level, offering options for grading, credit hours, and class scheduling is often beneficial.

See Chapters 9 through 11 for strategies.

## Parent Concerns About Inclusion

Parents have mixed views of the benefits gained from integration programs (Myles & Simpson, 1990). On one hand, some parents see integration as a positive step (Hanline & Halvorsen, 1989). Many may have watched their sons or daughters in self-contained classrooms be ridiculed by other students. They feel pain when their children are called dummy or retarded. Although it is not universally accepted among parents, these parents share the view that full inclusion is a viable option for their children, believing that segregated or even so-called mainstreamed programs would provide fractionated instruction and fewer alternatives (Stainback & Stainback, 1984) and reduce their children's likelihood of being integrated more completely later in life (Reynolds, Wang, & Walberg, 1987; Sailor et al., 1989). Hence, these parents may surmise that an integrated program with general education students would offer their children multiple advantages. First, they may believe that ridicule would decrease, since their children would be participating in a general education curriculum. Second, they may believe that the general education students would be a good influence (Hanline & Halvorsen, 1989). They envision their children's exposure to the appropriate academic and social behavior of students in regular classes as a beneficial experience. Finally, some may view the integration process as valuable for the regular students, as well. These parents anticipate that the general education student will become sensitive to the individual differences of students and grow to view exceptional children as "children with disabilities" rather than as "disabled children." In the former case, the disability is one aspect of the child; in the latter case, the child's total being is defined by the term disability.

For one mother's perspective on full inclusion, see Carr (1993); for a teacher's response to Carr, see Taylor (1994).

Conversely, some parents are apprehensive about inclusion programs, especially when their recommendations for adapting the curriculum, reducing class size, consulting with staff, and accessing support personnel are not considered (Myles & Simpson, 1990). Soodak and Erwin (1995) report that school programs and goals do not always match parent perceptions or expectations, even when IEP goals have been developed jointly. Parents continue to feel alienated from teachers and perceive that school personnel do not listen to their needs and that they receive suggestions for counterproductive methods and growth experiences for their children. According to Soodak and Erwin, "When parents disagree with what schools recommend, they are harshly reminded that schools are the experts in educational decisions" (p. 273).

Further, parents know that general education students may not accept their children, and they are aware that their children may precipitate problems in the regular classroom because of immaturity, lack of social skills, or the nature of their disabilities (Gresham, 1982). Parents are also concerned that, given the increased ratio of students to teacher, their children may not receive the individualized assistance and special instructional programming they receive in the self-contained special education classroom. Closely related to this concern is parents' apprehension that their children may not have the same response opportunities as other children in the classroom. Parents acquainted with classroom interaction realize that teachers are more apt to reinforce the student with the fastest answer, who is passive and compliant in the room, and who reinforces the teacher (Brophy & Good, 1974). Parents of students with disabilities who have characteristics different from those valued by teachers are likely to be apprehensive about mainstreaming.

Palmer, Borthwick-Duffy, and Widaman (1998) conducted a survey of almost 500 parents of children with disabilities from an original pool of 3,300 to determine parent perceptions of the effects of inclusion on (a) the quality of educational services, (b) general education students, and (c) acceptance of a student with a disability within the general education classroom. In the main, results showed that parents' perceptions of benefits were positive with respect to acceptance and treatment, and less positive regarding quality of instruction. Results suggest that parents who claim to value inclusion as an overall methodology may do so through a complicated analysis of the tradeoffs of social benefits for their children versus perceived academic gains. Further, time-based measures of inclusion (i.e., full versus selective) may not impact parent perception of determined benefit as much as other variables, namely, the presence of a caring teacher and their children's sense of well-being.

Finally, Turnbull and Ruef (1997) provide data from an interview study of 17 families of children, youth, and adults with serious and challenging behavior problems. When examining "lifestyle issues associated with inclusion" (e.g., issues associated with family life, friendship, school, community, and supported living), parents and family members reported that they had to be the "initiators" and "catalysts" for attaining assistance. In short, if the family member did not initiate a change in favor of a more supportive and inclusive lifestyle, it did not happen.

According to Turnbull and Ruef (1997) and Bennett, DeLuca, and Bruns (1997), several perceptions and themes were evident from the parent responses; however, two points are most germane to consultants:

• Parents believe that they spend considerable time and energy informing teachers and administrators about their children's special needs, thus becoming exhausted and frustrated about having to be always in the forefront to obtain supportive services. Also, an inverse relationship appears to exist: as child advocacy by parents increases, positive relationships with school members decrease (Bennett et al., 1997).

• Parents believe that teachers lack competence in dealing with their children's programmatic needs. In effect, parents report that they are tired of having to be the advocate and the agent of change. To paraphrase former president Lyndon B. Johnson, they believe that they are in a hailstorm where they can't get in, they can't get out, and they can't make it stop.

## Student Concerns About Inclusion

Vaughn and Klingner (1998) analyzed eight studies of students with learning disabilities to determine overall perceptions on inclusion. A total of 442 students were involved across six elementary and two high schools. Their synthesis of the data showed that students did not prefer one model (full-inclusion or pull-out) over another but were able to discriminate among the advantages of each model.

For instance, on one hand, they saw pull-out programs as a way to obtain more individual help. Likewise, some, but certainly not all, students viewed the social aspects of the resource room as positive (i.e., providing more opportunity to make and keep friends). Conversely, special and general education students perceived the inclusion setting as being a positive environment because another teacher was in the classroom, rendering assistance to *both* general and special education students.

Lovitt, Plavins, and Cushing (1999) conducted a 3-year longitudinal study of a cross section of high school students with disabilities (learning disabilities, developmental delays, mental retardation, and health and hearing disabilities) regarding their perceptions of their high school experience. With respect to specific concerns about inclusion, a total of 270 students were either interviewed or surveyed. Of these, an almost even split existed between those preferring general education classrooms (N = 130) and those preferring special education placements (N = 110), with the remaining preferring both (N = 29) or neither (N = 1). According to Lovitt et al., students preferred special education because of the availability of teacher help, fewer students, and perceived easier curriculum, the last finding replicating Vaughn and Klingner's (1998) results. With respect to socialization, mixed results were reported. Some students preferred the general education classroom because of feelings of being normal (". . . it's one of these standards where if you're in a normal class, everybody thinks you're normal . . ." [p. 76]), while other students continued to be ridiculed ("I've been made fun of ever since I can remember, and they still do it today" (p. 76).

Habel, Bloom, Ray, and Bacon (1999) conducted semiformal, small group or individualized interviews with 17 Native American students placed (or at risk of placement) in programs for severe behavior disabilities. While the intent of the survey was to obtain a holistic view of their total experiences in school, the students' perceptions about inclusion could be extrapolated from the data. Basing part of their analysis on Mouton, Hawkins, McPherson, and Copley's (1996) observation that a student's sense of belonging, network of friends, and perceived value of learning content in school were critical variables to success, Habel et al. suggest that students with severe behavior disorders may face difficulty in this regard:

> The movement to include student's with disabilities in general education settings presents special challenges to students with behavior disorders. These students by definition lack prosocial skills, engage in aggressive and externalizing behaviors, and have difficulties establishing and maintaining relationships. Furthermore, they are more likely to be rejected or neglected by peers and general education teachers. . . . When students with behavior disorders are included in general education classes, the number of peers from which to choose friends increases, but the number of interactions is not likely to increase, because the structure of the classroom typically limits the opportunities for interaction among students. Even when unstructured opportunities for interaction do occur in inclusive settings, students with behavior disorders are more likely to be rejected or neglected. (p. 103)

Salend and Duhaney (1999), in a review of the literature on the impact of inclusion on students with disabilities, found mixed results on academic and social performance measures. In some cases, enhanced performance occurred in the general education classroom; in other cases, special education placements were more beneficial. With respect to students without disabilities and their concerns, research suggests benefits from inclusion (e.g., increased acceptance and better tolerance of students with disabilities and wider social relationships). However, as Salend and Duhaney point out, mere placement is not sufficient; proactive plans to improve social and behavioral interactions must be integrated into the plan.

Vaughn and Klingner (1998), although referring to students with learning disabilities, may sum up the research on most students' with disabilities concerns about inclusion and the benefits of a continuum of services when they state: "The important lesson is that no one educational model will meet the needs of all students . . . thus there is an advantage to providing a range of educational models" (p. 86).

For a synthesis of research on student perceptions of inclusion, see Vaughn and Klingner (1998) and Salend and Duhaney (1999).

# Variables Affecting Exceptional Students in General Education Classrooms

## Composition of the Inclusive Classroom

Inclusive classrooms include one or more students with disabilities. Seldom does the general education teacher find more than 10% of a class identified as disabled. The high ratio of general education students to students with disabilities may be deceiving, however. At first glance it might appear as though only a small percentage of a class will need individualized programs or assistance. Unfortunately, the reverse is usually true. Within any general education classroom, even those without children with disabilities, a wide range of abilities, skills, and interest levels exists. For example, in a fifth-grade classroom the appropriate instructional level for some students will be seventh grade, while for others it will be third grade or lower. The majority of the class, however, will fall somewhere in between, as average fifth graders. So, even if children with disabilities were never integrated into regular classrooms, the student body would be heterogeneous. Cook and Semmel (1999) suggest another important point relative to the heterogeneity of a classroom, especially regarding the relationship of a student's disability to his or her social acceptance within the classroom.

> Students with severe disability do not stand out as considerably in heterogeneous classrooms. Thus, peers' expectations are not uniformly adjusted, resulting in rejection when atypical behavior occurs. Alternatively, in classrooms with relatively low student heterogeneity, individuals with severe disabilities readily stand out as markedly different, prompting differential expectations among peers. . . . Hence, classroom composition appears to have a qualitative impact on the role and acceptance of included students with severe disabilities. In contrast, peer acceptance of students with mild disabilities suggests that it may have a quantitative and less extreme impact on the role and acceptance of these students. (p. 57)

The important point here is that the inclusion of a student with disabilities may or may not extend the heterogeneity of the class. In many cases, students are integrated for only those subject areas in which they can be successful. The teacher may be less challenged instructing a student with disabilities than instructing a low achiever who has been in the classroom all along. A student with physical disabilities who has no loss of cognitive functioning would be able to perform the intellectual tasks, and perhaps some of the motor tasks, with normal amounts of teacher direction.

Another consideration is that children with unidentified disabilities may be in the classroom already. The teacher must address the individual learning needs of such students regardless of whether they have been labeled "disabled."

## Teacher Attitudes

An attitude is a predisposition to behave in a certain way. In any classroom, the teacher's attitude toward a student with disabilities greatly influences the success or failure of mainstreaming in that classroom. Numerous researchers have discussed the effects of teacher attitude on inclusion (e.g., Scott, Vitale, & Masten, 1998; Soodak et al., 1998; Wong, Kauffman, & Lloyd, 1991). These authors indicate that when a student with disabilities is placed in the general education classroom, if the teacher is pessimistic about the student's chance for academic or social success or doubts the efficacy of the integration, a climate may be established for a self-fulfilling prophecy (Jackson, 1968). That is, the student with disabilities may do poorly in the general education classroom simply because the teacher acts differently toward him or her as a result of the teacher's expectations. For example, if the student has a learning disability, the teacher might provide fewer learning trials, thereby precipitating lower performance.

## Changing Teacher Attitudes

One of the more difficult tasks that consultants face is changing a teacher's attitude toward having a student with disabilities in the classroom. This is a challenging task because the teacher may not have much experience with individuals with disabilities or, even if he or she does, may not use that experience to the benefit of the student (Schumm, Vaughn, Gordon, & Rothlein, 1994). Although many elementary and secondary teachers are required to complete courses on educating students with disabilities, such courses may not involve direct interaction in classroom settings with these students.

Consultants have a number of options for changing the attitudes of the regular educator. Recommended methods for influencing attitudes include: using the building principal as a resource, conducting a pilot study, implementing co-teaching, generating parent support, performing inservice training, and employing countercontrol and recruitment measures.

***Using the Building Principal.*** By virtue of the principal's position as administrative and instructional leader, he or she has achieved status with respect to the teachers. In many cases, principals are perceived as trustworthy individuals, and teachers are usually willing to follow their lead. A consultant can capitalize on this status by asking the principal to approach the teachers and listen to their concerns about students with disabilities. The principal can reassure the teachers that support services and instructional materials are available to assist with the process. Further, after inclusion has occurred, consultants could recommend that the principal visit the regular educator's classroom to reinforce teacher efforts. The visits need not be long, but they would confirm in the teacher's mind the personal commitment of the principal to see that inclusion succeeds.

***Conducting a Pilot Study.*** The consultant may choose to implement a pilot study, a small-scale investigation, to demonstrate to the general education teacher that he or she has the instructional knowledge to teach students with disabilities successfully. For example, the consultant and the regular educator might agree to conduct a short-term study to determine if a particular student with disabilities could function competently in a reading group. If the general educator had serious doubts, the study might persuade him or her that the student with disabilities could indeed function successfully in the reading group. This might change the teacher's attitude. Precedent for changing teachers' attitudes as a function of providing successful experiences has been reported by Larrivee and Cook (1979).

*Implementing Co-Teaching.* Co-teaching is a common instructional strategy. It involves two or more teachers sharing the planning and instructional and evaluative responsibilities for students. By pairing an experienced teacher of students with disabilities with a less experienced one, the less experienced teacher could gain the skills of the more experienced teacher. The veteran teacher could model appropriate planning, teaching, and managing techniques and provide opportunities for the less experienced teacher to practice those skills in a supportive environment. After gaining confidence and experience in teaching the student with disabilities, the teacher's attitude toward inclusion might be more favorable. Also, the teacher might be more likely to maintain a positive attitude after the formal team teaching component concluded. Finally, peer collaboration can improve a teacher's intervention problem-solving skills (Johnson & Pugach, 1991).

See Chapters 3 and 4 for additional discussion of co-teaching and strategies to improve problem solving.

*Generating Parent Support.* Many educators feel isolated from parents. They perceive the tasks the student completes in school as separate from tasks completed at home. By establishing lines of communication between teachers and parents, consultants can bridge gaps in the student's program and foster respect between teachers and parents (cf. Alessi, 1985; Weiss et al., 1983).

See Chapter 6 for a discussion of tactics to improve teacher-parent positive interaction and communication.

*Performing Inservice Training.* Inservice training of teachers can have a beneficial effect on a teacher's predisposition toward students with disabilities (McDaniel, 1982). When designing inservice programs, consultants would be well advised to work closely with teachers, administrators, parents, students, and university faculty to plan and deliver programs that participants view as meeting their immediate needs. Emphasis should be placed on presenting factual information, models, practice, and feedback in a systematic way (Joyce & Showers, 1980). Such programs should provide ample opportunity for participants to ask questions related to their own experiences and interactions with students with disabilities (Skinner, 1979). Follow-up consultation in the classroom can help solidify the connection between theory and practice.

See Alber, Heward, and Hippler (1999), in the "research" section of this chapter for a description of a recruitment strategy.

*Employing Countercontrol and Recruitment.* Countercontrol refers to a procedure whereby students are trained to use behavioral principles systematically to change teacher behavior (Graubard, Rosenberg, & Miller, 1971). Specifically, students with disabilities might be taught ways to increase the rate of praise by a teacher or decrease the rate of criticism or warnings. In short, they would reinforce the teacher for attending to them in a positive fashion. While we acknowledge that countercontrol raises a number of ethical issues, we suggest that consultants might want to use modified versions of it where teacher resistance has to be changed by a subtle, cost-effective, and systematic procedure.

In summary, consultants have a variety of options for changing teachers' attitudes toward students with disabilities. Consultants should not hesitate to use these techniques individually or collectively.

# Research on Inclusion

Sale and Carey (1995) conducted a sociometric study of students with disabilities. Their findings show that students with disabilities experience differential acceptance in inclusive settings. Placing students with disabilities in general education classrooms did not seem to improve social acceptability. While the authors concede that other measures of social adjustment were not assessed (e.g., teacher-student interaction and student-student interaction), nevertheless, on questions such as "Who would you most like (or least like) to work with in the class?" students with disabilities did not seem to fare as well as general education students.

Salisbury, Gallucci, Palombaro, and Peck (1995) suggest that social relationships between elementary students with and without disabilities can be enhanced by actively facilitating social interactions (cooperative grouping, tutoring, collaborative problem solving), using role release methods ("Turn it over to the kids."), building a sense of community within the classroom (climate concerns and social responsibility), and modeling acceptance and organizational influences (arranging multiage groupings and clusters). From a cost-based perspective, these researchers suggest that strategies to improve social relationships build on the skills that teachers currently possess and fall within the culture of the school.

Alber, Heward, and Hippler (1999) conducted a study with four middle school students with disabilities who were attending an inclusive classroom to demonstrate the effects of teaching the students to recruit positive attention on their academic performance. Briefly, students were trained to ask their teachers, "How am I doing?" about two to three times per class as a method to improve student recruiting, teacher praise, instructional feedback, and student productivity during seatwork. Results showed improvements for teachers and students across all dimensions, supporting previous research that showed a functional relationship between training students to recruit teacher attention and productivity (Craft, Alber, & Heward, 1998). In effect, the study showed that at least some students with disabilities can be taught to take an "active" role in shaping the nature and quality of their program within the inclusive setting.

See Lloyd, Forness, and Kavale (1998) for a discussion of other effective instructional methods.

Sharpe, York, and Knight (1994), in a preliminary study of the effects of inclusion on one general education student's performance, found no decline in either academic or social performance measures subsequent to inclusion, a finding consistent with social measures obtained by other researchers (cf. Staub & Peck, 1994; York et al., 1992).

Taylor, Richards, Goldstein, and Schilit (1997), surveying a combination of experienced teachers and undergraduate preservice teachers, noted that the majority of general and special education teachers viewed the principle of inclusion as positive and beneficial. However, with respect to the placement of certain types of students with disabilities (e.g., students with moderate to severe educational, behavioral, or emotional disabilities), most general education teachers did not favor inclusion in *their* classroom. Essentially, the teachers believed that the principle was acceptable as a social goal, but they did not want the students in their rooms. Schumm, Vaughn, Gordon, and Rothlein (1994) examined veteran general education teachers known to be skilled in working with students with disabilities. In the main, the authors found that even among highly skilled general education teachers, long-range planning, adapting course content, and adapting tests presented real challenges and these tasks were less likely to happen. Even when general education teachers knew

Revisit Turnbull and Ruef (1997) to note parent perceptions about their frustration in dealing with teachers and seemingly intractable school systems.

adaptations were necessary and desirable and they had the perceived skills to make the adaptations, implementation was still low. Teachers claimed that they did not have the time to meet all the needs of the students. Interestingly, whereas elementary teachers were more likely to adapt instruction and curriculum, middle and high school teachers tended to reflect perhaps a larger societal attitude that upon graduation fewer supports were going to be available to these students and that therefore nothing was going to be adapted. The students would need to make it on their own. This changing attitude from elementary to middle to high school perhaps explains, in part, why parents feel so enervated when it comes to advocating for change in their children's program.

Waldron and McLeskey (1998) examined the effects of an inclusive school program (ISP) on reading and math achievement of students with mild to severe learning disabilities. Two groups of elementary students participated. The experimental group (N = 71) included LD students from three schools using the ISP program (i.e., a combination of team teaching, general education curriculum, and instructional assistants within the classroom but no self-contained class placement). The other group of LD students (N = 73) used a curriculum-based approach but not ISP. Results showed that students with learning disabilities using ISP made more progress in reading than the controls did but only comparable progress in math. Also, students with severe learning disabilities made less progress. The authors sum up the research this way:

> Placement in an inclusive setting does not provide a panacea for students with learning disabilities, and the necessity remains to develop and implement effective instructional methods to increase the opportunities that these students have for learning important academic material, as well as for increasing the rate at which these skills develop. (p. 403)

Ivory and McCollum (1999), working with early education populations, found that the type of toy (social versus isolate) can make a difference with respect to the level of observed interaction in an inclusive classroom. Cooperative play occurred more often when social toys were made available rather than isolate toys.

Little and Witek (1996) call for an evaluation of inclusion that includes social validity measures and functional outcome analysis (cost-benefit with respect to time, space, training needs, teacher's sense of accomplishment, and student self-efficacy).

Pearl et al. (1999) examined the social interaction patterns of 1,538 elementary students with mild disabilities across three types of school systems (urban, large city; rural; and small city) to determine the relationship among peer group membership, peer-assessed behavioral characteristics, and peer-assessed behavioral characteristics of association. Using a survey method, Pearl et al. found that students with mild disabilities were overrepresented in social isolate groups and underrepresented in prosocial groups. Furthermore, students tended to affiliate more often with other students in the class who reflected similar behavioral patterns, meaning, for example, that students with prosocial behavior characteristics tended to interact more often with prosocial students without disabilities. The reverse was also true. One implication of Pearl et al.'s findings is that low prosocial students with disabilities who affiliate with other students with behavior problems may exacerbate these problems.

Still, some studies have shown that exceptional students are (a) accepted in general education class placements and (b) indistinguishable from peers on some measures (Roberts, Pratt, & Leach, 1991; Sabornie & Kauffman, 1985; Sabornie & Kauffman, 1986). In the Sabornie and Kauffman (1986) study, an assessment of social acceptance was administered to 46 LD students in grades 9 through 12 and a matched sample of students. The data indicated that the sociometric status of these adolescent students (LD and general education) did not differ significantly and that the LD students were as well known as their peers. Sabornie and Kauffman concluded:

> Our results should give educators hope that at least for some LD students the mainstream of education is socially meaningful and not rife with ostracism. . . . The picture of the LD adolescent's social skills is not as bleak as it once appeared—some exceptional students can find their appropriate social place in regular classrooms. Strategies have been devised to help mildly handicapped students become more socially adept in their relations with NH [nonhandicapped] peers. (pp. 59–60)

Roberts et al.'s 6-month observational study of 190 elementary students (95 students with learning disabilities and 95 general education students) ages 8 to 13 in integrated classrooms and the playground showed that similar patterns of low-level disruptive behavior existed in the classroom, but differential patterns existed on the playground. Compared to the general education students, students with learning disabilities interacted less with peers, engaged in more solitary play, and interacted with adults more often. These results suggest that setting has a significant effect on student-student interactions, a finding that apparently holds true even with preschool populations (Burstein, 1986).

One strategy that consultants might be well advised to recommend to improve the social behavior and perception of students with disabilities is role-taking training (i.e., having the general education peer assume the mannerisms or characteristics of the student with disabilities (Kitano, Steihl, & Cole, 1978). This training is designed to foster better social relationships between general education and exceptional students. Role-taking training may increase student sensitivity toward the needs and feelings of each group and improve self-esteem and social relationships between general education students and their peers with disabilities. Further, consultants might be able to assist students with disabilities, either directly or indirectly, to discover their social status within the classroom, develop specific behaviors that would positively affect their status, and learn to regulate their behavior.

A compelling body of literature indicates that the verbal and nonverbal behaviors of students with learning disabilities affect their status and acceptability adversely in the classroom (Bruininks, 1978b; Kitano et al., 1978; Bryan, 1977; Stone & La Greca, 1990; Vaughn, Elbaum, & Schumm, 1996). Thus, consultants and general education teachers need to examine the nature of verbal and nonverbal exchanges between general education students and students with disabilities. After data analysis, they could plan and implement joint programs to teach both groups to recognize and engage in socially acceptable and positively reinforcing verbal and nonverbal exchanges (Strain, Odom, & McConnell, 1984). Presumably, if students with mild disabilities were taught to use verbal and nonverbal signals in a constructive fashion, their status within the classroom would be enhanced.

Finally, although presenting information to general education students regarding disability characteristics can help change students' attitudes (Fiedler & Simpson, 1987), and attending to the seating arrangements for high- and low-achieving students may increase verbalizations (Fox, 1989), stronger interventions may be needed to actually shift behaviors in the desired direction. Planned social skills training programs and using peers as collaborative change agents may facilitate the rate of change (Hollinger, 1987). McIntosh, Vaughn, & Zaragoza's (1991) review of social intervention training programs revealed that the more successful interventions were cognitive-behavioral, conducted with individuals or small groups, and designed for long-term periods.

# Keys to Successful Inclusion

Also see Chapter 4 for elaboration on problem-solving approaches.

In our view, three variables provide the keys to successful inclusion: collaboration, teacher acceptability of educational intervention, and knowledge of the specialized health needs of students.

## Collaboration

Chalmers and Faliede (1996) emphasize that successful inclusion is not likely to occur in the absence of collaboration between general and special education teachers. Further, specific factors likely to facilitate successful inclusion are: preplanning with staff and students, developing a functional communication system and teamwork, structuring collaborative relationships, gaining administrative support, including parents, and refining the grading system to reflect the actual or modified curriculum (Mamlin, 1999). Elliot and McKenney (1998) note that in addition to collaboration, team teaching is essential so that general and special education teachers can learn from each other. Fox and Ysseldyke (1997), extrapolating from research efforts and experience, indicate that inclusion is more likely to be successful if collaboration also addresses adequate leadership, training, and administrative issues. Staff must have a vested interest in the process, share a vision for their school as a community, and involve parents actively in the process. Consultation efforts across faculty, staff, and parents can help in this regard (Stanovich, 1996). Conversely, inclusion is not likely to be successful in situations where faculty, staff, and administrators reluctantly and grudgingly acquiesce because of pressure, where adequate supports are not in place, and where meaningful participation across parties is not engaged (Giangreco et al., 1995).

## Educational Intervention

See *Intervention in School and Clinic* (1996), *31*(3) for a rich source of ideas about grading, homework, and testing accommodations. Also, see Scott, Vitale, and Masten (1998) for a review of the literature on implementing instructional adaptations.

Polloway, Bursuck, Jayanthi, Epstein, and Nelson (1996) make the point that teacher acceptability of interventions is important if inclusion is to become a viable option for all parties involved in the process. In their view, *teacher acceptability* of educational intervention means "the likelihood that certain specific classroom interventions—particularly those that involve adaptation or modification—will be accepted by the general education teacher" (pp. 133–134). Of particular interest to general education teachers are issues such as grading, homework, and testing. In the end, teacher acceptability of select field-tested strategies will be determined by his or her collegial relationship with the consultant, and more important, by the dimensions of utility, ease of implementation, and fairness (Polloway et al., 1996).

# Knowledge of the Specialized Health Needs of Students

Given improved morbidity for children with what once were catastrophic illnesses (e.g., childhood leukemia, cystic fibrosis, acute respiratory illness), an increased number of these children are being maintained in public school, some in inclusive classroom situations. Hence, consultants must be knowledgeable about such children's conditions and any specialized treatments that might be involved in their care.

Wadsworth and Knight (1999) suggest that the *Classroom Ecological Preparation Inventory* (CEPI) might serve as a mechanism to determine the health-related needs of students across medical access, physical environment, assistive equipment, instructional adaptation, and social and behavioral management concerns. For students who are medically fragile, with moderate to severe disabilities, or who might otherwise require specialized health accommodations for whatever reason (e.g., asthma, catheter implant), the consultant's knowledge about the full array of treatments, adaptations, and supports would enhance the likelihood of success.

Readers might refer to Chapter 2's discussion of the Tatro case, in which intermittent catheterization during school hours was deemed appropriate and necessary for a child to take full advantage of the educational opportunity afforded by the school.

# Multipronged Approach

Bassett et al. (1996) suggest that a multipronged approach is likely to be needed in any situation where inclusion programs are implemented. Not only will strategies, materials, and resources be required on site, but teacher education programs will need to gear up to train general education teachers who are capable of managing a fuller range of students in their classrooms. Bassett et al. hit the issue squarely on the head when they state:

> Real change will not take place unless it is rooted in the notions that all teachers and schools must become more accommodating to diverse learners, that all children should be prepared to participate in living and working in their communities, and that our children must be helped to care enough to value all types of people as members of a community. (p. 377)

# A Decision-Making Model

Heron (1978a) constructed a decision-making model that consultants, supervisors, principals, and teachers can use to address issues related to integrating students with disabilities. The intent of the model is to preclude the premature removal of a student with disabilities from a general education setting before a series of alternatives has been attempted systematically. Essentially, this model outlines hierarchically arranged strategies that consultants can employ with general and special needs students and their teacher. The least intrusive technique is listed first, followed by more intrusive measures. More important, the strategies proposed are field tested and data based. All have been demonstrated to be effective in a variety of settings, and all are relatively easy to implement. Finally, the strategies can be implemented across elementary, middle, and high school levels.

Practitioners interested in other strategies and guidelines for including students with special needs in general education classrooms are referred to Friend and Bursuck (1996).

# Gaining Perspective on Inclusion

Other resources can be found in *The Journal of Special Education* (1997, *31*[1]).

Kauffman and Hallahan (1993) indicate that a research base favoring full inclusion does not exist. Some researchers, notably Mills, Cole, Jenkins, and Dale (1998), who replicated earlier findings, have shown that at least for preschool children, differential effects can be obtained. That is, while both higher- and lower-performing preschoolers may benefit from some inclusion, their data seem to show that higher-functioning students benefited more from full inclusion setting; whereas lower-performing students derived more benefit from partial inclusion. The implication of Mills et al.'s research, if further replicated,

is: (a) one size of special education programming does not fit all students, and (b) the differential effect of full inclusion versus a continuum of service options probably depends on the individual student. In other words, consultants trying to meet the philosophical, legal, educational, and social mandates of IDEA '97 would probably be on safer ground recommending placement and program options that meet the individualized needs of students, rather than trying to meet an "abstract" standard for political purposes.

Issues related to inclusion will no doubt continue to surface as a growing number of students across a range of disability areas find their way into the general education setting. Philosophical, programmatic, legal, and research issues are likely to be hotly debated well into the next millennium as practitioners and parents continue to struggle with challenging questions about how to educate and train students with disabilities in an appropriate setting and environment. Simpson (1996) sums up the situation relative to inclusion in this way:

> Accordingly, debate over integration and inclusion of students with disabilities has largely come from individuals' and organizations' values related to inclusion. That is, the full inclusion debate has been characterized by arguments over who is right, who is ethical and moral, and who is a true advocate for students with special needs. Of course this situation has forced educators and parents into difficult educational placement decisions, and this challenge will likely continue as a major special issue into the foreseeable future. (p. 22)

Still, while there does not appear to be (a) any single philosophy, program, or research study that provides convincing evidence on the benefits or disadvantages of inclusion, or (b) consistent methodological rigor across all areas of disability to the point that unanimity of opinion can be achieved, the field has reached tentative "consensus" on the following points related to inclusion:

• More research needs to be conducted to determine the variables operating in the environment (school and home) that promote inclusion success. These variables relate to level of disability, type of inclusion program, training and sensitivity of the teachers, parent involvement, and administrative and financial support.

• The more severe the disability (physical, sensory, or orthopedic), the more difficult it becomes to integrate students into the broader academic and social milieu afforded students without disabilities.

• Despite massive efforts at the national, state, and local levels, many parents continue to feel disenfranchised, frustrated, and fed up with the lack of support they receive at the school level.

    • General education preservice teacher training programs do not prepare teachers adequately to meet the increasing challenges of students with special needs.

# Helping Teachers To Develop and Evaluate Individualized Education and Family Programs

With the changes in IDEA '97 regulations, the role of the general education teacher will become more prominent with respect to developing, implementing, and evaluating the Individualized Education Program and the Individualized Family Services Plan. Consultants can serve as a knowledgeable resource for faculty, staff, and administrators on these changes.

    IEPs and IFSPs can be considered from two perspectives: (a) the conference where parents and professionals begin the process of forging the program for the child, and (b) the document itself that represents the record of the program and specifies the course of action (Heward, 2000). In both cases, consultants must ensure that this conference and this document reflect and are sensitive to the culture, language, values, socioeconomic background, and ethnic group of the student (Bailey & Simeonsson, 1988; Ortiz & Wilkerson, 1989). Ortiz and Wilkerson include a model IEP form that provides for the specialized needs of limited-English–proficient students. Consultants should be aware that the IEP document is continuing to evolve. Figure 5.1 shows the range of information that must be included on the IEP for a language-minority student.

> For a copy of an *IEP Team Guide* (1998), contact the Council for Exceptional Children, 1920 Association Drive, Reston, VA.

    Before an IEP or IFSP can be implemented successfully, three procedural steps must be taken. First, initial assessment of the student's performance levels must take place. Second, assessment data must be analyzed so that annual goals and short-term objectives can be prepared and resources identified to meet those goals. Third, an IEP or IFSP meeting must be planned and conducted to develop the specific program that will be aimed at remediating the student's deficits, rearranging the student's environment, or adjusting the curriculum.

    Consultants can be of service to special educators in each of these areas. For example, the consultant might (a) recommend specific assessment procedures or protocols, (b) co-evaluate formal and informal data with the teacher to determine goals and objectives, and (c) assist with organizing the IEP or IFSP conference. With respect to the last point, the consultant can recommend that a draft of the IEP or IFSP be mailed to the parents prior to the meeting so that they can share the teacher's view of the program. In a cover letter to the parents it must be made clear that the proposed plan is intended to set the occasion for discussion at the meeting. Affleck, Lowenbraun, and Archer (1980) make this point succinctly in reference to the IEP process:

> In preparing for the IEP meeting, participants should not only collect and summarize information on current functioning level, but they should also determine potential areas that might require special service programming. Written drafts of portions of the IEP, especially the long-term goals and short-term objectives, may be outlined before the meeting. While the process of participatory planning and collecting information from all parties should not be circumvented by signing of a pre-written document, we

## Individual Education Program

Student _____ Sex _____ ID# _____
(Last)                (First)              (Middle)

Date of birth: _____ Place of Birth: _____ School _____ Grade _____

Current handicapping condition(s) _____

Program placement:  Reg Ed _____ Bi Ed _____ Migrant Ed _____ ESL _____

Other _____ Teacher _____

If applicable, percent of English instruction _____ Native language instruction _____
ESL instruction _____

Number of years in bilingual education program _____

English as a second language program _____

Purpose(s) of meeting: ____ Admission ____ Dismissal ____ Review ____ Other _____

Language of meeting: English _____ Native language _____ Other _____

Interpreter used: _____ Yes _____ No

I. ELIGIBILITY DETERMINATIONS (Record language(s) of testing as appropriate):
A. Information reviewed by the committee:

| | Date of Report | Lang of Testing | | Date of Report | Lang of Testing |
|---|---|---|---|---|---|
| Referral folder information | | | Comprehensive individual assessment | | |
| Group achievement/aptitude | | | Related services assessment | | |
| Language proficiency | | | Attendance history | | |
| Parent information | | | Prior school history | | |
| Other: | | | Other: | | |

B. Based on the information indicated above, the committee decided that the student:

DOES/DOES NOT meet eligibility criteria for _____|_____
Primary Handicap      Other Handicap(s)

C. Based on above information, committee ensures that this decision was not primarily due to criteria based on:

Date Source(s)        Justification

____ Command of the English language _____
____ Different cultural lifestyle _____
____ Lack of educational opportunity _____

II. PLACEMENT DECISIONS: Amount of Time (min/hrs per day/wk)
Voc. Ed. _____ Spec. Ed. _____ Other _____
Regular education ____ Bi. Ed ____ ESL ____ Migrant Ed ____ Other (specify): _____
Instructional arrangement (Indicate bilingual special education if appropriate):
Itinerant ____ Resource ____ Partially self-contained ____ Self-contained ____ Other ____

| SUBJECT | TIME/DAY Reg Voc Sp | DATES Beg End | MODIFICATIONS NEEDED (IF ANY) (facility, equip. method, material) | LANGUAGE OF INSTRUCTION |
|---|---|---|---|---|
| | | | | |
| | | | | |
| | | | | |

(continues)

Figure 5.1. Individualized Education Program for language-minority students. From "Adapting IEPs for Limited English Proficient Students," by A. A. Ortiz and C. Y. Wilkerson, 1989, in *Academic Therapy, 24*(5), 564–566. Reprinted with permission.

recommend prior preparation of portions of the IEP. It is important that any prepared drafts be presented only as proposals on which additional input and modifications will be accepted. (p. 27)

In other situations, parents might be contacted by telephone to solicit their ideas and/or to share preliminary goals. Timely notification may provide the opportunity for teachers to conduct further probes or assessments in response

| RELATED SERVICES | POSITION RESPONSIBLE | LANGUAGE OF SERVICE | AMT TIME PER DAY | DAYS PER WK | DATES Beg   End |
|---|---|---|---|---|---|
|  |  |  |  |  |  |
|  |  |  |  |  |  |
|  |  |  |  |  |  |

| GROUP ACHIEVEMENT TESTING | | | | |
|---|---|---|---|---|
|  | Yes | No | For Experience Only | Language of Testing |
| READING |  |  |  |  |
| MATH |  |  |  |  |
| (other) |  |  |  |  |

| Limited English Proficient (LEP) Student? Yes No | | |
|---|---|---|
| Dominant Language English ____ Native Lang. ____ | | |
|  | Most Recent | Date |
|  | Test Score | |
| English |  |  |
| Native Lang. |  |  |

Date parent notified of mtg.: _____ Date of mtg: _____

This educational placement is in the least restrictive environment and is appropriate to meet the needs of the student. The student is being educated to the maximum extent appropriate with students who are nonhandicapped.

Alternative placements reviewed and reasons rejected: _____

_____

Services reviewed and reasons rejected: _____

_____

III. COMMITTEE SIGNATURES:    Indicate area represented (e.g., representative of administration, instruction, appraisal, special education, vocational education). Continue on reverse if necessary.

| VOTING MEMBER | AGREE | DISAGREE* | SIGNATURE | POSITION | PROGRAM ASSIGNMENT (e.g., Bi. Ed. ESL) | Bilingual? Yes   No |
|---|---|---|---|---|---|---|
|  |  |  |  | Parent/Legal Guardian |  |  |
|  |  |  |  | Parent/Legal Guardian |  |  |
|  |  |  |  |  |  |  |
|  |  |  |  |  |  |  |
|  |  |  |  |  |  |  |

*If disagreeing, indicate area(s) of disagreement on the back.

**Figure 5.1.** Continued.

to parental questions (White & Calhoun, 1987). In addition, the consultant can indicate to teachers how complex, and sometimes confusing, information can be integrated so that a functional program can be developed and presented to the parents. The consultant can assist with assuring that all components of the IEP or IFSP, including transition plans where appropriate, are recorded on the IEP form, a procedural step that often has been ignored or neglected, especially across types of settings (Grigal, Test, Beattie, & Wood, 1997; Smith, 1990a, 1990b). Finally, the consultant can assist in recommending related services and can provide technical assistance with developing and evaluating the IEP long- and short-term goals and transition plans. As Grigal et al. indicate, while transition goals may appear on the IEP, they must also be written in such a way as to ultimately provide benefit to the individual. Compliance with a statutory regulation to include a statement does not necessarily mean that best practice methods will be used to achieve the goal.

With respect to designing the IFSP, Wolery (1991) suggests that the curriculum content be specified, the match between the student's need and that content be clarified, changes in the environment be documented, and procedures for generality and transition be recorded.

## Conducting the Initial Assessment

See Chapter 8 for a discussion on assessment.

Assessment refers to the range of tasks a teacher performs to obtain data to enhance instruction (McLoughlin & Lewis, 1990; Taylor, 1997). These tasks include administering and interpreting unbiased, nondiscriminatory norm- and criterion-referenced tests; conducting observations in the classroom; assessing student performance using curriculum-based measures; interviewing the students, the teacher, or the parents; and using analytic and precision teaching approaches.

Since each of these methods for obtaining reliable and valid assessment data has been discussed comprehensively by other authors (e.g., Cooper et al., 1987; McLoughlin & Lewis, 1990; Taylor, 1997), the rest of this chapter focuses on the ways a consultant can assist special and general educators with integrating assessment data, writing goal statements, planning individual programs, monitoring and evaluating programs, and promoting generality and maintenance.

## Integrating Assessment Data

A preliminary objective for the consultant might be to generate a diagnostic summary sheet for a student—let's call her Arlene—that might be used ultimately as a mechanism to write her IEP (see Table 5.2 and Figure 5.2). Conducting the assessment is only half the battle; the other half is to integrate the data so that a functional program can be written and ultimately delivered in the inclusion classroom. Assume that the data portrayed in Tables 5.3 through 5.5 represent reading, math, and spelling scores, respectively, obtained for Arlene, a 10-year-old student with suspected learning disabilities, during the course of an initial assessment. In addition to listing items common to the IEP, the summary sheet profiles Arlene's level of performance and her learning style, preferred reinforcers, objectives for instruction, materials and techniques, and evaluation measures. Data listed for these items may well come from a range of other sources: criterion-referenced assessments, functional assessments, curriculum-based measures, and student interviews.

### Determining Strengths

An academic or social strength is the skill or cluster of skills that allows the student to perform independently. That is, he or she is able to complete 90% to 95% of assigned tasks without assistance. The term *mastery* is usually reserved for completed tasks that are above 99% correct. Strengths can be delineated using a variety of formats. For example, Arlene is able to read competently at the 1.5 reading level on word recognition and comprehension. (A general rule of thumb is that the independent level is approximately two grade levels below the grade equivalent score on the test.) Also, she has mastered two vowel sounds and one half of the consonants (Table 5.2).

### Determining Areas of Need

Technically speaking, performance at an 80% success criterion could be considered an instructional level. This means that the student has sufficient knowledge or skill to profit from instruction. The cutoff score to determine a level is somewhat flexible and depends upon the skill to be mastered and the teacher's

## Table 5.2
### Diagnostic Summary Sheet for Arlene

Student's Name: Arlene M.          Birthdate: April 23, 1989
Date: December 14, 1999            Grade level: 5th (Inclusion)
Teacher's Name: Ms. Marge H.

Reading Strengths                 Reading Weaknesses

- Mastered two vowel sounds       - Difficulty w/ word identification
  (a and e) and 1/2 of consonants
                                  - Unable to identify word parts
- Motivated
                                  - Difficulty w/ all aspects of reading
- Enjoys listening to stories       comprehension

*Learner Style*

Arlene's performance is enhanced when tasks are issued one at a time rather than all together. She seems to rely heavily on visual cues, enjoys having stories read to her. Providing modes of response that allow her to write or demonstrate might be helpful.

*Preferred Reinforcers*

Arlene clearly enjoys free time in class. Throughout the assessment, she stated that games (Battleship, checkers, bingo) were her favorite activities.

*Annual Goals*

1. By June 1, Arlene will be able to read CVC words correctly.
2. By June 1, Arlene will be able to comprehend literally a one-paragraph story.
3. By June 1, Arlene will be able to comprehend figuratively a one-paragraph story.
4. By June, Arlene will be able to identify 20 Dolch words.

*Short-term Objectives*

1. By November 30, Arlene will be able to read 10 CVC words correctly.
2. By December 19, Arlene will be able to answer (orally) 5 out of 5 literal and figurative comprehension questions.
3. By March 31, Arlene will be able to identify 20 Dolch words with 100% correct.

*Materials and Techniques*

1. Direct instruction (DI).
2. Practice DI worksheets.
3. Visual presentations combined with multiple opportunities to respond.

*Evaluation Measures*

1. Tracking sheet showing date of mastery of each short-term objective.
2. Direct and daily measures.

criterion for success. The 80% criterion level is appropriate for most activities but would probably be in the frustration range for reading words in context, which usually requires 95% success.

Areas of need are, in a practical sense, those skills that may not be fully developed and may need further remediation and instruction. In the example shown in Table 5.2, Arlene has difficulty with word identification. In addition, she has difficulty with word parts and reading comprehension.

Student's Name: _Arlene H_

Primary Language: _English_

IEP Meeting Date: _1/4/00_

Duration of Services: _One School Year_

Physical Education Program: _General program_

Assessments: _Woodcock Reading Mastery Test–Revised;_

_Diagnostic Achievement Battery–2; Test of Written_

_Spelling–4_

Medical: _Vision/hearing w/in normal limits; no medications_

Disability Classification: _Specific Learning Disability_

Date of Birth: _4/23/89_

Date of Assessment: _12/14/99_

CA: _10-7_

General Education Class Participation: _1/2 day_

Resource Room: _1/2 day_

Related Services: _None_

Performance Strengths (Only reading shown):
- Mastered two vowel sounds (a and e) & 1/2 of consonants
- Motivated
- Enjoys listening to stories

Access to General Education Program: 1/2 of school day for general curriculum

Performance Weaknesses (Only reading shown):
- Difficulty w/ word identification
- Unable to identify word parts
- Difficulty w/ all aspects of reading comprehension

Effect of disability on access to GE curriculum:

Arlene's reading disability may make it difficult for her to participate in some reading group work. Her high motivation to succeed may compensate.

| | | |
|---|---|---|
| Annual Goal: By June 1, Arlene will be able to comprehend literally a one-paragraph story. | General and Special Education Teachers | Classroom Observation; Criterion-referenced testing |
| Benchmark: By December 19, Arlene will be able to answer (orally) 5 out of 5 literal comprehension questions. | | |
| Annual Goal: By June 1, Arlene will be able to comprehend figuratively a one-paragraph story. | General and Special Education Teachers | Classroom Observation; Criterion-referenced testing |
| Benchmark: By December 19, Arlene will be able to answer (orally) 5 out of 5 figurative comprehension questions. | | |
| Annual Goal: By June, Arlene will be able to identify 20 Dolch words. | General and Special Education Teachers | Assessment based on Dolch word list. |
| Benchmark: By March 31, Arlene will be able to identify 20 Dolch words with 100% correct. | | |

**Figure 5.2.** Arlene's Individualized Education Program.

## Table 5.3
### Arlene's Reading Performance on the Woodcock Reading Mastery Test–Revised

| Subtest | Grade Equivalent | Age Equivalent | Percentile | Standard Score |
|---|---|---|---|---|
| Word Identification | 1.9 | 7–2 | .3 | 59 |
| Word Attack | 1.6 | 6–10 | 3 | 72 |
| Word Comprehension | 1.7 | 6–11 | .1 | 54 |
| Passage Comprehension | 1.8 | 7–1 | .4 | 61 |
| Basic Skills Cluster | | | .5 | 61 |
| Reading Comprehension Cluster | | | .1 | 55 |
| Total Reading Cluster | | | .3 | 58 |

## Table 5.4
### Arlene's Math Performance on the Diagnostic Achievement Battery–2

| DAB–2 | Raw | Grade Equivalent | Percentile Score | Standard Score |
|---|---|---|---|---|
| Math Reasoning | 16 | 2.2 | 5 | 5 |
| Math Calculation | 10 | 3.0 | 5 | 5 |

## Table 5.5
### Arlene's Spelling Performance on the Test of Written Spelling–3

| TWS–3 | Raw Score | Spelling Age | Grade Equivalent | Percentile | Standard Score |
|---|---|---|---|---|---|
| Predictable Words | 1 | <5–0 | <.5 | 1 | 65 |
| Unpredictable Words | 5 | 6–3 | .5 | 1 | 66 |
| Total Words | 6 | 5–3 | <.5 | <1 | <60 |

## Learning Style

Learning styles are considered to exist in four modes: visual, auditory, kinesthetic, and mixed. While conducting assessments the teacher should note the mannerisms or behaviors the student displays when completing the task, because such information can be used in educational programming. Further, teachers need to consider the number of tasks that are assigned to students and the rate and mode with which those tasks are to be completed. Students unable to complete a task presented in one fashion might be able to do it when it is presented differently. For example, a student with learning disabilities may be unable to supply an answer that requires filling in the blank. However, if the student is provided with several visual alternatives, his or her performance may improve.

Other behaviors to look for might be: If a student is asked to pronounce a word, does he or she attempt to sound it out? Does the student seem to look at only the first part of the word and then guess at the rest? If a student consistently uses one modality (visual, auditory, or kinesthetic) to solve problems on the assessment, the teacher might infer that that sensory channel is the preferred learning modality. However, the consultant must caution the teacher against wholeheartedly assuming that it is the preferred modality. The research data on the effects of teaching to a child's modality strength are not convincing. Kavale and Forness (1987) make this point:

> Although the presumption of matching instructional strategies to individual modality preferences to enhance learning efficiency has great intuitive appeal, little empirical support for this proposition was found from the quantitative synthesis of the extant literature. Neither modality testing nor modality teaching were shown to be efficacious. (p. 237)

According to the teacher's perception, Arlene's performance is enhanced when tasks are well paced. Giving too many assignments at one time apparently results in a poorer performance. Also, providing Arlene with writing or demonstration responses seems to increase her accuracy.

### Preferred Reinforcers

*Preferred reinforcers* are consequences that students choose more frequently than other reinforcers. Teachers can determine preferred reinforcers in three ways. First, the teacher can ask the students what they like. Valuable time and energy can be saved when teachers ask students what they would prefer to do contingent upon task completion. Second, the teacher can watch students to see what they like to do during free time. Third, teachers can set up a forced-choice situation (Cooper et al., 1987). For example, the teacher might say, "John, you can play a game, read a book, or help Mark with his math." If John chooses to read a book, the teacher might infer that reading was the most reinforcing activity given those options. The other two activities might also be reinforcing, but the teacher now knows which is the most powerful of the three. The teacher was able to determine that Arlene's preferred reinforcers included Battleship, checkers, and bingo.

## Writing Goal Statements

After the assessment data have been collected and analyzed, the next step in preparing an appropriate IEP or IFSP for a student is to establish goals, both long and short term. In addition, it is important to check periodically to ensure that those goals are being achieved.

### Annual Goal

An *annual goal* is defined as a statement of the behavior the student is expected to achieve within a calendar year. It is anticipated that annual goals for each major need identified in the evaluation procedures will be attained through implementation of the IEP or IFSP. Consultants should note that annual goals should be written for every major critical need identified under present levels of performance; they must be measurable, and they must enable the child to participate and make progress in the general curriculum (cf. IEP Team Guide, 1999). Examples of annual goal statements are found on the Diagnostic Summary Sheet for Arlene (Table 5.2).

## Table 5.6

### Criteria for Prioritizing Annual Goals

1. Will the child be able to use the skill in his or her immediate environment?
2. Is it a functional, useful skill?
3. Will the child be able to use the skill often?
4. Has the child demonstrated an interest in learning this skill?
5. Is success in teaching this skill likely?
6. Is the skill a prerequisite for learning more complex skills?
7. Will the child become more independent as a result of learning this skill?
8. Will the skill allow the child to qualify for improved or additional services, or services in a less restrictive environment?
9. Is it important to modify this behavior because it is dangerous to the child or others?

Turnbull, Strickland, and Hammer (1978) state the purpose of the annual goal:

> The annual goals, by necessity, must be somewhat global in nature so they may encompass the entire spectrum of short-term or intermediate objectives in a given area. They must, however, describe the educational performance to be achieved by the end of the school year. Each student must be considered individually in formulating annual goals so that realistic goals may be set and relevant teaching strategies may be determined to improve the child's functioning. (p. 71)

Given that annual goals are global in nature, a point Fuchs, Fuchs, and Hamlett (1990) underscore, the question of relative importance of one annual goal over another is raised. Consultants can assist the IEP or IFSP team to develop jargon-free, prioritized annual goals by applying appropriate criteria (Hughes & Ruhl, 1987; Pasanella & Volkmor, 1981). Dardig and Heward (1981b) suggest a 6-step process to prioritize annual goals. After introducing team members and establishing rapport (step 1), the team lists as many IEP goals as possible (step 2). Next, criteria for arranging the goals are applied (step 3). Table 5.6 shows a 9-item checklist for prioritizing the goals. These questions will provide the team with the basis for arranging goals in a hierarchical order. Steps 4 and 5 are concerned with rating the goals and synthesizing responses. The matrix shown in Figure 5.3 illustrates the outcome of this process. Finally, in step 6 a prioritized list of goals is produced. Examples of annual goals for Arlene are included on the Diagnostic Summary Sheet (Table 5.2).

Bailey and Simeonsson (1988) indicate that plans for early childhood intervention programs may be facilitated if goal attainment scaling (GAS) is used. In this procedure, goals are set, prioritized, and placed on a continuum from best outcome to worst outcome. Then intervention services are provided, and child performance is measured. Table 5.7 shows an example of a Goal Attainment Scale for five family-related behaviors.

## Benchmarks

Simply stated, a *benchmark* is a *short-term objective* or an intermediate step between the child's current level of performance and the annual goal. These steps are measurable and act as milestones for indicating progress toward the annual goal. Short-term objectives are less detailed than daily instructional objectives, which usually require more specific outcomes or products (Pasanella

The terms *short-term objective* and *benchmark* can be used synonymously, although benchmark is a broader-based designation representing major milestones of achievement (cf. IEP Team Guide, 1999).

**INDIVIDUAL RATING SCALE**
(Sample)

Child's Name _____

Team Member Name and Position _____

Date _____

Key:
1 = No or Never
2 = Rarely — Lowest Priority
3 = Maybe or Sometimes
4 = Usually
5 = Yes or Always — Highest Priority

Fill in Goals (in abbreviated form)

A. grooming—hair and nails
B. table manners
C. sight word recognition
D. leisure time crafts
E. pre-voc.-sorting
F. comparative social interaction
G. independent bus travel
H. exercise
I. oral communication
J. reduce self-stimulation
K. money handling skills
L. fine motor skills
M. housekeeping—cooking
N. completing tasks on time
O.

1. is skill useful in immediate environment?
2. is skill functional?
3. would skill be used often?
4. has child demonstrated interest?
5. is success likely?
6. is skill prerequisite?
7. will child become more independent?
8. will child quality for additional services?
9. is behavior dangerous to self or others?

TOTALS:

**TEAM RATING SCALE**
(Fill in Scores Given by Each Team Member)

Child's Name _____

Date _____

Fill in Members
1 2 3 4 5 6 7 8    TOTALS

Fill in goals (in abbreviated form):
A.
B.
C.
D.
E.
F.
G.
H.
I.
J.
K.
L.
M.
N.

Figure 5.3. Individual Rating Scale. From "A Systematic Procedure for Prioritizing IEP Goals," by J. C. Dardig & W. L. Heward, 1981c, *The Directive Teacher*, 3(2), 8. Copyright 1981 by The Directive Teacher. Reprinted with permission.

## Table 5.7
### Sample Goal Attainment Scale for Family-Related Goals

| Program Families Project | | Goal Attainment Scale for Jason | | Date of Program Plan 9/23/84 | |
|---|---|---|---|---|---|
| Scale Attainment Levels | Goal 1 Quality of Handling (W1 = 3) | Goal 2 Awareness of State (W2 = 2) | Goal 3 Community Resources (W3 = 3) | Goal 4 Implementing Training (W4 = 3) | Goal 5 Sibling Relationship (W5 = 1) |
| 2 Best expected outcome | Father almost always handles child in sensitive fashion. Never rough or abrupt. | Mother almost always differentiates states when child is receptive for social/educational interactions. | Family always accesses needed community resources independently. | Mother follows training program steps with accuracy of at least 90% (A). | Sibling often participates in a positive fashion in interactions between handicapped child and parents. |
| 1 More than expected outcome | Usually sensitive handling of child. | Usually differentiates states (A). | Usually accesses community resources independently. Occasionally needs help. | Mother follows training program steps with accuracy of at least 80%. | Sibling sometimes participates in a positive fashion in interactions between handicapped child and parent. |
| 0 Expected outcome | Sometimes sensitive handling, about half the time (A). | Sometimes differentiates states, about half the time. | Sometimes accesses needed community resources, about half the time (A). | Mother follows training program steps with accuracy of at least 70%. | Sibling rarely interferes with parent-child interactions (A). |
| −1 Less than expected outcome | Occasionally sensitive handling. | Occasionally differentiates states and responds appropriately. | Family rarely accesses community resources independently. | Mother follows training program steps with accuracy of at least 60%. | Sibling sometimes interferes with parent-child interactions. |
| −2 Worst expected outcome | Father never handles child in sensitive fashion, almost always rough or insensitive (I). | Mother never differentiates states when child is receptive to social/educational interactions (I). | Family always depends on others to access community resources (I). | Mother follows training program steps with less than 60% accuracy (I). | Sibling almost always interferes with parent-child interactions (I). |

*Note.* W = weights, I = initial performance, A = attained performance. From "Family-Focused Intervention: A Functional Model for Planning, Implementing, and Evaluating Individualized Family Services in Early Intervention," 1986, by D. B. Bailey, R. J. Simeonsson, P. J. Winton, G. S. Huntington, M. Comfort, P. Isbell, K. J. O'Donnell, and J. M. Helm, 1986, *Journal of the Division for Early Childhood, 10,* 156–171. Copyright 1986 by *Journal of the Division for Early Childhood.* Reprinted with permission.

& Volkmor, 1981). Short-term objectives specify the expected behavior, the conditions under which the behavior should occur, the criterion for success, and the anticipated completion date (Strickland & Turnbull, 1990). The number of short-term objectives that are identified depends on several factors, including the number of annual goals, the complexity of the task to be learned, and the criteria established for success. Short-term objectives are written to project meaningful and realistic student accomplishment within a specified unit of time (e.g., a report card period, quarter, or semester). Examples of short-term objectives are shown on Arlene's Diagnostic Summary Sheet (see Table 5.2). A generic example of the relationship between an annual goal and a short-term objective (benchmark) can be seen in the following illustration:

▶ **Present Level of Performance (Determined September 1)**

- Sean can spell one-syllable words (consonant-vowel-consonant) correctly in isolation.

▶ **Annual Goal**

- Sean will spell two-syllable words correctly in isolation and context by June 1.

▶ **Short-Term Objectives (Benchmarks)**

- By November 30, Sean will spell (write) two-syllable words correctly in isolation.
- By March 31, Sean will spell (write) two-syllable words correctly in isolation and in context (with prompts).
- By June 10, Sean will spell (write) two-syllable words correctly in isolation and in context (without prompts).

## Materials/Approach

After conducting an assessment, the teacher must make a decision about the method, duration, and location of instruction; the materials that will be used; and the process that will be used during the instructional program. Since Arlene has difficulty with all basic reading skills, the teacher has elected to use a direct instruction approach. The general education classroom may be selected as the site for reading instruction because the student's IEP calls for her to participate in reading in this location.

Reisberg (1990) provides a format for materials and curriculum that includes an analysis of their scope and sequence, organization, presentation, guided practice, independent practice, and periodic review (see Figure 5.4). Consultants, in conjunction with teachers, could analyze programs for individual students, a class, or the district based on these criteria.

## Evaluation

Evaluation of all short-term objectives should be based on measurable performance levels. Cooper et al. (1987) recommend that continual or direct and daily measurement be employed in cases where systematic data collection is warranted. Reviewing short-term objectives on a periodic basis will help to ensure student progress. According to Sugai (1985):

> Short term objectives that have been mastered should be probed regularly and systematically to evaluate how well their achievement has been

# Material Evaluation Form

Name of curriculum or material _____

_____

Copyright date _____ Publisher _____
Area of instruction _____
Intended audience (age and/or grade) _____
Date of evaluation _____
Evaluator _____

Rate each of the questions with the following scale:
1. Material meets the intent of the statement.
2. Material would be appropriate with modifications.
3. Material does not meet the intent of the statement, and alternative materials should be found.

|  | Ratings | | | Comments |
|---|---|---|---|---|
| **I. Scope and Sequence** | | | | |
| 1. The declarative knowledge included in this material is appropriate for the students. | 1 | 2 | 3 | |
| 2. The procedural knowledge included in this material is appropriate for the students. | 1 | 2 | 3 | |
| 3. The stated objectives taught in the program seem to be sequenced correctly. | 1 | 2 | 3 | |
| 4. The material includes all objectives necessary for the mastery of the content. | 1 | 2 | 3 | |
| 5. The material includes objectives focusing on higher-order skills (application and generalization). | 1 | 2 | 3 | |
| **II. Organization** | | | | |
| 1. Data-based evaluation | | | | |
| A. The material includes pre- and posttests. | 1 | 2 | 3 | |
| B. Criteria for mastery levels are clearly noted, including acquisition, proficiency, and automaticity. | 1 | 2 | 3 | |
| C. Suggestions for branching and acceleration are included. | 1 | 2 | 3 | |
| 2. Appropriate time lines and pacing | | | | |
| A. Time alloted for each lesson is appropriate. | 1 | 2 | 3 | |
| B. Pacing for each objective is appropriate for students. | 1 | 2 | 3 | |
| 3. Input and output requirements are appropriate. | 1 | 2 | 3 | |
| **III. Presentation** | | | | |
| 1. Lessons begin with a daily review. | 1 | 2 | 3 | |
| 2. The objective for each lesson is clearly presented to the students. | 1 | 2 | 3 | |
| 3. An overview of the lesson and activities is presented. | 1 | 2 | 3 | |
| 4. The presentation follows a clear format. | 1 | 2 | 3 | |
| 5. Student attention and interest is maintained. | 1 | 2 | 3 | |
| 6. Skills are modeled for students. | 1 | 2 | 3 | |
| 7. Instruction progresses from concrete to abstract examples. | 1 | 2 | 3 | |
| 8. Frequent and varied questions are posed. | 1 | 2 | 3 | |
| 9. Clear correction procedures are described. | 1 | 2 | 3 | |
| 10. Presentation is at appropriate instructional level. | 1 | 2 | 3 | |
| **IV. Guided Practice** | | | | |
| 1. Provides sufficient practice opportunities. | 1 | 2 | 3 | |
| 2. Sets mastery levels at the proficiency level. | 1 | 2 | 3 | |
| **V. Independent Practice** | | | | |
| 1. Includes active seatwork practice. | 1 | 2 | 3 | |
| 2. Sets mastery at the automatic stage. | 1 | 2 | 3 | |
| 3. Focuses on generalization. | 1 | 2 | 3 | |
| **VI. Periodic Review** | | | | |
| 1. Presents skill in both familiar and novel situations. | 1 | 2 | 3 | |

**Figure 5.4.** Form used in evaluating and adapting curriculum materials. From "Curriculum Evaluation and Modification: An Effective Teaching Perspective," by L. Reisberg, 1990, *Intervention in School and Clinic*, 26(2), 101. Copyright 1990 by PRO-ED, Inc. Reprinted with permission.

maintained and generalized. . . . The teacher should identify the conditions under which the behavior is to be demonstrated by the student and the criterion level at which the behavior is to occur. When an objective is mastered, the date of completion is noted. (p. 235)

## Planning the Individualized Education Program

According to McDaniels (1980), the IEP serves six important functions. First, it is a communication vehicle for the parents and the school. Each party helps to write the IEP, and each understands the needs of the child and the goals of the program. Second, the IEP serves as the basis for resolving conflicts between the parents' desires for programs and the school's wish to serve the child. Third, resources are allocated based on the prescription in the IEP. Fourth, the IEP is a management tool for teachers; it enables them to provide appropriate education and related services. Fifth, the IEP is a compliance and monitoring document. It allows parents, schools, and government agencies to determine whether the child is receiving the appropriate service. Finally, the IEP can serve as an evaluation device to determine student progress, although teachers are not held accountable if IEP annual goals or short-term objectives are not reached by prescribed time lines.

The first three and the sixth functions of the IEP listed above are important for the consultant to stress to special and general education teachers (Polloway, Patton, Payne, & Payne, 1989). However, the consultant must also emphasize to teachers that parents must be active members of the process. Swick, Flake-Hobson, and Raymond (1980) state that the key element in the IEP conference is parent participation:

> Parents must have the opportunity to contribute their unique perspective of the child at home. To achieve a successful conference, teachers and specialists must communicate clearly and effectively with parents and make them feel that they are important members of the team. Information shared by teachers can be threatening, anxiety producing, or intimidating to parents if it is not presented in the proper atmosphere. If parents are uneasy or overwhelmed by the conference they may not be willing or able to share important information about their child. (p. 144)

Too often, parents attend an IEP meeting only to find the document has already been completely prepared without them. Either directly or indirectly they get the message that the educators have decided on the best course of action and parental input is not needed. Anecdote 5.1 is an example of how a consultant helped a special education high school teacher plan how to include parents in developing an IEP for a student named Fred.

### Anecdote 5.1

CONSULTANT: I understand that you'll be meeting with the Wilson family next week to discuss Fred's IEP.

TEACHER: That's correct. I was hoping that you might be able to give me some suggestions on the best way to approach the parents with the IEP goals.

CONSULTANT:  I'd be glad to help. Let's start by reviewing Fred's progress.

TEACHER:  (handing the Diagnostic Summary Sheet to the consultant): I've already begun to list what I believe are appropriate long-term goals and short-term objectives, as well as the instructional approach and materials I'd like to use.

CONSULTANT:  Good.

TEACHER:  I don't want to complete the entire IEP document, because I'm afraid the parents might feel that I don't want their suggestions.

CONSULTANT:  I couldn't agree with you more. Maybe we could outline the program, the services to be rendered, and their duration on the IEP for the parents. Put it in the mail along with a short cover letter explaining the draft so that they can review it before the meeting. Any changes that the parents recommend could be added, and if they felt strongly that any of our plans were inappropriate, we'd be able to discuss our reasoning.

TEACHER:  That sounds fine.

CONSULTANT:  I'd like to suggest that the annual goals and short-term objectives we list for Fred be written so that the emphasis is on application of skills and concepts in real-life situations. I think the parents would appreciate the career education emphasis and goals that will lead to better survival skills for Fred.

TEACHER:  I hadn't thought of that. We have units on careers, community living, and leisure, but I've never written them directly into an IEP.

CONSULTANT:  It's certainly something to consider, especially in Fred's case. He'll be graduating from high school this year, and it will be important for him to be able to apply the skills you are teaching to many situations. A career education emphasis might increase his chances of getting a job.

TEACHER:  What happens if the parents refuse to sign the IEP?

CONSULTANT:  You've raised a good question. The parents are not obligated to sign the IEP. Many do, of course, but there is no rule that says they must. What is required is that both parties—parents and educators—agree on the most appropriate program. Hopefully, if both parties are prepared for the meeting, we'll be able to reach consensus. We inform the parents that they'll receive a copy of the IEP for their records.

TEACHER:  Thanks so much for your help.

CONSULTANT:  I'll try to attend the meeting, but sometimes too many professionals at the IEP meeting inhibit communication. If you have any questions before or after the meeting, please feel free to give me a call. Remember, it's important for the parents to have the opportunity to express their views. Let them talk.

TEACHER:  I'll do that. Thanks again.

In this anecdote the consultant provided three key recommendations that should greatly enhance the productivity of the conference team and strengthen Fred's performance after the conference as well. First, the consultant suggested that a working draft of the IEP be mailed to the parents so that they would be better prepared to discuss Fred's program at the conference. Some school districts provide this service, and according to anecdotal information, parents are responsive to this approach. Second, the consultant suggested that the annual goals and short-term objectives for Fred be written with a career education focus. Given Fred's impending graduation, it was critical that he have an opportunity to practice the survival skills he would need after leaving school. Finally, the consultant reminded the teacher to give the parents an opportunity to talk. Goldstein, Strickland, Turnbull, and Curry (1980) indicate that the two most frequent speakers at IEP conferences are the resource room teacher and the parent. However, resource room teachers speak twice as often as parents. Parents must be given every opportunity to discuss their concerns, especially as they relate to placement, curriculum, and instructional method (Hammill & Bartel, 1990). The consultant can encourage parents whose verbal participation is low to express themselves by carefully constructing questions that seek additional information or allow them to expand upon previous remarks.

## Monitoring and Evaluating the IEP

Consultants can provide a great deal of assistance to teachers and parents by helping to monitor and evaluate the IEP. According to Strickland and Turnbull (1990), the monitoring process can include an evaluation of whether the goals and objectives are being met and the timetable for their completion. Lynch and Beare (1990) suggest monitoring IEPs to determine the generality, functionality, and age-appropriateness of the document and whether the goals and objectives are actually being addressed in the curriculum. Margolis (1994) recommends that monitoring can be accomplished successfully when objectives are measurable, scheduled meetings are held periodically to review data, objective and impartial experts participate in classroom observations, and frequent communication occurs between teachers, parents, and students.

Safer and Hobbs (1980) indicate that the majority of IEPs contain criteria for determining the accomplishment of goals and/or short-term objectives. Typically, the criteria refer to performance measures on standardized, criterion-referenced, or classroom-designed instruments.

Howell and McCollum-Gahley (1986), for instance, documented a 5-step curriculum-based measurement (CBM) system for monitoring student progress. The steps are: selecting the short-term objective, developing a measurement procedure, setting a performance level criterion, initiating instruction and plotting progress, and reviewing achievement and adjusting the curriculum. Figure 5.5 shows a performance and progress aim chart. The dots represent rate performance, and the diagonal line shows the expected (predicted) progress, given current performance. Point A represents the aim point and expected date of completion. As long as student progress maintains a positive ascending trend along the line, the method of instruction and/or materials can be continued. If progress fails to match the expected rate of acquisition, a change in instructional programming would be warranted.

Maher and Barbrack (1980) formalized the monitoring and evaluation process for the IEP (Table 5.8). Their system, termed a Framework for Comprehensive Evaluation of the Individualized Education Program, is designed to

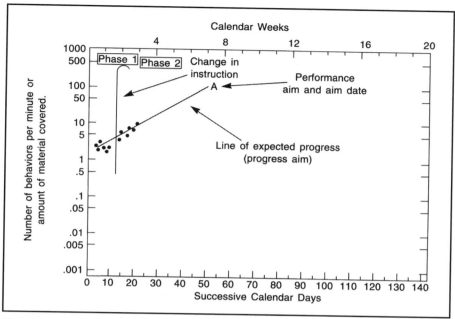

**Figure 5.5.** Performance and progress aim chart. From "Monitoring Instruction," by K. W. Howell & J. McCollum-Gahley, 1986, *Teaching Exceptional Children, 19*(1), 47. Copyright 1986 by The Council for Exceptional Children. Reprinted with permission.

### Table 5.8
#### A Framework for Comprehensive Evaluation of the Individualized Education Program

| Evaluation Strategy | Area of Evaluation | Evaluation Issue | Decision Maker |
|---|---|---|---|
| Evaluability Assessment | Program Design | Program Evaluability | Planners |
| Process Evaluation | Program Implementation | Program Operations | Implementers |
| Outcome Evaluation | Pupil Progress | Goal Attainment | Planners and Implementers |
| Consumer Evaluation | Program Satisfaction | Program Utility | Planners |

*Note.* From "A Framework for Comprehensive Evaluation of the Individualized Education Program (IEP)," by C. A. Maher and C. R. Barbrack, 1980, *Learning Disabilities Quarterly, 3*(3), 50. Copyright 1980 by *Learning Disabilities Quarterly*. Reprinted with permission.

ensure that all aspects of the IEP or IFSP (e.g., student outcomes, consumer satisfaction, concurrence with legislative rules) are evaluated. As a global source for evaluating all aspects of the IEP or IFSP, the framework is helpful because it encompasses all of the critical variables required for compliance with legal statutes.

At a more specific level, however, consultants can help teachers determine on a day-to-day or month-to-month basis whether IEP objectives are being met. Sugai (1985) proposed the Daily Monitoring Sheet as one method to monitor student progress on IEP objectives (see Figure 5.6). For instance, the chart

| | Student Name | *J. Caesar* |
| | Teacher Name | *Ms. Augustus* |

**Daily Monitoring Sheet**

| Date | Obj. # | Plan/Schedule | Behavior | Condition | Criteria | Data | Comments |
|---|---|---|---|---|---|---|---|
| 2/17 | 1.1 | Meet with Ms. Patrick and J. to discuss J.'s progress in her classroom | Raise hand. | When teacher asks a question. | 75% 2 consecutive days 4/5 classes | 80–83% 4/5 classes | "*Good* job in Ms. Patrick's class. Your objective was *met!*" |
| 2/18 | 1.1 | Phone J.'s parents and discuss fading of tokens and pairing more verbal praise and home activity reinforcers. | Raise hand. | When teacher asks a question. | 75% 1 day 4/5 classes | 85–87% 5/5 classes | "Another *great* day. Objective *met* again!" |
| 2/19 | 1.1 | Observe in Ms. Patrick's classroom. | Raise hand. | When teacher asks a question. | 85% 4 consecutive days 5/5 classes | 86–88% 4/5 classes | "Almost did it today. Try again tomorrow." |
| 2/22 | 1.1 | Meet with J. at 8:30 A.M. Go over progress thus far. Discuss Ms. Patrick's question-asking strategies and J.'s answering behaviors. | Raise hand. | When teacher asks a question. | 85% 4 consecutive days 5/5 classes | | |

**Figure 5.6.** Daily Monitoring Sheet. From "Case Study: Designing Instruction from IEPs," by G. Sugai, 1985, *Teaching Exceptional Children*, 17(3), 237. Copyright 1985 by The Council for Exceptional Children. Reprinted with permission.

shows the date on which individual objectives were addressed, a description of the teacher's activity, a description of the desired response, the conditions under which the behavior is to occur, and the criterion for success. The chart also provides space for recording actual student performance and anecdotal comments.

According to Sugai (1985), "The Daily Monitoring Sheet serves as the lesson plan. When maintained on a daily basis by the resource room teacher, it functions as a dynamic record of the student's progress toward the completion of short-term objectives and as a systematic structure for sequencing instructional activities" (p. 236).

Monitoring need not be a labor-intensive proposition. Useful data can be obtained in as little as 1-minute probes, and students can be responsible for charting their own work, thus relieving the teacher of that task. Potter and Wamre (1990) reassure teachers of the beneficial effects of such probes with respect to reading:

> Considering the complexity of a skill like reading, it does seem somewhat contrary to logic that a task as simple as having the student read for 1 min from a classroom text can provide much information about that student's ability to read. Our sense is that skepticism about CBM is not overcome until teachers use it with students for a reasonable period of time and see for themselves that this measure or oral reading fluency really does give them a good sense of students' general reading skills. (p. 17)

Price and Goodman (1980) suggest that another important area to consider when evaluating IEPs is the cost. According to these authors, the average amount of time required to prepare an IEP for an exceptional student was 6.5 hours (4.5 hours at school, 2.0 hours personal time). Data such as these can be useful for the consultant because excessive amounts of time expended to prepare the IEP may mean: (a) less direct instruction will be provided to students; (b) inservice training may be needed for staff on procedures for developing IEPs; and (c) district resources may need to be reallocated during peak IEP development times (e.g., fall and spring quarters). By gathering these data a consultant would be able to address IEP preparation needs that otherwise might go unnoticed.

## Generality and Maintenance of Skills

Another way a consultant can help after the IEP conference is to consult with the inclusion teacher on effective ways to promote generality and maintenance of the student's skills. This is an important task, because the student needs to use the academic or social behavior learned in the classroom in other areas or settings.

Since many learners with disabilities need specially designed materials and have to function in a variety of home and school settings, it is imperative that built-in instructional strategies for promoting generality and maintenance be in place. The consultant can help to increase the general educator's awareness that generality and maintenance can be part of the overall plan. The first step toward increasing a teacher's awareness is to let him or her know that generality can be considered in two ways: stimulus generality and response generality.

### Stimulus Generality

According to Cooper et al. (1987), *stimulus generality* occurs "when a target behavior is emitted in the presence of stimulus conditions other than those in which it was directly trained. . . . The setting in which stimulus generality is desired can contain some components of the behavior change program that was implemented in the training environment, but not all of the components. If the complete program is required to produce behavior change in a different environment, then no stimulus generality can be claimed" (p. 556).

Consultants working with preschool teachers would find the study conducted by Ducharme and Holborn (1997) a practical illustration of how stimulus generality can be assessed as part of an overall social skills training program. In their study, the effects of a social skills training program on the social interaction behaviors of 5 preschool children with hearing impairment were assessed. While the training setting was a special class for children with hearing impairment, the generality setting resembled an inclusive environment insofar as children with normal hearing and social and behavioral skills were present. The social skills targeted for improvement included sharing and cooperating, play organizing, and assisting. During Treatment 1, explicit training in social skills occurred through modeling, instruction, prompting, and reinforcement. An implicit component during Treatment 1 included play coupled with teacher prompts and reinforcement. During Treatment 2, Treatment 1 conditions plus generalization programming occurred. That is, new teachers, peers, and materials were introduced, thereby changing the environment to resemble a more typical preschool setting. Furthermore, the schedule of reinforcement (teacher praise) was thinned considerably.

The data for the 5th student, not reported on Figure 5.7, match the data path for "Tony."

Figure 5.7 shows the results of the multiple baseline design for 4 of the 5 students. The data show an immediate and dramatic effect of Treatment 1 on the percentage of social skills emitted by the students. However, little evidence of generalization occurred during this phase (see open circles). When Treatment 2 was initiated, in which generalization was more specifically programmed, capitalizing on the natural reinforcers and new exemplars in the classroom, generalization was boosted. The authors attributed the marked generalization to the use of multiple exemplars in the generality setting (new teachers, peers, and materials, respectively).

Ducharme and Holborn's (1997) study is important for consultants because it underscores the point that simulated training, delivered by the classroom teacher as part of the instructional program, may not be sufficient to produce generalized behavior. Specific and planned generalization programming in a natural setting may also be needed if lasting behavior change is to take place. Consultants working with teachers and parents are encouraged to work jointly with these agents to assess the effects of training in nontrained settings.

## Response Generality

Cooper et al. (1987) define *response generality* as "the extent to which the learner performs a variety of functional responses in addition to the trained response; that is, responses for which no specific contingencies have been applied are altered as a function of the contingencies applied to other responses" (p. 558). For example, suppose a teacher as part of an art project taught students how to shoot photographs with a 35mm camera at a fixed distance using fixed settings. Each clear image obtained by the students produced teacher praise (e.g., "Christine, that's a clear photo with nice sharp edges"). If Christine then produced clear pictures at varying distances and settings without specific training, then response generality would have occurred. Cooper et al. summarize the key point for consultants who are helping other practitioners reinforce new forms of a behavior: "Reinforcing a few members of the response clues of

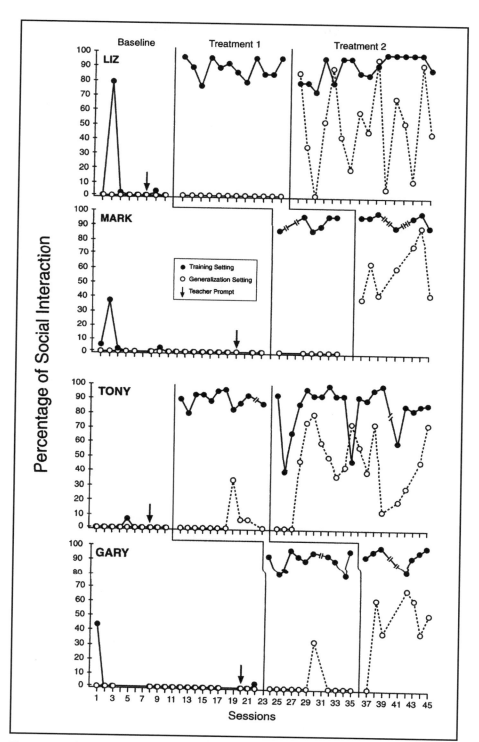

**Figure 5.7.** Percentage of social interactions in training and generalization settings for Liz, Mark, Tony, and Gary across experimental phases. From "Programming generalization of social skills in preschool children with hearing impairments," by D. E. Ducharme and S. W. Holborn (1997) in *Journal of Applied Behavior Analysis, 30*(4), 639–651. Copyright 1997 by the Society for the Experimental Analysis of Behavior, Inc. Reprinted with permission.

new forms *resulted* in other members of the class being strengthened as well" (p. 560, italics added).

## Maintenance

*Maintenance* of behavior change means that the individual continues to perform the desired behavior after training has terminated. According to Koegel and Rincover (1977), for maintenance to occur it has to be programmed into the intervention by thinning the schedule of reinforcement of desirable responses and occasionally delivering noncontingent reinforcement.

Baer (1989) provides several suggestions for programming maintenance into the intervention. For example, she recommends that administrators receive more direct training on management issues so that they can (a) model these skills to teachers, and (b) organize systematic programs across the school. Second, programs that are likely to be maintained are relatively easy to learn by staff and not prohibitively expensive. Third, if key personnel are necessary for the program to work, then a systematic plan must be developed to transition to other personnel before the key person leaves. Finally, practical and logistical obstacles must be overcome (e.g., having maintenance data collected on a periodic basis).

Minner, Minner, and Lepich (1990) concede that maintaining substantial amounts of data on student performance can be an overwhelming task for teachers. However, they also assert that teachers who collect periodic data on student performance, and who make instructional decisions based on student performance with curriculum-based measures, are more effective. While data can be obtained through charting, audio or videotapes, or student self-recording, Minner et al. have used a 3-step process that provides a useful alternative for teachers. Essentially the steps are: (a) determining the number of short-term objectives for each student in the program, (b) duplicating that number of data maintenance sheets (Figure 5.8), and (c) recording each student's progress toward that goal on a sheet. The data can be transposed to a graph that immediately shows the trend in the student's performance (see Figure 5.9). Minner et al. suggest that teachers begin the process by charting and recording one objective per student. Consultants can assist with modifying the form to meet individual student needs and evaluating the effects of instruction.

## Promoting Generality of Behavior Change

Cooper et al. (1987) cite several steps and strategies that can be used to improve the likelihood of generality of behavior change. The strategies are divided into two major categories—planning and implementing—and draw on the often cited work of Stokes and Baer (1977).

### Planning

As part of any behavior change program, consultants should work with teachers and parents to plan for generality of behavior change. Three questions should be asked at this phase: What are the behaviors to change? In what environments should the new behaviors occur? What will be required of practitioners in those environments to support and maintain performance?

To illustrate, these questions might be addressed when planning for generality of behavior change with a student with learning disabilities who is engaged

1.  Student: _Greg Prater_
2.  Teacher: Allan Beane—LD Specialist
3.  Data collected   From: _9-12-90_    To: _12-18-90_
4.  Annual Goal: _To improve social interactions with peers_
5.  Short-Term Objective: _During free time periods in the resource room_ _Greg will engage in zero aggressive acts (kicking, hitting)._
6.  Method of Data Maintenance (check all that apply)

    work samples: _____

    audiotapes: _____

    videotapes: _____

    frequency recording: ___X___

    duration recording: _____

    interval recording: _____

    time-sampling: _____

    other (specify): _____
7.  Date Objective Met: _12-18-90_
8.  Notes: _first intervention began on 9-26; intervention_ _consisted of a verbal reminder at beginning of period_ _and frequent praise for appropriate behavior._

### SUMMARY OF STUDENT'S PERFORMANCE

| Date | Performance | Notes | Date | Performance | Notes |
|------|-------------|-------|------|-------------|-------|
| 9-14 | 6 acts | — | | | |
| 9-18 | 8 acts | — | | | |
| 9-21 | 7 acts | — | | | |
| 9-26 | 3 acts | started 1st intervention | | | |
| 10-11 | 3 acts | | | | |
| 10-17 | 2 acts | | | | |
| 10-24 | 1 act | | | | |
| 11-8 | 1 act | | | | |
| 11-15 | 1 act | | | | |
| 11-20 | 1 act | | | | |
| 11-29 | 2 acts | | | | |
| 12-6 | 1 act | | | | |
| 12-13 | 1 act | | | | |
| 12-18 | 0 acts | | | | |
| 12-20 | 0 acts | follow-up | | | |

**Figure 5.8.** Daily maintenance sheet. From "Maintaining Pupil Performance Data: A Guide" by S. Minner, J. Minner, and J. Lepich, 1990, in *Intervention in School and Clinic,* 26(1), 34. Reprinted with permission.

in a work study program. Consultants and teachers might begin by focusing on all behaviors (academic and social) that are likely to be required in both settings (i.e., school and work). Further, an examination of both settings should be conducted to determine if the trained behavior would have to be evident

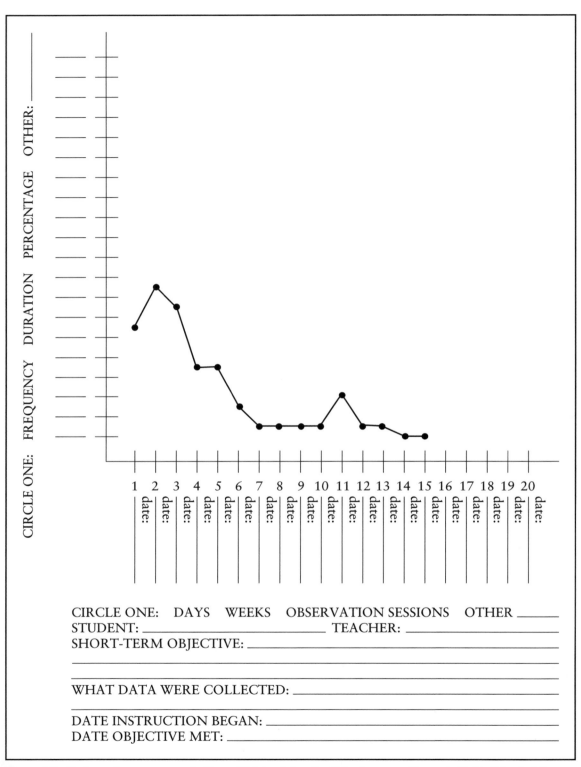

**Figure 5.9.** Daily maintenance graph. From "Maintaining Pupil Performance Data: A Guide," by S. Minner, J. Minner, and J. Lepich, 1990, *Intervention in School and Clinic, 26*(1), 35. Copyright 1990 by PRO-ED, Inc. Reprinted with permission.

within the same setting but in a different location. For instance, would the behavior need to be evident at school, in the classroom, hallway, cafeteria, or gymnasium? Finally, all personnel in the school and on the job site who might come into contact with the student should be aware of, and actively support, the desired behavior change. The more people who can respond to the student with an appropriate consequence (e.g., feedback or reinforcement), the more likely it is that generality will occur.

Vaughn, Bos, and Lund (1986) provide an illustration of a generalization plan/record that shows how a teacher planned a lesson on place value with 2-digit numbers across four instructional environments with three different teachers. Note that the materials, directions, criteria, reinforcers, and performance standards are specified (see Figure 5.10).

## Implementing

Stokes and Baer (1977) and Cooper et al. (1987) list six strategies for promoting generality of behavior change. While it might be impossible for the consultant to set the occasion for all six of these strategies to be used in any given situation, the more of them that can be introduced, the more likely it is that generality will occur.

*Aim for the Natural Contingencies of Reinforcement.* Using the natural contingencies of reinforcement means that events that might occur in any setting can be used to reinforce behavior. Events like teacher recognition, parental praise, or peer acceptance are consequences that qualify as natural contingencies of reinforcement. Teachers might have to provide extra training to students to prime these natural contingencies. For instance, a student might have to be taught to show his preoccupied father how well he did on his math paper so that his father can deliver an appropriate comment.

> Recall that in the Ducharme and Holborn (1997) study, a plethora of teachers, peers, and materials were introduced, and the schedule of reinforcement was thinned systematically.

*Teach Enough Examples.* A common mistake that teachers and parents make is to teach a skill using only one or two examples and expect the behavior to change over time, settings, and situations. While some authors have shown that generality of behavior change can be produced with as few as two examples (cf. Stokes, Baer, & Jackson, 1974), the more likely scenario for ensuring that generality takes place is to provide a sufficient subset of important stimuli and response examples. But how many examples are enough? Cooper et al. (1987) provide a disclaimer:

> The number of examples that must be taught before significant generality occurs varies considerably. It is a function of such variables as the target behavior(s) being taught, the instructional procedures employed, the subject's opportunities to emit the target behavior under various conditions, the existing natural contingencies of reinforcement, and the learner's history of reinforcement with regard to generality. (p. 572)

*Program Common Stimuli.* Several stimuli are common across special and general education settings. Consultants working with teachers in inclusive classrooms would be advised to focus on skill building, the time and length of instruction, and the type of reinforcement so as to enhance the likelihood of a successful transition.

With respect to skill building, for example, assume that a student with learning disabilities could perform 2-digit by 2-digit multiplication with regrouping and the teacher wanted to extend the skill to 3-digit by 3-digit multiplication.

**Name:** _Gerald General_

**Task:** _Place value with two-digit numbers_

**Targeted Strategies:** _Change teachers, settings, materials, cues, and reinforcer(s)_

| Date | Teaching Situations | Instructor | Setting | Materials | Directions/Cues | Criteria | Reinforcer(s) | Performance |
|---|---|---|---|---|---|---|---|---|
| 10-6 | 1 | Resource teacher | One to one at small table in corner of resource room | Cuisenaire—"Powers of Ten" blocks with 1's, 10's, 100 chart | "Use the blocks to make the number chart." | Given 10 two-place numbers, Jerry will complete task with 90% accuracy. | Teacher gives verbal praise at the end of each item. Jerry marks number of problems correct on bar graph | Eight out of ten problems correct. Jerry had difficulty with 97 and 92. |
| 10-10 | 2 | Teacher aide | Small group at horseshoe table in resource room | Same | "Show me the number ____ with your blocks." | Same | Same | Nine out of ten problems correct. Jerry is working well with small group. |
| 10-11 | 3 | Resource teacher | Independent seat-work—resource room | Ditto sheet of place Value problems | "Work these problems here." "Raise your hand if you need help." | 85% accuracy with 20 problems | Teacher gives praise as Jerry completes entire assignment. | Seventeen out of twenty problems correct. Jerry asked for teacher help to get started. |
| 10-17 | 4 | Phase into second-grade math class for mainstreaming—Regular class teacher | Large group instruction—regular classroom | Math workbook place value page of 20 problems | "Open your math workbook and do the problems on page 42." | 80% accuracy | Teacher gives intermittent verbal praise. | Sixteen out of twenty problems correct. Jerry had to be reminded to get to work. |

**Figure 5.10.** Generalization plan/record. From "But They Can Do It in My Room: Strategies for Promoting Generalization," by S. Vaughn, C. S. Bos, & K. A. Lund, 1986, _Teaching Exceptional Children, 18_(3), 179. Copyright 1986 by The Council for Exceptional Children. Reprinted with permission.

The teacher, by focusing on the elements common to each problem (arranging the numbers according to place value and correctly multiplying and adding the columns), would be training the student for a higher-order skill using a specific response generalization approach.

Likewise, general education teachers who have students with disabilities in their classrooms would be wise to consider several variables common to each setting that may affect the success of the program. For example, one of the most useful pieces of information a student needs is the classroom rules (i.e., what is permitted and what the consequences are for rule infraction). Often students with disabilities break rules and suffer the consequences because the rules were not explained clearly or were not well understood.

The consultant can assist the teacher with becoming aware of the type and complexity of instructional materials that are used in the general education class. Matching the materials that the student used in the special education class with those used in the inclusive class with respect to interest, readability, level of difficulty, and skills to be learned is likely to improve generality.

Two other factors that can be equated across settings are the time and length of instruction and the type of responses that students make (active versus passive). Many youngsters with disabilities have short attention spans and require their instruction in small doses over longer time periods. Also, some students with disabilities perform much better in the morning than they do in the afternoon. In such a case, heavy academic instruction should probably be scheduled in the morning rather than later in the day. Further, the data are clear and compelling that when students make active responses (actually say the response rather than just attending to a model), performance improves (Sterling, Barbetta, Heward, & Heron, 1997).

A final factor to promote generality is the type of reinforcement the student receives. For example, if an adolescent with developmental disabilities receives points at school for appropriate behavior, a similar system could be established at home. If verbal praise is given in the special class for appropriate behavior, then verbal praise should be included as one method of reinforcing appropriate responses in the inclusive classroom.

*Train Loosely.* To train loosely means that a wide variety of stimuli should be present at the time of training so that no one stimulus or format of instruction gains exclusive control over the behavior. The use of multiple teachers, multiple locations for lessons, multiple types of examples, and variable noise and light levels are examples of how to train loosely (cf. Ducharme & Holborn, 1997).

*Use Indiscriminable Contingencies.* Essentially, the consultant who recommends indiscriminable contingencies would advocate the use of *intermittent schedules of reinforcement* or delayed reinforcement. Intermittent schedules of reinforcement fall between continuous reinforcement (all responses produce reinforcement) and extinction (no response produces reinforcement). With either of these two contingencies (all or none), behaviors originally acquired under continuous reinforcement are more likely to occur when reinforcement is no longer available for each response. Reinforcing student performance on an intermittent schedule is more advantageous to the teacher if stimulus or response generality is desired.

A consultant working with a classroom teacher in an inclusive setting should, at the least, increase the teacher's awareness of four intermittent schedules of reinforcement that can benefit the student as he or she advances from one skill or one setting to another. The first two schedules (fixed interval and variable interval) are time related. That is, reinforcement is issued for a response after a given time period has passed. The second two schedules (fixed ratio and variable ratio) are response related. That is, the student has to perform the desired behaviors to earn reinforcement.

*Fixed Interval.* A fixed-interval (FI) schedule of reinforcement is said to be in effect when the first correct response following a specific time period is reinforced (Cooper et al., 1987). For instance, a student with physical disabilities who is reinforced on a fixed-interval schedule of 3 minutes (FI 3) for appropriate object sorting would receive reinforcement for the first appropriate object-sorting behavior he or she completed following the 3-minute time frame. If the behavior did not occur immediately after the 3 minutes, reinforcement would be withheld until it did.

While there are a few advantages the consultant could cite to the teacher interested in this schedule (e.g., it might be easier logistically), there are several distinct disadvantages the consultant needs to point out. First, the schedule may become too predictable. Students may figure out when reinforcement is likely to occur and work only at that time. Second, because the schedule may be predictable, little work may be evident soon after reinforcement has occurred. This characteristic pause tends to produce a curve, referred to as a "scallop," which shows little or no work soon after reinforcement but steady increases in performance toward the end of the interval. Finally, the student can make a great many errors during the interval for which no corrective feedback is obtained. If a student with behavioral disorders were on a fixed interval of 20 minutes (FI 20) for appropriate social behavior, not only would the teacher have to wait at least 20 minutes to deliver reinforcement, but inappropriate social behavior might go undetected during the 20-minute interval. In effect, the student might practice inappropriate behavior and receive reinforcement (perhaps from a peer in the form of attention) and completely compromise the system.

Consultants should recommend FI schedules to inclusive teachers with the proviso that the intervals be short. Increases in the time of the interval should be extended as the student's behavior improves.

*Variable Interval.* When a variable-interval (VI) schedule is used, reinforcement is delivered for the first correct response following the passage of a varying amount of time (Cooper et al., 1987). For example, a student with learning disabilities in a self-contained classroom who is on a VI 10 schedule for assignment completion would receive reinforcement for the first correct or appropriate response that occurred following the passage of 10 minutes *on average*. The student might be reinforced after 2 minutes, 6 minutes, 20 minutes, or 12 minutes—as long as he or she performed the desired response after the passage of that time limit and the intervals averaged 10 minutes.

The striking advantage of a VI schedule over a FI schedule is that it is unpredictable. Reinforcement can occur at any time—varying around a specific average amount of time—and the behavior targeted for change is more likely to be sustained during the interval. This is in contrast to the FI schedule, where the target behavior may not be as evident during the entire interval, only at the end of the interval.

*Fixed Ratio.* A fixed-ratio (FR) schedule simply requires the student to perform a set number of responses before reinforcement is delivered (Cooper et al., 1987). For instance, a student with behavioral disabilities on an FR 14 for math would have to complete 14 math calculation problems before reinforcement would be delivered; on an FR 27, the student would have to do 27 problems before earning reinforcement.

One advantage of FR schedules that the consultant can indicate to the inclusive teacher is that they are used in many classes. It is common to hear a teacher say, "When you are finished with your math worksheet, you can have free time." For the student who is likely to be included in the general education classroom, the consultant might recommend that an FR schedule be introduced with low response requirements (e.g., FR 5), which could be later expanded to more closely match the response requirements of the inclusion classroom (e.g., FR 30).

*Variable Ratio.* A variable-ratio (VR) or "gambler's" schedule provides reinforcement for a varying number of responses (Cooper et al., 1987). The number of responses required to earn reinforcement varies around a specific average. For instance, a student with speech and language disabilities who is operating under a VR 7 schedule for verbal initiations in an inclusion class would receive reinforcement following an average of 7 participatory responses. Since the student is just as likely to earn reinforcement after 1 response as he or she is after 7 or 10 or 100, very high rates of responding occur.

One distinct advantage of the VR schedule is its unpredictability. Students might emit a large number of responses anticipating that the very next response will be reinforced. The primary reason for suggesting this schedule is that reinforcement occurs at unpredictable times in the inclusion classroom, and if the student is already operating under a VR schedule (say in a resource room), it is less likely that appropriate behavior learned in the resource room will be extinguished in the inclusive setting. More important, generality and maintenance will be enhanced.

**Teach Self-Management.** If self-management skills are taught to individuals, the cue or prompt to occasion a behavior resides with that person. Also, when different stimulus conditions are present, or when different responses are required, a person who has an available cue to use is more likely to emit the appropriate, generalized behavior.

See Chapter 12 for a more complete discussion of self-management and self-monitoring.

According to Cooper et al. (1987), self-management can be taught to students in 5 steps: (a) selection and definition of behaviors to change; (b) self-observation and recording of the behavior; (c) specification of the behavior change procedure; (d) implementation; and (e) evaluation. Cooper et al. provide a thorough description of how to design, implement, and evaluate self-management programs.

Several educators emphasize the importance of programming for generality of behavior change (Colvin & Lazar, 1997; Kerr & Nelson, 1998; Walker & Shea, 1999; Zirpoli & Melloy, 1997). Vaughn et al. (1986) underscore the importance of generalization programming, and they provide consultants with a method-example matrix that illustrates how to program for generalization across reinforcement, prompt, materials, response set, stimulus, setting, and teacher changes (see Figure 5.11).

# Conclusion

Consultants who work with teachers in self-contained classrooms often have to extend their services in two directions. First, they must be able to assist the self-contained teacher with tasks that are required to meet the instructional

## Change Reinforcement

| Description/Methods | Examples |
|---|---|
| Vary amount, power, and type of reinforcers. | |
| • Fade amount of reinforcement. | • Reduce frequency of reinforcement from completion of each assignment to completion of day's assignments. |
| • Decrease power of reinforcer from tangible reinforcers to verbal praise. | • Limit use of stars/stickers and add more specific statements, e.g., "Hey, you did a really good job in your math book today." |
| • Increase power of reinforcer when changing to mainstreamed setting. | • Give points in regular classroom although not needed in resource room. |
| • Use same reinforcers in different settings. | • Encourage all teachers working with students to use the same reinforcement program. |

## Change Cues

| Description/Methods | Examples |
|---|---|
| Vary instructions systematically. | |
| • Use alternate/parallel directions. | • Use variations of cue, e.g., "Find the . . ."; "Give me the . . ."; "Point to the . . . ." |
| • Change Directions. | • Change length and vocabulary of directions to better represent the directions given in the regular classroom, e.g., "Open your book to page 42 and do the problems in set A." |
| | • Move from real objects to miniature objects. |
| • Use photograph. | • Use actual photograph of object or situation. |
| • Use picture to represent object. | • Move from object/photograph to picture of object or situation. |
| • Use line drawing or symbol representation. | • Use drawings from workbooks to represent objects or situations. |
| • Use varying print forms. | • Vary lower- and upper-case letters; vary print by using manuscript, boldface, primary type. |
| | • Move from manuscript to cursive. |

## Change Materials

| Description/Methods | Examples |
|---|---|
| Vary materials within task. | |
| • Change medium. | • Use unlined paper, lined paper; change size of lines; change color of paper. |
| | • Use various writing instruments such as markers, pencil, pen, typewriter. |
| • Change media. | • Use materials such as films, microcomputers, filmstrips to present skills/concepts. |
| | • Provide opportunity for student to phase into mainstream. |

## Change Response Set

| Description/Methods | Examples |
|---|---|
| Vary mode of responding. | |
| • Change how student is to respond. | • Ask child to write answers rather than always responding orally. |

*(continues)*

**Figure 5.11.** Generalization strategies. From "But They Can Do It in My Room: Strategies for Promoting Generalization," by S. Vaughn, C. S. Bos, and K. A. Lund, 1986, *Teaching Exceptional Children, 18*(3), 177–178. Copyright 1986 by The Council for Exceptional Children. Reprinted with permission.

- Change time allowed for responding.

- Teach student to respond to a variety of question types such as multiple choice, true/false, short answer.
- Decrease time allowed to complete math facts.

### Change Some Dimension(s) of the Stimulus

*Description/Methods*

Vary the stimulus systematically.
- Use single stimulus and change size, color, shape.

- Add to number of distractors.

- Use concrete (real) object.
- Use toy or miniature representation.

*Examples*

- Teach colors by changing the size, shape, and shade of "orange" objects.
- Teach sight words by increasing number of words from which child is to choose.
- Introduce rhyming words by using real objects.
- Use miniature objects when real objects are impractical.

### Change Setting(s)

*Description/Methods*

Vary instructional work space.
- Move from more structured to less structured work arrangements.

*Examples*

- Move one-to-one teaching to different areas within classroom.
- Provide opportunity for independent work.
- Move from one-to-one instruction to small-group format.
- Provide opportunity for student to interact in a large group.

### Change Teachers

*Description/Methods*

Vary instructors.
- Assign child to work with different teacher.

*Examples*

- Select tasks so that child has opportunities to work with instructional aide, peer tutor, volunteer, regular classroom teacher, and parents.

**Figure 5.11.** Continued.

needs of students within the class. They must be able to play an active role in the IEP or IFSP process, recommending assessments, providing technical assistance with administration of the tests, and interpreting the results. Also, the consultant must be familiar with the scope and sequence of the curriculum so that instructional strategies that are jointly determined by the teacher and the consultant facilitate generality and maintenance. Several key strategies are mentioned in this chapter that a consultant can use to accomplish each of these objectives.

A second task that a consultant might have to perform with the self-contained teacher would occur when a student is to be integrated into a general education classroom. The consultant can provide the needed support for the self-contained teacher in terms of preparing the student for the new environment. For example, the consultant might recommend that a different schedule of reinforcement be used, or that instructional materials be aligned more closely with the materials in the general education classroom. The important point for the consultant to remember is that he or she is serving four agents: the student or child, the parents, the special teacher, and the general education teacher. The strategies the consultant recommends must meet with the approval of each teacher and address the instructional needs of the student.

This chapter distinguished among the terms *mainstreaming, inclusion,* and *least restrictive environment.* Next, the chapter addressed teacher, parent, and student concerns about inclusion as well as several factors that affect exceptional students within a general education classroom. These factors included: the composition of the mainstreamed classroom, the teacher's attitude, teacher-student interaction, and student-student interaction. Keys to successful inclusion were noted. Further, methods for planning, developing, and evaluating IEPs were presented. Finally, the chapter presented strategies for promoting generality and maintenance.

# Summary of Key Points

## Inclusion, Mainstreaming, and the Least Restrictive Environment

1. Multiple definitions of the term inclusion exist in the literature. Broadly defined, inclusion spans "full inclusion" (in which all students with disabilities are integrated within the general education classroom) to "selective inclusion" (in which only some students with disabilities are integrated into the general education classroom under some conditions).

2. The term *inclusion* also has connotations with respect to professional development, curricular modifications, and integrating a richer and more diverse ethnic and cultural population within the general education classroom.

3. Mainstreaming refers to the temporal, instructional, and social integration of eligible exceptional children with general education peers based on an ongoing, individually determined, educational planning and programming process and requires clarification of responsibility among regular and special education administrative, instruction, and supportive personnel.

4. The term mainstreaming is not synonymous with the term inclusion.

5. The term least restrictive environment has essentially two components. First, to the maximum extent possible the student is to be educated with his or her general education peers; and second, the student should be removed from that setting only when the nature of his or her disability precludes an adequate educational experience even when supplementary learning aids are used.

6. The term least restrictive environment may also relate to opportunity to respond, proportional interaction, and social relationships.

7. Many regular educators believe that they lack the specialized training needed to teach academic, social, or adaptive behaviors to students with disabilities.

8. General educators' attitudes about accepting students with disabilities into their classrooms are also related to their competence and willingness.

9. The more knowledgeable teachers are with respect to adapting instructional and behavioral strategies, and the more highly developed their personal self-efficacy skills, the more willing they are to participate in inclusion.

10. Many general educators are concerned that exceptional students will be "dumped" in their classrooms and they will be held accountable for lack of student progress.

11. Most teachers agree with the philosophical purposes of inclusion, but only a slight majority are willing to implement inclusion in their classrooms, especially in cases where the perceived intensity of the inclusion effort would be high.

12. Parents have mixed views of the benefits gained from inclusion programs. Some see inclusion as a positive step. Many may have watched their sons or daughters in self-contained classroom be ridiculed by other students.

13. Other parents are apprehensive about inclusion programs, especially when their recommendations for adapting the curriculum, reducing class size, consulting with staff, and accessing support personnel are not considered.

14. Time-based measures of inclusion (i.e., full versus selective) may not impact parent perception of determined benefit as much as the presence of a caring teacher and their children's sense of well-being.

15. As child advocacy increases by parents, positive relationships with school members decrease.

16. Parents believe that teachers lack competence in dealing with their children's programmatic needs. In effect, parents report that they are tired of having to be the advocate and the agent of change.

17. Students did not prefer one model (full-inclusion vs. pull-out) over another, but they are able to discriminate the advantages of each model.

18. Some, but certainly not all, students viewed the social aspects of the resource room as positive. Conversely, special and general education students perceived the inclusion setting as positive insofar as team teaching was possible in the classroom, rendering assistance to *both* general and special education students.

19. Some students preferred the general education classroom because it made them feel more normal.

20. With respect to students without disabilities and their concerns, research suggests that the benefits of inclusion include increased acceptance of others, better tolerance, and wider social relationships.

## Variables Affecting Exceptional Students in General Educational Classrooms

21. The inclusion of a student with disabilities may or may not extend the heterogeneity of a general education class.

22. A teacher's attitude is defined as a predisposition to respond in a certain way. Teacher attitudes about the presence of a student with disabilities in

the classroom may be changed by using the principal, implementing team teaching, generating parent support, performing inservice training, and using countercontrol.

23. Students with disabilities experience differential acceptance in inclusive settings.

24. Social relationships between elementary students with and without disabilities can be enhanced by incorporating active facilitation of social interactions, role release, community building, modeling acceptance, and organizational influences.

25. Some students with disabilities can be taught to take an "active" role in shaping the nature and quality of their program within the inclusive setting.

26. The majority of general and special education teachers view the principle of inclusion as positive and beneficial. However, most teachers did not favor the placement of challenging students with disabilities in their classrooms.

## Keys to Successful Inclusion

27. The keys focus on several variables: collaboration, teacher acceptability of treatment, training, financial resources, specialized health needs of students, parent cooperation, and solid decision-making and problem-solving approaches.

## Helping Teachers To Develop and Evaluate Individualized Education and Family Programs

28. Consultants can assist special education teachers develop and evaluate the IEP or IFSP by helping with any of the following functions: the initial assessment, integrating the assessment data, writing goal statements, planning the IEP, and monitoring and evaluating the IEP process. The consultant can assist with assuring that all components of the IEP or IFSP are recorded, including transition plans, where appropriate, and that no procedural step has been ignored or neglected.

29. When integrating assessment data, consultants should help teachers determine each student's strengths and weaknesses, learning style, and preferred reinforcers. When writing goal statements, consultants can help in arranging annual goals; determining short-term objectives; selecting appropriate instructional materials, strategies, and reinforcers; and designing effective evaluation procedures.

## Generality and Maintenance of Skills

30. Stimulus generality occurs when a target behavior is emitted in the presence of stimulus conditions other than those in which it was directly taught.

31. Response generality is defined as the extent to which the learner performs a variety of functional responses in addition to the trained response.

32. Maintenance is defined as the performance of the target behavior after training has been terminated. Maintenance can be improved by including

administrators in planning, ensuring that interventions are relatively easy to implement and cost efficient, and planning for the replacement of key personnel.

## Promoting Generality of Behavior Change

33. Generality of behavior change can be promoted by focusing on planning and implementing prior to the initiation of treatment. When planning for generality, focus on what behavior will be changed, where the new behaviors will occur, and what will be required of individuals within the environment. During implementation, focus on developing the natural contingencies of reinforcement, teaching enough examples, programming common stimuli, training loosely, using indiscriminable contingencies, and teaching self-management.

# Questions

1. Distinguish between the terms *inclusion, mainstreaming,* and *least restrictive environment.*

2. List and explain the three dimensions of Heron and Skinner's (1981) conceptualization of least restrictive environment.

3. Summarize the major concerns that teachers, parents, and students have with respect to inclusion.

4. Identify four keys to successful inclusion.

5. How does your personal perspective on inclusion match those of major professional organizations (e.g., TASH, CEC)?

6. State the major components of an IEP given the revised requirements of IDEA '97.

7. Identify and describe two types of generality.

8. Indicate procedures to follow to facilitate generality. Give a classroom-related example of each.

9. Assume that a student is to be moved from a self-contained classroom to a general education classroom. Why is it important for the two environments to be somewhat similar?

10. Define four basic schedules of reinforcement and provide an applied example of each.

# Discussion Points and Exercises

1. Pick a child with a learning problem in your school and identify that child's preferred reinforcers.

2. How would service delivery to students with mild disabilities be enhanced (or impeded) if Heron and Skinner's (1981) definition of the least restrictive environment were employed?

3. It is sometimes said that general education teachers, though competent with general education students, lack the skills to serve students with disabilities. What skills and attitudes are essential for teachers if mainstreaming is to be a successful educational alternative?

4. The following represents an annual goal for a 6-year-old student with multiple disabilities: Sue Ellen will acquire prerequisite skills necessary for handwriting. Develop appropriate short-term objectives and indicate how those objectives might be evaluated.

5. Prepare a 15-minute videotape depicting a teacher who has conducted a lesson that was programmed for generality. Identify key elements in the generality training. Solicit ideas on how this approach could be used in classrooms.

6. Conduct a sociometric analysis of a general education classroom using a peer-nominating procedure to determine the degree of social acceptance and rejection within the class. Compare these data with classroom observations. With the teacher, design an intervention to reduce or eliminate the degree of social rejection. Consider using modeling and integrated working groups for your intervention.

7. Devise a plan to maintain student academic and social gains across time.

8. Counter an argument offered by a general educator who stated that students with disabilities should be educated in separate facilities using specially trained teachers and unique equipment.

9. Present a 15-minute videotape to a group of general educators, perhaps junior high science teachers, depicting a student with disabilities in a science class. Ask the teachers to identify the positive teaching behaviors (prompts, reinforcers, etc.) that the instructor uses and state how the lesson could have been presented differently. Focus the teachers' attention on specific instructional techniques that were used to enhance the lesson.

# Consulting with Parents and Families

# 6

This chapter addresses factors that affect parent and family member participation in the consultation process, including ecological, systems, and empowerment issues that inhibit even the best-intended parent and family-centered programs. The chapter also elaborates on ways that parents of students with disabilities can assume the role of home-based manager, behavior educator, tutor in the classroom, and partner in the Individualized Education Program or Individualized Family Service Program for their children. The chapter discusses ways in which consultants can access and involve parents in this important process.

A comprehensive parent program means that all parents are involved at some level of participation (Kroth, 1980). Consultants, however, should remember that not all parents will be able or willing to participate in every facet of a home-school program (Callahan, Rademacher, & Hildreth, 1998). The consultant must be cognizant of the fact that a parent's primary responsibility is to be a parent, not a clinician, educator, or therapist (McLoughlin, 1978). Furthermore, several key assumptions are made when practitioners consult with parents and family members. First, the family and the teacher are part of a larger system—an ecology—the balance of which can be affected by interventions introduced into the system. Second, interventions should attempt to develop (or restore) a healthy equilibrium in family dynamics consistent with the child's, parents', and family members' culture (Voltz, 1994), sibling relationships (Caro & Derevensky, 1997; Cramer et al., 1997), the expectations of school personnel and the community, and the present and future needs of the child (Apter, 1982). Quick fixes are not often possible. Finally, the consultant must recognize that the challenges that face at-risk families, particularly those where poverty, substance abuse, violence, and disability intersect, often last a lifetime (Hanson & Carta, 1996). Solutions to systemic problems necessarily require interactive, coordinated, and multilevel approaches. Consultants should recognize that there are data to suggest that at least for families of children with emotional disturbances, parents perceive present professional services to be helpful but also fragmented, difficult to access, and unresponsive to their complex and multiple needs (Lehman & Irvin, 1996).

This chapter was written with two basic assumptions. First, consultants need to consider the family ecology system factors affecting parent involvement and multiple assessment and intervention perspectives as they engage in collaborative interactions with parents and family members. There appears to be growing support in the literature, especially at the early intervention stages, that family-centered service delivery pays large dividends with respect to increasing parent empowerment (Thompson et al., 1997).

Readers interested in resources for siblings should see Cramer et al. (1997).

See William Bennett's *The Index of Leading Cultural Indicators: Facts and Figures on the State of American Society* (1994) for additional technical information on crime, families and children, youth pathologies and behavior, education, and popular culture.

See Bailey et al. (1998) for a discussion of program evaluation and efficacy research related to family-centered early intervention programs.

For a review and discussion of how conjoint behavioral consultation can be employed between teachers and parents, refer to Sheridan and Colton (1994).

Second, there are at least three reasons for consulting and working with parents: (a) parents can help to jointly design programs that achieve generalization; (b) parents can be trained to interact effectively with their children in a manner that is consistent with their culture and also likely to facilitate their child's inclusion; and (c) it is cost effective (Noel, Hess, & Nichols, 1996).

## Objectives

After reading this chapter, the reader will be able to:

1. cite the four levels of Kroth's (1980) Mirror Model of Parental Involvement from the professional and familial perspective;

2. cite three ways consultants can assist parents to become better home-based managers;

3. state several methods of initiating and maintaining home-school communication programs with parents;

4. list several principles of an effective communication program;

5. describe how a home-school communication program using a telephone answering device could be established and maintained;

6. identify key aspects in the development of parent education or training programs;

7. state four phases of a parent conference and describe the function of each phase;

8. identify nine variables to consider when establishing parent education or training programs;

9. explain two advantages of using parents as tutors in the classroom.

## Key Terms

empowerment

Mirror Model of Parental Involvement

home-based educator

home-school communication

parent conference

parent training program

coincidental teaching

## Consulting with Parents of Inclusion Students

Educational consultants who consult with parents of children enrolled in inclusive settings need to understand the parental, familial, cultural, and societal contexts within which they carry out their responsibilities. Further, consultants must recognize the distinction between the phrases working with and consulting with parents. Fine (1990) brings this difference into sharp focus. He claims that these two phrases are synonymous only when they are anchored within the concept of collaboration, empowerment, and enablement. Furthermore, consultation must be based on a family orientation, meaning that the consultant needs to be sensitive to family issues, interactions, and pressures. Sensitivity, however, must focus on the individual family member as well as the ethnic or cultural group to which the member belongs (Fine & Gardner, 1994). Contacts that do not consider the contemporary family, cultural-ethnic considerations, language, and life-cycle factors, and which are not embodied within a consultative relationship, may ultimately fail. The educational consultant's understanding of these situations is crucial so that supports can be provided for the parents and the family. Consultants can provide special assistance in such areas as communication, behavior management, and guidance with the Individualized Education Program or the Individualized Family Services Plan.

Educational researchers and practitioners have stated consistently that parent involvement in the educational process is critical (Cooper & Nye, 1994; Heward, 1996; Shea & Bauer, 1985; Simpson, 1990, 1996). Christenson and Cleary (1990) state this point concisely: "Outcomes of educational and psychological consultation are likely to be more successful when there is an effective parent-educator partnership" (p. 219). Public Law 105-17 and Public Law 99-457 assure the opportunity for parent involvement in the education process, including the preschool levels, by (a) mandating that identification and placement decisions be made that involve parents as decision makers (Felber, 1997), (b) ensuring that parents' and children's rights to due process are protected (Turnbull & Turnbull, 1998), and (c) acknowledging that "individual families, as well as individual children, have unique strengths and needs that should be considered in developing intervention plans" (Sussell, Carr, & Hartman, 1996, p. 54).

Consultants might experience more success when interacting with parents and family members if additional consideration is given to three factors: family ecology, impediments to family participation, and empowerment.

For a discussion of integrating education, health, and social services, see Short, Talley, and Kolbe (1999).

## Family Ecology

Schoor (1988) asserts that "successful [consultation] programs see the child in the context of family and the family in the context of its surroundings" (p. 257). Hence, it should be apparent that one-shot interventions aimed at one member or another in the family and designed to rectify chronic and systemic problems are not likely to be successful. Consultants need to become more aware that as children and parents interact across environments (e.g., home, school, community), events, individuals, and systems within those settings shape their behavior (Christenson & Cleary, 1990).

Falik (1995) makes the point that when a disability is identified, the family as a whole reacts and attempts to adjust to the situation. In his view, the adjustment can take the form of two polar reactions: mobilizing or freezing. In the latter case, parents might perceive individuals outside the family system (e.g., consultants, teachers, psychologists) as judging the acceptability of their child's behavior, and by implication, their own ability to serve as parents. Parents might further perceive that these individuals will require them to "do something" on a time schedule not within the family's control. Falik asserts that consultants who are aware of family dynamics and ecological issues related to acceptance of the disability, resistance to treatment, or potential compliance with interventions might be in a better position to recommend a mediational approach to address those issues. Smith et al. (1997) underscore the importance of keeping an ecological perspective, especially one that considers a full range of home, school, and community partnerships, coupled with multilevel consultation, to increase the likelihood of success with parents and families.

Otherwise, well-intended but poorly planned programs that focus exclusively on the parents are likely to miss the mark. Fine and Gardner (1994) put it succinctly: "How the parents and other family members view the individual with special needs and the appropriateness of treatment recommendations will influence the course of treatment and the quality of relationships" (p. 287).

## Impediments to Family Participation

Numerous barriers affect family member participation in a full range of educational or home-based programs. Fine (1990) categorizes those factors into school and home elements. With respect to school factors, Fine contends that the teacher's perception of parental incapability, feelings of parental intrusiveness within the school program, different value systems, use of jargon, policy statements, or ability of school personnel to respond to individual circumstances (e.g., one-parent families) affect parents' degree of participation. Likewise, parents' perception of their own prior school experiences, distrust of the school system, discomfort with the changing technology of instruction, defensiveness, linguistic and cultural background and values, lack of interaction skills, and day-to-day time, economic, and logistical demands set the occasion for them to be unresponsive when interacting with teachers (O'Shea, O'Shea, & Nowocien, 1993; Salend & Taylor, 1993; Voltz, 1994).

Adelman (1994) suggests that barriers to parental involvement can be conceptualized by type (i.e., institutional, impersonal, or personal) and form (i.e., negative attitudes, lack of mechanisms or skills, and practical deterrents) (see Figure 6.1). Consultants who are familiar with the types and forms of teacher and parental barriers that reduce involvement are in a better position to devise a continuum of counteractive measures and tasks, such as institutional organization, inviting involvement, general welcoming, special invitations, and co-advocacy relationships to overcome the barriers (Adelman, 1994; O'Shea, O'Shea, & Nowocien, 1993).

Beckman and Pokorni (1988), in summarizing a study with infants and their parents, indicate that family stress is linked to the complexity of a child's problem, and that parental stress levels and the factors that contribute to the stress change over time. In a study involving children with learning disabilities and family members, Dyson (1996) administered three types of questionnaires to 19 parents and 19 siblings of children with specific learning disability (SLD) and 55 normal-achieving children and their parents. They also administered two open-ended questions that asked parents and siblings to describe how the presence of the learning disability in the family affected them. Quantitative results indicated that parents of the students with SLD experienced more stress and had more difficulties adapting to school issues but also showed a positive family relationship and coherence to family routines when compared to the nondisabled group. Qualitative verbal comments by parents indicated that they were generally not satisfied with their child's academic and social progress in school, suggesting that continued support is warranted.

Further, Johnson (1993) speaks eloquently of the effects of stress when she reminds us:

> Since the parents of young children who are experiencing stress are frequently under a great deal of stress themselves, they may be less able to focus on their children's needs, and their perception of their children's

| | | Negative Attitudes | Lack of Mechanisms/ Skills | Practical Deterrents |
|---|---|---|---|---|
| **TYPES OF BARRIERS** | Institutional | e.g., school administration is hostile toward increasing home involvement | e.g., insufficient staff assigned to planning and implementing ways to enhance home involvement; no more than a token effort to accommodate different languages | e.g., low priority given to home involvement in allocating resources such as space, time, and money |
| | Impersonal | e.g., home involvement suffers from benign neglect | e.g., rapid influx of immigrant families overwhelms school's ability to communicate and provide relevant home involvement activities | e.g., school lacks resources; majority in home have problems related to work schedules, child care, transportation |
| | Personal | e.g., specific teachers and parents feel home involvement is not worth the effort or feel threatened by such involvement | e.g., specific teachers and parents lack relevant language and interpersonal skills | e.g., specific teachers and parents are too busy or lack resources |

**Figure 6.1.** General types and forms of barriers to home involvement. From "Intervening to Enhance Involvement in Schooling, " by H. S. Adelman, 1994, *Intervention in School and Clinic, 29(5),* 278. Copyright 1994 by PRO-ED, Inc. Reprinted with permission.

functioning may be distorted . . . it is important to recognize and acknowledge the pressures they themselves are experiencing, and to focus on the common interest in enhancing the child's development. (p. 170)

Dunst, Leet, and Trivette (1988) caution that parental nonconformity with school participation may not be related to "contempt for professional opinion" but to lack of consensus on the problem, treatment procedures, or outcome expectations. "A family's failure to adhere to a professional prescribed regimen may not be because its members are resistant, uncooperative, or noncompliant, but because the family's circumstances steer behavior in other, more pressing, directions" (p. 110).

Parental expectations for lower achievement may negatively influence parents' ability to cooperate with well-meaning consultants. Tollison, Palmer, and Stowe (1987), for example, showed that mothers of children with specific learning disability held lower expectations and had more pronounced negative affective responses with their child than did parents of nondisabled children, a finding confirmed by previous research on this subject (Pearl, Donahue, & Bryan, 1986). Still, these differences, when viewed from an interactionist perspective, may point to specific adaptation responses of parents based on the child's behavior, and vice versa.

Finally, the method by which consultants seek to involve parents may be a root cause for noninvolvement. Downing and Bailey (1990) maintain that the procedure that professionals use (i.e., of collecting data, writing formal reports, and presenting a program or solution to parents in the absence of direct parental input) may sow the seeds of noninvolvement because the parents are not invested in the process from the beginning. In Downing and Bailey's view, the subordinate role that the parents play in the process might produce the expectation that the experts will take care of everything. Learned helplessness is the byproduct. In short, the parents do not become empowered to prevent or solve their own problems.

Voltz (1994) concurs with Downing and Bailey's (1990) assessment for parental noninvolvement. In Voltz's (1994) and Dyson's (1996) view, consultants may engage in at least three counterproductive behaviors that reduce the likelihood of involvement: (1) they either implicitly or explicitly assign predetermined roles to family members, thereby limiting their options (Dyson, 1996); (2) they perceive and treat parents differently, thereby creating potential self-fulfilling prophecies; and (3) they are not sensitive to or able to accommodate cultural diversity.

## Empowerment

Enablement, a term often used in conjunction with *empowerment,* refers to the process of providing learning experiences to parents. See Dunst and Trivette (1987) for additional information.

*Empowerment* refers to the parents' perception that they have the necessary capability and skill to make a significant difference in their child's life (Dunst & Trivette, 1987). Thompson et al. (1997) define empowerment from a personal and community perspective. At the personal level, empowerment "occurs when individuals are confident they have the information and problem-solving skills necessary to deal with challenging situations . . . [at the community level]. Social movements emerge from the education and empowerment of people who collectively attempt to change institutions whose values differ from their own" (p. 100).

When parents have to struggle at every turn to obtain needed services, or when they believe that their input during IEP or IFSP conferences is perfunctory, they are less likely to feel empowered (Downing & Bailey, 1990). Dunst (1985) states that parent empowerment must be based on a family systems model, meaning that parents make informed decisions, take control over environmental events, and focus interventions on family strengths. Proactive social supports, especially during early intervention programs, can help parents build competencies and a sense of empowerment (Mowder, 1994). Consultants can develop such supports in at least three ways: by connecting parents to support groups, by setting the occasion for parents to become more active in research efforts, and by developing ownership.

### Support Groups

See Anderson and Anderson (1997) for helpful Web-based sites to support parents of children with disabilities.

Miller and Hudson (1994) suggest that parent support groups serve three purposes: information dissemination, a forum to share experiences, and team-partnership building and/or problem solving. While parent support meetings can be conducted in a variety of formats, Miller and Hudson suggest that they be conducted for approximately 1–1½ hours during which a guest speaker provides the context for the meeting (e.g., dealing with attention deficit disorder), that small breakout sessions be convened to provide parents with the chance to share their own experiences on the topic and to brainstorm solutions, and that they conclude with facilitator remarks to sum up key points and chart a possible course of action. Evaluation can be conducted with short, Likert-scale ratings to assess parents' view on their effectiveness. Other types of evaluative instruments (e.g., the *Family Empowerment Scale* [Cheney, Manning, & Upham, 1997] may also be employed to determine parents' perceived empowerment across three levels: family, services, and community factors.

## Research Partners

Donley and Williams (1997) describe a model research-partnership program conducted at the Fred Keller School that embraces parents as full partners in conducting action research with their children. In Donley and Williams' model, "the parents *are* the scientists, and they conduct empirical studies under the supervision of the school's parent educators" (p. 46). Briefly, in the Keller model, a collaborative research effort between teachers, parents, therapists, and students is conducted on an annual basis during which data are collected and evaluated within the team. Their program is conducted in five phases: recruitment, parent assessment, learning objectives, parental instruction, and summative evaluation. The experience culminates with a "poster session presentation" at the end of the school year during which academic, social, and affective gains are displayed. Parents are also connected with a paid parent educator who assists them with learning a variety of parenting behaviors (e.g., how to call the school to request information, effective communication techniques with the teacher, self-sufficiency at home, verbal behavior, evaluating performance data, and so forth). Donley and Williams recognize that every school program may not have the resources to hire a parent educator. However, in their view, the program can be adapted to other situations.

Kay and Fitzgerald (1997) concede that involving parents in home-based research experiences can, at times, be overwhelming. Still, they view the benefits as far outweighing the disadvantages. Their motto might best be summarized by the title of their article: "Parents + Teachers + Action Research = Real Involvement." Parents conduct action research by engaging in the following steps: generating a research question, collecting data, reflecting on the data, analyzing the data, brainstorming ideas, planning a course of action, obtaining necessary permissions, and conducting the study. Action research fosters a closer bond between teacher and parent, provides parents with the satisfaction of knowing what works and why, and increases the functional communication between teacher and parent.

Regardless of whether the parent educators are paid or volunteer, the key point is that parents are involved in collecting performance data on their children, talking about those data on a regular basis with other parents, and displaying the data in an informal and supportive environment at the end of the year.

Of course, dominating many applied research efforts between home and school may be cultural factors, which may be further complicated by disability, poverty, and minority status. Consultants must be sensitive to these factors and recognize that their role as a researcher—alone or in combination with parents—may be affected by them (Harry, 1996).

## Developing Ownership

Developing ownership essentially means that parents, consultants, and teachers work together to design, implement, and evaluate programs. If consultants attempt "top-down" models, whereby they provide well-intended but unilateral programs, parents are less likely to embrace them. Further, ownership implies that parents become more independent of the consultant's assistance, better problem solvers, and more self-directed (Friedman, 1994).

The term *empowerment,* however, has another connotation for the consultant. In this context, the term refers to how and under what conditions the consultant attempts to solve the seemingly endless tangle of problems that are associated with some cases. Baer (1987) states that at least three barriers inhibit professionals from applying techniques to solve chronic, deep-rooted problems: (a) consultants may not have the technical ability or the job responsibility to solve the larger problems, (b) an analysis is lacking on how consultants can empower themselves to try to solve those problems, and (c) a systematic task analysis for problem solving does not exist.

For the consultant to be empowered means that he or she is aware of the existence of weak controls, and that attempts to alter behaviors are often muted by the influence of more persistent ecological variables. This does not mean that systemic problems cannot be attacked, only that the procedures employed will need to overcome strong environmental factors and that considerable time might be needed to find solutions. Empowerment is not "bestowed" but must be programmed into the intervention (Baer, 1987). Friedman (1994) reminds consultants that there is probably no single solution to problems. In her view, consultants need to create interventions that offer reciprocal assistance, promote parents' natural resources and supports, involve team effort, and ensure family ownership of change. Further, consultants must be able to tell when their involvement with the family would shift from less intrusive levels (diagnostician and communication facilitator) to more intrusive levels (consultant and counselor).

Assuring the opportunity for parent participation and actually obtaining it are two different things. Participation cannot be mandated; it must be nurtured, encouraged, and reinforced. Kroth's (1980, 1985) Mirror Model of Parental Involvement provides the consultant with an excellent perspective on the reciprocal nature of the parent-professional partnership. Also, it provides an index to determine the level of parent involvement.

## Mirror Model of Parental Involvement

Figure 6.2 shows Kroth's (1980) *Mirror Model of Parental Involvement.* Essentially, the model is divided into two major areas: professional service and parental service. Within each area are four levels of participation designated by the terms *all, most, some,* and *few.* According to Kroth (1980, 1985), lower levels of participation need to be firmly established before higher levels of involvement can be expected. For example, all parents could probably provide information regarding the child's preschool medical and social history. Most parents could provide relevant information during the IEP or IFSP process or help with an occasional field trip (e.g., prepare snacks, donate equipment, or volunteer to assist teachers). Some parents might become strong advocates for services for disabled students. They may attend legislative hearings, initiate parent advisory groups, or volunteer as teacher's aides. Finally, only a few parents might become involved enough to form active parent groups and conduct parenting workshops themselves.

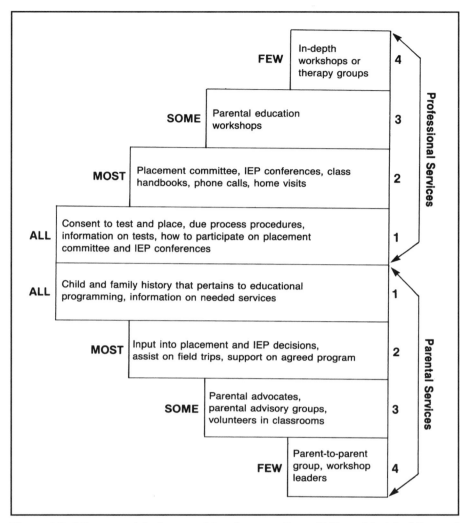

**Figure 6.2.** Mirror model of parental involvement. From "Mirror Model of Parental Involvement," by R. L. Kroth, 1980, *The Pointer, 25*(1), 19. Copyright 1980 by Heldref Publications. Reprinted with permission.

Conversely, all professionals (e.g., teachers, school psychologists) would be able to provide parents with information relative to standardized and norm-referenced tests used with their child. Most teachers are willing to call parents on the telephone to discuss pertinent happenings in school. Some teachers conduct parent education training programs to help improve the quality of service their school provides. Finally, a few teachers conduct in-depth workshops for parents and colleagues that go beyond the single-session programs usually offered through districts.

How is this information helpful to a consultant? First, it may dramatically change the way a consultant communicates to a teacher the expectations for a successful parent-teacher partnership. Too often a consultant hears from teachers that the parents are not interested because they do not attend meetings or scheduled conferences. Teachers may interpret nonattendance as a lack of interest, or they may form stereotypic, culturally biased opinions, and, in turn, become frustrated because they feel that they are working alone to help the student (Thorp, 1997). These feelings of frustration can build to resentment toward the child, the parent, and the family ("If the parents do not care how their child is doing in my class, why should I?"). If these doubts are translated into social rejection, the student's educational program may be compromised.

Parental nonattendance at scheduled meetings could be for several reasons. In addition to the major reasons cited earlier—family ecology, dynamics, and empowerment—logistical factors can affect attendance. For instance, the time selected for the conference may be inconvenient. Both parents may work, or they may work different shifts. Also, the parents may believe they need to strike a balance between the help they give their disabled child and the time they share with each other or other family members. Finally, if the distance is too great to travel or provisions cannot be made for competent child care, then attendance at meetings might decline. Thorp (1997) suggests that consultants take a proactive view and engage in "reframing" (taking a different perspective) that does not lead to immediate, negative conclusions about nonattendance.

Second, conducting a needs assessment of parent and professional concerns, strengths, and time restrictions will help the consultant structure a comprehensive parenting program. Cone, DeLawyer, and Wolfe (1985) designed an easy-to-administer, 63-item measure to assess parent participation in the educational process. Their assessment instrument was predicated on the assumptions that overall involvement must be determined, specific types of involvement (fund raising, volunteering in the classroom) must be indexed, and that parents must be assessed separately. Bailey and Simeonsson (1988) designed a 35-item survey that assessed the functional needs of family members individually and collectively. Consultants might also consider designing parallel surveys to compare reported behavioral correspondence between parents and teachers (Handon, Feldman, & Honignan, 1987). Levels of agreement (or disagreement) could be used for subsequent decision making, intervention, or resource or time allocation. Assessment considerations aside, consultants should recognize that most of the organization and implementation tasks will have to be performed by them until such time as a "few" parents are able to carry on.

Third, when trying to determine the effectiveness of a school-, district-, or county-wide parent involvement program, single measures of evaluation (e.g., attendance at meetings or numbers of parents who volunteer as teacher aides or home-based educators) could be abandoned in favor of a more comprehensive index, the percentage of parents who participated at any level in the model. In effect, 100% of the parents could have been involved, with differing ratios of parental involvement at each level.

Anecdotes 6.1 and 6.2 describe how a consultant attempted to increase the level of participation of two parents. The first parent was already at the *most* level of participation; she provided extensive input for her child's IEP. The second parent was at the *some* level; she had experience providing testimony to state legislative committees. In both cases, the consultant attempted to move the parents' involvement to the next higher level.

In Anecdote 6.2, the consultant achieved his objective of having Lee serve as a workshop presenter. Lee was reinforced for her expertise, and her cooperation was obtained for the presentation. Lee may have been inclined to accept the consultant's offer because the time commitment was short or because she felt a social obligation to help. Regardless of why, the consultant attained his goal.

## Anecdote 6.1

| | |
|---|---|
| CONSULTANT: | (a week after the IEP conference) Mrs. Kempe, you provided several excellent recommendations during Sal's IEP conference. |
| PARENT: | It's important to me that Sal receives all the necessary services. He is already so far behind. I am especially eager to see him in the tutoring program. |
| CONSULTANT: | I was quite impressed with your knowledge of school services. In fact, the reason I'm calling you is to see if you would be interested in helping Sal's teacher implement some of the objectives for Sal and for other children. |
| PARENT: | You mean help out at school during the day? |
| CONSULTANT: | Yes. Sal's teacher indicated that he would love to have you as an assistant. |
| PARENT: | I'm afraid that I will not be able to accept. At the time of the conference I was interviewing for a part-time job, and yesterday I was offered the position. |
| CONSULTANT: | Congratulations! I can see where your time will be limited during the day. |
| PARENT: | Yes, it will. Is there anything I could do for the teacher short of coming to the school? |
| CONSULTANT: | Maybe we could set something up with you and Sal at home. I'm thinking of a program that would help him with school-related tasks but would require only a few minutes each night. |
| PARENT: | I already do that, but I'm open to ideas on specific things I can do. I often feel lost. |
| CONSULTANT: | I'll set up a meeting with you, the teacher, and me if you can give me a few open dates. (The parent provides the dates.) Again, good luck with your new job. I'm looking forward to working with you and the teacher on Sal's home program. |

This scenario illustrates several positive consulting behaviors. First, the consultant reinforced the parent for her previous participation at the IEP conference. Second, she included the teacher in the discussion by stating that he was eager to have the parent assist in the classroom. Third, she reinforced the parent for getting a job offer. Instead of ignoring the parent's success, the consultant expressed congratulations and empathy for the parent's limited time during the day. Finally, the consultant ended the conversation by reiterating that she still believed the parent's participation was of value and that a home-based program could be explored.

## Anecdote 6.2

| | |
|---|---|
| CONSULTANT: | Lee, I read in the newspaper last night that you provided testimony to the House Education Committee on a bill dealing with special education funding. |

LEE:            That's right. It is important that the bill go to the Senate with the amendments I proposed.

CONSULTANT:    I realize that you are busy, but I wanted to talk to you because I'd like to capitalize on your experience in an upcoming series of workshops that I'm offering.

LEE:            What could I do?

CONSULTANT:    I'd like for you to present your ideas on the topic of working with legislators to a group of parents who will be attending the workshop. I'd like them to have the total view of educating students with disabilities, including the role of the legislator.

LEE:            If the presentation can be scheduled at a time when I'm not required to be in session with the legislators, I'll be glad to do it.

CONSULTANT:    Thank you. I appreciate your help.

See Anderson and Anderson, 1997, for helpful Web-based sites to support parents of children with disabilities.

In sum, Kroth's (1980, 1985) model can enhance communication with regular and special education teachers and parents. Feelings of isolation and disillusionment might be prevented when teachers understand that parents need not participate in all levels of the model for the total parent involvement program to be successful. Also, when Kroth's model is used with a needs assessment, the consultant is in a better position to recommend parenting resources. Traditional networks of communication (e.g., the school newspaper, Parent Teacher Association meetings, or regional newsletters) as well as emerging networks (e.g., fax, email, Web sites) can be used to disseminate information about the program. Finally, once success has been achieved with a parent at one level of participation, increased involvement at a higher level is more likely.

# Parents as Behavior Managers

O'Dell (1985) provides a review of programs in which parents have learned to use behavior management approaches in the home.

All parents change child behavior. They permit some behaviors, inhibit or prevent others, and punish still others. Some parents, however, are more consistent than others about the behaviors they allow, inhibit, and punish. As a result, they become more effective behavior managers and more effective parents. Learning to become a better manager is not an impossible task for parents, and parents can learn to use complex behavior-change procedures previously thought to be reserved for professionals alone. Cooperatively developed plans between professionals and parents have been implemented across a wide range of behaviors (Hall, Cristler, Cranston, & Tucker, 1970; Lazarus, 1986; Weiss, 1984) and age groups, including preschool children (Cordisco & Laus, 1993).

Numerous studies have been conducted that demonstrate that parents can serve as effective home-based managers and that their efforts can be generalized to other settings and across noncompliance (Richman, Harrison, & Summer, 1995); task fluency (Lasater & Brady, 1995); disruptive behavior and engagement (Vaughn, Clarke, & Dunlap, 1997); communication training (Derby et al., 1997); chronic food refusal (Werle, Murphy, & Budd, 1993); and a host of other behaviors.

Niemeyer and Fox (1990), for example, demonstrated that parents could implement a program designed to reduce the aggressive hitting, biting, and grabbing of their son during rides from school to home. In this study, a 17-year-old adolescent with moderate mental retardation and autistic behavior engaged in repeated acts of aggression toward his mother or father when either of them drove him home from school. The adolescent was also self-abusive and engaged in perseverative questioning, meaning that he continued to ask questions that the parent had just answered. Baseline data were collected during the car ride by means of an audiotape. The parent-driver recorded an "A" (for aggression) or a "P" (for perseverative talk) at each occurrence and noted the geographic location (e.g., Clymer Lane) for later review. Parent training, which occurred subsequent to the baseline, consisted of one formal instructional session during which the parents learned about differential reinforcement of other behaviors (DRO) and the procedural application of tokens. A question-and-answer period was provided. Training also included modeling and feedback during actual rides in which the experimenters used the first half of the ride to show parents how to implement the procedures, and the second half of the ride to provide feedback on the accuracy of their implementation. When the DRO procedure was in effect, the parent-driver delivered a token to the adolescent contingent on the absence of aggressive behavior during any of the five predetermined segments of the ride. Tokens were exchanged for backup reinforcers at home. The criterion for exchange was increased over the course of the study from two to four tokens per ride. Ultimately, the number of tokens needed to earn a reinforcer was increased from four to five, signifying no aggressive behavior of any kind during any portion of the ride. Further, the number of occasions for token delivery was reduced. Toward the end of the program (session 61), no tokens were delivered at all, and the absence of inappropriate behavior was maintained by praise.

Figure 6.3 shows the results of this parent-implemented behavior management program. The frequency of aggression was reduced dramatically during the DRO contingency, was maintained during the fading condition, and follow-up data obtained 2 and 3 months after cessation showed continued low levels of aggressive behavior.

There are five implications of this study for consultants. First, parents can learn to change dangerous and aggressive behaviors using positive reductive procedures (PRO). Second, behavior change programs can be applied to older individuals with success, eliminating the misperception that behavior-change programs are reserved only for the young. Third, training programs need not be elaborate and time consuming. Even though this research program was conducted over an extended time period, only two sessions were used for training. Fourth, behavior change programs applied consistently can produce long-lasting results. Finally, this study demonstrates that observing behavior in the actual situation in which it occurs is central to the intervention's success. A considerable challenge parents face is planning a family outing to a restaurant. These occasions can produce stress, friction, and loss of parental and/or child control. Home-based behavior management practitioners have explored this topic using a variety of "how-to" (McMahon & Forehand, 1981) and "advice-package" (Risley, Clark, & Cataldo, 1976) approaches.

Bauman, Reiss, Rogers, and Bailey (1983) used an advice package to assist four families with reducing the percentage of incidents of pre-meal inappropriate behavior across four categories of behavior: verbal (crying, demanding); motor (leaving the seat, reaching across the table); food/utensils (playing with utensils, food); and noncompliance (not following parent redirective statements). The advice package consisted of behavior specifications for the parents to follow (e.g., finding a table in an uncrowded section of a restaurant, seating

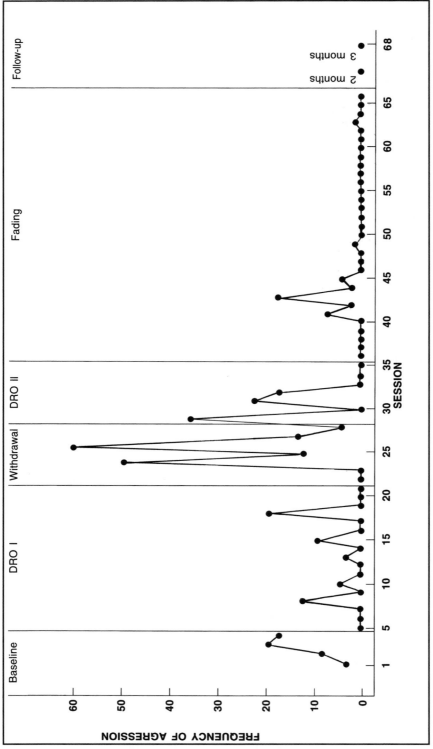

Figure 6.3. Frequency of aggression during car riding. From "Reducing Aggressive Behavior During Car Riding Through Parent-Implemented DRO and Fading Procedures," by J. A. Niemeyer and J. Fox, 1990, *Education and Treatment of Children, 13*(1), 26. Reprinted with permission.

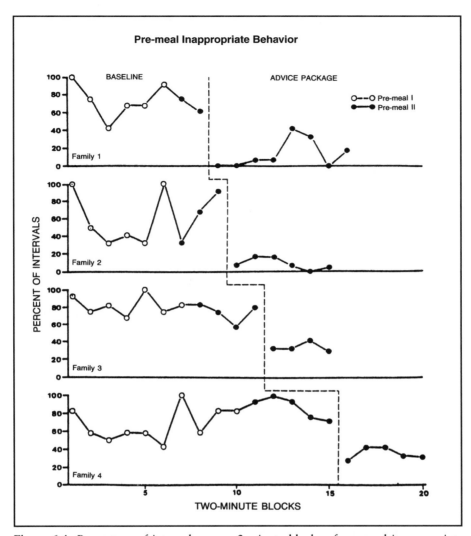

**Figure 6.4.** Percentage of intervals across 2-minute blocks of pre-meal inappropriate behavior by target children during baseline and advice package conditions. From "Dining Out with Children: Effectiveness of a Parent Advice Package on Pre-meal Inappropriate Behavior," by K. E. Bauman, M. L. Reiss, R. W. Rogers, and J. S. Bailey, 1983, *Journal of Applied Behavior Analysis, 16*(1), 60. Copyright 1983 by Journal of Applied Behavior Analysis. Reprinted with permission.

the child in an inside seat near the wall, separating the children, providing crackers while waiting for the order, ordering the child's favorite foods, providing an object to play with while waiting, removing utensils, and praising appropriate behavior).

Figure 6.4 shows the results of the multiple baseline study. At baseline, the percentage of intervals of inappropriate behavior was high for all families. When the advice package was introduced, inappropriate behavior decreased markedly across all families, averaging a 51% reduction.

A lesson from this study for the consultant is that intervention programs for families should not explore consequence strategies exclusively, but instead should examine the full range of environmental variables that contribute to a problem. In this study, significant gains were achieved by restructuring the restaurant setting. In a subsequent part of the experiment, parental praise for compliant behavior was removed, and inappropriate behavior continued to remain low. Parents reported that they liked the advice package and planned to use it in the future.

Consultants do not always work with "compliant" parents who are skilled at serving as home-based managers, however. Such circumstances can present unique difficulties to field-based practitioners.

Powell (1990) reported on two 18-week, home-based, pilot studies that were conducted with two parents of preschool children with emotional disturbance and autism. Using a multidisciplinary approach, the team informed the parents of the availability of services, conducted home visits, assisted the parents with prioritizing goals, and generated an Individualized Family Service Plan (IFSP) with them. During the intervention phases, the team modeled strategies using behavior rehearsal and role playing, provided feedback and reinforcement, and evaluated parent-child interactive behavior.

Powell reported that the comprehensive nature of the service assisted one parent with finding a part-time job, securing child care, and managing child behavior in the home more effectively. While the second parent continued to be resistant to some aspects of the program, the team's focus on modifying the child's behavior helped to reduce her concern about the intrusiveness of the approach. She came to realize that a change in her child's behavior did not occur in the absence of a change in her own behavior, a point that she was perhaps not willing to concede during the early stages of the project.

Muir and Milan (1982) conducted a training program with parents of three preschool children that reinforced the parents for using a lottery system for their child's achievement of receptive and expressive language skills. Parents were provided with a lottery coupon, exchangeable for donated merchandise, contingent upon the number of language tasks that the child performed during the week. The results across all three families showed that when the lottery system was in effect, the cumulative number of language tasks mastered by the children increased significantly and that the parents preferred the program. The distinguishing feature of this study was that parents earned reinforcers for child behavior improvement, not just for participating in training sessions or program planning sessions.

Consultants can assist parents who are interested in becoming better behavior managers in a number of ways. First, specific workshop programs can be established that provide the parents with the skills they seek. The focus of the workshop might be to train parents to assess the current levels of their children's behavior, plan and execute effective interventions, and analyze the results. More important, the inservice training should provide opportunities for parents to practice the skills being taught, receive constructive feedback from a skilled supervisor or consultant, and obtain praise for improved performance.

Second, consultants can provide indirect service to parents by referring them to other sources of support or other resources.

Many parent associations (e.g., the Learning Disabilities Association ) have "parent assister" programs established to help parents who have child-rearing problems or problems related to their child's performance in school. The parent assister can serve as a liaison between the parents and another agency (the school) or simply provide information, support, or formal counseling to the parents.

Consultants interested in a range of organizations, print material, government agencies, clearinghouse and information centers, and publishers may refer to the National Information Center for Children and Youth with Disabilities (NICHCY) News Digest issue titled "Parenting a Child with Special Needs: A Guide to Reading and Resources," 2nd edition, February 1997.

Finally, consultants do not always need intrusive programs to assist parents. Gmeinder and Kratochwill (1998), for example, demonstrated the effects of a self-help program to increase child compliance with parental requests (brushing teeth, cleaning room, doing chores, etc.). An inexpensive training manual (*The Good Kid Book*, Sloane, 1988) and minimal consultant time (brief home visits to conduct consultation interviews and discuss data collection) constituted the major treatment. Parents read the manual step by step, essentially learning how to give instructions to their children, select goals, record behavior, and distribute reinforcers. Consultant visits were distributed over the course of the study. Figure 6.5 shows a multiple baseline graph of the percentage of compliance

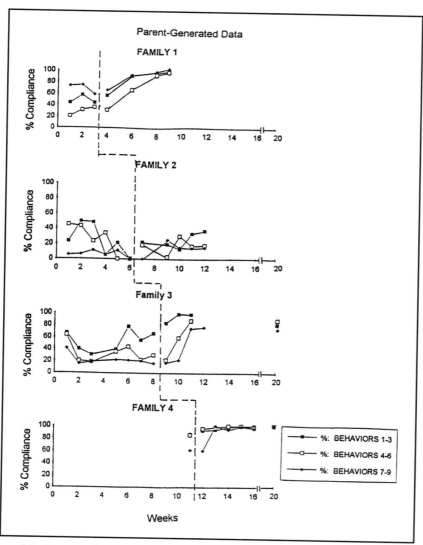

**Figure 6.5.** Parent-collected compliance data during baseline and treatment phases. From "Short-Term, Home-Based Intervention for Child Noncompliance Using Behavioral Consultation and a Self-Help Manual," by K. L. Gmeinder and T. R. Kratochwill, 1998, *Journal of Educational and Psychological Consultation*, 9(2), 106. Copyright 1998 by Lawrence Erlbaum Associates, Inc. Reprinted with permission.

across four families for nine different behaviors. Three of the four families showed clear improvement; those families turned out to have the highest level of integrity in implementing the program. Family 2, with 28% implementation of the program, produced the lowest levels of compliance. Gmeinder and Kratochwill make the point that a correlation appeared to exist between parent integrity in implementing the program and outcome. Better outcomes were achieved by parents who implemented the program on a regular basis.

When the behaviors to be changed are chronic and severe, assessment-based interventions within the family context may be required (Vaughn, Clarke, & Dunlap, 1997). In Vaughn, Clarke, and Dunlap's study, an 8-year-old child with chronic disruptive and aggressive behavior served as the subject. After conducting a functional assessment of environmental demands in the home (bathroom) and at a fast-food restaurant, a family-centered intervention was implemented that consisted of (a) in the home, showing the child the sequence of events that would follow compliance (e.g., access to a preferred toy) and (b) at the restaurant, providing an adapted menu for increased participation during wait time in line and a photograph of a preferred toy that would be provided in the car during the ride home contingent on compliance. The child's mother implemented all intervention components. Figure 6.6 shows the results of the family-centered intervention on disruptive and engaged behavior. During baseline for both bathroom and restaurant settings, disruptive behavior occurred at moderate to high levels and engagement occurred at low to moderate levels. However, during the family-centered intervention, the levels were reversed. Follow-up data collected over several weeks and in novel settings continued to show improved performance.

An important point for consultants to remember is that they can assist parents to become more effective managers by helping them initiate home-based behavior management strategies. The intent, of course, would be to provide a consistent approach in both settings—school and home.

A final point needs to be stated regarding the maintenance of home-based parent management programs subsequent to the termination of formal training, support, or monitoring by the consultant. That is, improved parent-child interaction will not in itself guarantee the maintenance of the program in the future. Wahler (1980) demonstrated a therapeutic effect with 18 mother-child dyads with respect to the mother's aversive behavior toward the child and the child's oppositional behavior to the mother. Clear and impressive gains were achieved during intervention. However, at a 1-year follow-up, those gains had returned to baseline levels. Wahler speculated that the loss of effect may have been due to the "insular" circumstances of the mothers. That is, the mothers' pattern of few and aversive extra-family contacts may have indirectly affected their child-rearing practices, suggesting that establishing community-based friendships for these individuals may have provided the occasion for more sustained positive mother-child interactions.

## Parents as Home-Based Educators

Teachers and administrators frequently state that there is only so much that can be done to develop systematic methods for establishing and maintaining parental assistance. While reasons for the lack of home-school cooperation are numerous (e.g., working parents, single-parent families, multiple family commitments, and lack of parental enthusiasm), it is still possible to devise useful

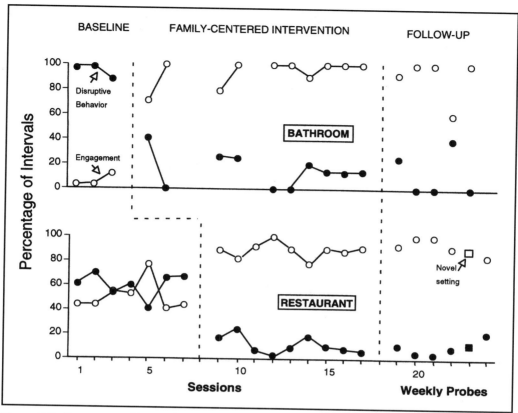

**Figure 6.6.** Percentage of intervals with disruptive behavior and engagement across bathroom and restaurant routines. Connected data points represent sessions that occurred approximately two times per week. Disconnected points span a period of at least 1 week. The square data points during follow-up in the restaurant routine depict a probe session that was conducted in a different restaurant environment. From "Assessment-Based Intervention for Severe Behavior Problems in a Natural Family Context," by B. J. Vaughn, S. Clarke, and G. Dunlap, 1997, *Journal of Applied Behavior Analysis*, 30(4), 715. Copyright 1997 by Journal of Applied Behavior Analysis. Reprinted with permission.

methods that give parents the opportunity to assist in their child's academic and social development as a *home-based educator*. Further, there is some exploratory data that suggests that even untrained parents may be able to create home-based effective learning environments, with high levels of engaged time, to teach academic skills (Dowds, Ness, & Nickels, 1996; Duvall, Ward, Delquadri, & Greenwood, 1997).

In recent years, partly stimulated by changes in federal law (e.g., P.L. 105-17, P.L. 99-457, P.L. 101-476) and the heightened realization of the necessity of extending school-based programs to other settings in the child's environment, increased attention has been paid to designing home-based interventions. For instance, successful home-based programs have been reported to teach personal safety (Miltenberger & Thiesse-Duffy, 1988), identification and reporting of child illness (Delgado & Lutzker, 1988), infant care by fathers (Dachman et al., 1986), mother-child interactions (Feldman et al., 1986), dental care (Dahlquist & Gil, 1986), multiplication facts (Stading, Williams, & McLaughlin, 1996), study skills (Hoover, 1993), and tutoring (Mehran & White, 1988; Thurston & Dasta, 1990).

**Table 6.1**

Homework Guidelines Across Assignment, Management, and Parent Areas

*Assignment Considerations*

1. Recognize the purpose of homework and establish its relevance for each assignment.
2. Select appropriate activity to complete task.
3. Ensure high chance of success.
4. Avoid using homework as punishment.

*Management Considerations*

5. Assess homework skills.
6. Assign homework early.
7. Establish a routine for assigning, collecting, and evaluating homework.
8. Coordinate with other teachers.
9. Verify assignments using a buddy system. The buddy system confirms that assignments have been copied.
10. Allow students to start homework in class.
11. Use assignment books and logs.
12. Evaluate and provide feedback.

*Parent Considerations*

13. Create a supportive environment and encourage and reinforce child's effort.
14. Maintain involvement and communicate with teachers.
15. Seek additional training.

*Note.* From "Home and School Partnerships: Parent as Teacher," by P. Hudson and S. P. Miller, 1993, *LD Forum, 18*(2), 32. Copyright 1993 by the Council for Learning Disabilities. Reprinted with permission.

## Parents as Tutors

Assuming that tutoring is valued by all family members, and that teacher assistance is possible, some parents may be able to serve as home-based tutors (Hudson & Miller, 1993). These authors recommend, however, that the parent and child establish the nightly schedule; that appropriate tutoring activities are employed; that materials be age and skill appropriate; and that parents receive training on how to tutor, collect data, and interface with the teacher on effectiveness. Table 6.1 provides guidelines for parents with respect to assignments, management, and parental considerations.

One tutoring method that has worked well is for parents to follow the teacher's instructional methodology but to do so using a game-like approach for brief periods (10 minutes) each night. Barbetta and Heron (1991), for instance, successfully implemented a home-based education program with parents of students with learning disabilities over the summer months. Project SHINE (*Systematic Home Instruction and Evaluation*) was conducted in 4 steps: identifying and training parent-child teams, programming home-based tasks, and evaluating the program. Identification, training, implementation, and evaluation were adapted from a field-tested peer-tutoring system model (Cooke, Heron, & Heward, 1983) and therefore had built-in features of high opportunity to respond (OTR), reinforcement, and instructional consistency. Parents used a self-contained folder to store materials and graph daily achievement

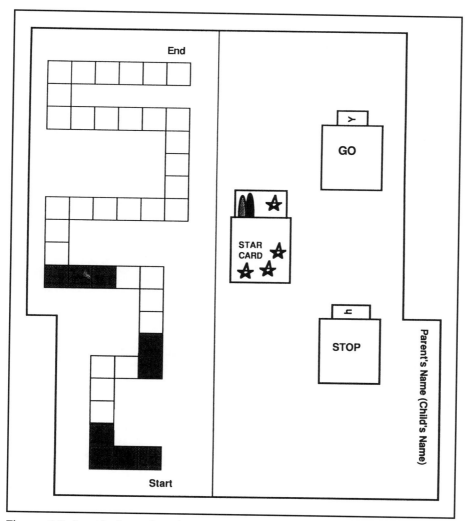

**Figure 6.7.** Sample home-based tutoring folder. Adapted from "Project SHINE: Summer Home Instruction and Evaluation," by P. Barbetta and T. E. Heron, 1991, *Intervention in School and Clinic, 26*(5), 278. Copyright 1991 by PRO-ED, Inc. Reprinted with permission.

(see Figure 6.7) and a daily progress form (see Figure 6.8) to report progress to consultant personnel. At the conclusion of the program, not only did students master and maintain their skills, but also parents reported that they were satisfied with their child's progress and that their parent-child interactions were constructive and positive.

## Helping with Homework

Numerous educators have reported on the challenges that students with special needs have when it comes to completing homework. For example, Epstein, Polloway, Foley, and Patton (1993) indicated that students with disabilities, as compared to their nondisabled peers, are more likely to procrastinate, become distracted, and need frequent reminders and supervision with respect to homework. Kay, Fitzgerald, Paradee, and Mellencamp (1994), while conducting a

```
┌─────────────────────────────────────────────────────────────────┐
│                   Project SHINE Daily Progress Form               │
│                                                                   │
│   Date: ___8/4/89___   Session number ___4___  Tutoring Time _10_ minutes │
│                                                                   │
│   ───────────────────────────────────────────────────────────── │
│                                                                   │
│   Flashcards mastered in session (put in the "Stop" pocket) ____6____ │
│                                                                   │
│   Mastered complete set this session (underline one)     YES      NO │
│                                                                   │
│   Extra Activities:                                               │
│   Sarah wrote sentences using her vocabulary words, and then we   │
│   read a story from a book she selected from the library.         │
│                                                                   │
└─────────────────────────────────────────────────────────────────┘
```

**Figure 6.8.** Project SHINE daily progress form. From "Project SHINE: Summer Home Instruction and Evaluation," by P. Barbetta and T. E. Heron, 1991, *Intervention in School and Clinic, 26*(5), 279. Copyright 1991 by PRO-ED, Inc. Reprinted with permission.

study with parents of students from rural areas, identified five themes from their research:

1. Parents believed that they were not prepared to help their children with homework.

2. Parents needed and wanted more information about teacher expectations and their role in fulfilling those expectations.

3. Parents wanted the teachers to provide individually prescribed homework for their children.

4. Parents valued family-oriented homework assignments.

5. Parents wanted a functional, two-way communication system to enhance the home-school partnership.

See Cooper and Nye (1994) for a review of the homework literature as it applies to students with learning disabilities. Also, see Chapters 9, 10, and 11 for related treatment of this topic.

Jenson et al. (1994) also recommend using "Sanity Savers" for parents who wish to help with homework. Their article provides a 5-week method for parents.

The beneficial gains to be achieved when parents, or other family members, help with homework have also been documented (Callahan, Rademacher, and Hildreth, 1998; Cooper & Nye, 1994; Jenson, Sheridan, Olympia, & Andrews, 1994; Bryan & Sullivan-Burstein, 1997). Since for many students with special needs as much as 20% of their quarterly grade may be earned by homework compliance, it is to the consultant's advantage to be well versed in strategies and procedures to improve student performance in this area. Bryan and Sullivan-Burstein (1997) suggest that teachers use innovative homework assignments, coupled with "planners" that assist students in knowing when assignments are due. Further, they recommend that parents and teachers develop a log of assignments so that each party knows which assignments have been completed and which assignments are outstanding. Callahan, Rademacher, and Hildreth (1998) have demonstrated that improved performance can be facilitated with self-management approaches. Weaver and Heron (1998) suggest United States postcards as one tool that teachers can use to keep parents informed of homework completion (see Figure 6.9). Enlisting peer support within cooperative learning groups can be successful (O'Malia & Rosenberg, 1994). Finally, Jenson et al. (1994) highly recommend the use of validated training packages that incorporate easy-to-read and nontechnical manuals to assist parents.

```
Date: _____ Teacher: _____
Subject: _____
Total points (cumulative) earned/possible so far this semester (quarter):
____ / ____
Present grade (circle one): A  B+  B  B–  C+  C  C–  D+  D  D–  F
(_____'s) overall work this week has (improved, stayed the same,
deteriorated)(circle one). The circled item represents the number of missing
assignments: 0, 1, 2, 3, 4, more than 4 (circle one).
```

**Figure 6.9.** Sample postcard wording (preprinted). To be copied and pasted on multiple U.S. postcards.

With respect to home-based tutoring programs, it should be noted that not all educators favor working and consulting with parents in this manner. Barsch (1969) and Kronich (1969), for example, suggest that parents should not attempt home-based education programs. In general, those authors believe that parents of children with disabilities may be too anxious, may lack the proper education skills, or simply may not have the time to do an adequate job. Further, Callahan, Rademacher, and Hildreth (1998) suggest that parents may be unwilling or unable to help with homework. Finally, it is believed that parents may impede the learning process by drifting unintentionally from a role of parental assistant to parental interference (Cooper & Nye, 1994).

We are convinced that overwhelming research evidence shows that parents can and should serve as home-based educators if guidance, sufficient training, and feedback are provided. Also, parents must be comfortable with the task. If parents want to engage in home-based instruction to improve the academic, social, self-care, or motor skills of their child, the consultant should facilitate the process at every opportunity.

## Early Intervention Applications

Working in a home-based early intervention program, Anderson, Avery, DiPietro, Edwards, and Christian (1987) showed that the systematic use of behavioral teaching and extensive parent training in the home produced marked changes in language, self-care, social, and academic development of children with autism. Fourteen children, ages 64 months to 18 years, participated with their parents, who received 10 hours of direct training with a skilled therapist per week and were involved in training activities for another 5 to 15 hours per week. Parents were trained using modeling, feedback, training manuals, and games. Results, over a 2-year period, showed that parents improved their ability to provide prompts and reinforcement for their child's appropriate behavior, and they maintained their skills over time. Further, parents were satisfied with the service they received, indicating that it contained an essential component of social validity (Wolf, 1978).

Lubeck and Chandler (1990), however, caution that a necessary prerequisite for home-based educational interventions, especially with infants and preschool populations, is to conduct an assessment of the caregiving environment. In their view, a basic caregiving setting should "ensure the nutrition, health, and safety of the child . . . and provide opportunities for learning, positive parent-child relationships, and predictable child care routines" (p. 349).

Consultants can work together with parents in a manner, consistent with cultural factors, to enhance their understanding of concepts related to balanced meals, routine health care, home safety, and play. Once these fundamental health, medical, and safety issues have been addressed, direct and specific home-based educationally oriented programs for the infant or preschooler can be presented. Mowder (1994) and Hadden and Fowler (1997) recommend that consultants team with early education and intervention specialists to coordinate administrative, curriculum, instruction, and related services provisions, especially during critical transition ages (i.e., early intervention to early childhood special education programs, or preschool to school age).

# Communication Techniques with Parents and Family Members

Readers interested in learning more about communication techniques with parents can consult Kroth and Edge (1997).

Lovitt (1989) states that communication with parents can occur at the information, advocacy, or training level. Consultants working with parents at each of those levels could provide parents with specific types of information (e.g., school progress, nature of the disability); procedures for securing their rights (referral and placement alternatives); and methods for improving parenting skills (training packages or manuals). Ironically, however, Arnold, Michael, Hosley, and Miller (1994) caution that just providing parents with information may affect attitudes negatively, whereas the more frequently consultants engage parents in useful activities and exchanges, the more likely parents are to view communication interactions positively.

Regardless of the level of consultation, for a functional home-school relationship to develop, effective and engaged two-way communication must exist. Wilson (1995) reminds us that effective communication is rooted in the following principles: accepting what is being said, listening, questioning appropriately, encouraging, staying directed, and developing a working alliance.

## Accepting Parental Statements

Accepting parents' statements means that the consultant conveys to the parents through verbal and nonverbal means that what is being said is valued. Parents are provided with the opportunity to speak freely and openly, and they perceive that what they are saying is respected in a nonthreatening manner (Wilson, 1995). Accepting parents' statements does not mean that the consultant must agree with everything they say. It is one thing to convey the message "I understand and appreciate your point of view." It is quite another to have to agree with it.

## Listening

According to Wilson (1995), good listeners attend to content, feelings, and tone in a sincere and genuine manner. They attend to what is said, how it is said, and by whom it is said. For example, in a conference attended by extended family members (e.g., grandparents), a consultant engaged in active listening would assuredly notice if a grandmother was speaking for the mother, or a mother was speaking in a tone different from the father.

# Questioning

To the extent possible, consultants should use open-ended questions as opposed to closed-ended ones when communicating with parents, especially during conferences. An open-ended question sounds like this: "Tell me, how does your son use his leisure time on the weekend?" A closed-ended question goes like this: "Is it true that your son has difficulty using his leisure time on the weekend?" The former question is likely to produce a good description of the child's leisure behavior. The response to the latter question can almost be predicted: a one-word reply (yes or no).

# Encouraging

In most non-crisis conferences or interactions, parents need to hear that their son or daughter is making progress, even if the progress is incremental. To accomplish this goal, it is helpful to use a "sandwich" technique whereby items (academic or behavioral) that need to be addressed come between a layer of comments describing any positive steps that the student has made.

# Staying Focused

Consultants must ensure that during conferences or other verbal interactions with parents that the conversation stays on track, while recognizing that in some cultures it is customary to engage in lengthy greetings and pleasantries before getting down to business (Wilson & Hughes, 1994). Consultants must recognize this distinction and be able to tell when extended "small talk" is cultural and when it is drifting off target. Consultants must also recognize when a parent or other family member starts to divert the conversation to other tangential subjects (e.g., the need for marriage counseling, unemployment benefits, projections for college while the student is in first grade, etc.). Surely, parents may need a safety valve to vent their concerns or frustrations with these topics; however, consultants should recognize that parents are not likely to address main agenda items if they stray too far off base with a personal agenda.

# Developing a Working Alliance

A working alliance essentially means that all parties perceive that they are a part of a collaborative and cooperative team, a partnership, that is focused on addressing the student's main problems in an accepting and nonthreatening manner (Bedard, 1995).

In the larger sense of the term, *home-school communication* is defined as a broad range of oral or written messages between parents and teachers for the purpose of exchanging information and providing training to the parents. Consultants, especially those working with multicultural populations, must realize that significant barriers to effective communication can exist aside from the normal logistical difficulties of work schedule conflicts or transportation problems (Wilson & Hughes, 1994). Lynch and Stein (1987), for instance, conducted a comparative study with Hispanic, Black, and Anglo parents whose children received special education services. An analysis of their interview data showed that all groups were satisfied with the services their children were receiving, but the Hispanic parents were less knowledgeable and less involved in the program. Further, the lack of bilingual skills and general communication problems between the dominant and nondominant cultural agents (teachers and parents) were cited as factors affecting closer exchanges. When homework is the focus of the communication, Jayanthi, Nelson, Sawyer, Bursuck, and Epstein (1995) report that at least six problem areas can be identified: initiations, frequency, timing, consistency, follow-through, clarity, and usefulness. Contributing factors to these communication problems included time, lack of awareness, varying expectations, and attitudes and beliefs. Jayanthi et al. recognize correctly that in inclusive situations, communication problems may be compounded because of the triangulated nature of the communication: parent, general education teacher, and special education teacher.

Most of the literature on effective communication between parents and teachers focuses on school-age populations, a defensible posture given the numbers of students in school. Hill, Seyfarth, Banks, Wehman, and Orelove (1987), however, examined parents' attitudes with respect to services for vocational training for their adult children. As a rule, parents expressed low interest in their adult child's working conditions or wage levels. Most were satisfied that their son or daughter was working, albeit at a low-paying wage. Only 12% of the parents indicated a preference for a competitive employment situation that would improve working conditions or wages. Hill et al. state that an effective parent-professional partnership is rooted in explicit communication:

> If an effective communication process can be established between parents and professionals on vocational issues, parents will once again be called upon to assume the role of advocate for improved vocational services for handicapped adults—the same role they held over a decade ago for free and appropriate public school services for all handicapped children. (p. 22)

Meyers and Blacher (1987) found that 47% of the families with severely handicapped children that they surveyed were involved at some level in parent-school communication, but, strikingly, in one-third of the families, home-school communication was rare or nonexistent. In an ex post facto study of 129 randomly selected high school special education student graduates, Haring, Lovett, and Saren (1991) found that 23% of parents indicated that they were not involved at all in their child's school program.

Hughes and Ruhl's (1987) and Hughes, Ruhl, and Gorman's (1987) survey data of preservice and inservice training programs suggest that the low levels of parental contact or involvement may be explained, in part, by the inadequate training teachers receive to occasion such participation. In their view, teachers are not adequately prepared to engage parents: (a) during the IEP meeting, (b) through a variety of written and oral communication methods, or (c) in organized parent support groups.

The following section will describe a number of field-based methods for improving the quality and frequency of home-school communication. Documentation to support each method is provided.

## Telephone

Nearly every American family has a telephone or lives close to someone who does. Gartland (1993) states that telephone conversations, especially brief contacts, can be very effective for maintaining parental involvement. Further, short calls help to reduce the parents' sense that calls from school always mean that something is wrong. Surprisingly, however, it has been only within the recent

See Gartland (1993) for suggestions on improving written, telephone, and newsletter communications with parents. Jayanthi, Bursuck, Epstein, and Polloway (1997) offer recommendations for teachers, administrators, parents, and students to improve communication, especially with respect to homework.

past that the telephone has come to play an important role in the home-school communication network.

A number of researchers (Alessi, 1985; Heron & Axelrod, 1976; Heron & Heward, 1982; Heward & Chapman, 1981; Lazarus, 1986; Weiss, 1984) have used the telephone to increase parents' knowledge of school-related activities or as a method to structure home-based instruction. Heron and Axelrod (1976), for example, used a telephone to reinforce inner-city parents for assisting their children with work recognition assignments. The procedure involved calling the parents each day to tell them how well their child had done on the previous day's word recognition task and to ask them to provide the opportunity for their child to learn the next day's 10 target words.

The results of the study demonstrated that when parents were given feedback via the telephone for helping with their child's work, the child's performance improved. Conversely, when the parent did not receive such feedback, word recognition performance worsened. Also, the parents reported that they liked the telephone calls. In the past, the only time that school personnel had called them was when a son or daughter was in trouble. This positive telephone approach was welcomed. Also, it should be noted that the parents did not receive explicit instructions on how to teach the target words to their children. Yet at least one parent stated that she told her daughter to "look for little words in the big word, write the words in the air with her eyes closed, and finally write the words in sentences." The latter two decoding strategies are commonly recommended by reading specialists.

If the telephone system is to have maximum advantage on a school- or district-wide basis, consultants need to find ways to extend this support to more parents. One way is with a telephone answering service (Alessi, 1985; Bittle, 1975; Heward & Chapman, 1981; Lazarus, 1986; Weiss, 1985).

Bittle (1975), for example, demonstrated that a telephone answering service installed in the school and preprogrammed with information on school-related subjects could be used as a low-cost method to establish and maintain a parent-teacher communication network and to improve student performance in school. As one part of the study, students were instructed to take a list of four spelling words home to their parents. The students were scheduled to be tested on the words the following day. In the next step of the study, the teacher not only sent the words home with the student but also recorded the words on a nightly phone message for the parents to retrieve. In the third phase, the word-list-only condition was reinstated for 7 days. Finally, the word-list-and-telephone-message phase was repeated for 6 days. The results indicate a functional effect between the phone message and student performance. When the spelling words were on the phone message, the level of student performance increased. When the spelling words were removed from the telephone answering service, student performance level dropped.

Heward and Chapman (1981) replicated Bittle's (1975) study. Their procedure involved taping instructions, requests, and progress notes for the parents on the school telephone answering service. The parents were free to call after school each day to obtain the data. The results of Heward and Chapman's study indicated that more telephone calls were made to the school each day when the messages were available than when they were not. Parents reported that they liked the system, because it provided them with essential information on school events.

Hassett et al. (1984) used a home-school communication system during summer vacation to improve the written language expression of three adolescent students with learning disabilities. Essentially, the procedure involved having students listen to a daily "story starter" and then write for 10 minutes about the topic suggested by the story starter. Parents were instructed to count the number of words produced by their child during the 10-minute session. After 12 days of collecting baseline information on the number of words produced, parents attended a workshop where they learned how to recognize action words and adjectives and to record the total number of words written by their child. Parents also learned how to access a story starter via a teacher-produced audiotape connected to a telephone answering system, how to explain the target behavior (e.g., defining an action word or adjective) to their child, how to record the results of their child's daily written work, and how to evaluate their child's writing. Parents also learned how to award coupons, exchangeable for free or inexpensive reinforcers, contingent upon improved production of action words, adjectives, or total words.

The results of the 9-week multiple baseline study showed that the summer writing program was successful in increasing the number of action words and adjectives used by the adolescents. When the home-school communication program was in effect, the number of action words and adjectives increased. When it was not in effect, the number of action words and adjectives was lower. Also, Hassett et al. (1984) indicated that the parents liked the program and that they were able to conduct it at home without problems.

Weiss (1984) conducted a study using a home-school communication program combined with home tutoring to improve the academic performance of 11 students with learning disabilities attending a private elementary school. During baseline, students were pretested by the teacher on their sight words, spelling words, and math facts. Prior to initiating the home-school program via the telephone, parents attended a 2-hour workshop to learn how to carry out the procedures of the study (e.g., accessing words and facts via the telephone, procedures for tutoring their child, suggestions for reinforcing learning). Next, parents had access to sight words via the telephone. Each night they tutored their child on words presented by the tape and reported the results of their teaching on the "message" side of the tape. Home tutoring using the audiotape was introduced sequentially for sight words, spelling words, and math facts.

The results of the study showed that phone messages produced an increase in student performance on sight words, spelling words, and math facts recognition during daily and weekly assessments (Figures 6.10 and 6.11). Further, the results showed that parents could function as home-based tutors and that parents viewed the program as successful.

Alessi (1985) conducted an interesting variation of the home-school communication program with six parents of students with learning disabilities. The students were enrolled in a self-contained classroom and mainstreamed in third or fourth grade for some academic skill areas. After teaching the students to correctly identify nouns, adjectives, and verbs in a story they had written in response to a story starter and setting a criterion for each variable, students learned how to make an audiotape that their parents would later hear by calling on the telephone. For instance, students made announcements like: "Hi, Mom! This is [name]. I made my goal today. I wrote 8 nouns, 5 adjectives, and 6 verbs, and 43 total words today. I hope you are proud of me!" During the home-school communication phases of the program, students made audiotapes contingent upon completing their story starters at criterion with the designated number of nouns, adjectives, and verbs. Parents left a message for their child to hear the next day prior to writing that day's story (e.g., "[Name], I am proud of all the words you wrote yesterday. Keep up the good work.").

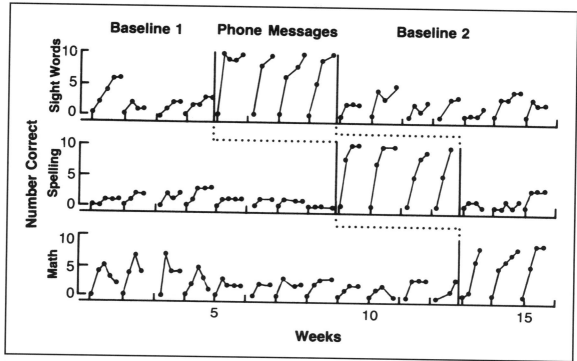

**Figure 6.10.** Number of items answered correctly on daily in-class assessments during baseline and phone messages. From "The Effects of a Telephone-Managed Home-School Program Using Parents as Home-Based Educators on the Academic Achievement of Learning Disabled Students," by A. B. Weiss, 1984, unpublished doctoral dissertation, The Ohio State University, Columbus. Reprinted with permission.

Alessi's (1985) study showed that student production of nouns, adjectives, and verbs increased during home-school communication. Also, students and parents indicated on an exit interview that they enjoyed the program and found it useful, practical, and convenient. Finally, it should be mentioned that Alessi's study was conducted over a 75-day period, indicating that a home-school communication program can be carried out over extended periods of time.

Lazarus (1986) conducted a study that merged a home-school communication program with home-based education. Specifically, parents of seven children who attended a private preschool program participated in a study of their child's ability to identify word parts and sight vocabulary. During a 2-hour workshop, parents learned how to access information via a telephone answering device, tutor and test their child at home, and report the results through the answering device. Nightly tutoring at home followed the same format as described by Cooke, Heron, and Heward (1983) and included six components: obtaining tutoring material, word-part and word practice, practice word testing, "bonus" word testing, recording, and reporting. After calling a designated school phone number to receive their child's word parts, practice words, and bonus words for the week, parents conducted tutoring in a three-part sequence. During "Practice: Get Ready," parents presented word parts (e.g., *ab*) and words containing those word parts (e.g., *absent*). The parent would say, "This says *ar* as in *car.*" As the parent said this statement, she or he would flip the flash card over to show the word *car*. The child imitated the parent's vocalization. During "Practice: Sequential Order," the word parts were again presented

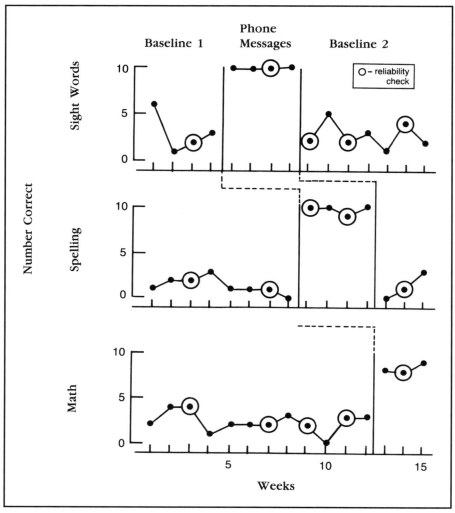

**Figure 6.11.** Number of items correctly answered on weekly in-class posttests during baseline and phone messages (open circles represent scores obtained by second observer). From "The Effects of a Telephone-Managed Home-School Program Using Parents as Home-Based Educators on the Academic Achievement of Learning Disabled Students, by A. B. Weiss, 1984, unpublished doctoral dissertation, The Ohio State University, Columbus. Reprinted with permission.

but the parent's verbal model was omitted. If the child said the word part and corresponding word correctly, he or she would be praised. If an incorrect response was made, the parent would say, "Try again." This phase of tutoring lasted 4 minutes. During "Practice: Random Order," the parent shuffled the cards and re-presented them to the child. Practice word testing consisted of having the parent present practice words to the child without prompts, scoring each verbal utterance as correct or incorrect by placing an X (incorrect) or a ☺ (correct) on the back of the card. Bonus word testing was conducted in a similar fashion, only those words were not exposed to the child beforehand and served as a measure of response generality. Finally, the parent reported the results of the testing each night via the telephone answering device.

The results of the withdrawal design study indicated that during the parent-tutoring, home-school communication phase, each of the seven students' word part and word recognition ability improved significantly. When that phase was not in effect, word part and word recognition performance dropped. The data also indicated that parents consistently reported their child's performance accurately, left comments for the teacher on the audiotape, and found the system a convenient and efficient means to maintain home-school communication.

Overall, the telephone system offers consultants a novel way to enlist the cooperation of parents, and it has a number of distinct advantages. First, it is flexible. Daily tapes can be generated and updated in a matter of minutes, and single-parent families or families in which both parents work can gain access to information after school without having to contact the teacher personally. Second, it is a low-cost item. The cost of the answering service, including installation, is within the budget of most school systems, and maintenance and tape costs are low. Third, it is reliable. Handwritten notes are often lost, and parents do not receive the information. Fourth, it is functional. The data indicate that parents will use the telephone to obtain important information about their child's program and may use that information in a structured home-based tutoring program. Fifth, since data on individual students are not reported on the tape, confidentiality is assured. Reporting data to parents is reserved for either a private conference or written correspondence. Finally, parents view the telephone-managed system in a positive way, perceiving that it opens another avenue for home-school communication.

## Notes and Notebooks

Another low-cost technique that teachers have used repeatedly over the years is to send notes or notebooks home with students. The notes or notebooks, unless of a disciplinary nature, usually aim at informing parents of a student accomplishment in school (Williams & Cartledge, 1997).

Hawkins and Sluyter (1970) conducted a study that demonstrates the effectiveness of sending notes home to indicate appropriate student academic performance in school. When notes were sent home, student performance improved, and when the notes were later used as tokens, exchangeable for a variety of reinforcers in the home, student performance improved even more. Privileges (e.g., staying up later, going to a movie) or the removal of certain tasks (e.g., putting out the trash) can serve as reinforcers for the notes.

Sending notes or notebooks home with students has a number of advantages (Williams & Cartledge, 1997). First, it is a tangible reminder from the teacher that the student's performance was acceptable. Second, the note acts as a prompt to the parents to comment on their child's performance. Finally, the note can be used as a token. When notebooks are sent home on a regular basis, parents can see their child's daily work and ascertain progress more readily.

## Video

Alberto, Mechling, Taber, and Thompson (1995) suggest that consultants might find videotape to be a useful addendum to their repertoire of communication techniques. Videos might help with progress reports, IEP or IFSP meetings, summer programming, integration efforts, transition programming, and home use. Specifically, by showing parents a videotape of their child's interactions in school, parents might gain a greater appreciation of their child's performance in demand, leisure, group, and individual work situations. The video segments can help with assessing the child's current levels of performance. Furthermore, when a behavioral or educational intervention needs to be applied, consultants can show parents how it works, rather than just talk about it or provide print materials.

## Parent Conferences

Additional information on conferencing can be obtained in Simpson (1996).

A fourth opportunity for home-school communication is through the parent conference. Polloway, Patton, Payne, and Payne (1989) state that a *parent conference* can occur in one of three contexts: procedural meetings such as the IEP conference, crisis sessions occasioned by an emergency of some sort, or routine meetings (e.g., 9-week report card period). Jordan, Reyes-Blanes, Peel, Peel, and Lane (1998) state that there are two types of conferences: casual and formal. Regardless of the type of conference, Jordan et al. emphasize that consultants must be sensitive to the rich diversity that parents of different cultures bring to the conference and to be prepared to stimulate interaction within the conference irrespective of the ethnic and cultural background of participants.

Stephens (1977) and Jordan et al. (1998) contend that a parent conference should be a goal-directed session that provides for the exchange of information between teacher and parent to enhance educational programming. The parent conference, especially one conducted in the formal sense of the term, should not be considered a social visit, but rather should aim to accomplish specific objectives.

To enhance the effectiveness of parent conferences and to support the development of parent-professional partnerships, Jordan et al. suggest that educators must recognize (a) their attitudes toward people of diverse cultures; (b) the roles of respective members (e.g., grandparents, extended family members) within the culturally diverse family; (c) perceived differences in academic or social expectations between themselves and the family members; (d) sensitive issues associated with potential denial of the disability, treatment confusion, embarrassment, etc.); and (e) educational language differences, their use of educationese (i.e., terms such as IEP, ADA, IFSP, and so forth) that can serve to befuddle and further confuse parents. Jordan et al. (1998) express our view succinctly when they state:

> Communication about disabilities can become complex, not only due to the use of technical language, but also because of one's view of the disability. In some cultures, a child's disability is viewed as a parent's punishment or curse; in other cultures, disability is seen as a challenge. . . .
> A family's reaction to a disability may be based on tradition, religion, economic level, or prior knowledge and experiences. Teachers who have explored the family's view of disabilities will be able to convey the information in a sensitive manner. (p. 144)

One method that educators might employ to assess the degree to which their communication is being effective is to use a self-monitoring checklist (Perl, 1995). Figure 6.12 shows six skills that educators or consultants might employ: caring, building rapport, listening, empathizing, reflecting affect, and clarifying statements.

Stephens (1977) indicates that parent conferences should be conducted in four phases: (a) establishing rapport, (b) obtaining information, (c) providing information, and (d) summarizing. To establish rapport it is imperative for the teacher to be able to place the parents at ease immediately. Teachers are advised

Checklist for Self-Monitoring

MY LEVEL OF COMPETENCE *(Check One)*

| SKILL | Adequate | Needs Improvement | GOALS |
|---|---|---|---|
| Caring | | | e.g., I will monitor my reactions to parents after each meeting. |
| Building Rapport | | | e.g., I will offer coffee or water to parents before each conference. |
| Listening | | | e.g., I will respond more often to concerns that parents express to me. |
| Empathizing | | | e.g., I will notice parents' nonverbal cues to help in perceiving their feelings. |
| Reflecting Affect | | | e.g., I will more often reflect feelings I perceive parents to be expressing. |
| Clarifying Statements | | | e.g., I will use clarifying statements when these can help parents improve their focus in conferences. |

**Figure 6.12.** Checklist for self-monitoring. From "Improving Relationship Skills for Parent Conferences," by J. Perl, 1995, *Teaching Exceptional Children, 28*(1), 31. Copyright 1995 by the Council for Exceptional Children. Reprinted with permission.

to make general statements regarding neutral topics that give the parents an opportunity to speak. For example, the teacher might say, "I'm so glad we have this opportunity to meet. Were you able to find the school without much trouble?" Opening statements to avoid would include teacher questions on private family matters or controversial school or community issues. Also, to make parents more comfortable the teacher should offer them a beverage and an adult-sized chair. The teacher must remember that parents may feel intimidated in the school, and every effort should be made to reduce their anxiety. Anecdote 6.3 illustrates how a regular education teacher established rapport with the parent of a handicapped student who attends her class.

## Anecdote 6.3

TEACHER: Welcome to King Avenue School. It's so nice that you were able to come.

PARENT: Thank you. I have been looking forward to the meeting.

TEACHER: (offering the parent a cup of coffee) Did you have any difficulty finding the school?

PARENT: No. The map you included in the announcement letter was perfect.

While a teacher conference usually is scheduled so that the teacher can inform the parent of the student's progress, it would be premature to begin documenting the student's performance right after establishing rapport. A better option for the teacher would be to obtain information from the parent on how the child feels about school, how the child performs at home on school-related tasks, and how he or she gets along with neighborhood children. It is imperative for the teacher to have these data if successful programming is to be accomplished. Of course, the teacher need not continue to ask leading questions of parents to obtain every bit of information possible. Rather, the teacher should wait until there is a natural break in the conversation to provide school-related information to the parents. Anecdote 6.4 describes a scenario where such a break occurs.

## Anecdote 6.4

TEACHER:    How does Sally handle money while she is shopping alone? (teacher obtaining information)

PARENT:    Not too well. She often does not count her change, and I'm afraid to trust her with large bills.

TEACHER:    Yes, I've observed a similar pattern in the classroom while we were working on paper money, coins, and giving change. Hopefully, we'll begin to see a turnabout in this area, because I've introduced a store in the classroom. Students can buy things from the store—pencils, chalk, and erasers—with play money. To keep what they buy, they have to be able to count the change correctly, name the coins they get as change, and give an equivalent value for the coins. (teacher providing information)

PARENT:    That sounds like the kind of practice she needs.

Parents and teachers should be aware that parent conferences that address challenging issues will require more time.

The dialogue continues with teacher and parent exchanging information until all the teacher's objectives (outlined prior to the conference) are met. Parents should be given every opportunity to ask questions, provide alternatives, and challenge the type of programming their child receives. Teachers need not feel defensive about the educational experiences they are providing; rather, they should state as clearly and as straightforwardly as possible the rationale for their approach. If parents object, the teacher should pursue a line of questioning that will elicit from the parents their specific objections. Anecdote 6.5 provides such an example.

## Anecdote 6.5

TEACHER:    Are there other questions you have regarding Paco's achievement?

PARENT:    Yes, I don't feel that the math instruction he is receiving is doing him any good. He seems to be going nowhere.

TEACHER    (reflecting the parent's statement) You feel that your son has not made adequate progress in math?

PARENT:    That's right. He continues to have trouble telling time, measuring distances, and dealing with money.

TEACHER: Let's just explore one of these areas. When Paco arrived in the class in September, he could not tell time to the hour, half hour, or quarter hour. Presently, he is able to tell time to the hour and half hour. Have you noticed this at home?

PARENT: Well, yes, but he still cannot tell time.

TEACHER: If I understand you correctly, you mean Paco cannot tell time to the quarter hour and the minutes. Is that correct?

PARENT: Yes.

TEACHER: I wish we had been able to make faster progress, Mrs. Gomez, but, as I think you see, Paco has made some progress, although not as fast as we would like.

PARENT: Yes, that's right.

TEACHER: Since I've had some success with Paco teaching him time to the hour and half hour, I think I'll continue a similar technique with the quarter hour and minutes. Maybe we can work out a program for Paco at home.

---

The final phase in the parent conference is the summary. It is important that the parents hear a review of the major points discussed in the conference prior to their departure. The summary provides an opportunity to bring closure to the meeting by restating all the important items of discussion.

More important, perhaps, than simply recounting the major discussion points of the conference, the summary allows the teacher to perform two additional tasks. The first is to provide training for the parents so that they will be better able to carry on the school program at home, especially if computers, assistive technology devices, or reporting forms are part of the IEP or IFSP (Hourcade, Parette, & Huer, 1997; Margalit, Rochberg, & Al-Yagon, 1995; Parette, Brotherson, Hourcade, & Bradley, 1996; Perry & Garber, 1993). For example, the teacher may need to show the parents how to change a battery in a hearing aid, use a communication board, access a Web site, teach their child to tell time using a digital clock, or make interesting word or sound games. Further, the teacher may demonstrate how to set up a contingency contract with a child so more productivity is achieved in the home (see Chapter 12 for more details on contingency contracting).

The second task is for the teacher to set a firm plan for follow-up consultation. The follow-up plan need not be elaborate and need not occur immediately. After the initial consultation, the teacher should mention to the parents when they can expect the plan. In those instances in which the teacher has demonstrated a new strategy to the parent, or when a different course of action is being engineered, it is critical that the follow-up occur soon after the conference. It might be as early as the next day. If the problems are not pressing, the follow-up could be postponed a little while. Whatever the case, follow-up should not be put off too long as delay can weaken credibility. Anecdote 6.6 shows how the last two items of the parent conference—training and follow-up—can be incorporated in the summary of the conference.

The conference in Anecdote 6.6 was closed in a nonthreatening manner for the parents. The teacher did not tell the parents what to do; rather, she suggested alternatives for the parents to consider (word bingo, lotto games, etc.). Finally, the teacher made it clear that follow-up contact would be made in

2 weeks. The parents' perception of this meeting more than likely was positive. One could speculate that the parents perceived the teacher as very interested in the development of their child, knowledgeable about instructional activities, and willing to assist them to ensure that progress would be made. It is likely that a joint strategy could be achieved without too much difficulty.

### Anecdote 6.6

TEACHER: Unfortunately, we're running short of time, but before you go let me take a minute to summarize what we've discussed so far.

PARENT: Fine.

TEACHER: One point of concern for both of us is Richie's need to learn more sight vocabulary words. While he's made progress, his reading recognition and comprehension might be increased if he had more knowledge of basic sight vocabulary.

PARENT: That's right. He seems to miss many words that I feel he should know by the beginning of the third grade.

TEACHER: (about to provide a minitraining session): Agreed. One of the activities I've found successful with Richie is a word game. He seems to like this type of game. Let me take time to share with you some of the games you can play at home to complement what I'm doing at school. (Teacher shows the parents how they can play word bingo, concentration, and lotto games. Then she goes on to share another observation.) Another item that we discussed was Richie's unwillingness at times to follow instructions. While I don't consider this a chronic problem, it seems to be occurring with sufficient frequency to call attention to itself.

PARENT: That's true. We've noticed similar behavior at home. We figured that he was imitating his friends in the neighborhood, because in the past he would usually follow instructions without too much fuss.

TEACHER: Well, why don't we just wait awhile to see what happens. If possible, let's say that we arrange a follow-up contact in 2 weeks. If Richie's performance with following directions has not improved, we might be able to plan a joint strategy to resolve the problem. In the meantime, would you be able to count the number of times per day Richie is given an instruction and the number of times he fails to carry it out in a reasonable amount of time? I'll do the same with him in school. In 2 weeks I'll call you and we can compare notes to see if the trend is increasing, decreasing, or staying the same.

PARENT: Fine. That sounds like an excellent idea. We'll do our best.

TEACHER: Very good. Do you have any additional questions you'd like to bring up at this time?

PARENT: That just about covers it.

TEACHER: O.K. If you have any questions or if you would like any additional suggestions on sight vocabulary games, please feel free to call me. If not, you can expect a telephone call from me 2 weeks from today. Would 7:30 P.M. be a good time to call?

PARENT: That would be fine.

TEACHER: Again, I appreciate your willingness to come in for the conference. I learned a great deal. I hope you have a nice day.

PARENT: Thank you. I learned quite a bit as well. We'll hear from you in 2 weeks. Good-bye.

Underscoring any successful parent conference and family-school partnership is communication (Jordan et al., 1998; Perl, 1995). When educators are sensitive to verbal and nonverbal communication patterns across cultures, parents and other family members are more likely to feel at ease, interact positively, and enhance the relationship.

## Student-Led Conference

A relatively new phenomenon in schools is for educators to structure a student-led conference. Picciotto (1996) describes a student-led conference as one in which the student takes the lead during the conference to recount progress with class projects, individual assignments, or independent work. Further, the student might outline upcoming events, state future goals and objectives, and describe measures that he or she will take to improve academic or social behavior.

Picciotto (1996) outlines the benefits of student-led conferences for parents, teachers, and the students themselves. Essentially, a student-led conference provides an occasion for parents to see and hear the child describing progress in the day-to-day environment, and for teachers to see parent-child interactions in a way not normally afforded to them. Students benefit by reviewing their work for potential display, thinking about how they might present their samples to their parents, and judging areas that need further improvement. Picciotto cautions, however, that a student-led conference must be planned as carefully as a teacher-led conference—maybe more so—insofar as students may need a list of prompts or cues to review relevant materials and encouragement to participate, as well as reinforcement during the conference. From an experimental perspective, the effectiveness of student-led conferences has not been determined.

## Home Visits

Home visits can be an excellent way for consultants to learn more about a child's skills and abilities. Parents may be more comfortable in their homes, logistical problems associated with child-care or transportation are eliminated, and a more informal, but informative, conference could occur. Still, home visits should be considered in light of other factors, notably safety concerns in the neighborhood, cost-benefit (in terms of distance traveled per child), and contractual issues associated with the district or county program. Edens (1997) outlines several cultural issues that consultants should keep in mind for home visitation programs with ethnic minority families. For example, it may be inappropriate to suggest interventions using behavior analysis or behavior modification techniques if the cultural values of the family hold that such approaches are intrusive. Edens states: "Parents may not be receptive to such conceptualizations of their child's behavior or to the use of what may appear to be intrusive treatment programs, particularly when espoused by persons with little understanding of the relevant cultural issues and constraints affecting such families" (p. 375).

## Parent Training

Numerous publications, workshops, and commercial materials are available to help parents rear their children from birth to adulthood. Kramer (1990) and Elksnin and Elksnin (1991), in discussing best practices in parent education and training, report that short-term workshops, published training packages, hand-outs and manuals, training modules and videotaping, modeling, rehearsal, group counseling and support models, and direct instruction constitute the more popular methods for parent training. Other strategies have been advanced as well, including mentoring (Searcy, Lee-Lawson, & Trombino, 1995); spousal feedback (Harris, Peterson, Filliben, Glassberg, & Favell, 1998); and clinical intervention (Eiserman, Weber, & McCoun, 1995).

Dunst et al. (1991) categorize the range of intervention options for a *parents training program* into four models:

1. *Professionally centered:* The professional is the expert in determining parent (family) needs.

2. *Family-allied:* The professional is the expert in determining parent (family) needs, but the parents implement the program.

3. *Family-focused:* The professional outlines options for the parents (family) and assists them in selecting among alternatives.

4. *Family-centered:* The professional is the broker for the family, assisting them to meet individualized and flexible family goals.

Trivette, Dunst, Boyd, and Hamby (1996), investigating parents' assessment of help-giving practices and personal control appraisals across these models, found that "adherence to particular kinds of family-oriented models [are] associated with differences in program (helpgiving) practices and a number of family outcomes . . . demonstrating that adoption of particular helpgiving models can be expected to have differential influences on the people participating in human services programs" (p. 243).

A number of authors with a behavioral orientation (e.g., Cooper & Edge, 1981; Dardig & Heward, 1981a; Heward, Dardig, & Rossett, 1979) have outlined specific strategies for parents to address common problems that arise in the home. Dardig and Heward (1981a), for example, offer parents and children the opportunity to learn contracting strategies. The major theme of their book is that many home-based problems can be prevented or overcome if parents and children establish and implement effective contingency contracts.

Cooper and Edge (1981) offer specific suggestions to the parents for problems such as toileting, noncompliance at mealtime, discipline, and a host of others. In their text is a discussion of the principles of learning as well as case studies in which those principles were applied.

Rivera and Rogers-Adkinson (1997) emphasize that when consulting with families of the four largest minority groups in the United States (Hispanic Americans, African Americans, Asian Americans, and Native Americans), consultants engaged in training programs would be well advised to recognize the role of culture within the family before training begins. Further, they suggest that consultants should become keen discriminators of student behaviors that might be acceptable (or even rewarded) at home but be deemed inappropriate (and perhaps punished) at school. To reduce the likelihood of judgment errors, Rivera and Rogers-Adkinson (1997) suggest that programs: (a) be offered in culturally

Some authorities (e.g., Brazelton, 1983; Spock, 1976) provide not only medical information, but also information about developmental milestones and behavior to be expected at each stage of maturation.

sensitive ways, (b) build on family strengths, (c) recognize the structure of the family decision-making process (e.g., autocratic, democratic), (d) consider value conflicts between home and school, and (e) consider other options for training (e.g., support and group models versus consultant-directed model).

Sileo, Sileo, and Prater (1996) suggest that the European-derived cultural values of efficiency, independence, and equity—even though they exist in other cultures—may not operate in the same way within those cultures. Salend and Taylor (1993) emphasize that cultural, linguistic, and economic considerations can affect parent-teacher interactions. They advise that educators should adjust training methods to meet unique family needs across these dimensions to reduce the potential for conflict between the consultant and the family.

Table 6.2 shows a three-column matrix that represents a way for consultants to become more sensitive to families from diverse cultures.

Regardless of model or method to train parents, Alper, Schloss, and Schloss (1996) remind consultants of two key points regarding programs for families of children with disabilities:

> (a) The entire family, not just the person with a disability, needs services and supports to meet their needs and avoid loss of control and responsibility. Families, not professionals, should ultimately decide what specific resources and services they need. . . . (b) The roles and needs of children with disabilities and their family evolve and change over time . . . we must consider the needs of all family members at each stage of the life cycle. (pp. 261–262)

## Establishing Family Education and Training Programs

Anastopoulos, DuPaul, and Barkley (1991) outline 10 specific steps for conducting parent training (see Figure 6.13). Although intended for parents of children with attention deficit-hyperactivity disorder (ADHD), the applicability of these procedures by consultants to other parent and family groups seems appropriate. Anastopoulos et al. indicate that adherence to the program is enhanced by between-session assignments, review, and avoidance of professional jargon. Stoddard, Valcante, Roemer, and O'Shea (1994) further suggest that issues of family support and home-school partnerships become embodied within a college or university preservice and inservice curriculum. Collaborative relationships among college or university faculty, teachers, student teachers, and family members offer a good chance for success.

In situations where time constraints or heavy consultation loads prevent the design and implementation of multiple sessions for training, consultants might consider *coincidental teaching* as a method to improve parent skills (Schulze, Rule, & Innocenti, 1989). Coincidental teaching can be conducted in a 1-hour session during which the consultant assists parents with selecting a behavior to change, prompting opportunities to occasion the behavior, reinforcing the behavior when it occurs, and scheduling daily routines. Parents can keep the consultant informed of progress by weekly contacts. Parents like coincidental teaching because it is easy to learn and carry out, and the program benefits the children.

Consultants, however, cannot design, implement, and evaluate parenting programs exclusively. Their job responsibilities call on them to perform a myriad of other tasks. Consequently, establishing, maintaining, or connecting parents

## Table 6.2
Three Column Matrix Representing a Way for Consultants to Become More Sensitive to Families from Diverse Cultures

| Western culture/values | Family culture/values | Strategies |
|---|---|---|
| *Efficiency* | | |
| Value/use time wisely; quality of task may be secondary. | Efficient use of time not as important; OK to be late. | Avoid scheduling parent-teacher conferences too closely together. |
| Direct approach; get right to the subject; solve problem. | Indirect approach; discuss related issues; "talk story." | Avoid "quick fix"; respect quality of the interaction. |
| Tend to rush, fast-paced. | More slowly paced, need time to think. | Slow pace of meetings with parents; allow "thinking time." |
| *Independence* | | |
| Prefer to make own decisions. | Interdependence, decisions are made as a family; natural family supports in place. | Encourage extended family involvement; work with extended family members. |
| Individual right to privacy of feelings. | Strong family ties; open sharing of personal feelings; actions of individual reflect on entire family. | Respect sense of family; identify cultural attitudes toward or religious beliefs about disabilities. |
| Parental responsibility for raising child. | Extended family, shared responsibility of child rearing. | Identify authority figures; respect deference to authority; allow parents time to take decision to others. |
| *Equity* | | |
| Parents are equal partners in team. | Perceive professionals as "above" family. | Professionals need to be aware of and "read" parent perceptions; recognize parents as experts. |
| Prefer active parent involvement (e.g., input at meetings, work with child at home). | Accept teachers' opinion; teachers are experts. | Decrease control of interaction; involve parents in planning, implementing, and monitoring programs. |
| Information sharing. | Passive reception of information. | Elicit wants, hopes, and concerns of parents; information sharing versus information giving and question asking; use parent suggestions when possible; provide timely feedback. |
| Democratic family decision making. | Matriarchal or patriarchal family structures. | Respect lines of authority. |

*Note.* From "Parent and Professional Partnerships in Special Education: Multicultural Considerations," by T. W. Sileo, A. P. Sileo, and M. A. Prater, 1996, *Intervention in School and Clinic,* 31(3), 152. Reprinted with permission.

1. Orient parents to the nature of the disability.
2. Provide understanding of parent-child relationship; teach behavioral principles.
3. Enhance parental attending skills.
4. Catch the child being good.
5. Establish a home-token system.
6. Use response-cost and time-out procedures.
7. Extend time-out to other behaviors.
8. Manage behaviors in public effectively.
9. Handle future behavior.
10. Provide booster sessions.

**Figure 6.13.** Ten specific steps for conducting parental training. Adapted from "Stimulant Medication and Parent Training Therapies for Attention Deficit–Hyperactivity Disorder," by A. D. Anastopoulos, G. J. DuPaul, and R. A. Barkley, 1991, *Journal of Learning Disabilities, 24*(4), 215–216. Copyright 1991 by PRO-ED, Inc. Reprinted with permission.

to support groups can go a long way toward extending initial training because it provides a network within which parent skill development and emotional support can be maintained (Bedard, 1995; Hallenbeck & Beernick, 1989; Margolis & Brannigan, 1986).

Assuming that a formal, multisession parent training program is being considered, Stephens, Blackhurst, and Magliocca (1982) offer the following guidelines: (a) use a consistent theoretical model, (b) determine parental skills to be mastered in advance, (c) allow for varying rates of learning by parents, (d) employ a systematic and functional approach, and (e) provide follow-up.

By using Stephens et al.'s guidelines a consultant can provide an individualized parent training program, based on the assessed needs of each parent and tailored to their individual learning styles and rates. Providing follow-up training, booster sessions, or a refresher course is essential if the skills acquired during the initial training are to be maintained. While Stephens et al.'s suggestions are consistent with a behavioral orientation, the success or failure of parent training programs rests to a large extent on the variables listed below.

## Time of Meeting

Meeting times should be scheduled so that the maximum number of parents can attend consistently. Meeting times set on different days from week to week often lead to poor attendance and a lack of continuity in the program. If possible, parents should have a choice of times to accommodate their particular needs. Consideration should also be given to scheduling meetings during the day so that single-parent families or parents who work nights can attend.

## Length of Sessions

Each instructional session should range from 1 to 2 hours. The length of meetings should be based on the number of parents there and how far they have to travel to attend. If parents have to travel a considerable distance, it would be better to schedule longer meetings. Obviously, parents would think twice about attending if the meetings were too brief to appear worthwhile.

## Number of Sessions

For a general guide on the number of sessions to use, the content to cover in each session, and the instructional and evaluation materials to employ, the reader is referred to Cooper and Edge (1981).

Patterson's (1975) training program is accomplished within a 5- to 15-week period. The total number of sessions may be determined by a needs assessment, a procedure to decide the number of skills to be mastered by parents. Keeping in mind Stephens et al.'s (1982) point that parents will learn the skills at different rates, the consultant can establish a flexible schedule with respect to the number of sessions required. To do this the consultant can give the parents a pretest on the course syllabus at the first session. Based on the data obtained in the test, the consultant can then calculate the number of sessions he or she believes will be required to achieve competency. Kramer (1990) provides the best advice, however, with respect to scheduling sessions:

> Perhaps in our efforts to train parents as behavior change agents the single most important step we can take towards assuring learning is to operationalize the skills we want parents to learn and continue to provide training and feedback until parents achieve stipulated levels of competence. That is, it is much more important to continue to provide training to parents until they are able to consistently use the skills being trained than it is to only provide training during an 8-week workshop or to use a commercially available program because it is convenient. (p. 527)

## Location of Sessions

To the maximum extent possible, the location of the training sessions should be central and easily accessible to the participants. School buildings, churches, or community auditoriums provide the consultant with an optimum amount of flexibility. For example, if meetings are held in a school or community facility, there is usually access to audiovisual equipment, chalkboards, and ample space. Although the informal atmosphere in someone's home may initially be more conducive to discussion, one should also consider the disadvantages that can occur in someone's home (e.g., potential distractions, the logistical problems of transporting equipment and materials).

## Grouping

Although there are no clear rules on the optimum number of people in a parent training group, experience seems to indicate that small groups, ranging from 8 to 12 people, are best. Small groups based on common need offer more opportunity for each parent to participate (Elksnin & Elksnin, 1991). Further, if role playing and behavior rehearsal are part of the training—and they should be—small groups facilitate those exercises. Frequently, people who are meeting to discuss problems become inhibited if the group is too large. Also, larger meetings can be dominated by a few outspoken parents, and less verbal members may not participate as much.

Finally, groups should remain intact for the length of the training program. The rationale, of course, is that personal relationships have a chance to develop among the parents, and they become more willing to confide in each other.

## Cost of Sessions

There are a number of ways to reduce or eliminate the cost of parent training programs to the school: First, obtain the training through a university or college.

Frequently, colleges offer course work or practica that require graduate students to actively engage in parent programming. Under the supervision of faculty members, parent training is offered at minimal cost or no cost at all. Second, apply for grant money. Many national, state, and local sources offer grant money to organizations involved in parent training. A reference list of sources can be obtained at a public library. Third, seek funds through corporations or private individuals. Many national and local corporations have funds budgeted for community projects. Guidelines are often available to help organizations apply for these sources of money, and private individuals have been known to donate funds for parent training programs. Fourth, secure volunteer assistance. Teachers or administrators interested in establishing parent education and training programs can often be enlisted to run the groups without charge.

## Structure of Sessions

While the topics will vary from session to session, it is important that the structure of the sessions remain consistent. During each session the parents should receive information that will help them at home; have the opportunity to ask questions and discuss issues; practice skills taught in the session; and receive feedback, reinforcement, and support. It is one thing for parents to gain cognitive or affective knowledge; it is quite another for them to gain the practical skill needed to apply that knowledge at home. Training sessions that emphasize the former at the expense of the latter provide the parents with only half of the skills they need. "Rap" sessions and home visits also have a useful place in the overall structure of parenting programs. Both can provide the means for personal sharing and emotional support. Consultants would be advised, however, to balance these types of sessions against the overall goals of the program.

The initial session should be devoted to having the parents get to know one another. Effective consultants typically use "icebreakers" to encourage parents to talk to one another. For example, the consultant might have everyone mingle, introducing themselves, saying where they live, and sharing other basic, but nonintrusive information.

## The Final Session

The final session should be reserved for distributing certificates of achievement (Figure 6.14) and answering any questions that parents may have. Plans for follow-up can be discussed, and individual parent concerns can be addressed.

## The Team Leader

To a large extent the success or failure of a parent training program can be traced to the effectiveness of the team leader (Kramer, 1985). Just as teachers are willing to accept the suggestions of supervisors they perceive as competent, parents are likely to accept the recommendations and suggestions of a parent trainer they believe is trustworthy and expert. Parents must feel that the trainer cares about their problems and is a person in whom they can confide. Also, parents must feel that the trainer has had experience with the types of problems they are encountering. If parents do not have confidence in the trainer's ability to help them, little progress is likely to be made.

# THE OHIO STATE UNIVERSITY
## COLLEGE OF EDUCATION
## SCHOOL OF PHYSICAL ACTIVITY AND EDUCATIONAL SERVICES

Hereby acknowledges that

*Christine Tanner*

Has successfully demonstrated the competencies of the

***Parenting and Family-Skills Workshop***

**Parenting and family-skills acquired:**

➤ Pinpointing Specific Child Behaviors
➤ Observing and Recording Child Behaviors
➤ Graphing Behavioral Data
➤ Selecting and Using Strategies for Increasing, Decreasing, Maintaining, and Generalizing Behaviors
➤ Using Contingency Contracting
➤ Evaluating the Effects of Parenting

*March 17, 2000*
Awarded on

*Mike Sherman*
PAES School Director

*Marge Campiglia*
Workshop Leader

*Kathy Q. Wojan*
Education and Training Coordinator

**Figure 6.14.** A sample certificate of achievement that could be presented to parents at the completion of a parental education and training program.

As with any type of training program, consultants must weigh expected benefits against the cost of implementation. If time or resources permit, extensive training programs that sequence technical parenting skills can be implemented (Feldman et al., 1986; Dachman et al., 1986; Kohr, Parrish, Neef, Driessen, & Hallinan, 1988). In situations where time or support are scarce or logistical impracticality exists, consultants must fashion training programs that might focus on specific skill acquisition (Schulze et al., 1989), rely on the support of parent relationships (Harris et al., 1998), or be limited to information and/or advocacy training (Lovitt, 1989).

Finally, consultants must take the long view, meaning that any functional and comprehensive parent training program might take up to 5 years to develop fully (Wolf & Stephens, 1990). Most social or institutional change takes time (Fullen, 1982), and if consultants give up during the initial stages of implementation because of poor attendance at meetings or lack of apparent parental support, they may be sowing the seeds of their downfall. It simply takes time, consistent and systematic planning, and parent investment to affect large-scale change. Consultants must recognize the needs that most parents have for their children—personal and social adjustment, accommodation, independence, literacy, and a supportive environment (Lange, Ysseldyke, & Lehr, 1997)—and fashion programs to meet those needs.

# Parents in the Classroom

Until recently the classroom was thought to be the exclusive domain of the classroom teacher. The teacher was responsible for planning and teaching lessons and evaluating the performance of each student. Clearly, these are teacher responsibilities, but just as clearly some duties can be accomplished by parents who volunteer in the classroom.

Parent volunteers, though they require instruction and supervision by the teacher, can perform essential jobs for the teacher. For example, parent volunteers can write or explain directions to students, correct papers and provide reinforcement, or give one-to-one remedial instruction. However, without a well-thought-out plan for working with parents as paraprofessionals, many of the possible benefits will be lost.

Fortunately, a number of educators have recognized the need to provide training for parents who assume the duties of a paraprofessional. Strenecky, McLoughlin, and Edge (1979), for example, identified guidelines for a parent tutoring program. In general, those authors feel that potential parent tutors should receive an inservice orientation, support from the school administration, and supervision from the teacher or consultant. Further, they recommend that parents not tutor their own children.

Many parents would be unable to participate in such a program because of family or work responsibilities, but even if a few parents were able to volunteer, the teachers, pupils, and parents would gain the following advantages: (a) given a reduced teacher-student ratio, the teacher would be free to provide more direct remedial assistance to the students most in need; (b) parents would become better acquainted with the problems of exceptional students and more knowledgeable about methods for remediating or coping with those problems; (c) parent input in the IEP and IFSP process would be enhanced; and (d) if the program incorporates "foster grandparents," capable senior citizens would have the opportunity to contribute their time and talents in a worthwhile project (Jones, 1986)—for them, an increased feeling of self-worth could be a valuable spin-off advantage.

# Conclusion

This chapter suggested a number of ways in which practitioners can consult with the parents and families of children with disabilities. A model was presented that describes the types of services professionals and parents can perform and the levels of those services. Techniques for increasing parent involvement as behavior managers and home-based educators were presented. Using a telephone answering service and several other methods were suggested as a means by which consultants can help to increase home-school communication and student academic performance. Procedures for conducting effective parent conferences were described, and several recommendations were proposed for establishing and implementing functional parent training programs. Finally, the use of parents as in-school tutors was discussed.

# Summary of Key Points

## Consulting with Parents of Inclusion Students

1. When consulting with parents, practitioners must be aware of ecological factors, parental and familial barriers, and empowerment issues.

2. There are at least three reasons for consulting and working with parents: (a) parents can help with programming for generalization; (b) parents can be trained to interact effectively with their children in a manner that is likely to facilitate their inclusion; and (c) it is cost effective.

3. Parent-professional interactions that do not consider the contemporary family, cultural-ethnic considerations, language, and life-cycle factors, and which are not embodied within a consultative relationship, are not likely to be successful.

4. Consultants can develop such supports in at least three ways: connecting parents to support groups, setting the occasion for parents to become more active in research efforts, and developing ownership.

## Mirror Model of Parental Involvement

5. The Mirror Model of Parental Involvement is divided into two reciprocal areas: professional services and parent services. Within each area are four levels defined by the terms *all, most, some,* and *few.*

6. The Mirror Model of Parental Involvement is helpful to the consultant because it affects teacher expectations of a successful parent training partnership. Also, it shifts the emphasis of evaluation from single measures to multiple measures.

7. The Mirror Model of Parental Involvement can serve as a communication vehicle for teachers and parents.

# Parents as Behavior Managers

8. Consultants should examine the full range of environmental variables that contribute to problem resolution. For example, antecedent and consequence strategies should be considered.

9. Consultants can assist parents to become better behavior managers in three ways: First, workshop programs can be offered that provide parents with skills. Second, consultants can refer parents to support groups (e.g., LDA). Third, consultants can serve as mediators between the home and the school.

10. Maintenance of parent skills may be difficult as behavior manager due to the insular circumstances of the parents. Community-based friendships may reduce this effect.

# Parents as Home-Based Educators

11. Parents serve as home-based educators when they supplement the instruction their child receives during the day.

12. Parents can serve as appropriate home-based educators if guidance and/or mini-training sessions are provided to them.

# Communication Techniques with Parents and Family Members

13. Communication with parents can occur at the information, advocacy, or training level.

14. Effective communication is rooted in the following principles: accepting what is being said, listening, questioning appropriately, encouraging, staying directed, and developing a working alliance.

15. Home-school communication techniques with parents can be facilitated using the telephone, notes and notebooks, videos, parent conferences, student-led conferences, home visits, and parent training. Each of these techniques has advantages, and techniques can be combined.

16. The range of intervention options for parents can be categorized into four models: professionally centered, family-allied, family-focused, and family-centered.

17. Home-school communication programs managed by a telephone answering device offer consultants several advantages not available through conventional avenues.

# Establishing Family Education and Training Programs

18. Coincidental teaching may be an effective alternative for consultants who do not have the opportunity to offer long-term family-training programs.

19. To establish an effective family-training program, consultants should use a consistent theoretical model, determine the parental skills needed, allow for varying rates of learning, employ a systematic approach, and provide for follow-up.

20. Effective family-training programs must also consider variables such as the time of the meeting; the length, number, location, and structure of sessions; grouping; cost; and qualifications of the team leader.

## Parents in the Classroom

21. Parents can be effective assistants in the classroom by helping with one-to-one instruction, giving feedback to students orally and in writing, and preparing materials.

22. Parents in the classroom reduce teacher-student ratios; acquaint parents with remedial strategies for exceptional students; potentially improve the IEP process; and permit senior citizens to engage in a meaningful activity.

23. Foster grandparents or senior citizens can contribute time and talent to assist mainstream students.

## Questions

1. Describe the ecology—parental, familial, and societal—that affects consulting interactively with parents. What steps need to be taken to "empower" parents to be more effective?

2. Identify the four levels of parent involvement in Kroth's (1980, 1985) Mirror Model of Parental Involvement. What types of activities could professionals and parents do at each level?

3. Provide two examples that show how parents use behavior management techniques to change inappropriate child behavior. What are the advantages and disadvantages of these tactics?

4. How can consultants develop proactive social supports for parents and family members?

5. List three advantages of using the telephone to enhance student academic achievement. Cite variations of how a home-school communication program could be used with a telephone answering device.

6. Parent conferences can occur across three contexts. Give an example of each context and the consultant's potential role within each.

7. According to Stephens (1977), what are the key phases or components of an effective parent conference?

8. What guidelines do Anastopoulos et al. (1991) offer for establishing an effective parent training program?

9. Name two ways to help reduce the cost of parent training programs.

10. What advantages can be obtained from having parents participate as in-class tutors?

# Discussion Points and Exercises

1. Argue for or against the use of parents as in-school tutors. State your reasons and provide documentation for your positions.

2. Conduct an inservice training program based on the recommendations of Cooper and Edge (1981); Heward, Dardig, and Rossett (1979); or Anastopoulos et al. (1991). Note the effects. Rewrite inservice training components based on your experience.

3. Conduct an informal meeting with teachers, parents, and administrators. The topic of the meeting is "Managing Students' Behavior at School and at Home." Record comments from each participant. Obtain consensus on a course of action with a current problem.

4. Discuss the special problems students with disabilities have inside and outside the general education classroom. Identify at least three recommendations that you could offer to teachers and other support personnel for dealing more effectively with these students.

5. Present a videotape of a parent conference. Have teachers identify the four phases outlined by Stephens (1977) (rapport building, obtaining information, providing information, and summarizing). Follow-up the videotape training by observing teachers during a conference. Provide appropriate praise and feedback.

6. Conduct parent education or training programs using textual, modular, and video formats with a direct instruction framework. Note the effects of each format with respect to acquisition, maintenance, generality, and social validity.

# Multicultural Considerations in Educational Consultation

7

The authors recognize that one's culture is influenced by a variety of factors, some of which are religion, age, gender, abilities, ethnicity, and language. In this chapter, the focus is on working with people who can help consultants deal with the language differences exhibited by students and their families. Language differences can result in substantial changes in the way educational assessment and instruction are delivered. Therefore, after discussing demographic considerations, the characteristics of culturally and linguistically diverse (CLD) students, and educational service delivery models for these students, we will discuss professional competencies for working with culturally and linguistically diverse exceptional (CLDE) students and their families. Examples from the literature and the authors' experiences related to these topics are provided.

## Objectives

After reading this chapter, the reader should be able to:

1. describe demographic trends in the United States;

2. describe the characteristics of culturally and linguistically diverse students;

3. describe three educational service delivery models for culturally and linguistically diverse exceptional (CLDE) students;

4. identify professional competencies for working with CLDE students;

5. identify strategies and resources for accommodating the culture of CLDE students;

6. distinguish two key features of second-language acquisition;

7. identify strategies and resources for enhancing second-language acquisition;

8. identify strategies for understanding the language and culture of culturally and linguistically diverse families;

9. identify strategies to facilitate communication with culturally and linguistically diverse families;

10. identify strategies for involving culturally and linguistically diverse families in the school programs of their children;

11. identify assessment techniques to assist in determining a student's language proficiency;

12. describe the principles that should provide the foundation of an appropriate curriculum for culturally and linguistically diverse students;

13. identify strategies for collaboratively planning for the language and culture needs of culturally and linguistically diverse students;

14. describe modifications that are sensitive to language and culture;

15. identify criteria to evaluate the appropriateness of curriculum materials for culturally and linguistically diverse students;

16. identify strategies to promote understanding of one's own and others' cultures;

17. identify strategies to enhance cross-cultural interactions;

18. identify strategies for working with interpreters;

19. describe school personnel and programs that are resources for CLDE students.

## Key Terms

limited English proficient (LEP)

culturally and linguistically diverse (CLD) students

culturally and linguistically diverse exceptional (CLDE) students

integrated bilingual special education model

bilingual support model

coordinated services model

cultural identity

assimilation

acculturation

second-language acquisition

basic interpersonal communication skills (BICS)

cognitive academic linguistic proficiency (CALP)

comprehensible input

sheltered instruction

cross-cultural competence

language proficiency

language dominance

symbols of respect

interpreters

bilingual education

transition program

maintenance program

two-way enrichment bilingual education programs

English as a Second Language (ESL)

## Demographic Considerations

More and more, schools are charged with educating increasingly diverse student populations. Of the 45 million students now enrolled in public and private elementary and secondary schools, over 30% are from groups designated as racial or ethnic minorities. This diversity will increase, as it is anticipated that by the year 2050, only 50% of the total population of the United States will be non-Hispanic whites (Gonzalez, Brusca-Vega, & Yawkey, 1997). Conversely, because the majority of general and special educators appear to be Euro-American, monolingual speakers of English, the composition of the population of educators may not reflect the changing ethnic and language composition of the population of the children they may eventually serve (Obiakor & Utley, 1997).

Linguistically different individuals are scattered throughout the country, with heavier concentrations in the Southwest and the Northwest. Thirty-one states have at least 25,000 children and youth who are not native English speakers (Baca & deValenzuela, 1998). Location aside, the largest single group of linguistically different students is Hispanic, representing approximately 75% of the *limited English proficient* (LEP) population of students (i.e., those students who have limited skills in English reading, writing, speaking, and understanding). The number of Hispanic students increased from 9.9% of the public school student population in 1986 to 12.3% in 1992 (Baca & deValenzuela, 1998).

Considering the overall size of the culturally and linguistically diverse population, another important question is How many of these children also have special needs? Baca and deValenzuela (1998) estimate that approximately 1.2 million children are both culturally *and* linguistically different *and* exceptional. These students are entitled to receive services under bilingual legislation and special education legislation. However, historically, culturally and linguistically diverse children have been misplaced and overrepresented in special education programs (cf. Baca & deValenzuela, 1998). Due to biased assessment practices, many more culturally and linguistically diverse students have been placed in special education programs than would be expected. Interestingly, underrepresentation has also become an issue. Some parents and educators are reluctant to identify linguistically diverse students as in need of special education since special education services that appropriately address the needs of these students is not always available. It is important that consultants facilitate the appropriate education of these students by considering the role language education programs can take in the instruction of CLDE students. Educators are encouraged to collaborate with school district personnel who work with culturally and linguistically diverse students and to examine the writings of authorities in the field to best understand how to coordinate services for these students.

Some resources that readers may find useful are the following: Baca & Cervantes, 1998; Cummins, 1981a, 1981b, 1984, 1986; Echevarria & Graves, 1998; Esquivel & Yoshida, 1985; Fradd & Tikunoff, 1987; Garcia, 1982; Gersten & Jiménez-Gonzalez, 1998; Gonzalez et al., 1997; Jones, 1988; Krashen, 1981, 1982, 1985, 1999; Lynch & Hanson, 1998; Ortiz, 1988; Ovando & Collier, 1985; Terrell, 1981; Willig & Greenberg, 1986. Readers are also encouraged to access the Web site of National Clearinghouse for Bilingual Education (NCBE) (*http://www.ncbe.gwu.edu*). NCBE collects, analyzes, synthesizes, and disseminates information related to linguistically and culturally diverse students.

## Characteristics of Culturally and Linguistically Diverse Students

*Culturally and linguistically diverse students* are those whose culture and/or language background at home is different from the culture of the school. Most typically, they are not members of the predominant Euro-American culture. There are at least three categories of difference—physical, linguistic, and behavioral—that CLD students have to deal with as students in U.S. schools (Leung, 1990). For instance, CLD students have visibly different physical features and skin color that distinguishes them from Euro-American students (Leung, 1990). Young children attending school must deal with developing self-image and social status. CLD students must also deal with what Guskin and Guskin (1970) call the "psychology of difference." CLD students may become distressed when they realize how others perceive them and that they cannot change their physical differences or social status. However, not all CLD students are physically different, nor is the impact of being physically different uniformly debilitating. Generally, perceived physical and cultural differences have less potential risk in cosmopolitan areas, where diversities are prevalent. However, it may be an issue to address for a sensitive CLD student going to school in a provincial or closed community (Leung, 1990).

Consultants also need to be aware of and accommodate for the linguistic differences of CLD students. Differences may include not speaking any English; speaking little English and consequently not communicating well; communicating adequately in English but not speaking English well enough to think and learn in English; and speaking a dialect—like the Black dialect—that makes their speech different from standard English and may cause them difficulty in communicating (Leung, 1990). Consultants should help educators to become aware of the individual linguistic variations among their students, understand the implications of those differences, and help all students use language for communication and learning.

A third difference identified by Leung (1990) is culture-based behavior. According to Leung, "Behaviors are governed by culture. They manifest cultural norms, values, beliefs, and practices. Therefore, behavioral characteristics of one culture group can be markedly different from those of another. . . . Statistically, culturally diverse children's behaviors cannot be normal, unless their cultures approximate mainstream culture" (pp. 40–41). Several authors have discussed differences in the behaviors of children who are representative of the Euro-American culture and the behaviors of children from other ethnic/racial groups. The following are some examples:

- "Most Afro-Americans . . . speak 'standard English' . . . in settings where it is appropriate to conform to the dominant society's norm. However, when socializing with less assimilated relatives and friends, they often use many words and phrases that linguists call 'Black English'" (Banks, 1984, p. 57).

- "Few Asians engage in free participation in group discussions" (Kitano, 1973, p. 14).

- "American Indian students learn more through observation or visual means rather than verbal" (Pepper, 1976, p. 140).

- "Hispanic students prefer cooperative activities, are concerned with immediate tasks, and are characterized by close family ties" (Aragon & Marquez, 1973, pp. 20–21).

Consultants are encouraged to work with teachers as they help CLD students deal with their differences, provide time for CLD students to accommodate to the norms of the classroom, and modify the norms of the classroom to incorporate CLD students. CLD students may be aware of their differences, experience shame and confusion, and withdraw from classroom activities until they learn what is culturally appropriate for the classroom. Older CLD students may show defiance or anger as a way to protect their self-esteem and cultural identity.

CLD students have many issues to deal with in school. Consultants should help classroom teachers to be aware of and accommodate for the social, psychological, and physical adjustments CLD students face in school as well as at home. Families, especially immigrant families, may be adjusting to experiences that are not common to them. For example, many family members must deal with a loss of social status after immigrating to the United States. CLD students may have difficulty developing their own identity, and, if these students also have disabilities, the impact of their special needs may become confounded. Consultants should take responsibility for informing classroom teachers about the culturally and linguistically diverse students in their classes and their indi-

*Though behavioral descriptions of children representing various ethnic and racial groups are provided, the authors want to stress that consultants must guard against stereotyping children's behavior because of their ethnic or racial identity. Each individual constructs his or her own culture, and that culture may or may not be heavily influenced by ethnic or racial identity. Consultants must learn the individual cultures of those with whom they work and not make assumptions about behaviors, beliefs, or values based on ethnic or racial characteristics, socioeconomic status, or educational background.*

vidual characteristics. Most important, classroom teachers must be sensitive to the needs of these students. If teachers are not informed and sensitive, these students may fail in school and suffer socially and psychologically (Leung, 1990).

# Educational Service Delivery Models for CLDE Students

*Culturally and linguistically diverse exceptional students* are those students whose culture and/or language at home is different from the culture of the school and who have one or more disabilities (e.g., learning disabilities, mental retardation, visual impairment). Traditionally, there have been three models for providing educational services to CLDE students: the Integrated Bilingual Special Education Model, the Bilingual Support Model, and the Coordinated Services Model (Ambert & Dew, 1982). We shall discuss each of these models and how they relate to inclusive instruction.

## Integrated Bilingual Special Education Model

In the *integrated bilingual special education model,* the bilingual special education teacher provides all the educational services for the CLDE student in a self-contained special program. To offer this program, the teacher must be fluent in the languages of all the children in the class as well as knowledgeable and sensitive to all the children's various cultural and linguistic differences. The teacher's professional training must include bilingual and special education methodologies appropriate for the levels of language proficiency for all the students in the classroom and the types of exceptionalities the children represent. Even when there is a teacher with all the necessary expertise to conduct such a program, the self-contained nature of the program limits the contact CLDE students will have with their same-age, nondisabled peers. Therefore, this type of program, though appropriate for some students, may not be considered the least restrictive environment for all CLDE students. Consultants are encouraged to consider other types of service delivery options that promote the inclusion of CLDE students with CLD students who do not have disabilities.

## Bilingual Support Model

In the *bilingual support model,* instruction is also delivered in a self-contained setting. However, this model is used when the teacher is trained in special education but not in bilingual education and is not proficient in the languages of all the children in the class. In this situation, a bilingual special education paraprofessional provides native language support for the instruction that the special education teacher provides in the self-contained class. Besides limiting the contact CLDE students have with their nondisabled peers, this model does not provide for an individual trained in bilingual education to deliver bilingual services to students.

This model is seldom appropriate with CLDE students. Monolingual English-speaking special education teachers certainly have much to offer CLDE students; however, it is suggested that they and their bilingual paraprofessionals work closely with educators trained to teach CLD students, provide services within those teachers' classrooms, and coordinate their efforts with those teachers.

## Coordinated Services Model

See Chapters 3 and 4 for a discussion of those skills.

In the *coordinated services model,* the special education teacher and the teacher of CLD students combine their expertise to serve the CLDE student. In this way, the CLDE student has the benefit of the services of two well-trained individuals. It is also possible that CLDE students can receive these services with nondisabled peers in the classrooms of the teachers of CLD students, thereby receiving services in an inclusive environment. However, to implement a coordinated services model, all teachers providing services must have the skills necessary for effective collaboration.

A continuum of services for CLDE students could include the following:

- full-time bilingual special education;
- bilingual or general education with ESL and pull-out special education;
- inclusive classroom with special education consultant;
- general education with ESL and modifications for disabilities;
- bilingual education and modifications for disabilities.

Coordinated services for CLDE students should be offered in all placements.

# Professional Competencies for Working with CLDE Students

The authors would add that these areas are equally important when consulting with faculty, staff, and parents.

In her summary of the literature, Harris (2000) identified the following areas every educator needs to develop to work successfully with CLDE students: culture, language, families, assessment, curriculum, instructional planning, instruction, materials, and consultation and collaboration. Consultants should take responsibility for helping educators to develop competencies in each of these areas.

## Culture

When developing an individualized program for a CLDE student, it is necessary to remember that the student's language is inextricably bound to his or her culture. Culture provides meaning for verbal communication. Consultants should help educators to understand the historical origins of local communities, as well as the socialization systems and differences in attitudes toward education and motivation (Baca & Almanza, 1991).

Franklin (1992), in her discussion of culturally sensitive instructional practices for African American learners with disabilities, identified several assumptions that should be the basis for culturally sensitive practices and are applicable to students from a variety of cultural backgrounds. First, instruction should incorporate resources from the learner's environment outside the school, i.e., the home and the local community. Second, culturally sensitive teachers should identify and build on their students' strengths and interests.

Third, culturally sensitive teachers should realize that language and dialectical differences are important cultural influences that affect not just communication, but also interaction between the teacher and the learner. Teachers should learn different interpretations of classroom activities based on how the students view the world. Finally, culturally sensitive instruction should be an integral part of activities that provide learners with the opportunity to learn and practice new skills.

Harris (2000) suggests that consultants must develop the personal and professional competencies to work with individuals whose culture differs from theirs and to respect the development of these individuals' identities within their own culture. *Cultural identity* is one's identifcation with a cultural group. Franklin, James, and Watson (1996) discuss strategies that educators should use at various stages of a student's development of cultural identity. For example, at the beginning stage of cultural identity development, the student tends to reject his or her cultural values and prefer those of the dominant culture. In this case, educators should use multicultural content to help the student develop cultural awareness and appreciation. When a student is confused about the importance of his or her culture in relation to that of other cultures, educators should design instruction that reflects the contributions of the student's culture to society, as well as the contributions of other cultural groups. As collaborators develop interventions, it is important that they assess the cultural identity of each student. According to Lynch and Hanson (1998) getting to know the students and their families as individuals can be the basis for this assessment. In this way, educators can ascertain the values of the children and their families and not just assume that they identify with particular values because they belong to a particular ethnic group.

In summary, consultants must consider the cultural background these students bring to the educational setting. The consultant should help educators to develop a curriculum in consideration of the following characteristics of the child: (a) What is the student's familiarity and identification with the Euro-American culture? (b) What is the student's familiarity and identification with his or her own traditional culture? (c) What is the student's contemporary culture? (d) What is the student's expectation of the educational environment? and (e) Has the student been successful in becoming part of the educational community? Consultants should be aware of the distinction between cultural *assimilation* and *acculturation*. Assimilation "holds that diverse cultures should be merged into a single homogeneous society with common lifestyles, language and cultural practices" (Winzer & Mazurek, 1998, p. 27). Assimilation is not consistent with a culturally pluralistic philosophy. Acculturation, or the degree to which an individual develops his or her own culture based on an integration of dominant and home cultures, reflects cultural pluralism or the belief that a "society is strengthened and enriched by the contributions of different cultural groups" (Winzer & Mazurek, 1998, p. 28). We encourage consultants to help teachers and their students acculturate. Table 7.1 provides a list of questions that should be addressed when instructing culturally and linguistically diverse students.

## Language

Several researchers have documented the value of the family's native language in the education of students. The Ramírez report is probably the most noteworthy, documenting the results of an 8-year study commissioned by the U.S.

## Table 7.1

Questions to Identify Cultural Practices That Influence Students' Behaviors

| Topic | Questions |
|---|---|
| Family Dynamics | • What are the important family rules?<br>• What are the primary disciplinary methods used at home and the student's reactions to those methods?<br>• Is the student praised, corrected, or criticized? How often and by whom?<br>• What are the behavioral expectations for children toward elders and teachers?<br>• What emotions are expressed openly?<br>• What emotions are never expressed?<br>• What messages are communicated to children nonverbally?<br>• Are shame and guilt used as disciplinary techniques? |
| Misperceptions About Student Behavior | • What roles do silence, questions, and responses play in the student's culture?<br>• How do the student's quiet and obedient behaviors affect the teacher's perceptions?<br>• Do student's inappropriate behaviors result from a lack of language proficiency or misunderstanding?<br>• Does the teaching style differ from the student's accustomed learning style? |
| Student Characteristics | • Do students question or obey authority figures?<br>• Do students assume a competitive or a cooperative posture in their leaning and interactions with other students?<br>• Do students put their needs and desires before those of the group or vice versa?<br>• What are the students' beliefs regarding sharing belongings with others? How do those beliefs affect rules, classroom organization, and expectations?<br>• Do boys and girls demonstrate different behavioral expectations in their interactions with each other or with adults? Do students' perceptions about gender influence grouping patterns in the classroom or their interactions with and respect for authority figures?<br>• Do students maintain personal space or distance different in their interactions with other students of the same gender, students of the opposite gender, or adults? |
| Disciplinary Style | • What are the acceptable and unacceptable ways to motivate or change students' behavior based on their perceptions of positive and negative consequences?<br>• What are acceptable ways to provide feedback to students about their academic and social behaviors?<br>• How do students' perceptions about rights influence their willingness to change behavior to benefit their peers? |

*Note.* From "Creating Classroom Environments That Address the Linguistic and Cultural Backgrounds of Students with Disabilities," by T. W. Sileo and M. A. Prater, 1998, *Remedial and Special Education, 19*(6), p. 329. Copyright 1998 by PRO-ED, Inc. Reprinted with permission.

Department of Education. The study was designed to provide definitive answers to a controversial question in American education: What types of programs work best in helping Latino students succeed in school? Both opponents and proponents of bilingual education accept the report as methodologically valid.

In Cummins's (1992) summary of the Ramírez report, he stated that Latino students who received sustained instruction in their home language throughout elementary school had better academic prospects than those who received most or all of their instruction in English. Cummins (1991) also documented the development of a second language through instruction in the first or native language. In his longitudinal study of Portuguese-speaking children, he found that literate and conversational skills in the home language were significantly related to development of literate and conversational skills in a second language.

Lack of native language development can affect student learning at school and at home. Wong Fillmore (1991a) conducted a large-scale study of at-home language use patterns among non-native English-speaking families and documented the tragic consequences of the breakdown of communication between parents and children. If parents do not receive instruction in the English language, they frequently attain only limited command of English. Their children rapidly lose facility in the native language because instruction and usage are not present. The parents and their children then have difficulty communicating in a language they both can understand and use proficiently. Wong Fillmore (1991b) argues strongly for provision of home-language preschool programs that reinforce children's identity and conceptual foundation in the first language. Her data suggests that such programs can increase academic achievement significantly at no cost to English-language proficiency.

Since there is considerable research to suggest that inclusion of students' home language and culture into the school program is a significant predictor of academic success, all educators working with CLDE students should have a basic understanding of the nature of language, as well as an understanding of the principles of first- and second-language acquisition. They should also, as with culture, understand regional, social, and developmental varieties in language use (Baca & Almanza, 1991).

Two key features of *second-language acquisition* warrant emphasis. First Cummins (1981a, 1984) suggests that language proficiency is composed of two distinguishable components: everyday conversational skills (*basic interpersonal communication skills,* BICS) and abstract skills characteristic of academic instruction (*cognitive academic linguistic proficiency,* CALP). It is important for the teacher to know the level and type of proficiency (e.g., BICS or CALP) of a student to decide which language to use when providing different types of instruction. If a student has mastered BICS in English but not CALP, the student may be able to converse in English but unable to learn academic content in English. CALP seems to be acquired only after a 5- to 7-year exposure to the new language, in this case, English.

A second feature of second-language acquisition relates to the process whereby students acquire a second language. According to Krashen (1982), a second language is acquired when the student receives *comprehensible input* (i.e., students understand the meaning of the content being taught) in a low-anxiety situation. Terrell (1981) provides the following suggestions for teachers to provide comprehensible input: "(1) create a necessity for communication of some message, (2) communicate a message, and (3) modify (simplify) their speech until the students understand the message" (p. 123).

Comprehensible input is necessary but not sufficient. One must reduce anxiety so that comprehensible input will not be blocked. Terrell (1981) provides the following suggestions to teachers to create an atmosphere low in anxiety: "(1) the emphasis should be on the use of language in interpersonal communication (i.e., the focus is on students and their needs and desires as individuals), (2) all attempts at language use should be accepted and encouraged without overt correction of form, and (3) no attempt should be made to force production before acquirers are ready" (p. 125).

Several strategies have been developed to enhance second-language acquisition (cf. Asher, 1977; Krashen, 1985; Terrell, 1981). An important strategy that should be used by all educators to enhance the comprehensibility of content is *sheltered instruction* (Echevarria & Graves, 1998): "The primary goal of sheltered instruction is to teach academic subject matter to English-language learners using comprehensible language and context, enabling information to be understood by the learner" (p. 8). When using sheltered instruction, teachers provide assistance to learners through visuals and modified texts and within the context of each student's proficiency in English. Planning a sheltered lesson involves identifying critical content and presenting it in meaningful units. In a sheltered lesson, there is a high level of student interaction and a student-centered focus to the instruction in addition to high-context clues provided through visuals and other concrete materials. It is important to explicitly make the connection between students' knowledge and experience and the lesson. The teacher must also be aware of her or his speech (e.g., adjusting it to an appropriate rate) as well as body language and gestures that are used to enhance meaning.

> Readers are encouraged to consult Echevarria and Graves (1998) for a thorough discussion of sheltered instruction as well as practical guidelines and lesson plans.

Educators are urged to determine the student's mastery of CALP before relying upon English as the language of instruction for complex academic subjects like those usually found in secondary classes. If Cummins's (1981a, 1984) estimate of a 5- to 7-year exposure to the new language is correct, secondary educators should seriously question the extent of each secondary Limited English Proficient (LEP) student's English language mastery when developing appropriate educational programs for those students. Given the importance of the students' native language at elementary and secondary levels, if educators are not fluent in that language, they will need to become fluent or work in collaboration with teachers of CLD students who are fluent.

## Families

To work effectively with CLD families, consultants must develop *cross-cultural competence.* As Lynch and Hanson (1998) indicate, cross-cultural competence in our multicultural society is important and yet not easy to define. However, the following are common characteristics of a person who has cross-cultural competence: respects others; makes continued and sincere attempts to take others' points of view; is open to learn; is flexible; has a sense of humor; and can tolerate ambiguity (Lynch & Hanson, 1998).

Campinha-Bacote (1994) provides a mental health perspective of cultural competence. In her view, a culturally competent model of care views cultural awareness, knowledge, skill, and encounter as the necessary components of cultural competence. Cultural competence is viewed as a process, not something that is ever finished. This perspective also helps with understanding the multiple steps of the process. Not only must we become culturally aware, but we must also seek sound cultural knowledge and then act accordingly with this awareness and knowledge. That is, we must develop cultural skill (i.e., an ability to assess the cultural perspectives of those with whom we work). Finally, it is imperative that we have cultural encounters, allowing direct engagement in cross-cultural interactions. Campinha-Bacote (1994) asserts that "the failure to directly interact with another cultural group only serves to stereotype that culture" (p. 6).

We will adopt the definition provided by Lynch and Hanson (1998) and promote the process of cultural competence described by Campinha-Bacote insofar as cross-cultural competence is described as "the ability to think, feel, and act in ways that acknowledge, respect, and build upon ethnic, (socio)cultural, and linguistic diversity" (p. 50). As further emphasized by Lynch and Hanson (1998), "This definition assumes that all individuals and groups are diverse and does not imply that one group is normative. It also acknowledges that sociocultural factors often play as great or greater a role in people's shared or unshared experience as their ethnicity, language, or culture" (pp. 49–50). In sum, cross-cultural competence addresses two elements: one's own skills and also developing skills within society at large so that other cultures are not measured against a norm (Lynch & Hanson, 1998).

When working with families of CLDE students, consultants are encouraged to be aware of verbal as well as nonverbal communication. Edens (1997) has found that lack of cultural knowledge and lack of the use of common patterns of communication were barriers to developing relationships with culturally diverse families. The family members may feel uncomfortable, tire quickly, and/or need time to reflect, thereby influencing how they communicate with the consultant. The consultant should be aware of family members' behaviors and feelings, especially if an interpreter is being used, as the interpreter may also serve to "filter" those feelings. Consultants should also be aware of their own nonverbal behavior and its cultural implications. For example, closeness and body contact are common in Hispanic cultures. However, diversity is the rule rather than the exception among ethnic groups. For example, an American Latino family that has been in the United States for several generations may have very different customs when compared to a recently emigrated family. This is particularly important to keep in mind to avoid assuming that bicultural consultants can easily identify with family members. They may speak the same language as a Latino family, but, depending on their own cultural identity, they may or may not share the same cultural practices as that family. Therefore, the consultant's distance when speaking with another person, his or her body posture, use of hands, and dress may have different meanings to families of other cultures with regard to formality, level of authority, and respect (Brandenburg-Ayres, 1990). According to Edens (1997) the following interpersonal and communication behaviors are useful in working with culturally and linguistically diverse families: (a) promoting a collaborative and supportive relationship; (b) respecting the knowledge base and experience of the parents; (c) developing a "common language" and facilitating communication between the family and the school system; and (d) identifying mutually acceptable methods of assessment and intervention. To practice these interpersonal and communication behaviors, it is essential for consultants, bicultural or unicultural, to carefully examine their biases and assumptions, a topic which is discussed later in this chapter. Table 7.2 provides communicative guidelines for professionals when consulting with families of CLDE students.

Often, communication with parents of children with disabilities occurs through parent conferences. Consultants should consider several factors when

Consultants should strive to become competent and comfortable in the cultures of the families with whom they work. Jordan et al. (1998) suggest strategies for developing cultural competence, including learning about the family's customs and traditions. While some skills within this domain may be acquired by reading books and articles, more important skills can be learned only by interacting with family members and/or other members of the culture (e.g., clergy, community employers) who serve as cultural informants and/or colleagues (e.g., teacher, paraprofessional). Behring and Gelinas (1996) offer suggestions for consulting with Asian American children and families. Lynch and Hanson (1998) provide a useful resource across a variety of ethnic and racial groups for the school professional working with children with disabilities and their families.

For an example of a cross-cultural conference, see Jordan et al. (1998).

## Table 7.2

### Communication Guidelines for Educators Consulting with Families of CLDE Students

- Speak to family members as adults, as collaborators with valuable information.
- Use comprehensible language.
- Teach the interpreter the use of professional vocabulary.
- Begin with student's good points.
- Be certain of comprehending the family members; if they have accents, ask them to repeat and speak more slowly.
- Be certain family members understand you; repeat, speak clearly.
- Remain calm, keep voice at an even level.
- Consider cultural and linguistic implications. A rising voice may not indicate emotion in another culture; more response "wait time" may be appropriate.
- If the interaction seems to fail, it may not signal the end of communication.

*Note.* From "Working with Parents" (p. 68), by S. Brandenburg-Ayres, 1990, in V. I. Correa and S. H. Fradd (Eds.), *Bilingual/ESOL Special Education Collaboration and Reform Modules,* Gainesville, FL: University of Florida. Adapted with permission.

conducting conferences with culturally and linguistically diverse parents of children with disabilities. One factor is the definition of disability that the family members maintain. Harry, Grenot-Scheyer, Smith-Lewis, Park, Xin, and Schwartz (1995) found that families from culturally and linguistically diverse backgrounds generally have a broader definition of disability than that of the school professional. Family members define a child's disability in terms of the child's functioning in the home environment as well as their expectations for the child's future. Another factor to consider is the possibility that families may be confusing special education services with other support services in the school.

To deal with these factors as well as to promote effective conferencing with culturally and linguistically diverse families, Jordan et al. (1998) offer the following suggestions:

- Have frequent casual conferences with families to build rapport and increase knowledge about one another.

- Use purposeful conferences when a particular topic needs to be addressed such as Individualized Education Program or Individualized Family Service Plan changes.

- Use multiple methods to encourage communication (e.g., phone calls, informal notes).

- Be sure to invite both parents and other significant members of the family to any conference, consistent with any legal guidelines regarding parent custody and/or release of information.

- Allot more time for the conference than you think you may need to maintain rapport and show respect for the family.

Home visits are effective ways to promote understanding of home culture among educators. Once educators understand the culture that exists within the home, they can incorporate culturally appropriate activities and language into the school environment. However, home visits should be conducted within local school guidelines. For example, many school districts have a community liaison that can assist consultants with home visits and provide them with entry into different neighborhood communities.

To facilitate communication with culturally and linguistically diverse families, consultants are encouraged to consider home visits. According to Brandenburg-Ayres (1990), home visits may have the following advantages: "(1) parent difficulties with transportation and child care are resolved, (2) parents may be favorably impressed by the willingness of the school to meet their needs, (3) parents are more comfortable in their own home and may discuss issues with more freedom, (4) much useful information regarding the structure and needs of the family may become evident during the visit, and (5) students often have positive reactions toward the teachers who know and are supportive of their families" (p. 83).

Edens (1997) has found that home visits generally have two purposes: (1) presenting new information as a way to affect change; and (2) developing the relationship between the parents and the consultant as the source of change. If the consultant focuses on presenting information as a way to affect change, several problems may emerge as a result of a cultural mismatch. If using this approach, the consultant must consider the importance of psychosocial influences, including the family structure, the cultural value system, interactional patterns, and adaptive coping strategies that may be different from those of the consultant.

For those consultants focusing on the second purpose of home visits, i.e., developing relationships, Edens (1997) identifies several barriers that can impede the consultant's ability to forge a good relationship. These barriers include perceived lack of respect for parents, failure to trust parents, too strong a focus on children's deficits, failure to show appreciation for parenting styles, and failing to deal successfully with resistance. For example, among some Hispanic and Asian cultures, family problems are viewed as issues to be resolved by the family, not outside professionals. Guidelines for visiting the homes of families of CLDE students are provided in Table 7.3.

Conferences and home visits are two strategies for involving families in the educational programs of their children. However, consultants should be aware of reasons that parents from diverse cultural populations may not be involved in school activities. For example, a parent who is not a fluent English speaker or is unfamiliar with the educational system in this country may be reluctant to participate in school-sponsored activities. There may also be a specific cultural value in conflict with Euro-American expectations for parental participation. Ortiz and Yates (1989) state that "among some traditional Hispanics, there is a transfer of authority to the teacher . . . parents perceive teachers and other school personnel as experts in academic matters and, once they have transferred their responsibility to the educational expert, they feel it is not their prerogative as a parent to interfere or to question decisions or actions of school authorities" (p. 187).

### Table 7.3
Guidelines for Visiting the Homes of CLDE Students

- Ascertain whether or not the visit will be considered threatening or intrusive (use cultural informant or interpreter).
- Dress professionally.
- Be aware of the symbolic importance of offered food and drink; refusal may signal rejection of hospitality.
- Be complimentary of food, drink, and children (in some cultures a host may feel obligated to present an admired object to the visitor).
- Be prepared for the presence of extended family (you may wish to conduct highly confidential discussions in another setting).

*Note.* From "Working with Parents" (p. 84), by S. Brandenburg-Ayres, 1990, in V. I. Correa and S. H. Fradd (Eds.), *Bilingual/ESOL Special Education Collaboration and Reform Modules,* Gainesville, FL: University of Florida. Adapted with permission.

### Table 7.4

#### Strategies for Involving Culturally and Linguistically Diverse Parents of Children with Disabilities in Educational Activities

- Translate written information into home language(s) of families.
- Distribute translated written information to bilingual educators with instructions to relay information to families who may find the information relevant.
- Meet with bilingual educators and see how special and bilingual educators can work together to gather and sustain culturally and linguistically diverse family participation.
- Distribute translated written information to community resource agencies (e.g., clinics, libraries, parks, Planned Parenthood, HMOs).
- Send a press release to churches for their Sunday bulletin.
- Send a press release to local cultural radio stations.
- Put a notice on cultural cable TV stations.
- Get parent volunteers to phone parents of the same cultural group.
- Have alternatives to formal meetings and conferences at school sites.
- Sustain this activity throughout the year.

*Note.* From *Spanish-Speaking Families with Special Needs Members,* by B. C. Goldstein, 1996, unpublished manuscript. Adapted with permission.

Another reason for lack of parental participation may be environmental constraints. Parents in lower socioeconomic classes may have duties and responsibilities that take immediate priority over their child's education. Parents' low income may result in transportation or babysitting problems as well as a lack of time to participate (Ortiz & Yates, 1989).

For additional resources for facilitating family involvement, see Sileo, Sileo, and Prater (1996).

Goldstein (1996) discusses several strategies to involve working poor (below minimum wage and with limited native language literacy) and Spanish-speaking families in a local educational conference (Fiesta Educativa). She noted that word of mouth is always better than written information and that participation means different things to different people. Her strategies are listed in Table 7.4.

In summary, when working with culturally and linguistically diverse families, consultants should strive to become culturally competent. They should use appropriate communication and interpersonal skills, conduct informal and formal meetings in culturally appropriate ways, and establish rapport with families through a variety of activities, including home visits. Consultants should devise culturally appropriate ways to involve families in the education of their children.

## Assessment

See Chapter 8 for further discussion of assessment issues and strategies.

As indicated by Reisberg and Wolf (1988), educators need more than a passing familiarity with a variety of assessment and instructional options to be helpful to exceptional students. Alternative assessment models have been developed in response to the inconsistencies found when assessing students from culturally and linguistically diverse backgrounds (Mercer & Rueda, 1991). These assessment models focus on the use of authentic sources of information about a student's performance, such as culturally appropriate work and language samples. Educators not only must be aware of these alternative assessment models, but they must also be able to use them when determining a CLDE student's academic performance, behavior, intellectual functioning, adaptive behavior, and language development levels. To work within a multicultural society, consultants need to understand assessment issues as they apply to students who are culturally and linguistically diverse and work with consultees to use appropriate assessment strategies.

Since language assessment is key to documenting the difference between language difference and language disability, educators should know assessment procedures for determining *language proficiency* (i.e., level of functioning) and *language dominance* (i.e., which of two—or more—languages in which the student is most proficient). González, Bauerle, and Féliz-Holt (1994) make several points regarding the appropriate assessment of language development in bilingual children. First, they emphasize the importance of having a first language administration. Also, they suggest the use of verbal and nonverbal assessment materials because other languages (e.g., Spanish) have dimensions different from those found in English (e.g., linguistic gender assignments). They emphasize the need to assess children in both languages, a recommendation supported by Ortiz and Garcia (1995). Ortiz and Garcia also caution against the use of language assessments that are older than 6 months, because of the developmental nature of language. Before primarily English instruction is provided to a student, Ortiz and Garcia (1995) recommend that a language assessment provide evidence that the student has the cognitive academic language proficiency (CALP) required for mastery of literacy skills (e.g., narrative skills, story retelling, ability to use language abstractly) in both his or her native language and English. A specific challenge in assessing language proficiency, relative to instruction, is obtaining information regarding a student's ability to learn in English and in the native language. This can be ascertained by engaging the student in academic tasks that focus on the attainment of concepts and assessing the student's ability to learn those concepts in English and in the native language.

In summary, consultants are urged to help professionals collect as much information as possible concerning students' language use in home, school, and community situations. Consultants should help educators to apply knowledge of second-language acquisition in determining the language of instruction for a CLDE student. They should also help professionals collaborate in conducting appropriate assessment strategies, as people who speak the student's native language may need to be involved in conducting assessments.

See our discussion later in this chapter on working with interpreters.

## Curriculum

Cummins (1986) suggests four components that should be incorporated in an appropriate curriculum for a multicultural society. First, students' native language and culture should be incorporated into the curriculum. Second, families and communities should be involved in collaboratively developing the school's mission and activities. Third, student assessment should focus on identifying ways to support learning rather than on documenting student deficits. Finally, the instructional approach used in schools should be interactive and experiential because that approach facilitates language development and higher-order thinking.

Tharp (1994) further discusses ways to establish an appropriate educational curriculum in a multicultural society. He argues that cultural compatibility should be established between students' actual learning styles and the teaching style that is operational in schools. Therefore, if in the students' culture knowledge is developed through conversation, then in the school, linguistic competence should be developed through functional language use and purposeful conversational interactions. For example, to provide effective instructional conversation in Native American classrooms, educators should (a) extend the wait time for processing of verbal input; (b) maintain low conversational tones and student-paced activities; (c) present information in a holistic, rather than an analytic, learning style (e.g., have Navajo third-grade children read or listen to an entire story before discussion); and (d) organize instruction consistent with home culture (e.g., devote the majority of the school day to individual or small-group activities in which peers work together and teachers move among students and involve them in quiet discussion). There should also be adequate opportunity for cooperative work to solve problems or make projects that involve the teacher, as in the Native American home culture with elders (Tharp & Yamauchi, 1994).

## Instructional Planning

Instructional planning is important for all educators but particularly for educators working with CLDE students. Given the language needs of these students, many educators will find it necessary to plan instruction collaboratively with teachers of CLD students. It is also important for educators to be able to use language proficiency and dominance assessment information to plan appropriate instructional goals and objectives for students.

Fueyo (1997) provides the following suggestions when planning instruction. First, consider the kind of language that will be required of the students. Incorporate language requirements that will enable students to use their conversational fluency, but also develop their language skills. Second, clearly identify the language of classroom instruction and match it to students' needs. If there are many English-language learners, the third step will need to be addressed; i.e., What will the teacher need to do to maximize students' comprehension? What sheltered instruction techniques will be most effective? The fourth aspect the teacher should consider is if the level of teacher language is appropriate for students' levels of proficiency. If there are students at low levels of English proficiency, sheltered instruction will be essential. Fueyo suggests that when planning, teachers new to teaching culturally and linguistically diverse students prepare a script. During instruction, teachers may find it useful to record their lessons on videotape or audiotape to analyze their own and their students' language. Some strategies for using teacher language include:

- Slow down the rate of speech during instruction.
- Articulate clearly.
- Use longer pauses.
- Use high-frequency words.
- Use fewer pronouns.
- Use gestures and visuals to accompany words.
- Use short, simple sentences.
- Increase repetition and rephrasing.
- Add context to learning activities to increase understanding.
- Provide visual supports.
- Put labels everywhere.

- Emphasize comprehension.

- Use signals to help students make transitions, e.g., "Let's begin," "Let's put our books away" (Fueyo, 1997, p. 65).

Tables 7.5 and 7.6 provide examples of co-teaching lesson plans. These plans incorporate strategies for collaborative planning discussed in Chapter 4. Plans are provided for the elementary and secondary levels in native language instruction and sheltered instruction in English.

## Instruction

Typically, educators implement the instructional plans they develop. This requires them to be familiar with linguistically and culturally appropriate adaptations and behavior management strategies as well as sheltered language techniques. Educators should strive to establish a classroom climate that promotes success for *all* students (Baca & Almanza, 1991).

Optimal instructional strategies for students from non-native, English-speaking groups should be based on the principle that "language learners are active learners who, when exposed to sufficient language input from others, devise hypotheses about rules, test them out, modify them, and gradually construct their own language" (Willig & Ortiz, 1991, p. 291). Consultants should help educators develop instructional strategies that build on this principle. In general, it is recommended that educators (a) assess and secure resources for providing appropriate language instruction, (b) determine the level of congruence between the teacher's views and expectations of CLD students and the students' educational needs, (c) develop congruence between the culture and language of the home and those of the school, and (d) use instructional strategies that are effective with CLD students (e.g., sheltered instruction).

In deciding how to instruct a CLDE student, the language of instruction is an important consideration. If it is decided that the student should be taught using two languages (i.e., English and the student's native language), language can be used in various ways (Baca, 1998). For instance, the teacher can alternate the times when a given language is used in the classroom. In the alternate-day plan, the native language is used one day and English is used the other day. The half-day plan involves the use of the native language for one part of the school day and the use of English for the other part of the school day. In a mixed schedule some subjects are taught in the native language and other subjects are taught in English. The authors have found that teachers of CLDE students prefer the mixed schedule. The teachers found that if they were able to select the language of instruction for specific subjects, it was more likely that they would be able to make a match between the student's language proficiency and the language of instruction.

If a teacher does not have mastery of a student's native language, it is essential that the teacher use sheltered instructional techniques that incorporate many modalities in presenting content. In this way, the learning experience for the student is maximized. If the student does not clearly understand the language of instruction and the teacher demonstrates the skill to be mastered using auditory, visual, and concrete materials, the student has a greater chance of grasping the concept. Further, if a teacher uses many modes in presenting content, he or she has a better chance of matching the learning style of the student with the mode of presentation. However, teachers are urged to consider individual

## Table 7.5
### Co-Teaching Plan for Native Language Instruction

*Program*

- *Objective:* Native English speakers acquiring Spanish in an integrated program with native Spanish speakers who are acquiring English.
- *Challenge:* Support fluent acquisition of Spanish by native English speakers and prevent native language attrition of Spanish speakers.
- Instructional strategies include cooperative learning.
- Academic curriculum is consistent with the general education curriculum.
- Target language is used approximately 50% of the time.

*Key Participants*

*Lucy:*

- Special education teacher, English speaker, late 20s, energetic;
- 5 years' teaching experience in special education resource programs and special education–general education co-teaching;
- has taught in this school for 2 years.

*Ida:*

- First-grade bilingual teacher, Spanish speaker, late 20s, energetic, no co-teaching experience;
- about 5 years' teaching experience in kindergarten and first grade;
- has taught in this school for last 4 years (last year taught these same students in kindergarten).

*Amelia:*

- Bilingual teaching assistant, Spanish speaker, mid 40s, mature, motherly.

*Students:*

- 25—13 Spanish speaking, 12 English speaking; most are nonreaders.
- Of the 13 Spanish speaking, 2 are students with learning disabilities.
- Of the 12 English speaking, 3 are students with learning disabilities.
- The students with learning disabilities are nonreaders, have short attention spans, and exhibit disorganization and poor motivation.

Objective

Lucy and Ida are interested in co-teaching during language arts (about 1 hour). They feel that the two of them working together can better meet the reading objectives of this diverse group of students, especially those students with learning disabilities.

After meeting and talking about the students, they decided that their learning goal for all the students was to pronounce words with short-vowel sounds. Ida organizes her language arts class into centers, and the teachers want to maintain that structure. They want to make a plan that would develop skills in three areas based on individual student needs: blending, practice in using blends, and developing a sight word vocabulary. These three needs cut across native Spanish-speaking and native English-speaking students.

*(continues)*

learning styles as well as cultural learning styles. For example, if the teacher is presenting a lesson that requires student initiation for participation, the lesson may not be consistent with an Asian American student's response mode. Teachers should not automatically attribute lack of participation by a CLDE student to a lack of interest. Rather, teachers should carefully consider the response modes of students in light of their cultural identity. Teachers are also urged to use

## Table 7.5 (*Continued*)

| What | Co-Teaching Technique | When | Language of Instruction | Specific Teacher Tasks | Materials Needed | Evaluation |
|---|---|---|---|---|---|---|
| Short *a* CVC words | Station teaching | After Ida introduces short *a* CVC words through a story read in Spanish and English | *Ida:* Spanish & English<br><br>*Lucy:* English<br><br>*Amelia:* Spanish | *Ida & Lucy:* Identify English and Spanish words and materials.<br><br>*Lucy:* Adapt materials for 4 stations for (students with LD) Spanish & English sight words, Spanish and English blending.<br><br>*Ida:* Supervise student activities across 3 stations, i.e., Spanish blending, Spanish sight words, English blending practice.<br><br>*Amelia:* Supervise student activities at Spanish blending practice station.<br><br>*Lucy:* Supervise student activities across 2 stations, i.e., English blending, English sight words. | pictures of short *a* words<br><br>word labels<br><br>picture directions for each station<br><br>scissors<br><br>glue<br><br>crayons<br><br>paper<br><br>tape recorder & tapes | Student Activities<br><br>Be sure to put name and date on each student product |

good judgment, however, and recognize the dangers of stereotyping and over-generalizing cultural characteristics to all children from a particular group.

In keeping with cultural and individual learning styles, consultants should help teachers to use grouping strategies appropriately. Cooperative grouping techniques can be appropriately used across all age groups. Teachers must decide how to form peer and/or cooperative learning arrangements so as to meet the needs of all students, including CLDE students.

In Chapter 11, the use of peer tutoring and cooperative learning strategies is discussed.

## Materials

It is often necessary to modify materials to meet the needs of exceptional learners. When modifying materials for CLDE learners, it is also necessary to consider language and culture. The following characteristics may be considered when deciding the appropriateness of curriculum material: (a) difficulty levels relative to language levels of the student, (b) pacing of the material, (c) format and readability, (d) use and control of complex language, (e) cultural relevancy and level of interest, (f) potential for independent use (Hoover & Collier, 1998).

When determining if the material is comprehensible, the educator must determine if the language level of the material matches the language proficiency of the student. It is also necessary to determine if the language concepts expressed in the material are consistent with the language concept development of the student. For example, in some languages there is no distinction between sexes. Sex is determined by the sensitivity of the culture to different sex roles, not by a word to denote sex. There, the teacher will need to incorporate culturally appropriate activities and teach the concepts of *he* and *she;* otherwise, the student may become confused.

## Table 7.6

Co-Teaching Plan for Sheltered Instruction

*Program*

- English language development is a goal.
- Requisite terminology for content areas is a focus.

*Key Participants*

*Nancy:*

- English language development teacher, English speaker, limited Spanish, 30s, no co-teaching experience;
- 10 years teaching experience in English-language development programs, secondary level;
- has taught in this school for last 7 years.

*Betty:*

- Special education teacher, English speaker, 30s;
- 15 years' experience in secondary special education resource programs and special education–general education co-teaching;
- has taught in this school for last 5 years.

*Ramon:*

- Teaching assistant, bilingual in English and Spanish.

*Students:*

- 16—mixture of Spanish-, Portuguese-, and Vietnamese-speaking students;
- Time in U.S. ranging from 2 weeks to 3 years;
- Three students receiving special education services are in this ESL class:
  - *Marcel* is a recent immigrant who speaks very little English and is withdrawn. He does not seek help. Academic success is limited.
  - *Avina* is from a rural area in Vietnam. Her parents are not literate, and there have been limited literacy experiences at home. She exhibits behavior problems in school, e.g. fighting.
  - *Luisa* is friendly but quiet. Spanish is her first language, but both English and Spanish are spoken at home. She speaks English and Spanish quite well. Written expression is poor.

*Objective*

Nancy and Betty are interested in co-teaching during the English language development reading class. Nancy usually structures the reading class as follows: 10 minutes of silent reading; students write the answer to a specific comprehension question followed by discussion; students break into groups and teachers read aloud; this is followed by discussion on meaning, interpretations, and feelings connected to students' experiences. Nancy determines their comprehension by asking them to write about their thoughts and opinions about the people and events in the book. Betty feels that she can develop Marcel's social interaction skills, Avina's coping skills, and Luisa's writing skills by working with Nancy in Nancy's English language development class.

*Co-teaching Instructional Plan*

English-Language Development Teacher: <u>Nancy</u>
Special Educator: <u>Betty</u>   Bilingual TA: <u>Ramon</u>
Student Objectives: Read, discuss, and retell a story.

*(continues)*

**Table 7.6** (*Continued*)

| Students | What | Co-Teaching Technique | Specific Teacher Tasks | Materials | Evaluation |
|---|---|---|---|---|---|
| All students; some students (especially Avina, Marcel, and Luisa) can select to listen to the story. | 10 minutes silent reading | Supportive learning activities | *Nancy & Betty:* Choose books with moral specifically relevant for Avina. <br><br> *Betty:* Provide audiotapes and supervise student use of them. | Book or tape <br> Tape recorders and headsets | |
| Almost all students | Comprehension question | Station teaching | Students break up into 3 groups & discuss question—Nancy, Betty, and Ramon each facilitate a group discussion. | | |
| Some students, i.e., Marcel | | | *Betty:* Takes groups with Marcel & encourages and reinforces social interaction. | | Chart # of student-initiated statements. |
| All students | Read aloud | Station teaching | Students remain in their group—*Ramon* with Luisa, *Betty* with Marcel, *Nancy* with Avina (teachers will switch groups so that all will have an opportunity to work with all students at another time). | | |
| Almost all students; <br><br> Marcel, Luisa, and a few other capable students. | Written retelling <br><br> Dictate retelling | Alternative teaching | *Nancy & Ramon:* Circulate around the room. <br><br> *Betty:* Takes the retelling dictation of this small group. | Paper and pencil or computer and printer | Collect student work samples <br><br> Name and date each student's work and notes. |

In addition to determining if the language is comprehensible, the educator should determine if the curricular material is culturally sensitive. For example, many materials depicting different cultural groups may present general stereotypes. The teacher should be careful to discuss materials from the perspective of those that are indicative of modern-day cultural groups and those that are not. The teacher should encourage the students to help identify and explain the cultural values depicted in curricular materials.

The educator should also use curricular materials in a culturally sensitive fashion. As discussed by Hoover and Collier (1998), the educator should not assume that what is true in one culture is true in another. For example, in teaching the colors white, black, and brown, the teacher might consider using different groups of people as examples. However, in many non-Western cultures, the words for white, black, and brown are never applied to human beings.

In summary, the modification of curricular materials requires the educator to be sensitive to the learning, language, and cultural characteristics of students. It requires the educator to know about content areas, learning problems, and compensatory strategies as well as language and cultural characteristics. Educators should consult with one another to increase their knowledge in areas of weakness as well as to determine the individual needs of CLDE students. General suggestions for teachers of CLDE learners are provided in Table 7.7.

### Table 7.7

#### General Suggestions for Teachers of CLDE Learners

- Match teaching-learning activities with cultural preferences, unique behavior characteristics, and specific learning needs.
- Provide bilingual and/or English language development education based on students' needs.
- Use instructional materials that reflect diversities and provide an identity for the CLD student.
- Model an understanding and acceptance of difference.
- Use instructional strategies that will promote the active participation of all students and provide opportunities for all students to experience positive social roles.
- Be prepared to deal with the social-emotional problems faced by CLD students.
- Cultivate open communication, trust, and respect with parents and the extended family of the CLDE student.

*Note.* From "Early Risks: Transition from Culturally/Linguistically Diverse Homes to Formal Schooling," by E. K. Leung, 1990, *Journal of Educational Issues of Language Minority Students, 7,* 35–51. Copyright 1990 by *Journal of Educational Issues of Language Minority Students.* Reprinted with permission.

Educators must be familiar with culturally appropriate materials. Consultants can be a great help in providing resource materials that are appropriate for students from various cultural and linguistic backgrounds. Consultants can also help educators evaluate the cultural appropriateness of the materials they plan to use with specific students. The materials educators use should promote the active and meaningful participation of students (Baca & Almanza, 1991).

## Consultation and Collaboration

For an interesting application of these competencies in bicultural communities, see Goldstein (1998).

Based on a review of the educational consultation and bilingual special education literatures, Harris (1991) developed a set of generic and specific consultation competencies needed by educators who serve CLDE students as consultants. Four general competencies emerged from this literature review: (a) understanding one's perspective; (b) using effective interpersonal, communication, and problem-solving skills; (c) understanding the role(s) of collaborators; and (d) using appropriate assessment and instructional strategies. The last competency has been discussed in the preceding sections. The first three competencies will be discussed below. The competencies discussed below are not meant to be all inclusive; rather, they represent areas that consultants need to develop to work successfully with a diverse community.

### Understanding One's Culture and Its Relationship to Others' Cultures

Understanding one's own perspective is a necessary prerequisite to any collaborative activity. To engage in a consultation activity, it is necessary for collaborators to understand their own attitudes, values, needs, beliefs, skills, knowledge, and limitations (Kurpius, 1978; West, Idol, & Cannon, 1989). This understanding is necessary to establish a climate for the collaboration that will foster growth and change. According to Gibbs (1980), collaborators have an ethical responsibility to be aware of their own culture, values, and beliefs, as well as to understand how they differ from those of others.

It is important for bicultural consultants to engage in this activity as well. Bicultural consultants can't assume that because they share the same ethnicity and/or language of a family, they share the same perspective. Neither can bicultural consultants assume that a community views them as sharing its perspective just because of their ethnicity. Bicultural consultants must examine their assimilation and acculturation experiences as influences on their perspectives, especially when working with people who share their ethnicity and language.

Using Hall's (1976) broad view of culture (i.e., personality, modes of expression, ways of thinking, ways of moving, and ways of resolving problems), consultants can identify activities they can conduct to help them and their consultees understand their own cultures and how they relate to the cultures of others. According to Lynch and Hanson (1998), "Cultural self-awareness begins with an exploration of one's own heritage. Issues such as place of origin or indigenous status, time of immigration, reasons for immigration, language(s) spoken, and the place of the family's first settlement in the United States all help to define one's own cultural heritage. The political leanings, religion, jobs, status, beliefs, and values of the first immigrants provide a sketch of one's family and heritage. Information about the economic, social, and vocational changes that subsequent generations have undergone complete the picture" (pp. 51–52).

Euro-Americans, who make up the mainstream culture in the United States, may be the least aware of the way their culture influences their behavior and interactions, perhaps owing to the dominance of their culture and to the melting pot theory that restricts acknowledgment of diversity among immigrant Americans (Lynch & Hanson, 1998). Hyun and Fowler (1995, p. 25) suggest that educators ask themselves questions such as, "When I was growing up, what did my family say about people from different cultures?" as a first step in understanding one's culture. They also suggest that educators examine common sayings as a way to understand their culture. As they state, "If you have been raised in beliefs like 'Where there is a will, there is a way,' your views about disabilities may be very different from those of a person who has heard that 'It's God's will' or 'It's my fate'" (p. 26).

Recognizing one's culture and how it influences one's behavior is the first step. It is then necessary for consultants to assess how their perspective differs from that of the people with whom they are working. Consultants can learn about other cultures through reading, interaction, and involvement. However, as pointed out by Lynch and Hanson (1998), assuming that the culture-specific information one learns from books or a study of the language applies to all members of a cultural group is not appropriate and can be dangerous, as it can lead to stereotyping that actually reduces understanding. It is best to learn about the culture of others by getting to know them as individuals rather than as members of a group. Home visits, as stated previously, are helpful, as are friendly conversations in which consultants and consultees share information about such topics as favorite activities and people they know in common.

In Table 7.8 are the kinds of questions educators should ask themselves when striving to understand their culture and its relationship to other cultures, assessing their beliefs regarding culturally and linguistically diverse individuals and individuals with disabilities, determining the basis for those beliefs, determining their expectations for educators serving CLD students, and ascertaining their willingness to learn from as well as share expertise with those educators. Each professional must determine the degree of congruence between his or her own beliefs and values and the beliefs and values of family members of individuals with disabilities and other professionals.

Readers are encouraged to consult the following works for an elaboration on this topic: Darder, 1995; Darder, Torres, and Gutierrez, 1997; Villenas, 1996.

A multicultural pie graph is a tool that facilitates personal awareness of cultural heritage. Readers are referred to Gollnick and Chinn (1990) for a discussion of that technique.

Soo-Hoo (1998) provides an interesting discussion of reframing techniques that are useful for all consultants as they attempt to understand the consultee's frame of reference.

# Table 7.8

## Consultation Competencies for Educators Serving CLDE Students

### Use appropriate assessment and instructional strategies.

- Do I know and am I able to use assessment techniques that describe and measure educational environments as well as attitudes and behaviors of CLDE students and teachers?

- Do I know how curricula are developed and adapted in cross-cultural settings?

- Can I obtain the necessary information to incorporate language and cultural considerations when making decisions about assessment, curriculum, and instruction for CLD students?

- Am I familiar with and to what extent can I use instructional strategies that will enhance the learning of CLDE students as well as their social and emotional growth?

### Understand one's culture and its relationship to others' cultures.

- What are my goals and expectations in consulting?

- Am I willing to learn from professionals who serve CLDE students (e.g., bilingual/ESL educators, general educators, and special educators) as well as share my expertise with them?

- What are my beliefs regarding the abilities of various ethnic minorities? What is the basis for those beliefs, and do I expect all educators serving CLDE students to share those beliefs and values?

- What are the beliefs of my collaborators regarding the abilities of various ethnic minorities? What is the basis for those beliefs?

- What are my beliefs and values regarding exceptional students? What is the basis for those beliefs, and do I expect all educators serving CLDE students to share those beliefs and values?

- What are the beliefs of my collaborators regarding exceptional students? What is the basis for those beliefs?

### Use effective interpersonal, communicative, and problem-solving skills.

- Can I exhibit the ability to be caring, respectful, empathetic, congruent, and open in cross-cultural consultation interactions?

- Can I interview effectively to elicit information, explore problems, and set goals and objectives?

- Can I exhibit the ability to grasp and validate overt and covert meaning and affect in cross-cultural interactions?

- Am I able to establish and maintain sensitive and responsible cross-cultural interactions with family members of CLDE students as well as professionals of diverse disciplines and ethnic groups who might serve CLDE students?

- Am I able to work effectively with an interpreter to facilitate clear and effective communication in oral and written form?

### Understand the roles of collaborators.

- Am I familiar with individual and institutional objectives relevant to CLDE students?

- What is the purpose of the collaborative consultation?

- What activities must be conducted to accomplish the intended purpose?

- Can I identify the skills and individuals needed to address the situation?

- Am I familiar with the skills that can be contributed by those who serve CLD students (e.g., bilingual/ESL educators, general educators, special educators, school psychologists, speech and language therapists)?

- Are the roles of participants clearly understood by all collaborators?

*Note.* From "An Expanded View on Consultation Competencies for Educators Serving Culturally and Linguistically Diverse Exceptional Students," by K. C. Harris, 1991, *Teacher Education and Special Education, 14*(1), 25–29. Copyright 1991 by *Teacher Education and Special Education.* Adapted with permission.

## Using Effective Interpersonal, Communicative, and Problem-Solving Skills

Using effective interpersonal, communicative, and problem-solving skills is essential for the consultant because the consultation process is based upon communication and problem-solving skills (Harris, 1996). As discussed by Raffaniello (1981), all individuals engaged in problem solving must be multicultural. Goodenough (1976) argues that since role expectations differ with different social situations, each set of expectations constitutes a different culture to be learned. Therefore, educators consulting with one another in a teaming situation must learn the culture of the team; educators engaging in cooperative teaching must learn the culture of that teaching situation; and educators consulting with families must learn the cultures of the families. It can be even more challenging consulting with CLDE students, as there are many cultures that can impact the interaction. In the previous examples, it is the culture of the school that is paramount. When consulting with CLDE students and their families, ethnicity or race may be a factor, as may disability, country of origin, and familiarity with U.S. educational programs, to name just a few variables. As Daniels and DeWine (1991) suggest, consultants and consultees can work to establish the same interpretation and meaning of issues that are addressed. In this way, through their interpersonal communicative interactions, the consultant and consultee develop a common culture for collaborative activities.

As indicated in Table 7.8, the kinds of questions consultants can ask themselves regarding using effective interpersonal, communicative, and problem-solving skills, include the ability to engage in effective cross-cultural interactions as well as the ability to work effectively with an interpreter. Educators may find it necessary to work in several different types of cross-cultural situations (e.g., when gathering information from CLD students and their families, when conducting meetings with CLD students and their families, and when meeting with professionals from other disciplines who represent a different cultural orientation and/or ethnic or racial background). Table 7.9 provides an elaboration of the interpersonal and communication skills presented in Chapter 4. It also includes several specific skills consultants should use to develop their cross-cultural competence.

Interpersonal skills are important to develop a trusting relationship, the essence of any communication. Fradd (1990) addresses the interpersonal

### Table 7.9
Specific Interpersonal and Communication Skills for a Multicultural Society

*Interpersonal*

- Respect individuals from other cultures.
- Identify needed multicultural knowledge base.

*Communication*

- Work effectively with an interpreter or translator.
- Acknowledge cultural differences in communication and relationship building.
- Ensure that the problem identification does not conflict with cultural beliefs.

*Note.* From "Collaboration Within a Multicultural Society: Issues for Consideration," by K. C. Harris, 1996, *Remedial and Special Education, 17*(6), 357. Copyright 1996 by PRO-ED, Inc. Adapted with permission.

characteristics educators should exhibit when engaging in cross-cultural interactions. She contends that if school professionals are approachable, patient, and trustworthy, cross-cultural communication will be successful. Behaviors representing these characteristics are provided in Table 7.10.

Another important aspect of cross-cultural communication is selecting sensitive *symbols of respect* when interacting with people from cultures other than the mainstream Euro-American culture. Symbols of respect are nonverbal communications and, therefore, must be selected carefully. According to Tyler (1987), any symbol of respect is more valuable when given with more thought than money: "Giving respect by giving of yourself is essential to intercultural protocol" (p. 56). However, to do this successfully, the giver should learn the customs that are practiced by the recipient as well as allowing the recipient to reciprocate. In addition, the giver should identify the motive for giving so that the recipient will understand that the gesture is a symbol of respect and not a bribe (Tyler, 1987). Questions to help guide respectful symbols are provided in Table 7.11.

In addition to interpersonal and nonverbal skills, the consultant must use appropriate verbal skills. Often, when consultants do not speak the language of the consultee and rely on the use of interpreters, they do not focus on their use of verbal skills. However, using culturally appropriate pragmatic skills as well as eliminating demeaning or disabling linguistic practices is essential for effective cross-cultural communication.

## Table 7.10
### Interpersonal Characteristics That Facilitate Cross-Cultural Communication

*Approachable School Personnel*

- Encourage family members of CLDE students to speak even when their English is limited.
- Show genuine interest in all team members.
- Take the first step in meeting others.

*Patient School Personnel*

- Remain calm.
- Have time to listen and reflect.
- Realize that not all concerns can be met at once.
- Are willing to take the time to be a team member.

*Trustworthy School Personnel*

- Are consistent in their approach.
- Are fair in considering information presented by others.
- Are agreeable in decision making.
- Are able to demonstrate firsthand knowledge of the CLDE student.
- Are clear about the overall goals of fair and nondiscriminatory assessment, appropriate placement, and an instructional plan that incorporates aspects of language and culture.
- Are free of cultural and racial bias in their educational decision making.

*Note.* From "Transdisciplinary Teaming," by S. H. Fradd, 1990, in V. I. Correa and S. H. Fradd (Eds.), *Bilingual/ESOL Special Education Collaboration and Reform Modules* (p. 127), Gainesville, FL: University of Florida. Copyright 1990 by S. H. Fradd. Adapted with permission.

## Table 7.11

A Checklist for Using Respectful Gestures in Cross-Cultural Interactions

1. How is this symbol a compliment or tribute? (Is it lavish or insufficient?)
2. In what ways are different relationships implied: business, friendship, concern?
3. To whom is the symbol of respect offered: mother, father, sibling, other?
4. When is an indirect show of respect (through an intermediary in private) more acceptable than a direct or personal approach?
5. Will the recipient see the symbol as something that can be reciprocated? How?
6. If there has been an apparent mistake, when is it best to correct it? (Immediately? Privately?)

*Note.* From *Intercultural Interacting* (p. 59), by V. L. Tyler, 1987, Provo, UT: Brigham Young University, David M. Kennedy Center for International Studies. Copyright 1987 by BYU, David M. Kennedy Center for International Studies. Adapted with permission.

Harris (1996) provides an example of the impact of language practices that Euro-American consultants, familiar with the field of special education, will recognize. If one traces the use of terms used over the years to refer to people with disabilities, one can see the impact of language. Historically, people with cognitive delays were referred to as imbeciles and idiots. However, those are now considered pejorative terms that define the individual in a substandard and inhumane way. As the educational rights of such people have been acknowledged, other terms related to their ability surfaced. For example, people with cognitive delays were later referred to as educable mentally retarded or developmentally delayed. As society members recognized such people as human beings, preferred terminology stressed the importance of their individuality (e.g., an adolescent with behavior problems). This language usage connotes a different way of viewing people and, subsequently, of developing appropriate interventions for them.

The consultant should also become aware of the meaning of language practices that is interpreted for non-English-speaking consultees and strive to use language practices that demonstrate respect for the consultee's culture. For example, it may be disrespectful to ask family members a direct question and more appropriate to encourage the family to share information through an open-ended conversation.

Readers are encouraged to learn about the linguistic practices of the people with whom they work, i.e., students, families, and colleagues. We have discussed general verbal and nonverbal skills in Chapter 4, but readers are encouraged to learn about verbal and nonverbal practices across cultures. Lynch and Hanson (1998) provide a list of resources that offer a good beginning for the educational consultant.

In addition to the special, general, and bilingual education staff, the CLDE student may need to receive services from *interpreters*. Interpreters generally facilitate communication by interpreting during the following activities: communications with families via the telephone and formal and informal meetings; communications with students through instructional activities; informal communications, and assessments; communications with school staff through informal discussion about family or student concerns; community meetings; inservice training; hearings, etc. (Fradd, 1990). Bilingual paraprofessionals, secretaries, and other staff members may be asked to serve as interpreters for monolingual English-speaking teachers and students who do not speak English. According to Plata (1993), "Interpretation is not simply a matter of substituting a word/phrase/clause/sentence in the listener's language for the speaker's word/phrase/clause/sentence. Interpreters must be prepared to circumvent problems that occur during or because of the interpretation process" (p. 20). However, as Jordan et al. (1998) caution, consultants should avoid using the student as interpreter for his or her parents because this may distort the roles of parent and child.

Readers should be aware that the educational and certification requirements for interpreters for deaf students and interpreters for students whose native language is not English are often very different. Both interpreters can help students participate in educational activities by interpreting what they want to say to professionals and classmates as well as what the professionals and other students want to say to them. However, though the educational and certification requirements for interpreters for students with hearing impairments vary from state to state, there *are* educational programs available and certification is generally required. People who interpret for non-native English speakers often receive no specific training and no certification is required. As a consequence, parents and professionals working with people who interpret for non-native English speaking students and family members need to be familiar with the interpreter's background and skills and strive to help the interpreter become part of the educational team so that the intent of the communication is accomplished.

It is important for consultants to be familiar with the skills needed by interpreters and the skills needed by consultants to work successfully with anyone who is interpreting. Brandenburg-Ayres (1990) suggests the following for choosing an interpreter: (a) select someone who has served before and is trained, (b) select someone preferably in education, (c) select someone who is bilingual and familiar with the community, (d) select someone who is willing to help and expresses personal warmth, (e) select someone who can control his or her responses, (f) select someone who talks easily and answers well, and (g) select someone who is respectful of family confidentiality.

Medina (1982) lists several minimal qualifications that interpreters should have. She states that the interpreter should be bilingual and biliterate with proficiency in English and the target language. Proficiency in the target language includes the ability to speak and understand the pragmatics and nuances of the target language (Plata, 1993). The interpreter should also be able to adjust to different levels of language use (i.e., the interpreter should be able to function whether the situation involves colloquial language or literary language). The interpreter should realize that there are people who have varying degrees of training and varying degrees of understanding about the educational process and interpreters should be able to deal with them (Plata, 1993). This also necessitates that the interpreter be familiar with the appropriate educational terminology, the culture of the school, and the culture of the student. Familiarity with the culture of the student includes understanding the impact of the culture upon the student and family (Plata, 1993). This is necessary to interpret cues, to be sensitive to the family's needs, and to understand family members' nonverbal language (Brandenburg-Ayres, 1990). Finally, and most important, the interpreter should be familiar with the ethics of interpretation. This includes maintaining the confidentiality of information and interpreting responses and questions without elaboration. As stressed by Plata (1993), interpreters must be willing to take a secondary role and strive to relay information, not initiate or change it.

According to Plata (1993), interpreters have responsibilities to a variety of people. First, they have a responsibility to the listeners. The interpretation should be conducted so that listeners are not affected by the mediation of the interpreter. Second, they have a responsibility to the speaker. They must communicate clearly the speaker's message. Third, they have a responsibility to the language. If an interpreter is not proficient in the target language, a message of disrespect may be communicated. Fourth, interpreters have a responsibility to their colleagues. They must be sure to just interpret and not infringe on the rights of the families or the school. Finally, interpreters have a responsibility to themselves. They should know their skills and limitations and not accept assignments just to be helpful—they could do more harm than good.

The following represents a modification of Langdon's (1983) discussion of the skills one should have when working with interpreters. First, the consultant should be familiar with the dynamics of interpretation. This includes familiarity with the procedures for establishing rapport with multicultural participants, knowledge of the kinds of information that can easily be interpreted and not be lost in the interpretation process, understanding of the authority position of the educator, use of appropriate and culturally sensitive nonverbal communication methods, and understanding of the need for translations that do not include the personal input of the interpreter. Second, the consultant should be able to plan and conduct pre- and post-sessions with the interpreter. During these sessions, the consultant orients the interpreter to the purpose and procedures of a given educational situation. Third, the consultant should be able to help the interpreter follow ethical procedures of interpretation. When briefing an interpreter, the educator should do the following: state the purpose of the interaction, stress confidentiality, inform the interpreter about the student and/or family who will be involved in the interaction, explain and share any information about technical aspects of the interactions (e.g., reliability and purpose of tests), discuss verbal and nonverbal communicative strategies with the interpreter, and request the interpreter to be conscious of his or her own nonverbal behavior and note all behaviors observed (Brandenburg-Ayres, 1990). The consultant should also seek input from the interpreter about the most culturally appropriate way to accomplish the tasks listed above—for example, information about how given terms might be interpreted in the target language, guidance in communicating concepts that might not translate easily into the target language, and/or a process for problem solving that might be most effective in the target culture.

In addition to conducting a briefing session, the consultant and the interpreter must also conduct a debriefing session. They should discuss the information collected, any problems relative to the activity (e.g., the interpreter gave the student more time than warranted for responding to test items), and any problems relative to the interpretation process (e.g., the consultant used terminology that the interpreter found difficult to communicate in the target language). What is learned during the debriefing session can help the consultant to assess the information obtained realistically. It can also help the consultant and the interpreter to improve their collaboration. Interpreters are team members. Guidelines for working with team members are certainly applicable to interpreters. Table 7.12 lists some situations that might occur when working with interpreters.

See Chapters 3 and 4 for details on working within a team.

Plata (1993) emphasizes that a management system and a training program should be in place for interpreters. It is important to note that, even though interpreters share the same language as a student's family members, they might not share the nationality or socioeconomic status of those family members. Therefore, interpreters need training in dealing with their own perspectives and biases regarding people within their own ethnic groups. According to Plata (1993), there should also be guidelines that outline the interpreter's role and guidelines and procedures for selecting and working with interpreters. The guidelines and training should be followed for all personnel involved in the interpretation process, including consultants. It is important to plan carefully for the use of

Please see Lynch and Hanson (1998) for generic interpretation guidelines as well as specific suggestions for various ethnic groups.

## Table 7.12
### Things Nobody Ever Told You About Working with Interpreters

- Expect difficulties in communication and address them openly.
- Expect the interpreter to identify with the students of the target language and culture and to want to assist them in producing the correct answers. Be prepared to show the interpreter when such assistance is beneficial and when it is not.
- Expect families and children to unburden their tragedies on the interpreter, and be prepared to provide emotional support when that happens.
- Expect the interpreter to wonder if you can be trusted. Be prepared to have your behavior and motives questioned and to show over and over that you are a person who is worthy of respect.
- Expect to learn about inhumanities as well as kindnesses and triumphs in ways you never dreamed possible, and be prepared to confront these insights realistically.

*Note.* From "Transdisciplinary Teaming," by S. H. Fradd, 1990, in V. I. Correa and S. H. Fradd (Eds.), *Bilingual/ESOL Special Education Collaboration and Reform Modules* (p. 160), Gainesville, FL: University of Florida. Adapted with permission.

interpretation services to avoid the pitfalls of interpretation, including the possibility that interpreters may develop hostile feelings toward monolingual English-speaking school personnel. Hostile feelings can develop if interpreters believe that they are performing the work of highly paid professionals without adequate compensation, if they are asked to interpret in addition to their normal work load without compensation, and/or if they are asked to interpret in areas in which they are not competent (Plata, 1993). Table 7.13 provides a list of points to address when training all staff in the use of interpreters.

## Understanding the Role(s) of Collaborators

See Chapters 3 and 4 for a discussion of cooperative teaching and teacher assistance teams.

Opportunities for collaboration exist within a number of different organizational structures in schools (e.g., teams, committees, working groups). Students who are at risk for educational failure are supported by professionals who work within these different organizational structures.

The roles the consultant assumes usually depend upon the purpose of the collaboration. Therefore, it is important for educators to clearly define the purpose of each collaboration and identify the appropriate role to accomplish that objective. When applying this competency to CLDE students, educators must be familiar with objectives that are relevant for CLDE students. For example, in addition to developing or implementing individual educational objectives for CLDE students, educators are in a position to effect personal and institutional change (Idol & West, 1987; Kurpius & Lewis, 1988; Reisberg, 1988; Reisberg & Wolf, 1988; West et al., 1989). Institutional change for CLDE students should address issues such as the incorporation of their language and culture into the school program, promoting local community participation, and advocating for appropriate assessment and quality instruction for them (Cummins, 1986).

As indicated in Table 7.8, the kinds of questions that consultants should ask themselves regarding understanding the roles of collaborators include

### Table 7.13
Areas to Address When Training in the Use of Interpreters and Translators

- The need for precise translation in written documents.
- The important role of the interpreter as an objective assistant, not as an advocate of parents or of school personnel.
- The need for the interpreter to maintain a respectful and positive stance with the parents.
- The need for the translator to prepare a reverse translation for school personnel when precise translations are difficult.
- The training of translators and interpreters in the use of specialized vocabulary (e.g., Individual Educational Program).
- The need for school personnel to speak directly to the parents, not to the interpreter, during exchanges.
- The need for confidentiality of student and family information.
- The importance of the translator and interpreter in establishing positive parent-school relationships.
- The need for translators and interpreters to remain in that role and not become the primary source of information.

*Note.* From "Working with Parents," by S. Brandenburg-Ayres, 1990, in V. I. Correa and S. H. Fradd (Eds.), *Bilingual/ESOL Special Education Collaboration and Reform Modules* (p. 79), Gainesville, FL: University of Florida. Adapted with permission.

determining the consultant's level of familiarity with individual and institutional objectives relevant to CLDE students; understanding the purpose of the consultation; identifying the skills and individuals needed to address the situation, especially the skills that can be contributed by bilingual and ESL educators; and assuring that they understand the roles of all the collaborators. However, it is important that collaborators learn about one another's values and not assume that the values and roles of each collaborator are based on ethnicity or job title (Harris, 1996). In working with bilingual special education teacher assistance teams, Harris (1995) found that team members often approached their roles in the school differently, and the roles assumed were not always dictated by ethnicity. Ortiz and Garcia (1995) caution that, though bilingual educators have been trained in bilingual methodology specific to a target language group (e.g., Spanish), just being bilingual does not ensure that one has knowledge of a student's culture or skills in bilingual educational methodology. The skills that can be contributed by bilingual educators include the ability to speak, read, and write the target student's native language; provide instruction in the native language across all content areas; and assist the target student with the transition from the native language to English. These skills enable them to conduct bilingual education programs and English as a Second Language (ESL) programs. A description of various types of bilingual education programs, based on the information presented in Baca and Cervantes (1998) is provided below.

*Bilingual education* is an educational program in which the teacher uses two languages to provide instruction. The process of providing effective bilingual education is controversial, and not all educators agree on the most effective process. However, bilingual education programs have been found to be effective in developing students' academic achievement, social and emotional development, and English language skills (cf. Baca & Cervantes, 1998). These goals are reflected in a number of different bilingual program designs.

*Transition programs* use the native language and culture of a student to teach that student how to function in a general school curriculum and ultimately to become proficient in English. Students are taught basic skills in their native language with ESL instruction. When students demonstrate English proficiency, they are moved to general education programs where instruction is provided in English. Typically, students in these programs exit within 2–3 years; therefore, these programs are sometimes called "early exit" bilingual programs.

*Maintenance programs* promote English-language proficiency as well as literacy in the student's native language. An example of a maintenance program is one that continues to provide native language instruction after the student demonstrates English proficiency and is receiving instruction in English. Many families now send their children to "culture schools" to achieve the goals of maintenance programs. In these programs, students continue to receive instruction in their home culture and language.

*Two-way enrichment bilingual education programs* are different from transition and maintenance programs because in them native English speakers acquire a second language while native speakers of that language acquire English. These programs are designed to foster bilingualism and biliteracy in students from both language backgrounds. They must be constructed carefully, as the methodology is different for native English speakers (the dominant language group in U.S. schools) than for those acquiring English. In addition, students' varying levels of native and second-language acquisition need to be accommodated. Therefore, scheduling must be coordinated carefully so that the needs of both groups are balanced across language use and integrated

For a summary of bilingual education and a discussion of how bilingual services could be delivered through collaboration and co-teaching, readers are referred to Bahamonde and Friend (1999).

instructional time needs. However, this type of bilingual program is gaining in popularity in many school districts.

*English as a Second Language* is not a bilingual approach per se because it relies exclusively on English as the language of teaching and learning. In schools, ESL instruction can be offered as an independent program, or it can be incorporated as a method of promoting English fluency in bilingual programs. Bilingual education and ESL are compatible, and, if possible, both programs should be used in developing an appropriate educational program for a CLDE student. At times, however, it is not possible to provide bilingual instruction for students who are non-native English speakers. For example, if only a few students speak a particular language (e.g., Samoan) in the school, the school may not have the resources to provide bilingual instruction. In such cases, an ESL program and modifications to make instruction comprehensible (sheltered techniques) may be the only option.

Shaper-Walters (1998) reviewed the research on bilingual education of the last 3 decades. Most research findings have failed to demonstrate the superiority of transitional bilingual programs, which are the most common programs in U.S. public schools. A long-term view is warranted; there is no one answer to the question of how long it takes for a non-English speaker to become fluent enough in English to benefit from instruction that is provided in English. In fact, some research has concluded that the specific models and languages of instruction are less important than the quality of the teaching that linguistically diverse students receive. Ruiz (1995) reports a similar theory that is gaining prominence among educators, i.e., "that the context of interaction dramatically affects the children's abilities and disabilities" (p. 491). If this is so, consultants have an incredibly important mission to help all teachers to provide appropriate interaction that addresses the language and culture needs of their increasingly diverse students.

As reported by Markham, Green, and Ross (1996), ESL, bilingual, and special education teachers have many similarities. Both groups of teachers face challenges in preparing students for inclusive, integrated classrooms. Both groups are successful when their target students no longer need them. The researchers suggest that bilingual and ESL teachers consult with special educators about strategies for inclusive instruction. Consultants should be aware that ESL and bilingual teachers have a unique responsibility as the bridge between the LEP student's home culture and the culture of the school. Unless there are bilingual administrators and counselors or other bilingual support personnel, bilingual and ESL teachers often act as cultural liaisons and social workers for LEP students.

Salend, Dorney, and Mazo (1997) report on the roles of bilingual special educators in creating inclusive classrooms. Specifically, those educators share responsibility for helping others understand the rationale for bilingual and multicultural education. Also, they are often consulted when others are having difficulty understanding a student's behavior from a sociocultural perspective. For instance, the researchers provide the example of the second-language learner who appeared to have become tired and lost concentration after about 10 minutes of instruction. The bilingual special education teacher helped the general education teacher to understand that instruction in a second language requires intensive concentration that can be maintained only for a brief period of time. Consultants who are knowledgeable about bilingual education can also help teachers prepare students to transition into more English instruction as well as help teachers diversify the curriculum to meet the cultural needs of their students. When bilingual educators function as co-teaching team members with general educators, they may need to reconcile differences in their own cultural and experiential backgrounds with those of their colleagues. That is why it is imperative that consultants learn about the cultural perspectives of others.

# Conclusion

Providing appropriate services for CLDE students requires sensitivity to the language and culture of the student and to the student's learning strengths and needs. Educators have an obligation to consult with the families of CLDE students as well as to collaborate with one another, sharing their expertise. To work effectively with CLDE students, educators need to develop specific multicultural competencies in a number of different areas, including culture, language, families, assessment, curriculum, instructional planning, instruction, materials, and consultation and collaboration. To effect successful multicultural collaboration, educators need to understand their own culture and the cultures of their collaborators, use effective multicultural interpersonal and cross-cultural communicative skills, and understand the roles of their collaborators. Consultants should be prepared to help educators develop these multicultural competencies.

# Summary of Key Points

## Demographic Considerations

1. It is anticipated that by 2050, only 50% of the total population of the United States will be non-Hispanic white.

2. The single largest group of linguistically different students is Hispanic, and demographic trends suggest that there will be increasing numbers of Hispanic children in our schools.

3. Culturally and linguistically diverse exceptional students are entitled to educational services under bilingual and special education legislation.

## Characteristics of Culturally and Linguistically Diverse Students

4. CLD students usually differ from Euro-American students in their physical appearance, language, and culture-based behavior.

## Educational Service Delivery Models for CLDE Students

5. Traditionally, there have been three models for providing educational services to CLDE students.

6. In the Integrated Bilingual Special Education Model, the bilingual special education teacher can provide all educational services for the CLDE student in a self-contained special education setting.

7. In the Bilingual Support Model, instruction is delivered in a self-contained special education setting by a monolingual, English-speaking, special education teacher and a bilingual special education paraprofessional.

8. In the Coordinated Services Model, a special education teacher and a teacher of CLD students combine their expertise to serve the CLDE student. The location of educational services is not dictated by this model; therefore, students can be served in an inclusive setting.

9. A continuum of least restrictive environment placements includes bilingual and English language development classes as inclusive or mainstream classes for CLDE students.

## Professional Competencies for Working with CLDE Students

10. To effectively work with CLDE students, professionals should develop competence in the following areas: cultural awareness, language, understanding families, assessment, curriculum, instructional planning, instruction, selecting materials, and consultation and collaboration.

11. Educators are encouraged to avoid stereotyping and consider culture as a continuum, with people demonstrating traits ranging from those traditionally attributed to the target group to those of a person with no apparent target group status.

12. Educators are encouraged to conduct an analysis of the home and community of each student to determine each student's cultural characteristics.

13. To develop cultural awareness, educators should understand how their own cultural perspective affects the ongoing teaching-learning relationship, should promote an atmosphere in which cultural differences can be explored and approached intellectually as well as attitudinally, should draw upon the cultural experiences of students and parents, and should help students expand their knowledge of their own culture as well as the cultures of other students.

14. Culturally sensitive teachers should incorporate resources from the learner's home and local community environment, identify and build on their students' strengths and interests, realize that language and dialectical differences are important cultural influences that affect not just communication but also interaction between the teacher and the learner, learn different interpretations of classroom activities based on how the students view the world, and provide students with the opportunity to learn and practice new skills.

15. Since there is considerable research to suggest that inclusion of students' language and culture into the school program is a significant predictor of academic success, all educators working with CLDE students should have a basic understanding of the nature of language as well as an understanding of the principles of first- and second-language acquisition.

16. Language proficiency is composed of two distinguishable components: everyday conversational skills (basic interpersonal communication skills, BICS) and abstract skills characteristic of academic instruction (cognitive/academic linguistic proficiency, CALP).

17. Second languages are acquired when the student receives comprehensible input in a low-anxiety situation.

18. Educators are encouraged to determine the student's mastery of CALP before relying upon English as the language of instruction for complex academic subjects.

19. An important strategy that should be used by all educators to enhance comprehensibility of content is sheltered instruction. When using sheltered instruction, teachers provide assistance to learners through visuals, concrete materials, modified texts, teaching in light of each student's proficiency in English, providing a high level of student interaction, making connections between students' knowledge and experience and the lesson, and adjusting communication patterns by using an appropriate rate of speech as well as body language and gestures to enhance meaning.

20. Professionals working with culturally and linguistically diverse families should promote a collaborative and supportive relationship, respect the knowledge base and experience of the parents, develop a "common language," facilitate communication between the family and the school system, and identify mutually acceptable methods of assessment and intervention.

21. Consultants, when conferencing with family members, should have frequent casual conferences to build rapport and increase knowledge about one another; use purposeful conferences when a particular topic needs to be addressed (e.g., the IEP); use multiple methods to encourage communication (e.g., phone calls, informal notes); invite both the parents and other significant members of the family to any conference; and allow more time than might be necessary to maintain rapport and show respect for the family.

22. Home visits are useful to present information to family members and, more importantly, to develop a relationship between the consultant and the family members. The consultant must be sure, when developing a relationship with family members, to show respect for and trust of the parents, to focus on the child's strengths, and to deal with resistance adequately.

23. Consultants should generate a variety of strategies to involve family members in the education of their children so as to overcome some of the reasons that parents of CLDE students become only minimally involved in their child's education. For example, in some communities, word of mouth is much more effective than a written notice. Consultants may also want to elicit the support of other parents, as well as community radio and television stations.

24. Consultants should be aware of alternative assessment models that have been developed in response to the inconsistencies found when assessing students from culturally and linguistically diverse backgrounds and that focus on the use of authentic sources of information about a student's performance such as culturally appropriate work and language samples.

25. Since language assessment is key to documenting the difference between language difference and language disability, educators should be familiar with first- and second-language assessments to determine language proficiency as well as language dominance.

26. Consultants should obtain as much information as possible concerning the student's language use in home, school, and community situations.

27. The appropriate curriculum for CLDE students should reflect cultural compatibility between the students' actual learning styles and the teaching style.

28. To address the language needs of CLDE students, consultants should be prepared to help special, bilingual and ESL educators collaboratively plan lessons.

29. When planning lessons, educators should incorporate language requirements for practice and language development as well as sheltered instruction techniques to increase comprehensibility.

30. Educators should strive to establish a classroom climate that promotes success for *all* students.

31. Consultants should assess and secure the resources for providing appropriate language instruction, determine the level of congruency between the teacher's views and expectations of CLDE students and their educational needs, develop congruence between the culture and language of the home and those of the school, and use instructional strategies that are effective with CLDE students (e.g., sheltered instruction, effective grouping strategies).

32. When modifying materials for the CLDE student, the educator must determine: if the language level of the material matches the language level of the students, if the language concepts expressed in the material are consistent with the language concept development of the students, if the curriculum material itself is culturally sensitive, and if the use of the curriculum material is culturally sensitive.

33. One competency that consulting educators should develop is an ability to understand their own culture and its relationship to other cultures. To address this competency, ask yourself the following questions: What are my own goals and expectations? Am I willing to learn from professionals who serve CLD students as well as to share my expertise? What are my beliefs and the beliefs of my collaborators regarding CLD and CLDE students?

34. Another important competency for consulting educators is to be able to use effective interpersonal, communicative, and problem-solving skills. To address this competency, ask yourself the following questions: Can I exhibit the ability to be caring, respectful, empathetic, congruent, and open in cross-cultural interactions? Can I interview effectively to elicit information, explore problems, and set goals and objectives? Can I exhibit the ability to grasp and validate overt and covert meanings and affects in cross-cultural interactions? Am I able to establish and maintain sensitive and responsible cross-cultural interactions with culturally and linguistically diverse family members and colleagues? Am I able to work effectively with an interpreter to facilitate clear and effective communication in oral and written form?

35. A consultant must assume a dual perspective, that is, be able to operate from the culture within which he or she has been socialized professionally as well as understand the cultures of the individuals with whom he or she is interacting.

36. The following situations should be avoided in cross-cultural communications: dominating the conversation, talking too fast, being too intent, talking down, and being boisterous.

37. The following conditions should be developed in cross-cultural interactions: allow extra time, avoid situations with many people interacting at one time, talk openly about communication and discrimination, seek help, and learn to accept and appreciate differences.

38. Consultants involved in cross-cultural interactions should be approachable, patient, and trustworthy.

39. When giving a symbol of respect, educators should select one thoughtfully, allow the recipient to reciprocate, and identify the motive for the symbol.

40. Educators engaged in cross-cultural interactions are encouraged to obtain the training they need so that they feel comfortable with, can enjoy, and can learn from cross-cultural interactions.

41. A third competency for consulting educators is to understand each other's roles during consultation activities. The kinds of questions that consultants should ask themselves regarding this competency include determining their level of familiarity with individual and institutional objectives relevant to CLDE students; understanding the purpose of the collaboration; identifying the skills and individuals needed to address the situation, and assuring that each collaborator understands the roles assumed by all other collaborators.

42. Interpreters should be bilingual and biliterate, knowledgeable in educational terminology and culture as well as the culture of the student, flexible, and ethical.

43. The primary role of the interpreter is to facilitate communication. Interpreters should be proficient in the target language and familiar with procedures for establishing rapport, with using nonverbal communication, and with using colloquial expressions.

44. When working with interpreters, educators should be able to establish rapport with all participants, use appropriate nonverbal communication, and conduct pre- and post-sessions with the interpreter.

45. Bilingual education involves the use of two languages to provide instruction.

46. Transition bilingual education programs teach students basic skills in their native language while developing English-language proficiency. Typically, students in these programs are exited within 2–3 years; hence, these programs are sometimes called "early exit" bilingual programs.

47. Maintenance bilingual education programs provide native language instruction even after a student demonstrates English-language proficiency.

48. Two-way enrichment bilingual education programs provide English speakers with an opportunity to acquire a second language while native speakers of that language acquire English while learning the general education curriculum.

49. English as a Second Language (ESL) is not a bilingual approach because it relies exclusively on English as the language of teaching and learning. It focuses on the development of English-language skills.

# Questions

1. How can inclusion serve to celebrate, not obliterate, differences among individuals?

2. Whenever there is difference, there is conflict and tension. Describe such a situation. Discuss the ways that participants can positively engage the tension that results from these differences, and examine their assumptions and perspectives.

3. What is the advantage to the CLDE student if he or she receives instruction in a bilingual classroom?

4. Describe an educational situation that would necessitate use of a bilingual paraprofessional. How could the teacher work with the bilingual paraprofessional to provide appropriate instruction for a CLDE student?

5. Describe the characteristics of a group of students who represent more than one culture and language. How could you choose assessment techniques to determine the appropriate curriculum and instructional strategies to use with these students? Why would you use those techniques?

6. Describe a situation that would involve the family of a CLDE student. How could you work with this family to increase their involvement in the educational program of the CLDE student?

7. Describe a situation that would involve the need for collaborative instructional planning between a special educator and a bilingual or ESL educator. Develop a collaborative lesson plan that would address the situation.

8. Describe an educational situation that would require the modification of instructional materials for CLDE students. What kinds of modifications would you make and why?

9. Obtain a lesson plan for a general education classroom. Now, modify it to incorporate sheltered instruction techniques for a hypothetical group of CLDE students.

10. Why is it important for all children, including CLDE children, to be able to use language for learning?

11. How do you think educational services for CLDE students could be improved?

# Discussion Points and Exercises

1. Develop a special education referral process for students in your school or agency who are not members of the majority culture.

2. Tape cross-cultural communications between educators and parents and/or among culturally diverse school personnel. Critique the interaction based upon the cross-cultural communication suggestions offered in this chapter.

3. Design a program for the families of the CLDE students in your school that will increase their participation in school-based programs.

4. Design a cultural awareness training program for the monolingual, English-speaking special educators in your school.

5. Consider several "differences" CLDE students can experience. Construct an activity sensitive to students' feelings that will help students and educators understand these differences.

6. Coordinate a training program designed to develop curriculum and instructional modification skills among special educators, bilingual educators, ESL educators, general educators, and paraprofessionals.

7. Drawing upon the information presented in this chapter and in Chapter 4, make a list of generic communication strategies for effective consultations and specific communicative strategies for cross-cultural interactions.

# Section IV

---

*Effective Assessment, Instruction, and Management Strategies*

# Assessment Strategies for the Educational Consultant

8

onsultants are called upon frequently to gather information about a variety of individuals and situations. Within a consultation problem-solving framework, data are usually collected for any of the following purposes: to identify a problem, to develop an intervention plan, to monitor implementation, or to evaluate the program. With the passage of IDEA '97, functional assessment data may also be required to address pressing questions regarding a student's behavior.

This chapter discusses several methods for conducting a comprehensive assessment within a problem-solving framework. Qualitative and quantitative techniques for gathering information are discussed and examples are provided to use with these techniques. Next, three primary methods for conducting functional assessments are provided. Advantages, disadvantages, and examples of each method will be presented as well. The chapter concludes with a discussion of monitoring implementation and evaluating student progress, as well as evaluating the consultation process itself.

## Objectives

After reading this chapter, the reader should be able to:

1. distinguish between qualitative and quantitative data collection strategies;

2. describe the general purposes of assessment;

3. distinguish between survey-level and specific-level assessment;

4. identify assessment techniques useful for the consultant when identifying a problem, developing interventions, monitoring implementation, and evaluating intervention plans;

5. recognize situations appropriate for each of the following techniques: case study, structured interview, unstructured interview, ecological assessment, checklist, rating scale, curriculum-based assessment, and sociometric assessment;

6. distinguish between formative and summative evaluation;

7. identify three methods for conducting a functional assessment;

8. describe the advantages and disadvantages of using an indirect, descriptive, or functional analysis method;

9. specify considerations for planning and implementing program evaluation activities.

## Key Terms

| | |
|---|---|
| qualitative information | curriculum-based assessment |
| quantitative information | sociometric assessment |
| survey level | sociogram |
| specific level | functional assessment |
| case study | indirect method |
| multimodal data | descriptive method |
| narrative recording | functional analysis |
| structured interview | monitoring plan implementation |
| unstructured interview | evaluation |
| ecological assessment | formative evaluation |
| checklist | summative evaluation |
| rating scale | evaluating the consultation process |
| performance assessment | |

# Assessment Frameworks

There is much controversy in the field regarding the use of qualitative and quantitative information (Howe & Eisenhart, 1990). Our goal is not to engage in debate about the relative merits of an ethnographic (qualitative) approach versus a psychometric (quantitative) approach, but to present each of these orientations accurately. Further, we intend to show how each approach might be used to assist the consultant with the important task of gathering useful information for the purpose of education decision making.

Simply put, *qualitative information* is a narrative source of report designed to describe and understand a given situation from the perspective of the participants in that situation. Therefore, the important aspects to describe are often identified by the participants and not predetermined by the data gatherer. In contrast, *quantitative information* or data are numerical indices designed to portray the occurrence of specific behaviors. Educators disagree as to whether these two approaches to obtaining information should be distinct or should be combined (Smith, 1983a, 1983b). We take the position that each approach provides practical information, depending upon the assessment purpose, and each can be used to observe process and product variables (e.g., consultant-consultee interactions or achievement scores, respectively).

Within an educational setting, a consultant will have occasion to gather information about a variety of individuals and situations. For example, if a student is experiencing difficulty in a particular educational placement, a consultant might collect information about the student's behavior to determine the nature of the problem and, thereby, play a role in solving it.

On the other hand, a consultant may be required to gather information about groups rather than individuals. For example, a school administrator may be interested in assessing the effects of inclusion on an individual student and the general education teacher. In addition to deriving information about individuals and groups, a consultant may assume program assessment responsibility within the school (e.g., evaluating an inservice teacher program, assessing a specific educational intervention, and/or determining the effectiveness of the educational consultation program). We shall consider the process a consultant may use to gather information within the following 4-stage problem-solving sequence: identifying a problem, developing an intervention plan, monitoring implementation and student progress, and evaluating treatment.

# Identifying a Problem

Traditionally, special educators, resource specialists, and school psychologists have been responsible for the diagnosis and assessment of students referred for special education services. This chapter, however, will not focus on using assessment tools per se for diagnosis and assessment. Instead, we will focus on the strategies the educational consultant could use to help teachers prevent and solve the problems they experience.

For an in-depth treatment of assessment topics, see Maddox (1997); Taylor, (2000).

Two levels of identification can be defined: survey and specific. At the *survey level,* a consultant attempts to identify the problem. The focus can be an individual, a classroom, or the whole school. Sometimes the referral a consultant receives is worded vaguely—for example, "Sally misbehaves." Here it is necessary to observe the situation before the consultant can specify the exact nature of the misbehavior. Only after the problem has been identified accurately can information be gathered and procedures initiated to remedy the situation. To cite another example, a teacher may complain that students in the classroom always fight. Through observation, the consultant may discover that a few students instigate most of the fights and that the problem is not as widespread as the teacher believes. After observing the classroom of the frustrated teacher and talking with that teacher about the observed events, the consultant may find that the teacher attends to the few students who misbehave far more frequently than she attends to the appropriate behavior of the rest of the class.

It is at the *specific level* that the consultant tries to collect information about the factors contributing to the problem. A necessary consequence of this process is the development of a program designed to improve the situation. The strengths and weaknesses of students with disabilities are routinely assessed to develop appropriate individual educational or family services programs for them. If a student with disabilities displays maladjusted behavior in class, the consultant may observe the student to determine the nature and degree of the inappropriate behavior. For example, a secondary-level student may be described by the algebra teacher as having a "poor attitude." During observation, the consultant may note that the teacher provides few initiations to the student, waits only a short period of time for oral responses, and does not use prompting procedures effectively.

The consultant might then observe the frequency of both teacher and student behaviors in the algebra class. After obtaining the data, a program could be developed and implemented to improve the student's attitude. Subsequent observation of both student and teacher would reveal whether the attitude had indeed been changed and whether there was any change in the teacher's reaction to the student. Thus, the systematic use of case studies, interviews, ecological assessments, checklists and rating scales, and curriculum-based assessments can help a consultant assess current levels of performance and ultimately evaluate the success of an intervention program.

## Case Study

A *case study* is a qualitative approach that has also been referred to by educators as educational ethnography, participant observation, qualitative observation, field study, and field observation (Harris & Smith, 1996, 1998a, 1998b). It is useful when a consultant wants to understand the perspective of the participants, the context in which specific behaviors are being measured, and/or to define problems or behaviors to be measured. Holmes (1991) discusses the use of case study to understand the vantage points from which children view their social world. She took the role of a nonauthoritarian adult whom she termed the child's aide. As the child's aide, she observed, played, and interacted with children to obtain the child's, not the teacher's, perspective on the classroom environment. The nature of the descriptions and conclusions that might be drawn from a child's behavior as assessed by a child's aide using participant observation techniques can be found in Table 8.1.

A case study may involve a considerable investment of time and energy. Therefore, it is used most efficiently when important judgments or decisions need to be made or when nebulous problems have to be clarified. The case study is based on the assumption that human behavior is significantly influenced by the settings in which it occurs (Wilson, 1977). Its purpose is to provide an on-site, holistic study of a group, program, or individual that furnishes a rich description of the situation. This description can be used to generate further observation and measurement of relevant specific behaviors.

### Table 8.1
#### Field Observation Conclusions of a Child's Aide

Bryan was one of the most physically active children in either (kindergarten) class, and he demanded persistently to be the center of attention. His behavior, unlike that of his classmates, was both verbally and physically aggressive, and his actions were often misinterpreted by his peers. His behavior neither affected nor precluded his ability to form friendships, but he did have difficulty maintaining them. The problem was due in part to his aggressiveness and his unwillingness to share with his classmates. At times he was classified behaviorally as "bad" by the teacher and his classmates, but Bryan could also be quite charming, lovable, and congenial with his classmates.

One particular play episode involved a group of boys who were building a garage. Bryan was often a sought-after playmate, and he and his "best friend" Patrick were building in the back of the room. But when it came time to share building materials, Bryan grabbed the blocks from Patrick. When Patrick responded by taking the blocks away from Bryan, Bryan pushed him aggressively and knocked down the building they had built together. Patrick ended the episode by telling Bryan, "You're not my friend anymore."

This incident could obviously be interpreted in several ways. Nevertheless, the perspective of an adult who has played with the children has several important advantages. My relationship with the children gave me the opportunity to see how they negotiated, shared, and resolved conflict. An adult who understands the importance of children's acts in their own terms is able to assist them in resolving the problem using their rules rather than simply altering the children's behavior through adult intervention.

Sharing was an important obligation and expectation between "friends," and the children often used this rule of behavior to resolve conflict. By employing the children's rules of behavior, for example, sharing a toy with a friend, a teacher could easily explain to a child that an aggressive act was not necessarily the best means of resolving a situation ridden with conflict. Thus rather than classify Bryan as "aggressive," perhaps he was simply unskilled in the social technique of negotiation.

*Note.* Excerpted from "A Lesson Learned: Teacher's Aide or Child's Aide," by R. M. Holmes, 1991, *Intervention in School and Clinic, 26*(3), 160. Excerpted with permission.

## Essential Elements

There are three essential elements of the case study. First, the focus of observation—a person, an institution, or a program—must be identified (Stake, 1978). The purpose is not to measure prespecified behaviors, but to identify behaviors to be measured. What is happening in the environment and deemed important with respect to the person, institution, or program determines what is measured.

Second, it is essential that the observations be conducted on site (i.e., at the school). As the purpose of the case study is to identify behaviors in need of further assessment, the consultant draws upon observations to determine any additional information that must be collected to understand the situation under study.

Finally, the data are based upon a narrative description, but the approach is constructed to allow and actually foster *multimodal* data collection. That is, one may begin with a narrative description of what is happening in a given situation for a period of time, similar to an anecdotal record. Observations are usually conducted over a long enough period of time (hours and weeks as opposed to minutes and days) to ascertain patterns of behavior. The descriptive narrative then provides the basis for other means of data collection. *Narrative recording* is used to generate questions and to help the consultant learn what additional data will be necessary to answer questions. Since multimodal data come from many sources, they provide the consultant with a wider database and lend objectivity to this method.

## Procedure

Wilson (1977) describes the procedure generally used in case study. First, the consultant, acting as observer, must establish a role within a particular situation. For example, if the consultant intends to study an elementary, self-contained, special education classroom for students with learning disabilities, he or she would first establish a role in the classroom as an unobtrusive observer. An educational consultant can become an accepted part of the classroom environment in many ways. For example, the consultant could model the behavior of other adults in the classroom (e.g., aides or parent volunteers) who are there to assist the teacher and students. The consultant needs to use verbal and nonverbal communication skills effectively to enter and gain acceptance into the classroom. The reader is encouraged to review the work of experts regarding entry into field study situations (e.g., Dobbert, 1982; Erickson, 1973; Spindler, 1970; Spradley, 1980). Consultants are urged to carefully consider appropriate entry and acceptance into an educational environment when conducting any of the many varied activities they are called upon to perform.

Second, the data must be collected. Since the data are multimodal, the consultant may attempt to describe the physical setting; describe how that setting changes with modification in activity or personnel; and describe both the form and content of verbal as well as nonverbal interactions between participants. The various modes of data collection evolve from the basic narrative in the field notes. The consultant develops questions based on those notes and, in the process, develops additional sources of data to answer the questions. For example, the consultant might record activities that the classroom aide performs. After reflecting on the descriptions of the activities, the consultant may question whether the teacher uses the aide primarily for instructional or clerical assistance. The consultant may then decide to ask the teacher how she would plan for the same class at a similar time during the year but without the aide's assistance. Or the consultant may decide to ask the teacher about the aide's duties in the classroom. Either informal interview would provide an additional data source to the field notes about the role of the aide in the room.

Third, a representative sampling of information is obtained to achieve objectivity. It is established by using long-term and multimodal data collection and interpreting the data in terms of the context in which they were gathered. The observer must be sure to conduct field observations in all relevant situations and over a sufficient period of time to detect behavior patterns. For example, in a field observation of an elementary class with mainstreamed exceptional students, the physical setting of the classroom, playground, lunchroom, and gym, as well as various aspects of the teacher-student and student-student interaction, the amount of time spent on academic tasks, and the nature of the educational program should be observed.

Boehm and Weinberg (1977) suggest conducting observations about the physical features—objects, people, and activities—for any given situation as a means of obtaining information about the key components of a setting. Such an initial observation could be used by the consultant for many different purposes (e.g., to determine specific activities to be observed at later dates, to generate questions for the teacher regarding material and equipment use in the room, and/or to provide preliminary information about the educational environments for a specific student who had been referred due to a behavior problem).

Fourth, the data are analyzed. Data analysis involves a logical comparison of information and can reflect a variety of approaches (Miles & Huberman, 1984). Smith (1979) describes a process of analyzing the field observation data that incorporates: (a) comparing and contrasting information, and (b) looking for antecedents and consequences. Smith searches actively for overall patterns, and the final analysis of the field observation involves understanding the particular situation in comparison to his general knowledge of all situations of this type.

## Example of Case Study

The field note excerpt found in Table 8.2 was taken from observations conducted by a junior high school resource teacher (Harris, 1981). This excerpt demonstrates the process of case study (i.e., describing what is observed and noting questions and additional information that must be explored to understand the situation under study). In the field note excerpt, a consultant was observing a resource teacher during a math period. The consultant described what was said and recorded questions to ask the teacher at a later date (e.g., "Comment: How are schedules arranged for students?" "Comment: Explore basis and importance of grades;" "Comment: What happens tomorrow? Planning for this lesson—does it represent a modification of plan?") as well as impressions to be confirmed or negated by additional observation (e.g., "Comment: Does not seem that aide is given much instructional responsibility").

Consultants should be aware that qualitative techniques such as case study can be used successfully to identify problems in education, particularly those in which an understanding of a situation is needed. If, for example, school district personnel believe that the mainstreaming program is not working based on measures of the number of students reintegrated and their grades, there is still a need to identify why the program is not working. One cannot develop an intervention, or even measure the problem behavior, if that behavior is not

**Table 8.2**

Example of a Field Observation

---

*Situation:* Third period, 10:00 A.M.

Six students around table with teacher. Tony and Nate (students) each at separate tables. (COMMENT: How are schedules arranged for students?)

> TEACHER *(passes out paper)*: "Are we ready to begin?"
>
> SUE *(student)*: "Won't be ready until the end of the period."
>
> TEACHER *(writes math problem on board)*: "I'm going to count this as a quiz, OK? For a grade, OK?"

Boy reading out loud to aide at back table Station 3. This is one of Sharon's (another teacher's) students. Prior to this there was some discussion between two teachers and aide about what aide should do. Sharon made a comment about having plenty for the aide to do, starting with the bulletin board, the one that had been decorated by one of the students, Tom. (COMMENT: Does not seem that aide is given much instructional responsibility.) Students finish papers independently. As students state that they're finished, teacher takes their papers and grades them.

> TEACHER: "Careless mistake here, Marvin—multiply."
>
> MARVIN *(student)*: "Don't mark it wrong."
>
> TEACHER: "2 times 8 is not 10."
>
> JIMMY *(student)*: "Don't mark it wrong, please!" *(whining)* (COMMENT: Explore basis and importance of grades.)
>
> TEACHER: "Fair is fair. I'll give you another chance tomorrow."
>
> TEACHER: "Good job, people. Very good, Tony, one or two careless errors. Don't mess up tomorrow." (COMMENT: What happens tomorrow? Planning for this lesson—does it represent a modification of plan? Look at yesterday's assignment.)

---

defined clearly. It may be possible to define the variables affecting the mainstreaming program by using qualitative approaches. Once variables have been identified and defined, then measurement of their effect can occur.

## Interview

An interview allows an individual, usually the participant in a given situation, to express his or her perceptions. An interview is often used during field observation to obtain a more in-depth understanding of a situation. Interviews can be constructed along a continuum from structured to unstructured. A structured interview should be used to provide relevant information once there is a thorough knowledge of the problem or situation under study (McCallon & McCray, 1975). Pugach and Johnson (1988) use a structured interview to elicit information during the prereferral consultation process that maximizes introspection and self-questioning and minimizes advice giving. You will recall from Chapter 3 that prereferral consultation is a process by which two or more educators mutually identify a problem; consider a variety of potential interventions; and select the most appropriate approach to be implemented, monitored, and evaluated (DeBoer, 1986). In Pugach and Johnson's approach, classroom teachers are paired and follow a systematic, highly structured dialogue about the problems they are facing, working toward a greater comprehension of those problems before they try to solve them.

Welch, Judge, Anderson, Bray, Child, and Franke (1990) developed a form to be used for the *structured interview* in the prereferral consultation process. The questions in this structured interview are provided in Table 8.3. The questions are designed to target variables influencing behavior, to target alternative intervention strategies, to define the mission and responsibility of each educator for systematic implementation of the strategy, and to identify strategies and techniques for monitoring and evaluating learner progress.

To understand a given situation, an unstructured interview is most appropriate. An *unstructured interview* uses a conversational approach. It permits a discussion of those aspects believed to be important by the interviewee. Spradley (1979) describes a form of unstructured interview called the ethnographic interview. The educational consultant may want to use an ethnographic interview as an aid in understanding the social system of a given school. For an educational consultant, the ethnographic interview would be most useful when trying to work within a school environment that is new. By using ethnographic interview techniques and effective communication skills, the educational consultant can obtain a greater understanding of the perceptions of the

## Table 8.3
### Structured Interview—Questions for Prereferral Consultation

*Targeting Variables Influencing Behavior*

1. How would the situation or behavior be described? What are the antecedents to and consequences of the behavior?
2. What has been tried to resolve the situation or problem, and what was its effect?
3. Where and when does the situation or behavior take place, and for how long has it been occurring?
4. What is (or has been) an area of strength or success for this person?
5. What appears to motivate this person, and can it be used as a reinforcer?
6. What others are involved, and how are they involved?

*Techniques for Monitoring and Evaluating Learner Progress*

7. What options for intervention have been identified through brainstorming?
8. Which options are likely to have the most desired results?
9. What is the behavioral objective of the chosen option?
10. What are the evaluation criteria for the targeted outcome?
11. How and when will progress be measured and recorded?
12. What roles and responsibilities will each participant have for implementing the option?
13. When and where will the next meeting take place, and who should attend?

*Note.* From "CO-OP: A Tool for Implementing Prereferral Consultation," by M. Welch, T. Judge, J. Anderson, J. Bray, B. Child, and L. Franke, 1990, *Teaching Exceptional Children*, 22(2), 31. Reprinted with permission.

people who function within the school and, therefore, a greater understanding of the school as a social system. Such an understanding is essential if the consultant wishes to help produce change within the school.

Spradley (1979) describes the ethnographic interview as a series of friendly conversations. The interviewer introduces new elements slowly to obtain further information from interviewees. It is suggested that this process be unhurried and friendly so as to establish and maintain rapport. According to Spradley, there are three important elements: explicit purpose, explanations, and questions.

## Explicit Purpose

When the interviewer and the interviewee meet to conduct an ethnographic interview, the situation is informal and conversational. However, if the interviewer wants to know the interviewee's perceptions about a given topic, it is the responsibility of the interviewer to introduce the topic. For example, without sounding authoritarian, the consultant may ask about the grading system at the school. The consultant would engage the teacher in conversation about the grading system and also be responsible for keeping the conversation focused upon the grading system of the school.

## Explanations

In an ethnographic interview, the interviewee is essentially informing the interviewer about the culture or social system in question. The interviewer, then, must help the interviewee with this process. Explanations as to why one is engaged in this conversation help. For example, the consultant may want to make general statements concerning the reason for engaging the teacher in conversation (e.g., "I'm new in this school, and I really want to know how things operate"). Or the consultant may want to understand the terminology the teachers use related to grading or other activities. In addition, to clarify understanding of the topic being discussed, the consultant may ask the teacher to show examples of grade cards and how they are completed.

## Questions

The type of questions the consultant asks helps to establish an environment for communication. Spradley (1979) discusses three main types of ethnographic questions: descriptive, structural, and contrast. Descriptive questions help the interviewer to obtain the interviewee's perspective on the situation as well as identify terminology the interviewee uses in discussing the topic. An example of a descriptive question might be "Could you tell me what you do when grading?" Structural questions show how the interviewee organizes the topic under discussion. For example, the consultant may ask, "What are the steps involved in completing a grade for a student?" Sometimes, structural questions are repeated to facilitate understanding of the situation (e.g., "Can you think of any other things to do to get the grade card completed?"). Contrast questions help the interviewer to understand the terminology used in the discussion. For example, the consultant may ask, "What is the difference between an $S$ and an $S+$?"

There are other situations when the consultant may want to conduct an interview for more specific purposes. For example, the consultant may want to engage a student in discussion about a given learning situation as part of a clinical teaching method (Opper, 1977). Or the consultant may want to engage a teacher in discussion about a given teaching technique as part of a study of that teacher's classroom. In both of these situations, the purpose of the interview is narrower than that of the ethnographic interview, and, understandably, the interview process can usually be completed within a shorter period of time (i.e., one or two brief sessions).

### Example of an Unstructured Interview

Table 8.4 provides an example of an actual interview conducted with a resource teacher (Harris, 1981). This excerpt was selected to illustrate the consultant's reliance upon the teacher's comments when formulating questions during an interview. The purpose of the interview was to understand the teacher's use of standardized assessments. The reader should be aware that other issues raised during the conversation (e.g., the importance of spelling in an academic curriculum) were later addressed by the consultant.

After explaining the purpose of the interview, the consultant asked a few predetermined questions (e.g., "How did you determine what Kottmeyer to give?" "O.K., could you talk with me about your use of the Woodcock in first period today?"). However, many more questions were asked by the consultant (e.g., "Why is that test used?" "What happens if you have kids who you think are at a higher level?"). These questions were suggested by the teacher's responses to predetermined questions and provided information the consultant needed to understand the teacher's use of standardized assessments. This type of unstructured interview is a communicative activity in which the consultant actively participates in the conversation.

Regardless of the purpose of an unstructured interview, it is suggested that the consultant carefully communicate the purpose of the interview, engage the interviewee in conversation that will allow the identification and pursuit of topics deemed important by the interviewee, and ask questions that will help to clarify the interviewee's intent. The effective use of communication skills will greatly facilitate this process.

## Ecological Assessment

*Ecological assessment* tends to be a quantitative approach that addresses the same purpose as the case study. Ecological assessment can be defined within two broad perspectives. First, the individual's behavior is considered interactive. That is, a change in performance of one behavior may affect other behaviors. Second, behavior is viewed in relation to its environmental context. That is, a change in one setting or context may produce changes in other environments and, in turn, affect an individual's performance (Heron & Heward, 1982). Ecological assessment analyzes different types of quantitative information to identify problems. The consultant, using ecological assessment techniques, raises the questions and seeks answers to those questions. In contrast, the qualitative concepts previously discussed (i.e., case study and ethnographic interview) allow for participants to identify what is important to them, and the questions are generated by the participants in the situation as well as the person gathering information.

Ecological assessment is usually conducted when a sample of a student's behavior and environment that extends beyond the classroom is desired (Glass, Christiansen, & Christiansen, 1982). As Heron and Heward (1982) suggest, before an effective intervention can be conducted, the student and his or her relationship to the environment must be assessed.

## Table 8.4
### Example of an Unstructured Interview

---

***Situation:*** Interview

***Purpose:*** Use of standardized assessments, basis for teacher's decision making

| | |
|---|---|
| CONSULTANT*: | How did you determine what Kottmeyer to give? |
| TEACHER: | There's the two levels. *(pause)* I figured all our kids fit into the above. *(pause)* |
| CONSULTANT**: | Why is that test used? |
| TEACHER: | Gee, I don't know. *(pause)* It's the one Sharon had in there to *(pause)* ascertain a grade level. *(pause)* |
| CONSULTANT**: | I think that only goes up to the sixth grade. What happens if you have kids who you think are at a higher level? |
| TEACHER: | We do have a couple, Donna and Tommy, above a sixth-grade level. |
| CONSULTANT**: | What happens with them? |
| TEACHER: | Well, at that point, levels aren't that important; spelling is not that important, I guess, in how it relates to the kid's expression. For example, Tommy can express himself clearly in writing. |
| CONSULTANT*: | O.K., could you talk with me about your use of the Woodcock in first period today? |
| TEACHER: | Yeah. I looked in the Woodcock just to see if I could pick up any patterns of theirs. *(pause)* |
| CONSULTANT**: | Did you look at the tests that the kids from the first period took? |
| TEACHER: | Yeah. I picked up Piccolo's, Votor's, and Zap's. I didn't pick up Tommy's. *(pause)* |
| CONSULTANT**: | Any reason for that order? |
| TEACHER: | No, just the first one I came to. The first thing I put on the board, *slip* and *slap,* was something that Votor had missed last week in the World of Vocabulary . . . |
| CONSULTANT**: | The *bite–site* stuff from the Woodcock? |
| TEACHER: | Yeah, and Rick said *invited* for *inventor.* |
| CONSULTANT**: | This was on the Woodcock? |
| TEACHER: | Yeah, so I wanted to set that pattern. I just felt like teaching them something after all that testing. |

---

*Note.* From *The Classroom Program of a Special Education Teacher: A Case Study,* by K. C. Harris, 1981, unpublished doctoral dissertation, Temple University, Philadelphia. Reprinted with permission.

*Predetermined questions
**Generated questions

A basic assumption in an ecological approach is that there is an intrinsic order to human events and that behaviors occur within and in response to the surrounding environment (Gutmann, 1969). As Brandt (1975) notes, it then becomes the task of the data collector to gather enough information to make this order and behavioral consistency apparent.

There are many situations in which a consultant may conduct an ecological assessment. Lowenthal (1991), for instance, discusses the use of ecological assessments with preschool children and identifies four areas that must be assessed: (a) determining the major environmental settings for the child (e.g., home, preschool classroom, day-care center, church); (b) establishing the behavioral expectations of significant people in those settings (e.g., the parent of a hyperactive preschooler might expect the child to sit quietly through a long church service); (c) assessing the child's ability to meet those expectations; and (d) estimating the preschooler's tolerance of specific settings.

## Procedure

Due to the comprehensive nature of an ecological assessment, the consultant should consider the student's behavior in several settings. Wiederholt, Hammill, and Brown (1978) have identified the school, the home, and the community as the major environments in an ecological assessment. Harris and Little (1982) suggest that the student, peers, family, employers, community members, teachers, school administrators, and school staff be considered when conducting an ecological assessment. For example, the consultant may assess a student's behavior in the general education classroom, the special education setting, the gym, the lunchroom, and the playground. Heron and Heward (1982) note the possible importance of the physical aspects of a given classroom: that is, the amount of space each student has, how the seating is arranged, the amount of classroom lighting, and the noise level. These variables have been shown to affect student performance. In addition, academic response time (i.e., the time during which a student is actively performing academic tasks such as reading, writing, and asking or answering questions) has been found to be positively correlated with academic achievement (Heward, 1994).

Heron and Heward (1982) also identify other factors that seem related to student performance. These include student physiological aspects (e.g., medical history, medication, and diet), the nature of student-student interaction, the nature of teacher-student interaction, and the previous reinforcement history of the student.

To conduct a comprehensive ecological assessment, several sources of information may need analysis. One readily available source of information is the student's permanent record. According to Heron and Heward (1982), student records should indicate the level (and possibly the rate) of student achievement as well as provide important information on pertinent physical or psychological characteristics. Such records should not be viewed as the sole source of information, nor should they be viewed as verification of a student's problem. Rather, student records should serve as a stimulus to continue the inquiry.

A consultant can probe areas identified through student records by interviewing relevant individuals, such as teachers, students, parents, and physicians. Through interview, the consultant can confirm, clarify, and possibly add to information in the student records.

Another useful way to investigate student behavior and the environment is by direct observation. Direct, daily observation can be used to assess physical aspects of an environment, such as the amount of space in the room, as well as the behavioral aspects of an environment, such as the frequency and duration of a student behavior. The consultant can select among several observation techniques when conducting an ecological assessment.

When is it appropriate to conduct a full-scale ecological assessment? Heron and Heward (1982) suggest that two criteria be employed before using this time-consuming assessment procedure. First, ecological assessments should be undertaken only when a planned intervention has the potential to produce unexpected consequences that could presumably be jeopardized if salient ecological variables were ignored. Second, this assessment procedure should be employed when behavior change procedures would be successful when viewed in isolation but when viewed in their larger context are not likely to produce desired outcomes.

### Example of an Ecological Assessment

Evans, Evans, and Gable (1989) provide an example of an ecological survey of student behavior (see Figure 8.1). This survey covers a wide range of variables that can influence a student's behavior. It may not be necessary to complete the survey to identify the problem behavior. However, this survey attempts to identify a range of factors that could be assessed when attempting to identify a problem behavior. The survey is the data collection sheet and may be used to record information from school records, direct observation, and interviews.

## Checklists and Rating Scales

A *checklist* reflects the presence or absence of a particular characteristic accord-ing to some predetermined set of categories, and a *rating scale* represents an estimate of the degree to which a particular characteristic is evident along a basic continuum. Therefore, if the degree or frequency of behavior is impor-tant, a checklist would not be appropriate. Checklists covering the varieties of observable behavior among children in special education are available com-mercially and are also being developed locally by teachers and consultants (Bush & Waugh, 1982). To maximize reliability of checklists and rating scales, consultants should use operational definitions for behaviors to be measured, request that individuals complete checklists at the time behavior occurs, and provide training and enough time for the completion of rating scales.

Checklists and rating scales can be used by consultants for identifying problems in a number of different areas. Perhaps the most frequent use of checklists and rating scales for problem identification is for the measurement of the environmental demands experienced by mainstreamed students with dis-abilities. Bender (1988) suggests that teaching strategies, instructional modifi-cations, and unusual aspects of the curriculum (e.g., reading level of the whole school, reading level of the texts in mainstream classrooms) should be exam-ined. Fad (1990) reports that sociobehavioral competencies are clearly linked to students' performance in mainstream environments and may be more criti-cal determinants of the success of special education students in general educa-tion classrooms than academic achievement and demographics. Table 8.5 lists the 10 most critical skills in each of the sociobehavioral areas that Fad identi-fies as clearly related to success in inclusive environments, i.e., ability to cope, ability to work successfully, and ability to form effective peer relationships.

**ECOLOGICAL SURVEY OF STUDENT BEHAVIOR**

Name of person(s) completing form _____ Date(s) _____

**I. General Information**
Name of child _____ Address _____
Telephone number _____ Date of birth _____ Age _____ Sex _____
School _____ Teacher _____ Grade _____
Who does the child live with and for how long? (List parent, siblings, others.) _____
_____
Mother's and/or father's place of employment _____
Mother _____ Father _____
Language spoken in the home _____
What present problems (academic and/or social) does the child have? _____
What do you think is causing these problems? _____
What expectations do you have of your child? _____

**II. Educational Information**
Previous psychological and/or educational testing:
Test _____ Date _____ Results _____
Educational history:　　preschool _____
　　　　　　　　　　　　elementary _____
　　　　　　　　　　　　secondary _____
Does the child enjoy reading? _____
Does the child read at home? _____ If yes, list types of materials read at home _____
What academic areas does the child like? _____ dislike _____
How well does the child adjust to school situations? _____ very well _____ fairly well _____ poorly
How would you describe the child's performance in school? (In terms of grades earned and behavior.)
_____
How would you describe the conditions in the classroom and school that could influence this child?
(Classroom discipline, size of classes, and instructional factors, etc.) _____
_____
Does the child regularly complete homework? _____
Has the child ever been retained? _____ What grade? _____
Is the child absent or tardy frequently? _____
Has the child ever been suspended? _____ Explain _____
Has the child ever been in or referred to a special education clasroom? _____ What type?_____
Has the child ever had special reading instruction or any special adaptations in instruction? _____
What grade? _____
Explain _____
Have any of the child's brothers or sisters had problems in school? _____ Explain _____

**III. Home/Community Information**
How would you describe the conditions in the home and community that might affect this child? (Adequacy of housing, basic needs, significant events such as divorce, etc.) _____
_____
Is the child involved in regular activities in the community? (Recreational, religious, etc.) _____
_____
_____

**Figure 8.1.** Ecological survey of student behavior. From "An Ecological Survey of Student Behavior," by S. S. Evans, W. H. Evans, & R. A. Gable, 1989, *Teaching Exceptional Children, 21*(4), 14–15. Copyright 1989 by The Council for Exceptional Children. Reprinted with permission.

## Table 8.5
Ten Most Critical Sociobehavioral Skills

*Coping Skills*

1. Is able to express anger without physical aggression or yelling.
2. Copes appropriately if someone insults him or her.
3. Copes in acceptable ways if someone takes something that belongs to him or her.
4. Copes in an acceptable way when someone gives orders or bosses him or her around.
5. Avoids an argument when another student is provoking one.
6. Can handle being lied to.
7. Copes with being blamed for something he or she did not really do.
8. Can cope appropriately if someone is upset with him or her.
9. Copes with aggression in an appropriate way (walking away, seeking assistance, or defending himself or herself).
10. Is able to cope with someone calling him or her a name.

*Work Habits*

1. Completes homework assignments on time.
2. Completes classwork on time.
3. Is on task most of the time.
4. Pays attention during class discussions.
5. Uses class time efficiently.
6. Listens carefully to teacher directions.
7. Listens carefully during direct instruction.
8. Follows written directions.
9. Is an independent worker.
10. Promptly follows teacher's requests.

*Peer Relationships*

1. Knows how to join a group activity already in progress.
2. Develops and maintains individual friendships with more than one significant peer.
3. Maintains friendships over an extended period of time.
4. Interacts with a variety of children on a regular basis.
5. Shares laughter and jokes with peers.
6. Will initiate conversations with peers.
7. Initiates play activities with other children.
8. Can express feelings of affection or friendship toward peers.
9. Appears to make friends easily.
10. Regularly compliments others.

*Note.* From "The Fast Track to Success: Social-Behavioral Skills," by K. S. Fad, 1990, *Intervention in School and Clinic, 26*(1), 41. Copyright 1990 by PRO-ED, Inc. Reprinted with permission.

Fad (1990) provides a teacher rating scale to assess a student's mastery of social competencies. A portion of this rating scale in presented in Figure 8.2. This rating scale measures the teacher's perceptions of a student's social competence. It can be used to help determine what the teacher feels are the student's behavioral problems.

---

**Instructions**

The following pages contain a number of statements describing an individual student. Please (a) read each statement and (b) rate the student whose name is on the front of this form on each statement by putting a number in the blank on the right side of the page. It is very important that you *rate each student on each item. Do not omit any items. It is also important that you use only whole numbers. Do not use any fractions, decimals, or zeros.*

| 1 | 2 | 3 | 4 | 5 |
|---|---|---|---|---|
| Never | Rarely | Sometimes | Often | Always |

**This student . . .**
1. follows classroom rules.                                     1. _____
2. is able to cope with teasing.                                2. _____
3. appears to make friends easily.                             3. _____
4. promptly follows teacher requests.                          4. _____
5. is able to cope with someone calling him or her a name.     5. _____
6. is included in activities.                                  6. _____
7. keeps his or her desk or work area neat.                    7. _____
8. can accept not getting his or her own way.                 8. _____
9. is sought out by other children to involve him or her in activities.  9. _____
10. comes to class prepared to work.                          10. _____
11. speaks to the teacher respectfully.                       11. _____
12. chooses to interact with peers during recess and free time.  12. _____
13. is on task most of the time.                              13. _____
14. accepts responsibility for his or her own behavior.      14. _____
15. initiates play activities with other children.           15. _____
16. feels that he or she has control of his or her behavior in academic activities.  16. _____
17. accepts constructive criticism.                          17. _____

**Figure 8.2.** Excerpts from Teacher Rating Scale. From "The Fast Track to Success: Social-Behavioral Skills," by K. S. Fad, 1990, *Intervention in School and Clinic,* 26(1), 42. Copyright 1990 by PRO-ED, Inc. Reprinted with permission.

Another aspect of determining the demands experienced by mainstreamed students is to assess the instructional environments that support learning activities. Hudson and Fradd (1990) provide a checklist for determining mainstream setting demands (see Figure 8.3). They report the use of this checklist by teams of educators who are working together to facilitate the transition of exceptional students with limited English proficiency into regular classes. This checklist can be used to identify the specific task demands of the classroom. It can give a rough estimate of the language and cognitive demands of individual activities and the cumulative demands of the setting. However, Hudson and Fradd caution that the information obtained through the checklist may have to be verified by classroom observations, as many teachers are unaware of the linguistic and cognitive demands they place on their students.

Wood and Miederhoff (1989) discuss a checklist they have designed to measure several aspects of mainstreamed environments (e.g., classroom instructional methods and materials; course content; evaluation techniques; classroom management; interpersonal and social relations; and related school environments such as the cafeteria, gym, etc.). Excerpts from this checklist are presented in Figure 8.4. The checklist is designed to determine which characteristics apply to the general education setting as well as the student's performance in relevant

*Mainstream Setting Demands*

Teacher _____    Student _____
Subject _____    Date _____

| Class Activities | Instructional Arrangement | | | | | Language Requirements | | | | | | |
| --- | --- | --- | --- | --- | --- | --- | --- | --- | --- | --- | --- | --- |
| | whole group | small group | peer tutor | cooperative designs | individual | oral directions | written direct | read | write | listen | oral participate | other |
| Reading + assignment | | | | | | | | | | | | |
| Lecture & discussion + assignment | | | | | | | | | | | | |
| Demonstration + assignment | | | | | | | | | | | | |
| Drill & practice | | | | | | | | | | | | |
| Projects | | | | | | | | | | | | |
| Audio-visual materials | | | | | | | | | | | | |
| Worksheets | | | | | | | | | | | | |
| Tests | | | | | | | | | | | | |
| Objective | | | | | | | | | | | | |
| Essay | | | | | | | | | | | | |
| Homework | | | | | | | | | | | | |

Priority    Discrepancies

Figure 8.3. Mainstream setting demands. From "Cooperative Planning for Learners with Limited English Proficiency," by P. Hudson & S. Fradd, 1990, *Teaching Exceptional Children*, 23(1), 19. Copyright 1990 by The Council for Exceptional Children. Reprinted with permission.

areas. For example, if the teacher indicated a use of large, small, and one-to-one grouping patterns, a rating of the student's performance in all three types of grouping patterns as well as the student's ability to adapt to various group settings could be conducted with this checklist.

## Developing an Intervention Plan

Often consultants use the information gathered during the problem identification stage to assist in determining what variables need to be altered for a successful intervention. To develop an intervention plan, it is necessary to obtain in-depth

**CLASSROOM**

Student: _____

Teacher: _____ Subject: _____

Grade or Type of Class: _____ Date: _____ Teacher Completing Observation: _____

Directions: Mainstream teacher: Check the items in the Characteristics column that describe the mainstream setting.
   Special classroom teacher: Check the appropriate items in the Student's Present Performance Level column.

| CHARACTERISTICS OF MAINSTREAM SETTING | Check if It Applies | STUDENT'S PRESENT PERFORMANCE LEVEL | Has Mastered Skills | Is Working On Skills | Is Unable to Perform Skills |
|---|---|---|---|---|---|
| I. CLASSROOM | | | | | |
| A. Physical Variables | | | | | |
| 1. Grouping for instruction | | | | | |
| a. Large group | | Works well in large group | | | |
| b. Small group | | Works well in small group | | | |
| c. One-to-one | | Works well one to one | | | |
| | | Adapts to various group settings | | | |
| 2. Sound | | | | | |
| a. No talking allowed | | Works silently | | | |
| b. Minor distractions (some interaction) | | Works with minor distractions | | | |
| B. Instructional Variables | | | | | |
| 1. Teaching Techniques | | | | | |
| a. Lecture | | Retains material from lectures | | | |
| b. Explanation | | Comprehends group explanations | | | |
| c. Audiovisual presentation | | Retains audiovisual presentations | | | |
| d. Discussion | | Participants in class discussion | | | |
| 2. Media | | | | | |
| a. Notetaking | | | | | |
| (1) Copied from board | | Can copy notes from chalkboard | | | |
| (2) Prepared by teacher | | Can read teacher-written notes | | | |
| (3) From lecture | | Can take organized lecture notes | | | |
| b. Equipment | | Student learns from varied media: | | | |
| (1) Overhead projector | | Overhead projector | | | |
| (2) Filmstrip projector | | Filmstrip projector | | | |
| (3) Tape recorder | | Tape recorder | | | |
| (4) Computer | | Computer | | | |
| 3. Materials | | | | | |
| a. Textbook used | | Can read textbook at grade level | | | |
| Grade level of text _____ | | Needs text adapted to _____ level | | | |
| b. Supplementary handouts | | Reads most handouts | | | |
| 4. Content | | | | | |
| a. Homework | | | | | |
| (1) Assignments copied from chalkboard | | Copies accurately from chalkboard | | | |
| (2) Written assignments provided | | Reads written assignments accurately | | | |
| b. Modifications | | | | | |
| (1) No modifications made in subject matter | | Needs no modification | | | |
| (2) Some modifications made (List) | | Requires some modifications (List) | | | |
| (3) Peer tutors used | | Requires assistance of peer tutor | | | |
| c. Class procedure | | | | | |
| (1) Students read aloud | | Reads text aloud | | | |
| (2) Students present projects/reports orally | | Presents materials orally | | | |
| 5. Evaluation | | | | | |
| a. Test format used | | Can take tests in these formats | | | |
| b. Test given orally | | Can take oral tests | | | |
| C. Counseling | | | | | |
| 1. Teacher frequently counsels students | | Is able to seek guidance as needed | | | |
| 2. Little time provided for student counseling | | Is able to express personal and/or academic problems appropriately | | | |

*(continues)*

**Figure 8.4.** Transition checklist. From "Bridging the Gap," by J. W. Wood and J. W. Miederhoff, 1989, *Teaching Exceptional Children, 21*(2), 67–68. Copyright 1989 by The Council for Exceptional Children. Reprinted with permission.

## INTERPERSONAL/SOCIAL RELATIONS

Student: _____

Teacher: _____ Subject: _____

Grade or Type of Class: _____ Date: _____ Teacher Completing Observation: _____

Directions: Mainstream teacher or appropriate personnel: Check the items in the Characteristics column that describe the mainstream setting. To evaluate the student, check the appropriate items in the Student's Present Performance level column.

| CHARACTERISTICS OF MAINSTREAM SETTING | Check if It Applies | STUDENT'S PRESENT PERFORMANCE LEVEL | Has Mastered Skills | Is Working On Skills | Is Unable to Perform Skills |
|---|---|---|---|---|---|
| II. INTERPERSONAL/ SOCIAL RELATIONS<br>  A. Student Interaction<br><br>    1. Individual<br>    2. Cooperative<br>    3. Competitive<br>  B. Regular students have positive attitude toward handicapped<br><br>  C. Dress/Appearance<br>    1. Dress code applied<br>    2. Concern given to appearance by most students | | Can interact appropriately in the following ways:<br>    Individual<br>    Cooperative<br>    Competitive<br>Has positive attitude toward self<br>Has positive attitude toward regular students<br><br>Dresses appropriately<br>Follows dress code<br>Presents neat appearance | | | |

## RELATED ENVIRONMENTS

Student: _____

Teacher: _____ Subject: _____

Grade or Type of Class: _____ Date: _____ Teacher Completing Observation: _____

Directions: Mainstream teacher or appropriate personnel: Check the items in the Characteristics column that describe the mainstream setting. To evaluate the student, check the appropriate items in the Student's Present Performance level column.

| CHARACTERISTICS OF MAINSTREAM SETTING | Check if It Applies | STUDENT'S PRESENT PERFORMANCE LEVEL | Has Mastered Skills | Is Working On Skills | Is Unable to Perform Skills |
|---|---|---|---|---|---|
| III. RELATED ENVIRONMENTS<br>  A. Cafeteria<br>    1. Procedures for purchasing lunch ticket/token posted or explained<br>    2. Lunchroom routine explained/posted<br><br><br>  B. Physical Education<br>    1. Uniform required<br><br>    2. Showering required<br>  C. Music/Art<br>    1. Students move to class independently<br>    2. Rules of classroom explained/ posted<br>    3. Grading system used<br>      a. Letter grade<br>      b. Pass/fail<br>      c. Other_____ | | Follows correct procedure for purchasing lunch ticket/token<br><br>Follows lunch routine:<br>    Purchases lunch<br>    Finds assigned table<br>    Returns tray<br><br>Purchases appropriate uniform<br>Brings clean uniform once/week<br>Changes uniform under time pressure<br>Showers independently<br>Moves to nonacademic classes independently<br>Follows orally presented rules<br>Follows written rules<br>Works best under following system:<br>    Letter grade<br>    Pass/fail<br>Adapts to various grading systems | | | |

**Figure 8.4.** Continued.

information about child and environmental factors. If descriptive information has been obtained at the problem identification stage through observation and/or interview, it may be necessary to measure specific behaviors before an intervention plan can be developed.

In developing an intervention plan, it is important for consultants to recognize their own perspectives regarding instruction and learning. The fundamental assumptions consultants hold regarding knowledge will influence how that knowledge is assessed. This issue has been discussed over the last decade (cf. Fuchs & Deno, 1991; Heshusius, 1986, 1991; Kimball & Heron, 1988) and is also reflected in the increasing "effort to break free of the artificial knowledge evaluated in many standardized tests" (Wolf, Bixby, Glenn, & Gardner, 1991, p. 55).

As Heshusius (1991) discusses, educators hold different assumptions regarding the teaching and learning process, and those assumptions may not be compatible. Many of the assumptions held by the proponents of holistic education are reflected in *performance assessment*. In performance assessment, students are asked to demonstrate basic skills in genuine rather than artificial ways and in integrated rather than isolated tasks. For example, students may be presented with the task of designing a playground of the future. To accomplish this task, they are given the area and the total budget. As students work through this type of assessment, they produce a portfolio that reveals their skills in numbers, measurement, geometry, patterns and relations, data analysis and probability, and analytical reasoning.

Many of the assumptions held by proponents of direct instruction are reflected in curriculum-based assessment. According to Taylor (2000), curriculum-based assessment "involves the measurement of the level of a student in terms of the *expected curricula outcomes of the school*" (p. 114, italics in original).

The next section will describe and provide examples of three assessment procedures: curriculum-based assessment, sociometric assessment, and functional assessment. Included within the discussion of functional assessment will be a thorough presentation of functional analysis, the experimental component of functional assessment.

## Curriculum-Based Assessment

*Curriculum-based assessment* (CBA) uses the student's performance on daily, weekly, or mastery test items as the basis for making instructional decisions. Typically, teachers using CBA measure student performance with 1-minute probes, short quizzes, or daily proficiency tests to determine performance relative to curriculum goal achievement.

### Purpose

The major purpose of curriculum-based assessment is to obtain a quick, reliable, and useful measure of student mastery of the content to be learned (McLoughlin & Lewis, 1991). As an informal strategy, the teacher can integrate CBA-obtained data with information gathered from other sources to determine an appropriate course of remediation. Likewise, teachers can use these data to launch extension or enrichment exercises for students who have mastered the basic content.

## Procedure

A curriculum-based measure can be achieved easily when the teacher gives an instruction to the students to complete an assignment that is directly related to the content to be learned. Anecdote 8.1 illustrates how a teacher directed a class of students to write a short passage using their weekly spelling words. The purpose of this assignment was to assess the ability of the students to integrate spelling with written language production.

**Anecdote 8.1**

| | |
|---|---|
| TEACHER: | After clearing your desk, please take out a sheet of paper and a pencil. |
| CLASS MEMBER: | Are we going to do math problems? |
| TEACHER: | I would like you to write a passage that describes your feelings about going on our class field trip to the aquarium. Instead of just using any words, however, I want you to include at least 15 of your 20 weekly spelling words in the selection. You can use more than one spelling word in a sentence if you like. |

After collecting the written language passages, the teacher counts the number of spelling words each student used in his or her passage. These data serve as a curriculum-based measure of student spelling accuracy as well as their correct usage of words. These data could be averaged, and an individual student's performance could be compared with the class performance. More importantly, given this repeated exercise, the teacher could compare an individual student's performance with his or her past performances.

## Example of Curriculum-Based Assessment

Lindsley (1990) provides a convincing example of how curriculum-based assessment occurs, and how teachers can use direct measures to improve student performance. Figure 8.5 shows the basic math fact performance of a second-grade student over a fall semester. Data were generated during one-minute time probes. Dots show correct responses; x's indicate errors. Slope is shown by examining the trend line through data points. Note that Hollie's performance changed across the five phases of the study. Her performance on +5 and +6 facts improved considerably when the order of these problems was changed.

Two examples of assessment activities conducted for reading can be found in Tables 8.6 and 8.7. These two samples demonstrate possible differences when gathering information from different perspectives. An important component of developing an effective intervention plan is to determine the assumptions of instruction and learning that are held by the participants and to use assessment procedures that are appropriate for those assumptions.

In addition to information about the student, data about the environment also need to be gathered. The Instructional Environment Scale (TIES) developed by Ysseldyke and Christenson (1987) provides a framework for assessing variables in the instructional environment of a student. The major purposes for using TIES are: "(a) to systematically *describe* the extent to which a student's academic or behavior problems are a function of factors in the

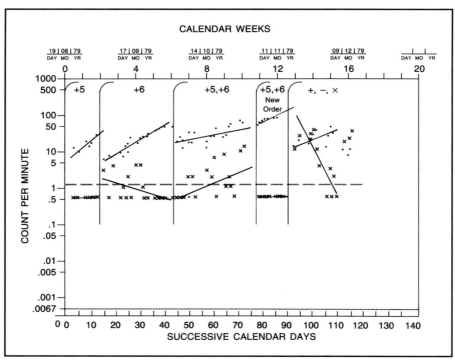

**Figure 8.5.** Hollie's mathematics chart. From "Precision Teaching: By Teachers for Children," by O. R. Lindsley, 1990, *Teaching Exceptional Children, 22*(3), 15. Copyright 1990 by The Council for Exceptional Children. Reprinted with permission.

instructional environment and (b) to identify starting points in designing appropriate interventions for individual students" (Ysseldyke & Christenson, 1987, p. 3, emphasis in original). The TIES uses a structured teacher interview, a structured student interview, and guidelines for classroom observation that are derived from the following components of effective instruction: instructional presentation, classroom environment, teacher expectations, cognitive emphasis, motivational strategies, relevant practice, academic engaged time, informed feedback, adaptive instruction, progress evaluation, instructional planning, and student understanding. A description of each of these components of effective instruction is provided in the TIES to assist in completing the interviews and observations (see Table 8.8 for a sample of a TIES data record).

According to Polsgrove and McNeil (1989), when devising an acceptable intervention plan, in addition to obtaining information about the variables that must be altered, one should also obtain information about what needs to be done to establish cooperative working relationships, including the identification and resolution of any resistance. It is essential that the psychological climate for the intervention be positive; otherwise, the plan has little chance for success.

Sources of possible resistance include adults and students. As indicated by Jenkins and Heinen (1989), it is important to consider students' perspectives when deciding upon placement options, especially placement in mainstream settings. There are various ways to obtain information about adult and student attitudes. One can use the observation and interview techniques previously discussed; another procedure is sociometric assessment.

## Table 8.6
### A Sample Holistic Approach to Assessment in Reading

*Sample Goal*

Assessment of constructing meaning from text

*Sample Activities*

- Predict what they expect to find in a text, given a short preview (the theme, the title, or a few pictures).
- Students write down ideas that occur to them.
- Students rate the likelihood (yes, maybe, or no) that a stated idea might be included in such a selection.
- Given a multiple-choice semantic map, they rate the relatedness of a set of concepts (closely related, somewhat related, and not at all related) to the topic of the passage.
- At predetermined points, students are asked to revise their predictions based upon the information they have acquired so far.
- Culminating activity is discussion about how and why their ideas changed along the way.

*Measurement*

What can the students do without help, and what can they do with help (i.e., dynamic assessment)? Analyze student responses; watch their behaviors as they try to find the answer to a question; observe them engaged in dialogue with peers as they try to determine the author's point of view; observe strategies used as teacher intervenes with social support, modeling, and/or cognitive scaffolding.

*Note.* From "Principles for Classroom Comprehension Assessment," by S. W. Valencia and P. D. Pearson, 1988, *Remedial and Special Education, 9*(1), 26–35. Copyright 1998 by PRO-ED, Inc. Reprinted with permission.

## Table 8.7
### A Sample Curriculum-Based Assessment in Reading

*Sample Goal*

Given a passage from Level 9, Ginn 720, student will read 70 words per minute correctly with no more than 8 errors.

*Related Test Item Pool*

200-word passages from Level 9, Ginn 720, without poetry, exercises, and/or excessive dialogues.

*Measurement Procedure*

Randomly select a passage from the goal-level material; place it in front of and facing the pupil; keep another copy in front of the examiner; provide directions; have the student read orally for 1 minute; score performance in terms of numbers of words correct and errors.

*Note.* From "Program Development," by L. S. Fuchs, 1987, *Teaching Exceptional Children, 20*(1), 42. Copyright 1987 by The Council for Exceptional Children. Reprinted with permission.

## Table 8.8

Data Collected with The Instructional Environment Scale (TIES)

*Teacher Interview—Sample Questions*

1. To what extent was (student's name) performance on (day) typical?
2. What are your expectations for (student's name)?
3. How do you plan instruction for (student's name)?

*Observation—Sample Areas*

1. Instructional Presentation
   lesson development
   clarity of directions
   checking for student understanding
2. Classroom Environment
   management
   time-use
   climate
3. Relevant Practice
   opportunity
   task relevance
   materials

*Student Interview—Sample Questions*

1. I want you to tell me what you needed to do on these assignments.
   a. What did your teacher want you to learn?
   b. What did your teacher tell you about why these assignments are important?
   c. What did you have to do?
   d. Show me how you did the work.
2. I am going to ask you several questions. In each case, I want you to tell me your answer by using this scale, where 1 means "not very much" and 4 means "very much."
   a. Sometimes students understand their assignments. Sometimes they don't. Show me how well you understand the assignment.
   b. How much did you believe you could do the assignment?
   c. How interesting is this work for you?
3. What did your teacher tell you about:
   a. Completing your work?
   b. Getting the answers correct?
   c. Having neat papers?

*Note.* From *TIES: The Instructional Environment Scale,* "Data Record Form," by J. E. Ysseldyke and S. L. Christenson, 1987, Austin, TX: PRO-ED. Copyright 1987 by PRO-ED, Inc. Reprinted with permission.

## Sociometric Assessment

*Sociometric assessment* provides data about the attitudes of group members toward one another and is often used for finding out how well special students are accepted by peers (Asher & Taylor, 1981). Students may be asked to rate their classmates, choose between pairs of students, or nominate a peer. In the peer-nominating technique, each child's social position in the class is determined by analyzing his or her responses to specific questions. For example, each student might be asked to name someone with whom he or she would like to play. It is assumed that the student who is named most frequently enjoys the highest status in the class.

Sociometric measurements can provide information useful for understanding classroom dynamics or interactions because it focuses on student-student interaction in the classroom. However, collecting sociometric data is not without its challenges and shortcomings. Practitioners should be sensitive to the type of questions asked as well as the format of the questions. For example, it would be inappropriate to ask a student to respond to the question "Who would you least like to play with?"

## Procedure

In a sociometric assessment, each student may be asked to choose two or three children in the class with whom he or she would most like to play or most like to work on a project. The students' responses are confidential. Students are not asked to make their nominations aloud but usually write the names of their choices on pieces of paper. An alternative is to assign a number to each child. Then each student, in response to a question, writes on paper the number of the selected child. It is also possible to provide a multiple-choice situation. That is, for each question, the students may have the names or numbers of the other students before them, and then indicate their selections by circling or underlining the appropriate name or number. Whatever the method, it should take into account each student's response capability.

Once the peer nominations have been made, they are plotted on a *sociogram*. A sociogram is a schematic representation of all student responses. Figure 8.6 shows a schematic representation of the responses by a third-grade class to the question "Who would you most like to sit next to?" This sociogram shows us that Yolanda was not picked by any student, nor did she select any student to sit near. Irene chose two students, Sean and Lynn, but was not chosen herself. Also, one may suspect that Kathleen and Christine, Blaine and Marge, and Lee and Lynn are close friends, since they chose each other.

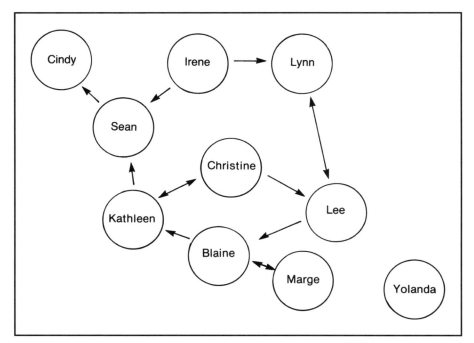

**Figure 8.6.** Example of a sociogram.

After the sociogram is analyzed, the consultant might help the teacher plan a program to change for the better the social relationships of the students in the classroom.

### Example of Sociometric Assessment

It is apparent from Figure 8.6 that Yolanda is isolated in this class. If Yolanda also exhibits withdrawn behavior (e.g., she does not participate in class discussions, raise her hand, or talk with her teacher or classmates outside the classroom), the results of this sociometric analysis might confirm why and help the consultant understand how Yolanda's peers feel about her and she about them. Steps could then be taken to engineer positive social interactions between Yolanda and one or two selected classmates. A subsequent sociometric analysis could measure any change that might result in the social status of Yolanda with respect to her peers. In this way, some estimate as to the success of the intervention plan for Yolanda and her classmates could be made.

# Functional Assessment

Of all the behavior change methods published within the past 20 years, functional assessment ranks as one of the more significant advancements (Neef, 1994; Wacker, Berg, Cooper, Derby, Steege, Northup, & Sasso, 1994). It is precisely because functional assessment permits an examination of contextual variables that affect behavior that it has become so popular in the field. In large measure, the shift from examining the topographical features of behavior (i.e., its form with respect to frequency, intensity, and duration) to assessing its function has spurred research and pragmatic interest in this important assessment area.

See Chapter 2 for a discussion of the procedures employed to make this determination.

Further, with the passage of IDEA '97, the imperative to be skilled with functional assessment is even more evident. Final rules and regulations published in IDEA '97 now mandate that functional assessment be employed, especially in situations where practitioners must wrestle with the thorny issue of whether a student's behavior is a "manifestation" of a disability or not.

Hence, from a practitioner-interventionist perspective, and certainly from a mandated federal perspective, consultants who are well versed in how and under what conditions to conduct functional assessments will provide a great benefit to those they serve.

## Definition of Functional Assessment

*Functional assessment* is designed to determine the contextual variables that occasion, reinforce, or maintain behaviors, thereby enabling the practitioner to select appropriate interventions (Conroy, Fox, Crain, Jenkins, & Blecher, 1996; Gast & Wolery, 1987). Functional assessment assumes that environmental variables affect behavior, that events can be determined through the assessment process, and that by later arranging alternative responses, the challenging behavior that may have prompted the assessment can be reduced or minimized (Iwata, Dorsey, Slifer, Bauman, & Richman, 1994).

Reed, Thomas, Sprague, and Horner (1997) indicate that functional assessment includes the following steps:

1. defining the target behavior (e.g., reducing aggressive behavior);

2. identifying the antecedent stimulus to the target behavior (e.g., math worksheet, demand situation), setting event (e.g., male teacher), or establishing operation (e.g., undetected or diagnosed medical condition);

3. determining the consequences that maintain the behavior (e.g., attention or escape);

4. generating hypotheses to test variables that seem to control the behavior (e.g., Mark's aggression seems to occur in the presence of math assignments issued by male teachers and is maintained by negative reinforcement [escape]); and

5. collecting relevant data (e.g., interview responses, scatter plots, permanent product measures).

Operationally, functional assessment can be viewed as occurring along a continuum that extends from an indirect assessment to a descriptive level to ultimately an experimental level (Flannery, O'Neill, & Horner, 1995; Sasso et al., 1992; Symons, McDonald, & Wehby, 1998). Figure 8.7 shows a schematic of this continuum and depicts the indirect and descriptive methods (left and center positions) as having less ability to determine controlling variables because the data are correlational in nature. The right side of the continuum, technically referred to as the functional analysis method, provides more experimental control because variables are tested empirically to determine their effects. The distinguishing feature between indirect or descriptive methods and functional analysis methods relates to the degree of control over the determinant variables. In any case, functional assessment is based on "conditional probability." According to Gable, Hendrickson, and Sasso (1995), conditional probability is "our ability to predict one event from knowledge of another event or variable" (p. 227).

> Functional analysis is the experimental component of functional assessment.

Clearly, the emergence of all functional assessment approaches—indirect methods, descriptive methods, functional analysis—is linked to the movement

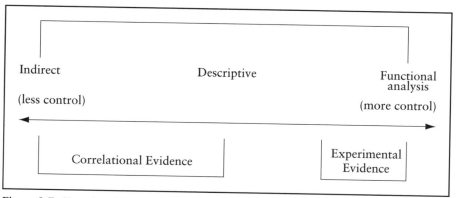

**Figure 8.7.** Functional assessment continuum showing indirect and descriptive methods as being primarily correlational in nature (left and center positions), with functional analysis being primarily experimental in nature (right position).

within special education and applied behavior analysis to examine behavior based on its function, not just its topography. Flannery et al. (1995) make this point succinctly:

> Interventions are now developed based upon the function of the behavior (e.g., to get someone's attention, to get out of activity demands) rather than its topography (e.g., biting, head banging, throwing items . . .). Functional assessment and analysis information should guide us in developing support plans that include: (a) changes in setting or antecedent variables; (b) teaching of new skills that are alternatives to the problem behaviors (e.g., communication behaviors); and (c) arranging positive outcomes for appropriate behaviors and minimizing or removing positive outcomes for problem behaviors. (p. 500)

## Functional Assessment Methods

Three broad functional assessment methods have been identified in the literature: indirect methods, descriptive methods, and functional analysis (Steege & Northup, 1998). Each of these methods has general characteristics, procedural variations, strengths, limitations, and recommended procedures for implementation.

### Indirect Method

See Chapter 12 for more discussion of the advantages and disadvantages of checklists and rating scales.

The *indirect method* of functional assessment is characterized as being informal, subjective, and based primarily on the verbal or anecdotal reports of others (e.g., teachers, parents, other students). Typically, when the indirect method is employed, either a checklist, rating scale, or interview is used to determine possible variables in the environment that seemingly occasion, reinforce, or maintain the behavior of interest. Although an indirect method is relatively easy to conduct in applied settings, the student is not involved directly. Hence, the information that a consultant might gather is filtered through the perspective of other agents (teachers, parents, other students). As a general guide, however, indirect methods may provide *de minimus* levels of information that could be helpful with identifying variables that themselves could be the subject of more experimental analysis.

For a discussion of student-guided functional assessment interview procedures, see Reed, Thomas, Sprague, & Horner (1997).

Lawry, Storey, and Danko (1993) provide a list of recommended questions that consultants might use when conducting a functional assessment interview (see Table 8.9). These questions attempt to probe the conditions under which behaviors occur, the controlling variables across the three-term contingency, and other possible factors associated with the behavior (e.g., alternative behaviors that could be substituted during a subsequent intervention). Flannery et al. (1995) suggest a similar type and level of questions; however, they recommend a categorical approach that examines the student's behavior across the possible changing dimensions of (a) sequence or order (does the inappropriate behavior occur when a change in routine or classroom structure takes place?); (b) content or material (has the level of math changed? is the vocabulary now more difficult?); (c) novelty (has a new student or teacher entered the class?); and (d) time (has a once short, daily assignment now become a longer one?).

---

## Table 8.9
### Selected Interview Questions

- Describe the behaviors of concern.
- Describe the extent to which you believe activities that occur during the day are *predictable* for the person. To what extent does the person know the activities that will be happening, when they will occur, and the consequences?
- About how often does the person get to make choices about activities, reinforcers, and so forth?
- *When* are the behaviors most likely? Least likely?
- *Where* are the behaviors most likely? Least likely?
- *With whom* are the behaviors most likely? Least likely?
- *What activity* is most likely to produce the behavior? Least likely?
- Identify the "function" of the undesirable behavior(s). What consequences maintain the behavior(s)?
- What events, actions, and objects are perceived as positive by the person?
- What "functional alternative" behaviors are known by the person?

*Note.* Adapted from O'Neill et al. (1990), cited in "Analyzing Problem Behaviors in the Classroom: A Case Study of Functional Analysis," by J. R. Lawry, K. Storey, and C. D. Danko, 1993, *Intervention in School and Clinic, 29*(2), 97. Reprinted with permission.

### Descriptive Method

The *descriptive method* of functional assessment is characterized as being a direct and observational system that relies primarily on observation within the natural setting under conditions in which the relevant contextual variables of interest are present. When the descriptive method is employed, quantifiable data in the form of frequency counts, time samples, or duration measures are obtained to determine relationships between variables. While the descriptive method allows for observation and yields quantifiable data, it is limited, insofar as the behavior of interest may not occur during the observation cycle, or the teacher (or parent) may inadvertently change the environment during the observation in such a way as to mask accurate measurement. While descriptive methods provide quantifiable measurement, these data may still be only correlational in nature. Correlational data cannot be used to make cause-effect determinations. Common descriptive methods include time sampling, ABC (antecedent-behavior-consequence) analysis, and scatter plot.

Symons et al. (1998) provide an example of scatter plot analysis data that were collected by a special education teacher in her classroom using a hand-held counter (see Figure 8.8). Aggregate data were tallied at the end of the interval and marked with a symbol representing the rate of a student's (Ryan's) shouting and talking out of turn. Note that in this scatter plot analysis baseline data were collected for 5 weeks and intervention data for approximately 4 weeks. Each day was divided into 30-minute intervals, beginning at 8:30 A.M. Patterns of occurrence become clearly visible by examining the scatter of symbols across time and day. In Ryan's case, most of the behaviors occurred during the 8:30 A.M. to 11:30 A.M. time slot (weeks 1 through 3) and continued during the 8:30 A.M. to 9:00 A.M. slot for all 5 weeks of baseline.

Next, the teacher, in consultation with team members, conducted an analysis of the data by further searching for corroborative factors that could account for his behavior. They asked questions such as: Under what circumstances did the

See Chapter 12 for more discussion of the types of measurement systems that can be used during descriptive functional assessment.

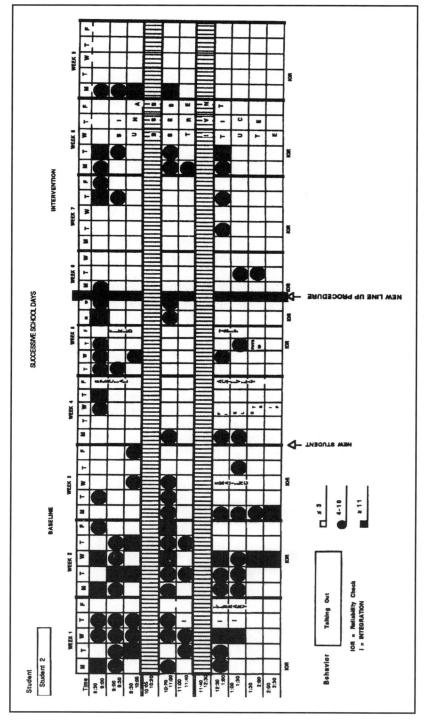

Figure 8.8. Ryan's scatter plot with talk-outs plotted across time. Open squares represent a rate of fewer than 3. Shaded circles indicate occurrences ranging from 4 to 10 per interval. Filled squares reflect 11 or more occurrences of talking out during that interval. From "Functional Assessment and Teacher Collected Data," by F. J. Symons, L. M. McDonald, and J. H. Wehby, 1998, *Education and Treatment of Children*, 21(2), 145. Reprinted with permission.

behavior occur? What was the nature of the activity at the time of onset? Subsequently, a hypothesis was generated and tested by rearranging one element within the day (e.g., the nature of the activity). In Ryan's situation, it was hypothesized that the "morning routine" of lining up was occasioning his shouting behavior. So, during the intervention, a different line-up procedure was employed that provided separation between students as they entered the classroom, included more individual teacher-student interaction time, and prompted more effective teacher direction on the upcoming morning assignments. During intervention, scatter plot data show fewer shouting episodes (i.e., fewer closed squares and circles are marked on the scatter plot). This design, although "pre-experimental" (baseline-treatment), did permit the teacher to identify a factor that was apparently correlated with Ryan's behavior and take effective steps to reduce it.

## Functional Analysis Method

*Functional analysis* is defined as the experimental component of functional assessment. Kahng and Iwata (1998) provide a technical definition that should serve consultants well as they pursue experimental manipulations to determine the effects of controlling variables:

> In the typical functional analysis, behavior is observed under several test conditions (in which the variable of interest is present) and is compared with that observed under a control condition (in which the variable is absent). . . . A common control condition found in many studies has been described as the "play" or "leisure" condition and is characterized by the absence of demands, the continuous availability of leisure activities, and the frequent delivery of attention on a noncontingent (response independent) basis. (p. 669)

Functional analysis is characterized as also being direct and observational, but a distinguishing feature of functional analysis is that comparisons can be made between experimental and control conditions. Because direct, systematic, and replicable comparisons are made within the natural or analog setting under conditions in which relevant contextual variables of interest are both present and absent, empirical control is established. When the functional analysis method is employed, multiple probes across attention (praise), demand (escape), alone, and play (control) contingencies are typically obtained, and those data are plotted on a reversal, multi-element, or combined design that shows the pattern or trend of the data under each condition. Hence, across and within condition performance can be ascertained. While the functional analysis method allows for empirical analysis of quantifiable data, it is time consuming and usually requires tight control of environmental variables. Still, the effort may be worth the price—a cost-benefit decision—insofar as more conclusive statements can be made at the level of proof with respect to variables controlling the behavior. Two procedural variations of functional analysis have been described in the literature: full, and brief and analog.

See Chapter 12 and Cooper et al. (1987), for more discussion of the types of designs and data interpretation procedures.

For a discussion of how parents can implement functional analysis or how this approach can be applied in a clinical setting, see Cooper, Wacker, Sasso, Reimers, and Donn, 1990.

*Full Functional Analysis.* A distinguishing feature of full functional analysis is that repeated measures are taken across multiple conditions to ascertain the contributing effects of suspected variables. Iwata, Dorsey, Slifer, Bauman, and Richman (1994) provide an excellent illustration of how a full functional analysis could be conducted using any of three types of designs: multi-element, reversal, or pairwise test-control (see Figure 8.9).

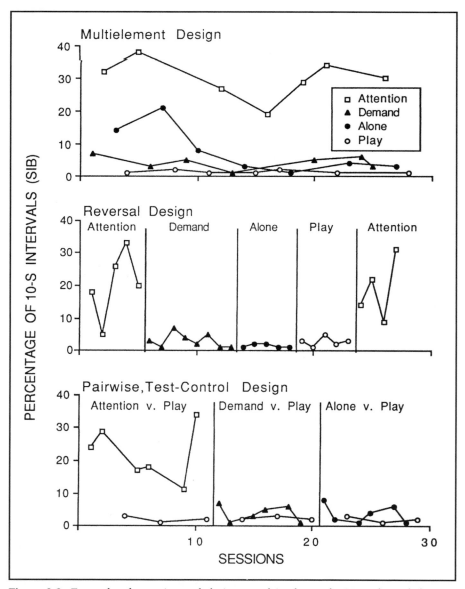

**Figure 8.9.** Example of experimental designs used in the study. Hypothetical data represent an individual whose SIB is maintained by contingent attention (social-positive reinforcement). From "The Functions of Self-Injurious Behavior: An Experimental-Epidemiological Analysis," by B. A. Iwata et al., 1994, *Journal of Applied Behavior Analysis, 27*(2), 223. Copyright 1994 by *Journal of Applied Behavior Analysis.* Reprinted with permission.

Note that in the upper tier (multi-element design) repeated measures taken across alternate and random sessions show data fractionation in favor of the attention condition as producing more self-injurious behavior (SIB). Likewise, the data paths for the other variables (demand, alone, and play) show little if any difference. Hence, knowing that SIB might be maintained by attention—and discounting demand, alone, and play factors—an intervention could be designed to counter attention as a consequence following SIB episodes. Extinction, differential reinforcement of other behavior (DRO), differential reinforcement of alternative behaviors (DRA), or differential reinforcement of incompatible behaviors (DRI) could be initiated to determine relative effects. The middle and lower tiers show hypothetical data being plotted on reversal and pairwise designs to further illustrate that SIB could be plotted in alternative ways. Still, the interpretation—and ultimate course of intervention—would be the same.

Nevertheless, interpretation of functional analyses should proceed cautiously, and consultants would be well advised to heed disclaimers voiced by Hagopian, Fisher, Thompson, Owens-DeSchryver, Iwata, and Wacker (1997) and Kahng and Iwata (1998) when it comes to analyzing these data. For instance, Kahng and Iwata report data on the percentage of intervals of self-injurious behavior (SIB) for a participant in a study (see Figure 8.10).

Note that under the alone condition, the percentage of SIB was low, while under the play and demand conditions, SIB was differentiated; but this clearer picture of the data fractionation occurs only after session 12. The data for the demand condition rise noticeably while the data path for the play condition continues a strong downward trend. Here's the point: Had this experiment been terminated on session 12, having accrued approximately 4 data points per the demand and play conditions respectively, clear differences between demand and play would not likely have been identified and the course of treatment could have been affected adversely (Kahng & Iwata, 1998). Specifically, the consultant may have concluded (mistakenly) that there was no difference between play and demand when there actually was a difference. To avoid misinterpretations, functional analysis data should be analyzed following generally accepted guidelines for decision making.

*See Cooper et al. (1987); Kahng and Iwata (1998); and Hagopian et al. (1997), for data interpretation rules and guidelines.*

***Brief and Analog.*** *Brief functional analysis* refers to how long an assessment is scheduled, whereas an *analog assessment* represents the conditions under which the assessment is conducted (natural setting versus clinical setting versus simulated conditions).

*For a discussion of how brief functional analysis can be used to select reading interventions, see Daly, Martens, Dool, and Hintze (1998).*

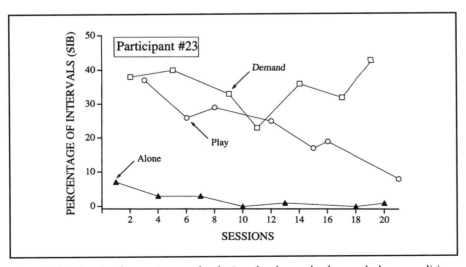

Figure 8.10. Session-by-session results during the demand, play, and alone conditions for Participant 23. From "Play Versus Alone Conditions as Controls During Functional Analyses of Self-Injurious Escape Behavior," by S. W. Kahng and B. A. Iwata, 1998, *Journal of Applied Behavior Analysis, 31*(4), 671. Copyright 1998 by *Journal of Applied Behavior Analysis*. Reprinted with permission.

According to Conroy et al. (1996):

> Analog assessment consists of experimental probe sessions designed to systematically present different classes of antecedents and/or consequences which are suspected of maintaining challenging behavior. These probes are conducted under highly controlled and counterbalanced presentations of different events and are typically done outside of the person's natural environment. A comparison is then made of the relative rates of challenging behavior under these different analog probe conditions. (p. 234)

An analog assessment can be a time-efficient method for obtaining relevant functional analysis data, especially under time-limited conditions or clinical circumstances. Essentially, during the analog procedure, multiple probes are taken across the same conditions as might be used during a full functional analysis: attention, demand, alone, and play. However, the time frame is greatly reduced, usually with 90 to 120 minutes being the norm. We'll now turn to discussing the major variables used to conduct a functional analysis: attention, demand, alone, and play.

*Attention.* During a contrived attention condition, the consultant and the student occupy a room and the student is told to engage in an activity (nondemand) for a period of time. Occurrences of the target behavior produce attention of some sort (physical proximity, verbal comments, or social disapproval statements). Other behaviors are ignored.

*Demand.* The demand condition is the escape condition. Here, the student is provided with challenging, but doable, tasks and is directed by the teacher or consultant to complete the tasks. If the student fails to comply, a series of verbal, modeling, and physical prompts are provided to cue the response. If the inappropriate behavior occurs, the teacher or consultant stops the task and walks away (terminating the session briefly). When the inappropriate behavior ceases, the teacher or consultant reengages the student.

*Alone.* In the alone condition, the student is left by him- or herself; no other people are present in the room. As Gable, Hendrickson, and Sasso (1995) state, "If the frequency of the target behavior is high in this condition, sensory reinforcement is inferred" (p. 234).

*Play.* The play condition represents the control condition. That is, the teacher or consultant is present in the room, and the student is encouraged to play with available toys, games, or objects. The teacher provides noncontingent reinforcement, meaning she or he emits praise statements on a specific schedule (e.g., every minute).

Figure 8.11 shows the results of Gable et al.'s (1995) analog assessment of a student's aggressive behavior. Data were collected within a 10-minute period for each condition. Results, interpreted by visual inspection of the data, indicate that the escape condition (demand) produced the highest percentage of aggressive activity. With these data, an appropriate treatment can be devised that would counteract escape behavior during demand situations.

Likewise, Tincani, Castrogiavanni, and Axelrod (1999) show that the results of brief and extended functional analyses produce similar interpretations (see Figure 8.12). That is, "the same maintaining contingencies for each response class of maladaptive behavior" (p. 335) were revealed. In this case, the percentage of 10-second intervals of aggression were clearly apparent under tangible reinforcement contingencies for both the brief and extended

---

*Clinicians and/or consultants who work in hospital- or clinic-based treatment centers can read Harding, Wacker, Cooper, Milliard, and Jensen-Kovalan (1994) and Cooper et al. (1990) to learn how to set up brief, analog functional analyses in hospitals, which may include parents as the therapists.*

*An ignore condition is a variation of the alone condition insofar as the consultant remains in the room but does not attend to the target behavior whatsoever.*

*See Cooper et al. (1987) for a discussion of how to conduct a visual analysis of the data.*

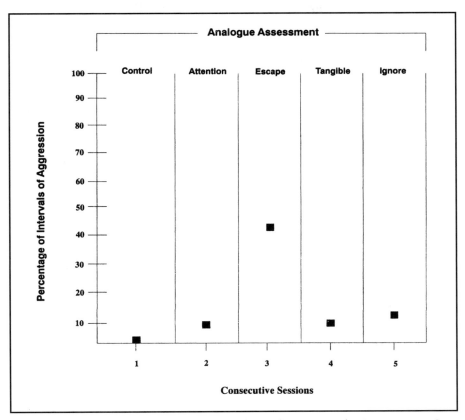

**Figure 8.11.** Standard clinical functional analysis of aggression for Susan across Control, Attention, Escape, Tangible, and Ignore Conditions. From "Toward a More Functional Analysis of Aggression," by R. A. Gable, J. M. Hendrickson, and G. M. Sasso, 1995, *Education and Treatment of Children, 18*(3), 235. Copyright 1995 by *Educational and Treatment of Children*. Reprinted with permission.

functional and analyses. Tincani et al. remind practitioners of two important points. First, whereas brief functional analysis may determine controlling variables as effectively as extended analysis, preexisting establishing operations should also be examined in different settings or across various time periods so as to render brief and/or extended analyses the more desirable option. Stated differently, a brief functional analysis may be more susceptible to establishing operations confounds because the practitioner has only the one data point with which to interpret results. Performing the brief functional assessment in more than one setting or across different time periods may help to control for possible establishing operation interplay. Alternatively, where establishing operation confounds are known to exist—and the likelihood of being able to control them is minimal—an extended functional assessment may be warranted. Second, interventions focused on teaching alternative responses should not be ignored.

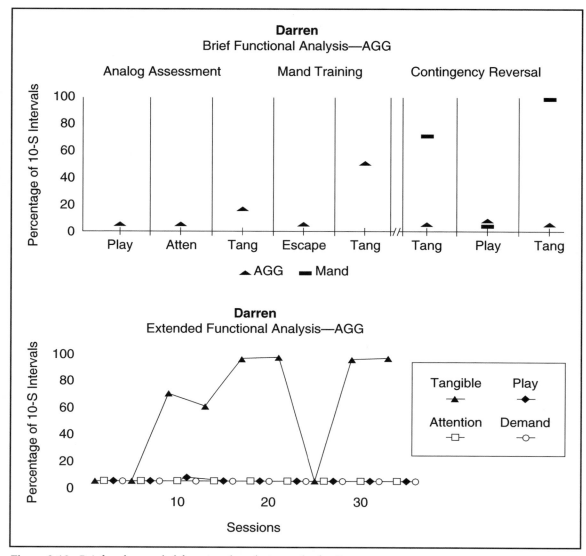

**Figure 8.12.** Brief and extended functional analysis results for Darren.

## Deciding on Functional Assessment and Analysis Methods

It is clear that exigent circumstances are likely to arise within a school district that would prompt consideration of one form or another of functional assessment. For instance, it is within the realm of possibility that an identified special education student will violate one of the school's policies. If the student acts aggressively toward a classmate, for example, and injures that student, the school cannot unilaterally expel the student. First, district personnel must make a determination as to whether the aggressive act was related to the disability. If the student does not have an existing behavior intervention plan (BIP), and if the student has never received a functional assessment, one must be conducted within 10 days of the aggressive episode. With this short time line to complete a useful functional assessment, consultants would be wise to have a decision plan in hand for complying with this IDEA '97 requirement.

Figure 8.13 shows a decision model that consultants might employ to address this important and time-limited question.

Essentially, the model begins at the point when a behavioral episode or problem is noted and the consultant or the multifactored evaluation team must conduct a functional assessment. The consultant would initially conduct either an indirect or a descriptive analysis with the intent of determining relevant controlling variables, and then appropriate hypotheses would be generated regarding the role of those variables. For example, if the target student's aggressive behavior is attention driven, the BIP would be rewritten to withhold attention for aggressive behavior (extinction) while simultaneously adding a DRO and/or a DRA procedure.

However, if the indirect or descriptive analysis fails to identify and ultimately fix the situation, then a "brief" analog or clinical assessment might be conducted, holding as many relevant variables constant as possible to determine the controlling variables. If this method fails to resolve the problem, a full-scale functional analysis would be required to determine the contributing factors experimentally.

How confident could a teacher or consultant be that a brief or analog assessment would yield data representing the actual level of the behavior as a full functional analysis would? Kahng and Iwata (1999) report that "brief and within session analyses correspond with those of the full functional analyses in 66% and 68% of the cases, respectively" (p. 149). They go on to state:

> Although the hit rate (proportion of true positives and true negatives) obtained with the brief analysis was not exceedingly high, it was sufficient to provide justification for its use when time constraints are paramount, especially when the alternative consists of verbal reports measures whose reliability has been shown to be generally poor. (p. 158)

Also, Sasso et al. (1992) demonstrated that out-of-class analyses conducted by an experimenter were as useful with respect to identifying controlling variables of aggression as in-class analyses conducted by the teacher. In short, functional analysis can be conducted with confidence across settings, situations, and teachers and consultants; and interventions based on those analyses can produce desired outcomes.

Finally, Watson and Sterling (1998) demonstrated that a brief functional analysis based on a prior descriptive assessment was effective in reducing the attention-getting coughing habit of a 4-year-old child with a history of repeated, nonmedically based coughing.

## Monitoring Implementation and Student Progress

When *monitoring plan implementation,* the consultant's chief goal is to determine whether (a) the jointly developed program is being implemented the way it was designed, and (b) the program is producing the intended effect. One effective technique for monitoring plan implementation is to check whether the plan is being implemented as designed. Usually 1–2 days after intervention begins is

---

*Margin notes:*

This model could be employed preemptively during the multifactored evaluation (MFE) so as to further refine the behavior implementation plan for the student before an episode transpires.

See Frea and Hughes (1997) for suggestions on how alternative responses (DRA) can be used to address social communication behaviors of adolescents with developmental disabilities.

For a discussion of evaluating analog assessments, see Conroy et al. (1996).

When a behavior (e.g., aggression) may have a medical origin (e.g., otitis media), functional analysis may reveal the cyclic nature of the behavior, meaning that the medical problem may act as an establishing operation or a biological setting event (O'Reilly, 1997) for the aggression. When the medical problem is present, higher levels of aggression are noted; when it is absent, levels are lower.

Consultants desiring to learn more about conducting interobserver agreement checks are referred to Cooper et al. (1987).

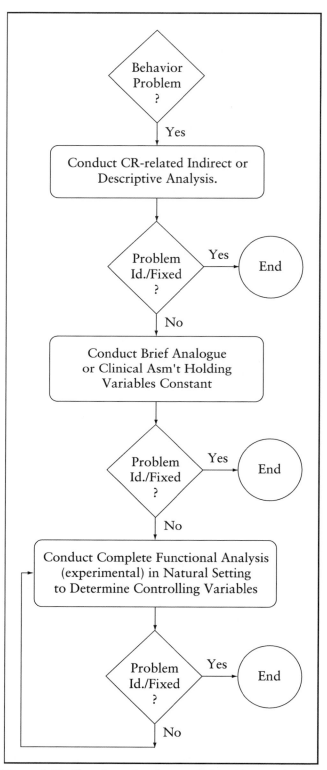

**Figure 8.13.** Flowchart showing procedures for conducting a comprehensive functional assessment of a challenging behavior.

sufficient. Another purpose of this check is to ascertain whether performance growth is evident.

When monitoring student progress, Brophy and Alleman (1991) suggest that feedback should be provided that includes not only information about the quantitative aspects of performance (i.e., correct and incorrect responses), but also, and most importantly, information about the qualitative aspects of errors (i.e., how the errors may be corrected and how specific aspects of performance may be improved). Brophy and Alleman emphasize the need to provide immediate feedback while students are actively engaged. This would require consultants to work with teachers to provide ongoing analysis and feedback to students during learning activities.

Readers interested in a comprehensive treatment of feedback are referred to Van Houten (1980, 1984).

Reflecting the direct instruction/curriculum-based assessment approach toward teaching and learning, Fuchs (1986) states that formative evaluation is a methodology for monitoring student progress. Fuchs provides three critical dimensions to address in monitoring student progress, i.e., the focus of measurement, the frequency of measurement, and the type of data display.

Fuchs (1986) furnishes questions to be asked when deciding upon the focus of measurement. What simple, observable behaviors are critical indicators of student performance? What is an appropriate scope for a goal statement? What principles are useful for determining mastery criteria? Fuchs suggests that twice-weekly measurement is satisfactory, considering the time constraints upon practitioners. Fuchs encourages displaying data on graphs as a way to organize the information, provide a quantitative summary, and assist in communicating the results. Figure 8.14 and Figure 8.15 show noncumulative and cumulative representations of data.

A more complete illustration of student performance, however, can be achieved using a standard celeration chart (West, Young, & Spooner, 1990). A standard celeration chart is produced on a logarithmic scale and permits the

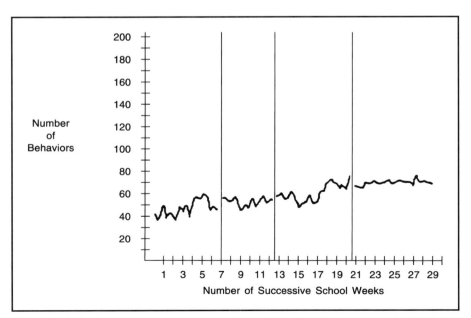

**Figure 8.14.** Performance monitoring chart. From "Graphing Performance," by G. Tindal, 1987, *Teaching Exceptional Children, 20*(1), 45. Copyright 1987 by The Council for Exceptional Children. Reprinted with permission.

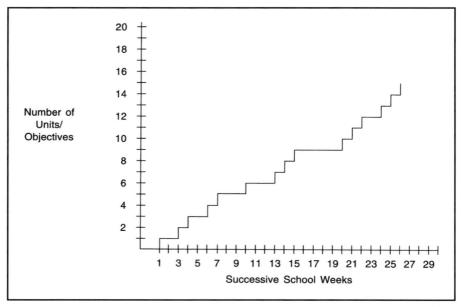

**Figure 8.15.** Mastery monitoring chart. From "Graphing Performance," by G. Tindal, 1987, *Teaching Exceptional Children, 20*(1), 45. Copyright 1987 by The Council for Exceptional Children. Reprinted with permission.

---

**OBSERVATION OF INSTRUCTIONAL TIME**

Student _____    Date _____

Observer _____    Class _____

Directions: Record in each column for every activity, including math, reading, recess, lunch, and others. Indicate if the major lesson format was teacher-directed (TD), seatwork (SW), or nonacademic instruction (NA). Use the formulae at the bottom to calculate desired information.

| Time Begin | Time End | Activity | Minutes | TD/SW/NA | Major Student Tasks and Observer Comments |
|---|---|---|---|---|---|
| 8:00 | 8:15 | Homework | 15 | TD | Checking math problems |
| 8:15 | 8:17 | Transition | 2 | NA | Putting away homework; getting into reading groups |
| 8:17 | 8:35 | Reading | 18 | TD | Teacher directing student's reading group |
| 8:35 | 9:15 | Reading | 40 | SW | Silent reading & workbook; teacher is with other groups |

Total TD minutes           _____
Total SW minutes           _____
Total TD plus SW minutes   _____
Total NA minutes           _____

**Figure 8.16.** Observation of instructional time. From "Direct Observation of Academic Learning Time," by R. Wilson, 1987, *Teaching Exceptional Children, 19*(2), 14. Copyright 1987 by The Council for Exceptional Children. Reprinted with permission.

uniform graphing of behaviors ranging from 1 response per day (.0007 responses per minute) to 1,000 responses per minute, all with equal intervals. Consultants working with teachers can see at a glance how a student's correct and incorrect responses are accelerating or decelerating with respect to target floor and ceiling projections. Likewise, phase changes shown on the graph show instantly the results of successive treatments, allowing for the comparative analysis of treatments (refer to Figure 8.5). According to West et al., "A given instructional strategy is presumed to be effective if the learning slopes (or best fitting lines) are steeper in the desired direction when the strategy is used than when the strategy is not used. When a learning slope is nearly flat or is going in the wrong direction, different teaching strategies must be tried until one is found that reverses the trend" (p. 8).

Clearly, what the consultant monitors is dependent upon program goals. Wilson (1987) argues that academic learning time—i.e., "the amount of time students spend successfully performing relevant academic tasks" (p. 13)—should be monitored, as it is highly related to academic achievement. According to Wilson, the three observable components of academic learning time are: student engagement rate or time on task; amount of instructional time; and student success rate, or the percentage of correct responses. Using applied behavior analysis techniques, observation guidelines for measuring each of these areas are provided in Figures 8.16, 8.17, and 8.18. Applied behavior analysis techniques provide

For the distinctions between academic learning time, allocated time, opportunity to respond, and active student response, see Heward (1994).

For a thorough discussion of applied behavior analysis techniques, see Cooper et al. (1987).

**OBSERVATION OF ON-TASK BEHAVIOR**

Date ______________________

Student ______________________

Class ______________________

Observer ______________________

Directions: Determine the content (e.g., reading or math) and the format of the activity (either seatwork [SW] or teacher-directed [TD]). At 10-second intervals, record a + if the student is on-task, a – if off-task. On-task means the student is watching an appropriate instructional object or person.

Activity: ______________________ SW TD

Time Begin ______________ Time End ______________

Total Time ______________________

| *Minutes* | *Seconds* 00 | 10 | 20 | 30 | 40 | 50 |
|---|---|---|---|---|---|---|
| 1 | | | | | | |
| 2 | | | | | | |
| 3 | | | | | | |

Totals for Activity* ______________________

Comments: ______________________

*Totals represent time on-task and are determined by the following formula:

$$\frac{+\text{'s}}{+\text{'s} + -\text{'s}} \times 100\%$$

**Figure 8.17.** Observation of on-task behavior. From "Direct Observation of Academic Learning Time," by R. Wilson, 1987, *Teaching Exceptional Children, 19*(2), 15. Copyright 1987 by The Council for Exceptional Children. Reprinted with permission.

**STUDENT SUCCESS RATE**

Student _____  Date _____

Observer _____  Class _____

Directions: Record in each column for every instructional activity. Record oral and written responses separately. Use a "+" to indicate a correct student answer, a "0" to indicate an incorrect answer. Calculate success rate for each category, activity, and the entire day using the examples and formula provided in the first 2 entries below.

| Activity | Oral Responses | Success Rate | Written Response | Success Rate |
|---|---|---|---|---|
| Homework | None | None | ++++00+++0 ++000++00+ | 12/20 = 60% |
| Math class | +0++ | 3/4 = 75% | ++++00++0++ 00 | 7/12 = 58% |

Total Daily Success Rate = $\dfrac{\text{Total Correct Responses (+'s)}}{\text{Total Correct Plus Incorrect Responses (+'s and 0's)}}$ x 100% = _____

Figure 8.18. Student success rate. From "Direct Observation of Academic Learning Time," by R. Wilson, 1987, *Teaching Exceptional Children, 19*(2), 16. Copyright 1987 by The Council for Exceptional Children. Reprinted with permission.

measurements of discrete behaviors and represent an assessment approach that provides information regarding the performance of specific behaviors.

Consultants may also be asked to assist students in monitoring their performance. Agran, Martin, and Mithaug (1989) and Schloss (1987) are just a few professionals who have developed procedures for students to monitor their own performance in transition programs. According to Mithaug, Martin, and Agran (1987), students in a transition program should record information and make comparisons between actual and expected behavior in the following areas: being on time, task selection and set-up, and task outcomes. Figure 8.19 depicts a self-evaluation tool a student could use in a maid service job.

Schloss (1987) provides another approach toward student self-evaluation of transition skills. In Figures 8.20, 8.21 and 8.22, Schloss outlines a procedure for students to identify and monitor appropriate job behavior.

# Evaluating Intervention Plans

## Basic Considerations

There are many issues to consider when conducting program evaluations, including: influence of professional and personal viewpoints in deciding what is of value in a program (Caro, 1971); the match of evaluator with program clients and implementers (North Dakota Study Group on Evaluation, 1977); and the effect of evaluation at both the individual and program levels (Angrist, 1975). The importance of classroom evaluation cannot be overemphasized. As stated by Crooks (1988), classroom evaluation "affects students in many different ways . . . it guides their judgment of what is important to learn, affects their motivation and self-perceptions of competence, structures

```
┌──────────────────────────────────────────────────────────────────────┐
│                    DAILY  ADAPTABILITY  CONTRACT                        │
│                           MAID SERVICE                                  │
│      NAME _____     DATE _____     │
├──────────────────────────────────────────────────────────────────────┤
│                              PLAN                                       │
│                                                                        │
│   Time to Start                                    Time to End          │
│      ┌─────┐                                          ┌─────┐           │
│      │ 12  │                                          │ 12  │           │
│      │     │     Number to Do   1  2  3   4  5  6     │     │           │
│      │9   3│                                          │9   3│           │
│      │  6  │                                          │  6  │           │
│      └─────┘                                          └─────┘           │
├──────────────────────────────────────────────────────────────────────┤
│                              WORK                                       │
│                                                                        │
│  Time Started                                       Time Ended          │
│      ┌─────┐   Rooms Completed  1   2   3   4   5   6  ┌─────┐          │
│      │ 12  │        Floors      __  __  __  __  __  __ │ 12  │          │
│      │     │        Beds        __  __  __  __  __  __ │     │          │
│      │9   3│        Bath        __  __  __  __  __  __ │9   3│          │
│      │  6  │        Toilet      __  __  __  __  __  __ │  6  │          │
│      └─────┘        Sink        __  __  __  __  __  __ └─────┘          │
│                     Mirror      __  __  __  __  __  __                  │
│                     Waste       __  __  __  __  __  __                  │
│                     Dust        __  __  __  __  __  __                  │
├──────────────────────────────────────────────────────────────────────┤
│                            EVALUATE                                     │
│              Begin Work on Time?      Yes      No                       │
│              Work Expected Number?    Yes      No                       │
│              End Work on Time?        Yes      No                       │
├──────────────────────────────────────────────────────────────────────┤
│                             ADJUST                                      │
│  Next Time:   Begin Work    Earlier    Same    Later    Time?           │
│               Complete      Fewer      Same    More     Rooms?          │
│               End Work      Earlier    Same    Later    Time?           │
└──────────────────────────────────────────────────────────────────────┘
```

**Figure 8.19.** Daily adaptability contract—maid service. From "Achieving Transition Through Adaptability Instruction," by M. Agran, J. E. Martin, and D. F. Mithaug, 1989, *Teaching Exceptional Children, 21*(2), 6. Copyright 1989 by The Council for Exceptional Children. Reprinted with permission.

```
┌──────────────────────────────────────────────────────────────────────┐
│                            SELF-AUDIT                                   │
│   1. The behavior that my boss, other workers, or the customers do     │
│      not like is                                                        │
│   _____         │
│   2. Good workers behave this way _____ times a day or _____ minutes a day. │
│   3. I show this behavior about _____ times a day or _____ minutes a day.    │
│   4. I want to show this behavior _____ times a day or _____ minutes a day.  │
└──────────────────────────────────────────────────────────────────────┘
```

**Figure 8.20.** Self-audit. From "Self-Management Strategies for Adolescents Entering the Work Force," by P. J. Schloss, 1987, *Teaching Exceptional Children, 19*(4), 41. Copyright 1987 by The Council for Exceptional Children. Reprinted with permission.

---

**CRITICAL EVENTS LOG**

Date:_____

| | What Critical Events Happen Before the Behavior? | Can These Events Be Avoided? |
|---|---|---|
| Write the Behavior | | |

_____No
_____Yes

If the critical events can be avoided, state how._____

---

**Figure 8.21.** Critical events log. From "Self-Management Strategies for Adolescents Entering the Work Force," by P. J. Schloss, 1987, *Teaching Exceptional Children, 19*(4), 41. Copyright 1987 by The Council for Exceptional Children. Reprinted with permission.

---

**SELF-MONITORING REPORT**

1. The behavior I will change is _____

2. I will count or time the behavior: _____

Date                                                     How Often or How Long?

---

**Figure 8.22.** Self-monitoring report. From "Self-Management Strategies for Adolescents Entering the Work Force," by P. J. Schloss, 1987, *Teaching Exceptional Children, 19*(4), 43. Copyright 1987 by The Council for Exceptional Children. Reprinted with permission.

---

their approaches to and timing of personal study, consolidates learning, and affects the development of enduring learning strategies and skills. It appears to be one of the most potent forces influencing education" (p. 467). However, the concern here is with methodological issues. Several program evaluation models have been developed over the years (e.g., DEM, *Discrepancy Evaluation Model,* Yavorsky, 1978; GAS, *Goal Attainment Scaling,* Maher, 1983). Field and Hill (1988) suggest that the key concept to maintain is an ecological model of schools. That is, one needs to recognize that there are interrelationships among students, teachers, activities, and resources, as well as different purposes for schools, e.g., schools are workplaces for adults, learning places for children, objects of legislation, etc. Regardless of the evaluation model, one must determine program evaluation activities. The following suggestions for planning and conducting program evaluation activities are offered:

1. Clearly identify program goals (Knowlton, 1983; Maher, 1983).

2. Clearly identify desired outcomes of the program (Knowlton, 1983) as well as the process of program implementation.

3. Specify measurable objectives that will reflect desired program outcomes as well as the process of program implementation.

4. Evaluate the usefulness of program evaluation activities, that is, the extent to which efforts serve the program development and improvement needs of users (Maher & Bennett, 1984).

5. Assure the propriety of evaluation activities, that is, the legal and ethical considerations (Maher & Bennett, 1984).

6. Assure the accuracy of program evaluation data collection activities, that is, that activities are technically defensible (Maher & Bennett, 1984).

7. Identify the resources available within or outside the institution to conduct program evaluation (Knowlton, 1983).

8. Include, as a source of evaluative information, consumers of the program (Field & Hill, 1988).

In addition to gathering information for identifying problems and developing intervention plans, a consultant may also be asked to evaluate students and programs in the school. *Evaluation* provides the means to determine the effectiveness of a given course of action. In tracing the trends in evaluation, House (1990) states: "Between 1965 and 1990, the methodology, philosophy, and politics of evaluation changed substantially . . . moved from monolithic to pluralist conceptions, to multiple methods, measures, criteria, perspectives, audiences, and even multiple interests. Methodologically, evaluation moved from a primary emphasis on quantitative methods . . . qualitative methods became acceptable . . . [and] useful for obtaining the views of participants" (pp. 24–25).

Program evaluation can provide valuable information for decision making (Angrist, 1975). Traditionally, program evaluation has relied on the use of standardized measures of student achievement, such as test scores. Usually, a pretest of either the children or the teachers is made, the innovative program is implemented, and a posttest is administered at the conclusion. However, there has been a growing dissatisfaction among educators with this approach. Perhaps one of the most vocal protests was made by parents, teachers, and evaluation researchers during the First Annual Conference on Educational Evaluation and Public Policy (North Dakota Study Group on Evaluation, 1977). An opinion frequently expressed at that conference was that the trend in evaluative practices tends to discount educational outcomes that are not easily quantified through standardized testing. A plea was made for the use of evaluation measures that are sensitive to the goals of each program. Therefore, a need for a wide variety of evaluation methods to match the wide variety of program goals is apparent.

For an extensive treatment of program planning and evaluation, especially as it relates to principles, procedures, and planned change, see Illback, Zins, and Maher (1999).

Many programs attempt to affect the process of teaching (the interaction between teachers and students) and not just the products (test scores). Therefore, the evaluation of process variables becomes as important as the evaluation of product variables. Techniques can be employed to measure a host of process variables that, in turn, may lead to a more refined picture of the teaching act. Evaluation, therefore, can be conceptualized as part of an ongoing feedback loop in which program outcomes are judged against both process and product program goals (Angrist, 1975).

## Formative Evaluation

*Formative evaluation* is conducted during the actual implementation of the program (the intervention mutually agreed upon by the teacher and the consultant). In formative evaluation, the consultant determines whether a plan is being implemented as intended and considers the effectiveness of the plan for changing behavior. Formative evaluation allows for "midcourse correction." If the plan is implemented as intended, yet no functional effect on the targeted behavior is noted, another strategy can be initiated immediately.

Three general arguments have been advanced to support formative evaluation: (a) formative evaluations are necessary to better understand and avoid the pitfalls of previous outcome evaluations; (b) traditional outcome evaluations (i.e., experimental and quasi-experimental designs involving groups of students) require large-scale interventions to show statistically significant effects; and (c) formative evaluation approaches yield more useful information for decision making (Gersten & Hauser, 1984).

## Summative Evaluation

*Summative evaluation* is conducted at the end of an intervention. The question the consultant seeks to answer then is, did the plan have a functional effect? If the teacher's (or student's) behavior changed a significant amount in the desired direction and adequate controls were used to eliminate competing explanations for the change, then the consultant can be reasonably confident that the plan accounted for the change.

## Combined Approach

Gersten and Hauser (1984) contend that evaluations of special education programs should produce information useful for program improvement. Measurements should be used that are sensitive to the process as well as to program outcomes. These authors discuss the use of behavioral observations and teacher ratings as viable outcome measures. They argue that two critical areas need to be assessed to improve evaluation results: program implementation and measurement of outcome. Assessing program implementation is important for two reasons: (a) it provides information on the extent to which the program was implemented as intended; and (b) the information can be used to establish the relationship between the program and its intended—outcome, that is, how much or what quality of the intervention is associated with what level of outcome?

This combination of formative and summative evaluation can be used for groups and individuals. For example, the IEP or IFSP process demands a yearly or summative evaluation. However, short-term objectives for each annual goal and methods for evaluating those objectives are also written into an IEP or IFSP. If during implementation, it is found that these short-term objectives are not being met, steps can be taken to modify the educational program. The appropriateness of the instructional methodology or the measurement technique itself may be examined. Rather than waiting a year to determine whether the IEP or IFSP has been successful for the student, a formative evaluation of short-term objectives can indicate program success (or failure) and suggest alterations in the IEP or IFSP that could increase the probability of overall success.

# Evaluating the Consultation Process

When *evaluating the consultation* process, practitioners may need to gather information regarding the success of one-to-one interactions as well as the success of team functioning. When evaluating the intervention designed through any consultation activity, Phillips and McCullough (1990) suggest that the following feasibility issues be considered: (a) the degree of disruption to school and classroom procedures and/or teacher routines; (b) the side effects upon students, peers, home and family, and faculty and staff; (c) the degree of support services needed to implement the intervention; (d) the competencies and philosophical biases needed to implement the intervention; (e) the probability of the intervention achieving the student goal; (f) the immediacy of results; (g) the consequences of no intervention; and (h) the generality of the intervention.

Landerholm (1990) considers the following areas essential to determining the success of the consultation process of transdisciplinary teaming in infant intervention programs: interpersonal relations, developmental process, whole team structure, and role release. Consultants can use a case study or ecological approach to determine effective team functioning.

When assessing interpersonal relations, it is useful to ascertain whether any teachers or parents are viewed as inferior by other team members. This can be determined by observing team member behaviors and communication styles. To determine the effectiveness of the developmental process, a consultant can examine team records for lack of time for team building, staff turnover, and minority opinions. To ascertain effectiveness of team structure, one can observe meetings for flexibility and rigidity as well as clarity of roles of members. Finally, team members sometimes have problems in role release, i.e., sharing and exchanging information and skills across disciplinary lines. One can determine the ease of role release by talking with team members as well as exploring collective records regarding the roles the participants assume during the team meetings and the responsibilities peers assume in the action plan.

Other types of team efforts include interagency collaborative programs. Flynn and Harbin (1987) identify three areas to consider when evaluating the effectiveness of interagency efforts. They suggest an evaluation across three continua: climate, resources, and policies. When determining the climate for coordination, information should be gathered regarding the degree of support for the collaborative effort. This can be done by noting recognition of need, degree of support, and degree of collaboration and leadership for coordination and widespread cooperation among agencies and private providers. In assessing resources, consultants would want to determine the economic base, fiscal resources, amount of appropriately trained personnel, and adequacy of specialized facilities. Policy evaluation would include an inspection of mandates, written agreements, and the degree to which interagency cooperation has been institutionalized.

Heron and Kimball (1988) discuss an ecological approach for evaluating the success of any type of consultation activity. It is their recommendation that information be gathered about the logistics of consultation activities and the team process, the fiscal and time cost, organizational factors such as the consultant's skill, and the degree to which consultation outcomes are generalized (see Table 8.10).

Pryzwansky and Noblit (1990) assert that a case study approach should be used to evaluate the consultation process:

> Case studies that involve an evaluation component can be an invaluable part of a plan to assess the efficacy of consultation services in a system and serve a case related accountability purpose. Similarly, as part of the strategy to improve one's own service, an a priori planned case study can provide valuable insights into the ongoing consultation process, contribute to a self or peer critique of the consultant's work, as well as serve

## Table 8.10

### Ecological Variables for the Evaluation of Consultation Activities

1. **Intervention Management:** Arranging space and facilities for implementation, record keeping, establishment of evaluation procedures, and maintenance of intervention integrity.
2. **Logistics of Team Process:** Coordinating schedules and responsibilities of general program teachers, special educators, school psychologists, administrative staff, and other participants.
3. **Fiscal Cost:** Personnel compensation, training needs, instructional materials, caseload size, required facilities.
4. **Time Cost:** Completions of consultation activities (e.g., clarifying the problem, developing and implementing interventions, and determining the extent of program monitoring and adjustments).
5. **Organizational Factors:** Written policies legitimizing consultation services and documenting administrative support; clarity of roles; consultation skills of the consultee; referral patterns; support of consultation by parents, students, and paraprofessionals.
6. **Generality of Consultation Outcomes:** Consultee application of strategies across students, student use of interventions across curricular areas, and consultant recognition of appropriate models or processes.

*Note.* From "Gaining Perspective with the Educational Consultation Research Base: Ecological Considerations and Further Recommendations," by T. E. Heron and W. H. Kimball, 1988, *Remedial and Special Education, 9*(6), 26. Reprinted with permission.

to influence intervention decisions regarding a particular consultation case. Such a case study would also seem to have potential for enhancing one's future consultation. . . . Finally, the contributions of case studies to hypothesis generation may be significant given the small number of data-based guidelines for consultation practice (pp. 294–295).

See Miles and Huberman (1984) for suggestions related to data analysis.

In using a case study approach to document and evaluate the consultation process, consultants are encouraged to follow the guidelines for conducting a case study described earlier in this chapter, i.e., observe the consultation process; take notes regarding the consultation; question it; inspect documents related to it; and note changing actions, perceptions, emotions, and thoughts. Doing this for each consultation will provide a corpus of data that can be analyzed. The conclusions generated through a reading and rereading of data should be confirmed by supportive information in all the types of data collected.

Pryzwansky and Noblit (1990) encourage consultants to write their case studies for conference presentation or journal publication. Writing sets the occasion for consultants to consider their work and its implications for practice; they should write throughout the consultation process. "It is during the writing phase that design, data collection, and data analysis come together to form a coherent whole" (Pryzwansky & Noblit, 1990, p. 306). If writing is not possible, consultants are urged to tape-record their notes and listen to their tape-recordings repeatedly, noting changes that occur. Merriam (1988) provides the following guidelines for writing a case study: Discuss what led to the study, the context of the consultation, the dynamics of the consultation, the processes and beliefs that were present during the consultation, the key aspects that were explored, and the conclusions regarding procedures to follow in the future.

# Conclusion

This chapter discussed comprehensive assessment techniques that could be used throughout the consultation process. Examples from our experience and the literature have been provided to assist consultants in making decisions about the assessment techniques that they might employ throughout the consultation process.

Regardless of the approach selected, consultants are encouraged to: (a) match the philosophy of instruction and assessment with the approach; (b) announce their intention to gather information beforehand; (c) be as unobtrusive as possible; and (d) provide appropriate feedback to all interested parties.

# Summary of Key Points

## Assessment Frameworks

1. Distinctions between qualitative and quantitative data were presented.

2. Qualitative data was defined as narrative designed to describe and understand a given situation from the perspective of the participants in that situation.

3. Quantitative data are data reduced to numerical representation and are designed to measure the occurrence of specific predetermined behaviors.

4. A consultant may gather information about individuals (e.g., student success in a mainstream placement), groups (e.g., the effect of mainstreaming upon mainstream teachers, and processes (e.g., the process of developing a consultation program in a school).

## Identifying a Problem

5. In problem identification, the consultant may be asked to define the problem (survey level) or to measure the factors contributing to the problem (specific level).

6. A *case study* is useful in problem identification when the consultant wants to obtain information that the participants identify as important, wants to understand the perspective of the participants, wants to understand the context in which specific behaviors are being measured, and/or wants to specify problems or behaviors to be measured.

7. Case study is based upon narrative recordings conducted on site. However, additional information, suggested by the field observation, is also collected, characterizing this approach as multimodal.

8. To successfully conduct a case study, the consultant must take care to enter and become accepted into the environment about which information is being gathered.

9. Interview allows an individual to express his or her perceptions.

10. Interviews can be constructed along a continuum from unstructured to very structured.

11. Structured interviews are used to gather information about predetermined variables.

12. Unstructured interviews are useful when one wants to gather information about what is of importance to the interviewee.

13. Ecological assessment is useful in problem identification when one wants to obtain information about a broad range of predetermined variables.

14. In an ecological assessment, all environments related to the behavior in question are assessed using a variety of assessment techniques.

15. A checklist reflects the presence or absence of a particular characteristic according to some predetermined set of categories.

16. A rating scale represents an estimate of the degree to which a particular characteristic is evident along a basic continuum.

17. To maximize reliability of checklists and rating scales, consultants should use operational definitions for behaviors to be measured, request that individuals complete checklists at the time behavior occurs, and provide training in and enough time for the completion of rating scales.

## Developing an Intervention Plan

18. To develop an intervention plan, it is necessary to obtain in-depth information about child and environmental factors.

19. An important component of developing an effective intervention plan is to determine the assumptions of instruction and learning that are held by the participants and to utilize assessment procedures that are appropriate for those assumptions.

20. Performance assessment reflects a holistic approach to education. Students are asked to demonstrate basic skills in genuine rather than artificial ways and in integrated rather than isolated tasks.

21. Curriculum-based assessment reflects a direct instruction approach to education. Student achievement is measured by operationalizing a sequence of behaviors and measuring student performance in each behavior. The behaviors measured are directly related to the program of study of the student.

22. Curriculum-based measures are a source of information relative to the student's performance with content-related skill acquisition.

23. Sociometric assessment provides information about the attitudes of group members toward one another.

24. In a sociometric assessment, individuals belonging to a group are asked a question about the group (e.g., "Who would you most like to sit next to?"). Results are plotted on a sociogram and visually inspected.

# Functional Assessment

25. Functional assessment can be conducted using any one of three methods: indirect method, descriptive method, and functional analysis.

26. Indirect and descriptive methods yield correlational evidence of contributing factors associated with the target behavior.

27. Functional analysis yields experimental evidence of contributing factors associated with the target behavior.

28. Brief and analog measures may yield sufficient data for practitioners to proceed with interventions, especially when time constraints are paramount and where the alternative is a less desirable interview or descriptive method.

# Monitoring Implementation and Student Progress

29. Plan implementation is monitored to ascertain whether the intervention is being implemented as intended and whether the program is having the desired effect on student performance.

# Evaluating Intervention Plans

30. Evaluation provides a means of determining the effectiveness of a given course of action.

31. Formative evaluation is conducted during the implementation of the program and allows for "midcourse correction" (i.e., changes in the program before the program has been completed).

32. Summative evaluation is conducted at the end of the program, and it is designed to measure the effect of the program.

33. Consultants are encouraged to combine formative and summative evaluations into the activities of a program evaluation.

34. When planning and implementing program evaluations, consultants should clearly identify program goals; clearly identify desired outcomes as well as the process of program implementation; evaluate the utility and propriety of program evaluation activities; assure the accuracy of program evaluation data; and include as a source of evaluation the consumers of the program.

35. When measuring student progress, immediate feedback should be provided to students that includes information about the correctness of their work as well as their errors, which will clarify how their performance may be improved.

36. When evaluating the success of consultation efforts, one may need to gather information regarding the success of one-to-one interactions between consultants and consultees, as well as the success of team functioning.

37. A variety of techniques can be used to evaluate consultation activities, including interview, checklist, rating scale, case study, and ecological assessment.

## Evaluating the Consultation Process

38. When evaluating the consultation process, practitioners may need to gather information regarding the success of one-to-one interactions as well as the success of team functioning.

39. Ecological and case-study approaches are two primary methods by which the consultation process are evaluated.

## Questions

1. What are the distinctions between qualitative and quantitative data?

2. What are the general purposes of assessment?

3. Distinguish between survey and specific levels of assessment.

4. Discuss how the case study approach would be useful to the consultant in the problem identification stage of the consultation process.

5. In what situations would structured interview be useful to the consultant?

6. What are some of the factors that should be considered in an ecological assessment?

7. What is the basic difference between a checklist and a rating scale?

8. Describe three methods for conducting a functional assessment of student behavior.

9. State the advantages and disadvantages of conducting a functional assessment with respect to the identification of critical and controlling variables, cost, and time.

10. What is an important consideration when developing an intervention plan?

11. State how curriculum-based assessment might be incorporated into a qualitative assessment gathering plan.

12. Define an indirect functional assessment procedure and provide an applied example.

13. Define a descriptive functional assessment procedure and provide an applied example.

14. Define a functional analysis procedure and provide an applied example.

15. State the conditions under which an indirect, descriptive, or functional analysis method might be the preferred option for a school-based consultant? A clinic-based consultant?

16. Distinguish between formative and summative evaluation.

17. Identify considerations when planning, implementing, monitoring, and evaluating program activities.

# Discussion Points and Exercises

1. Interview and observe the consultants in your school district to determine the purposes of gathering information. Identify the types of information gathering techniques used and find out what the consultants feel are the strengths and weaknesses of those techniques.

2. Based on a teacher referral of a student who exhibits problems in the school, design an information gathering strategy that will identify and measure the problem. If possible, develop an intervention plan and evaluate the success of that plan.

3. Identify a curriculum or instructional program that teachers have been asked to implement in your school. Design an information gathering strategy that will be sensitive to the way each teacher is implementing that program. Using the information gathered, explain why the program is being implemented in this fashion.

4. The principal has informed you, the educational consultant, that the special education program in the school has a bad reputation. The principal wants you to do something about it. Develop a plan that will help you to assess the situation.

5. Conduct a functional assessment of student behavior using the three methods outlined in the chapter. Discuss the results with respect to the quality of the data, the cost-benefit ratio of collecting the data, and the usefulness with respect to implementation.

6. Devise an information gathering strategy that will provide data regarding the process of your consultation activities as well as their effects.

# Modifying Environmental, Instructional, and Reinforcement Strategies at the Elementary School Level

*9*

This chapter has a twofold purpose for consultants: (1) to provide field-tested methods to assist teachers with individualizing an adapted curriculum, and (2) to address how these strategies can be juxtaposed within an environmental, instructional, and reinforcement context during preteaching, teaching, and postteaching phases of instruction. Recent research has shown that if general education teachers receive appropriate training, they can meet broader student needs in the classroom successfully (Stainback, Stainback, Courtnage, & Jaben, 1985; Wood, 1998). At the elementary level, consultants and teachers are encouraged to work collaboratively to develop skill-based teaching methodologies that achieve that objective. While it is beyond the scope of this chapter to describe every possible adaptation that could be considered, a sampling of strategies will be presented that have been field tested and found to be effective.

## Objectives

After reading this chapter, the reader should be able to:

1. define adapted instruction and state how adaptations should be designed to meet the individualized needs of students;

2. provide exemplars of adaptations that could be jointly designed across preteaching, teaching, and postteaching areas considering environmental, instructional, and reinforcement factors.

## Key Terms

adapted instruction

lesson plans

large-group instruction

small-group instruction

individual contingency

group contingency

proactive feedback

# Adapted Instruction

*Adapted instruction* is an approach that accommodates the unique learning needs of individual students within every classroom (Wang, Reynolds, & Schwartz, 1988; Wood, 1998). Research on effective adapted instructional programs suggests that such programs have incorporated the following features: flexible scheduling, individual diagnosis and prescription, mastery learning, large- and small-group instruction, individual tutorials, and cooperative learning (Wang & Lindvall, 1984; Wang & Walberg, 1985; Wood, 1998).

While variety exists among adapted programs in terms of goals and strategies, all adapted instruction programs share the common characteristic that accommodations are conducted in ways that best suit individual student needs (Walberg & Wang, 1987; Wang & Lindvall, 1984; Wang & Walberg, 1985; Waxman, Wang, Anderson, & Walberg, 1985; Wood, 1998). To design and implement an adapted instruction program requires knowledge of a substantial array of modifications. To assist in matching adaptations to student needs, Cohen and Lynch (1991) developed an instructional modification process, which is presented in Table 9.1.

According to Cohen and Lynch (1991), each step in this process exists along a continuum of options. Decisions are made at each step. Actions made at the low end of the continuum further define the step; actions at the high end lead toward the next step.

Recall the data reported on teacher perceptions found in Chapter 6.

In our view, teachers should identify those elements that they are willing and able to change, with technical assistance, whenever the need occurs. One reason a teacher may be reluctant to teach a student with disabilities in the elementary classroom is that the teacher might believe that she or he is unable to meet the student's learning needs. The teacher might believe that the time required to teach 30 or more students will preclude individualizing instruction. A teacher who expresses negative feelings about "having to go it alone" can be helped. A consultant can increase the teacher's awareness of effective teaching strategies, curriculum adaptations, and technological hardware. Ultimately, a consultant's objective would be to help the elementary teacher develop the necessary knowledge and confidence to direct a well-organized program.

For a comprehensive treatment of adaptations that general education teachers can employ in the classroom, the reader is referred to Scott, Vitale, and Masten (1998) and Wood (1998).

Consultants are encouraged to collaborate with teachers to develop modifications across environmental, instructional, and reinforcement areas within the contexts of three critical phases of instruction: preteaching, teaching, and postteaching. Table 9.2 shows a matrix representing a sample of possible strategies for each. This matrix is not intended to describe every strategy that might be included; however, it is intended to show a representative range of field-tested options that can serve as the launching point for other possibilities. Given deBettencourt's (1999) point that "general educators [may] not use . . . strategies that research suggests facilitate academic achievement for students with mild disabilities" (p. 33), consultants may be in a position to explore research-based, field-tested options with general education teachers.

# Preteaching: Environmental Adaptations

There are a host of preteaching strategies that consultants can recommend to increase the likelihood of a successful accommodated program at the elementary level. We'll focus on six common preteaching areas where adaptations can

## Table 9.1
### Instructional Modification Process

| Action To Be Taken | Modification Process | | Action To Be Taken |
|---|---|---|---|
| | *LOW* | *HIGH* | |
| Hold off on modifications until factors under teacher's control are delineated. | *Step 1.* Clarification of elements under teacher control. ←——→ | | Continue to review elements for control criteria. Move to Step 2. |
| Make additions to menu by literature search, information from other teachers, alternatives you've seen or tried in the past, etc. | *Step 2.* Development of a modification menu. ←——→ | | Review periodically to increase familiarity with options. Move to Step 3. |
| Concentrate on elements more directly under the teacher's control. | *Step 3.* Decision about whether or not a problem exists. ←——→ | | Determine immediacy and severity of the problem. Move to Step 4. |
| Rewrite problem statement to be more specific and objective. | *Step 4.* Development of problem statement. ←——→ | | Accept problem statement. Move to Step 5. |
| Peruse other sources of information. Too few options may mean that the menu is not varied enough to include the needed problem solutions. | *Step 5.* Selection and grouping of modifications. ←——→ | | Too many options may indicate that the problem statement is not focused enough. Review and clarify the problem statement if necessary. Move to Step 6. |
| Consider low-ranked options only if no other options appear viable. | *Step 6.* Ranking of modification options. ←——→ | | Consider options with high rankings as primary focus for change. Move to Step 7. |
| Review steps 1–6. | *Step 7.* Selection of modification option and implementation. ←——→ | | Evaluate modification results. |

*Note.* From "An Instructional Modification Process," by S. B. Cohen and D. K. Lynch, 1991, *Teaching Exceptional Children, 23*(4), 13. Reprinted with permission.

make a difference: lesson plans, scheduling, group considerations, materials, media and technology, and rules.

## Lesson Plans

According to Polloway, Patton, Payne, and Payne (1989), *lesson plans* are written documents that contain four major elements: objectives, materials, method of presentation, and evaluation. Clearly, consultants can increase a teacher's awareness of these elements and of how they can be modified to meet

## Table 9.2

Matrix of Environmental, Instructional, and Reinforcement Adaptations
Across Preteaching, Teaching, and Postteaching Phases

| | Preaching (planning) | Teaching (instructional and management adaptations) | Postteaching (evaluation) |
|---|---|---|---|
| Environment | • Lesson plan<br>• Schedule<br>• Grouping<br>• Materials<br>• Media and technology<br>• Rules | • Seating arrangements<br>• Creating a rich learning environment<br>• Establishing multiple groups | • Homework<br>• Testing<br>• Grading |
| Instruction and Management | • Mode of presentation<br>• Mode of response | • Correcting student errors<br>• Changing cues and response modes<br>• Managing behavior | |
| Reinforcement and Feedback | • Individual<br>• Group<br>• Continuous v. intermittent | • Proactive reinforcement<br>• Recruiting teacher praise and attention<br>• Changing schedules<br>• Charting performance | |

the individual needs of students. For example, Table 9.3 shows a sample lesson plan for a science objective at the elementary level and how it was adapted to meets the needs of a student with specific learning disabilities. The objective was changed to learning only 5 "key terms" in the chapter as opposed to the 10 terms planned for other students. Further, while the general education students might receive the instruction through a lecture-discussion method coupled with a teacher-directed overhead transparency presentation, the adapted version would incorporate specially designed flashcards, guided notes, and response cards to enhance the lesson. Finally, the general education students might be evaluated by a written, timed test. The student with specific learning disabilities might receive an oral, untimed test covering the same content but conducted by the resource room teacher. A lesson plan for a student with disabilities should be based on the IEP, and there should be a linear relationship between the annual goals, the short-term objectives (benchmarks), and the lesson plan.

## Scheduling

For a detailed explanation of direct instruction, see Carnine (1983), Heron (1983), and Stein, Silbert, and Carnine (1997).

Scheduling individualized lessons can be arranged in several ways. For instance, in a direct instruction classroom, lessons follow a specific sequence that builds upon prior skill acquisition. Further, lessons are scripted to maximize directions, exemplars, active student responding, reinforcement and feedback, and practice. Future lessons are not begun until mastery of previous lessons has been demonstrated. The goal for direct instruction lessons is not to teach rote, mechanical skills, but to teach *explicit* skills (Heward, 2000; Stein et al., 1997).

**Table 9.3**
Science Lesson Plan with Adaptations

| Regular | Adapted |
|---|---|
| Objective: | Objective: |
| • To learn 10 terms and definitions associated with the chapter on the life cycle. | • To learn 5 "key terms" and definitions associated with the chapter on the life cycle. |
| Materials: | Materials: |
| • Teacher overhead transparency | • Teacher overhead transparency<br>• Flashcards (w/ terms & definitions) |
| Method of presentation: | Method of Presentation: |
| • Lecture and discussion | • Lecture and discussion<br>• Guided notes<br>• Response cards |
| Evaluation: | Evaluation: |
| • Posttest on stated objectives (written and timed) | • Posttest on stated objectives (oral and untimed, conducted by the resource room teacher) |

Following a direct instruction lesson schedule and format ensures that skills are not presented in a random manner.

Other scheduling formats that consultants are likely to encounter are subject- and/or time-based approaches and block scheduling. In subject- or time-based approaches, the teacher allocates a specific number of minutes for instruction (e.g., reading: 45 minutes, 9:00 to 9:45 daily; math: 45 minutes, 9:45 to 10:30 daily; etc.). Some subjects within this approach may be relegated to every other day or once per week (e.g., spelling: Monday, Wednesday, Thursday; civics, Friday only). Polloway et al. (1989) suggest that schedules should take into account the scope and sequence of the material, student preferences for subject matter (high or low), and opportunities for reinforcement and feedback.

## Group Considerations

Polloway, Cronin, and Patton (1986) discuss the positive benefits of grouping for instruction. Grouping generally promotes better use of teacher time and more efficient management of students, increases instructional time and peer interaction, and facilitates overlearning and generalization. Polloway et al. (1989) suggest that any individualized instruction arrangement can be assessed by examining its effectiveness, efficiency, and social benefits. Providing individualized instruction in group arrangements, however, requires the application of various types of grouping techniques. Whether the teacher is introducing a skill, reviewing previously taught skills, or providing guided practice dictates whether a whole-group, cooperative learning, or dyadic arrangement will be used. In this chapter, we'll discuss two major grouping arrangements: large-group and small-group instruction. More specialized grouping arrangements (e.g., tutoring, cooperative learning groups) will be presented in Chapter 11.

See Chapter 11 for grouping strategies that apply across a range of elementary (and secondary) levels.

See English, Goldstein, Kaczmarek, and Shafer (1996) and English, Goldstein, Shafer, and Kaczmarek (1997) for information on promoting "buddy systems" with preschool populations.

## Large-Group Instruction

*Large-group instruction* occurs when one teacher directs a lesson with the whole class simultaneously, usually with 30 or more students. Many general educators may believe (mistakenly) that it is impossible to individualize within this context. This perception may help to explain Moody, Vaughn, and Schumm's (1997) findings that show that general education teachers use whole-class instruction most of the time to teach reading, even when students with disabilities are included in the classroom. That is, they may perceive that since they cannot deliver individualized instruction—meaning, in their view, 1:1 instruction—a group approach will have to suffice.

Consultants who collaborate with elementary teachers to plan large-group instruction must recognize that these teachers may not have received adequate preservice or inservice training to plan large-group instruction that maintains an individualized approach. To assist, consultants can show (model) how to plan a lesson within a large-group context that provides individualized instruction by using verbal, positional, or situational cues effectively.

## Small-Group Instruction

In elementary classrooms it is not surprising to find a wide range of student abilities, interests, and rates of learning. When faced with such heterogeneity, teachers usually organize students for *small-group instruction,* an arrangement whereby the teacher works with one group, while the other students are assigned seat work, board work, or independent activities. To meet the individual needs of all students, including students with disabilities, the teacher must be able to manage all groups simultaneously. Further, if the results of Elbaum, Vaughn, Hughes, and Moody's (1999) meta-analysis of grouping practices showing an average effect size for alternative/flexible groups are accurate, performance gains of nearly half a standard deviation higher than whole-class (large-group) instruction can be expected. Obviously, it would behoove the consultant to work more closely to provide additional training on how small groups can be used effectively and be modified according to individual needs. Anecdote 9.1 describes a conversation between a special education teacher and an elementary teacher who is having difficulty with her classroom, which included two students with developmental disabilities.

### Anecdote 9.1

| | |
|---|---|
| ELEMENTARY TEACHER: | (talking to special education teacher) Mr. Krebs, I'm having trouble with my reading groups, and I'm really lost for ideas on what to do with Dale and Joe while I'm with a reading group. They seem to demand so much attention. |
| SPECIAL EDUCATION TEACHER: | Tell me about it. |
| ELEMENTARY TEACHER: | Right after morning exercises and announcements I explain all the boardwork to the class, and I try to take extra time with Dale and Joe. I go over each assignment and ask if there are any questions. |

| SPECIAL EDUCATION TEACHER: | Do many students ask questions? |
|---|---|
| ELEMENTARY TEACHER: | A few do, but most wait until I take my first reading group. Then they'll raise their hand or come back to my desk to ask for help with a problem I just explained. |
| SPECIAL EDUCATION TEACHER: | I know what you mean. I used to have the same problem, and it wasn't just the students with disabilities who would interrupt. |
| ELEMENTARY TEACHER: | What did you do? |
| SPECIAL EDUCATION TEACHER: | Well, I started the morning the same way you do. But I told the students that I wasn't to be interrupted (unless, of course, it was an emergency) while I was with a reading group. If they had questions, they were to put their names on the board and continue with the work they could do. I made quick trips to a student who needed help when I thought it was necessary. |
| ELEMENTARY TEACHER: | How do you do that without interrupting the flow of instruction? |
| SPECIAL EDUCATION TEACHER: | Suppose the first group you have is reading a story. One thing you can do is have the students read the next paragraph of the story to themselves. Tell them to read to find out why something happened or to find out what the paragraph is about. While they are reading silently, slip off quickly to the student whose name appears first on the board to provide individual help. While you are at the student's desk and while you are returning to yours, praise students for their work. The system should reduce the number of interruptions you have, and the students' on-task behavior should improve because you will be praising their effort and achievement. |
| ELEMENTARY TEACHER: | That sounds like a great idea. I think I'll try it. |
| SPECIAL EDUCATION TEACHER: | It worked for me. I'm sure it will work for you. You may have to make extra trips to Dale's and Joe's desks initially to help them, but as you shape their work-duration behavior, fewer trips are likely in the future. |

In this case, the special education teacher provides a suggestion on how to handle small-group instruction in a classroom where students are having difficulty with their daily assignments. Further, the special education teacher indicates that although Dale and Joe might need more assistance initially, direct help to them could be reduced gradually over time.

For further discussion regarding effective group instruction to meet the needs of all students, refer to Chapter 11.

## Materials

Materials can be adapted in several ways during the preteaching phase. First, the scope and sequence of the material or its format might be redesigned to facilitate comprehension of the instructional sequence or to accommodate a student with limited comprehension skills. Second, supplemental aids (e.g., games, tapes, talking books) might be introduced to further develop or refine comprehension. Third, teachers might consider redesigning physical or spatial features. Fourth, the "look" of the materials may be modified. Finally, for preschool children or primary-level students, materials can be adapted to assist with grasping, manipulating, positioning, or stabilizing (Schaeffler, 1988).

## Redesigned Formats

Stein et al. (1997) state that "formats should reflect a carefully designed progression, beginning with a teacher demonstration of the strategy and followed by teacher-guided worksheet practice, worksheet practice with less teacher directions, supervised worksheet practice and finally independent work" (p. 21). At any point, adaptations in terms of time; the number of examples to be provided; the number of pictorial, verbal, or visual prompts anticipated; and/or the technical support from others (peers) may be planned to develop the skill. Of course, one of the best instructional design formats that teachers could elect comes from a direct instruction (DI) approach.

## Supplemental Aids

Most students enjoy playing games, and instructional games that focus on the content to be learned can be integrated into preteaching planning as one way to facilitate learning. For instance, when teaching the students a money skill, groups might play Monopoly. Likewise, a game like Scrabble might follow a lesson in which letter sounds or word parts were emphasized. Consultants can assist the teacher to determine what game to play and for how long. Tapes, talking books, and enrichment materials may also be introduced.

An elaborative map extends a mnemonic cue by providing more detail. For example, if the student was expected to recall that the Battle of Trenton occurred on Christmas Day by looking at a map, the key word for Trenton—"tent"—would be further elaborated by showing a tent decorated with Christmas ornaments.

***Changing physical or spatial features.*** Brigham, Scruggs, and Mastropieri (1995) showed that changing information on historical maps (e.g., maps of the Revolutionary War) from non-mnemonic to mnemonic to elaborative maps altered student ability to recall information (i.e., map features, important content). By organizing and planning linkages with prior knowledge or capitalizing on visual, spatial, or redundant cues, enhanced learning is achieved (Wood, Frank, & Hamre-Nietupski, 1996). An analog to visual and/or spatial displays when planning written language exercises might be to plan a lesson that ultimately would use story webs, story maps, or graphic organizers.

***Materials Design.*** In addition to how basic text might be changed, consultants may need to show teachers how to plan for the redesign or the "look" of materials (Friend & Bursuck, 1999). For example, Table 9.4 shows a two-column matrix with identical teacher-posed questions in each column. The differences between the columns is that in column B, the text uses a larger type font and the specific pages to find the answers are provided.

A Kurzweil reading machine is a computer that can scan print and read it aloud.

For a student with visual impairments or who is blind, Braille books, larger-print books, or a Kurzweil reading machine may be incorporated into the planning stage. Promising practices in hardware and software development may include voice-activated programs that would allow a student's dictated oral expression to be encoded automatically as "keyboarded" text on a computer. By considering these options during preteaching, the teacher will enhance the likelihood of the student benefiting from the lesson and reduce the chance of failure.

**Table 9.4**

Two-Column Matrix Showing Redesign Based on Font Size
and Answer Location in the Text

| Planned Teacher Questions (standard) | Planned Teacher Questions (adapted) |
|---|---|
| 1. Who discovered the New World? | 1. Who discovered the New World? (p. 1) |
| 2. How many ships did Columbus use when he set sail from Spain? | 2. How many ships did Columbus use when he set sail from Spain? (p. 2) |
| 3. Why did Columbus's sailors threaten mutiny? | 3. Why did Columbus's sailors threaten mutiny? (pp. 13–15) |

## Media and Technology

In the broadest sense, educational media includes any supplemental device, instrument, or instructional aid that the teacher uses to enhance the learning process. Heward (1994) separates media and technology into two distinct categories: high-tech and low-tech applications. High-tech applications include personal, desktop, or laptop computers, interactive video, and Web-based or Internet programs. Low-tech applications usually include overhead projectors, tape recorders, language masters, CD players, and so forth. The distinction between high- and low-tech devices is that low-tech devices are readily available, inexpensive, and require little set-up time or effort from the teacher (Heward, 1994). Consultants jointly planning a lesson with a general education teacher can show that teacher how to embed or extend a lesson by the appropriate integration of media and technology. Conversely, a key point that the consultant could communicate can be summarized in the phrase: "Just because you can, doesn't mean you should." In this context, the phrase is applicable where a general education teacher may wish to plan an expensive interactive video program to teach sight-word vocabulary, while the experienced consultant might suggest that a peer- or cross-age tutoring program could accomplish the same objective with far less cost and include a social benefit as well.

See Chapter 11 for more discussion of media applications across K–12 levels.

## Rules

Virtually every elementary classroom has rules that prescribe expectations and consequences for behavior. Rules, of course, can be generated by an administrator, teachers, students, or some combination. Our point in incorporating a "rules" section within a preteaching–environment component is to underscore the view that the consultant and the teacher must reach consensus on how rules will be formed; communicated to the students, especially students with disabilities; enforced; and reinforced. Rules that are defined haphazardly, articulated poorly, and enforced inconsistently are not likely to engender a positive classroom atmosphere. Furthermore, if rules are not clarified during preteaching, the chances for confrontation, rule breaking, and a chaotic classroom increase markedly.

For a complete discussion on establishing rules and procedures of conduct, the reader is referred to Cangelosi (1993).

# Preteaching: Instructional Adaptations

Individualized instruction can be provided when the modes of presentation and expected student response are anticipated. For instance, suppose that a teacher in an elementary school class plans to introduce a geography unit on the Nile Valley. He or she might design tasks so that some students in the class are required to provide oral responses to questions while others are directed to demonstrate or point when making a response.

Also, the teacher should plan the level of supplementary prompts or cues that might be needed during instruction if the critical initial prompt or cue does not produce an appropriate response. For instance, if the critical prompt is "Joan, what is the capital of Ohio?" the teacher, during this preteaching phase, should have prepared possible supplemental questions such as "Joan, let me try again. Is the capital of Ohio: Harrisburg, Phoenix, or Columbus?" Likewise, if a comparative question was the critical question: "Christine, how might Columbus's voyage to the New World be similar to a modern-day astronaut's voyage?" the planned supplemental question might be "Christine, compare how you felt when you went to summer camp not knowing what might happen, with what you think Columbus's sailors felt on their adventure?" The point is that the teacher anticipates possible changes in the mode of presentation or the mode of response so as to ensure successful student participation.

# Preteaching: Reinforcement Adaptations

See Chapter 12 for a complete discussion of how to select and implement appropriate behavior management strategies to increase, decrease, maintain, and generalize behavior.

Consultants are generally aware of the power that reinforcement has to increase the probability of behavior. During the preteaching planning phase, the consultant can assist the general education teacher with deciding under what conditions (group or individual) and on what schedule (continuous or intermittent) reinforcement is to be delivered.

## Individual Contingency

Actually, it is a "response class" of behaviors that is being reinforced, not the just performed behavior. See Chapter 12 and Cooper et al. (1987) for more details on this point.

An *individual contingency* can be defined as the relationship between a single student's behavior, an event presented subsequent to that behavior, and the future probability of that behavior. Individual contingencies are the hallmark of applied behavior analysis and special education insofar as the behavior of the individual determines the consequences that are delivered (Cooper et al., 1987). Consultants should impress upon the teacher that the target behavior to be changed, the criterion for success, and the reinforcer(s) should be included in the overall lesson plan.

## Group Contingency

See Chapter 12 for more details on how to arrange a group contingency.

A *group contingency* can be defined as the relationship between a single student's or multiple students' behavior, an event presented subsequent to that behavior, and the future probability of that behavior. During preteaching, the consultant and the teacher should determine which of the three primary ways of arranging a group-oriented contingency might apply. Such contingencies can be arranged on a dependent, independent, or interdependent basis.

| Student's Name | Daily Assignments Completed (Best Possible/Day = 6) | | | | | Weekly Total | Weekly Average | Best Score | Best Ever Score |
|---|---|---|---|---|---|---|---|---|---|
| | M | T | W | R | F | | | | |
| Marge | 6 | 6 | 6 | 6 | 6 | 30 | 6 | 6 | 6 |
| Kathy | 5 | 6 | 6 | 6 | 6 | 29 | 6 | 6 | 6 |
| Christine | 6 | 5 | 6 | 6 | 6 | 29 | 6 | 6 | 6 |
| Bill | 4 | 5 | 5 | 6 | 6 | 26 | 5.2 | 6 | 6 |
| John | 4 | 5 | 5 | 6 | 6 | 26 | 5.2 | 6 | 6 |
| Theresa | 2 | 3 | 2 | 1 | 3 | 11 | 2.2 | 3 | 4 |
| Denise | 3 | 2 | 1 | 3 | 2 | 11 | 2.2 | 3 | 4 |

**Figure 9.1.** Feedback chart showing the number of daily assignments completed as well as weekly total, weekly average, best score, and best ever score by each student.

Finally, although not a reinforcement principle or procedure per se, the use of feedback for student performance can be an appropriate method for improving behavior. At this stage, planning how feedback is to occur and the format for the feedback should be considered. Figure 9.1 shows a feedback chart that provides information about the daily assignment completion of an entire class. The chart shows the number of daily assignments completed as well as the weekly total, weekly average, best score, and best ever score for each student. Within this framework, the teacher can provide feedback for the total class, a group within the class (e.g., those with 5 or more assignments completed), or provide individual contingencies to select students (e.g., Theresa and Denise), depending upon other management issues occurring at the time.

Readers are referred to Van Houten (1980) for additional information on feedback systems.

## Continuous Versus Intermittent Schedules

During the acquisition phase of learning, it is desirable to use continuous schedules of reinforcement initially. That is, to "catch the students being good" every time. Failure to follow this basic procedure will likely place students' behavior on "extinction," thereby reducing its future likelihood. Once behaviors have become more firmly established, the teacher can move to an intermittent schedule in which some, but not all, behaviors are reinforced.

# Teaching: Environmental Adaptations

General education teachers may need additional technical assistance when conducting a lesson, especially in a heterogeneous, multicultural classroom. Assistance might be rendered with seating arrangements, creating a rich learning environment, and establishing multiple group configurations.

## Seating Arrangements

The physical size, configuration, and arrangement of seats within a classroom may be an important factor in learning new behaviors. This may be especially true for students with low achievement or disabilities. Low achievers, for example, may improve academically as their seats are moved from the back of the room toward the front. As a rule, the closer students with learning problems are to the teacher and to the stimuli to which they have to attend, the better their performance becomes (Wood, 1998).

If teachers are interested in increasing the verbal behavior of students with disabilities during "show and tell" or classroom discussion times, consultants might suggest that students with high verbal ability sit across the table from those with low verbal skills. In this configuration, the low-verbal student may pick up gestural, facial, and verbal messages more readily from the high-verbal student, thereby increasing the likelihood of a reciprocal oral response.

## Creating a Rich Learning Environment

Wall and Dattilo (1995) suggest that creating rich learning environments facilitates the self-determination of individuals, especially within multicultural settings. A rich learning environment means that the classroom is attractive, and that supplies, books, and educational support materials are readily available. Further, the teacher presents lessons with enthusiasm, and students participate in the process. As Wall and Dattilo state:

> Modifications can . . . be made in the physical and social environments to enhance growth in interdependence and self-determination within the appropriate cultural context. . . . As participants obtain ownership in the design of their program they can become more thoughtful participants in their own education. (p. 284)

## Establishing Multiple Group Configurations

Teachers, especially teachers in inclusive classrooms, must be able to establish and manage multiple groups simultaneously. Setting up the classroom to facilitate teacher-directed instructional lessons, independent work, and/or student-directed cooperative learning teams or tutoring dyads must be considered as an important environmental task. Attending to details such as the length of time each group will work before rotating to another group, the composition of group members, and the mechanics of how students can receive assistance if they become stalled are further considerations that should be addressed at this stage.

# Teaching: Instructional and Management Adaptations

## Correcting Student Errors

Of all a teacher's behaviors during an instructional lesson, how he or she handles a student's errors ranks as one of the more important. If a student error is not managed appropriately, the student may be embarrassed or humiliated and become frustrated or confrontational. In any case, the result is usually a deterioration of future performance. Heward (2000) provides three guidelines that teachers can implement to reduce the likelihood that errors will produce counterproductive consequences: reduce opportunities for students to practice errors, provide effective and efficient error correction, and evaluate the effects of error correction strategies.

## Reduce the Chances of Students Practicing Errors

Classrooms are busy environments, and teachers cannot reasonably be expected to catch every instance of students' mistakes. However, teachers should be aware that during the acquisition phases of learning—when students are being exposed to a skill for the first time—the chances for errors are higher than they are during a practice or proficiency stage of learning. Consequently, teachers should execute more personal, peer (Miller, Barbetta, Drevno, Martz, & Heron, 1996), self-checking, and self-correction checks (McGuffin, Martz, & Heron, 1997; Okyere, Heron, & Goddard, 1997) so that errors are not practiced.

> When students who are acquiring a second language make errors, teachers are encouraged to model the appropriate language forms. For more information related to second-language and multicultural issues, see Chapter 7.

## Provide Effective and Efficient Error Correction

Several experimental studies have examined how error correction affects future student performance. When errors are corrected immediately (within seconds or minutes of the error), briefly (with as few words, models, or guides, as necessary), and directly (focusing on the target behavior) and allow an active correct response before proceeding to the next step, performance improves (Barbetta, Heron, & Heward, 1993; Barbetta, Heward, & Bradley, 1993; Barbetta, Heward, Bradley, & Miller, 1994; Heron, Heward, Cooke, & Hill, 1983).

## Evaluate the Effects of Error Correction Techniques

Consultants can assist teachers by assessing the relative effectiveness of various types of error correction procedures on a student's performance. Working jointly, they can decide to examine questions that further explore the timing, nature, and quality of error correction procedures, with student performance being the key marker for choosing or abandoning any error correction procedure.

# Changing Presentation and Response Modes

Despite the best planning possible, teachers will ask students questions during an instructional lesson that produce blank stares, no response, withdrawal behavior, and a host of other undesirable outcomes. In such situations, teachers will have to recast their questions if the student is to have a chance to make an appropriate response. Anecdote 9.2 illustrates how a planned geography lesson actually unfolded, with the teacher alertly making changes in the method of presentation and the expected mode of response.

### Anecdote 9.2

| | |
|---|---|
| TEACHER: | (calling on April) April, why is the Nile River important to the economy and well-being of Egypt? |
| APRIL: | The river is important because it provides water for irrigation and transportation for people up and down the valley. |
| TEACHER: | Yes. Since much of Egypt is arid, the Nile provides the necessary water to raise crops and livestock. Very good. |
| TEACHER: | (calling on Joan, who is an at-risk student in the class) Joan, by the way, what is the capital of Egypt? |
| JOAN: | (surprised by her name being called): Uh, I don't know. I forgot. |

| | |
|---|---|
| TEACHER: | (wishing to continue with Joan to boost her self-confidence and participation) Joan, let me ask it this way: Is the capital of Egypt Moscow, Belgrade, or Cairo? |
| JOAN: | (sitting just a bit taller in her seat) I think it's Cairo. |
| TEACHER: | I think you are correct. Good job of sticking with the questions. |
| TEACHER: | (calling on Richard, a student with cerebral palsy) Richard, please turn on the overhead projector. You'll notice that an outline map of Egypt and a grease pencil are on the overhead. Richard, please do the following: first, draw a line where the Nile is located; second, shade the area around the Nile that was once known as the flood plain; and last, put an X where the series of dams were constructed along the river to prevent flooding and provide hydro-electric power. |
| RICHARD | takes the grease pencil in his hand and performs the tasks. |
| TEACHER: | Excellent! Class, notice that Richard has shaded a large area of the river valley. Prior to dam construction projects, this shaded area represented the land that was flooded annually by the Nile. (Teacher continues with the rest of the lesson.) |

The teacher in this anecdote attended to the individual needs of two students with disabilities in a large-group setting. She knew the content she wanted to teach, and she changed the expected mode of student response when necessary given a student's initial response. Joan may have been caught off guard by the teacher's question, or she may not have known the content at the level of recall. In changing the mode of her response to a recognition level, the teacher provided a successful opportunity for Joan to participate. While April and Joan had to supply answers orally, Richard's participation in the same activity was tailored to promote success using a drawing mode. He did not say a word, yet he performed exactly what was required. The teacher's verbal praise not only reinforced all three students' performances, but also announced their success publicly to the class. Especially for elementary students, public recognition for acceptable performance can be a definite boost to confidence and can enhance performance.

An effective way to individualize instruction is to vary the type and level of questions asked, essentially varying the level of presentation. For instance, Table 9.5 provides suggestions for questioning techniques. Technique number 3, "Adapt questions to student ability level," is a necessary strategy for heterogeneous groups of students. For some students, teachers can use simple language and concrete terminology and require a yes or no response. For other students, requiring a verbal description as a response may be more appropriate. The key principle is to adapt questions to the student's receptive and expressive skills.

## Managing Behavior

Managing behavior while teaching is an extremely labor-intensive and difficult task. The more management issues can be resolved before instruction begins, the more likely instruction is to be successful. Typically, however, in inclusive classrooms where students of varying ability levels and cultural backgrounds reside, it is hardly possible to address all of those issues beforehand. Two key issues pertain to managing noncompliance and dealing with confrontational situations.

Abrams and Segal (1998) and Meece (1997) provide suggestions on being a positive therapeutic teacher and for establishing and maintaining a positive classroom climate. Also, Carpenter and McKee-Higgins (1996) provide recommendations for improving classroom atmosphere.

Readers are referred to Chapter 12 for more in-depth treatment of management issues.

## Table 9.5

### Questioning Techniques

1. *Plan key questions to provide lesson structure and direction.* Write them into lesson plans, at least one for each objective—especially higher-level questions. Ask some spontaneous questions based on student responses.

2. *Phrase questions clearly and specifically.* Avoid vague or ambiguous questions such as "What did we learn yesterday?" or "What about the heroine of the story?" Ask single questions: avoid run-on questions that lead to student frustration and confusion. Clarity increases probability of accurate responses.

3. *Adapt questions to student ability level.* This enhances understanding and reduces anxiety. For heterogeneous classes, phrase questions in natural, simple language, adjusting vocabulary and sentence structure to students' language and conceptual levels.

4. *Ask questions logically and sequentially.* Avoid random questions lacking clear focus and intent. Consider students' intellectual ability, prior understanding of content, topic, and lesson objective(s). Asking questions in a planned sequence will enhance student thinking and learning.

5. *Ask questions at a variety of levels.* Use knowledge-level questions to determine basic understandings and to serve as a basis for higher-level thinking. Higher-lever questions provide students with opportunities to practice higher forms of thought.

6. *Follow-up student responses.* Develop a response repertoire that encourages students to clarify initial responses, lift thought to higher levels, and support a point of view or opinion. For example, "Can you restate that?" "Could you clarify that further?" "What are some alternatives?" "How can you defend your position?" Encourage students to clarify, expand, and support initial responses to higher-level questions.

7. *Give students time to think when responding.* Increase wait time after asking a question to 3 to 5 seconds to increase number and length of student responses and to encourage higher-level thinking. Insisting upon instantaneous responses significantly decreases probability of meaningful interaction with and among students. Allow sufficient wait time before repeating or rephrasing questions to ensure student understanding.

8. *Use questions that encourage wide student participation.* Distribute questions to involve the majority of students in learning activities. For example, call on nonvolunteers, using discretion for difficulty level of questions. Be alert for reticent students' verbal and nonverbal cues such as perplexed look or partially raised hand. Encourage student-to-student interaction. Use circular or semicircular seating to create an environment conducive to increased student involvement.

9. *Encourage student questions.* This encourages active participation. Student questions, at higher cognitive levels, stimulate higher levels of thought essential for the inquiry approach. Give students opportunities to formulate questions and carry out follow-up investigations of interest. Facilitate group and independent inquiry with a supportive social-emotional climate, using praise and encouragement, accepting and applying student ideas, responding to student feelings, and actively promoting student involvement in all phases of learning.

*Note.* From *Questioning Skills, for Teachers* (2nd ed., p. 10), by W. W. Willen, 1987, Washington, DC: National Education Association. Copyright 1987 by the National Education Association. Reprinted with permission.

## Managing Noncompliance

Noncompliance can appear in any of four guises: passive noncompliance, refusal, direct defiance, and negotiated statements (Walker & Sylwester, 1998). Consultants can assist the general education teacher with recognizing each of these facets and providing appropriate responses to them. Briefly, a student who exhibits passive noncompliance is not likely to become aggressive, whereas a student who is directly defiant may become aggressive. A strategy that might work in the first situation may be totally inappropriate in the second. Walker and Sylwester (1998) make the point, however, that teachers cannot merely look to students as the "cause" of the problem. They state: "If student resistance or refusal is a persistent problem in your classroom, seriously examine what *you* might be doing, if anything, to aggravate the problem" (p. 56, emphasis added).

### Defusing Potential Confrontations

The specter of having to deal with a classroom confrontation haunts virtually every general and special education teacher. Explosive situations do arise in classrooms, and teachers must be prepared to deal with them. Colvin, Ainge, and Nelson (1997) provide the teacher with ways to adapt instruction during teaching that can help defuse confrontations. For example, suppose that Joe is frequently out of his seat and the teacher is about to lower the boom on him by saying: "Joe, get back to your seat, now!" Instead, the teacher might adapt this action by (a) using proximity control—getting closer to Joe; (b) verbally reinforcing students who are in their seats; (c) redirecting Joe privately with a two-part directive ("Joe, it's time to sit. Please do so now." And, if followed by more noncompliance, "Joe, you've been asked to sit. Decide to sit now please, or risk losing your recess."); and (d) ultimately placing Joe in a brief time-out. In any case, where potential confrontation is likely, teachers should be reminded to think in terms of prevention, defusion (reducing the degree of escalation), and follow-up (reinforcing the student when compliance is noted) (Colvin et al., 1997; Gilliam, 1993).

## Teaching: Reinforcement Adaptations

As Kameenui and Darch (1995) indicate, "When teachers are primarily positive in their interactions with students, the stage is set for increased academic achievement and improved student conduct. Teachers who fail to use reinforcement as part of their instructional routine or those who rely substantially on punishment to control the behavior of students will in the end create disruptive, underachieving, and resentful students" (p. 104). Four techniques can be applied to increase the likelihood that reinforcement will prevail over punishment: proactive feedback, recruiting teacher praise and attention, shifting schedules of reinforcement, and charting performance.

## Proactive Feedback

By providing *proactive feedback*—that is, cues during the actual lesson—teachers can learn to shift their praise ratio in the direction that is more likely to build positive student repertoires. For example, Van Houten and Sullivan (1975) showed that providing a brief, auditory "beep" over the classroom's public address (PA) system served as an effective reminder to teachers to praise students in the class, even when self-recording of praise statements had failed to demonstrate an improvement. When auditory cueing using the PA procedure was in effect, teacher praise statements increased; when it was not in effect, teacher praise statements fell. As Van Houten and Sullivan state, "In the absence of cues, teachers may become so busy with other activities that they forget to praise" (p. 200).

## Recruiting Teacher Praise and Attention

Another proactive and innovative way to improve the ratio of praise statements or attention is to teach the students themselves to *recruit* praise and attention from the teacher. Alber and Heward (1997) and Craft, Alber, and Heward (1998), for example, demonstrated the effectiveness of this technique. Essentially, students were taught a series of recruitment behaviors such as: when to recruit (as substantial work is completed); how to recruit (hand raising or some other signal); how often to recruit (enough to maintain performance but not so much as to be a pest); what to say while recruiting ("How am I doing?"); and how to respond ("Thanks for stopping by my desk to check my work."). In a teacher-recruitment scenario, students use a method that is consistent with a well-structured and efficient classroom to further increase their chances of responding correctly and being noticed by the teacher in a positive way.

## Shifting Schedules of Reinforcement

An important consideration for general education teachers is to recognize when to shift from a continuous schedule of reinforcement to an intermittent schedule. When to shift should be determined by examining student performance. As students begin to acquire skills, the timing or ratio of reinforcers can be thinned (Cooper et al., 1987). Practitioners should realize that when shifting from a continuous to an intermittent schedule, the art and science of teaching intersect. That is, move too fast, and learner performance will deteriorate; move too slowly, and progress will be stilted. To determine how best and when to shift, consultants should reiterate the importance of keeping daily or weekly records of student performance and monitoring the outcomes of reinforcement schedule changes.

## Charting Performance

According to Cooper (2000), precision teachers are guided by four main principles: counting student responses when teaching, displaying response performance, using a frequency (rate) measure to record student performance, and recognizing that the learner knows best. Using direct and daily measures during instruction helps to ensure formative evaluation, which means that midcourse corrections can be made rapidly. Probes of student performance, taken daily, can provide teachers with sufficient data on which to make sound instructional decisions (Cooper et al., 1987).

# Postteaching Adaptations

Three postteaching adaptations are relevant for consultants and teachers to explore: homework, testing, and grading.

## Homework

General education teachers assign homework to students with increasing regularity. Ratnesar (1999), citing a University of Michigan study, reported data showing that the number of minutes of homework for younger children had

For a discussion of the policies, advantages and disadvantages, and recommendations on homework, see Black (1996); Patton (1994); Roderique, Polloway, Cumblad, Epstein, and Bursuck (1994).

increased from 44 minutes per day in 1981 to 120 minutes in 1997; for older students the increase went from 2 hours, 49 minutes, to almost 3.5 hours daily. Homework is typically assigned to provide additional practice with concepts, assist with the synthesis and refinement of skills, provide practice toward fluency, and help students develop personal responsibility (Corno, 1996). While it is beyond the scope of this chapter to address all the arguments for and against regular homework, suffice it to say that general education teachers assign homework, and consultants can provide technical assistance with designing, implementing, and evaluating homework practices. Given that consultants and general education teachers might collaborate on homework practices, the guidelines provided in Table 9.6 might warrant consideration.

## Testing

See Bursuck, Polloway, Plante, Epstein, Jayanthi, and McConeghy (1996) and Jayanthi, Epstein, Polloway, and Bursuck (1996) for results of national surveys on report card grading, adaptation practices, and testing accommodations.

General education teachers are legitimately concerned about how to assess the learning outcomes of their students, including students with disabilities. Typically, general education teachers use daily, weekly, or mastery test scores to determine end-of-semester grades. However, a frequent concern expressed by general education teachers is how and under what conditions students with disabilities will be tested (Bursuck et al., 1996). That is, what accommodations or adaptations will be necessary to measure a student's performance, and what does one student's performance mean in relationship to other students under nonadapted conditions?

At the elementary level, three types of test modifications are typically exercised: personnel, time, and presentation-response accommodations.

### Personnel Accommodations

In this arrangement, the student takes the test with another teacher (e.g., the resource room teacher). Hence, while the general education teacher gives the weekly spelling test to the rest of the class, in this variation the resource room teacher might dictate the test to the student with special needs. By prior arrangement and with consultation from the general education teacher, the resource room teacher might provide explanations or clarifications for some test items, but without sacrificing the integrity of the test. Scoring and other grading procedures (applications of a rubric), however, remain identical.

### Time Accommodations

In this test variation, the student is allowed extra time or more frequent breaks during the test (Thurlow, Ysseldyke, & Silverstein, 1995). For instance, if the general education students have 30 minutes to take a social studies quiz or test, the student with special needs may have 45 to 60 minutes. This accommodation is often coupled with an accommodation of location. That is, the student may take the test in a quiet corner of the library or during the teacher's preparation time in a different classroom. However, this accommodation should be considered carefully, as it may be perceived by the students in a stigmatizing way (Jayanthi et al., 1996).

### Presentation-Response Accommodations

Presentation-response accommodations occur when the manner in which the test item is presented or the manner in which the response is made changes. For

## Table 9.6
### Homework Guidelines

1. Ensure that the students have the prerequisite skills to complete the homework. It will do little good for students to take work home and not have the skills to complete it. In short, assign homework well within the students' instructional repertoire (Epstein, Polloway, Foley, & Patton, 1993).

2. Be reasonable with respect to the amount of homework assigned. Consider the developmental age, cognitive skills, and endurance of the student. While it can be a difficult task to *a priori* know how long an assignment may take, it would be helpful to have parents keep a record of the duration of homework so that future adjustments can be made based on those data (Salend & Gajria, 1995).

3. Assign homework early in the instructional period to maximize the student's ability to copy it and ask questions about it. Also, providing an early assignment allows time to practice homework examples while the teacher can still supervise (Epstein et al., 1993).

4. Provide a backup mechanism so that parents can get a heads-up on at least the general areas. Establishing functional home-school communication programs can be one step in this direction (Jayanthi, Nelson, Sawyer, Bursuck, & Epstein, 1995; Weiss, Cooke, Grossman, Ryno-Vrabel, Hassett, Heward, & Heron, 1983).

5. Provide extra assistance with homework where appropriate. Assigning a buddy or peer to help record the homework, seeing that it gets in the book bag for going home, and allowing alternative response modes may help (Polloway et al., 1994; Salend & Gajria, 1995).

6. Use homework logs to record work (Epstein et al., 1993; Shields & Heron, 1989; Stormont-Spurgin, 1997). Shields and Heron (1989), for example, indicate that homework logs allow parents to have more direct input into their child's behavior. By initialing completed homework, parents verify that they have proctored the homework assignment. Teacher initials show that the homework has been submitted (see Figure 9.2). Communication between parent and teacher is essential (Jayanthi et al., 1995; Salend & Gajria, 1995).

7. Establish a routine and ritual for homework assignments, submission, and recording (Epstein et al., 1993; Patton, 1994; Stormont-Spurgin, 1997). Integrate self-scoring and self-monitoring into the process.

   See Chapter 12 for additional details on how to establish self-monitoring programs.

8. Consider a weekly homework report card (see Figure 9.3). This card is affixed to a U.S. postcard and mailed to parents on Friday each week so that they can have up-to-date information on homework that was or was not submitted. A homework report card can help to keep parents apprised of their child's progress on a week-by-week basis.

9. Use negative reinforcement procedures occasionally (Cooper et al., 1987). That is, remove a homework assignment, contingent on improved performance. When a student completes 90% of homework assignments during the week, a future homework assignment is removed.

10. Provide positive reinforcement for homework completion. In short, if you're going to assign it, reinforce it (Patton, 1994; Shields & Heron, 1989).

instance, the student may be presented with a large-print test to which he or she can make an oral response. Likewise, a test item may be signed through an interpreter and a signed or demonstration response provided (Thurlow et al., 1995).

An essay titled "Why Johnny Can't Fail" (Jesness, 1999) reminds us that misplaced sentimentality or a floating standard of acceptability can creep into our analysis of student performance. Substantial drifts can occur so that student performance, no matter how poor, is judged to be higher than it merits. The author warns that floating standards may be politically motivated (administrators hear fewer parent complaints when students receive passing, albeit

| Subject Assignment | Today's Date | Date Due | Parent Initials | Teacher Initials | Date Submitted |
|---|---|---|---|---|---|
| Reading: Answer questions 1–4 (p. 20) | 4/23 | 4/24 | MH | HRH | 4/24 ☺ |
| Math: Complete problems on p. 37 | 4/23 | 4/24 | MH | HRH | 4/24 ☺ |
| Social Studies: Draw a map showing the main rivers of Ohio | 4/23 | 4/25 | (pending) | (pending) | (pending) |

**Figure 9.2.** Homework log issued on April 23 and checked on April 24.

Date: _____    Teacher: _____

_____' overall work this week has:

improved, stayed the same, deteriorated

(circle one)

The circled item represents the number of missing homework assignments this week:

0,  1,  2,  3,  4,  5+

(circle one)

**Figure 9.3.** Sample preprinted postcard. To be copied and pasted on multiple U.S. postcards.

undeserved, grades) or considered cost effective (schools do not have to run summer and/or remedial programs or do warranty work). His indictment of testing—perhaps shared by many in the educational community and expressed most clearly below—must be addressed by consultants at some point:

> If the students will not or cannot read the play, read it to them. If they will not sit still long enough to hear the whole play, consider an abridged or comic-book version, or let them watch the movie. If they cannot pass a multiple-choice test, try a true-or-false or a fill-in-the-blank test that mirrors the previous day's study sheet. If they still have not passed, allow them to do an art project. . . . If all else fails, try group projects. That way you can give passing grades to all the students, even if only one in five produces anything. . . . Keep dropping the standard, and sooner or later everyone will meet it. If anyone asks, you taught *Hamlet* in a nonconventional way, one that took into account your students' individual differences and needs. (pp. 23–24)

While Jesness's position may echo the frustration of many teachers, it misses a fundamental mark in how tests for students with disabilities should be adapted. As Thurlow et al. (1995) remind us, the Standards for Educational and Psychological Testing adopted by the American Psychological Association (1985) make it clear that just not *any* accommodation or change in a test is acceptable:

> When a test user makes a substantial change in test format, mode or administration, instructions, language, or content, the user should revalidate the

use of the test for the changed conditions or have a rationale supporting the claims that additional validation is not necessary or possible. (cited in Thurlow et al., 1995, p. 262)

In short, it becomes the general education teacher's and the consultant's responsibility, working collaboratively, to ensure that test standards are met, even when accommodations are made as to personnel, timing, or presentation-response modes. Ease of implementation must be balanced against measuring the target behavior, as well as teacher, student, and parent perceptions of the usefulness and fairness of the adapted strategy (Bursuck, Munk, & Olson, 1999; Jayanthi et al., 1995).

See Wood (1998) and Christiansen and Vogel (1998) for suggested procedures for testing and grading students with disabilities.

## Grading

Assigning grades based on student performance can be accomplished using product, process, and progress measures (Bradley & Calvin, 1998). For example, scores on weekly test items might yield a percentage-correct ratio that, in turn, could be converted to either a numerical coefficient or a letter grade (product). A process grade might be assessed based on how the student went about solving a problem. Finally, a progress grade might be awarded based on the student's performance relative to past performance (Bradley & Calvin, 1998).

Likewise, other forms of evaluation have been advanced as a way to broaden the range of options for measuring student performance. Portfolio assessment, proficiency tests, skill demonstrations, and the like have emerged as possible methods for determining student skill acquisition and maintenance. Whereas general education teachers prefer numerical or letter grades for students without disabilities, they also find it helpful to use multiple measures (portfolios, pass-fail arrangements, effort grading) for students with and without disabilities (Bursuck et al., 1996).

For a description of how to use portfolios to develop independent thinking, the reader is referred to Duffy, Jones, and Thomas (1999). For a discussion of how to establish the reliability and validity of portfolios and how to include students in the process, refer to Carpenter, Ray, and Bloom (1995); Salend (1998); Swicegood (1994).

According to Bursuck et al. (1996), the five methods that general education teachers find most helpful when grading work for students with disabilities are: (a) considering the amount of improvement the student makes, (b) deciding if IEP objectives are met, (c) separating grades based on process (effort) versus grades based on product (skill acquisition), (d) using weighted grades for projects, and (e) using adjusted grades based on ability. Consultants should be aware that teachers will need to have technical assistance with deciding which options should be exercised for grading, developing "adapted" tests, and using homework, projects, and other assignments appropriately in the grading process (Bursuck et al., 1996; Cooper & Nye, 1994). In the end, however, the relative effects of adapted grading systems on students with disabilities is still an empirical question. Bursuck et al. (1996) conclude: "Nonetheless, the impact that the various types of grades and grading systems have on students with disabilities is largely unknown" (p. 316).

For a discussion of how students perceive grade adaptations, see Bursuck, et al. (1999). While the students in that study were secondary level, possible parallel implications for elementary students may be drawn.

## Conclusion

An elementary teacher who has students with disabilities in the classroom must be able to attend to the individual needs of the students. In large part, the success of any child's program will be determined by the teacher's ability to adapt instructional techniques across preteaching, teaching, and postteaching, considering environmental, instructional, and reinforcement factors. The strategies discussed in this chapter address each of these important areas.

# Summary of Key Points

## Adapted Instruction

1. Adapted instruction is an instructional approach that accommodates the unique learning needs of individual students within every classroom.

2. To design and implement an adaptive instruction program, educators should be familiar with a wide array of instructional modifications, notably, flexible scheduling, individual diagnosis and prescription, mastery learning, large- and small-group instruction, individual tutorials, and cooperative learning.

3. Consultants can collaborate with teachers to develop modifications across environmental, instructional, and reinforcement areas within the contexts of three critical phases of instruction: preteaching, teaching, and post-teaching.

## Preteaching: Environmental Adaptations

4. Six common preteaching environmental areas where adaptations can make a difference are: lesson plans, scheduling, group considerations, materials, media and technology, and rules.

## Preteaching: Instructional Adaptations

5. Teachers and consultants can plan instructional adaptations at the preteaching level by anticipating teacher mode(s) of presentation and student expected mode(s) of response.

## Preteaching: Reinforcement Adaptations

6. The consultant can assist the general education teacher with deciding under what conditions (group or individual) and with what schedule (continuous or intermittent) reinforcement is to be delivered.

## Teaching: Environmental Adaptations

7. Environmental adaptations at the teaching level might include changing seating arrangements, creating a rich learning environment, and teaching and monitoring multiple groups simultaneously.

## Teaching: Instructional and Management Adaptations

8. Correcting student errors, changing presentation and response modes, and managing student behavior are techniques that teachers and consultants might consider.

## Teaching: Reinforcement Adaptations

9. Several techniques can be used to adapt reinforcement: providing proactive feedback, recruiting teacher praise and attention, shifting the schedule of reinforcement, and charting performance.

## Postteaching Adaptations

10. Three postteaching adaptations are relevant for consultants and teachers to explore: homework, testing, and grading. Within each area, consultants can collaborate with colleagues to develop adaptations that are appropriate to the student's developmental, cognitive, and skill levels.

# Questions

1. What might a consultant say or do to help allay the fears of an elementary-level teacher who does not believe that she is capable of adapting instruction for students with special needs?

2. Of the six common environmental preteaching areas cited in the text, identify challenges that might need to be overcome by the consultant and the teacher. What tactics might address the challenges?

3. Aside from those mentioned in the text, what are useful ways for the consultant and the teacher to plan for mode of presentation and mode of response changes during the preteaching phase?

4. Under what conditions might a teacher and a consultant decide whether an individual or group, or a continuous or intermittent adaptation should be planned?

5. How might changing a student's seating arrangement, creating a rich learning environment, or managing multiple groups simultaneously be easier or more difficult in an urban, multicultural classroom?

6. State three positive ways to manage student academic errors and non-compliant or confrontational behavior.

7. How might reinforcement or feedback adaptations be included in a teacher's repertoire during the teaching phase?

8. From your own experiences, state arguments for and against the assignment of regular homework.

9. Identify the functional methods that can be used to conduct test and grading accommodations.

10. Determine the possible responses to a general education teacher who believes it is unfair to revise the standards for assigning letter grades to students with disabilities.

## Discussion Points and Exercises

1. Conduct a meeting with the special and general education teachers to determine how existing curricula materials in both classrooms could be adapted to meet the needs of a specific student with disabilities.

2. Conduct a pilot study with a group of elementary education teachers to determine how jointly agreed upon adaptations changed student academic performance.

3. Show a videotape of a teacher instructing a class in social studies, science, or math using the techniques suggested in the text. Obtain audience views from general and special teachers on how the lesson's goals were achieved.

# Effective Instructional Strategies at the Middle and High School Levels

10

Providing appropriate instruction for secondary-level students with disabilities can be a challenging task for general education teachers. Unlike their elementary colleagues, who are responsible for instructing one class of students, teachers at the secondary level are usually responsible for several cohorts of students, many of whom face major life transitions such as moving into the workforce, attending college, or joining the military. Consultants working collaboratively to assist secondary educators who teach students with disabilities need a thorough understanding of the learning environments at this level.

The purpose of this chapter is to examine ways that consultants and secondary professionals, family members, and community members together can provide appropriate and effective instruction for students with learning problems. The chapter provides a framework for educational consultation at the secondary level by identifying and discussing the people in the adolescent's community, the structure of current secondary school programs and home/community programs, and issues regarding individualized programs for youth with disabilities. The discussion focuses on collaborative opportunities for consultants at the secondary level.

## Objectives

After reading this chapter, the reader should be able to:

1. identify and describe the perspectives of people in the adolescent's community;

2. describe the structures of secondary school programs including comprehensive high schools, middle schools, and vocational schools;

3. identify and describe the main components of home/community programs;

4. discuss curricular options for individualized programs for youth with disabilities;

5. identify and describe the key components of transition programs.

## Key Terms

| | |
|---|---|
| transition coordinator | tutorial curriculum |
| schools-within-a-school | locational study skills |
| block scheduling | organizational study skills |
| middle school | functional curriculum |

| | |
|---|---|
| tech-prep programs | transition |
| career pathways | transition services |
| career academies | transition team |
| connecting activities | self-determination skills |
| school-to-work programs | transition assessment |
| remedial curriculum | vocational assessment |
| compensatory techniques | career assessment |
| learning strategies curriculum | |

Consultation at the secondary level involves the facilitation of individualized programs that integrate school, home, and community resources. Although the same process occurs at the elementary level, consultation at the secondary level often involves more people and more complex interactions. Instruction is no longer restricted primarily to one general or one special education teacher who implements the basic curriculum. It involves several content-oriented teachers, curriculum and instructional modifications, varied levels of family and community involvement, and adolescents with disabilities. With IDEA '97, teachers must now work with students to ensure that they have access to and experience success in the general education curriculum. Consulting at this level involves designing and implementing programs collaboratively that accommodate individual learning problems within the general education curriculum, attend to the professional concerns of content-area specialists, meet the expectations of the family, and provide transition services using a realistic curriculum that prepares students for post-secondary demands.

# People in the Adolescent's Community

People in the adolescent's community include the adolescent, secondary professionals, the youth's family, and community members. To establish a basis for consulting with these people, it is helpful to know who they are and understand their perspectives.

## The Adolescent

In societies everywhere, the onset of adolescence is synchronized closely with the biological changes of puberty. Early adolescence extends from approximately age 10 through age 14. Middle adolescence covers ages 15 to 17. Late adolescence stretches from age 18 into the 20s. Young adolescents are barely out of childhood and often need special nurturing and protection; older adolescents share many of the attributes of adults (Carnegie Council on Adolescent Development, 1995).

Readers are referred to the report of the Carnegie Council on Adolescent Development (1995) for an extensive discussion of the educational and health risks of the 10- to 14-year-old population. Readers may cross-reference William Bennett's text *The Index of Leading Cultural Indicators* for additional information.

Adolescents confront many challenges, including alcohol, tobacco, drugs, and sex. Many can be depressed, especially during critical times of adolescence (e.g., important school events, growth spurts, family trauma). About a third of adolescents report that they have contemplated suicide. Others grow up lacking the ability to handle interpersonal conflict without resorting to violence. By age 17, about a quarter of all adolescents have engaged in behaviors that are harmful or dangerous to themselves and/or others (e.g., becoming pregnant, using drugs, committing crimes, and failing in school). Altogether, nearly half of American adolescents are at high or moderate risk of seriously damaging their life chances (Carnegie Council on Adolescent Development, 1995).

Early adolescents are changing rapidly, from the physically smaller stature and more typically docile temperament of earlier childhood to a taller and typically more variable temperament. There are many adjectives used to describe these adolescents (e.g., in-betweeners, pubescents, middlers, emerging adolescents, and early adolescents, among many other descriptors). They are experiencing the transition from childhood to full adolescence during this time. Sweeping generalizations of who they are, how they are, and what they care about should be treated with caution (Stevenson, 1998).

What is normal and predictable during early adolescence is that there are many changes, and, though all adolescents experience these changes, they vary in timing and intensity across individuals (Stevenson, 1998). As discussed by Stevenson, important influential variables in the adolescent's development are home, neighborhood, prevailing gender roles, and racial and ethnic identity. We should also realize that the influences and effects of early adolescence are long lasting.

For a thorough discussion of these variables, readers are referred to Rice (1996).

During adolescence, complex interactions of biology (primary changes) occur with context (settings) and adolescent developmental tasks (secondary changes). Adolescent developmental tasks include changes in attachment (i.e., the transformation of bonds between children and parents to bonds between parents and their adult children) and intimacy (e.g., the transformation of acquaintanceships into friendships).

For a better understanding of adolescent development, readers are referred to Hill (1980).

Like all adolescents, those with disabilities are expected to forge new and mature relationships with peers, develop emotional independence from adults, and accept their sexuality (Havighurst, 1952). There is an expectation that secondary students will be more involved than they were at the elementary level in all aspects of their education. However, a disability often makes the accomplishment of these developmental tasks extremely difficult. For example, young adolescents have a developmental need to socialize with a wide variety of others (National Middle School Association, 1995; Stevenson, 1998). This can be particularly challenging for a student with disabilities who has poor social skills.

A singular alarming fact about students with disabilities in high schools is their dropout rate. Kortering and Braziel (1999) report that youth with disabilities drop out of school at a much higher rate than their nondisabled peers. The National Longitudinal Transition Study of Special Education Students found that dropout rates were high: 30% of students with disabilities dropped out of high school, and another 8% dropped out before entering high school. The average dropout with disabilities was 18 years old at the time of leaving but had earned less than half the credits needed to graduate (Blackorby & Wagner, 1996). Follow-up studies of individuals leaving school report that dropout rates for students with learning disabilities range from 36% to 56% (Adelman & Vogel, 1990; Edgar, 1987; Malcolm, Polatajko, & Simons, 1990). When a student believes that a current program is not meeting his or her needs, a satisfactory alternative must be developed as part of transition planning if the student is to be motivated to remain in school. In essence, if a student is to remain motivated to stay in school, the relevance and feasibility of the school program for attaining that student's long-range transition goals must be evident (Halpern, 1994).

Recent studies of the impact of special education programs for those who graduate are also disappointing, documenting that young adults with disabilities frequently experience significant difficulty making the transition into adult life (Blackorby & Wagner, 1996; Edgar, 1991; Halpern & Benz, 1987; Love & Malian, 1997; Wagner et al., 1991). The results of the National Longitudinal Transition Study of Special Education Students found that employment successes were strongly related to taking a concentration (four courses) in vocational education. Youths with learning disabilities or speech impairments were most likely to approach the rate of employment found in the general population. Postsecondary education rates were low: 37% of high school graduates with disabilities had attended a postsecondary school, compared with 78% of high school graduates generally. Students with hearing or visual impairments were most likely to attend college; course failure and dropping out were most common for students with serious emotional disturbances. There is apparently an increase in the incidence of serious emotional disturbance among older students. It seems that this disability is more likely than any other to surface in adolescence (Wagner & Blackorby, 1996).

## Secondary Professionals

The professionals who work with youth with disabilities in secondary schools can be numerous depending on the needs of the student. For example, in addition to a special educator, students with disabilities may require the services of related-service personnel such as physical or occupational therapists or social workers. Given the need to ensure that students with disabilities have access to the general education curriculum, it is likely that secondary general educators will also be involved in their education.

### High School General Education Teachers

In high school, students usually attend different content-area classes taught by different teachers who have little time for joint planning and coordination. Their primary aim is student mastery of specific content matter. High school teachers are content-area experts. They generally organize their content in a way appropriate for late adolescent students, who are often able to think like adults (Stevenson, 1998).

### Middle School General Education Teachers

For more information on teaming in middle schools, readers are referred to Arnold and Stevenson (1998) and Dickinson and Erb (1997).

Middle school teachers provide instruction to early adolescents, who are going through a variety of developmental changes. As a consequence, teachers must address the developmental needs of these students while teaching them content. A primary structural difference between middle and high schools is the interdisciplinary team organization at the middle school. Middle school teachers who teach different disciplines team together to deliver instruction to a cohort of students. Adults and children come to know each other in these circumstances, and teachers are inclined to understand and accommodate the needs and circumstances of their students (Stevenson, 1998).

### Secondary Special Education Teachers

The teaming and problem-solving skills addressed in Chapters 3 and 4, as well as the strategies discussed in Chapters 5 and 11, are skills that all secondary special educators should develop.

As we have seen, there are many individuals at the secondary level with whom special education teachers work to develop indivudalized programs for students with disabilities. The secondary special education teacher must assure that each student's individualized program addresses the needs of that student, including two major concerns: the student's access to the general education curriculum and the student's transition into adulthood.

Consultants should be aware that it may be necessary to help secondary special educators assume the role of *transition coordinator,* a person who helps a student pass from youth to adult, by providing community-based vocational education experiences, collaborating with vocational educators to interpret assessment data, and developing and implementing transition plans (Asselin, Todd-Allen, & deFur, 1998). We will discuss these responsibilities in this chapter.

For a discussion of the many roles a transition coordinator might assume, readers are referred to Asselin, Todd-Allen, and deFur (1998).

## Family Members

The following discussion reflects the work of Turnbull and Turnbull (1990) and Alper (1994) in tracing the historic roles family members have assumed in the lives of their children with disabilities. When the child's disability is first identified, some family members assume that they are the source of their child's problem. This can be a devastating role for many family members, and the skills discussed in the text (especially those found in Chapter 6) will help consultants work with families in addressing that role. As the child with disabilities grows older, family members may find themselves becoming members of support or advocacy groups. Family members often assume this role when services for the child with disabilities are difficult to obtain. Family members are often in the role of recipient of professional decisions as professionals share their findings and recommendations through the IEP or IFSP process. Family members may also find themselves in the roles of learner and teacher. They may be a learner through professional training they receive and then a teacher as they teach what they learn to their child. Family members are also in the role of decision makers, for example, regarding the IEP or IFSP. Finally, parents, siblings, grandparents, and significant others in the child's life assume the role of family members for the child with disabilities. For example, parents have to help siblings understand the needs of their sister or brother with a disability and work to assimilate those needs into the family system.

Although families of adolescents with disabilities seek to develop independence in their child, sometimes that independence is modified by their child's ongoing need for support and assistance (Hanley-Maxwell, Pogoloff, & Whitney-Thomas, 1998). Students with disabilities often continue to have active involvement with their families after they have moved out of their family home. Many of these students actively acknowledge the need for family as a source of social support as well as a primary source of assistance in planning for their futures (Morningstar, Turnbull, & Turnbull, 1996). Because other family members, such as brothers and sisters, often assume future responsibility for or with the family member with a disability, they should also be included in this process (Brotherson, Backus, Summers, & Turnbull, 1986; McLoughlin & Senn, 1994). Consultants may be able to help family members assume some of the following roles: guide and role model for career selection, helper in planning for the future, mediator with different service systems, teacher of adult support skills, de facto case manager, and primary caregiver (Hanley-Maxwell et al., 1998). According to Hanley-Maxwell, Whitney-Thomas, and Pogoloff (1995, pp. 12–13), families identified the following broad categories of need to help with these roles:

- reliable, accessible, and high-quality services that address all aspects of adult life (e.g., transportation, adult education, recreation, housing, employment);

- physical separation of adult child from family through the provision of home-like residential alternatives;

- support networks for parents, families, and adult children (e.g., respite, friendships, natural supports, parental assistance);

- service systems that respond to family and individual needs and goals in the time frame determined by the family and the adult with a disability (e.g., flexible service, beginning and ending time frames, broadening the definition of transition beyond the employment focus, increasing availability of services, providing nontraditional supports to families, refocusing the end goal to be the happiness and fulfillment of the adult with a disability); and

- multiple and diverse experiences for students prior to leaving high school.

The kind of information consultants should provide to families to help them during this transition include the following:

- role descriptions of IEP committee members (especially parents and students);

- criteria for evaluating the IEP;

- identification of postsecondary options and connection strategies;

- agency access information (including eligibility requirements and contact people);

- social security (including eligibility and access information);

- legal issues of guardianship and estate planning;

- assistive technology information (including legal mandates and resources);

- example forms used for evaluation and planning; and

- list of addresses and phone numbers for local, regional, and state "disability" services (Quadland, Rybacki, Kellogg, & Hall, 1996).

It is apparent that, at the secondary level, consultants may need to assist families in working with a variety of people inside and outside the school system. Consultants must encourage families to become involved in their young adult's education, as the reported passivity of families in the special education process—and this seems to be even greater among families from minority backgrounds (Harry, Allen, & McLaughlin, 1995)—will not serve them well as their children become young adults.

## Community Members

All adolescents, including those with disabilities, deal with members of the community (e.g., customer service staff and employers). We sometimes believe that all the needs of people with disabilities should be addressed within the context of agency programs and services, accompanied by family supports. However, a wide variety of community services exist for the benefit of all people. Consultants should help the adolescent and young adult with disabilities to access those general services, including churches and community recreation facilities that can be found in almost any community (Halpern, 1994).

Consultants must realize that educators alone cannot provide the necessary services to help a student with disabilities make the transition into adulthood. It takes the cooperation of many, including family members, educators, repre-

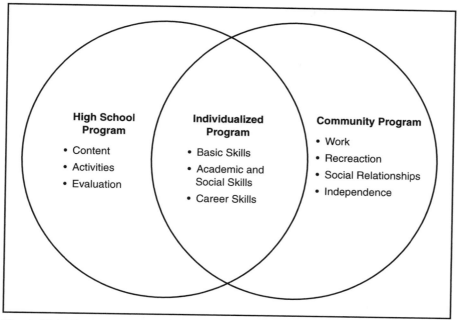

**Figure 10.1.** Environments of adolescents with disabilities.

sentatives from rehabilitation services and social services, employers, tribal and religious leaders, directors of recreation programs, mental health personnel, and community college and university representatives. The consultant can play a valuable role in helping those people to collaborate effectively with one another.

## Programs for All Adolescents

Students function within two general social systems: the school and the home/ community. To provide consulting services effectively within these settings, three factors generally need to be considered: (a) the content of the setting, (b) the activities of the setting, and (c) the evaluation of success in the setting. Figure 10.1 pinpoints the environments to consider when implementing programs for a student with disabilities, as well as the more critical features of those environments. Failure to address all of these environments is likely to result in difficulty in school, at home, or in the community.

## Secondary Schools

Cobb and Neubert (1998) state that very little has changed in the design of high schools. Over the last few decades, vocational schools and vocational high schools have developed, but the comprehensive high school is still the prevalent structure. In his extensive study of U.S. high schools, Boyer (1983) acknowledges that each secondary school is unique in that it is designed to serve a specific population in a given geographic area. However, most comprehensive high schools share many features. Their content reflects a comprehensive curriculum (i.e., academic programs, vocational education programs, and general studies programs). Students usually have access to traditional academic courses (e.g., English, mathematics, science, and social studies), vocational courses (e.g., agriculture, distribution and marketing, health, business and office occupations, industrial arts, trades and industry, and consumer and homemaking), and general courses, often described as personal service and social development (e.g., music) (Boyer, 1983). Courses are generally offered in high schools serving approximately 1,000 students, although much larger populations can be identified, with a faculty of approximately 50 to 60 teachers. Earning a diploma is a major indicator of success for the high school student.

Though the design of high schools has not changed dramatically, two major secondary reforms have dramatically affected how instruction is delivered at the secondary level, i.e., schools-within-a-school and block scheduling. We describe these two movements as they will affect how consultants work with secondary professionals to deliver services to students with disabilities.

Copa and Pease (1992) discuss how comprehensive high schools are dealing with the effect of size. To reduce the complexity of managing the movement of large numbers of students, some high schools are organized as schools-within-a-school. The *schools-within-a-school* concept establishes basic learning subcommunities of approximately 400 students each. As of 1994, this schools-within-a school reform has been realized in at least 15% of American high schools (Lee & Smith, 1994).

Another reform movement that is evident in secondary schools is *block scheduling*. In the traditional high school setting, students attend a six-, seven-, or eight-period school day, with periods lasting approximately 50 minutes each. With block scheduling, these periods are combined into three or four periods per day of approximately 80 to 120 minutes each (Canady & Rettig, 1996; Santos & Rettig, 1999).

There are two commonly used models of block scheduling (Santos & Rettig, 1999). One model is referred to as an A/B-day, alternate-day, odd/even-day, or day1/day2 schedule. In this model, classes meet every other day for 80 to 120 minutes. This plan can be adapted for six, seven, or eight courses. The second most common model is called a 4/4 semester plan or an intensive schedule. This model enables 4-year-long classes to meet for approximately 90 minutes every day for a semester.

Several benefits for students and teachers have been attributed to block scheduling. First, with fewer classes per day to manage, scheduling a speech therapist or special education teacher to support included students may be easier. Second, general education teachers can modify their teaching strategies so as to keep a 85-to-90-minute class, where students with disabilities are included, more interesting. Third, instructional time may increase and distractions decrease when the number of classes to change is reduced. Fourth, there are fewer discipline problems in the hallways between classes (less tardiness, fights, and discipline referrals to the office). Fifth, teachers may focus on trouble spots and difficult concepts for longer periods of time. Sixth, teachers work together for longer periods of time and have more opportunities to collaborate with each other (Inclusive Education Program, 1997).

Accommodations have been made in block scheduling for students with disabilities. For example, special education students can be given one full block for working with their resource room teacher to support their academic coursework. In another example a study skills class for students with special needs immediately follows their English block; conducted by a special education teacher, the class supports what the students learned in the English class (Inclusive Education Program, 1997).

To be successful, teachers must reexamine the curriculum, redefine priorities, pace the class, make effective transitions from one activity to another, and maintain student engagement using a variety of activities (Inclusive Education Program, 1997).

## Middle Schools

One third of all the students in public schools may be referred to as being in the middle level or middle grades (5 to 9). Since the mid-1960s, a gradual but steady reform has been taking place in the design and practice of education for these students (Lounsbury, 1984). However, they attend schools that are organized according to a variety of configurations (e.g., K-6, 7-12, K-8, K-12, 7-9) (Stevenson, 1998).

A *middle school* is organized to include some combination of grades 5 through 9. The junior high school movement of the late 1920s and early 1930s was previously the most focused attempt to create distinctive schooling for the middle grades. However, because there was not a clear understanding of what 10- to 14-year-olds needed, and because the junior high schools were modeled on their senior high counterparts, the junior high school concept did not last. In contrast, the middle school movement has a specialized mission for 10- to 14-years-olds, and it is anticipated that the organization of middle schools will enhance that mission (Stevenson, 1998).

Inclusion of students with special needs is facilitated in middle schools because it is consistent with the need of those schools to embrace diversity (National Middle School Association, 1995; Stevenson, 1998). The kinds and degree of physical, emotional, and academic diversity among students with learning disabilities are often not that different in nature (though they may be different in intensity) from what is found in the mainstream young adolescent population, so it makes sense for an all-inclusive educational context to be the norm (Deering, 1998).

As students with disabilities progress from elementary school to high school, their need for independent living skills and preparation for work increases greatly. Elementary programs provide students with a functional knowledge base in reading, math, and social skills. Middle school students should build on this knowledge and learn a set of strategies and adaptations for living in the real world. Students need to acquire as much independence as possible to be prepared for a high school program rich in vocational and work-related activities (Beakley & Yoder, 1998).

## Vocational Education

According to Cobb and Neubert (1998), current practices in vocational education, largely in response to the Perkins Amendments of 1984 and 1990 and the School to Work Opportunities Act of 1994, include school-based learning, work-based learning, connecting activities, programs and services for students at risk for school failure, and performance standards and measures. In the area of school-based learning, several practices can be found, including: tech-prep, the integration of academic and vocational education, career pathways, and career academies.

*Tech-prep* programs in vocational education provide a way to increase academic and vocational skills development and bridge the gap between secondary

For block scheduling resources on the Internet, see the following: block scheduling at Wasson High School, http://www.class room.net/classweb/myhome .html; block scheduling at the University of Virginia, http://curry.edschool.vir-ginia.edu/~dhv3v/block/ BSintro.html; "Primer: Extended-Period Schedules," University of Minnesota, http:// carei.coled.umn.edu/ bsmain.htm; Ask ERIC InfoGuideon—block scheduling, http://ericir.syr.edu/ Virtual/Infoguides/ Alphabetical List of Infoguides/Block Scheduling-05.97.html; Cooperating School District, Lutheran North, http://info/ csd.org/WWW/Schools/luth eran/Block.html; also see the National Association of Secondary School Principals Web site at: http:// nassp.org/ nahs/ nahs_frm.htm.

For an annotated bibliography of publications concerning the education of young adolescents, see Lawton (1989) and Totten et al. (1996).

and postsecondary training. An example is a student taking a sequence of vocational and academic coursework in high school and at the community college, culminating with an associate degree or a certificate of completion at the community college.

The integration of academic and occupational learning has received increased attention in vocational education and other school-to-work programs as a way to bridge the separation between vocational education, general education, and the workplace. Some methods of integrating academic and vocational education make applied academic course materials available from commercial vendors, provide inservice training for vocational educators and academic teachers, and offer technical assistance for administrators on the topic (Cobb & Neubert, 1998).

For research regarding the effectiveness of career academies, see Linnehan (1996).

*Career pathways* are broad clusters of occupations that revolve around a theme (e.g., health occupations). Many vocational education programs use a career pathway approach. Career academies probably represent the best-researched form of school-based learning (Cobb & Neubert, 1998). Cobb and Neubert (1998) report that *career academies* contain the following components:

- a school within a school, spanning grades 9 to 12, and offering classes that are conducted by a small group of teachers from a variety of disciplines;

- application required for admission to the academy;

- focus on a career theme; and

- a combination of technical and academic content.

Often the academy maintains an option for the student to attend college, and students are employed in jobs related to the career theme.

It is likely that consultants working in secondary situations will also become involved in *connecting activities,* i.e., those activities that link school-based and work-based learning (Cobb & Neubert, 1998). The connecting activities that were perceived to be most effective by Kopp, Kazis, and Churchill (1995) were:

- regular, formal relationships between school and work site personnel;

- opportunities for teachers to learn about modern work settings and for work site personnel to learn about the realities of high school;

- explicit and clearly delineated expectations of the learning that is likely to take place; and

- classroom-based activities that draw upon and reinforce work site learning.

Consultants may also become involved in securing instructional support services for students with disabilities. Support services can vary greatly but include tutors, aides, interpreters, instructional material and curriculum modifications, equipment modifications, and referral assistance to other programs and agencies (Cobb & Neubert, 1998).

## Home/Community Programs

The content of the home/community program usually includes maintenance of family and friend relationships and work. The activities related to this content are usually job related, self-maintenance, and/or recreational. Success in the home/community is usually measured by sustained social relationships, independent functioning, and the acquisition of financial resources.

Benz, Yovanoff, and Doren (1997) report that interest in improving the school-to-work transition process for *all* students has reached critical mass, and states and local communities are engaged actively in building such programs and incorporating them into their larger education reform efforts. *School-to-work programs* are secondary programs that help all adolescents make the transition from school to the workforce by involving their families, educators, and members of the community in planning and implementing programs for them. The inclusion of students with disabilities in these efforts is a priority in the school-to-work movement and the special education community. Local programs should include the following features:

- options for multiple pathways and time frames,
- reasonable accommodations and support services,
- relevant performance indicators, and
- adequate training of and technical assistance for all personnel (Benz, Yovanoff, & Doren, 1997).

Consultants can help professionals in the school-to-work movement to work together to ensure that career exploration and planning provide the necessary foundation and framework for the student's school-based and work-based activities. Educators should take advantage of the emphasis in the school-to-work movement on integrating academic and occupational instruction, teaching that content in contextual settings and holding students accountable for high standards of achievement in those areas. Students with disabilities will need strong academic skills to access the higher-skill, higher-wage jobs being targeted by the school-to-work movement.

With the School to Work Opportunities Act of 1994, it is imperative that schools develop a school-to-work system that will help *all* students make the connection between school and work. So, Charner, Fraser, Hubbard, Rogers, and Horne (1995) suggest that school-based learning provide multiple points of connection between schools and the work setting. They suggest that schools use alternative strategies for teaching and learning that include work-based, computer-assisted, and other innovative approaches. They also strongly emphasize the need for cross-sector collaboration. To accomplish effective collaboration, all stakeholders—schools, businesses, postsecondary institutions, and community partners—must be engaged in an active and ongoing partnership and be willing to reform all aspects of the system. This requires a variety of individuals from different disciplines and organizations to work together to implement effective programs for students. For example, under the Individuals with Disabilities Education Act and the Rehabilitation Act Amendments of 1992, collaboration is needed between schools and vocational rehabilitation agencies to implement school-to-work programs effectively for students.

Benz, Johnson, Mikkelsen, and Lindstrom (1995) cite the following general barriers to collaboration in school-to-work programs. One barrier is the poor or inaccurate perceptions of vocational rehabilitation by school staff, students, and parents and the poor or inaccurate perceptions of secondary schools and students by staff of vocational rehabilitation agencies. A second barrier is nonexistent or ineffective procedures to structure the collaboration of school and vocational rehabilitation staffs throughout the referral, eligibility determination, and transition planning process. These barriers affect the assessment as well as the planning process for students. It is essential that consultants help school staff understand the vocational rehabilitation system and, conversely, that consultants help vocational rehabilitation staff understand the needs of adolescents. Benz et al. (1995) offer several suggestions, many of which would be helpful to consultants who are facilitating the development and implementation of school-to-work programs for students with disabilities. Among these suggestions are the following:

Readers are encouraged to review the discussion of interagency collaboration found in Chapter 3.

- Develop policy and practice guidelines to reduce differences in disability definitions and criteria between agencies.

- Provide materials that will help school staff summarize their knowledge of students in a way that will provide functional information for vocational agency staff.

- Establish one consistent person within the school who is knowledgeable about school and vocational agency practices to serve as a stable resource for students and parents.

Consultants should become familiar with career education and life-skill education models that develop the competencies needed for independent adult functioning. They are referred to Sitlington (1996) for a brief overview of these models and to Cronin and Patton (1993) for a practical curriculum. Consultants may also want to consider the role community service plays in preparing all students for adulthood (cf. Everington & Stevenson, 1994).

In addition to making a transition to the world of work, adolescents with disabilities need assistance making a transition to adult life. Sitlington (1996) argues that young people with disabilities, especially learning disabilities, need help moving into the following adult functions: maintaining a home, becoming appropriately involved in the community (including recreation and leisure activities), and experiencing satisfactory personal and social relationships. To help them accomplish a successful transition to work and postsecondary education as well as other adult functions, it is essential that life-skills training and transition to all aspects of adult life be integrated into general education programs.

## Individualized Programs for Adolescents with Disabilities

Because a litmus test of education is how well one functions in the community, and because so many students with disabilities have difficulty generalizing what they learn in class to the community, the individualized program should incorporate content, activities, and evaluation procedures that address students' needs in both the school and the community. To implement a successful individualized program at the secondary level, collaborators must function as problem solvers and problem preventers. Consultants at the secondary level must be skilled in problem resolution. Even more so, they must understand secondary environments and be able to orchestrate situations to *prevent* problems.

What do programs for adolescents with disabilities look like in secondary public schools? In the 1980s, Zigmond and Sansone (1986) identified six models that varied across two broad dimensions: (a) the amount of time that students received instruction from the special education teacher, and (b) the extent to which the curriculum was different from the general education curriculum. The six models were:

1. Resource Room Special Curriculum: Teach basic skills remediation, compensatory skills, learning strategies, or a combination of all three.

2. Resource Room Tutoring: Assist students with mainstreamed content subjects.

3. Self-Contained Class with Special Curriculum: Teach functional skills.

4. Self-Contained Class with General Education Curriculum (Parallel Alternate Curriculum): Maintain the general education curriculum but change the conditions under which the students learn.

5. Consultation Services: Provide consultation to general education teachers.

6. Work Study Program: Teach job skills and supervise on-the-job experiences.

The goals of many of these programs can still be found in secondary schools, though programs may be organized differently. For example, consultation services and instruction in the general education curriculum can be found in schools today through a different service delivery option. Many special education teachers provide consultation services and in-class support to general education teachers and their students, using co-teaching arrangements.

Curricula that could be implemented in the models identified above will be briefly discussed. Consultants should work with special educators to help them to choose the most appropriate model and curriculum for students and to coordinate their efforts with their colleagues in general education and vocational rehabilitation.

> Readers are referred to Chapter 3 for a discussion of co-teaching and resources to help them implement co-teaching models.

## Remedial Curriculum

In a *remedial curriculum,* teachers provide basic skills remediation for academic skill deficits (Deshler, Schumaker, Lenz, & Ellis, 1984). Basic skills in reading, writing, and mathematics are usually taught at a level commensurate with the achievement level of the student. For example, if a student in the 11th grade reads on a 5th-grade level, a remedial reading program would be designed to address the student's reading deficits. The reading ability of the student would be systematically developed according to a scope and sequence plan for each grade level.

Secondary educators who wish to implement a remedial curriculum should: emphasize mastery of the student's basic skills (Englemann & Carnine, 1982); provide an intensive remedial experience to maximize mastery of the basic skill (Meyen & Lehr, 1980); and use strategies that will motivate the student to engage in the remedial tasks (Cox, 1980). Students with learning disabilities, in particular, are noted for poor motivation in revising tasks that they have failed in the past.

If implementing a remedial curriculum, the special educator should consider the following two questions: Where should instruction begin? And what is the most appropriate teaching strategy to use? The strategies that are chosen depend on several variables, including the degree of disability exhibited by the student, the amount of time available for instruction, and the resources that can be mustered to provide supportive services in the general education classroom and the home and community.

If an adolescent with disabilities receives instructional support through a remedial model from a special educator, it is critical that general education teachers who also instruct the student understand the scope and sequence of the student's remedial program. Otherwise, they may make unrealistic or confusing demands and miss opportunities to help the student apply what he or she is learning in the remedial program in his or her general education classes. General educators should be helped to consider how they might modify their curriculum and assignments to help address the student's learning problems in their classes. Anecdote 10.1 presents a conversation between a special education resource teacher and an 11th-grade English teacher about Jerry, an adolescent with learning disabilities. Jerry's listening comprehension is adequate and his verbal skills are above average, but his written expression is poor. He has difficulty writing essays, themes, book reports, and narratives. He has trouble organizing his thoughts on paper, and he has little knowledge of punctuation and grammar. Consequently, he is at a severe disadvantage in the class. He does, however, maintain a C or better average in other assignments such as oral reports and group projects.

## Anecdote 10.1

| | |
|---|---|
| SPECIAL EDUCATOR: | (just finishing a description of Jerry's program in the special education classroom) Mr. Holbrook, do you have any questions about Jerry's program in the special education class? |
| MR. HOLBROOK: | No. It seems like a good idea. I just hope there's enough time left in the school year to see an improvement. |
| SPECIAL EDUCATOR: | I do, too. The year is going very fast, which brings up my reason to meet with you. As Jerry's English teacher, you can play an important part in his program. |
| MR. HOLBROOK: | Me?! I'm responsible for teaching junior English to 180 students. I don't have the time to teach Jerry the proper use of commas and periods. Besides, he can hardly write, anyway. |
| SPECIAL EDUCATOR: | (resolutely) I am well aware of the limitations on your time, Mr. Holbrook. You have a difficult job, and I don't mean to imply that you should take primary responsibility for Jerry's instruction. |
| MR. HOLBROOK: | (straightforwardly) Then what are you asking? |
| SPECIAL EDUCATOR: | I'd like to discuss some ways that you might individualize Jerry's instruction and at the same time reinforce the program we've established in the special education class. |
| MR. HOLBROOK: | Sounds like I am going to have to do more work. |
| SPECIAL EDUCATOR: | Maybe. But try to think in terms of helping Jerry. |
| MR. HOLBROOK: | I'm listening. |
| SPECIAL EDUCATOR: | I understand that Jerry, along with other students in the class, has written and oral assignments to complete each marking period. |
| MR. HOLBROOK: | That's right. |
| SPECIAL EDUCATOR: | One way to individualize Jerry's program would be to issue all, or most, of his writing assignments at one time. He could work on them in the resource room. Not only wound he be able to schedule his work over the marking period, but also the smaller group in the resource |

|                    |                                                                                                                                                                                                                                                                                                                                                                                                                                        |
|--------------------|----------------------------------------------------------------------------------------------------------------------------------------------------------------------------------------------------------------------------------------------------------------------------------------------------------------------------------------------------------------------------------------------------------------------------------------|
|                    | room would serve as a source of ideas for writing. Your assignments could be the basis of his remedial help.                                                                                                                                                                                                                                                                                                                            |
| MR. HOLBROOK:      | That doesn't sound too difficult. Anything else?                                                                                                                                                                                                                                                                                                                                                                                        |
| SPECIAL EDUCATOR:  | (feeling more confident) Yes. I understand students in your class earn extra points for additional work.                                                                                                                                                                                                                                                                                                                                |
| MR. HOLBROOK:      | That's right. I frequently give bonus points for extra assignments.                                                                                                                                                                                                                                                                                                                                                                     |
| SPECIAL EDUCATOR:  | Good. I'd like you to think about doing that in Jerry's case so that he could earn extra points when consecutive writing assignments improve.                                                                                                                                                                                                                                                                                            |
| MR. HOLBROOK:      | You mean, he wouldn't have to do extra work, just improve from assignment to assignment?                                                                                                                                                                                                                                                                                                                                                |
| SPECIAL EDUCATOR:  | That's right. That would really motivate him and reinforce him for what he needs to accomplish.                                                                                                                                                                                                                                                                                                                                         |
| MR. HOLBROOK:      | (hesitating) Well, that's a bit different from my normal procedure, but I guess I could work it out.                                                                                                                                                                                                                                                                                                                                     |
| SPECIAL EDUCATOR:  | Great! There are two more items that I'd like to discuss with you, namely, testing and evaluation. Until Jerry's writing begins to improve, I'd like to reduce the number of written tests he has to take. I realize it's not possible to eliminate all of them. But I think Jerry's attitude toward writing, evidenced by his procrastination, doodling, and poor performance, suggests that we should ease off on the number of writing tasks he has to complete—at least right now. |
| MR. HOLBROOK:      | Maybe you can help with some of the tasks.                                                                                                                                                                                                                                                                                                                                                                                              |
| SPECIAL EDUCATOR:  | Sure. I'd be glad to. Another consideration—is there any way that Jerry could be assigned to a discussion group for his writing tasks the same way he is in the special education room?                                                                                                                                                                                                                                                   |
| MR. HOLBROOK:      | I haven't used discussion groups lately. But come to think of it, it might be a good idea for all the students. The group might help to clarify topics.                                                                                                                                                                                                                                                                                  |
| SPECIAL EDUCATOR:  | That would be great. It would help Jerry and maybe some of the other students as well.                                                                                                                                                                                                                                                                                                                                                  |
| MR. HOLBROOK:      | I'll do what I can with the suggestions you've made.                                                                                                                                                                                                                                                                                                                                                                                    |
| SPECIAL EDUCATOR:  | I couldn't ask for more. I'll stop around next week to see how it's going. In the meantime, you have an open invitation to come over to the special education resource room and see just what Jerry's whole program is like.                                                                                                                                                                                                               |
| MR. HOLBROOK:      | Thanks. I'll see if I can get over next week during my planning period. That's fifth period.                                                                                                                                                                                                                                                                                                                                            |
| SPECIAL EDUCATOR:  | Great! I'm looking forward to your visit.                                                                                                                                                                                                                                                                                                                                                                                               |

## Compensatory Techniques

*Compensatory techniques* are survival strategies to overcome or circumvent the lack of a specific skill. For example, to compensate for a poor sense of direction, one might: develop map reading skills, always outline the route after referring to a map, follow the outlined route, and carry a map just in case one encounters a detour and needs to develop a new route. Use of compensatory techniques does not require extensive training. It does, however, require thoughtful planning to develop or modify materials.

Why would a teacher consider using compensatory techniques with adolescents with disabilities? Besides poor reading and writing skills, adolescents with disabilities often experience poor memory and organizational skills. Compensatory techniques can help secondary students compensate for such deficits. For example, to compensate for poor basic math skills, the student may be taught to use a hand-held calculator. By high school, the time remaining for formal instruction is short; therefore, the curriculum and instruction for the high school student with disabilities must be appropriate and efficiently and effectively delivered.

In addition to providing compensatory techniques to help students with academic skills, it is often critical to teach students to compensate for poor organizational skills. Many students experience problems with time management. Educators, therefore, may find it necessary to help adolescents structure time.

When developing a time schedule for adolescents with disabilities, it is important to accommodate need with simplicity and consistency. Without simplicity and consistency, students may not understand or be able to follow through with a plan. As many academic assignments are issued weekly or monthly, students may need assistance to develop weekly or monthly schedules. To give them that assistance, educators will have to work with them to determine what tasks need to be accomplished and to realistically estimate the time required to accomplish each one. Estimating the time to accomplish a new task is difficult. Nevertheless, it is a necessary skill for adolescents to develop. Consultants and teachers can help students estimate the time needed by reviewing with them how long it took to accomplish similar tasks in the past. If secondary students establish realistic goals and experience the efficient completion of tasks, they are likely to experience the benefits of completing a task in a timely fashion (e.g., more time for other activities) and experience increased motivation for task completion.

Figure 10.2 provides a sample time-management procedure developed by modifying a simple calendar. Fred goes to school and works 4 hours a day. His school assignments include daily homework as well as a weekly assignment (e.g., a book report). The management plan accommodates Fred's busy schedule by allotting time each day to work on daily homework assignments as well as the weekly assignment. In addition, the plan tries to accommodate his interests (e.g., by keeping Friday night free and planning minimum homework over the weekend). The comments section is provided to encourage Fred to note any problems he has and/or additional resources he needs to complete an assignment.

## Learning Strategies

The *learning strategies curriculum* was developed for adolescents with learning disabilities by researchers at the University of Kansas Institute for Research in Learning Disabilities (Schumaker et al., 1983). The approach was designed to

# WHAT NEEDS TO BE DONE THIS WEEK?

**SCHOOL**

| TASK | DUE | TIME TO DO IT |
|---|---|---|
| Book report | Friday | 6 hours |
| Math homework | Monday & Wednesday | 2 hours |
| Social Studies | Tuesday & Thursday | 2 hours |

**HOME**

| TASK | Due | Time |
|---|---|---|
| Clean Car | Sat. | 1 hr. |

**WORK**

| TASK | Time |
|---|---|
| McDonald's | 4–8 M–F |

| | MONDAY | DATE | TUESDAY | DATE | WEDNESDAY | DATE | THURSDAY | DATE | FRIDAY | DATE |
|---|---|---|---|---|---|---|---|---|---|---|
| **SCHEDULE:** | 7–8 am bus ride (homework) 8–3 pm school 4–8 pm work 8:30–10:00– homework | | | | | | | | | |
| **TASKS: Time:** | Math 1 hr. Book 1 hr. Report (w/Patty) | | Soc. St. 1 hr. Book 1 hr. Report | | Math 1 hr. Book 1 hr. Report (w/Patty) | | Soc. St. 1 hr. Book 1 hr. Report | | Clean 1 hr. car | |
| **comments:** | | | Have Patty proofread book report | | | | | | | |

| WEEKEND |
|---|
| **SCHEDULE:** |
| **TASKS: Time:** Book 2 hrs Report |
| **Comments:** Need help outlining Book Report– See Patty |

**Figure 10.2.** Sample time-management calendar. From "The Uncalendar," by People Systems, 1977. Copyright 1977 by People Systems. Adapted with permission.

address limited basic skills, deficiencies in study skills and strategies, and social skills deficits.

The learning strategies approach teaches students strategies for how to learn and how to use skills to perform academic tasks (Deshler et al., 1984). The approach assumes that (a) knowledge is transitory, (b) current educational practice fails to teach students how to relate what they know to real-life problems, (c) learning strategies can be taught directly, and (d) learning strategies can be demonstrated in the general education classroom.

The five essential features of the strategies intervention model are represented in Figure 10.3. These features are considered essential for preparing low-achieving students to function in general education environments. The first feature is that instruction occurs in many settings (e.g., the general and special education classrooms) under the guidance of teachers. Second, the roles of all those involved—teachers as well as students—are clearly specified. Third, instructors cooperatively plan and discuss results. Fourth, generalization of learning strategies by students is incorporated. Fifth, support is provided to ensure that success is achieved in general education environments (Deshler & Schumaker, 1988). Putnam, Deshler, and Schumaker (1993) suggest that strategies are selected given the characteristics of the student and the learning environment. Given the complexity of learning strategies programs, it is suggested that teachers who wish to use the learning strategies curriculum receive training.

## Tutorial Curriculum

In the *tutorial curriculum,* the emphasis is on teaching content, such as identifying the factors that led to the Civil War. Specifically, a special education teacher or tutor teaches students academic content. The goal of this approach is to help students with disabilities receive passing grades in general education classrooms. The tutor generally uses adapted general education materials with a variety of instructional methods. The tutorial curriculum may help teachers and students with disabilities address the goal of access to the general education curriculum.

If tutoring is deemed beneficial for adolescents with learning problems, it is recommended that secondary educators carefully select content that is relevant to success in the general education classes and incorporate instruction in study skills. Once essential content is identified, it is possible to make more responsive decisions about what to teach in the tutorial sessions. For example, if an adolescent with disabilities who is included in a middle school geography class is required to learn map reading, the tutor might concentrate instruction on the key skills of legend reading, orientation, direction, and distance. After basic map reading is acquired, more complex skills could be introduced. In addition, before instruction begins, the special educator and the tutor should know how the student will be tested in the general education class. Will the student have to answer questions in writing or orally? Will the student have to select the correct answers from alternatives? Will the exam be a true-false test? Answers to these questions will help determine how to prepare the student.

To master academic content areas, students need to apply study skills. It is suggested that tutors teach and demonstrate such skills to adolescents who lack them. Most adolescents with disabilities need instruction and reinforcement in the use of both locational and organizational study skills.

*Locational study skills* help students find and understand material that can help them master specific content. For example, a tutor may help a student

There are many learning strategy programs available that have been developed for specific skills. The following are a few that have been developed for reading: DISSECT is a strategy for decoding words (Lenz & Hughes, 1990); IT FITS (King-Sears, Mercer, & Sindelar, 1992) is a strategy for remembering unfamiliar words; and ASK-IT (Schumaker, Deshler, Nolan, & Alley, 1994) is a strategy to help students improve their comprehension of text. For a description of learning strategies that enhance reading development and the research to support use of those strategies, see Lebzelter and Nowacek (1999).

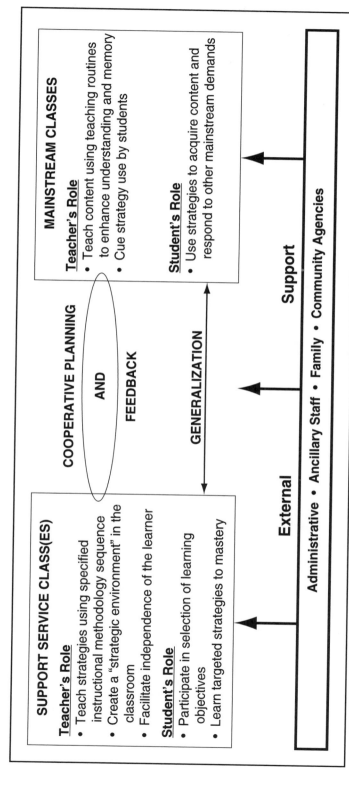

Figure 10.3. Strategies intervention model. From "An Instructional Model for Teaching Students How to Learn," by D. D. Deshler and J. B. Schumaker, 1988, in J. L. Graden, J. E. Zins, and M. J. Curtis (Eds.), *Alternative Educational Delivery Systems: Enhancing Instructional Options for All Students*, p. 395, Washington, DC: National Association of School Psychologists. Copyright 1988 by National Association of School Psychologists. Reprinted with permission.

determine where the different topics in a content area can be found by teaching the student to use the textbook's table of contents and index. The tutor may help the student locate definitions of unfamiliar words by teaching him or her how to use the textbook glossary or a dictionary. In addition, it is often helpful to teach students how to locate, read, and understand graphic aids such as tables, figures, and diagrams. Because graphic aids visually summarize larger volumes of information and show relationships between concepts, they can be very helpful to the student with disabilities (cf. Shields & Heron, 1989).

*Organizational study skills* that can be addressed in a tutorial approach include survey and note-taking skills. Survey skills are used to preview content material. It is suggested that students be taught to skim, use headings, interpret graphs, and read picture captions based on their own individual strengths and needs (Deshler, Ellis, & Lenz, 1996).

Note-taking skills are useful for all students. Generally, the use of some note-taking strategy is better than none. Kline (1986) compared high school students' performances on U.S. history daily and unit quizzes using a lecture-take-notes format and a guided-notes format. In the lecture-take-notes condition, students initially read assigned pages with the teacher. Then the teacher presented an overhead transparency of important information from the reading and provided the students with an opportunity to take notes from the overhead. Students in the guided-notes condition followed the same procedure, except that they had a copy of the information from the transparency on their desks and they filled in the key material as the teacher spoke. At the end of each session, a 10-point quiz was given on the material covered that day. Student performance was higher on daily and unit tests under the guided-notes condition than under the lecture-take-notes condition. Moreover, students preferred the guided-notes condition, saying that it helped them remain interested in the material.

Saski, Swicegood, and Carter (1983) suggest that effective note-taking formats help students incorporate print cues from the text with verbal cues obtained in class. They posit that note-taking formats be structured in consideration of space, subordination, division, questions, and connections.

For additional information regarding note-taking strategies and formats, readers are referred to Czarnecki, Rosko, and Fine (1998) and Wood (1998).

A spatially organized note-taking format facilitates efficient note-taking by carefully positioning information on a page so it is comprehensible later. Subordination and division help clarify the concepts and their relationships to each other. Questions are useful because they help students check their understanding of content as well as identify areas for which students require additional information. Questions also facilitate test preparation. Connections help students relate current information to previously learned concepts. Figure 10.4 illustrates a lesson plan for a tutorial session in which note taking is included.

## Functional Curriculum

A functional curriculum is designed to help students acquire independent-living skills. It is sometimes referred to as life-skills instruction. A functional curriculum delivers instructional content in the areas of personal-social, daily living, and occupational adjustment (Clark, 1994; Loyd & Brolin, 1997).

Valetutti et al. (1996) developed a functional curriculum for students with disabilities. The first volume addresses self-care, motor skills, household management, and living skills such as toileting, drinking and eating, dressing, undressing, personal cleanliness, grooming, operating simple appliances, planning meals, purchasing and preparing food and clothes, and caring for one's living

---

*Subject:* Political Systems

*Content Determination:* The student will be able to:

1. identify the presidency as the most important and powerful office in the political system of the United States.
2. define and discuss at least one role of the presidency.

*Tutoring Session Activities:*

1. Identify and discuss key vocabulary words, such as:

   president    chief executive    veto
   presidency   executive          role
   office       laws

2. Read the section from the text chapter "The Presidency," which discusses the roles of the presidency.
3. Outline one role of the presidency.

Outline

---

*Purpose:* define and discuss one role of the presidency

---

| Old Information | New Information |
|---|---|
| 1. Congress consists of senators and representatives. | 1. The president is the chief executive. |
| 2. Congressman make the laws. | 2. The current president is Ronald Reagan. |
| 3. The people are represented by Congress. | 3. The president executes the laws of Congress. |
| | 4. The president has the power to veto proposed laws before they are passed. |

---

*Questions/Answers*

1. What is the role of the presidency?
   (The president executes the laws of Congress.)
2. What is meant by the sentence: "The president executes the laws of Congress"?
   (The president is responsible for making sure laws are enforced.)
3. Why is the president more powerful than Congress?
   (The president has the power to veto a proposed law before the law gets passed.)

**Figure 10.4.** Example of a lesson plan for a tutorial session. From "Note Taking Formats for Learning Disabled Students," by J. Saski, P. Swicegood, and J. Carter, 1983, *Learning Disability Quarterly,* 6(3), 269. Copyright 1983 by *Learning Disability Quarterly.* Reprinted with permission.

quarters. The second volume addresses nonverbal and oral communication such as use of common gestures and appropriate responses to facial expressions. The third volume addresses functional academics. Functional reading skills include reading the time and understanding written information on safety signs and other common signs and labels. Functional mathematics includes cash transactions, measurement activities, and time management. Guidelines for instructional plans are provided for each of those areas.

Clark (1994) suggests a number of questions to determine what is functional knowledge or a functional skill, including the following: Is the instructional content of the student's current educational placement appropriate for meeting the student's personal-social, daily living, and occupational adjustment needs? Does the content provide a scope and sequence for meeting those future needs? And is the content appropriate for the student's chronological age and current intellectual, academic, or behavioral performance level(s)? Valletutti

Readers are encouraged to see volume 26, number 2 (1994), of *Teaching Exceptional Children* for a series of articles that deal with the topic of functional curriculum.

et al. (1996) recommend assuming a sociological perspective and first determining the environmental contexts within which an adolescent will function. Once the environmental contexts have been determined, one should determine the skills needed to function effectively in each of those environments, determine the skill deficits of the adolescent for each environment, and then develop an instructional plan that will remediate those skill deficits.

The types of individualized programs that can be constructed for students with disabilities vary. We have discussed a few options with which consultants should be familiar as they work with others to design appropriate programs. When designing programs for adolescents with disabilities, it is important to consider the voices of those students. Lovitt, Plavins, and Cushing (1999), in their study of what pupils with disabilities have to say about high school experiences, provide the following suggestions for teachers: assist students to be more independent (e.g., self-evaluate, self-chart, self-schedule); make students more aware of what is being done for them; present students with a wider array of postschool options; invest more time in teaching social skills; focus effort on a strength; and continue working on basic skills.

# Transition

*Transition* is a term used in the 1990 reauthorization of the Individuals with Disabilities Education Act (IDEA). At that time, a key provision of the act was that IEPs for students 16 years of age or older address the student's goals in the transition from adolescence to adulthood. In the 1997 reauthorization of IDEA, an IEP that addressed transition was required for all students with disabilities starting at age 14. The IEP must provide assistance in achieving goals when leaving secondary school whether that be obtaining a job or enrolling in a higher education program (O'Leary, 1998). The objective is for the IEP team to see the "big picture" for the student for the following 4 to 7 years.

The transition movement in education has been developing in light of the changes in people, programs, and individualized curricular options for adolescents with disabilities. Consultants working to effect appropriate transitions into adulthood for students with disabilities will find that they must work with a variety of people within and outside school programs and use a variety of individualized curricular options. Readers are encouraged to consider how to use the information discussed thus far in this chapter in designing and implementing effective transition services for adolescents.

*Transition services* are a coordinated set of activities for students with disabilities, designed within an outcome-oriented process that promotes movement from school to postschool activities, including but not limited to postsecondary education; vocational training; integrated, competitive employment (including supported employment); continuing and adult education; adult services; independent living; and community participation. The coordinated set of activities must be based on the individual student's needs, taking into account the student's preferences and interests, and including needed activities in the following areas:

- instruction;

- community experiences;

- the development of employment and other postschool adult-living objectives; and,

- if appropriate, acquisition of daily living skills and functional vocational evaluation (34 CFR 300.18).

# Transition Planning

Literature on best practices in transition suggests that three areas be addressed: planning, implementation, and follow-up services (Collet-Klingenberg, 1998). Planning for the transition of students with disabilities from a school environment to the community is a complex process, requiring the collaborative efforts of parents, students, school personnel, and community service providers (McDonnell, Wilcox, & Hardman, 1991). Students are leaving a relatively simple system and moving to a complex adult service system that offers a multitude of services, by a variety of agencies, with varying eligibility requirements (Gajar, Goodman, & McAfee, 1993). To be effective consumers of human services and knowledgeable self-advocates, students and their families should be familiar with local and regional agencies (Clark & Kolstoe, 1995). Being knowledgeable about Web-based sites can also help parents access up-to-date information on a variety of topics.

See Peters and Heron (1993) for a discussion of best practice.

Because of the various people and programs that could be involved in developing a transition plan, transition teams can usually provide transition services most effectively (Blalock, 1996). A *transition team* is a group of individuals responsible for planning and implementing transition services and should include all primary stakeholders, including the student and his or her family, educators, and other service providers. Consultants can help these transition teams focus on appropriate services by ensuring that students:

For a discussion of the kinds of teams and how they might be created and function, see Blalock (1996). For a discussion of the importance of communication and collaboration on transition teams and the implementation of planned transition activities, see Collet-Klingenberg (1998). For a discussion of team communication and collaboration skills, see Chapter 4 in this text.

- are aware of the complexity of adult services and have the skills to use those services;

- have access to quality vocational assessment, employment preparation programs, and functional academic and life-skills curricula; and

- have IEPs that include adult living outcomes and transition components (Asselin, Todd-Allen, deFur, 1998, p. 12).

The components that need to be addressed in planning include the following: parental involvement; interagency collaboration and service delivery; individual planning; interdisciplinary transition teams; employer input; vocational assessment; identification of vocational, residential, and social outcomes; transition inclusive IEPs; formal interagency agreements; and early transition planning (Kohler, 1993). Halpern (1994) identifies the following four major components of transition planning:

- an emerging sense of student empowerment;

- student self-evaluation, as a foundation for transition planning;

- student identification of post-school transition goals that are consistent with the outcomes of self-evaluations; and

- student selection of appropriate educational experiences to pursue during high school, both in school and within the broader community, that are consistent with self-evaluations and post-school goals.

As can be seen from Halpern's (1994) transition planning components, students and their families set the goals for transition planning (cf. Miner & Bates,

A number of approaches for planning are designed to provide students and their families with an assertive role. Some of these approaches are the Adapt-ability Model (Mithaug, Martin, & Agran, 1987); Lifestyle Planning (Wilcox & Bellamy, 1987); Personal Futures Planning (Mount & Zwernick, 1988); McGill Action Planning System (MAPS) (Vandercook, York, & Forest, 1989); Outcome-Based Planning (Steere, Wood, Pancsofar, & Butter-worth, 1990); Whose Future Is It Anyway? (Wehmeyer & Kelchner, 1995); the Self-Advocacy Strategy for Edu-cation and Transition Plan-ning (Van Reusen & Bos, 1994); TAKE CHARGE for the Future (Powers, 1996); and Essential Lifestyle Plan-ning (Smull & Harrison, 1992). Halpern et al. (1997), provide a curriculum to help adolescents, ages 14 to 21, with the transition process called Next S.T.E.P.: Student Transition and Educational Planning. Another program that helps get students involved in their planning, from the IEP through transi-tion is Choicemaker (Martin & Marshall, 1996). A char-acteristic of all these approaches is an emphasis on helping students and their families express their vision for the future and on the development of needed supports for realizing that vision.

The reader is referred to the following for transition models: Battle, Dickens-Wright, and Murphy (1998); Lombard (1994); Krieg, Brown, and Ballard (1995); Leconte, Castle-berry, King, and West (1994–95); Levinson (1993); Lombard, Larsen, and West-phal (1993); and Brandt (1994), which provide training workshops or self-study models on assess-ment and transition plan-ning designed for school psychologists and special educators.

1997). However, there are the situations that discourage students and their fam-ilies from having the main input into transition planning. First, transition plan-ning meetings are sometimes conducted without the student or the parents in attendance. Second, when the student and parents do attend, they may lack infor-mation about available services, and they may not have a clear understanding of their future goals. Third, students and parents may encounter professionals who fail to encourage them to express their preferences.

Still, programs have been developed to encourage student and family involvement in transition planning. Often such programs incorporate the devel-opment of self-determination skills. *Self-determination skills* provide the student with the opportunity to collect information and make choices. They include tracking skills such as developing self-management charts and progress port-folios, using assertive problem-solving techniques such as self-correction strate-gies and compensatory strategies, making decisions such as how to schedule activities and when to ask for help, and creating personal incentives such as selecting and planning rewards. Any instructional situation that encourages independent thinking is an opportunity to practice self-determination.

Lane (1995) offers the following recommendations for transition planning:

• Obtain the unabridged legislative guidelines regarding transition plan-ning and services. These would include definitions of transition services and vocational education, who should participate in meetings, transition services as a component of the IEP, transition services and agencies responsible, and an interpretation of the regulations.

• Identify the personnel and resources available for transition planning in the local school district. Possible transition planning service providers could include: the guidance counselor, the work-study program coordinator, the vocational program coordinator, the adult services representative, the commu-nity college representative, and the county recreation representative.

• Investigate the transition planning practices and high school curriculum options of other schools. One way to obtain and channel information efficiently is through a school-based committee composed of potential transition team members. The information, once interpreted, can be used to plan curricular changes and to channel support services accordingly.

• Promote family participation. This can be done by giving parents oppor-tunities to attend transition information workshops, giving parents written information on transition planning, and helping parents and students to develop the student's profile of strengths and priorities.

• Plan instructional activities that incorporate self-determination skills.

• Ensure that team members use a variety of assessment methods across all relevant academic, vocational, and social domains. The domains that should be addressed include academic achievement and performance, language and com-munication, independent living skills, career interests, vocational skills, adaptive behavior, and social skills. The measures that should be used include curriculum-based measures, ecological analyses, interviews, specific skills checklists, anec-dotal reports, and self-report inventories, as well as single-subject observations.

## Transition Assessment

According to Sitlington, Neubert, and Leconte (1997), the Division on Career Development and Transition (DCDT) "views *transition assessment* as an umbrella term that includes career assessment, vocational assessment, and ecological or functional assessment practices. . . . *Vocational assessment* relates to the role of worker. *Career assessment* relates to lifelong career development, which affects all life roles. Transition assessment relates to all life roles and to the support needed before, during, and after the transition to adult life" (p. 70, emphasis added).

See Chapter 8 for more discussion on functional assessment.

Assessment for transition can be divided into three levels though all three have the same purpose: to identify a student's potential, needs, functional abilities, interests, skills, aptitudes, and achievement relative to what is needed for success in both current and future environments (Thurlow & Elliott, 1998). Therefore, transition assessment is used to determine the nature of the transition program as well as what is working with the transition program that is implemented. Level 1 is the initial process of screening to arrive at a decision for providing transition services or instruction. The areas to be assessed are instruction, community experience, development of employment and/or postsecondary living objectives, and acquisition of daily living skills. Information about the student's interests, strengths, needs, and preferences is gathered. Level 1 assessment involves interviewing students, family members, and teachers and reviewing records. Often, information collected at this level is used for IEP development. Level 2 involves a more in-depth study of student needs, e.g., a vocational evaluation as well as the student's involvement in the community and with respective agencies. Level 3 is a systematic and comprehensive process that involves vocational assessment and should be performed by personnel trained in such assessment. The goal of a vocational assessment is to identify individual interests, strengths, and education and training needs. This information provides the basis for planning an individualized, comprehensive transition program.

For transition planning, assessment information should be obtained from students, families, and teachers, as well as people from a receiving agency such as community service personnel, admissions department personnel, and family services people. The people who are involved in providing assessment information depend on the comprehensiveness of the assessment, the transition goals, and the number of years the student will remain in the public school. It may be necessary to collect interview as well as observational data from real work environments. Sitlington et al. (1997) emphasize that assessment should occur in a variety of natural environments. It is important that special and general educators as well as related school personnel, community service providers, and students and their families work collaboratively to determine the assessment data that need to be collected and the best methods to collect that data. Sitlington et al. suggest that assessment methods must incorporate assistive technology or accommodations that will allow students to demonstrate their abilities and potential. Because assessment of students' needs and preferences is an important part of the transition process and because planning for transition is a process that occurs over a long period of time, assessment of students' preferences and needs and the monitoring of their transition plans should be conducted periodically (Cohen & Spenciner, 1996).

Readers are encouraged to review the assessment strategies presented in Chapter 8.

The transition planning process will be most effective when assessment data are formative as well as summative and when one person assumes the role for coordinating the collection of ongoing assessment information (Sitlington et al., 1997). The guidelines for formative and summative evaluation offered in Chapter 8 will serve consultants well when they are evaluating the effectiveness of transition programs. Consultants should strive to evaluate the overall transition-planning process, including collaboration, assessment, and the planning and writing of transition goals, as well as implementation of the plan (Thurlow & Elliott, 1998).

Though family members will have a longitudinal perspective on the transition process, they are not always in a position to assume the coordination role. Therefore, consultants should be prepared to assume that role initially or help other school or vocational staff to assume that role. Eventually, a family member can perform that function. Sitlington et al. (1997) identify the following competencies that are needed for successful transition assessment:

- skills related to assessing the individual's current and potential environments;

- skills in matching the culture and demands of the service environments with the strengths, needs, preferences, and interests of the individual;

- skills in using and communicating the assessment data to facilitate transition planning;

- skills in functioning as a member of an interdisciplinary team;

- the ability to recommend accommodations, assistive technology devices and services, and related services for students who require support to participate in inclusive work sites, vocational training programs, postsecondary educational programs, community settings, and social programs;

- skills to work in concert with students and parents throughout all phases of the assessment process to ensure understanding of assessment options and outcomes; and

- skills to train students and families to assume responsibility for ongoing assessment and transition planning.

For more information about transition, readers are encouraged to access the National Transition Alliance (NTA) home page: *http://www.dssc.org/nta/index.html*.

In summary, transition services are crucial for adolescents with disabilities. Transition programs should not be alternatives to the general secondary school curriculum as they have been in the past, resulting in attainment of vocational and social skills to the exclusion of academic skills. Rather, transition programs need to represent an integrated curriculum developed to address the appropriate goals and needs of each student. Consultants can facilitate the effective planning and delivery of transition services if they strive to develop and maintain transition teams and assist them in developing their assessment and planning skills.

# Conclusion

To provide a framework for consultation at the secondary level, the following components were discussed in light of current educational reforms: the people with whom the consultant will work in developing programs for adolescents with disabilities, the structure of school and home/community programs for adolescents and young adults, and a selection of curricular options available to design individualized programs for students with special needs. It is imperative for secondary consultants to realize that the goal for adolescents with disabilities is the successful transition to adulthood. To accomplish this goal, consultants will need to help adolescents and their family members take a pivotal role in planning the transition process. For the adolescent's transition plan to be successful, it will be necessary to coordinate activities across special, general, and vocational educators; social service providers such as rehabilitation counselors; and business and community leaders who will provide work-related training opportunities. For secondary consultants, then, establishing and maintaining transition teams will be a primary responsibility.

## Summary of Key Points

### People in the Adolescent's Community

1. Individuals involved in the life of secondary students include the adolescent, secondary professionals (e.g., general educators, special educators, vocational instructors, and related service personnel), family members, and community members.

2. Consultants can help secondary special educators prepare for their role as transition coordinators by helping them to collaborate with vocational personnel to provide community-based vocational education and interpret assessment data.

3. Consultants should be prepared to help family members assume a variety of roles, including guide and role model for career selection, helper in planning for the future, mediator with different agencies, and de facto case manager for the adolescent with disabilities.

### Programs for All Adolescents

4. Students function within two general social systems: the school and the home/community.

5. To provide effective consulting services within those settings, three areas generally need to be considered: (a) the content of the setting, (b) the activities of the setting, and (c) the evaluation of success in the setting.

6. Comprehensive high schools are the prevalent high school structure. They offer a comprehensive curriculum (i.e., academic programs, vocational education programs, and general studies programs).

7. Comprehensive high schools are using the concept of schools-within-a-school to transform the instruction of 1,000 or more students into basic learning subcommunities of approximately 400 students.

8. Secondary schools are using block scheduling to reduce the problems of short instructional periods. Instead of students attending a six-, seven-, or eight-period school day with each period lasting approximately 50 minutes, students attend three or four periods per day of approximately 80–120 minutes each.

9. The benefits of block scheduling include the use of diverse instructional strategies, fewer transitions between classes resulting in more instructional time, and the ability of teachers to address more difficult concepts because of longer time periods.

10. Middle schools are schools that are organized to include some combination of the grades five through nine.

11. The mission of middle schools is to address the diverse needs of the developing adolescent. Because diversity is acknowledged at the middle school, diverse instructional strategies are the norm rather than the exception.

12. Current practices in vocational education include school-based learning, work-based learning, and connecting activities.

13. Several practices can be found in school-based learning. Tech-prep programs provide a way to increase academic and vocational skills and bridge the gap between secondary and postsecondary training.

14. The integration of academic and occupational learning is another practice found in school-based learning. This practice often involves making available applied academic course materials from commercial vendors.

15. Career pathways are broad clusters of occupations that revolve around a theme (e.g., health occupations) and can be found in many school-based vocational learning approaches.

16. Career academies are another school-based learning approach in vocational education and often offer the following: schools-within-a-school, focus on a career theme, and a combination of technical and academic content.

17. Connecting activities are those that link school-based and work-based learning. Consultants should be involved in facilitating such activities. They include: opportunities for teachers to learn about modern work settings; opportunities for work site personnel to learn about the realities of secondary schools; regular and formal relationships between school and work site personnel; and classroom-based activities that draw upon and reinforce work site learning.

18. These home community programs are designed to help *all* adolescents move from the world of adolescence to the world of adulthood by involving their families, educators, and members of the community in planning and implementing programs.

19. Successful school-to-work programs use strategies for teaching and learning that use work-based and computer-assisted approaches as well as cross-sector collaboration.

20. Adolescents also need assistance making transitions into other aspects of adult life such as maintaining a home, becoming appropriately involved in the community, and experiencing satisfactory personal and social relationships.

## Individualized Programs for Adolescents with Disabilities

21. Individualized programs for adolescents with disabilities can vary across two broad dimensions: the amount of time students receive instruction from a special educator and the extent the curriculum is different from the general education curriculum. These individualized programs can be deliv-

ered in resource rooms or self-contained classrooms or through consultation and co-teaching.

22. In a remedial curriculum, teachers provide basic skills remediation for academic skills deficits (i.e., in reading, writing, and arithmetic).

23. When implementing a remedial curriculum, the special educator should answer the following two questions: Where should instruction begin? And what is the most appropriate teaching strategy to use?

24. Compensatory techniques are survival strategies that help people compensate for specific skills deficits. Examples of techniques to compensate for poor basic academic skills include the use of calculators. Techniques to compensate for poor organizational skills include note-taking formats and time-management calendars.

25. The learning strategies approach is designed to teach students how to learn. After specific strategies have been learned, they can be applied to any content area.

26. The tutorial curriculum helps students meet the needs of the general education curriculum through tutoring and developing study skills.

27. Functional curricula focus on developing basic skills needed to function within contexts that students will experience (e.g., the basic skills needed to be a member of a community, a contributing resident at home, and an enjoyable leisure activity partner).

## Transition

28. Transition is a term used in the 1990 and 1997 reauthorizations of the Individuals with Disabilities Act that require the IEP to address the student's goals of making the transition from adolescence to adulthood.

29. Transition services are a coordinated set of activities that promote movement from school to postschool activities such as vocational or further academic training or employment.

30. An effective transition requires planning, implementation, and follow-up activities.

31. Because of the various people and programs that could be involved in developing a transition plan, transition teams usually perform the services of planning, implementation, and follow-up effectively.

32. The students and their families are pivotal in the development of an effective transition plan. Programs to assist them in assuming this pivotal role address self-advocacy and self-determination skills. The common goal of these programs is to help students and their family members express their vision for the future and develop the supports needed to realize that vision.

33. Transition assessment is an important component of transition planning. It relates to all life roles and to the support needed before, during, and after the transition to adult life. It includes career assessment, vocational assessment, and ecological assessment.

34. Effective transition assessment requires skills to assess as well as skills to be part of an interdisciplinary transition team. Part of the role of the transition team members is to help family members assume the responsibility for ongoing assessment and transition planning as the student with disabilities moves into adulthood.

35. Transition programs should not be alternatives to the general secondary school curriculum. Vocational, general, and special education should merge to form an effective individualized program for each adolescent with disabilities.

# Questions

1. Describe the challenges faced by adolescents. What role should consultants take in helping adolescents address those challenges?

2. Describe the similarities and differences among high school general education teachers, middle school general education teachers, and secondary special education teachers.

3. Describe several strategies a consultant can undertake to help families cope with the transition of adolescents with disabilities into adulthood.

4. Discuss how the schools-within-a-school concept can alleviate problems of large school size.

5. Describe how block scheduling can accommodate the needs of an adolescent with disabilities.

6. What should be the focus of a middle school curriculum. Why?

7. How can the school-to-work programs for all students benefit adolescents with disabilities?

8. Describe and provide an example of each of the following: remedial curriculum, compensatory curriculum, learning strategies curriculum, tutorial curriculum, and functional curriculum.

9. Describe a hypothetical transition program for an adolescent with disabilities. Be sure your program addresses instruction, community experiences, the development of employment and other postschool adult living objectives, acquisition of daily living skills, and a functional vocational evaluation.

10. What are some strategies consultants should employ to promote the effective development and maintenance of transition teams?

# Discussion Points and Exercises

For examples of planning activities that teachers can use with Steve, see Ryan and Paterna (1997).

1. Steve is an eighth grader who attends his home junior high school in Alaska. He participates in the cross-country running club and enjoys computer and language arts classes. Steve receives special education services for autism and severe disabilities. His parents and teachers believe that school has

helped him develop self-esteem, friendships, personal management skills, and computer skills. His friends say that he has been an intricate part of their school. Steve participates in all general education classes with the benefit of supplemental aids and assistance through special education services. The eighth-grade teachers collaborate across subject areas and meet weekly to plan interdisciplinary units. Provide an example of an interdisciplinary unit that accommodates Steve.

2. DeShawn is a 16-year-old student who has a developmental disability and is enrolled in a suburban high school. His academic skills have developed steadily but slowly throughout his elementary and junior high years, resulting in a large gap between his achievement and that of his age mates. Socially, DeShawn is very immature. He has difficulty making and keeping friends, and his interactions with peers are tentative and awkward. What would you anticipate would be the transition plan for DeShawn? Why?

3. Visit a middle or high school to determine the curricular and instructional strategies that are used to accommodate adolescents with disabilities. Discuss with the principal, special educators, general educators, and vocational educators, their perceptions of the efficacy of the approaches in use.

4. Attend an IEP meeting for an adolescent with disabilities. Based on the student's current levels of achievement and future goals, discuss with team members an appropriate transition plan and instructional strategies to use with the student.

5. Conduct an interview with a high school student with disabilities. Determine from the student the type of program he or she is receiving and his or her role in the development of that program.

6. Interview secondary-level professionals who are functioning as transition coordinators. Identify their responsibilities and the strategies they use to facilitate the effective delivery of transition coordinator activities.

7. Interview community members (e.g., employers, rehabilitation counselors) who are involved in transition programs for adolescents with disabilities. Identify their perception of the school-based program and any activities they think would improve school-to-work programs.

# Implementing Instructional Strategies Across Grade and Skill Levels

# 11

Chapters 9 and 10 presented instructional strategies that can be used primarily at either the elementary or the secondary level. This chapter presents a number of instructional strategies that educational consultants can recommend with confidence from preschool through high school. Each strategy is anchored in "best practice" procedures (Peters & Heron, 1993), draws on the measurably superior instructional strategies found in Gardner et al. (1994), and includes meta-analysis recommendations based on Lloyd, Forness, and Kavale's (1998) work on effective methods.

Consultants armed with these strategies will be able to provide continuity of service within and across levels, thereby improving implementation. Further, consultants who work across levels will not have to adapt strategies radically from one level to another to accommodate the needs of students as they move from one level to another. To facilitate comprehension of chapter objectives, field-tested approaches will be divided into three major sections: teacher-directed, peer-mediated, and semi-independent and independent approaches.

For a complete discussion of effective strategies, readers are referred to Gardner et al. (1994); Lloyd, Forness, and Kavale (1998); Forness, Kavale, Blum, and Lloyd (1997); and Casto and Mastropieri (1986).

## Objectives

After reading this chapter, the reader will be able to:

1. define *best practice* and contextualize its use in applied settings;

2. recognize the characteristics of effective instruction;

3. define *measurably superior instruction* and provide examples from the literature;

4. list and describe the key elements of a tutoring system;

5. define *peer, cross-age, 1:1, small-group,* and *home-based tutoring;*

6. define and provide multiple examples of *cooperative learning arrangements;*

7. distinguish active student responding from passive student responding; provide examples of choral responding, write-on and preprinted response cards, and guided notes;

8. state how low, high, and assistive technology applications can be implemented to enhance semi-independent and independent performance.

## Key Terms

| | |
|---|---|
| best practice | tutoring systems |
| Daubert standard | class-wide peer tutoring |
| measurably superior instruction | class-wide student tutoring teams |
| teacher-directed approach | cross-age tutoring |
| direct instruction | small-group tutoring |
| early intervention | one-to-one tutoring |
| cognitive behavior modification | home-based tutoring |
| mnemonics | nontraditional applications |
| active student response | cooperative learning |
| choral responding | semi-independent and independent approaches |
| response cards | |
| guided notes | computer-assisted instruction |
| peer-mediated approach | assistive technology |

# Best Practice Strategy and Effective Instruction

What is a best practice strategy? How would consultants or teachers be able to recognize one if they saw it? The answer to these two important questions may be addressed by examining what constitutes a best practice and also by analyzing the research literature on effective instruction. That is, what works with students, especially students with disabilities included in general education classrooms. We'll contextualize our discussion by examining best practice and effective instruction briefly.

Peters and Heron (1993) state that for *best practice* to be claimed, five questions must be answered affirmatively:

- Does the practice have a sound theoretical base?
- Is the methodological integrity of the research convincing and compelling?
- Is there consensus with existing literature?
- Is there evidence that desired outcomes are consistently produced?
- Is there evidence of social validity?

See Chapter 7 to read parent, teacher, and student perspectives on inclusion programming and their views on the ineffectiveness of some instructional approaches.

Refer to Chapter 2 for discussion of the Daubert standard.

If consultants can answer yes to these questions, they will have more confidence in the recommended strategy. Unfortunately, in the past, many ill-conceived "bandwagon" or fad approaches have been implemented with students, with the resulting tragic outcomes of student failure, wasted time and effort, and parental alienation (Heward, 1999; Kauffman & Hallahan, 1995). Furthermore, consultants are ethically and legally bound—as are teachers—to use approaches that meet the *Daubert standard*. That is, consultants must use procedures that are reliable, valid, and state-of-the-art, not just those that are popular or favorites (Heron, Martz, & Margolis, 1996).

While clearly there are differences of opinion on what constitutes effective instruction, Lloyd, Forness, and Kavale (1998) conducted a meta-analysis of research studies to determine those strategies that produced robust effect sizes

## Table 11.1
### Matrix of Effective Strategies

| Teacher-Directed | Peer-Mediated | Semi-Independent & Independent |
|---|---|---|
| Direct instruction | Tutoring systems | Computer-assisted instruction |
| Early intervention | Cooperative learning | Assistive technology |
| Cognitive behavior modification | | |
| Mnemonic training | | |
| Active student response methods | | |

and that therefore would warrant adoption. Likewise, Gardner et al. (1994) identified *measurably superior instruction* practices across early childhood, school-age, and transition levels as being those strategies that produced viable and consistent outcomes for learners and that were conceptually and technologically intact. Table 11.1 shows a three-column matrix that divides these strategies into teacher-directed, peer-mediated, and semi-independent and independent categories. During the plan design and plan implementation phases of consultation, consultants might recall these strategies as one way to ensure that recommendations that are being proposed "fit" within the larger classroom ecology and the teacher's instructional repertoire.

For a complete discussion of effective strategies, readers are referred to Gardner et al. (1994); Lloyd, Forness, and Kavale (1998); Forness, Kavale, Blum, and Lloyd (1997).

# Teacher-Directed Approaches

In a *teacher-directed approach,* the teacher handles the primary tasks of delivering instruction and providing the prompts, cues, reinforcement, and feedback during each learning trial. Five teacher-directed methods will be presented here: direct instruction, early intervention, cognitive behavior modification, mnemonic training, and active student response methods.

For a discussion of the relationship between learning trials and achievement, see Heward (1994).

## Direct Instruction

*Direct instruction* (DI) involves the careful arrangement and orchestration of three main variables: organization of instruction, program design, and teacher presentation techniques (Carnine, Silbert, & Kameenui, 1997). Organization of instruction further involves the teacher (a) scheduling sufficient engaged time so that students come into contact with the content, and (b) arranging the physical setting and instructional materials in a logical and effective manner. Gersten, Carnine, and White (1984) capture the essence of DI when they state: "The key principle in the design of Direct Instruction programs is deceptively simple: For all students to learn, both the materials and teacher presentation of these materials must be clear and unambiguous" (pp. 38–39).

Program design involves multiple components. Carnine et al. (1997) believe that at least six elements constitute effective program design: (a) specifying objectives, (b) devising strategies, (c) developing teacher procedures, (d) selecting examples, (e) sequencing skills, and (f) providing practice and review. With respect to the latter three elements (selecting examples, sequencing skills, and providing practice and review), direct instruction provides teachers with "scripted lessons,"

For a distinction between allocated time, engaged time, opportunity to respond, and active student response, see Heward (1994). For a description of how DI was implemented in a Japanese junior high school, see Nakano, Kageyama, and Tsukuba (1993). For a description and synthesis of the National Longitudinal Evaluation Study, see Gersten, Carnine, and White (1984). For a synthesis of research findings on DI, see Becker (1992); Carnine et al. (1997); and Weisberg (1994).

which specify in detail how to present the skill, how many examples to provide, how much practice to allocate, and how to correct errors. Admittedly, the concept of scripted lessons has produced a great deal of debate in the field. Some teachers believe that scripted lessons rob them of creative opportunities to teach their students. Other teachers may believe (mistakenly in our view) that scripted lessons are dehumanizing and debasing because they create a stilted atmosphere within which otherwise heuristic learning would take place. Stein, Carnine, and Dixon (1998) correctly place the role of scripted lessons with the direct instruction program and may help to reduce teachers' misplaced fears regarding scripted lessons when they state:

> The greatest misconception derived from the use of scripts comes from the common confusion between rote instruction and explicit instruction. Direct Instruction programs teach generalizable strategies but do so in an explicit manner, scaffolding the instruction to meet the needs of students. Educators commonly confuse the step-by-step instruction found in the scripted lessons with approaches that require students to memorize answers and repeat them in rote-like fashion. It is important to note that scripts are only as useful as the strategies represented by the scripts. In other words, content of instruction matters. In fact, using scripted lessons would enable teachers to teach faulty strategies as easily as more useful ones. The script, in and of itself, is simply a tool that facilitates clear communication between teachers and students. (p. 228)

Finally, teacher presentation techniques embrace setting variables (large-versus small-group arrangements) as well as choral responding, wait time, corrective feedback, motivational techniques, and monitoring to best advantage. Gersten et al. (1984) make this point clearly:

> [DI] . . . is a behavioral orientation—in that the core of the model is precise analysis of the actual behavior of the teacher and the child. It differs from many other behavioral analyses of teaching and learning in that equal emphasis is put on exactly what the text says, and how the instructions or range of examples in the text could be improved or clarified. Similarly, while reinforcement of appropriate behavior is an essential component of teaching training, the Direct Instruction analysis does not stop there. A great deal of attention is given to how student errors are corrected. Whenever possible, the instructor gives the children a strategy and lets them work out the problem by themselves. The teaching materials offer precise guidelines for when explicit teacher guidance should be faded, and the stages in the fading process. (pp. 56–57)

According to Carnine et al. (1997), much academic failure can be prevented or minimized, and student achievement and self-esteem enhanced, by arranging, organizing, and sequencing instructional materials and directions properly. Direct instruction provides for such arrangements (Darch, Carnine, & Gersten, 1984; Patching, Kameenui, Carnine, Gersten, & Colvin, 1983), and innovative design principles such as programming "big ideas" offer consultants the basis for further curricular enhancements (Carnine et al., 1997).

For a meta-analysis review on the efficacy of early intervention programs, the reader is referred to Casto and Mastropieri (1986).

For a discussion of the importance of family members in planning, implementing, and evaluating programs, the reader is referred to Chapter 7.

## Early Intervention

"Early intervention consists of a wide variety of educational, nutritional, child-care, and family supports, all designed to reduce the effects of disabilities or prevent the occurrence of learning and developmental problems later in life for children presumed to be at risk for such problems" (Heward, 2000, p. 156). Despite concerns about the rigor of some early intervention programs and projects, there appears to be agreement that early intervention programs assist markedly with educational, social, and language-based communication skills of children (Casto & Mastropieri, 1986; Ramey & Ramey, 1992). Early intervention approaches and intervention benefit when family members are included in the program (Berry & Hardman, 1998; Sontag & Schacht, 1994).

While early intervention programs differ in terms of the range of services offered, their goals are generally based on decreasing the debilitating and immediate effects of a disability; empowering family members to assist in the cognitive, affective, and social development of their children; facilitating the transition from preschool to school-based programs; and reducing the potential cost of longer-term programs that otherwise might be required to achieve the same results. To achieve these goals, programs are often established on a center-based, home-based, or combination-based approach (Hardman, Drew, & Egan, 1999), the difference being essentially the location of the services, the on-site personnel available to deliver services, and the beneficial effects in favor of center-based approaches (Forness et al., 1997).

Consultants who are familiar with the beneficial effects of early intervention approaches are more likely to advocate for them in their districts, work to establish home-based or combination approaches, and have more effective transition programs than consultants who ignore this literature. Likewise, socializing parents to join educators in a collaborative effort while their children are still at the preschool or developmental age may help to reduce parental alienation and frustration in later school years. Finally, early intervention programs may have long-term benefits beyond academic achievement. Barnett and Hall (1990) suggest that early intervention programs may reduce referrals for later social or legal services and may have an effect on more chronic social problems among people with special needs (e.g., employment, legal transgressions, substance abuse).

Readers interested in learning about general curriculum and instructional strategies are referred to Wolery and Sainato (1996).

## Cognitive Behavior Modification

In a *cognitive behavior modification* program the practitioner "believes that faulty thinking is the cause of emotional and behavioral problems, and the primary focus of cognitive therapy is to change faulty thinking. Techniques for doing so can be described in three general classes: cognitive restructuring, self-instructional coping methods, and problem-solving strategies" (Martin & Pear, 1996, p. 355). Cognitive restructuring methods replace dysfunctional thinking with rational self-thoughts ("Things could be worse; I'll get by OK"). Self-instructional coping methods refer to self-talk on *how* to accomplish a desired behavior (taking deep breaths in an anxiety-producing situation, making positive affirmative self statements ("I can do this"), and issuing self-reinforcement statements ("I met my goals"). Finally, problem-solving strategies refer to learning how to think logically by defining problem elements, generating alternatives, making good decisions, and verifying outcomes (D'Zurilla & Goldfried, 1971). In the main, when cognitive behavior modification approaches are employed in school-based situations, they focus on the student's private verbal behavior and usually involve large doses of behavior modification. Clearly, the cognitive components of cognitive behavior modification refer to the self-statements to change irrational or maladaptive thinking, while the behavioral elements include modeling and imitation, behavioral rehearsal, reinforcement, and other operant procedures to increase, decrease, maintain, and generalize behavior (Martin & Pear, 1996). What is not clear from the literature are the relative contributions of the cognitive versus the behavioral components within cognitive behavior modification. Still, Martin and Pear (1996) provide some insight for consultants when evaluating such a program for students with disabilities is important:

> Cognitive therapies can be worthwhile, but they can be used most effectively when they are analyzed from a consistent behavioral view. A behavioral interpretation suggests (a) cognitive techniques rely largely on rule-governed behavior; (b) rules control behavior when they link the behavior to effective environmental consequences, and therefore (c) cognitive techniques will effectively change behavior if and only if there are sufficient links to the external environment." (pp. 363–364)

## Mnemonics

According to Heaton and O'Shea (1995), *mnemonics,* a memory-improving technique, is defined as "organizational or elaborative techniques used to improve retention . . . by relating [new sets of material] to some previous, well-learned set of materials" (p. 35). Mnemonic training is designed to provide students with a memory-aided strategy for recoding, relating, and retrieving information (Carney, Levin, & Levin, 1993). For instance, the simple acronym mnemonic SQ3R stands for: *s*urvey, *q*uestion, *r*ead, *r*ecite, and *r*eview, and might be taught to students to improve reading comprehension. COPS, a written-language mnemonic representing *c*apitalization, *o*verall appearance, *p*unctuation, and *s*pelling, might be employed to improve a student's written language by having that student focus on those critical areas prior to submitting an assignment.

However, mnemonic strategies can also involve keywords, pegwords, loci, and story-invention strategies. Two examples from the literature will illustrate these strategies. Suppose a teacher wanted to teach the names of the states and associated capitals. Carney et al. suggest that to learn Topeka, Kansas, using the keyword approach, the student would generate "a spinning *top* image" (keyword from *Top*eka) that would be superimposed over a picture of a *can* (keyword from *Kan*sas). When asked for the state and capital, the student would recall the image of a spinning top above a can. Other keywords and visual images would be generated for the remaining states.

Pegwords and loci (location) methods provide mnemonic reference to order by rhyming associations: one = bun; two = shoe; three = tree; and so forth. When serial order exceeds 10, more elaborate associations are produced, e.g., 21 = twin buns.

To learn the names and serial order of the presidents of the United States, a keyword-pegword approach might be combined. Mastropieri, Scruggs, and Whedon (1997) provide this example: As the first president, George Washington would generate the keyword *washing* (for *Washing*ton) as well as the pegword "bun" for one. Hence, students would generate a mental image of George Washington washing buns.

To remember a social studies association between frontier settlers and the Potawatomi Indians, Carney et al. suggest combining a keyword approach with story invention. In this illustration, the keyword *pot* (from *Pot*awatomi) would be generated, and a "story" describing Indians chasing settlers and flinging pots at them might be produced. Depending on the students and their needs, illustrations might be drawn physically or a mental image might suffice.

Heaton and O'Shea (1995) report that consultants interested in assisting teachers with the implementation of a mnemonic strategy in a class might use the acronym STRATEGY to accomplish this goal. Each letter of the word STRATEGY stands for a step the teacher would take to generate an appropriate mnemonic for her or his students:

- *Start* by choosing a learning or behavior outcome.
- *Task* analyze it.
- *Rearrange* the wording of the steps.
- *Ask* if you can make a word from the first letters.
- *Try* to find a word that relates to the task.
- *Examine* possible synonyms to be the first letter.
- *Get* creative!
- *Yes*, you can make your own strategies. (Heaton & O'Shea, 1995, p. 34)

Mastropieri et al. (1997) studied the effects of a traditional approach compared with a mnemonic approach on 19 inner-city students' ability to learn the serial order of U.S. presidents. Briefly, during the 3-week mnemonic condition, students used a keyword-pegword method to learn the associations. During the 3-week traditional approach, students simply practiced the names and order of the presidents, followed teacher-directed instruction using progressive disclosure on the overhead projector, and participated in a cumulative review. Results showed that under the mnemonic condition, students scored higher on weekly quizzes and delayed posttests.

In Carney et al.'s view, mnemonic strategies are effective because they add "meaningful connections to seemingly unconnected or arbitrarily connected pieces of information" (p. 25). Carney et al. report that mnemonics is useful during the acquisition phases of learning, especially for low-achieving students and students with disabilities, because these students typically have challenges with memory tasks.

*Readers interested in learning more about mnemonics and how it can be used across reading vocabulary, reading comprehension, math, and study skills are referred to Greene (1994) and Higbee (1988).*

Greene (1994) states that mnemonics assists the learner with acquiring abstract information by making it more concrete and incorporating multisensory modes as well as rhyme, rhythm, and repetition. Greene and Mastropieri et al. (1997) also assert that the visual imagery component of mnemonics, coupled with an auditory-visual link, is more effective than just a rote memorization strategy. Mnemonics might be particularly well suited for examination-type responses that teachers may demand on quizzes and tests. Hence, students armed with a well-functioning mnemonic repertoire might be able to perform better on such tests. Finally, mnemonics can be incorporated across grade and skill areas (Carney et al., 1993), but as Heaton and O'Shea (1995) state, "The key is to link the strategy to appropriate class tasks and activities, considering whether students' learning or behaviors can be aided more efficiently and effectively through mnemonics" (p. 34).

## Active Student Response Methods

*For reviews of research showing the relationship between student participation and achievement in general and special education settings, readers are referred to Brophy and Good (1974); Greenwood, Delquadri, and Hall (1984); and Greenwood et al. (1994).*

According to Heward (1994), *active student response* (ASR) methods comprise those instructional strategies in which students actually produce observable and measurable behavior. Instructional time, that is, the amount of time that the teacher might plan, allocate, or design, is of less importance from an ASR perspective than the time that a student is engaged actively in making academic responses.

Further, in Heward's view, opportunity to respond (OTR) and ASR procedures have been found to be effective in the literature (Greenwood, Hart,

Walker, & Risley, 1994), and they provide the teacher with useful information relative to the quality and quantity of student performance.

Heward (1994) has identified three "low-tech" but high-ASR strategies that teachers can employ across grade or skill levels. These include choral responding, response cards (preprinted and write-on), and guided notes.

## Choral Responding

In *choral responding,* all students respond together, in unison, to teacher-presented questions or items. For example, if an elementary teacher was reviewing math facts, she or he might say to the class, "Tell me the product of 5 × 5," and all the students would respond simultaneously, "25." In a high school health education class where students might be reviewing before a semester examination, the teacher might say, "Name a transmitted disease with which the HIV virus is associated," and students would respond in unison, "AIDS." According to Heward (1994) and Heward, Courson, and Narayan (1989), choral responding can be used with many curricular content areas during group instruction, especially when teacher presentations are lively, are well paced, provide ample models and cues for students, and are distributed throughout the day. Providing "response sprints" can assist with motivating students and presenting and/or firming-up content. The direct instruction approach, which was discussed earlier, clearly relies heavily on beneficial effects that choral responding produces.

## Response Cards

"Response cards are cards, signs, or items (such as felt boards) that are simultaneously held up by all students in the class to display their responses to questions or problems presented by the teacher" (Heward, Gardner, Cavanaugh, Courson, Grossi, & Barbetta, 1996, p. 5). Response cards come in two major forms: preprinted and write-on.

*Preprinted.* Preprinted response cards have either (a) discrete answers already encoded on the card (e.g., yes-no, true-false, or specific identifiable responses; see Figure 11.1), or (b) a range of responses that students select from by "pinching" one with a clothespin or some other attachment device (see Figure 11.2). For example, Figure 11.2 shows that in response to the teacher's question, "How many quarters does it take to make one dollar?" students pinched the number 4. If the teacher asked, "If I purchased an item for $.50 and gave the clerk $1.00, how many quarters would I receive in change?" students who pinched the number 2 would receive reinforcement.

Teachers can reinforce generality of responses by reinforcing any alternative correct responses. For instance, students who placed two clothespins on the number 1 would receive reinforcement. All correct variations equaling $.50 would be scored correct.

*Write-On.* "When using write-on response cards, students mark or write their answers to each instructional item on blank cards or boards that are erased between each question-and-answer trial" (Heward et al., 1996, p. 5). The board can be made of slate (chalkboard or bathroom board), making it usable with a dry eraser pen and eraser. In this format, the teacher would present an instructional cue, "What is ½ times ½?" and students would write the answer (¼) on their board and hold it up for the teacher (and other students) to see.

Cavanaugh, Heward, and Donelson (1996) provide a demonstration of how write-on response cards could be used during a lesson review with secondary-level students enrolled in an earth science class. Essentially, the study involved 23 ninth-grade students, including 8 students with special needs. Measures were obtained on next-day and weekly science tests. During a "passive review"

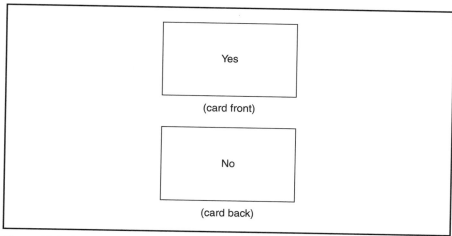

**Figure 11.1.** Preprinted response cards (specific items listed).

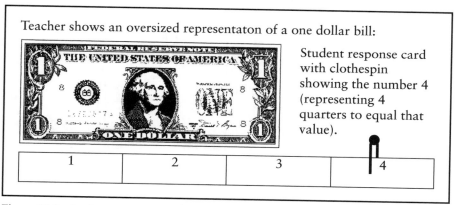

**Figure 11.2.** Student response card with clothespin indicating correct response. Teacher asks, "How many quarters does it take to make one dollar?"

component, students followed the teacher's presentation of key points using a progressive disclosure approach. During "response card" review, the teacher continued to use progressive disclosure, but a key point within each presented item was left blank intentionally. Students wrote a response to fill that blank on their response cards. Cards were raised, and teacher feedback and reinforcement were provided. Results showed that when write-on response cards were used, higher performance on next-day and weekly quizzes occurred, suggesting that students' active engagement was instrumental in producing the gain.

Likewise, Gardner, Heward, and Grossi (1994) showed that the number of responses that at-risk, inner-city elementary students make during whole-group instruction can be increased significantly during write-on response card conditions versus a more traditional hand-raising method. Figure 11.3 shows the results of five students' responses when hand raising (HR) was in effect versus response cards (RC). Gardner et al. report that an average of only 1.5 responses were made during the HR condition (an at-risk student raised his hand more often but was not called upon), whereas an average of 21.5 responses were made during the RC condition. Extrapolating these data over a semester (90 days) or a year (180 days) clearly would produce even higher margins of responding in favor of response cards.

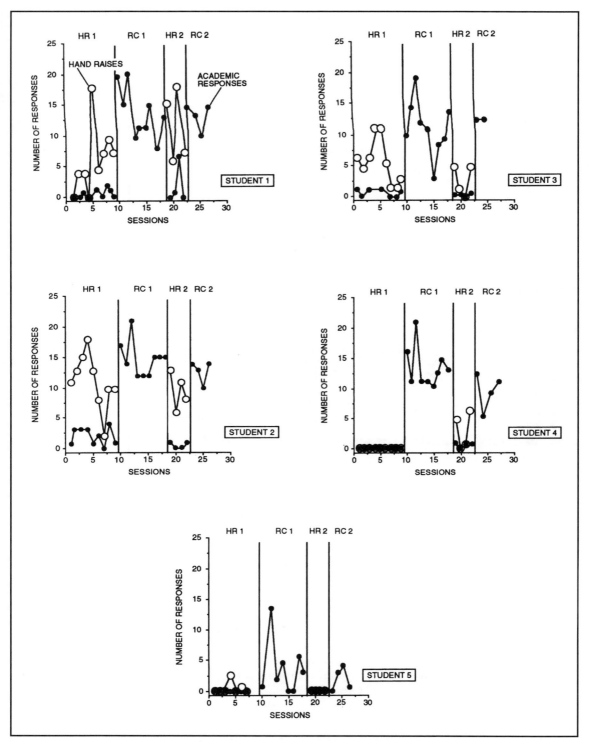

**Figure 11.3.** Number of academic responses and hand raises by students 1 through 5 during science lessons in which students participated by hand raising (HR) or response cards (RC). Breaks in data paths indicate student absences. From "Effects of Response Cards on Student Participation and Academic Achievement: A Systematic Replication with Inner-City Students During Whole-Class Science Instruction," by R. Gardner III, W. L. Heward, and T. A. Grossi, 1994, *Journal of Applied Behavior Analysis, 27,* 67. Copyright 1994 by *Journal of Applied Behavior Analysis.* Reprinted with permission.

Preprinted and write-on response cards provide the teacher and the learner with several advantages, including high ASR, modeling and imitation inter-actions, immediate reinforcement, and active teacher error correction (Barbetta, Heron, & Heward, 1993; Barbetta & Heward, 1993; Sterling, Barbetta, Heward, & Heron, 1997).

## Guided Notes

Heward (2000) provides a succinct definition of *guided notes* and their rela-tionship to the ASR and student achievement literature.

> Guided notes are teacher-prepared handouts that guide a student through a lecture with standard cues and specific space in which to write key facts, concepts, and/or relationships. (p. 274)

An emerging and increasing body of literature has demonstrated the effects of guided notes and guided notes used in combination with other teacher-directed review procedures on improved student achievement.

Lazarus (1993) demonstrated the effects of guided notes and guided notes plus a review by the teacher on the chapter test performance of two classes of students with special needs (LD and BD) enrolled in inclusive secondary-level history classes. During a baseline condition, students recorded notes in a tradi-tional fashion, meaning that they copied content that they believed to be relevant for later study. During guided notes, they were given a replica of the teacher's lecture notes from the prepared overhead transparency but with some key infor-mation missing. Students "filled in" these missing items (an active response) dur-ing the lecture. When guided notes plus in-class review was initiated, the guided notes continued as before, but now students were provided with a 10-minute period at the end of the class to examine and reread their responses to the guided notes until class time expired. Conditions were counterbalanced across the two classes. Overall results showed that during baseline, student per-formance never averaged higher than 50% on test items. When guided notes was instituted, student performance increased, ranging from 59% to 84%. When guided notes plus review was introduced, even higher levels were evident, with averages across the two classes ranging from 75% to 95%. Lazarus concluded that a functional relationship between guided notes and guided notes plus review existed, and that this strategy might be combined with other types of instructional arrangements (e.g., cooperative learning) to enhance the benefit.

See Heward et al. (1996) for a secondary-level example of how to integrate and incorporate choral responding, response cards, and guided notes into a science lesson.

# Peer-Mediated Approaches

In *peer-mediated* approaches, the students themselves, after training, take on the primary tasks of delivering instruction and providing prompts, cues, rein-forcement, and feedback during each learning trial. Two principal peer-mediated approaches will be presented: Tutoring systems and cooperative learning methods.

# Tutoring Systems

The research data on the beneficial effects of tutoring systems, especially within single-subject design and applied behavior analysis orientations, are over-whelming. Whether used as a stand-alone intervention or in combination with other procedures (Phillips, Fuchs, & Fuchs, 1994), tutoring systems have been shown to be effective in teaching functional math skills (Arreaga-Mayer, 1998; Harper, Mallette, Maheady, Bentley, & Moore, 1995; Schloss, Kobza, & Alper, 1997); social skills (Gumpel & Frank, 1999; Prater, Serna, & Nakamura, 1999); reading (Barbetta, Miller, Peters, Heron, & Cochran, 1991; Cooke, Heron, & Heward, 1983; Ezell, Kohler, & Strain, 1994); Spanish vocabulary (Wright, Cavanaugh, Sainato, & Heward, 1995); English as a second language (Houghton & Bain, 1993); basic math skills (Allsopp, 1997; Miller, Barbetta, Drevno, Martz, & Heron, 1996); and a wide variety of other academic and nonacademic behaviors across an even wider range of students with and without disabilities in different settings (Miller, Barbetta, & Heron, 1994).

*Tutoring systems* are defined as any formal and comprehensive approach to teaching students to prompt, praise, test, and chart the academic, social, or non-traditional skills of their partners on a daily basis. Schloss et al. (1997) indicate that "tutoring contributes to achievement outcomes in that students achieve a significantly higher rate of academic engagement . . . [and] . . . a higher rate of academic engagement has been linked to greater student learning" (p. 191).

## Classwide Peer Tutoring

*Classwide peer tutoring* (CWPT) involves having all students work in tutor-tutee pairs simultaneously (Cooke et al., 1983; Carta, Greenwood, Dinwiddie, Kohler, & Delquadri, cited in Greenwood, 1991). One goal of CWPT is to improve the basic skill performance of low-achieving minority or disadvantaged students or students with special needs within the general education classroom setting (Delquadri, Greenwood, Whorton, Carta, & Hall, 1986) and to increase the number of opportunities each child has to actively respond to academic materials (Greenwood, 1991). Individualization can take place for each student within the pairings.

There are various classwide peer tutoring systems (e.g., Heward, Heron, & Cooke, 1982; Maheady, Harper, & Sacca, 1986). We will discuss the multi-component system devised by Cooke, Heron, and Heward (1983) and Heward et al. (1982) because it (a) has been demonstrated to be effective, (b) can be used with general and special education students, and (c) requires minimal training. A key element in Heward et al.'s classwide peer tutoring system when a *nonreciprocal* approach is used is a procedure known as a tutor huddle. To form a tutor huddle, a class is divided into tutor-student pairs. Once pairs are formed, they are combined in groups of three to five pairs. For example, if there were 32 students in the class, 16 tutor-student pairs might be arranged into four tutor huddles with four tutors per huddle.

At the beginning of each tutoring session, the huddles meet for 5 minutes to review the concepts, facts, or terms listed on flashcards that will be presented to their partners during practice. Partners engage in teacher-assigned seatwork during this 5-minute period. As Figure 11.4 illustrates, tutors present sight-word vocabulary to one another, the same sight words that they will present to their partners (tutees) during the 5-minute practice session that follows. During the tutor huddle, the tutors confirm each other's correct responses to the sight vocabulary words by saying yes. If a tutor makes a mistake, the other tutors provide corrective feedback. If none of the tutors is able to provide the word, a tutor raises his or her hand to obtain teacher assistance.

At the teacher's signal, a 5-minute practice session begins. Each tutor is joined by his or her partner for drill (Figure 11.5). The tutor presents the cards

---

For a synthesis of four major tutoring centers' (Ohio State University, SUNY Fredonia, Vanderbilt University, and Juniper Gardens Children's Project) approaches to tutoring, the reader is referred to Maheady (1997).

A complete description of the classwide peer tutoring training package can be obtained by writing Dr. Timothy E. Heron, School of Physical Activities and Educational Services, The Ohio State University, 1945 N. High Street, Columbus, OH 43210.

For examples of how CWPT can be used in a game format in math, refer to Arreaga-Mayer, 1998; for a step-by-step method for using math CWPT, see Miller et al. (1996).

If a reciprocal method is used, then tutor and tutee switch roles for 5 minutes.

**Figure 11.4.** Four first-grade children participating in a tutor huddle.

**Figure 11.5.** A first-grade tutor presenting sight-word vocabulary to her student.

to the tutee as quickly as possible. If the tutee is not able to identify a word or says a word incorrectly, the tutor uses a 2-step prompting procedure to help. At the end of the 5-minute practice session, the tutee is tested by the tutor, and the results are graphed.

In a tutor huddle procedure, "a tutoring system within a tutoring system" is arranged (Heward et al., 1982, p. 121). Student's learn from one another, and the consequence of having to teach their partner may add an extra incentive to learn.

In a reciprocal approach whereby tutees and tutors switch roles within the instructional period, the tutor huddle component is not used. Instead, each tutoring dyad switches roles after practice so as to gain double exposure to items. If uncertainty occurs during practice, students are instructed to (a) raise their hands to seek teacher help, or (b) seek assistance from a neighboring tutor dyad.

Wright et al. (1995), for example, conducted a study of the effects of classwide peer tutoring on the Spanish vocabulary acquisition and maintenance of students identified as at-risk or learning disabled. After a brief training program, students engaged in CWPT daily for approximately 20 minutes by showing their partner a card with a picture on the front and the Spanish word for that picture on the back. After presentation, the tutee wrote the correct word on a response sheet. If the student wrote the correct response, praise was delivered. If the student made an error, the tutor provided on progressive trials a 2-, 3-, or 5-second delay before revealing the correct response for his partner to copy. Copying was accompanied by saying and spelling the word aloud so that the tutor could provide feedback and reinforcement. After 5 minutes of practice, the total number of responses was counted, and roles within the dyad were switched. Once both partners had practiced for 5 minutes, a daily test was administered. Maintenance tests were administered weekly and used as a basis for determining whether a word was "learned" or needed to be reinserted in the student's pocket of words to be learned. A long-term maintenance test was administered at the end of the program. Results showed that students learned and maintained the Spanish words after exposure to CWPT.

Readers interested in learning more about CSTT are referred to Harper and Maheady (1999).

A variation of CWPT, known as *classwide student tutoring teams,* or CSTT, (Harper & Maheady, 1999), combines CWPT with a teams-games-tournament cooperative learning approach described by Slavin (1990). Essentially, this procedure uses study guides, repeated active student practice, student learning activities, and high motivation during daily instructional sessions.

Arreaga-Mayer (1998) sums up the beneficial effects of CWPT when she states, "CWPT is consistent with the principles of effective instruction and inclusion. As a procedure, it has much to offer teachers and students looking for flexible, adaptable, motivating, and cost- and time-effective approaches to increasing active student responding and positive academic outcomes" (p. 94).

## Cross-Age Tutoring

*Cross-age tutoring* can be another effective method of providing individualized instruction (Gumpel & Frank, 1999; Schrader & Valus, 1990). It occurs when the tutor is approximately 2 or more years older than the tutee. Cross-age tutors often come from classes of older children within the same school. In some cases, junior high or high school students from campuses near an elementary school have been used (Barbetta et al., 1991). Some regular education teachers, especially those at earlier grade levels, may believe that the students within their classroom are not ready to teach one another, yet they still want a tutoring program. Cross-age tutoring effectively solves the teacher's problem. For example, a sixth grader could come in to tutor a second grader, and the teacher would merely have to resolve any scheduling conflicts for the sixth grader.

According to Jenkins and Jenkins (1981), the details that need to be worked out include: (a) where and when tutoring will take place; (b) which students will be tutors and how they will be selected and trained; (c) what materials will be used for tutoring and how they will be prepared; and (d) who will supervise the work of the tutors. Despite the logistical problems, the effort may be well worth it. A meta-analysis of cross-age tutoring programs conducted by Cohen, Kulik, and Kulik (1982) revealed that students who were tutored by older students outperformed those in comparison groups.

Some teachers may believe that peer or cross-age tutoring would be a beneficial experience but hesitate to do it because of the time it takes to prepare tutoring materials. This concern is clearly legitimate; however, the elementary teacher can be helped to identify those situations in which it would be appropriate for the students to prepare their own materials. Pierce and Van Houten (1984), for example, describe several situations in which it would be appropriate for students to prepare tutoring materials. For instance, students could construct their own flash cards. The teacher could make one sample set of cards and place each card at a separate work station. Students could move from station to station copying the cards. Elementary teachers should also establish criteria for successful task completion (e.g., neat flash cards, correct information recorded) and monitor students' activities while performing the task.

Cross-age tutoring can be used to teach more than just academics. Gumpel and Frank (1999), for example, demonstrated how cross-age tutoring can be used to improve the behavior of socially isolate students. Briefly, two sixth-grade students served as tutors for two kindergarten children on different components of a social competence model. When cross-age tutoring was in effect, the percentage of positive behaviors improved and the percentage of isolate behaviors decreased. Anecdotal reports from teachers indicated that a positive benefit was noted in the classroom.

## Small-Group Tutoring

In *small-group tutoring,* two procedural variations are possible. First, small-group peer tutoring can be used by students with disabilities who need additional (or remedial) practice with skills. Part of their independent seatwork time might be devoted to tutoring. In the second variation, the whole class would participate, but on a rotating basis. While the teacher worked with one instructional group, a second group would engage in small-group tutoring. Groups would rotate daily (or weekly) so that each group would engage in all activities.

## One-to-One Tutoring

In *one-to-one tutoring,* only select student dyads participate in 1:1 tutoring programs. Students needing remedial assistance usually work within 1:1 pairs using tutoring protocols similar to classwide, cross-age, or small-group arrangements.

## Home-Based Tutoring

In *home-based tutoring,* parents (or siblings) serve as tutors. Skill training typically involves showing parents how to manage the system, provide prompts and reinforcement to their child, evaluate the effects of sessions, and ensure a "game-like" atmosphere at home. Home-based tutoring programs have not been widely studied, but preliminary data show that parents can serve as effective tutors for their children (Barbetta & Heron, 1991; Elksnin & Elksnin, 1991).

## Nontraditional Tutoring Applications

*Nontraditional tutoring applications* refer to tutoring in subject or skill areas other than those that are academically oriented. For example, Heron and Welsch (1999) identify multiple uses of tutoring in subject matter other than academics (e.g., art, music, health education, and so forth). On the whole, data from nontraditional applications are entirely consistent with findings reported for academic subjects. That is, when tutoring is initiated, student performance improves and is more likely to be maintained and generalized and participants find it useful and enjoyable.

# Cooperative Learning

## Defining Cooperative Learning

"According to Artz and Newman (1990), *cooperative learning* is defined as small groups of learners working together as a team to solve a problem, complete a task, or accomplish a common goal" (p. 448). Goor and Schween (1993) identify several basic elements of cooperative learning. These include a shared purpose within the group, a classroom management system that supports cooperative learning activities, training to ensure that students have the prerequisites to function effectively, and a grouping arrangement that is consistent with the goals and objectives of the lesson.

All cooperative learning methods share the use of two essential elements to achieve academic and social goals: incentives and task structures. Marwell and Schmidt (1975) indicate that cooperation is not a single entity but a "set of relations among behaviors and their consequences" (p. 5), and different cooperative learning formats are derived from the variety of those relations (Sharan & Hertz-Lazarowitz, 1980). Madden and Slavin (1983) suggest that cooperative learning is an accepted practice in general education classrooms and would be considered a viable alternative for meeting the individual needs of special students in inclusive classrooms.

Johnson and Johnson (1989) indicate that cooperative learning is most effective when: (a) students perceive their positive interdependence (i.e., their need to depend on each other to complete the task); (b) students interact face to face; (c) individual accountability is clear (i.e., each student is responsible for the task); (d) the efforts of all members are needed for group success; (e) students have the skills they need for effective collaboration; and (f) students know how effectively their learning group is functioning. Further, the collaborative skills of leadership, decision making, trust building, communication, and conflict management are helpful to teach the students.

See Axelrod (1994) for a discussion of pedagogical issues related to cooperative learning. See Tateyama-Sniezek (1990) for a review of the effects of cooperative learning.

Carpenter, Bloom, and Boat (1999) suggest that cooperative learning may contribute to the achievement of socially valid outcomes by setting the occasion for students to belong to a group, participate in their own success, practice choice making, and experience empowerment through a sense of self-efficacy (i.e., their individual and collective perceptions that their efforts are recognized by the teacher and make a difference).

## Teacher's Role in Cooperative Learning

The teacher's role in cooperative learning includes specifying goals and objectives for the group; arranging teams and materials; clarifying the task, activity, and expectations; and monitoring and evaluating the group product (Johnson

& R.T. Johnson, 1987). Sapon-Shevin (1990) extends the role of the teacher in cooperative learning to eliminating competitive classroom symbols, using inclusive language, building the classroom community, and encouraging students to use one another as resources and to notice the accomplishments of others.

To develop cooperative skills, Johnson and Johnson (1975) indicate that students play a role in identifying the skills they think will be necessary, arranging situations to practice and receive feedback and reinforcement on the skills, and requiring that the skills be used frequently so that they become part of each student's behavioral repertoire.

Dugan, Kamps, Leonard, Watkins, Rheinberger, and Stackhaus (1995) conducted a study comparing the effects of cooperative learning with a teacher-directed lesson on the social studies skill acquisition of fourth-grade students. Cooperative learning groups included students with autism. During baseline conditions, the teacher used a lecture-discussion approach plus maps for a 40-minute lesson on social studies. During cooperative learning, the teacher conducted a 10-minute introduction to the lesson, followed by the formation of cooperative learning groups that implemented (a) peer tutoring on key words associated with the lesson, (b) a team activity, and (c) a wrap-up. Using an ABAB reversal design, Dugan et al. demonstrated that when cooperative learning was in effect, improved gains occurred on weekly tests and posttests for all students, including the students with autism. Further, increased levels of student engagement and the duration of their interaction favored the cooperative learning condition. Dugan et al. interpreted the findings to mean that (a) cooperative learning was superior to traditional, even for students with autism, (b) active student engagement was higher in cooperative learning than in traditional, and (c) high levels of student-student interaction during cooperative learning helped with the inclusive process, providing a social benefit that may not be derived from conventional teacher-directed approaches.

> See Pomplun (1997) for a discussion of how the presence of students with disabilities in a classroom may affect the level of cooperative interaction within a group, and Prater, Bruhl, and Serna (1998) and Fad, Ross, and Boston (1995) for methods to teach social skills within the group to enhance cooperation.
>
> In addition to social skills, consultants and teachers may consider teaching appropriate communication and trust-building skills.

## Cooperative Learning Methods

Bossert (1988) describes three procedures that have commonly been used, either separately or in combination, to set the occasion for cooperation: "instructing students to work together, varying the reward contingencies, and constructing tasks that are interdependent" (p. 227). Bossert states that the most debated differences between cooperative learning methods and other strategies concerns how task and reward structures are used to motivate students to cooperate or to compete. Within this context, cooperative learning research has focused on several well-developed models. The major cooperative learning models include: teams-games-tournaments, student teams and academic divisions, team-assisted individualization, cooperative integrated reading and composition, jigsaw methods I, II, and III, learning together, the group-investigation model, the group-investigation method, and peer tutoring in small investigative groups.

# Semi-Independent and Independent Approaches

In *semi-independent and independent approaches,* students by themselves, aided by computers or specialized teacher training, assume the primary responsibility for delivering their own instruction. Semi-independent and independent

> See Chapter 12 for a discussion of other semi-independent and independent approaches with respect to management.

approaches allow the student to practice skills at an independent level to develop proficiency and fluency, two critical components for skill mastery.

There is a major trend for microcomputers and related hard- and software to become smaller, more efficient, and less expensive and for publishers to offer semi-independent and independent activities and lessons on these applications (Rieth & Semmel, 1991). Still, microcomputers (or PCs) represent only one aspect of technology for improving instruction. In our view, technology refers to low- and high-tech applications, including educational media, materials, hardware, and software that can affect academic, social, and career education goals. Technology can also be formally referred to as *assistive technology,* meaning that instead of just making tasks, assignments, and projects less challenging, it also makes them feasible; they become accessible to people with disabilities (Bryant & Seay, 1998).

Readers interested in learning more about technological applications can consult the *Journal of Learning Disabilities,* 1996, *29*(4) and *Learning Disability Quarterly,* 1995, *18*(2). These special issues are devoted to a wide range of topics on technology, especially as they apply to people with learning disabilities.

## Low-Tech Applications

### Tape Recorders

The cassette tape recorder is excellent for individualizing instruction for later independent use by the student. It has several functions. Teachers can record review lessons, stories, tests, and directions for completing assignments. Students who have difficulty comprehending oral instructions can use the tape recorder effectively because they can replay an instruction several times. Further, the teacher can pace an exercise with the recorder so that students with lower rates of learning can be challenged while faster students can move ahead. Sample audiotaped teacher directions for a student practicing spelling are found in Anecdote 11.1.

### Anecdote 11.1

(Student turns tape recorder on.)

TEACHER: Good morning. Today we are going to take our practice spelling exam. I'll say one word at a time, use the word in a sentence, and then say the word again. After I pronounce each word the second time, turn off the recorder and write the correct spelling. Do this for each of the spelling words. When you are finished, see me for the answer tape. On the answer tape, I'll spell the word, and you can correct your own paper. Okay, get ready. The first word is *typhoon.* A typhoon is a fierce storm. Typhoon.

(Student turns off the tape recorder and writes the response. After completing the exam tape, the students shows his or her paper to the teacher, receives the answer tape, puts it in the recorder, and turns on the tape recorder to hear the teacher spell the words.)

TEACHER: This is the answer tape for your spelling words. Get ready to correct your own work. Write the correct spelling beside each word. The first word was *typhoon,* t-y-p-h-o-o-n.

(The student listens to the correct spelling for all 10 words.)

Now that you are finished listening to and writing down the correct spelling of each word, compare your spelling to my spelling.

> Write the number of words that are spelled correctly at the top of your paper. Bring the paper and tape back to me.

In this anecdote the teacher individualized the spelling words for the student as well as the response required, i.e., the student *wrote* the correct spelling word. For another student, the teacher may have requested an oral response, and the student would have spelled the word aloud directly onto the tape.

One potential disadvantage is that it takes time to produce the tapes. The teacher may seek the consultant's assistance with recruiting another person (e.g., a student, paraprofessional, or volunteer) to help make the tapes.

## Films, Videotapes, and Filmstrips with Recorders

For students with poor reading skills, films, videos, and filmstrip-tape packages offer the opportunity to participate in an individualized program or use them semi-independently as a follow-up to a main lesson. Students can view a film or video or listen to a tape of a story or lesson while simultaneously viewing an accompanying filmstrip. The auditory input carries information about sounds and expressive language and helps with interpreting the visual information. If viewed with a purpose stated by the teacher, students will attend thoughtfully (Kosma, 1991). Therefore, teachers should clearly establish a purpose for viewing. They can use this approach to review lessons or as an independent learning center assignment. If deaf or hard-of-hearing students are integrated into the general education classroom, a teacher of the deaf might collaborate with an elementary teacher and obtain captioned films or filmstrips so that those students will be able to participate as well.

## Overhead Projector

Aside from the tape recorder, the overhead projector is the most common piece of instructional hardware available for individual instruction. It can be used in a group lesson to introduce new skills, to review key points prior to an exam, or as a way to observe an individual student's response. One advantage of the overhead is its low cost. By using write-on transparencies and washable pens, teachers can reuse transparencies almost indefinitely. Like audiotapes, transparencies can be catalogued and filed by skill or content. Students can make responses directly on an overhead, thereby making them visible to the teacher and other students. Of course, consultants who might recommend that the overhead be used by students to make responses would further recommend that the teacher structure the question so as to ensure that it is within the student's repertoire. The whole idea of using the overhead is predicated on ensuring that correct responses are recognized by the group, not as a way to embarrass or humiliate a student by highlighting deficiencies in public.

# High-Tech Applications

Computer technology is becoming increasingly present throughout society. While district and school-wide adaptation of the more sophisticated aspects of computer technology has not received universal adoption or support in classrooms, a positive trend in that direction is evident. In the semi-independent and independent modes, the microcomputer can be used in computer-assisted formats to reteach, drill, simulate, and communicate. Microcomputer programs have been developed to teach new concepts and review previously taught ones,

With instruction, students can learn to access information on the Internet's World Wide Web, opening avenues for additional exploration during school hours or at home. Readers interested in exploring a variety of Web-based sites might preview the text *1001 Really Cool Web Sites* (Renehan, 1995).

and programs have been designed to provide the necessary drill and practice for students to overlearn and master concepts. Given the expanding array of user-friendly software programs available, teachers should be assisted in using a data-based evaluation guide to assess potential programs. Test (1985) outlined the following multistep procedure for evaluating programs:

Step 1. Read the documentation that accompanies the program carefully, paying attention to objectives, field-test data, and instructional claims.
Step 2. Use an evaluation form to document the assessment.
Step 3. Run the program and test how it responds to correct and incorrect responses.
Step 4. Observe a student as he or she completes the program to determine those features of the program that seem to set the occasion for and maintain responding.

Microcomputers can also be used to compensate for a skill deficit. For example, they can be used as word processors. Students who have difficulty writing, because of either poor motor coordination or poor organizational skills, can use the computer to complete written assignments. Students who experience disabling conditions, such as orthopedic, visual, or auditory impairments, can use the computer to help compensate for those disabilities. For example, a student with an orthopedic disability who does not have adequate fine-motor control or speech can, with a pointer applied to the keyboard, use a computer to receive instruction as well as to communicate with the teacher and other students in the class.

For the consultant, the essential point is to help the teacher integrate microcomputer technology with existing strategies—that is, to help the teacher recognize that a new strategy can be incorporated into his or her existing repertoire. The teacher does not have to abandon everything he or she has done to date to use this new instructional strategy effectively. For instance, the consultant could help the teacher apply the skills used to evaluate paper-and-pencil instructional materials to the evaluation of computer programs. First, the consultant should identify how the teacher currently evaluates materials. Once that is known, the consultant can help the teacher refine his or her criteria with microcomputer materials. Consultants are urged to help teachers answer two questions about microcomputer instructional uses: Does the computer program do what you want it to do well? And is the computer the best medium for the job?

When computer programs are used to provide instruction for students, there are several considerations to address. First, identify what the program is intended to do. For example, if the program is designed to provide drill and practice for mastery of multiplication facts, then evaluate it according to how well it helps the student master multiplication facts. Second, decide whether the lesson could be taught more effectively with another method. That is, in light of instructional objectives and individual students' needs, should textbooks, worksheets, manipulative materials, filmstrips, tape recorders, or some combination be used instead? Finally, consultants can help teachers develop and apply criteria that will effectively evaluate whether the computer program is well designed. Some of the items to consider in making this decision follow:

1. Is the software program user-friendly? For example, are sufficient prompts provided to students to operate the program semi-independently or independently? Is there a minimum number of keystrokes needed to execute the

program? How much time is taken in starting the program and moving to each of its parts?

2. Does the computer provide the student with sufficient opportunities to respond (OTR) and active student response (ASR)? For example, does the computer give the student more than one choice to respond to a given command? What is the computer's response when a student does not answer correctly? Does the computer provide hints? Does the computer model the correct response? Depending on the purpose of the lesson and the needs of the student, the teacher may want the instructional program to provide different types of responses to the student's response. Another question may then be asked about the program: Is the program modifiable? Is it possible for the teacher to override commands to the computer program to change the list of words that are practiced or to change parameters of the situation being simulated? Such modifications may be necessary to effectively use the program with some of the students in the class.

3. Does the computer program use graphics or sound? Is the intended reinforcement appropriate with respect to frequency and duration? Is it age appropriate? Is the reinforcement related to the skills to be learned in using the program, or is it external to the program's purpose? For example, some programs provide reinforcement in the way of a game. When students complete a lesson, they have some time away from the lesson and are provided with the opportunity to play a game. Other programs provide immediate reinforcement when a student responds correctly (e.g., a display of color graphics or sounds). The teacher needs to evaluate what type of reinforcement is appropriate for a given situation and whether the computer delivers that reinforcement satisfactorily.

## Computer-Assisted Instruction

*Computer-assisted instruction* (CAI) can be divided into broadly defined areas such as: drill and practice, tutoring, simulations and problem solving, and writing (Rieth & Semmel, 1991).

### Drill and Practice

Drill-and-practice software sets the occasion for students to achieve high levels of active student response, immediate reinforcement and/or error correction, feedback on the quality of the response, and self-paced lesson formats. However, as effective as drill-and-practice software might be, it may not be a panacea for *all* basic skill acquisition tasks.

Wilson et al. provide consultants with a valuable perspective on when to use CAI as an instructional method:

> The issue at hand, however, is not whether simple instructional procedures are effective for basic-fact acquisition. Rather, as special educators and general educators face increasing numbers of students with special needs . . . they must be able to match the instructional needs of students with the ecological needs of the classroom to design methods that optimize learning . . . instructional research must move beyond providing an either/or analysis of interventions and instructional practices, to specifying the conditions and effects of particular interventions. (p. 389)

See Wilson, Majsterek, and Simmons (1996) for an example of a comparison study between a computer-based drill-and-practice math software program (Math Blaster) and a teacher-directed instructional (TDI) approach. Their results showed that all students learned the facts under both arrangements but learned more facts and had more OTR under TDI.

## Tutoring

Unlike the tutoring systems discussed earlier in this chapter (e.g., CWPT), CAI tutoring refers to the computer taking the teacher's role to teach *new* skills to the students. In this application, students respond to computer-generated questions as the new content is presented. In CAI tutoring, it is important for the lesson objectives to be sequenced and modularized correctly, allowing for high rates of correct responses with ample reinforcement. CAI tutorials, although not without their critics, who may believe that they are electronic versions of flashcards (cf. Torgesen & Barker, 1995), do offer other benefits including potentially higher motivation to students, immediate feedback, game-like situations, graphic displays, and interesting screen designs unmatched by more traditional instructional strategies (Larsen, 1995). Further, tutoring can be combined with drill and practice to produce positive effects on student learning and fluency, even if the drill and practice and tutoring occur for short time periods (Hasselbring, Goin, & Bransford, 1988).

## Simulations/Problem Solving

According to Rieth and Semmel (1991), a simulation is "designed to model some reality" (p. 230). Usually, simulations are designed to provide students with an opportunity to solve problems. Simulations help the learner to experience a real-life situation without experiencing the cost, danger, or time-consuming effort of that situation.

Heretofore, high-tech and sophisticated simulations were available only to the military or other high-end users (e.g., airlines and private companies engaged in pilot training). Now, with increased computer capabilities coming within the financial reach of school districts, practitioners may have still another method of teaching. A promising area to explore is the use of virtual reality simulations (Muscott & Gifford, 1994). In virtual reality simulation programs, students experience a 3-D, computer-generated version of a real situation across passive (no control), exploratory (with movement through space), or interactive (movement plus dynamic interaction) environments. For example, students might be presented with a social situation involving peer pressure, and the simulation could vary the size of the antagonists or other environmental variables (e.g., the playground, classroom) in an effort to teach a cooperative, sharing, or interactive skill. Especially promising applications of interactive modes take advantage of the computer's multisensory ability and its ability to make changes in the virtual world by permitting multiple users, active problem solving, visualizations, complex dynamic processes (e.g., social interactions involving peer pressure), and cooperative learning arrangements (Muscott & Gifford, 1994).

## Writing

Using word and text processors offers practitioners a unique way to teach many of the editorial skills associated with written language (e.g., editing sentences, rearranging paragraphs, conducting spell checks). However, as some educators have indicated, the use of a computer may not help with generating original text. A promising adaptation that takes advantage of a student's oral language competence is that of voice-activated or speech-recognition computer programs. In these modes, the student's speech is recognized by the computer and encoded on the screen in real time for later manipulation. Since many students with learning disabilities experience significant challenges generating written language, speech-recognition programs offer them an attractive alternative (Higgins & Raskind, 1995).

In sum, research indicates that: (a) microcomputers can assist learners in reaching instructional objectives; (b) students who receive computer-assisted instruction can retain information after the CAI ends; (c) CAI can improve the speed at which students learn material; and (d) students react positively to well-designed CAI programs and tend to reject poorly designed ones (Edwards, Norton, Taylor, Weiss, & Van Dusseldorp, 1975; Gleason, 1981; Kulik, Bangert, & Williams, 1983).

These findings provide challenges to teachers, especially teachers who wish to incorporate students with special needs into the general education classroom, and suggest that the computer is a viable instructional tool in inclusive settings. For consultants to collaborate effectively with teachers in using the computer, the following questions should be addressed: What can a computer do? How much adaptation to the hardware or software will be necessary to use the system in the classroom? How can the computer be used to compensate for the challenges students with special needs experience in the inclusive classroom?

## Assistive Technology Applications

*Assistive technology* refers to any type of equipment or system that has been developed, has been modified, or is available commercially that can be applied to improve the independent functioning of students with disabilities (Parette, Brotherson, Hourcade, & Bradley, 1996). Hence, items such as augmentative communication devices, mobility aids, voice-based computer recognition systems, robotic applications, adaptive toys, adaptive switches, and keyboards all fall within the scope of assistive technology.

Parette et al. recommend that consultants be knowledgeable about and aware of how assistive technology can affect teachers, parents, families, and students. With respect to parents and families, they suggest that an assessment be conducted that seeks input on child needs, funding or cost issues, transportation or travel considerations, and training needs once an assistive technology device is secured. In their view, "Given the increasingly important role technology plays in the design and implementation of IFSPs, professionals must acknowledge and examine many evolving issues relating to the assessment of families' technology needs" (p. 110).

Blackhurst (1997) recommends, correctly in our opinion, that technology, especially assistive technology, be placed in its proper relationship to the needs of students as they interact with school and home environments. It does little good for a district to use scarce fiscal resources to purchase the latest piece of hardware or software only to determine later that it is (a) incompatible with the existing IFSP or IEP needs of the student; (b) incompatible with the "culture" of the school or family; (c) dependent on high start-up or maintenance costs (training or operating); and (d) unnecessary given other personnel, technical, or related services that could be provided instead. Blackhurst concludes that consultants, along with other researchers, must be on the forefront of taking state-of-the-art technology to the next level: state-of-the-science. That is, we must be able to integrate technology effectively in the classroom and the home (Smith, Martin, & Lloyd, 1998), render it accessible for all people with disabilities (Peters-Walters, 1998), and show at the level of objective proof that the assistive technology that we recommend produces the desirable outcome for each student with special needs.

Readers interested in learning more about World Wide Web applications of technology are referred to *Teaching Exceptional Children*, 1998, *30*(5). The articles in this special issue may be helpful to consultants as they work collaboratively with teachers to use Web-based strategies effectively with students in inclusive classrooms and other settings.

In sum, there are many issues to consider when deciding how best to use technology with students on a semi-independent or independent basis. Ultimately, the teacher must decide, based on the available technology, just what its use will be. Once that is determined for each situation, the teacher must decide whether the technology application meets that purpose well. It is important for teachers to make judgments based upon their knowledge of (a) the individual students' strengths and weaknesses, (b) the capability of technology, (c) best practice, and (d) effective instructional methodology. Consultants should help teachers to increase their skills in each of these areas as well as to evaluate the effectiveness of the technology.

# Conclusion

Consultants often work with case loads that span grade and skill areas. This chapter suggests that several effective and field-tested, teacher-directed, peer-mediated, and semi-independent and independent approaches can be used to meet the academic, social, and nontraditional needs of students. These approaches meet the standard for best practice, and they can be readily employed across subjects and settings. Finally, consultants might discover that the approaches that produced desirable outcomes at a younger age might also be called upon during transition years or later in a student's academic career.

# Summary of Key Points

## Best Practice

1. For best practice to be claimed, appropriate answers to the following questions must be addressed: Does the practice have a sound theoretical base? Is the methodological integrity of the research convincing and compelling? Is there consensus with existing literature? Is there evidence that desired outcomes are consistently produced? Is there evidence of social validity?

## Effective Instruction

2. What constitutes effective instruction is debatable, but one way to determine its parameters is to examine the robust effects that are produced as a function of the instruction. Do students learn?

3. Effective instructional strategies can be categorized into teacher-directed, peer-mediated, and semi-independent and independent approaches.

## Teacher-Directed Approaches

4. Five teacher-directed approaches are: direct instruction, early intervention, cognitive behavior modification, mnemonic training, and active student response modes. In a teacher-directed approach, the teacher assumes the primary role of delivering instruction, i.e., providing the prompts, cues, reinforcers, and feedback during each learning trial.

5. Three field-tested and validated approaches to using active student response include: choral responding, response cards, and guided notes.

# Peer-Mediated Approaches

6. In peer-mediated approaches, the students themselves, after training, assume the primary responsibility of delivering instruction, providing the prompts, cues, reinforcement, and feedback during each learning trial.

7. Peer-mediated approaches include tutoring systems (peer, cross-age, small-group, 1:1, home-based, and nontraditional applications). Cooperative learning approaches are also peer mediated.

# Semi-Independent and Independent Approaches

8. In semi-independent and independent approaches, the students themselves, after training, assume the primary responsibility of delivering their own instruction, providing the prompts, cues, reinforcement, and feedback during each learning trial.

9. Semi-independent and independent approaches can include low-technology, high-technology, and assistive-technology applications. Advances in microcomputer technology allow more opportunities for delivering instruction efficiently and effectively. For many people with disabilities, computer hardware and software offer additional prosthetic assistance that was not possible just a few years ago.

# Questions

1. What is a best practice strategy, and how would you recognize one if you saw it?

2. How does the Daubert standard apply to best practice approaches?

3. Distinguish between teacher-directed, peer-mediated, and semi-independent and independent approaches with respect to the person who assumes the primary responsibility for delivering instruction.

4. How might a direct instruction approach be combined with a mnemonics strategy for teaching a history lesson to students with learning disabilities?

5. Under what conditions might a teacher favor using choral responding over response cards or guided notes?

6. Discriminate between peer, cross-age, small-group, 1:1, and home-based tutoring approaches.

7. What function does a "tutor huddle" serve in a classwide peer-tutoring approach?

8. After defining *cooperative learning*, describe its various formats.

9. State how tape recorders; film, video, and filmstrip packages; and computer-assisted instruction could be used within an inclusive classroom to individualize instruction.

10. Give examples of assistive technology and state how that technology can be integrated into the IFSP or IEP.

# Discussion Points and Exercises

1. Conduct a meeting with special and general education teachers to determine how existing curriculum materials could be adapted, consistent with best practice methods, to meet the needs of students with disabilities.

2. Show a videotaped segment of a teacher instructing a class in social studies, science, or math using various teacher-directed, peer-mediated, or semi-independent or independent approaches. Obtain audience views on how the lesson could have been better individualized.

3. Conduct a pilot study with a group of elementary teachers to determine the efficacy of various pieces of instructional hardware (e.g., tape recorder, microcomputer). Include in the study a complete evaluation of how individualization was enhanced.

4. Obtain the IEPs for students across elementary, middle, and high school levels. Examine the annual goals, benchmarks, and suggested behavioral plans and determine an appropriate teacher-directed, peer-mediated, or semi-independent strategy to meet the IEP or IFSP goals.

5. Outline a home-based, peer-mediated, or semi-independent approach that could be implemented after school hours. Present this plan to the parents of a student with disabilities for their input. Consider implementation.

# Selecting and Implementing Appropriate Behavior Management Strategies

*12*

Each day teachers make innumerable decisions. They decide what lessons should be reviewed, what teaching material to use, what skills should be taught, and what behavior management strategies to employ. Similarly, parents and other caretakers within the family make multiple decisions. They decide what household responsibilities the child will have, what social experiences will be permitted, and what behaviors to discipline or ignore. For teachers, parents, and other caretakers within the family, these decisions are not always easy, but the decision-making process can be facilitated if a consistent management strategy is followed.

The emphasis of this chapter is on the management needs of students. Specifically, the purpose is to describe a number of procedures a consultant can recommend to teachers, parents, or other caretakers within the family to increase appropriate and decrease inappropriate behaviors. Ethical considerations related to the right to treatment and the right to education will be revisited. Training strategies are discussed along with a comprehensive decision model for changing behavior using the "least restrictive alternative" method. Examples from the authors' classroom teaching experience with students with and without disabilities as well as examples from research studies are presented.

## Objectives

After reading this chapter, the reader will be able to:

1. define the terms *positive reinforcement* and *positive reinforcer* and give an applied example of each;

2. outline five levels of reinforcers and give an applied example of each;

3. define the terms *negative reinforcement* and *negative reinforcer* and give an applied example of each;

4. describe the appropriate steps to use to establish, maintain, and thin a token reinforcement program;

5. write a functional contingency contract with task and components;

6. describe the Premack principle;

7. describe how a level system operates;

8. name two variables that enhance modeling and give an applied example of each;

9. define *self-management* and indicate how a teacher could teach this skill;

10. define the term *extinction;*

11. differentiate among several positive reductive procedures and give an applied example of each;

12. distinguish among the terms *punishment, overcorrection, time out from positive reinforcement,* and *response cost;*

13. discuss several ethical issues associated with using punishment in applied settings;

14. outline the key tenets of the right to treatment and the right to education position statements;

15. describe the components of a decision-making model for using punishment in applied settings;

16. define the term *group-oriented contingency,* indicate three procedural variations, and state the condition under which they should be used;

17. list several guidelines for using a group-oriented contingency.

## Key Terms

| | |
|---|---|
| positive reinforcement | self-management |
| positive reinforcer | self-monitoring |
| negative reinforcement | extinction |
| negative reinforcer | differential reinforcement of other behavior (DRO) |
| unconditioned reinforcer | |
| conditioned reinforcer | differential reinforcement of low rates of behavior (DRL) |
| edible reinforcer | |
| tangible reinforcer | differential reinforcement of incompatible behavior (DRI) |
| exchangeable reinforcer | |
| activity reinforcer | punishment by contingent presentation of a stimulus |
| social reinforcer | overcorrection |
| token reinforcer | time out from positive reinforcement |
| contingency contracting | response cost |
| Premack principle | Gaylord-Ross decision model |
| level systems | group-oriented contingency |
| modeling | good behavior game |

## Behavior Management: More Than Just Discipline

In our view, procedures to help prevent and solve behavior management issues rest squarely on the practitioners ability to establish functional proactive behavioral preintervention and classroom management tactics. Proactive approaches are not only required by law (IDEA '97), but also demanded by appropriate practice. According to Carpenter and McKee-Higgins (1996), proactive approaches embrace flexible instructional techniques, positive classroom conditions, dynamic and responsive management alternatives, and supportive collegial interactions that enhance practice and "significantly influence the behavioral and achievement outcomes for the individual child" (p. 202).

Further, we agree wholeheartedly with Murdick and Petch-Hogan (1996) when they assert, "[The] literature on effective teaching indicates that the *structure* of the classroom has a significant impact on the effectiveness of learning and the number of inappropriate behaviors that may occur. . . . True management includes all facets of the school environment, not just the control of students' inappropriate behavior" (p. 173, emphasis added).

## Preintervention Strategies

Preintervention strategies are composed of a wide variety of variables that the teacher manages to enhance learning and reduce behavioral disruptions. Physical setting, daily schedule, instructional delivery, precorrection, reinforcement and debriefing plans, classroom rules, and communication and cueing strategies (verbal and nonverbal) are but a few of the more salient items to consider when planning management options (Colvin, Sugai, & Patching, 1993; Daniels, 1998; Gardill, DuPaul, & Kyle, 1996; Marable & Raimondi, 1995; Murdick & Petch-Hogan, 1996; Sugai & Colvin, 1997).

Colvin et al.'s (1993) use of a precorrection checklist combines expectancy variables, context modification factors, reinforcement, prompting, and monitoring. Like the other preintervention strategies cited, precorrection is "based on the assumption that if effective preventative procedures are utilized, a number of desirable outcomes are possible . . ." (Colvin et al., 1993, p. 143). (See Figure 12.1.)

*Readers interested in guidelines for establishing classroom rules can consult Rademacher, Callahan, and Pederson-Seelye (1998).*

## Classroom Management Strategies

Classroom management strategies represent the full range of procedures that teachers may employ to increase appropriate academic and social behavior. Teachers, parents, and consultants have a number of *best practice* procedures at their disposal for improving academic and social behavior (Simpson, 1998). As stated previously, best practice is defined as one that focuses on: (a) the theoretical basis for a procedure; (b) the integrity of the research design and the extent of systematic replication; (c) consensus with existing literature; (d) process and product outcomes; and (e) evidence of social validity (Peters & Heron, 1993). The procedures that follow, largely drawn from the applied behavior analysis literature, are field-tested, have been used by the authors in many classroom and clinical settings, and meet Peters and Heron's criteria.

*Consultants interested in learning more about implementing classroom management strategies can refer to Cipani (1998); Colvin and Lazar (1997); Kerr and Nelson (1998); Sprick and Howard (1997); Walker and Shea (1999); Zirpoli and Melloy (1997).*

## Procedures To Increase Appropriate Academic and Social Behavior

It is important for consultants, especially consultants who work with teachers or parents of children with disabilities, to be well grounded in learning theory and applied behavior analysis because teaching children and youth with disabilities is challenging, and the teachers and parents must be prepared to meet this difficulty. A consultant who is skilled in applied behavior analysis, especially as

*See Daniels (1998) and the entire issue of Teaching Exceptional Children, 1998, Vol. 30(4) for a discussion of managing disruptive behavior in inclusive settings and of behavior and discipline respectively as regards IDEA '97.*

| **Precorrection Checklist and Plan** | Teacher: _____ Luis McGregor _____ <br> Student: _____ Alfonse Montague _____ <br> Date: __12__ / __2__ / __91__ |
|---|---|
| ☐ 1. Context | Students working at activity centers for 15 minutes. Activities involve manipulatives. |
| Predictable behavior | Alfonse runs to next center, grabs activity materials, and refuses to share with other students. |
| ☐ 2. Expected behavior | Play cooperatively for 15 minutes, share materials with three or four other students, walk to next center when prompted by teacher. |
| ☐ 3. Context modification | Teacher stands next to Alfonse just before announcing shift to next activity center and waits there until he begins to move to the next center. |
| ☐ 4. Behavior rehearsal | Just before announcing shift to next activity center, teacher asks Alfonse to tell him what he is going to do when he has to shift to the next center. |
| ☐ 5. Strong reinforcement | Teacher tells Alfonse that he can announce the next activity shift if he can play cooperatively for 15 minutes. He also provides specific verbal praise when Alfonse walks to the next center. |
| ☐ 6. Prompts | Teacher gets Alfonse's attention, points to the next activity center, and walks part of the way with Alfonse. |
| ☐ 7. Monitoring plan | The teacher counts the number of times Alfonse walks to the next activity center, and once every 3 minutes the teacher checks to see if Alfonse is playing cooperatively. |

**Figure 12.1.** Precorrection checklist and plan. From "Precorrection: An Instructional Approach for Managing Predictive Problem Behaviors," by G. Colvin, G. Sugai, & B. Patching, 1993 in *Intervention in School and Clinic, 28*(3), 149. Copyright 1993 by PRO-ED, Inc. Reprinted with permission.

those procedures are applied in inclusive classroom settings, will be able to assist teachers and parents competently as they jointly devise management programs.

## Positive Reinforcement

Positive reinforcement occurs when a behavior is followed immediately by the presentation of a stimulus or event, making that behavior more likely to occur again in the future (Cooper, Heron, & Heward, 1987). Actually, it's the response class that is more likely to increase rather than any individual behavior. Simply stated, positive reinforcement increases the likelihood of the occurrence of future behaviors within the response class. Catania (1984) specifies three necessary conditions for reinforcement to be claimed: (a) a response must have some consequence; (b) the response must increase in probability (i.e., the response must be more probable than when it does not have this consequence); and (c) the increase in probability must occur because the response has this consequence and not for some other reason.

The stimulus or event that follows the behavior (the consequence) is known as the *positive reinforcer.* For example, if Ray raises his hand to answer a question in class (the behavior), and the teacher praises him for his response (the reinforcer), the likelihood that Ray will raise his hand in the future is increased. Notably, a reinforcer can be so labeled *only* if it alone increases the likelihood of the behavior's recurrence. Table 12.1 contains a list of potential positive reinforcers. Whether any one stimulus or event is an actual reinforcer for an individual student depends solely on its effect on the student's behavior. Reinforcers are determined in a functional manner. What might be a reinforcer for one student may not work for another. What may be reinforcing for a student at one given time may not produce the same increase in behavior at another time (Justen & Howerton, 1993).

Consultants can assist teachers with identifying reinforcers in several ways. Students can be asked what events, activities, or stimuli they prefer; teachers can observe what events or activities students select when given the

### Table 12.1
Potential Positive Reinforcers for School-Aged Students

| Elementary-Level Students | Intermediate-Level Students | Secondary-Level Students |
|---|---|---|
| Popcorn | Graphs of behavior | Soft drinks |
| Soft drinks | Points/tokens | Radio listening time |
| Crayons | Calculators | Popular magazines |
| Comic books | Science activities | Free time in gym |
| Play money | Fast-food gift certificates | Romantic novels |
| Stars/stickers | Pictures of TV stars | Graphs of behavior |
| Graphs | Radio listening time | Praise |
| Toys | Structured free time | Rock star posters |
| Notes home | Sports and car magazines | T-shirts |
| Balls | Soft drinks | Plants |
| Raisins | Diary | Calculators |
| Chalkboard work | Games | Tickets to sports events |

option; or reinforcer sampling can be performed whereby students experience an unfamiliar stimulus in order for the teacher to determine its effectiveness in increasing future behavior. A forced-choice or choice-assessment procedure (Paclawskyj & Vollmer, 1995; Piazza, Fisher, Hagopian, Bowman, & Toole, 1996) might be used to determine which of two or three options students prefer or to assess the reinforcing properties of frequently selected items (e.g., reading, listening to a tape, quiet time, juice, praise, etc.) (Cooper et al., 1987; Paclawskyj & Vollmer, 1995).

Consultants and practitioners may want to go two steps further to determine (a) the relative quality of reinforcers, and (b) the controlling nature of a potential reinforcer. To accomplish the former, consultants might employ a concurrent operant paradigm (cf. Piazza et al., 1996), meaning potential reinforcers are made available concurrently and reinforcer effectiveness and suitability are determined systematically relative to high, medium, or low preference items. In the latter case, consultants might use: (a) a response-dependent, response-independent procedure (whereby the stimulus is presented contingently and noncontingently), (b) schedule control (whereby the potential reinforcer is paired with a known reinforcer), or (c) multiple procedures (whereby a combination of presentations and reversals is made) to determine the effect (Higgins & Morris, 1985).

Finally, consultants should include in their jointly developed programs with teachers practical procedures for determining the ongoing strength and usefulness of reinforcers in light of satiation and idiosyncratic student preference issues (Green et al., 1988; Mason, McGee, Farmer-Dougan, & Risley, 1989). Consultants should recognize that in some classroom situations at least, the level of reinforcement is low (Gunter & Coutinbo, 1997). Further, an overwhelming number of teacher-student interactions can be negative, a phenomenon that may have implications for programming changes with positive and negative reinforcement contingencies.

## Negative Reinforcement

Probably no term is misused or misunderstood more often than *negative reinforcement*. Simply stated, negative reinforcement occurs when a stimulus is removed contingent upon the performance of a particular behavior. Consequently, the likelihood of the behavior occurring in the future is increased. Negative reinforcement has the effect of increasing the desired behavior, not decreasing it. Negative reinforcement is not synonymous with punishment. In fact, it has the opposite meaning and effect (Justen & Howerton, 1993). Cooper et al. (1987) clarify the misconception regarding the terminology associated with positive and negative reinforcement:

> The term reinforcement always means an increase in response rate and the modifiers positive and negative describe the type of stimulus change operation that best characterizes the consequence (i.e., adding or withdrawing a stimulus). (p. 25)

Negative reinforcement can be used by skilled classroom teachers to improve student performance. For example, suppose a teacher says, "If each person in the class receives 85% or better on the first two math pages today, the third page of the assignment will be canceled." In effect, the teacher is removing the stimulus (the third page of math) contingent upon the successful completion of the first two pages. The *negative reinforcer,* the stimulus that is removed, is the third page of math. The behavior targeted for increase is a higher percentage of completion with assignments.

Consultants should not hesitate to recommend a negative reinforcement contingency to a regular classroom teacher. In many instances, the use of a negative reinforcement procedure can serve the teacher's purpose as well as a positive reinforcement procedure. For example, assume that a student with learning disabilities consistently returned homework that was sloppy and inaccurate. The consultant might suggest that the teacher set up a contingency whereby neater and more accurate papers were negatively reinforced by the removal of the student's homework requirements one day per week.

Consultants should be aware that the applications of positive and negative reinforcement procedures are not without shortcomings. In the former case, providing a superabundance of reinforcement—termed *satiation*—may lead to a subsequent deterioration of the behavior. Also, unplanned secondary effects may surface, insofar as reinforcement for the target behavior may suppress the future probability of other adaptive behaviors. Mace, McCurdy, and Quigley (1990) make this point:

> Individuals inevitably adjust their allocation of behavior according to the relative richness of reinforcement across response alternatives. Thus, increasing the rate of reinforcement for one response is likely to have undesirable effects on other behaviors that may be adaptive for the individual. (p. 203)

With respect to negative reinforcement, two disadvantages are apparent. First, a prior worsening of the environment is required. For example, a student may be directed to complete five pages of math problems, but if he achieves 80% correct on four of the pages, he does not have to do the fifth page. Negative reinforcement may produce escape and avoidance behavior (Gunter & Coutinbo, 1997; Iwata, 1987). Second, aggressive or emotional responses may be generated (Cooper et al., 1987).

In either case—positive or negative reinforcement—consultants should be aware that it is not the procedure per se that has the shortcoming; it is the application of that procedure. Epstein (1985) states, "Particular contingencies of reinforcement can strengthen and maintain 'lying, cheating, stealing, and conniving,' but reinforcement itself is not the culprit. It is, rather, poor contingencies that are at fault" (p. 74). Cipani (1995) provides consultants with direction insofar as determining whether behaviors are maintained by negative reinforcement. In his view, consultants should address the following three questions (a "yes" answer to each question would likely indicate that the behavior was being maintained by negative reinforcement):

1. Does the student's problem behavior effectively function to halt instruction or completion of the assignment?

2. Does the student feel competent to complete the task or assignment?

3. Does the rate of the student's problem behavior go up when certain instructional conditions are present?

To counter an existing negative reinforcement contingency, Cipani suggests increasing the level of positive reinforcement for the nonpreferred activity

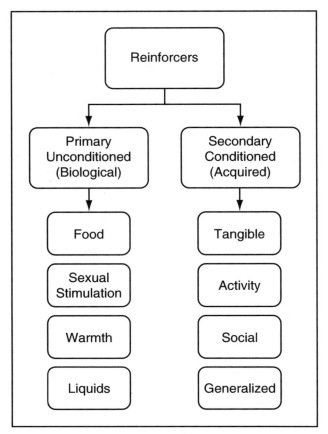

Figure 12.2. Types of potential reinforcers. From *Applied Behavior Analysis* (p. 261), by J. O. Cooper, T. E. Heron, and W. L. Heward, 1987, Columbus, OH: Merrill. Copyright 1987 by Merrill. Reprinted with permission.

and/or improving student skill performance levels to such a degree that the initial task is no longer aversive.

## Types of Reinforcers

Some reinforcers affect an individual's behavior without the individual having prior experience with them. The first type of reinforcer is termed an *unconditioned reinforcer.* An unconditioned reinforcer is biologically determined and tends to satisfy basic human needs. The great majority of reinforcers are of the second type: *conditioned reinforcers.* A conditioned reinforcer acquires its reinforcing capability when paired repeatedly with unconditioned reinforcers or previously acquired conditioned reinforcers. According to Cooper et al. (1987), the major types of unconditioned and conditioned reinforcers have associated subcategories (Figure 12.2).

It is important for the consultant to be aware of these types and subcategories so that he or she can contribute recommendations to the teacher or parent that will work within school or home settings. Further, the consultant must be able to recognize conditions in the classroom or home that would suggest a shift to more natural or generalized reinforcers such as social praise. The more commonly used subcategories of reinforcement are presented in this section. An analysis also illustrates the role of the consultant in dealing with a particular management problem in a classroom or home setting.

## Edible Reinforcers

An edible reinforcer can be defined as any food item that is delivered contingent on the occurrence of a particular behavior and that increases the likelihood that the behavior will occur again in the future. Willis, Hobbs, Kirkpatrick, and Manley (1975) used an edible reinforcer (snacks) to reduce the number of out-of-seat and talk-out behaviors of 27 highly disruptive seventh-grade students. Essentially, their reversal design study consisted of four conditions. During baseline 1 the number of out-of-seat and talk-out behaviors were measured. During treatment 1 students were informed that a 5-minute snack break would be available at the end of the class period if they did not leave their seats or call out during the first 15 minutes of class. Following treatment 1, baseline conditions were reinstated. During treatment 2, treatment 1 conditions were reinstituted. Finally, during treatment 3, students were told that snacks would still be provided contingent on the absence of out-of-seat and talking-out behavior, but the snack would not be provided every day. Students did not know from day to day whether a snack was going to be provided. The results of the study indicate that when the snack condition was in effect, the number of out-of-seat and talk-out behaviors was reduced to near zero. Likewise, the study showed that during the third snack condition, which provided reinforcement on a variable interval schedule, the reduced levels of out-of-seat and talking-out behavior were maintained.

Before implementing a program using edible reinforcers, the consultant should confer with the teacher, parent, and other significant family caretakers. First, from an ethical viewpoint, it is critical to make sure that there is no medical condition that might preclude the use of edible reinforcers. For example, if a student was allergic to chocolate or sugar and the teacher issued chocolate bits for appropriate behavior, a serious situation could develop. Second, edible reinforcers can lose their effectiveness quickly as the student becomes satiated—that is, if the student has received an overabundance of a reinforcer. A soda break is not as likely to be effective immediately after lunch as it might be during mid-afternoon. Finally, even though edibles can be used successfully to establish desired behavior and to maintain performance over long periods of time, it is usually advisable to switch to other reinforcers in the hierarchy, such as praise, that occur more naturally in the environment. The teacher should use edible reinforcers only in those situations where other reinforcers in the hierarchy are not likely to be effective.

## Tangible Reinforcers

A tangible reinforcer can be considered any type of physical object presented immediately subsequent to the occurrence of a behavior, which has the effect of increasing the future probability of that behavior. For example, if a student with a learning disability cleaned his or her desk each week, the teacher might reinforce that student with a puzzle or small trinket. Recall Table 12.1 and its list of potential reinforcers. Many of those reinforcers can be considered tangible, because the student receives a physical object contingent upon performance. Anecdote 12.1 describes how a general classroom teacher structured tangible reinforcers for two students with physical disabilities based on a prior discussion with the consultant.

## Anecdote 12.1

| | |
|---|---|
| TEACHER: | Nancy and Barbara, I've noticed that you have a difficult time getting your work completed each day. |
| NANCY: | That's for sure. There is so much to do, I barely have time to breathe. |
| BARBARA: | That's right. It seems like I am always working. |
| TEACHER: | Well, to help you complete the assigned tasks I want to present a plan to you. I've discussed the plan with Ms. Quatman, the consultant, and we both believe it's worth a try. When you complete your assigned tasks for the week, you'll earn a cassette tape on which I've recorded your favorite records. The tape will be yours to keep. |
| BARBARA: | That sounds great. |
| NANCY: | And we get to keep the tape? |
| TEACHER: | That's right, and to get things off to a good start, here is a cassette tape bin to store your tapes. I think you'll be earning a number of them. |
| GIRLS: | You bet! |

The consultant and teacher agreed jointly to use the cassette tapes because they knew the students enjoyed listening to music. They also chose tapes because they are powerful reinforcers, can be prepared easily, and can be used in other environments, such as the home. A teacher may want to issue a noncontingent reinforcer, one the students do not have to earn, to prime them to respond. In this case, the tape bin served as the noncontingent reinforcer. The teacher could just as easily have made the first few assignments simple enough so that the students could have earned the tape bin. Either strategy is acceptable.

### Exchangeable Reinforcers

A token, checkmark, or star that is earned by a student for appropriate behavior and later traded for another reinforcing object or event is considered an exchangeable reinforcer. Exchangeable reinforcers serve a dual function. First, they reinforce the target behavior immediately, and, second, they can be exchanged by the student for a stronger reinforcer in the future. Descriptions of token reinforcers and an illustration of how tokens serve as exchangeable reinforcers are found later in this chapter.

### Activity Reinforcers

An activity reinforcer can be defined as any game, free time, or social event that is used contingently to increase the future occurrence of the behavior that preceded it. McEvoy and Brady (1988) demonstrated that the academic performance of three students with severe behavior disorders could be improved when access to free time was made contingent on performance. Specifically, during baseline conditions the three students, ages 6 to 9 years old, were told to complete a math worksheet within their instructional repertoire. Prior to intervention, the students were shown a room that contained materials and activities. Then, the students were told that to have access to the materials for 5 minutes they needed to reach criterion and to work without disruption. Criterion levels were established by examining previous performance data and were differentially set for the students. Students were given 6 minutes to complete approximately 30 math calculations.

Figure 12.3 shows the rate of correct and incorrect performances across baseline and contingent access for the three students. The data show a functional

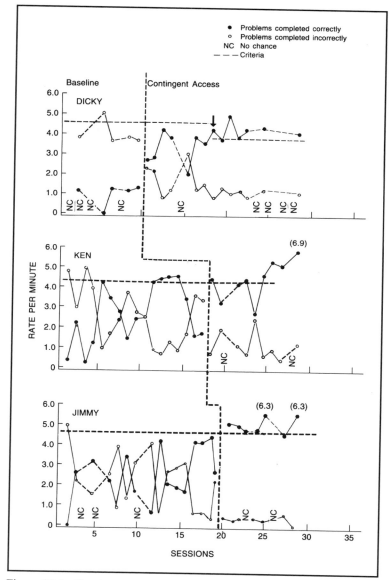

**Figure 12.3.** Contingent access to play materials. Daily rate of correct and incorrect math problems for Dicky (top graph), Ken (middle graph), and Jimmy (bottom graph) during baseline and contingent access conditions. Arrow (↑) in top graph indicates date of criterion change. From "Contingent Access to Play Materials as an Academic Motivator for Autistic and Behavior Disordered Children," by M. A. McEvoy and M. P. Brady, 1988, *Education and Treatment of Children, 11*(1), 15. Copyright 1998 by *Education and Treatment of Children*. Reprinted with permission.

relationship between the use of contingent access and improved rate performance. Two points of interest with respect to the data apply to consultants. First, the criterion level for Dicky was reduced after the seventh day of contingent access, indicating the formative use of the data for decision making. That is, when the initial contingency did not work, it was changed. Second, the variability of performance decreased from baseline to contingent access, indicating that the range of student performance became much more stable.

It is important to remember that when using activity reinforcers (free time, field trips, etc.), students should not have access to the activity at other times. It would hardly be effective to say to a student who had an articulation problem that contingent upon three correct verbal initiations to another student she would earn 15 minutes of free time, if access to free time were available at recess or lunch. Students will more likely perform under the stated contingencies if other sources of activity reinforcers are controlled.

Anecdote 12.2 shows how a consultant and general education teacher structured an activity reinforcer for a student with a hearing impairment who had been included in a general education junior high school class. The student experienced concomitant speech difficulties.

## Anecdote 12.2

| | |
|---|---|
| TEACHER: | Mrs. Bogan, I'm having a problem with one of my students. I thought you might be able to help me. |
| CONSULTANT: | I'll be glad to help if I can. What seems to be the difficulty? |
| TEACHER: | Megan, a student with a hearing-impairment in my class, has extreme difficulty talking to the other students. I think she's afraid they will either ignore her or make fun of her. |
| CONSULTANT: | I see. |
| TEACHER: | There are a few students who talk to her occasionally, but most of the students ignore her. |
| CONSULTANT: | I see. How about if we get together in a couple of days to discuss the situation? |
| TEACHER: | Okay. |
| CONSULTANT: | (meeting with the teacher a few days later) I recall you said that there were a few students who talked a little bit to Megan. |
| TEACHER: | Yes, that's right. |
| CONSULTANT: | How would you feel if we designed a program whereby those students could earn extra points if they interacted with Megan? |
| TEACHER: | That would be fine, since all of my students earn points for one thing or another in class. I'm sure we could extend the present program in that direction. |
| CONSULTANT: | Good. |
| TEACHER: | (approaching the two students who occasionally talk to Megan with the consultant) Chris and Bill, we have an idea that might interest the two of you. |

| BILL: | Really? What is it? |
|---|---|
| CONSULTANT: | As you know, Megan has difficulty talking to other students. |
| CHRIS: | We know. She's hard to understand sometimes. |
| TEACHER: | We realize that some of what Megan says is difficult to understand, but we'd like the two of you to make an effort to talk to her, maybe between classes or during project work in class. Whenever either of you says something to Megan, you'll earn one extra point toward your weekly total. |
| BILL: | That's all we have to do? |
| CONSULTANT: | That's right. Any time either of you begins a conversation with Megan, each of you will earn one extra point. |
| MEGAN: | (approaching the teacher some time later) Mrs. Jones, things have really improved. Two students in my classes are talking to me more and even listening to me when I talk. School isn't such a drag anymore. |

The consultant and the teacher could have arranged the contingency the other way around. That is, they could have made point acquisition for Megan contingent upon her initiating conversations with other students. The rationale for structuring the activity for the nondisabled students is that the teacher knew that the points would be a powerful reinforcer for Chris and Bill and that there might be more occasions for Chris and Bill to initiate a conversation with Megan than the reverse. Clearly, though, as time passed, the teacher and the consultant would continue to refine the program so that Megan would have more responsibility for initiating and maintaining interactions.

## Social Reinforcers

Social reinforcement is the least intrusive level of reinforcement that a classroom teacher can use to establish and maintain behavior. Praise is the foremost example of a social reinforcer. Other types of social reinforcement include smiles, pats on the back, facial gestures, and teacher attention. The use of contingent praise has been demonstrated for at least 30 years (Broden, Bruce, Mitchell, Carter, & Hall, 1970; Hall, Lund, & Jackson, 1968; Kazdin & Klock, 1973). Surprisingly, however, social praise is not given in the classroom with the frequency that one might expect, despite its demonstrated effectiveness. A practical guideline suggests that a functional ratio of about four praise statements to one disciplinary statement should be the goal of teachers in most learning settings.

Hall, Lund, and Jackson (1968) conducted a classic study showing the effects of praise on student behavior. When elementary-aged students engaged in study behavior, the teacher verbally praised them, patted them on the back, or came close to their desks. If a student was not studying, the teacher did not attend to him or her. Figure 12.4 clearly shows the effects of positive praise and attention on the study behavior of one of the students. When the contingency was in effect, study behavior increased. When it was not in effect, study behavior decreased.

The consultant recommending social praise as an alternative to building behaviors can remind the teacher that it is the most natural reinforcer that a teacher can use, and it has a number of distinct advantages over other levels of

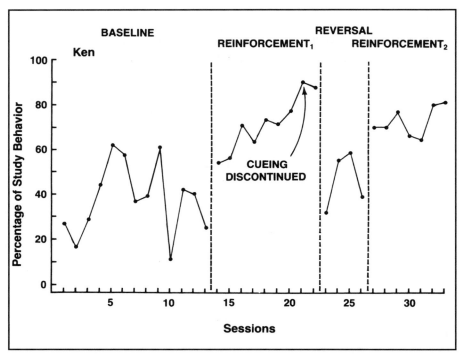

**Figure 12.4.** A record of study behavior for Ken. From "Effects of Teacher Attention on Study Behavior," by R. V. Hall, D. Lund, and D. Jackson, 1968, *Journal of Applied Behavior Analysis, 1*(1), 6. Copyright 1968 by Society for the Experimental Analysis of Behavior. Reprinted with permission.

reinforcement. First, given the variety of praising statements that teachers can use, satiation is unlikely to occur. Second, praise and attention are cost-effective. The teacher does not have to spend money to deliver the reinforcement. With other levels of reinforcers (edibles, tangibles, and exchangeables), the cost of purchasing items is a factor. Third, social reinforcers are convenient and efficient. Teachers do not have the potential messiness associated with edible reinforcers, nor do they have to be concerned with the potential delays in student response while the candy is eaten or the exchangeable reinforcers are handled. Finally, student performance is much more likely to be maintained in different learning settings under social reinforcement than under other levels of reinforcement.

## Token Reinforcers

For a complete description of the guidelines for establishing and maintaining token economy systems in the classroom, the reader is referred to Alberto and Troutman (1999); Cooper et al. (1987); and Myles, Moran, Ormslee, and Downing (1992).

According to Cooper et al. (1987), token reinforcers can be considered generalized reinforcers because they are associated with a large number of reinforcers. A token reinforcer can be a physical object, such as a chip or a star, or it can be a written symbol, such as a checkmark (Murdick & Petch-Hogan, 1996). Tokens can be reinforcing themselves, and they acquire stronger reinforcing capability when they are exchanged for back-up reinforcers, such as free time or activity reinforcers.

Tokens have been used to modify a broad range of academic and social behaviors (e.g., reading, math, social skills) across an even wider range of settings (preschools; elementary, middle, and high schools; homes; and clinics) (Cooper et al., 1987; Gardill, DuPaul, & Kyle, 1996; Myles et al., 1992). Overall, a convincing body of literature demonstrates the effectiveness of this procedure for changing behavior. Buisson, Murdock, Reynolds, and Cronin (1995) provide a contemporary demonstration of how tokens can be used to reduce the latency of responding with students with hearing impairments. Since latency of response (also known as procrastination) is a nagging problem for many practitioners, it would be informative to examine this application briefly. In the Buisson et al. study, two students who attended a deaf-education resource room experienced latencies of almost 8 and 3 minutes, respectively, between the time of a teacher direction and compliance. Using a 4-phase, step-down, changing criterion design, during which the students earned tokens for meeting reduced time-to-compliance requirements, Buisson et al. showed that compliance changed to less than 1 minute for both students using this simple, readily available procedure.

***Initiating and Maintaining a Token Economy in the Classroom.*** When initiating a token economy, the first step is to determine the target behavior to be modified. Once the target behavior has been identified in observable and measurable terms, the teacher describes the rules of the token economy. The teacher informs the students of the conditions under which tokens can be earned, the back-up reinforcers that are available, and the exchange procedure. Sometimes teachers combine game-like or real-life situations with their explanations, especially within inclusive settings, to further highlight how tokens are earned and lost. Finally, frequent token exchanges are recommended when initiating a token economy program (Anderson & Katsiyannis, 1997; Myles et al., 1992).

Cooper et al. (1987) suggest that consideration be given to selecting an appropriate token for the individual or group. The token should be safe (e.g., not likely to swallowed by young children) and not likely to be counterfeited. Also, it should be durable, reusable, and inexpensive. Anderson and Katsiyannis (1997), for instance, used the theme of a Speedway to show how mock license plates (the tokens) could be earned and revoked for a class of fifth-grade students.

Once the token system is established, maintaining it is a relatively simple task. The teacher needs only to follow the rules that were formed initially. Reinforcing students with the token immediately after the occurrence of the desired behavior, providing a variety of back-up reinforcers, and maintaining a functional exchange procedure are essential components of maintenance. Also, it is to the teacher's advantage to begin to increase the response requirements while simultaneously decreasing the amount of tokens earned. It is important to incorporate this strategy, because the primary goal of the token program should be to move to a higher level of reinforcement (e.g., praise) as soon as possible. By repeatedly pairing praise with the delivery of the token, the praise will acquire the reinforcing capability of the token.

***Financing a Token Economy.*** Consultants who recommend the use of token economies or other exchangeable systems must be able to suggest ways for teachers to finance such systems. A few alternatives are presented below.

*Grant-in-Aid.* Many state and local departments of education offer grants for teachers to develop, implement, and evaluate instructional approaches. If the tokens or exchangeable reinforcers are essential components of the overall instructional methodology, the cost of those items could be incorporated into the budget. The obvious disadvantage of this approach is that because competition for funding is often keen and many proposals have to be reviewed, there may be a considerable delay between the application and the reward of the grant. Waiting to implement the token program until a decision is rendered by the granting source may be counterproductive.

*District Support.* Some school districts allocate money each year for expendable items such as reinforcers. Often the principal has a petty cash account that might be used to reduce the cost of the token economy.

*Parent-Teacher Groups.* In many districts parent-teacher associations (PTAs) sponsor fund-raising events each year to reduce or eliminate costs for worthwhile school projects. Petitioning the PTA to sponsor a fund-raiser to support a token economy might help.

*Personal Expenditure.* Many teachers purchase exchangeable reinforcers with their own money. While this is an undesirable option from a cost standpoint, many teachers believe that the benefit the students derive from having the program outweighs the cost they incur. To avoid incurring expenditures for exchangeable reinforcers, teachers or parents should ensure that the available reinforcement menu includes a variety of no-cost options (e.g., free time, classroom privileges, donated fast-food coupons). If free time, classroom privileges, or coupons are reinforcers for the students, costs are eliminated.

## Contingency Contracting

Contingency contracting refers to a behavioral approach in which the criteria for task completion and conditions for reinforcement delivery are specified before the assignment is begun. According to Murphy (1988), the theoretical basis for contingency contracting is derived from the Premack principle. The *Premack principle* is often dubbed Grandma's law and is best explained in Grandma's own words: "When you finish your meat and beans, you will be able to have your ice cream." In such a context, the Premack principle means that access to a high-frequency behavior (eating ice cream) is contingent upon the performance of a low-frequency behavior (eating meat and beans). Once high- and low-frequency behaviors have been determined, the teacher (or parent) need only arrange them contingently. The contract provides the mechanism to accomplish that objective.

The use of contracts is frequent in our daily lives. Examples of contracts are mortgages, credit cards, and employment agreements. Although each of these items is different, a common feature exists. In any contract there are specifications about the terms of the agreement and the responsibilities of each party. According to Cooper et al. (1987), specifying the terms is an important consideration when establishing a contingency contract. Teachers, parents, and other family members who might use contracts must realize that the personal exchange between the parties is an important dimension of the process. Cooper et al. (1987) put it succinctly:

> The warning against the oversimplification of contracting is important. Contracting is not as simple as it is so often presented whether used with delinquent teenagers or well-behaved third graders. The negotiation/compromise process is not an adjunct to, but rather an integral component of contingency contracting as a behavior change intervention. (p. 16)

Educators (notably Cooper et al., 1987; Downing, 1990; Homme, Csanyi, Gonzales, & Rechs, 1969; Kelley & Stokes, 1982; Murphy, 1988) have outlined guidelines for using and negotiating contracts in school environments. Downing (1990), for example, outlined 15 specifications for contracts and suggested that contracts can be used with any population of students for any subject matter (Table 12.2).

## Table 12.2

Downing's List of 15 Guidelines

---

*Guidelines for Establishing and Maintaining Contingency Contracts*

1. Choose one behavior as the focus of the contract. Meet with parents and the student to discuss.
2. Determine the conditions under which the behavior occurs presently.
3. Determine who will use the contract and where; especially important if multiple parties are involved.
4. Determine the type of reinforcement to be applied.
5. Keep reinforcers small and easily managed.
6. Determine whether negative consequences will be applied and under what conditions.
7. Determine the schedule of reinforcement.
8. Assess the current level of the behavior.
9. Determine task expectations and goals.
10. Write the contract ensuring that task and reinforcement conditions are spelled out in detail.
11. Set daily expectations.
12. Discuss all provisions of the contract after it is written so that the student understands the provisions.
13. Sign the contract and provide each party with a copy.
14. After a week or so, convene the parties to review the contract; adjust if necessary.
15. Monitor the contract on a regular basis.

---

*Note.* From "Contingency Contracts: A Step-by-Step Format," by J. A. Downing, 1990, *Intervention in School and Clinic, 26*(2), 111–113. Copyright 1990 by PRO-ED, Inc. Reprinted with permission.

Taken as a whole, Downing's (1990) specifications provide the consultant with clear guidelines for assisting teachers in developing working contracts. Embedded in the rules, which are consistent with general guidelines for effective classroom management, are the behavioral procedures of immediate reinforcement, systematic application, fairness, and data sharing (Rademacher, Callahan, & Pederson-Seelye, 1998).

Teachers who use contingency contracting according to Downing's (1990) guidelines become more directive teachers, even for subject areas in which contracts are not employed. Teachers begin to recognize the value of positive directions, immediate feedback, frequent reinforcers, and consistency. In classrooms where students with disabilities are enrolled, teachers frequently report that the shared responsibility of developing the contract, in conjunction with the monitoring process, increases student academic and social performance.

Alberto and Troutman (1999), Cooper et al. (1987), Dardig and Heward (1976, 1981), and Murphy (1988) have indicated that contracts can be used with children in home or school settings to increase and maintain a wide variety of behaviors. These authors suggest that contracts be written so that the task and reinforcement components are clearly specified. Kidd and Saudargas (1988) suggest that to increase academic behavior in school, "positive" contracts be written that specify reinforcement contingencies, rather than "negative" contracts or a combination of positive and negative contracts. The latter two exemplars would specify that a punisher would be delivered if the contract was not fulfilled, or that the dual application of punishment and reinforcement would be applied for inappropriate or appropriate contract behaviors, respectively.

As Figure 12.5 shows, four items are completed under the task component portion: Who, What, When, and How Well. Under the reward component, the items Who, What, When, and How Much reinforcement are listed. In this contract, Ron must attend to his tasks each day with a minimum of two prompts from the teacher. When he does that, he will earn 10 minutes of free time from his teacher, Mrs. Pauley.

Ideally, contracts should be negotiated and written jointly with students. Students can specify tasks or reinforcers. For example, when beginning to contract with students, the teacher or the parent may specify the task components while the student completes the reinforcement categories. As the student develops more and more competence in task completion, the teacher or parent may have him or her suggest tasks as well. As a student becomes more self-directed—the ultimate goal of the procedure—more responsibility is provided for stating the terms of the contract.

Dardig and Heward (1976) suggest that contracts can also be employed across settings. For example, a student with disabilities who completes his or her work on time and at criterion in the regular classroom might have reinforcers issued at home. In a variation of home contracting, Trovato and Bucher (1980) found that reading-deficient, elementary-aged students made twice the achievement gains of peers participating in in-class tutoring when the in-class peer tutoring was supplemented with a home-based contingency contract. In their study, improved reading performance produced a variety of reinforcers specified by the contract, including preferred goods, being able to invite a friend to the house, or going out to eat dinner with the family.

Welch and Holborn (1988) have generated a 5-step decision-making flowchart of required negotiation behaviors that might be useful to novice contingency contracting managers.

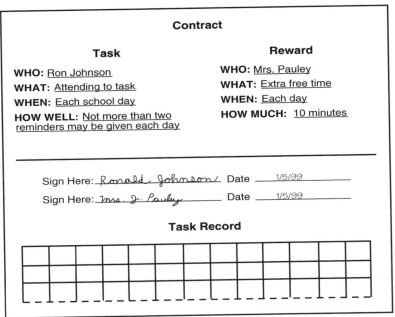

Figure 12.5. A sample contract. From *Sign Here: A Contracting Book for Children and Their Parents*, (2nd ed.) by J. C. Dardig and W. L. Heward, 1981, Bridgewater, NJ: Fournies and Associates. Copyright 1981 by Fournies and Associates. Reprinted with permission.

Contracts have been used at the elementary and secondary levels for students for whom previous types of reinforcement strategies have failed (Raimondi, 1994). Kelley and Stokes (1982) provide an excellent illustration of how contingency contracting was used with junior- and senior-level high school dropouts attending a vocational training center. During baseline conditions, the students earned money for attending daily class sessions. During contracting 1, students were paid for completing a negotiated amount of workbook items on a daily or weekly basis. For instance, their contract might require the completion of 5 daily assignments or 25 weekly assignments. Students earned their pay for attendance and work completion. Baseline conditions were reintroduced approximately halfway through the study, during which time the contingency contracts were removed. Finally, contingency contracting 2 was introduced.

Figure 12.6 shows that the contingency contracting was an effective procedure for improving the academic productivity of the students. During the contingency contracting condition of the study, the number of correct items completed by the students increased, whereas during baseline conditions the improvement was lost. Anecdotally, the students indicated that they preferred the contracts because they knew exactly how much work was expected of them to earn the reinforcer.

Consultants who recommend contingency contracting should emphasize that it may take a couple of trials with students before the contracting process is completely successful. They must also stress to teachers that contracting is a mechanism to increase student performance when other procedures have failed, as it provides students with a voice in determining either the tasks they have to perform or the reinforcement they will earn. For many students with disabilities, having a say about the curriculum can enhance their performance within it.

## Level Systems

An interesting combination of the token economy and contingency contracting merges with level systems, defined as "motivational plans for behavioral improvement based upon a graduated series of steps or levels . . . with increasing student responsibility at each step" (Reisberg, Brodigan, & Williams, 1991, p. 31). Table 12.3 shows the characteristics of level systems.

Essentially, level systems specify the steps, expectations, consequences and privileges, and transition rules for each level. Zirpoli and Melloy (1997) suggest that level systems are especially appropriate for teaching social skills. Level III, for example, would represent the entry level with the fewest expectations for behavior (e.g., earn 70% of the available merits [tokens]) and have the most restrictive privileges (e.g., stay in seat, supervised restroom breaks), while level I would have the highest expectations (e.g., earn 80% or more of the available merits) and the least restrictive privileges (e.g., leave seat without permission, unsupervised restroom breaks). Students proceed through the levels by calculating the ratio of merits to demerits. Figure 12.7 shows a daily recording sheet for noting the number of points earned and spent for five students enrolled in a class for students with behavioral disorders. The daily recording sheet shows performance across six periods as it relates to such behaviors as on time, academic responses, interactions, and rule following.

Consultants working with special education teachers who have students likely to be integrated into the general education curriculum might find level

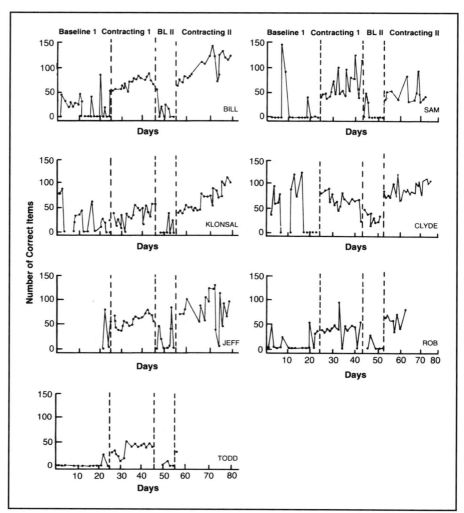

**Figure 12.6.** Number of items completed by students during baseline and contracting conditions. Missing data points represent student absences. From "Contingency Contracting with Disadvantaged Youths: Improving Classroom Performance," by M. L. Kelley and T. F. Stokes, 1982, *Journal of Applied Behavior Analysis, 15*(3), 452. Copyright 1968 by Society for the Experimental Analysis of Behavior. Reprinted with permission.

## Table 12.3

Characteristics of Level Systems

1. Define steps clearly.
2. Define observable, specific desired behavior.
3. Clearly define undesirable behavior.
4. Clearly define reinforcers.
5. Determine measurable criteria.
6. Measure and record student performance.
7. Include complementary systems.
8. Communicate frequently.

*Note.* From "Classroom Management: Implementing a System for Students with BD," by L. Reisberg, D. Brodigan, and G. J. Williams, 1991, *Intervention in School and Clinic, 27*(1), 35. Copyright 1991 by PRO-ED, Inc. Reprinted with permission.

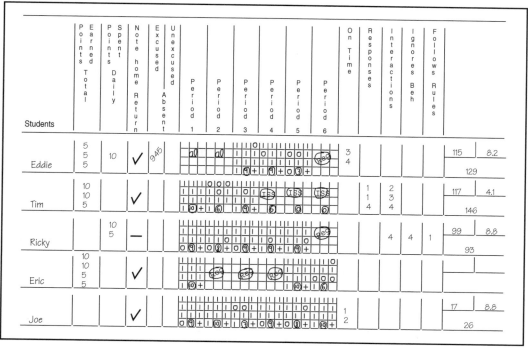

**Figure 12.7.** Daily recording sheet. From "Classroom Management: Implementing a System for Students with BD," by L. Reisberg, D. Brodigan, and G. J. Williams, 1991, *Intervention in School and Clinic, 27*(1), 35. Copyright 1991 by PRO-ED, Inc. Reprinted with permission.

systems beneficial for several reasons. First, the level system prescribes clear behaviors and outcomes for the students. For pupils about to be mainstreamed, increased practice with meeting behavioral standards could increase their successful integration. Second, when students earn merits (tokens), they can be exchanged for natural classroom privileges (e.g., earning access to free time) or for items on a reinforcement menu in a way described by McEvoy and Brady (1988). Hence, a system within a system can be configured to provide reinforcement for appropriate behavior and consequences for inappropriate behavior using least restrictive alternative strategies. Finally, a public record-keeping system and home-reporting component ensure that the program is visible, enabling students, parents, and other family members to contribute to decision making. Progress (or regression) can be discerned readily.

See Lyon and Lagarde (1997) for a description of a graduated reinforcement system (GRS) that includes a built-in level system for reinforcement.

## Modeling

In a modeling procedure, an antecedent stimulus is presented to the learner for the purpose of having him or her imitate it. The model can be a person or a behavior. Directing a student to watch the blackboard as the teacher solves a problem and then having the student imitate that behavior, would be an example of using a modeling procedure.

Striefel (1981) and Cooper et al. (1987) provide excellent guidelines for using modeling across a range of applied settings.

Despite the extensive literature that indicates the powerful effects modeling has on increasing student performance (cf. Cooper et al., 1987; Striefel, 1981), consultants sometimes overlook this procedure when recommending strategies to teachers or parents for solving problems because they do not fully understand how modeling can be used.

Espin and Deno (1989) demonstrated the differential positive effects of modeling over verbal prompting when teaching sight vocabulary to second-, fourth-, and fifth-grade students with learning disabilities. In this study, students were presented with sight vocabulary words on flash cards, and they had 3 seconds to make a response. In the *modeling condition,* if the 3 seconds passed without a correct response or if the student made an error, the teacher gave (modeled) the correct pronunciation of the word for the student to imitate. In the *prompting condition,* if the 3 seconds passed without a correct response or if the student made an error, the teacher gave part of the word for the student (e.g., said the first syllable). After repeating this cycle twice for the word lists, testing occurred. The results showed that the students learned more words that were modeled and that they retained their words 1 to 3 months after training. Further, the authors claimed that modeling consumed less instructional time, producing, in turn, more opportunities to respond to academic content.

A modeling strategy might also be applied to groups of students. Stainback, Stainback, Etscheidt, and Doud (1986) provided case study evidence that placing disruptive students into a group of well-behaved students who modeled appropriate behavior had a beneficial effect on the former group. Not only did the frequency of disruptive behaviors decrease, but the nature of the disruptions changed as well. Whereas before modeling, students were aggressive and argumentative, after modeling, the students were merely "off task," engaged in nonwork-related conversation. Stainback et al. attributed the radical change in behavior to the positive effects of the models.

When students possess many of the component skills required for a task, or when the teacher desires to use the beneficial influences of peers (cf. Werts, Caldwell, & Wolery, 1996), then a modeling procedure seems to be a powerful, yet nonintrusive, alternative. Werts et al. emphasize the positive effects of peer models when they state:

> The peer model procedure may hold advantages over one-to-one instruction of chained tasks. It may reduce the amount of teacher time and prompting required, allow students with disabilities access to more helpers, be easily embedded into ongoing classroom activities, and lead to more generalized observational learning. (p. 65)

## Self-Management

Readers interested in learning more about self-management and its application in applied settings are referred to Cooper et al.'s 1987 text, *Applied Behavior Analysis;* Lloyd, Hughes, and colleagues' (1993, 1994) three-part series, containing a total of 6 papers, published in the *Journal of Behavioral Education;* and Reid's 1996 review of research in the *Journal of Learning Disabilities.*

The goal for virtually every educative or habilitative program is to teach the individual to manage his or her own behavior independent of external controls. Self-management is an application designed to accomplish that purpose.

Cooper et al. (1987) define self-management as "the personal and systematic application of behavior change strategies that result in the desired modification of one's own behavior" (p. 517). Procedurally, self-management always requires two elements: the behavior to be managed (e.g., on-task, academic production), and the response that manages that behavior (e.g., graphing, tracking, or recording the behavior) (Lloyd & Hughes, 1993).

Consultants working with teachers (or parents and other family caretakers) who have exhausted other behavior management strategies may find self-management tactics appealing because they can (a) eliminate the necessity of an external observer; (b) be transported from one setting to another (e.g., classroom 1 to classroom 2); (c) be applied to a variety of behaviors; (d) be more effective than teacher-controlled strategies; and (e) produce a feeling of self-control not possible with other arrangements (Cooper et al., 1987).

Self-management and *self-monitoring,* the procedure to record targeted behaviors, have been used to increase on-task and academic productivity (Boyle & Hughes, 1994; Harris, 1986; Hughes & Boyle, 1991; Johnson, 1988; Seabaugh & Schumaker, 1994); independence (Dunlap, Dunlap, Koegel, & Koegel, 1991); on-task and written language behavior (Goddard, 1998; Harris, Graham, Reid, McElroy, & Hamby, 1994; Mathes & Bender, 1997; Wolfe, 1997); math performance (Dunlap & Dunlap, 1989; McDougall & Brady, 1998); work-related behavior and job success (Christian & Poling, 1997; Schloss, 1987); following directions (Agran, Fodor-Davis, Moore, & Deer, 1989); and social behavior during recess (Nelson, Smith, & Colvin, 1995).

For instance, in the Harris et al. (1994) study, experiment 2 focused on the effects of self-monitoring on on-task behavior and written language (i.e., the number of words produced in written stories). Students used a 5-step writing process that they had been taught. Self-monitoring of attention (SMA) and self-monitoring of performance (SMP) were introduced as separate conditions. Under SMA conditions, students recorded, tallied, and graphed whether they were on- or off-task at the sound of a tone. Under the SMP conditions, students counted and recorded the number of words written during the session. The results showed that self-monitoring increased on-task behavior, number of words written, and quality ratings of written work, and that neither condition was superior to the other (see Figure 12.8).

Young, West, Smith, and Morgan (1997) provide secondary-level teachers with a method for assisting students to track their performance (see Figure 12.9). In their view, the Classroom Performance Record (CPR) provides a mechanism for students to monitor a range of academic assignments, their status in completing these assignments, and their "citizenship" during the recording period. Further, an estimate of the student's academic and citizenship grade can be determined. Finally, the student completes the form by writing how the grades might be improved.

Wolfe (1997) used a self-monitoring procedure to determine the effects of self-monitoring and a changing-criterion-with-public-posting phase on student on-task behavior and written language performance. The subjects were four elementary school boys enrolled in an urban-based, elementary-level resource room for students with learning disabilities. Self-monitoring procedures for on-task behavior included the students listening to a tone recorded at 60-second intervals and responding to the question "Am I on-task?" Written language performance involved the students writing for a 10-minute session and counting and graphing the number of words written. During baseline conditions, student on-task behavior and written language performance were collected. During self-monitoring, students monitored their on-task behavior and written language performance simultaneously. In the changing-criterion-with-public-posting condition, the students received their goal for the day's session prior to writing, wrote, and recorded whether they met their goal.

While the overall results for the four target students showed a functional relationship between self-monitoring and on-task behavior (Figure 12.10 shows student 3's representative data), the data for the relationship between self-monitoring and written language performance were less compelling (see Figure 12.11 for student 3's representative data). A greater increase occurred when the changing-criterion-with-public-posting condition was introduced. Results

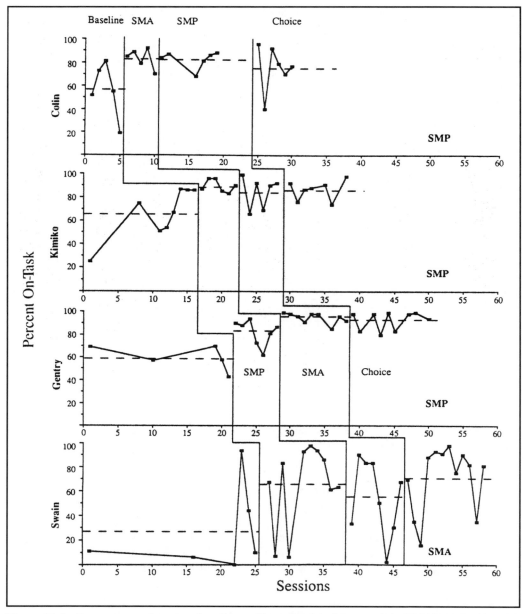

**Figure 12.8.** Percent on-task across baseline, self-monitoring for attention (SMA), and self-monitoring of performance (SMP). From "Self-Monitoring of Attention Versus Self-Monitoring of Performance: Replication and Cross-Task Comparison Studies," by K. R. Harris, S. Graham, R. Reid, K. McElroy, and R. S. Hamby, 1994, *Learning Disability Quarterly, 17*(2), 133. Copyright 1994 by *Learning Disability Quarterly.* Reprinted with permission.

| Day/Date | Absent/Tardy | Prepared | Tests and Assignments | Due Dates | Completed | Turned In | Points Possible | Points Earned and/or Grade | Student Rating Citizenship Grade |
|---|---|---|---|---|---|---|---|---|---|
| **Mon** 10/19 | – · | Yes | Page 66 1–10 | 10/20 | ✓ | ✓ | 10 | 10 | S |
| **Tue** 10/20 | T | No | Page 70 25–50 (odd) | 10/21 | ✓ | | 12 | 0 | U |
| **Wed** 10/21 | – · | Yes | Page 78 1–30 (even) | 10/22 | | | 30 | 0 | S |
| **Thu** 10/22 | A | | | | | | | | |
| **Fri** 10/23 | – · | Yes | Test | Today | | | 50 | 30 | S |

Name: John Doe  Subject: Math  Week: Oct. 19  Quarter: Fall

Estimated academic grade for this term ___D___

Estimated citizenship grade for this term ___S___

I could improve my grade by turning homework in and studying for tests.

**Weekly Total** — 102 | 40 | S Avg.

**Figure 12.9.** Classroom Performance Record (CPR). From *Teaching Self-Management Strategies to Adolescents* (p. 70), by K. R. Young, R. P. West, D. J. Smith, and D. P. Morgan, 1997, Longmont, CO: Sopris West. Copyright 1997 by Sopris West. Reprinted with permission.

suggest that self-monitoring changed on-task behavior, but that comparable effects for written language performance were not as evident.

Goddard (1998), who conducted a systematic replication of Wolfe's (1997) study, investigated the effects of self-monitoring (alone and in combination with changing criterion with public posting) and self-evaluation on the on-task and written language behavior of seven elementary students with learning disabilities. Self-monitoring included having the students graph the number of words, sentences, different words, and adjectives. Written self-evaluation involved having students evaluate the quantity and quality of their writing. The changing-criterion-with-public-posting condition involved the experimenter setting goals for each student, then posting total words produced each day. Also, students self-selected their writing target goals. Results showed an initial positive relationship between self-monitoring alone and number of words written for two students, although those results were not maintained at similar levels across self-monitoring phases. However, during the changing-criterion phase, a positive relationship was shown between self-monitoring when combined with targets and reinforcers and number of words written for four students. Results for self-evaluation were not compelling. There was no clear effect for on-task behavior associated with either self-monitoring or self-evaluation. Results suggest that self-monitoring may be an effective procedure for some students when combined

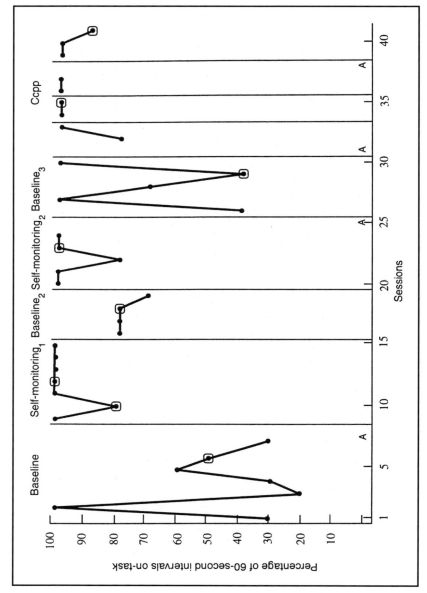

**Figure 12.10.** Percentage of 60-second intervals on-task for student 3 (representative of the four target students). Ccpp refers to changing criterion with public posting for written language performance; A refers to student absence, and the circled data represent interobserver agreement days. From "Effects of Self-Monitoring on the On-Task Behavior and Written Language Performance of Elementary Students with Learning Disabilities," by L. Wolfe, 1997, unpublished master's thesis, p. 58. Reprinted with permission.

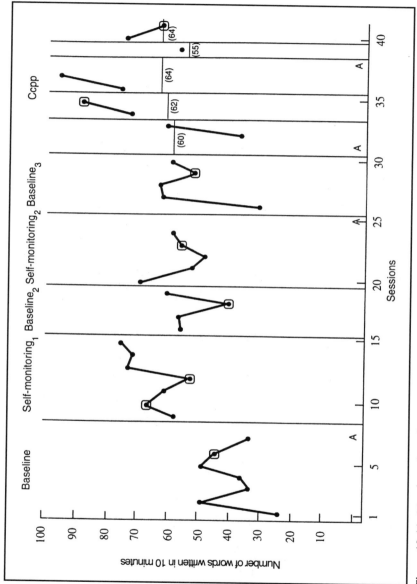

**Figure 12.11.** Number of words written in 10 minutes for student 3 (representative of the four target students). Ccpp refers to changing criterion with public posting for written language performance; A refers to student absence, and the circled data represent interobserver agreement days. From "Effects of Self-Monitoring on the On-Task Behavior and Written Language Performance of Elementary Students with Learning Disabilities," by L. Wolfe, 1997, unpublished master's thesis, p. 60. Reprinted with permission.

with goals for written language performance and reinforcement for meeting or exceeding those goals.

Goddard's (1998) results echo the findings of one student in McDougall and Brady's (1998) study insofar as positive gains in favor of self-monitoring were not always evident. McDougall and Brady (speaking of the nonresult with self-monitoring) stated, "Katy's results provide a reminder that even powerful self-management procedures can have limited impact, and that self-management components should be modified or combined with other techniques to meet the needs of individual students" (p. 163).

## Teaching Self-Management

Methodologically, to teach students to manage their own behavior, three configurations can be arranged. In a *pull-out program,* a target student learns to record his or her behavior separate and apart from the rest of the group. For instance, the teacher would take the student "down the hall" to teach him or her how to self-record, self-monitor, or self-reinforce. Then the student would return to perform the newly learned skills in the classroom. In a *small group arrangement,* the teacher would teach three to five students in the classroom how to perform the self-management behaviors (graphing, charting, etc.). Teaching would occur as part of their normal small group programming. Finally, the teacher could instruct the *whole class as a unit.*

Readers interested in learning about how to create charts and figures from word-processing programs, like Microsoft EXCEL, can consult Carr and Burkholder (1998).

Whether the teacher uses the first, second, or third option is dependent on the present rate of the target behavior, the number of students likely to benefit from instruction, how much instructional time the teacher can devote to the program, and the acquisition levels of the students. Regardless of the procedural variations, Lloyd and Hughes (1993) suggest that a direct instruction approach be employed to teach self-management skills. Marshall, Lloyd, and Hallahan (1993) add that explicit accuracy training also needs to be part of the program. "Through the use of direct instructional principles such as prompting, modeling, practice, and corrective feedback, people have been taught to observe instances of their undesired behavior and the environmental events affecting their behavior. The use of recording devices may help to make these events and their consequences more salient to the individual" (Lloyd & Hughes, 1993, p. 418).

Figure 12.12 shows the results of the Marshall et al. (1993) study, during which baseline data were collected on the percentage of on-task intervals by four students with learning disabilities who also had histories of low on-task performance and low accuracy with self-monitoring. During baseline, attention to task was registered for the four boys. Next, during self-monitoring (initial training), the teacher taught the boys to record a mark in a "yes" or "no" box, indicating their assessment of whether they were on- or off-task at the sound of a periodic tone. During the retraining condition (a so-called booster session), the teacher employed identical procedures as initial training for three of the students. Finally, during accuracy training, the teacher used a two-part role-play procedure whereby students first registered whether the *teacher* was on- or off-task during a simulated session, followed by the teacher and the student recording whether the *student* was on- or off-task during a simulated session. In both simulations, the teacher provided feedback. Results showed that percentage of attention to task levels increased during the accuracy training condition for all students.

Furthermore, the content of the self-management program might be taught using a "package" program. The package might include: individualized checklists or scales (Dunlap & Dunlap, 1989); a series of curriculum skills presented

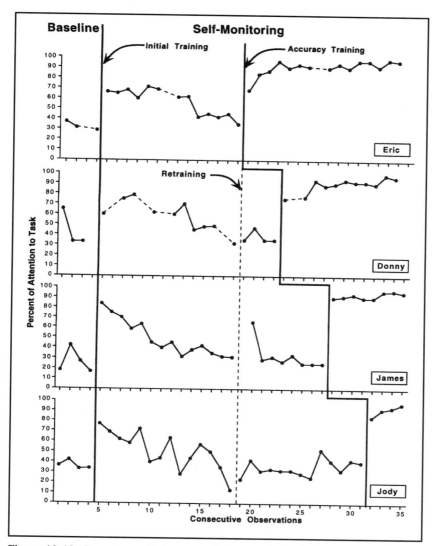

**Figure 12.12.** Percentage of time attending to task for four boys across conditions. Stippled lines in data path show absences. From "Effects of Training to Increase Self-Monitoring Accuracy," by K. J. Marshall, J. W. Lloyd, and D. P. Hallahan, 1993, *Journal of Behavioral Education*, 3(4), 453. Copyright 1993 by Plenum Publishing. Reprinted with permission.

sequentially session by session (Johnson, 1988); role play and self-verbalization (Agran, Fodor-Davis, Moore, & Deer, 1989); practice and feedback (Hughes, Ruhl, & Peterson, 1988); or contracting arrangements (Schloss, 1987). Consultants should also note that McDougall and Brady (1998) provide convincing evidence that once a "full-package" self-management program is initiated, components used to establish the program (e.g., audible cues, recording sheets, etc.) can be faded without loss of effect—a finding that replicated earlier results reported by Mathes and Bender (1997) and Boyle and Hughes (1994).

We agree with McDougall and Brady's (1998) endorsement of self-management when they state, "Practitioners should consider using multiple component self-management packages when immediate and robust improvements in students' performance during independent practice activities are desired" (p. 163).

Self-management and self-monitoring have been deemed "mature interventions" (Reid, 1996), meaning that the weight of evidence supporting their efficacy is virtually incontrovertible. Further, these strategies are viable alternatives for students, especially those involved in transition and/or inclusive settings where programming across environments (generality) is likely, where training materials are available, where consultation with other practitioners knowledgeable about self-monitoring exists, and where peers may need to implement the procedure without constant adult supervision (Frith & Armstrong, 1986; Hughes et al., 1988; McDougall & Brady, 1998; Nelson et al., 1995).

# Procedures To Decrease Inappropriate Behavior

Many behaviors that occur in school and home settings cannot be changed using reinforcement procedures alone. Oftentimes, a procedure is needed to weaken an inappropriate behavior. This section describes how extinction, positive reductive procedures, and punishment approaches can be used to reduce inappropriate behavior.

## Extinction

Extinction refers to the discontinuation of reinforcement for a previously reinforced behavior (Cooper et al., 1987; Justen & Howerton, 1993). Extinction (ignoring) generally produces desirable but gradual reductions in inappropriate behavior, especially if the other sources of reinforcement are eliminated.

The teacher's systematic use of an extinction procedure can have a dramatic effect on student performance in the classroom. Suppose that a teacher believes that he or she may be reinforcing undesirable behavior. For example, calling on students who shout their responses may reinforce shouting. To use extinction to reduce shouting behavior, the teacher would stop attending to students who shouted. The only students who would receive attention would be those who raised their hands quietly.

Iwata, Pace, Cowdery, Edwards, and Miltenberger (1994) make an important point regarding extinction:

> Ignoring misbehavior may represent extinction in some cases but not in others; conversely, the correct application of extinction may require termination of events in some cases but continuation in others. The procedures that define extinction in a given situation are determined by the specific nature of the reinforcement to be "discontinued." (p. 132)

Consultants working with practitioners who teach students with self-injurious behavior (SIB) problems need to recognize three functional variations of extinction: (a) withholding or terminating attention (as would be applied for behaviors maintained by positive reinforcement) [EXT (Attention)]; (b) preventing escape (for behaviors maintained by negative reinforcement) [EXT (Escape)]; and (c) attenuating consequences (for behaviors maintained by sensory stimulation) [EXT (Sensory)]. Iwata et al. (1994) provide an excellent illustration of expected outcomes when variations of extinction can be applied (see

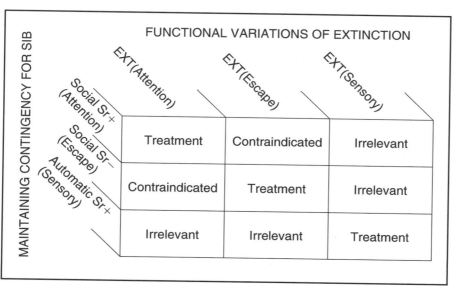

**Figure 12.13.** Expected outcomes when functional variations of extinction are applied to different maintaining contingencies. From "What Makes Extinction Work: An Analysis of Procedural Form and Function," by B. A. Iwata, G. M. Pace, G. E. Cowdery, G. Edwards, and R. G. Miltenberger, 1994, *Journal of Applied Behavior Analysis,* 27(1), 133. Copyright 1994 by Society for the Experimental Analysis of Behavior. Reprinted with permission.

Figure 12.13). Note that if EXT (attention) was applied to escape-maintained behavior, or if EXT (escape) was applied to attention-maintained behavior, a countertherapeutic outcome would be predicted. Consultants need to be aware of which procedure is being applied to a given situation.

While extinction can be a powerful technique for reducing inappropriate behavior, it has shortcomings. For example, it may take several sessions to be effective. For problems that require quick solutions, such as fighting, verbal abuse, or self-destructive behavior, the consultant is avised to recommend other alternatives to the teachers. Further, when extinction is introduced, the teacher may notice a temporary increase in the rate of the inappropriate behavior, called extinction burst (Cooper et al., 1987; Lerman & Iwata, 1995). Although not a universal phenomenon (perhaps occurring between 12% and 36% of the time), consultants need to advise teachers to prepare for such a temporary increase; otherwise, they may abandon the procedure prematurely.

## Positive Reductive Procedures

Students display a number of behaviors in the classroom that, while not totally disruptive, could be considered annoying or obnoxious. For example, a student who sings or hums to himself or herself may distract other students who are trying to complete their work. Under different circumstances, the humming and singing could be perfectly acceptable and even encouraged. Teachers are not interested in eliminating the singing; rather, they want to reduce the level of that behavior or teach the child when to sing and hum and when not to. Positive reductive procedures can be employed successfully when the teacher wants to reduce the level of behavior. Additionally, those procedures avoid the potential side effects associated with other, more restrictive techniques (e.g., punishment).

## Differential Reinforcement of Other Behavior

Differential reinforcement of other behavior (DRO), or omission training, is a relatively simple procedure to reduce unwanted behavior. Justen and Howerton (1993) state, "DRO can be conceptualized as a type of differential reinforcement techniques where positive reinforcement is contingent upon the omission, rather than the commission, of a behavior" (p. 38). Mazaleski, Iwata, Vollmer, Zarcone, and Smith (1993) add that DRO really combines two procedures: contingent reinforcement based on interresponse time and extinction (withholding reinforcement contingent on the occurrence of the target behavior).

To use a DRO procedure, (a) choose a target behavior; (b) establish a time interval for nonoccurrence of the behavior; and (c) deliver reinforcement if the time interval passes without the target behavior occurring. "The time intervals with 'zero undesired behavior' will gradually be increased until the student's behavior approximates that of an average peer in a regular classroom setting" (Webber & Scheuermann, 1991, p. 14). Initial interval size for the DRO should be based on baseline assessment data (Repp, Felce, & Barton, 1991). For example, if 20 disruptions occurred within a standard 50-minute class period, then the initial interval should be set at 2.5 minutes (50 minutes divided by 20 disruptions). Setting an interval that is longer, say 10 minutes, would be counterproductive.

Let's suppose that a fifth-grade teacher—Ms. Abbott—had a student with a learning disability in her classroom who did a competent job on assignments but often daydreamed. Ms. Abbott decided to reduce the amount of daydreaming. To accomplish her objective, Ms. Abbott discussed the situation with a consultant. At their meeting, they agreed that Ms. Abbott should collect baseline data on the student's daydreaming during the last 20 minutes of each period. The consultant, along with Ms. Abbott, established a series of four 5-minute intervals for each period. At the end of each 5-minute interval, a kitchen timer sounded. If daydreaming was not occurring, the student was reinforced. However, if daydreaming behavior occurred at the end of the interval, reinforcement was postponed. Any behavior that occurred at the end of the 5-minute period except daydreaming produced reinforcement. The intervals would gradually be increased from 5 to 10 minutes and beyond as the student's behavior improved.

One of the major shortcomings of the DRO procedure is that a wide range of behaviors could occur at the close of the interval, and the teacher would still provide reinforcement. This student, for example, might be sucking her thumb at the end of the 5-minute interval, but as long as she was not daydreaming, reinforcement would follow. Inappropriate behavior, therefore, could be reinforced.

Given the possibility of adventitious reinforcement of inappropriate behavior, and the fact that differential reinforcement of other behavior requires consistent observation, consultants might recommend a DRO procedure for those behaviors that can be clearly observed (e.g., talking-out, swearing) (Repp et al., 1991). While DRO procedures have been used to reduce aggressive behaviors (Niemeyer & Fox, 1990), caution should be applied to balance the need for a positive reductive approach with the challenge of suppressing the behavior quickly.

## Differential Reinforcement of Low Rates

Students who occasionally call out jokes, tell humorous anecdotes, or change the topic of discussion in class can help to maintain an informal atmosphere that makes learning more enjoyable. Students who engage in such behaviors constantly, however, can be annoying. To use a *differential reinforcement of low rates* (DRL) procedure, the teacher structures the management plan so that lesser amounts of the behavior lead to reinforcement.

Deitz and Repp (1973) used a DRL procedure to reduce the number of times high school girls changed the topic of conversation during a class discussion period. During baseline conditions, the number of subject changes was recorded. Then during phases 2, 3, 4, and 5, progressively fewer subject changes produced the reinforcer (free time on Friday). For instance, during phase 2, six or fewer changes earned free time; during phase 3, five or fewer changes produced reinforcement. Figure 12.14 shows how the DRL procedure produced a stepwise decrease in subject changes for the high school students.

According to Cooper et al. (1987), the DRL procedure has several advantages and disadvantages. First, it is positive. Students can earn reinforcers. Second, it is tolerant. It does not require the total elimination of a behavior; rather, DRL is designed to progressively reduce the inappropriate behavior. Third, it is convenient and effective. Teachers can incorporate DRL in the classroom without rearranging their entire management program.

On the other hand, DRL is slow. It takes time to reduce the inappropriate behavior to tolerable levels. Consultants would not recommend a DRL procedure to a teacher to reduce aggressive, violent, or dangerous behavior (Webber & Scheuermann, 1991). Also, this procedure focuses on the inappropriate behavior. Teachers who are not careful might fall into the trap of attending to undesirable behavior more than to desirable behavior and, in effect, inadvertently reinforce it.

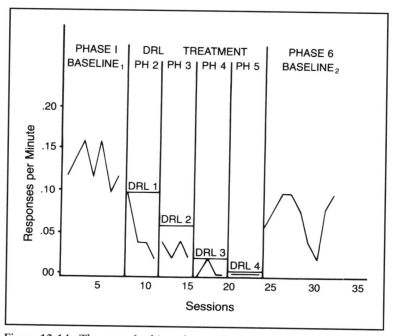

Figure 12.14. The rate of subject changes for a class of high school senior girls during baseline 1, treatment, and baseline 2 phases. From "Decreasing Classroom Misbehavior Through the Use of DRL Schedules of Reinforcement," by S. M. Deitz and A. C. Repp, 1973, *Journal of Applied Behavior Analysis, 6,* 461. Copyright 1973 by Society for the Experimental Analysis of Behavior. Reprinted with permission.

### Differential Reinforcement of Incompatible Behavior

When a teacher reinforces a behavior that is incompatible with another behavior, *differential reinforcement of incompatible behavior* (DRI) is in effect. Skilled consultants recommend DRI because they have learned that it accomplishes a threefold purpose: An inappropriate behavior is reduced or eliminated; an appropriate behavior is strengthened; and undesired side effects are not produced (Friman, 1990). Reinforcing incompatible behaviors blends the best features of reductive and reinforcement procedures (Cooper et al., 1987).

How does one choose an incompatible behavior? Usually, all that is required is to select a behavior that cannot physically occur at the same time as the target behavior. For instance, if a student with developmental disabilities roams around the room, in-seat behavior would serve as an incompatible response to reinforce. Likewise, if a student repeatedly blurts out answers, the teacher might choose quiet hand raising as the incompatible behavior. Friman (1990) found that the rate per minute of out-of-seat behavior of a 4-year-old hyperactive student decreased markedly when the student was consistently reinforced for appropriate in-seat behavior. Additionally, Friman noted a collateral benefit, in that the child care worker's use of physical restraint decreased as well under the DRI contingency.

Webber and Scheuermann (1991) provide several examples of positive incompatible behaviors that consultants could suggest to modify common classroom challenges (see Table 12.4).

## Punishment Procedures

Four common punishment strategies are used in applied settings: punishment by the contingent presentation of a stimulus, overcorrection, time-out from positive reinforcement, and response cost. The first two procedures are referred to as type I punishment, because a stimulus or event is presented immediately after the occurrence of a behavior. The last two are referred to as type II punishment, because they refer to the withdrawal of positive reinforcement. All punishment procedures have one feature in common: The future probability of a behavior (or response class of behavior) is reduced.

### Punishment by Contingent Presentation of a Stimulus

The SIBIS apparatus contains an adjustable sensor module applied to the subject's head to detect intensity of self-injurious behavior and a stimulus module, usually attached to the subject's arm or leg, to regulate the timing of the stimulation.

Punishment by contingent presentation of a stimulus means that a stimulus or event is presented immediately subsequent to the occurrence of a behavior, and the future probability of the behavior decreases (Cooper et al., 1987). Linscheid, Iwata, Ricketts, Williams, and Griffin (1990) provided a convincing experimental demonstration of the successful application of electrical stimulation by means of the self-injurious behavior inhibiting system (SIBIS) to virtually eliminate the chronic self-injurious behavior of five children with developmental disabilities. Johnny, one of the subjects in this investigation, was 11 years old with rates of 300 to 720 head-hitting episodes per hour during the previous three years. Differential reinforcement of other behavior, differential reinforcement of incompatible behavior, physical restraint, gentle teaching, and other strategies had been used unsuccessfully. During baseline, Johnny's self-injurious behavior was observed, and no treatment conditions were in effect. During helmet baseline, Johnny wore a hockey helmet only. In SIBIS-inactive, Johnny wore the SIBIS apparatus, but the stimulus connection was off. Finally, when SIBIS was

## Table 12.4
Positive Incompatible Alternatives for Common
Classroom Behavioral Problems

| Undesired Behavior | Positive Incompatible Alternative |
| --- | --- |
| Talking back | Positive response such as "Yes, sir" or "OK" or "I understand"; or acceptable questions such as "May I ask you a question about that?" or "May I tell you my side?" |
| Cursing | Acceptable exclamations such as "darn," "shucks." |
| Being off-task | Any on-task behavior: looking at book, writing, looking at teacher, etc. |
| Being out of seat | Sitting in seat (bottom on chair, with body in upright position). |
| Noncompliance | Following directions within _____ seconds (time limit will depend upon age of student); following directions by second time direction is given. |
| Talking out | Raising hand and waiting to be called on. |
| Turning in messy papers | No marks other than answers; no more than _____ erasures; no more than three folds or creases. |
| Hitting, pinching, kicking, pushing/shoving | Using verbal expression of anger; pounding fist into hand; sitting or standing next to other students without touching them. |
| Tardiness | Being in seat when bell rings (or by desired time). |
| Self-injurious or self-stimulatory behaviors | Sitting with hands on desk or in lap; hands not touching any part of body; head up and not touching anything (desk, shoulder, etc.). |
| Inappropriate use of materials | Holding/using materials appropriately (e.g., writing *only* on appropriate paper, etc.). |

*Note.* From "Accentuate the Positive . . . Eliminate the Negative," by J. Webber and B. Scheuerman, 1991, *Teaching Exceptional Children, 24*(1), 13–19. Copyright 1991 by The Council for Exceptional Children. Reprinted with permission.

in effect, the SIBIS apparatus delivered a brief electrical stimulus contingent on Johnny's head hitting.

Figure 12.15 shows the effect of SIBIS on Johnny's head-hitting responses per minute. During baseline, helmet, and SIBIS-inactive conditions, responses per minute were high. When SIBIS was in effect, head-hitting responses per minute dropped, regardless of whether Johnny was in alone, demand, or play situations. No negative side effects for Johnny, or the other subjects, were reported. Finally, Linscheid et al. appropriately suggest that SIBIS be considered only after other approaches have been assessed and only after compliance with behavioral treatment plans, due process, and consent has been achieved.

Another form of contingent presentation of a stimulus, corporal punishment (e.g., spanking, slapping, and hitting), has been ruled illegal in many states (Yell, 1994; Yell, Cline, & Bradley, 1995). Still, it is one of the more popular uses of punishment by the contingent presentation of a stimulus. In corporal punishment, the misbehaving student receives swats for rule infractions in the presence of a witness. According to Rose (1989), despite the long history of the use of corporal punishment in schools, there is little empirical evidence of its

For a review of case law on five categories of aversive interventions, including corporal punishment, see Lohrmann-O'Rourke and Zirkel (1998).

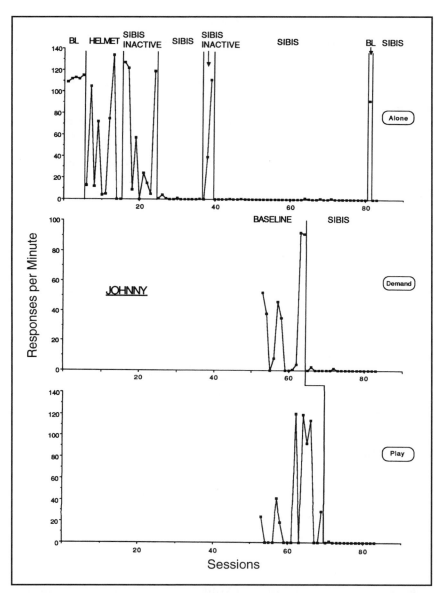

Figure 12.15. Head hits exhibited by Johnny during the treatment with SIBIS. From "Clinical Evaluation of the Self-Injurious Behavior Inhibiting System (SIBIS)," by T. R. Linscheid, B. A. Iwata, R. W. Ricketts, D. E. Williams, and J. C. Griffin, 1990, *Journal of Applied Behavior Analysis, 23*(1), 64. Copyright 1990 by Society for the Experimental Analysis of Behavior. Reprinted with permission.

effectiveness. Table 12.5 shows the Council for Exceptional Children's policy statement on corporal punishment.

Consultants are advised to be well versed on district policy relating to how and under what conditions corporal punishment can be administered (Daniels, 1998; Rose, 1989). A state board of education policy may include corporal punishment as a method, whereas local district policy may not. Consultants must be aware of *all* policies on its use. Further, as Yell et al., (1995) state, "OCR [Office of Civil Rights] has declared that in cases where students are

**Table 12.5**

Council for Exceptional Children's Policy Statement on Corporal Punishment

The Council for Exceptional Children supports the prohibition of the use of corporal punishment in special education. Corporal punishment is here defined as a situation in which all of the following elements are present: an authority accuses a child of violating a rule and seeks from the child an explanation, whereupon a judgment of guilt is made, followed by physical contract and pain inflicted on the child. The Council finds no conditions under which corporal punishment so defined would be the treatment of choice in special education.

*Note.* From "Corporal Punishment: What Teachers Should Know," by E. D. Evans and R. C. Richardson, 1995, *Teaching Exceptional Children, 27*(2), 33. Copyright 1995 by The Council for Exceptional Children. Reprinted with permission.

protected under Section 504, if schools administer corporal punishment, there must be a prior determination regarding whether the misbehavior and disability are causally related" (p. 303, brackets added).

Finally, an implication of Kennedy's (1995) study of teachers', student teachers', paraprofessionals', and college students' perceptions of when corporal punishment is deemed necessary in classrooms suggests that veteran teachers, over time, learn to use other options besides corporal punishment, whereas student teachers, first-year teachers, or paraprofessionals may resort to such punishment for challenging behaviors.

> Consultants should be prepared to provide support, additional inservice training, team-teaching methods, and modeling to demonstrate options to teachers who have an emerging repertoire of management skills.

## Overcorrection

According to Cooper et al. (1987), overcorrection consists of one or both of two components: restitutional overcorrection and positive practice overcorrection. In *restitutional overcorrection,* the individual must restore a damaged environment to a state better than existed prior to the disruption or infraction. For instance, if Lyle wrote his name on his desk with his pencil, he would be required to clean his own desk and all of the other desks in the room. *Positive practice overcorrection* means that the individual must engage in the appropriate behavior repeatedly. To continue with our example, under a positive practice overcorrection procedure the student would be required to write his name repeatedly on a piece of paper or on the blackboard.

Despite research that shows the efficacy of overcorrection for reducing inappropriate behavior (Cooper et al., 1987; Foxx, 1982; Foxx & Bechtel, 1983), consultants should not be too eager to recommend this form of punishment to teachers, parents, or other family caretakers. The need for adequately trained staff, the strong possibility of student resistance, the likelihood of inadvertent reinforcement of the inappropriate behavior, and the chance that collateral behaviors will be affected outweigh the wholesale endorsement of this reductive approach for all but the most serious of behaviors.

> Readers interested in learning more about this reductive approach are referred to Azrin and Besalel (1980); Cooper et al. (1987); and Foxx and Bechtel (1983).

## Time-Out from Positive Reinforcement

According to Cooper et al. (1987), time-out from positive reinforcement, or simply *time-out,* is defined as "the withdrawal of the opportunity to earn positive reinforcement or the loss of access to positive reinforcers for a specified period of time, contingent upon the occurrence of a behavior; the effect is to

> For a legal analysis of time-out, consult Budd and Baer (1976); Yell (1994); Yell, Cline, and Bradley (1995). For a discussion of procedures for using time-out, consult Bacon (1991); Brantner and Doherty (1983); Cooper et al. (1987); and Yell (1994).

reduce the future probability of that behavior" (p. 440). Procedurally, there are two types of time-out variations that can be considered: exclusion time-out and nonexclusion time-out.

*Exclusion Time-Out.* Exclusive time-out means that the student is removed from the classrooms. The physical removal of a student from the environment can be done successfully only under certain conditions. For example, the time-in environment (e.g., the classroom) must be positive and reinforcing. If the time-out environment is more appealing, it is unlikely that the procedure will be effective. If a teacher sends a student to the principal's office, for example, only to have the student talk with school staff, visitors, or other students, that time-out will be ineffective. Also, the time away from the classroom should be relatively short. Cooper et al. (1987) recommend time-out durations that do not exceed 15 minutes. Longer time-out intervals become self-defeating because students have the opportunity to engage in other behaviors that may not be desirable. Exclusion time-out, however, need not mean that the student is physically removed from the classroom (Yell, 1994). Foxx (1982) recommends using a partition to separate an offending student from his or her classmates for a brief period of time without being removed from the classroom. Based on court rulings, Yell (1994) warn consultants that prolonged use of time-out may violate student rights. In one case (cf. McCracken County School District, 1991), an untrained teacher used time-out everyday for 5 consecutive days to punish a student but made no corresponding attempt to change the student's behavior. Such usage was ruled a violation of Section 504. Yell (1994), extrapolating from case law, concludes that time-out is a "controlled intervention" that can be implemented given certain safeguards and procedural rules. He provides the seven guidelines found in Table 12.6.

*Nonexclusion Time-Out.* Planned ignoring, withdrawing a specific reinforcer, contingent observation, and time-out ribbon are four ways nonexclusion time-out can be delivered (Cooper et al., 1987). In each of these variations, the student remains in the setting but loses the opportunity to earn reinforcers or loses a specific amount of reinforcement. Nonexclusion time-out has the obvious advantage of reducing the risk of physical confrontations with students and can be conducted within the regular classroom.

Before a time-out procedure is implemented, the consultant should make sure that district policy does not preclude its use. Some school systems, reacting

*Consultants can provide effective service when time-out is to be implemented by insisting that the procedure be cited on the student's IEP, records of its use be kept, and data be maintained on its effectiveness and by showing that other positive approaches can be implemented to teach appropriate behavior.*

*School district policy references may be helpful in fashioning or redesigning time-out policy.*

## Table 12.6
### Seven Guidelines for Using Time-out

1. Be aware of local or state policies regarding time-out.
2. Have written procedures on the use of time-out.
3. Obtain permission prior to using time-out.
4. The IEP team should be involved in making decisions concerning the use of behavior reduction procedures such as time-out.
5. Time-out must serve a legitimate educational function.
6. Time-out should be used in a reasonable manner.
7. When using time-out, keep thorough records.

*Note.* From "Timeout and Students with Behavior Disorders: A Legal Analysis," by M. L. Yell, 1994, *Education and Treatment of Children, 17*(3), 293–301. Copyright 1994 by *Education and Treatment of Children*. Adapted with permission.

to public pressure and court mandates, have ruled that time-out cannot be employed. At least two court cases (*Morales v. Turman,* 1973, and *Wyatt v. Stickney,* 1972) have set mandatory guidelines and time limitations for physically secluding students from their normal environment. The *Honig v. Doe* (1988) case addressed the legality of expelling students with disabilities for behavioral reasons. Essentially, the court ruled that students cannot be expelled from school when the nature of the disruptive behavior is associated with their disability. Students can be expelled if it can be determined that the disruptive behavior was not related to their disability, a difficult task for the IEP team (Yell, 1991). Expulsion is an option for a student who has a disability, after due process has been served, but IEP services must still be rendered (Yell et al., 1995).

On the issue of suspensions, courts have ruled (e.g., *Honig v. Doe*) that students can be suspended for limited amounts of time (up to 10 school days) as that does not constitute a change in placement or a restriction of rights under the free and appropriate education (FAPE) provisions of the Education for the Handicapped Act, and it provides the school district and parents time to consider alternatives (Yell, 1994). In cases where clear and imminent danger exists, school district personnel can seek a temporary restraining order (TRO) from the court to bar a student from attending school. However, to be successful with a TRO, the district must show (a) that the student is "substantially likely to cause injury if he or she remains in the school environment . . . and (b) that it has done all it can to reasonably reduce this danger . . ." (Yell et al., 1995, p. 306).

## Use of Aversive Consequences

Given recent court decisions (e.g., *Honig v. Doe,* 1988; *Ingraham v. Wright,* 1977; *Wyatt v. Stickney,* 1972), school boards are more careful about condoning the use of any punishment contingency, especially ones that might involve aversives (corporal punishment, restraint), suspensions (time-out), or expulsions. Sometimes, however, student behavior can be physically harmful, and consultants may find themselves in the paradoxical—and unenviable—position of collaborating on a joint program that may involve the use of punishment contingencies while at the same time tempering their recommendations because of the potential for unpredictable effects. Being thoroughly familiar with the issues of effective behavioral and educational treatment and the case against "punishment" (Skiba & Deno, 1991; Yulevich & Axelrod, 1983) may be a functional sine qua non for consultants under such conditions.

## Response Cost

Response cost is defined as the loss of a specific amount of positive reinforcement contingent upon a behavior. The response or behavior "costs" the child a reinforcer. Like other forms of punishment, a response-cost contingency has the effect of temporarily reducing or suppressing the inappropriate behavior. Response cost does not involve the application of any physical stimulus; however, it can combine reinforcement for appropriate behavior with the loss of a reinforcer for inappropriate behavior (Gardill et al., 1996).

A number of examples demonstrate the efficacy of the response-cost procedure. For instance, Gallagher, Sulzbacher, and Shores (1976) and Leonardi, Duggan, Hoffheins, and Axelrod (1972) demonstrated how a response-cost technique can be used to reduce inappropriate behaviors in the classroom.

In both of these classic studies, the teachers wrote a series of numbers on the blackboard that indicated the amount of minutes available for free time. When a student disrupted the class, the teacher placed a slash through the highest remaining number on the blackboard, indicating that 1 minute of free time had been lost.

Anecdote 12.3 shows how a building principal worked collaboratively with a teacher who had two behaviorally disordered students mainstreamed into her junior high school classroom. In this case the principal recommended the response-cost procedure because the threat of student injury in the classroom was high. She made her decision knowing that the response-cost procedure has several possible advantages, including rapid suppression of the behavior, possible long-lasting effects, and ease of application for the teacher (Alberto & Troutman, 1999; Cooper et al., 1987).

## Anecdote 12.3

| | |
|---|---|
| TEACHER: | Mrs. Jackson, the two boys who are mainstreamed into my classroom have disrupted my regular program completely. |
| PRINCIPAL: | Does the problem lie only with those two students, or are there other students involved? |
| TEACHER: | Initially, it was just the two students, but the problem has spread to many others as well. I've tried talking to the boys, talking to their parents, and reinforcing them for their good behavior, but nothing seems to be working. I'm afraid someone is going to get hurt. |
| PRINCIPAL: | You feel there is a danger that someone might get injured? |
| TEACHER: | I do. Several arguments have already broken out. I'm afraid that a fight might break out at any time. |
| PRINCIPAL: | Given the circumstances, would you consider trying a response-cost procedure? |
| TEACHER: | At this point I'd be willing to try almost anything. Frankly, I have run out of ideas. |
| PRINCIPAL: | I know what you mean. I have days like those myself! Let me describe a procedure to try, and see what you think of it. |
| TEACHER: | Okay. |
| PRINCIPAL: | First, place the numbers 20 to 1 on the chalkboard so that everyone can see them. Then tell the students that anytime anyone in the classroom is out of seat or calls out the top number will be crossed off. Emphasize that the number left after the period is over indicates the amount of free time they'll have in class the next day, or that day, if possible. Teach the class as you normally do (i.e., continue to reinforce appropriate behavior), but make certain that every time one of the disruptive behaviors occurs, you cross off the highest remaining number. Any questions so far? |
| TEACHER: | What happens if the disruptive behavior continues? |

PRINCIPAL:   Let's wait to see what happens before we plan other alternatives. I'm prepared to recommend some options, but I'll hold off until after you've had a chance to try this procedure.

TEACHER:   I'm willing to try it for a day or so.

PRINCIPAL:   Let's meet again tomorrow.

While an informed principal would be aware of the disadvantages of response cost—it may generate escape or aggressive behavior—he or she might choose not to outline them to the teacher at the time. Perhaps here the principal believed that the teacher could implement the procedure more effectively if the possible disadvantages were outlined at a later time. Planning a meeting for the next day would give the teacher time to field-test the principal's recommendation and report the findings.

## Ethical Considerations

While it is beyond the scope of this chapter to discuss every ethical issue that may apply to consultants as they select management strategies, suffice it to say that two considerations seem paramount. First, what is the consultant's role in arranging situations that provide the teacher, parent, or student with choices or options for program selection? Second, how does the use of aversive consequences fit within the overall context of an educative or habilitative program?

### Options for Teachers, Parents, Family Caretakers, or Students

There is general consensus in the consultation literature that the client should be free to accept or reject the consultant's recommendations (West, 1988). Practically speaking, however, consultants may unwittingly gloss over this point as they assist teams with the design and implementation of IEP or IFSP goals. A good illustration occurs when the IEP or IFSP committee plans a program for the student—academics, social skills training, vocational programs—in the absence of student input. Since compelling arguments for and against student choice have been voiced (Bannerman, Sheldon, Sherman, & Harchik, 1990), consultants must decide where they stand on the questions that might surface. For instance, does a student with developmental disabilities, no matter the severity or degree of disability, have a fundamental right to participate in programs? Can a student choose not to participate in a program? Answers to these questions, of course, must balance basic human rights granted under the Constitution (life, liberty, and the pursuit of happiness) with societal need for an educated population and the teacher's duty to change behavior (academic, social, leisure, etc.). Bannerman et al. help to resolve these important ethical and philosophical questions when they state: "Habilitation and the right to choose need not be thought of as conflicting goals. . . . Choice making should be integrated into the habilitation process" (p. 85).

Procedurally, this balancing act might be accomplished by following a few guidelines. First, when targeting skills to be developed, consultants can assist the team, including the student, to choose behaviors that are independent and are likely to be sustained by the natural community of reinforcers. Second, student preferences for activities should be assessed before, during, and after program completion. Third, the act of decision making should be built into the curriculum. Instead of teaching academics, social skills, or vocational skills per se, those skills can be integrated into an overarching program of decision making. Finally, decision making should extend to the residential, community, school, and work settings (Bannerman et al., 1990). In the authors' view, decision making is an important and fundamental skill that consultants should not overlook in their quest to achieve other curriculum goals. Perhaps Bannerman et al.'s final commentary sums up their position explicitly:

> All people have the right to eat too many doughnuts and take a nap. But along with the right comes responsibilities. Teaching clients to exercise their freedoms responsibly should be an integral part of the habilitation [educational] process. While learning, clients [students] should be encouraged to make as many choices as their abilities allow, as long as these choices are not detrimental to the client or to others. (p. 86)

## The Right to Effective Treatment and Education

Several professional task forces have been outspoken about the individual's right to effective treatment. The Association for Behavior Analysis, for example, appointed a task force to consider a statement on the right to effective behavioral treatment as a guideline for ethical and applied use for the profession. Overall, the main points of the position statement relate to ensuring that the individual's rights to informed consent, proper treatment by a competent individual, access to functional programs, assessment and evaluation, and effective practice are not restricted (Van Houten, Axelrod, Bailey, Favell, Foxx, Iwata, & Lovaas, 1988). The major points of that position are found in column one of Table 12.7.

In 1991, the Task Force on the Right to Effective Education of the Association for Behavior Analysis published a parallel piece outlining its principal goals for effective education (Barrett et al., 1991). Its position, divided into six areas and written in the form of entitlements, is shown in column two of Table 12.7.

Furthermore, guidelines that would aid the consultants and teachers in deciding when and how to use punishment procedures with difficult-to-manage students have been published (Axelrod & Apsche, 1983; Cuenin & Harris, 1986; Heron, 1978b). Table 12.8 summarizes those guidelines.

From an ethical and legal perspective, consultants must be aware that punishment procedures to reduce behavior should be used only as a last resort and only after obtaining informed consent (Carr & Lovaas, 1983; Longo, Rotatori, Kapperman, & Heinze, 1981). Programmatically, before a punishment procedure is implemented, all other least restrictive alternatives—for example, extinction, differential reinforcement of incompatible behavior—should have been tried and have been shown to be ineffective.

## A Decision-Making Model for Using Punishment

The *Gaylord-Ross decision model* (Gaylord-Ross, 1980) provides an excellent illustration of procedures to consider when deciding the point at which punishment should be introduced. This model suggests that five areas be addressed before punishment is implemented (Figure 12.16).

*Assessment.* The assessment component of the model is designed to determine the severity of the inappropriate behavior. For example, is the behavior harmful to the individual or to others? If medical reasons are associated with the behavior, this stage allows for their identification and treatment without further steps.

## Table 12.7

Key Points Associated with the Right to Effective Behavioral Treatment and the Right to Effective Education

| Right to Effective Behavioral Treatment | Right to Effective Education |
|---|---|
| 1. An individual has the right to a therapeutic environment. | *Educational Context* |
| | 1. Academic achievement for students should be encouraged and maintained. |
| 2. An individual has a right to services with personal welfare as the overriding goal. | 2. Care and individual attention should be integrated into the curriculum. |
| | 3. Parent training should be included, as necessary. |
| 3. An individual has a right to treatment by a competent behavioral analyst. | 4. Communication between school and home should foster common programming. |
| | *Curriculum and Instructional Objectives* |
| 4. An individual has a right to programs that teach functional skills. | 1. Student instruction should be based on validated programs. |
| | 2. Proficiency should be prescribed. |
| 5. An individual has a right to behavioral assessment and ongoing evaluation. | 3. Personal and vocational objectives should be prescribed. |
| | 4. Maintenance and retention criteria should be prescribed. |
| 6. An individual has a right to the most effective treatment procedures available. | *Assessment and Student Placement* |
| | 1. Assessment should lead to appropriate decision making. |
| | 2. Placement should match entry-level student skills with prerequisite class skills. |
| | *Instructional Method* |
| | 1. Mastery of content should be self-paced. |
| | 2. Sufficient practice should be built into the program. |
| | 3. Error correction procedures should be established for each student. |
| | 4. Programs should be self-adjusting. |
| | 5. Equipment should be up to date and technically appropriate. |
| | 6. Teachers should receive feedback on their instructional performance. |
| | *Measurement and Summative Evaluation* |
| | 1. Educational decisions should be based on objective, curriculum-based measures. |
| | 2. Grading should be objective. |
| | *Assumption of Responsibility for Success* |
| | 1. Financial and operational consequences for teachers should be based on student learning. |
| | 2. Teachers and administrators should assume primary responsibility for student learning. |
| | 3. Students are entitled to change schools if their needs are not met. |

*Note.* From "The Right to Effective Behavioral Treatment," by R. Van Houten, S. Axelrod, J. S. Bailey, J. E. Favell, R. M. Foxx, B. A. Iwata, and O. I. Lovaas, 1988, *The Behavior Analyst, 11,* 111–114; and from "The Right to Effective Education," by B. H. Barrett et al., 1991, *The Behavior Analyst, 14,* 79–82. Copyright 1988 by the Society for the Advancement of Behavior Analysis. Adapted with permission.

## Table 12.8

Limitations of and Recommended Procedures for Punishment

*Limitations*

1. Disruptive or inappropriate behavior can be reduced using punishment procedures. However, if students are motivated to perform the punished behavior and have the opportunity to perform the punished behavior, it is likely that the inappropriate behavior will occur again.

2. If a teacher uses a punishment technique to remove an aversive stimulus (for example, yelling at students to be quiet), the teacher may be negatively reinforced. She may tend to use punishment again to reduce inappropriate student behavior.

3. Punishment may produce undesirable side effects. Student aggression, escape, or avoidance behavior may result. If punishment occurs in the same environment repeatedly (for example, in the classroom), the environment may become a conditioned aversive setting that students avoid.

4. Punishment may produce "spillover effects." That is, the behavior of nontarget students may be adversely affected by punishment directed toward target students.

*Procedures*

1. Vary the types of punishments that are used. If the same type of aversive stimuli are used repeatedly, the students may become satiated.

2. Use a high enough intensity of punishment to suppress the behavior but refrain from gradually increasing the intensity lest the student develop a tolerance for punishment.

3. Punishment delivered at the beginning of a sequence of disruptive or inappropriate behavior will often reduce the level of that behavior faster than punishment delivered at the end of the sequence.

---

*Reinforcement.* The purpose of this component is to determine if the inappropriate behavior is being maintained by reinforcement. If so, those reinforcers are identified, presented contingently, and/or withheld to determine if the behavior changes in the desired direction. Assuming that reinforcers cannot be identified or that the behavior cannot be altered measurably using a reinforcement approach (e.g., differential reinforcement of incompatible behavior), the next component of the model is introduced.

*Ecology.* Given that many educators have reported that ecological variables (e.g., noise level, seating arrangement) affect student performance (Heron & Heward, 1982), the practitioner at this stage searches for variables that might be setting the occasion for, or reinforcing, the inappropriate behavior. For instance, moving a student's seat from the back to the front of the room might reduce off-task or disruptive behavior by itself. Each suspected ecological variable should be altered before proceeding to the next step in the model.

*Curriculum.* The scope and sequence of the curriculum might set the occasion for inappropriate behavior. Changing the design of instructional materials (Vargas, 1984), the sequence of instruction (Engelmann & Carnine, 1982), or the pace of instruction (Carnine, 1976) might substantially reduce the occurrence of inappropriate behavior. Carnine (1976), for example, showed that when questions were asked at a fast pace (12 questions per minute), students answered correctly 80% of the time and were off-task only 10% of the time. Conversely, when a slow pace was used (5 questions per minute), the students answered correctly only 30% of the time and were off-task 70% of the time.

*Punishment.* The last phase in the Gaylord-Ross model prescribes punishment. To reiterate, this phase should be used only after the variables within the

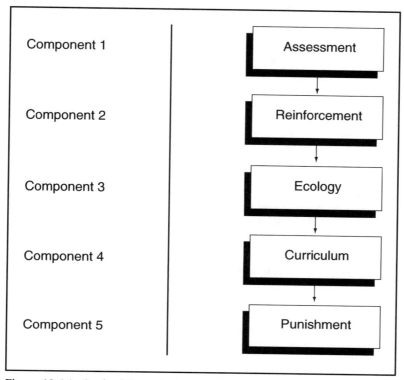

**Figure 12.16.** Gaylord-Ross decision-making model for punishment. From "A Decision Model for the Treatment of Aberrant Behavior in Applied Settings," by R. Gaylord-Ross, 1980, in *Methods of Instruction for Severely Handicapped Students* (p. 138), W. Sailor, B. Wilcox, and L. Brown (Eds.), Baltimore: Paul H. Brookes. Copyright 1980 by Paul H. Brookes. Reprinted with permission.

model discussed above have been investigated exhaustively. Even so, Gaylord-Ross (1980) recommends that the least restrictive form of punishment be used (e.g., type II) before more restrictive forms are initiated (e.g., type I). Furthermore, he recommends that punishment be combined with reinforcement for appropriate behavior or that punishment be reduced or eliminated as soon as the inappropriate behavior is under control.

## Group Contingencies in the Classroom

Thus far a number of procedures for increasing appropriate and decreasing inappropriate behavior in the classroom have been discussed. It should be noted that many of these procedures can be employed within a group context. Teachers who have serious problems with many students in the room, however, usually do not have the time to apply a series of individual contingencies. Teachers need an effective and convenient approach to deal with multiple misbehaviors. A *group-oriented contingency* serves this purpose, because the contingency is applied to the whole class regardless of individual behavior, and it allows the teacher to take advantage of peer group influences (Gardill et al., 1996; Slavin, 1991; Smith & Misra, 1994). Some authors have legitimately outlined the dangers of using peers as change agents (Sapon-Shevon, 1979); still, peers have been shown to be effective agents for constructive change (Gresham & Gresham, 1982).

## Advantages of Group-Oriented Contingencies

A group-oriented contingency has a number of advantages that teachers might find appealing. First, most students enjoy playing games, group games usually generate enthusiasm, and teachers can capitalize on student willingness to participate in games. Second, many student behaviors, appropriate and inappropriate, are the result of conformity to peer pressure. For older students, especially junior and senior high school students, performance of appropriate and inappropriate academic and social behavior may be reinforced by the peer group (Smith & Misra, 1994). Third, group contingencies are often easy to carry out in the classroom. Axelrod (1973), for example, compared individual and group contingencies in two classrooms to determine which would be more efficient in reducing disruptive behavior. He found that the techniques were equally effective, but that the group consequence was far easier to implement in the room since the consequence for any inappropriate behavior had to be administered only to the group rather than to each individual. Finally, simpler record keeping can be facilitated using group consequences. Individual data would not have to be gathered on 20 to 30 students; instead, the occurrence of each target behavior would be recorded for the class as a whole.

## Disadvantages of Group-Oriented Contingencies

The most obvious disadvantage for the use of a group-oriented contingency in the classroom is that all students, regardless of behavior, share the same outcome. For example, when a teacher uses a response-cost group contingency in a class to reduce call-outs, all students lose a minute of recess for each call-out. Students who do not call out receive the same punishment as those who do. However, if only a few students in the class are responsible for the call-outs, the teacher could set up a specific response-cost contingency just for them. In that case, the rest of the class would not be penalized for the inappropriate behavior of a few students.

Second, group procedures may not be sensitive to individual student performance. If a teacher uses only group data, individual student performance will be masked.

Finally, peer group pressure may be generated. Students who lose reinforcement because of a peer's behavior may threaten or intimidate that peer to force him or her to conform to group standards (Smith & Misra, 1994). Consultants who recommend a group-oriented contingency to teachers need to emphasize that peer pressure can work for and against them. All parties engaged in the design and implementation of a group-oriented contingency must be aware of the potential effects of this approach for all students.

Litow and Pumroy (1975) suggest that group-oriented contingencies can be arranged according to (a) dependent group-oriented systems, in which the whole class is reinforced if one student performs the stated behavior; (b) independent group-oriented systems, in which individuals are reinforced if they *each* perform the desired behavior; and (c) interdependent group-oriented systems, in which the whole class is reinforced when all students perform the acceptable behavior.

## Dependent Group-Oriented Systems

Gresham (1983) conducted a dependent group-oriented contingency study that would be of interest to consultants who must arrange management programs across home and school environments. Billy, the 8-year-old target of the study, earned good notes for nondestructive behavior at home (not setting fires, not destroying furniture). The notes, which served as a daily report card, were exchangeable at school for juice, recess, and tokens. After Billy earned five tokens, he was allowed to serve as the host for a class party. So Billy's good performance at home earned a reinforcer at school for him and his classmates. The results of the study indicate that Billy's destructive behavior at home was greatly reduced. A dependent group-oriented contingency is sometimes referred to as a "hero procedure" (Salend, 1987).

## Independent Group-Oriented Systems

Independent group-oriented procedures are most typically represented by token reinforcement or contingency contracting programs in which the performance of each student is independent of (i.e., does not depend on) the rest of the members of the group.

Robinson, Newby, and Ganzell (1981) provide a useful illustration of an independent group-oriented contingency to improve the academic performance of 18 hyperactive third-grade boys. Students earned colored disks (red, green, yellow, and white) for teaching themselves or a partner sight words or the use of the words in sentences. Each student could earn 15 minutes of free time after earning the red token, designating that he or she had taught another student to use words in a sentence. Using a reversal design, the data indicated that when the token system was in effect, student reading and math improved. When the independent group-oriented contingency was not in effect, performance decreased markedly (Figure 12.17). This example illustrates the point that classroom management procedures can and should be focused on academic outcomes as well as appropriate classroom behavior.

## Interdependent Group-Oriented Systems

An interdependent group-oriented contingency can be accomplished in one of four ways: (a) the group as a whole meets the criterion (Gola, Holmes, & Holmes, 1982); (b) reinforcement is delivered when a minimal group mean score is achieved (Baer & Richards, 1980); (c) a single student earns reinforcement for the group (Speltz, Shimamura, & McReynolds, 1982); and (d) the good behavior game is used (Barrish, Saunders, & Wolf, 1969; Cipani, 1998). Salend (1987) suggests that this variation be used when a behavior problem is prevalent with multiple members of the class. Of these four procedural variations, the good behavior game provides the consultant with the most flexibility for school or home application.

For an excellent description of how to establish a good behavior game in the classroom, readers are referred to Cipani (1998).

According to Barrish et al. (1969), the *good behavior game* begins by dividing the group into two (or more) groups or teams (see Figure 12.18). Each team is told that whichever team has the fewest marks against it, or against the established criterion, when the game ends is the winner (see Figure 12.19). The teams are also told that they can all win if they all meet the criterion specified by the teacher.

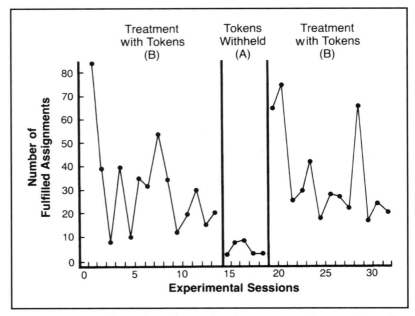

Figure 12.17. Total number of completed assignments for an 18-member class of hyperactive students. From "A Token System for a Class of Under-Achieving Hyperactive Children," by P. W. Robinson, T. J. Newby, and S. L. Ganzell, 1981, *Journal of Applied Behavior Analysis, 14,* 311. Copyright 1981 by Society for the Experimental Analysis of Behavior. Reprinted with permission.

| | Good Behavior Game Team Composition Chart | | | Notes |
|---|---|---|---|---|
| Team names | *Cougars* | *Lions* | *Dolphins* | |
| Students | 1._____ | _____ | _____ | |
| | 2._____ | _____ | _____ | |
| | 3._____ | _____ | _____ | |
| | 4._____ | _____ | _____ | |
| | 5._____ | _____ | _____ | |
| | 6._____ | _____ | _____ | |
| | 7._____ | _____ | _____ | |
| | 8._____ | _____ | _____ | |
| | 9._____ | _____ | _____ | |

Figure 12.18. Team composition chart. From *Classroom Management for All Teachers: 11 Effective Plans* (p. 85), by E. Cipani, 1998. Upper Saddle River, NJ: Merrill. Copyright 1998 by Prentice Hall. Reprinted with permission.

Figure 12.20 shows the results of the Barrish et al. (1969) study. When the good behavior game was in effect, the percentage of intervals of talking-out and out-of-seat behavior during reading and math decreased.

The good behavior game is an example of a "package" group contingency because it combines punishment, differential reinforcement of lower rates of behavior, stimulus control, and reinforcement. Its applicability in a wide vari-

---

**Good Behavior Game**
**Behavior Monitoring Chart**

Behavioral standard: _7 or fewer_ (see solid line)

Target behaviors: _out-of-seat, unauthorized talking_

Period: _9:15–10:30_ A.M.

| Cougars | Lions | Dolphins |
|---------|-------|----------|
| 1 | 1 | 1 |
| 2 | 2 | 2 |
| 3 | 3 | 3 |
| 4 | 4 | 4 |
| 5 | 5 | 5 |
| 6 | 6 | 6 |
| 7 | 7 | 7 |
| 8 | 8 | 8 |
| 9 | 9 | 9 |
| 10 | 10 | 10 |

---

**Figure 12.19.** Behavior monitoring chart. From *Classroom Management for All Teachers: 11 Effective Plans* (p. 85), by E. Cipani, 1998. Upper Saddle River, NJ: Merrill. Copyright 1998 by Merrill. Reprinted with permission.

ety of classroom situations makes it a desirable alternative for the consultant working with group problems.

Finally, Salend and Lamb (1986) provide a useful variation of the interdependent group-oriented contingency in their analysis of the effects of that arrangement on the number of inappropriate verbalizations of two groups of students with learning disabilities. The interesting variation adopted in this study occurred when students were directed to manage the contingency themselves. Specifically, when an inappropriate verbalization occurred during baseline, the teacher redirected the student in her usual manner. During intervention, when an inappropriate verbalization occurred, the student who committed the infraction, or one of the other students in a preassigned group, removed a paper strip (token) taped to an easel in the front of the room. A supply of tokens were pretaped to the easel. If tokens remained after the instructional session, students earned 15 minutes of free time. The criterion number of tokens was reduced over the course of the study as student performance improved. The results for both groups were significant. For instance, the number of inappropriate verbalizations for group 1 dropped from an average of 37 per session to 3.5, whereas group 2's verbalizations dropped from a mean of 28 per session to 2.2. In both cases, a ten-fold decrease in inappropriate verbalizations was noted, and those gains were maintained 2 months after training. The authors state that the results indicate that interdependent group-oriented contingencies can be useful for teachers because they reduce direct teacher involvement in the operation of the contingency, build independence, and promote maintenance.

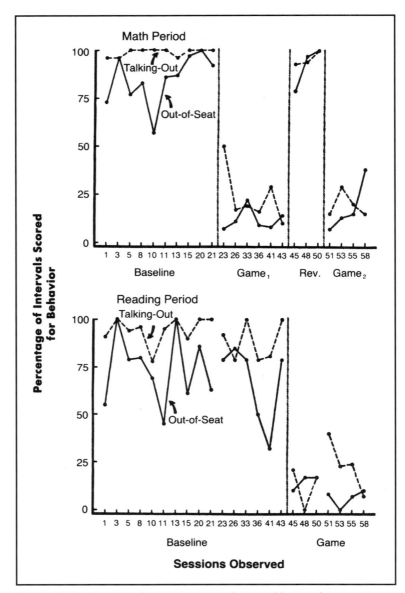

**Figure 12.20.** Percent of 1-minute intervals scored by an observer as con-taing talking-out and out-of-seat behaviors occuring in a classroom of 24 fourth-grade students during math and reading. From "Good Behavior Game: Effects of Individual Contingencies for Group Consequences on Disruptive Behavior," by H. H. Barrish, M. Saunders, and M. M. Wolf, 1969, *Journal of Applied Behavior Analysis, 2*(2), 122. Copyright 1969 by Society for the Experimental Analysis of Behavior. Reprinted with permission.

Whether consultants elect to assist teachers with dependent, independent, or interdependent group-oriented contingencies, it would be helpful to keep the following points by Rhode, Jenson, and Reavis (1998) in mind:

> Never use a group contingency if a student is learning a new behavior or skill . . . use group contingencies only for behaviors that a student can perform, but chooses not to perform . . . make sure that the criterion is

## Table 12.9
### Implementing a Group Contingency

1. Is a group contingency really necessary?
   a. Do peers contribute to the tough kid's misbehavior through encouragement or subtle behaviors?
   b. Is improved student cooperation necessary for this behavior?
   c. Have other positive approaches failed to change this behavior?
2. Define the target behavior. Is it observable, measurable, and easily tracked?
3. Is the student capable of the target behavior but unwilling to perform it?
   a. Make certain the student is not in the process of learning the behavior.
   b. Make certain the student can perform the behavior.
4. Define the group contingency criterion:
   a. Will the criterion be based on the total number of behaviors (e.g., total number of talk-outs)?
   b. Will the criterion be based on the average of the classroom (e.g., 80% of homework returned by the class)?
   c. Will the criterion be based on the performance of one student (e.g., if any student goes to time-out)? *Caution:* Because of the severity of this criterion, it is generally not advised.
   d. Will the criterion be based on an average of a set number of randomly selected students (e.g., three students will be selected at random and not identified; if they have handed in their homework and the work is 80% complete and 80% correct, then the class will be rewarded)?
5. Describe to the class the positive reinforcers that can be gained by the group. Ask for the group's input (e.g., class is permitted to select a reward from the reinforcer menu).
6. Describe to the class a mild reductive consequence if the criterion is not met (e.g., class loses free time period). *Caution:* Make sure the reductive consequence is not overly harsh or for too long a period (e.g., loss of privilege for a week is too long). The loss should be for a day or less.
7. Post the rules for the group contingency. These rules might include:
   a. No threats or making fun of a student who has difficulty will be allowed.
   b. Students may encourage others to do their best.
8. Publicly post the following group contingency information:
   a. the criterion for gaining a reward or losing a privilege—specific target behavior defined with the actual performance number (e.g., no more than five classroom talk-outs);
   b. how the students are doing (e.g., marks on the board for the number of talk-outs); and
   c. what the students will win or lose.
9. Plan a back-up procedure for a student who sabotages the group contingency—make the student a team by himself or herself.
10. Make certain that the group contingency plan is **written** and that:
    a. all classroom staff understand the program;
    b. all the students understand the program;
    c. the program is discussed with the school principal and has his or her support; and
    d. parents are informed.
11. Emphasize the positive and cooperative aspect of the group contingency.

*Note.* From "The Tough Kid Book: Practical Classroom Management Strategies," by G. Rhode, W. R. Jenson, and H. K. Reavis, 1998, Longmont, CO: Sopris West. Copyright 1998 by Sopris West. Reprinted with permission.

both explained well to students and is attainable . . . [and] publicly post feedback on how close students are to either gaining a reward or losing a privilege. . . . (p. 68)

Table 12.9 provides consultants with additional guidelines for implementing successful group-oriented contingencies, especially with difficult-to-manage students.

## Directing Consultation Efforts with Behavior Management

It is axiomatic to state that consultants need to be well versed in multiple behavior change procedures. Clearly, they will be called upon to assist with increasing, decreasing, maintaining, and generalizing academic, social, and vocational behaviors that have been resistant to previous efforts. They must also be realists, however. That is, they must recognize that consultees, in many instances, are not entirely interested in learning, or able to learn, contemporary behavioral procedures themselves; they simply are seeking a short-term solution to a problem. Staff development may not be a high priority for them. Still, consultants should use any problem-solving situation as an opportunity to introduce the use of innovative technologies, increase their involvement in the infrastructure of the school, become even stronger supporters of positive behavioral interventions, use the media to better advantage, and continue to work with parent groups to support school-based staff development and behavior change programs (Axelrod, Moyer, & Berry, 1990; Colvin, Kameenui, & Sugai, 1993; Lohrmann-O'Rourke & Zirkel, 1998). Colvin et al. (1993) put it succinctly:

If we have any hope of meeting the needs of all students in our public schools, especially students with learning and social behavior difficulties, our approach to behavior and classroom management must become more proactive and our staff development efforts must become more collegial and sustained. (p. 379)

## Conclusion

This chapter summarized a number of procedures for managing behavior, including the behavior of groups of individuals. Given that consultants are often called upon to assist with increasing or decreasing a wide range of responses, they must be skilled in the application of such procedures and principles. Even more so, they must recognize conditions under which certain procedures are warranted. The Gaylord-Ross (1980) model serves as one illustration of a decision-making process that is based on the concept of the least restrictive alternative. Finally, group-oriented contingencies offer the consultant another set of management procedures that can be applied in a variety of settings.

# Summary of Key Points

## Behavior Management: More Than Just Discipline

1. Behavior management involves more than just discipline; it includes a full range of proactive approaches embracing flexible instructional techniques, positive classroom climate conditions, dynamic and responsive management alternatives, and supportive collegial interactions.

2. Behavior management can be categorized into two clusters: preintervention approaches and classroom management tactics.

3. Common preintervention variables to consider include physical setting, daily schedule, instructional delivery, precorrection, reinforcement and debriefing plans, classroom rules, and communication and verbal and nonverbal cueing strategies.

4. Classroom management tactics include behavior modification principles and procedures associated with reinforcement, stimulus control, extinction, generality, and social validity.

## Procedures to Increase Appropriate Academic and Social Behavior

5. *Positive reinforcement* is defined as the presentation of a stimulus or event immediately subsequent to the performance of a behavior that increases the probability of the behavior (or response class of behavior) occurring again.

6. The stimulus or event that follows the behavior and is responsible for the increase in behavior is the *positive reinforcer*.

7. Consultants can provide technical assistance to teachers, parents, or other family caretakers by helping them to determine reinforcer preference or reinforcer quality.

8. *Negative reinforcement* is defined as the removal of a stimulus contingent upon a response and has the effect of increasing the probability of a desired behavior in the future.

9. The stimulus or event that is removed is the *negative reinforcer*.

10. Consultants should assist practitioners with determining whether behaviors are maintained by negative reinforcement (as opposed to some other contingency) so that the appropriate countermeasure can be applied.

11. Reinforcers can be of several types: edible, tangible, exchangeable, activity, or social. They are determined solely by their effect on behavior.

12. A token reinforcer is a physical object or symbol that is exchangeable for a back-up reinforcer.

13. Tokens can be employed in classroom situations where conventional reinforcers have been ineffective.

14. Token programs permit the teacher to use a wide variety of back-up reinforcers to establish and maintain behavior. Tokens should be paired with social praise so that when they are reduced or removed, student performance will be maintained by the praise.

15. To initiate a token economy: identify the target behavior; describe the rules for earning tokens; and ensure that the tokens are durable, reusable, and exchanged frequently.

16. Token programs can be maintained by following the rules designated for the program, providing a variety of back-up reinforcers, and using an intermittent exchange program.

17. A token economy might be financed through a grant-in-aid, district support, parent-teacher groups, or personal resources.

18. *Contingency contracting* refers to a behavioral approach in which the task and reinforcement components for the teacher and student are specified in advance.

19. Contracts should be written, and, if possible, students should help to write them. Contracts can be employed with individuals or groups of students and should be drawn using appropriate guidelines.

20. The Premack principle states that access to a high-frequency behavior is contingent upon the performance of low-frequency behavior.

21. High-frequency behavior can be determined by observing, asking, or arranging choices.

22. When a teacher wants to increase the performance of students who already possess many components of target behaviors, a modeling procedure may be effective.

23. Modeling can be employed for a wide range of academic or social behaviors.

24. Peer models can be effective agents for managing classroom behavior.

25. Self-management is the application of behavior change strategies that result in the modification of the individual's own behavior.

26. Self-management can be used to modify a variety of behaviors, and methodologically can be taught in three configurations: pull-out, small-group, and whole-class.

27. Two broad classes of self-monitoring exist: self-monitoring attention (SMA), and self-monitoring performance (SMP).

28. Self-management and self-monitoring skills can be taught using direct instruction, and when they are combined with self-graphing, a powerful management alternative can be produced.

29. Research demonstrates that once a "full" self-management program is introduced, elements of it can be faded without loss of effect.

## Procedures to Decrease Inappropriate Behavior

30. Extinction refers to the discontinuation of a previously reinforced behavior.

31. Extinction must be used cautiously in the classroom, because other sources of reinforcement for inappropriate student behavior might continue to be emitted.

32. Extinction usually has a delayed effect on behavior rather than an immediate one.

33. Three functional variations of extinction exist: (a) withholding or terminating attention (as would be applied for behaviors maintained by positive reinforcement) [EXT (Attention)]; (b) preventing escape (for behaviors maintained by negative reinforcement [EXT (Escape)]; and (c) attenuating consequences (for behaviors maintained by sensory stimulation) [EXT (Sensory)].

34. The temporary increase in the rate of the inappropriate behavior after onset of extinction is termed *extinction burst*.

35. There are three positive reductive procedures: differential reinforcement of other behavior, differential reinforcement of low rates of behavior, and differential reinforcement of incompatible behavior.

36. Punishment procedures can be divided into four categories: punishment by the contingent presentation of a stimulus, overcorrection, time-out from positive reinforcement, and response cost.

37. Punishment by the contingent presentation of a stimulus and overcorrection are referred to as type I punishments. Time-out and response cost are referred to as type II punishments.

38. Consultants are advised to recognize state and local policies on the use of corporal punishment in applied settings.

39. The prolonged and indiscriminate use of time-out, especially in the absence of an education program, may violate student rights.

40. Expulsion from school can be an option for students with disabilities in certain cases, but IEP services must nevertheless be rendered.

41. Punishment of any type should not be administered without informed consent or before all other nonintrusive approaches have been attempted.

42. Position statements published by respected professional associations have stated that each student's program must be delivered after informed consent has been reached, and treatment or education must be administered by a competent professional based on validated practices.

43. A 5-step decision-making model for using punishment specifies that before punishment is used, assessment, reinforcement, ecology, and curriculum variables must be considered. Only after these variables have been introduced and have been shown to be ineffective in reducing the inappropriate behavior should punishment be implemented.

44. A group-oriented contingency is designed to reduce the inappropriate behavior and increase the desirable behavior of a class as a whole.

45. A group-oriented contingency can be applied to a variety of academic and social problems.

46. Group-oriented contingencies can be classified into three categories: dependent, independent, and interdependent.

# Questions

1. Define and give one example each of positive reinforcement, negative reinforcement, punishment (including overcorrection, time-out, and response cost), and extinction.

2. Identify the components of a contingency contract. Why are contracts effective when other management procedures are sometimes not?

3. Provide a rationale for using self-management and/or self-monitoring as part of the overall behavior change program for a target student.

4. Explain why it is important to determine if disruptive behaviors are maintained by EXT (attention), EXT (escape), or EXT (sensory).

5. List three ways to decrease inappropriate social behavior. Focus your response on positive reductive procedures.

6. Why is it important for the consultant to be well versed with the ethical and right to treatment issues surrounding some types of behavioral interventions?

7. Assume that a student with disabilities brought a handgun to school. Outline the steps that would be needed to deal with that situation. Include a discussion of the student's rights, the teacher's rights, and the district's responsibility under two different scenarios: (a) bringing the gun to school was related to the disability; (b) bringing the gun to school was not related to the disability.

8. How can Gaylord-Ross's (1980) decision-making model be used at the elementary, middle, and senior high school levels? Would any modifications of the model need to be made at each level?

9. Describe three ways in which a group-oriented contingency could be placed into effect. What are the advantages and disadvantages of each approach?

# Discussion Points and Exercises

1. Discuss the value of objective data in teaching in terms of (a) deciding whether a problem exists; (b) determining appropriate intervention strategies; and (c) determining the effect of an applied intervention.

2. Identify your school system's procedures for dealing with truant students, students who abuse drugs and alcohol, and destructive students. Do the data indicate that existing procedures are effective?

3. How would you apply (a) a preintervention procedure or (b) a classroom management procedure with a student who is consistently late for class, a student who will not attempt assigned work, a student who has difficulty establishing and maintaining appropriate social relationships, and a student who sells narcotics on the playground?

4. List five potential reinforcers for students at each of the following grade levels: preschool, primary, intermediate, junior high, and high school.

5. Present regular teachers who have a student with disabilities in their classrooms with two blank contracts. Ask the teachers to complete a contract

for one student with disabilities and one student without disabilities in their classrooms. Check each contract for consistency against existing guidelines. Praise the teachers for correct performance.

6. During an inservice presentation, demonstrate how to pair social praise with the delivery of tokens. Stress how to remove tokens once performance begins to improve. Have teachers practice token delivery during inservice sessions and monitor their performances in the classroom.

7. Show a videotape of a skilled teacher using response-cost and time-out procedures with students with and without disabilities. Have teachers in attendance identify the specific teaching behaviors that make those approaches work. Solicit their opinions as to how those techniques could be used in their classrooms.

8. Compare and contrast the position statements related to the right to effective behavioral treatment with parallel statements cited in the right to effective education. What points overlap? Are there any points not included in either of the statements that should be provided?

# References

Abbott, S., Aro, M., Augsburger, H., Cordova, C., Edwards, J., McIntire, C., Roenker, C., Schwindt, D., & Heron, T. E. (1990). Ranger Bucks: A school-wide program to improve student social and interaction behavior. *Ohio Middle School Journal* (April), 4–6.

Abeson, A. (1976). Litigation. In F. J. Weintraub, A. Abeson, J. Ballard, & M. L. LaVor (Eds.), *Public policy and the education of exceptional children* (pp. 240–257). Reston, VA: Council for Exceptional Children.

Abeson, A., Bolick, N., & Hass, J. A. (1975). A primer on due process: Education decisions for handicapped children. *Exceptional Children, 42,* 68–74.

Abrams, B. J., & Segal, A. (1998). How to prevent aggressive behavior. *Teaching Exceptional Children, 30*(4), 10–15.

Adams, L., & Cessna, K. (1991). Designing systems to facilitate collaboration: Collective wisdom from Colorado. *Preventing School Failure, 35*(4), 37–42.

Adelman, H. S. (1994). Intervening to enhance home involvement in schooling. *Intervention in School and Clinic, 29*(5), 276–284.

Adelman, P. B., & Vogel, S. A. (1990). College graduates with learning disabilities—Employment attainment and career patterns. *Learning Disability Quarterly, 13,* 154–166.

Adler, A. (1964). *Social interest: A challenge to mankind.* New York: Capricorn Books.

Affleck, J. Q., Lowenbraun, S., & Archer, A. (1980). *Teaching the mildly handicapped in the regular classroom* (2nd ed.). Columbus, OH: Merrill.

Agran, M., Fodor-Davis, J., Moore, S., & Deer, M. (1989). The application of a self-management program on instruction-following skills. *Journal of the Association for the Severely Handicapped, 14*(2), 147–154.

Agran, M., Martin, J. E., & Mithaug, D. E. (1989). Achieving transition through adaptability instruction. *Teaching Exceptional Children, 21*(2), 4–7.

Alber, S. R., & Heward, W. L. (1997). Recruit it or lose it! Training students to recruit positive teacher attention. *Intervention in School and Clinic, 32,* 275–282.

Alber, S. R., Heward, W. L., & Hippler, B. J. (1999). Teaching middle school students with learning disabilities to recruit positive teacher attention. *Exceptional Children, 65*(2), 253–270.

Alberto, P. A., Mechling, L., Taber, T. A., & Thompson, J. (1995). Using videotape to communicate with parents of students with severe disabilities. *Teaching Exceptional Children, 27*(3), 18–21.

Alberto, P. A., & Troutman, A. C. (1999). *Applied behavior analysis for teachers* (5th ed.). Upper Saddle River, NJ: Merrill.

Alderman, G. L., & Gimpel, G. A. (1996). The interaction between type of behavior problem and type of consultant: Teachers' preferences for professional assistance. *Journal of Educational and Psychological Consultation, 7*(4), 305–313.

Alessi, C. (1985). *Effects of a home-school communication system on the writing performance of learning disabled students.* Unpublished master's thesis, The Ohio State University, Columbus, OH.

Algozzine, B., & Ysseldyke, J. (1981). Special education services for normal children: Better safe than sorry. *Exceptional Children, 48,* 238–243.

Allsopp, D. H. (1997). Using classwide peer tutoring to teach beginning algebra problem-solving skills in heterogeneous classrooms. *Remedial and Special Education, 18*(6), 367–379.

Alper, S. (1994). Introduction and background: The role of parents. In S. K. Alper, P. J. Schloss, & C. N. Schloss, *Families of students with disabilities: Consultation and advocacy* (pp. 1–16). Needham Heights, MA: Allyn & Bacon.

Alper, S., Schloss, P. J., & Schloss, C. N. (1996). Families of children with disabilities in elementary and middle school: Advocacy models and strategies. *Exceptional Children, 62*(3), 261–270.

Ambert, A., & Dew, N. (1982). *Special education for exceptional bilingual students.* Dallas, TX: Evaluation, Dissemination, and Assessment Center.

Amendments to the Education of All Handicapped Children Act of 1983, P.L. 98–199.

American Psychological Association. (1985). *Standards for educational and psychological testing.* Washington, DC: Author.

Americans with Disabilities Act of 1990, P.L. 101–336, July 26, 1990.

Americans with Disabilities Act of 1990: What you should know. Supplement to *Exceptional Children, 57*(2).

Anastopoulos, A. D., DuPaul, G. J., & Barkley, R. A. (1991). Stimulant medication and parent training therapies for attention deficit–hyperactivity disorder. *Journal of Learning Disabilities, 24*(4), 210–218.

Anderson, C., & Katsiyannis, A. (1997). By what token economy? A classroom learning tool for inclusive settings. *Teaching Exceptional Children, 29*(4), 65–67.

Anderson, K. M., & Anderson, C. L. (1997). Helpful Web sites for parents of children with disabilities. *Intervention in School and Clinic, 33*(1), 40–42.

Anderson, S. R., Avery, D. L., DiPietro, E. K., Edwards, G. L., & Christian, W. P. (1987). Intensive home-based early intervention with autistic children. *Education and Treatment of Children, 10*(4), 352–366.

Angrist, S. S. (1975). Evaluation research: Possibilities and limitations. *Journal of Applied Behavioral Science, 11*(1), 75–91.

Apter, S. J. (1982). *Troubled children, troubled systems.* New York: Pergamon.

Aragon, J., & Marquez, L. (1973). Highlights of institute on language and culture: Spanish-speaking component. In L. A. Bransford, L. Baca, & K. Lane (Eds.), *Cultural diversity and the exceptional child* (pp. 20–21). Reston, VA: Council for Exceptional Children.

Argyris, C. (1964). *Integrating the individual and the organization.* New York: Wiley.

*Armstrong v. Kline,* 476 F. Supp. 583 (E.D. PA 1979).

Arnold, J. F., & Stevenson, C. (1998). *Teachers' teaming handbook.* Fort Worth: Harcourt Brace Jovanovich.

Arnold, K. D., Michael, M. G., Hosley, C. A., & Miller, S. (1994). Factors influencing attitudes about family-school communication for parents of children with mild learning problems: Preliminary findings. *Journal of Educational and Psychological Consultation, 5*(3), 257–267.

Arreaga-Mayer, C. (1998). Increasing active student responding and improving academic performance through classwide peer tutoring. *Intervention in School and Clinic, 34*(2), 89–94, 117.

Artesani, A. J., & Mallar, L. (1998). Positive behavior supports in general education settings: Combining person-centered planning and functional assessment. *Intervention in School and Clinic, 34*(1), 33–38.

Artzt, A. F., & Newman, C. M. (1990). Cooperative learning. *Mathematics Teacher, 83,* 448–449.

Asher, J. J. (1969). The total physical approach to second language learning. *Modern Language Journal, 8*(1) 3–18.

Asher, J. J. (1977). *Learning another language through actions: The complete teacher's guide.* Los Gatos, CA: Sky Oaks Productions.

Asher, S. R., & Taylor, A. R. (1981). Social outcomes of mainstreaming: Sociometric assessment and beyond. *Exceptional Education Quarterly, 1*(4), 13–30.

Asselin, S. B., Todd-Allen, M., & deFur, S. (1998). Transition coordinators: Define yourselves. *Teaching Exceptional Children* (Jan/Feb), 11–15.

Aune, E. P., & Johnson, J. M. (1992). Transition takes teamwork! A collaborative model for college-bound students with LD. *Intervention in School and Clinic, 27*(4), 222–227.

Axelrod, S. (1973). Comparison of individual and group contingencies in two special classes. *Behavior Therapy, 4,* 83–90.

Axelrod, S. (1994). Cooperative learning revisited. *Journal of Behavioral Education, 4*(1), 41–48.

Axelrod, S., & Apsche, J. (Eds.). (1983). *The effects of punishment on human behavior.* New York: Academic Press.

Axelrod, S., Moyer, L., & Berry, B. (1990). Why teachers do not use behavior modification procedures. *Journal of Educational and Psychological Consultation, 1*(4), 309–320.

Azrin, N. H., & Besalel, V. A. (1980). *How to use overcorrection.* Austin, TX: PRO-ED.

Babcock, N. L., & Pryzwansky, W. B. (1983). Models of consultation: Preferences of educational professionals at five stages of service. *Journal of School Psychology, 21,* 359–366.

Baca, L. (1998). Bilingualism and bilingual education. In L. M. Baca & H. T. Cervantes (Eds.), *The bilingual special education interface* (2nd ed., pp. 26–45). Columbus, OH: Merrill.

Baca, L. M., & Almanza, E. (1991). *Language minority students with disabilities.* Reston, VA: Council for Exceptional Children.

Baca, L. M., & Cervantes, H. T. (1998). *The bilingual special education interface* (2nd ed.). Columbus, OH: Merrill.

Baca, L., & deValenzuela, J. S. (1998). Background and rationale for bilingual special education. In L. M. Baca & H. T. Cervantes (Eds.), *The bilingual special education interface* (2nd ed., pp. 2–25). Columbus, OH: Merrill.

Bacon, E. H. (1991). Using negative consequences effectively. *Academic Therapy, 25*(5), 599–611.

Baer, D. (1987). Weak contingencies, strong contingencies, and many behaviors to change. *Journal of Applied Behavior Analysis, 20*(4), 335–337.

Baer, G. G., & Richards, H. C. (1980). An interdependent group-oriented contingency system for improving academic performance. *School Psychology Review, 9,* 190–193.

Baer, R. A. (1989). Maintenance of child behavior change: What happens after the experimenters leave? *Education and Treatment of Children, 12*(2), 190–199.

Bahamonde, C., & Friend, M. (1999). Teaching English language learners: A proposal for effective service delivery through collaboration and co-teaching. *Journal of Educational and Psychological Consultation, 10*(1), 1–24.

Bailey, D. B., Jr., McWilliam, R. A., Darker, L. A., Hebbeler, K., Simeonsson, R. J., Spiker, D., & Wagner, M. (1998). Family outcomes in early intervention: A framework for program evaluation and efficacy research. *Exceptional Children, 64*(3), 313–328.

Bailey, D. B., Jr., & Simeonsson, R. J. (1988). Assessing needs of families with handicapped infants. *Journal of Special Education, 22*(1), 117–127.

Bailey, D. B., Jr., Simeonsson, R. J., Winton, J., Huntington, G. S., Comfort, M., Isbell, P., O'Donnell, K. J., & Helm, J. M. (1986). Family-focused intervention: A functional model for planning, implementing, and evaluating individualized family services in early intervention. *Journal of the Division for Early Childhood, 10,* 156–171.

Baldwin, D. S., Jeffries, G. W., Jones, V. H., Thorp, E. K., & Walsh, S. A. (1992). Collaborative systems design for Part H of IDEA. *Infants and Young Children, 5,* 12–20.

Ballard, J. (1976). Active federal education laws for exceptional persons. In F. J. Weintraub, A. Abeson, J. Ballard, & M. L. LaVor (Eds.), *Public policy and the education of exceptional children* (pp. 133–146). Reston, VA: Council for Exceptional Children.

Ballard, J., Ramirez, B., & Zantal-Wiener, K. (1987). *Public Law 94-142, Section 504, and Public Law 99-457: Understanding what they are and are not.* Reston, VA: Council for Exceptional Children.

Bandura, A. (1997). *Self-efficacy: The exercise of control.* New York: W. H. Freeman.

Banerji, M., & Dailey, R. A. (1995). A study of the effects of an inclusion model on students with specific learning disabilities. *Journal of Learning Disabilities, 28*(8), 511–522.

Banks, J. A. (1984). *Teaching strategies for ethnic studies* (3rd ed.). Boston: Allyn & Bacon.

Bannerman, D. J., Sheldon, J. B., Sherman, J. A., & Harchik, A. E. (1990). Balancing the right to habilitation with the right of personal liberties: The rights of people with developmental disabilities to eat too many doughnuts and take a nap. *Journal of Applied Behavior Analysis, 23,* 79–89.

Barbetta, P., & Heron, T. E. (1991). Project SHINE: Summer home instruction and evaluation. *Intervention in School and Clinic, 26*(5), 276–281.

Barbetta, P. M., Heron, T. E., & Heward, W. L. (1993). Effects of active student response during error correction on the acquisition, maintenance, and generalization of sight words by students with developmental disabilities. *Journal of Applied Behavior Analysis, 26,* 111–119.

Barbetta, P. M., & Heward, W. L. (1993). Effects of active student response during error correction on the acquisition and maintenance of geography facts by elementary students with learning disabilities. *Journal of Behavioral Education, 3,* 217–233.

Barbetta, P. M., Heward, W. L., & Bradley, D. M. C. (1993). Relative effects of whole-word and phonetic error correction on the acquisition and maintenance of sight words by students with developmental disabilities. *Journal of Applied Behavior Analysis, 26,* 99–110.

Barbetta, P. M., Heward, W. L., Bradley, D. M. C., & Miller, A. D. (1994). Effects of immediate and delayed error correction on the acquisition and maintenance of sight words by students with developmental disabilities. *Journal of Applied Behavior Analysis, 27,* 177–178.

Barbetta, P. M., Miller, A. D., Peters, M. T., Heron, T. E., & Cochran, L. L. (1991). TUGMATE: A cross-age tutoring program to teach sight vocabulary. *Education and Treatment of Children, 14,* 19–37.

Barnett, D. W., & Hall, J. D. (1990). Best practices in designing preschool interventions. In A. Thomas and J. Grimes (Eds.), *Best practices in school psychology II,* (pp. 309–321). Washington, DC: National Association of School Psychologists.

Barrett, B. H., Beck, R., Binder, C., Cook, D. A., Engelmann, S., Greer, R., Douglas, K., Jane, S., Johnson, K. R., Maloney, M., McCorkle, N., Vargas, J. S., & Watkins, C. L. (1991). The right to effective education. *The Behavior Analyst, 14,* 79–82.

Barrish, H. H., Saunders, M., & Wolf, M. M. (1969). Good behavior games: Effects of individual contingencies for group consequences on disruptive behavior in a classroom. *Journal of Applied Behavior Analysis, 2*(2), 199–224.

Barsch, R. H. (1969). *The parent teacher partnership.* Arlington, VA: Council for Exceptional Children.

Bassett, D. S., Jackson, L., Ferrell, K. A., Luckner, J., Hagerty, P. J., Bunsen, T. D., & MacIsaac, D. (1996). Multiple perspectives on inclusive education: Reflections of a university faculty. *Teacher Education Special Education, 19*(4), 355–386.

*Battle v. Commonwealth of Pennsylvania,* 629 (3rd Cir. 1980).

Battle, D. A., Dickens-Wright, L. L., & Murphy, S. C. (1998). How to empower adolescents: Guidelines for effective self-advocacy. *Teaching Exceptional Children* (Jan/Feb), 28–33.

Bauman, K. E., Reiss, M. L., Rogers, R. W., Bailey, J. S. (1983). Dining out with children: Effectiveness of a parent advice package on pre-meal inappropriate behavior. *Journal of Applied Behavior Analysis, 16*(1), 55–68.

Bauwens, J., & Hourcade, J. J. (1991). Making co-teaching a mainstreaming strategy. *Preventing School Failure, 35*(4), 19–24.

Bauwens, J., & Hourcade, J. J. (1995). *Cooperative teaching: Rebuilding the Schoolhouse for all students.* Austin, TX: PRO-ED.

Bauwens, J., & Hourcade, J. J. (1997). Cooperative teaching: Pictures of possibilities. *Intervention in School and Clinic, 33*(2), 81–85, 89.

Bauwens, J., & Korinek, L. (1993). IEPs for cooperative teaching: Developing legal and useful documents. *Intervention in School and Clinic, 28*(5), 303–306.

Beakley, B. A., & Yoder, S. L. (1998). Middle schoolers learn community skills. *Teaching Exceptional Children* (Jan/Feb), 16–21.

Becker, W. (1992). Direct instruction: A twenty-year review. In R. P. West & L. A. Hamerlunck (Eds.), *Designs for excellence in education* (pp. 71–112). Longmont, CA: Sopris West.

Beckman, P. J., & Pokorni, J. L. (1988). A longitudinal study of families of preterm infants: Changes in stress and support over the first two years. *Journal of Special Education, 22*(1), 55–65.

Bedard, E. (1995). Collaboration in educational planning: A parent's perspective. *LD Forum, 20*(3), 23–25.

Behring, S. T., & Gelinas, R. T. (1996). School consultation with Asian American children and families. *California School Psychologist, 1*, 13–20.

Bell, K. E., Young, R., Salzberg, C. L., & West, R. P. (1991). High school driver education using peer tutors, direct instruction, and precision teaching. *Journal of Applied Behavior Analysis, 24*, 45–51.

Bender, W. N. (1988). The other side of placement decisions: Assessment of the mainstream learning environment. *Remedial and Special Education, 9*(5), 28–33.

Bender, W. N., & Golden, L. B. (1988). Adaptive behavior of learning disabled and nonlearning disabled children. *Learning Disability Quarterly, 11*(1), 55–61.

Bennett, T., DeLuca, D., & Bruns, D. (1997). Putting inclusion into practice: Perspectives of teachers and parents. *Exceptional Children, 64*(1), 115–131.

Bennett, W. L. (1994). *The index of leading cultural indicators: Facts and figures on the state of American society.* New York: Simon and Schuster.

Bennis, W. G. (1969). *Changing organizations.* New York: McGraw-Hill.

Bennis, W. G. (1970). *Beyond bureaucracy.* New York: McGraw-Hill.

Benz, M. R., Johnson, D. K., Mikkelsen, K. S., & Lindstrom, L. E. (1995). Improving collaboration between schools and vocational rehabilitation: Stakeholder identified barriers and strategies. *CDEI 18*(2), 133–144.

Benz, M. R., Yovanoff, P., & Doren, B. (1997). School-to-work components that predict postschool success for students with and without disabilities. *Exceptional Children, 63*(2), 151–165.

Bergan, J. R. (1977). *Behavioral consultation.* Columbus, OH: Merrill.

Bergan, J. R. (1995). Evolution of a problem-solving model of consultation. *Journal of Educational and Psychological Consultation, 6*(2), 111–123.

Bergan, J. R., & Caldwell, T. (1995). Operant techniques in school psychology. *Journal of Educational and Psychological Consultation, 6*(2), 103–110.

Bergan, J. R., & Tombari, M. L. (1975). The analysis of verbal interactions occurring during consultation. *Journal of School Psychology, 13*, 209–226.

Bergan, J. R., & Tombari, M. L. (1976). Consultant skill and efficiency and the implementation and outcomes of consultation. *Journal of School Psychology, 14*(1), 3–14.

Berry, J., & Hardman, M. L. (1998). *Lifespan perspectives on family and disability.* Boston: Allyn & Bacon.

Bersoff, D. N. (1979). Regarding psychologists testily: Legal regulation of psychological assessment in the public schools. *Maryland Law Review, 39*, 27–120.

Bittle, R. G. (1975). Improving parent-teacher communication through recorded telephone messages. *Journal of Educational Research, 69*, 87–95.

Bjorck-Akesson, E., & Granlund, M. (1995). Family involvement in assessment and intervention: Perceptions of professionals and parents in Sweden. *Exceptional Children, 61*(6), 520–535.

Black, S. (1996). The truth about homework: What the research says might surprise you. *American School Board Journal, 183*(10), 48–51.

Blackhurst, A. E. (1997). Perspectives on technology in special education. *Teaching Exceptional Children, 29*(5), 41–48.

Blackorby, J., & Wagner, M. (1996). Longitudinal post-school outcomes of youth with disabilities: Findings from the National Longitudinal Transition Study. *Exceptional Children, 62*(5), 399–413.

Blalock, G. (1996). Community transition teams as the foundation for transition services for youth with learning disabilities. *Journal of Learning Disabilities, 29*(2), 148–159.

Blew, P. A., Schwartz, I. S., & Luce, S. C. (1985). Teaching functional community skills to autistic children using handicapped peer tutors. *Journal of Applied Behavior Analysis, 18*, 337–342.

*Board of Education v. Rowley,* 458 U.S. 176, 102 S. Ct. 3034, 73 L. Ed., 2nd 690 (1982).

*Board of Education of Sacramento City Unified School District v. Holland,* (1992). IDELR, 18, 761–767. U.S. District Court, Eastern District of California.

Boehm, A. E., & Weinberg, R. A. (1977). *The classroom observer: A guide for developing observation skills.* New York: Teachers College Press.

Bossert, S. T. (1988). Cooperative activities in the classroom. *Review of Research in Education, 15*, 225–250.

Boyer, E. L. (1983). *High school.* New York: Harper & Row.

Boyle, J. R., & Hughes, C. A. (1994). Effects of self-monitoring and subsequent fading of external prompts on the on-task behavior and task productivity of elementary students with moderate mental retardation. *Journal of Behavioral Education, 4*(4), 439–457.

Bradley, D. F. (1994). A framework for the acquisition of collaborative consultation skills. *Journal of Educational and Psychological Consultation, 5*(1), 51–68.

Bradley, D. F., & Calvin, M. B. (1998). Grading modified assignments: Equity or compromise? *Teaching Exceptional Children, 31*(2), 24–29.

Brady, M. P., McDougall, D., & Dennis, H. F. (1989). The schools, the courts, and the integration of students with severe handicaps. *Journal of Special Education, 23*(1), 43–58.

Bramlett, R. K., & Murphy, J. J. (1998). School psychology perspectives on consultation: Key contributions to the field. *Journal of Educational and Psychological Consultation, 9*(1), 29–55.

Brandenburg-Ayres, S. (1990). Working with parents. In V. I. Correa & S. H. Fradd (Eds.), *Bilingual/ESOL Special Education Collaboration and Reform Modules.* Gainesville, FL: University of Florida.

Brandt, J. E. (1994). *Assessment and transition planning: A curriculum for school psychologists and special educators.* Biddeford, ME: University of New England.

Brandt, R. M. (1975). An historical overview of systematic approaches to observation in school settings. In R. A. Weinberg & F. H. Wood (Eds.), *Observation of pupils and teachers in mainstream and special education settings: Alternative strategies* (pp. 9–37). Reston, VA: Council for Exceptional Children.

Brantner, J. P., & Doherty, M. A. (1983). A review of timeout: A conceptual and methodological analysis. In S. Axelrod & J. Apsche (Eds.), *The effects of punishment on human behavior* (pp. 87–132). New York: Academic Press.

Brazelton, B. (1983). *Infants and mothers.* New York: Delta/Seymour Lawrence.

Bridges, W. (1991). *Managing transitions: Making the most of change.* Reading, MA: Addison-Wesley.

Briggs, M. H. (1993). Team talk: Communication skills for early intervention teams. *Journal of Childhood Communication Disorders, 15*(1), 33–40.

Brigham, F. J., Scruggs, T. E., & Mastropieri, M. A. (1995). Elaborative maps for enhanced learning of historical information: Uniting spatial, verbal, and imaginal information. *Journal of Special Education, 28*(3), 440–460.

Brimer, R. W., & Barudin, S. I. (1977). *Due process, right to education and the exceptional child: The road to equality in education.* Unpublished manuscript, University of Missouri–Columbia.

Broden, M., Bruce, C., Mitchell, M. A., Carter, V. C., & Hall, R. V. (1970). Effects of teacher attention on attending behavior of two boys in adjacent seats. *Journal of Applied Behavior Analysis, 3,* 199–203.

Brophy, J. E., & Alleman, J. (1991). Activities as instructional tools: A framework for analysis and evaluation. *Educational Researcher, 20*(4), 9–23.

Brophy, J. E., & Good, T. L. (1974). *Teacher-student relationships: Causes and consequences.* New York: Holt, Rinehart and Winston.

Brotherson, M. J., Backus, L. H., Summers, J. A., & Turnbull, A. P. (1986). Transition to adulthood. In J. A. Summers (Ed.), *The right to grow up: An introduction to adults with developmental disabilities* (pp. 17–44). Baltimore: Paul H. Brookes.

Brown, D., Wyne, M. D., Blackburn, J. E., & Powell, W. C. (1979). *Consultation: Strategy for improving education.* Boston: Allyn & Bacon.

Bruininks, V. L. (1978a). Actual and perceived peer status of learning disabled students in mainstreamed programs. *Journal of Special Education, 12*(1), 51–58.

Bruininks, V. L. (1978b). Peer status and personality characteristics of learning disabled and nondisabled students. *Journal of Learning Disabilities, 11,* 484–489.

Bryan, T. H. (1977). Learning disabled children's comprehension of nonverbal communication. *Journal of Learning Disabilities, 10,* 501–506.

Bryan, T., & Sullivan-Burstein, K. (1997). Homework how-to's. *Teaching Exceptional Children, 29*(6), 32–37.

Bryant, B. R., & Seay, P. C. (1998). The technology-related assistance to Individuals with Disabilities Act: Relevance to individuals with learning disabilities and their advocates. *Journal of Learning Disabilities, 31*(1), 4–15.

Budd, K., & Baer, D. M. (1976). Behavior modification and the law: Implications of recent judicial decisions. *Journal of Psychiatry and Law* (Summer), 171–244.

Buisson, G. J., Murdock, J. Y., Reynolds, K. E., & Cronin, M. E. (1995). Effects of tokens on response latency of students with hearing impairments in a resource room. *Education and Treatment of Children, 18*(4), 408–421.

*Burlington v. Department of Education,* 105 S. Ct. 1996 (1985).

Burstein, N. D. (1986). The effects of classroom organization on mainstreamed preschool children. *Exceptional Children, 52*(5), 425–434.

Bursuck, W., Munk, D. D., Olson, M. M. (1999). The fairness of report card grading adaptations: What do students with and without disabilities think? *Remedial and Special Education, 20*(2), 84–92, 105.

Bursuck, W., Polloway, E. A., Plante, L., Epstein, M. H., Jayanthi, M., & McConeghy, J. (1996). Report card grading and adaptations: A national survey of classroom practices. *Exceptional Children, 62*(4), 301–318.

Bush, W. J., & Waugh, K. W. (1982). *Diagnosing learning problems* (3rd ed.). Columbus, OH: Merrill.

Callahan, K., Rademacher, J. A., & Hildreth, B. L. (1998). The effect of parent participation in strategies to improve the homework performance of students who are at risk. *Remedial and Special Education, 19*(3), 131–141.

Campinha-Bacote, J. (1994). Cultural competence in psychiatric mental health nursing: A conceptual model. *Nursing Clinics of North America, 29*(1), 1–8.

Canady, R. L., & Rettig, M. D. (1996). *Teaching in the block.* Larchmont, NY: Eye on Education.

Cangelosi, J. S. (1993). *Classroom management strategies: Gaining and maintaining student's cooperation* (2nd ed.). New York: Longman.

Caplan, G. (1970). *The theory and practice of mental health consultation.* New York: Basic Books.

Caplan, G. (1995). Types of mental health consultation. *Journal of Educational and Psychological Consultation, 6*(1), 7–21.

Caplan, G., Caplan, R. B., & Erchul, W. P. (1995). A contemporary view of mental health consultation: Comments on "types of mental health consultation" by Gerald Caplan (1963). *Journal of Educational and Psychological Consultation, 6*(1), 23–30.

Carnegie Council on Adolescent Development. (1995). *Great transitions: Preparing adolescents for a new century.* New York: Carnegie Corporation of New York.

Carney, I. H., & Gamel-McCormick, M. (1996). Working with families. In F. P. Orelove & D. Sobsey (Eds.), *Educating children with multiple disabilities: A transdisciplinary approach* (3rd ed., pp. 451–476). Baltimore: Paul H. Brookes.

Carney, R. N., Levin, M. E., & Levin, J. R. (1993). Mnemonic strategies: Instructional techniques worth remembering. *Teaching Exceptional Children, 25*(4), 24–30.

Carnine, D. (1983). Direct instruction: In search of instructional solutions for educational problems. In D. Carnine, D. Elkind, A. D. Hendrickson, D. Meichenbaum, R. L. Sieben, & F. Smith (Eds.), *Interdisciplinary voices in learning disabilities and remedial education* (pp. 1–51). Austin, TX: PRO-ED.

Carnine, D. W. (1976). Effects of two teachers' presentation rates on off-task behavior, answering correctly, and participation. *Journal of Applied Behavior Analysis, 9,* 199–206.

Carnine, D., Silbert, J., & Kameenui, E. J. (1997). *Direct Instruction reading* (3rd ed.). Upper Saddle River, NJ: Merrill.

Caro, F. G. (1971). Issues in the evaluation of social programs. *Review of Educational Research, 41,* 87–114.

Caro, P., & Derevensky, J. L. (1997). An exploratory study using the sibling interaction scale: Observing interactions between siblings with and without disabilities. *Education and Treatment of Children, 20*(4), 383–403.

Carpenter, C. D., Bloom, L. A., & Boat, M. B. (1999). Guidelines for special educators: Achieving socially valid outcomes. *Intervention in School and Clinic, 34*(3), 143–149.

Carpenter, C. D., Ray, M. S., & Bloom, L. A. (1995). Portfolio assessment: Opportunities and challenges. *Intervention in School and Clinic, 31*(1), 34–41.

Carpenter, S. L., & McKee-Higgins, E. (1996). Behavior management in inclusive classrooms. *Remedial and Special Education, 17*(4), 195–203.

Carr, E. G., & Lovaas, I. O. (1983). Contingent electric shock as a treatment for severe behavior problems. In S. Axelrod & J. Apsche (Eds.), *The effects of punishment on human behavior* (pp. 221–245). New York: Academic Press.

Carr, E. G., & Smith, C. E. (1995). Biological setting events for self-injury. *Mental Retardation and Developmental Disabilities Research Reviews, 1,* 94–98.

Carr, J. E., & Burkholder, E. O. (1998). Creating single-subject design graphs with Microsoft EXCEL™. *Journal of Applied Behavior Analysis, 31*(2), 245–251.

Carr, M. N. (1993). A mother's thoughts on inclusion. *Journal of Learning Disabilities, 26*(9), 590–592.

Carter, J., & Sugai, G. (1989). Survey on prereferral practices: Responses from state departments of education. *Exceptional Children, 55,* 298–302.

Casto, G., & Mastropieri, M. A. (1986). The efficacy of early intervention programs: A meta-analysis. *Exceptional Children, 52*(5), 417–424.

Catania, A. C. (1984). *Learning* (2nd ed.). Englewood Cliffs, NJ: Prentice-Hall.

Cavanaugh, R. A., Heward, W. L., & Donelson, F. (1996). Comparative effects of verbal and response card reviews during lesson closure on the academic performance of high school students in a ninth-grade earth science course. *Journal of Applied Behavior Analysis, 29,* 403–406.

Chalfant, J. C. (1994, April). *A new system for teacher support teams: Can we afford not to team?* Paper presented at the Annual Conference of Exceptional Children, Denver, CO.

Chalfant, J. C., Pysh, M. V., & Moultrie, R. (1979). Teacher assistance teams: A model for within-building problem solving. *Learning Disability Quarterly, 2,* 85–96.

Chalfant, J. C., & Van Dusen Pysh, M. (1989). Teacher assistance teams: Five descriptive studies on 96 teams. *Remedial and Special Education, 10*(6), 49–58.

Chalmers, L., & Faliede, T. (1996). Successful inclusion of students with mild/moderate disabilities in rural school settings. *Teaching Exceptional Children, 29*(1), 22–25.

Chandler, L. A. (1980). Consultative services in the schools: A model. *Journal of School Psychology, 18*(4), 399–401.

Charner, I., Fraser, B. S., Hubbard, S., Rogers, A., & Horne, R. (1995). Reforms of the school-to-work transition: Findings, implications, and challenges. *Phi Delta Kappan* (September), 40, 58–60.

Cheney, D., Manning, B., & Upham, D. (1997). Project destiny: Engaging families of students with emotional and behavioral disabilities. *Teaching Exceptional Children, 30*(1), 24–29.

Chesler, M. A., Bryant, B. I., Jr., & Crowfoot, J. E. (1981). Consultation in schools: Inevitable conflict, partisanship, and advocacy. In M. J. Curtis & J. E. Zins, (Eds.), *The theory and practice of school consultation.* Springfield, IL: Charles E. Thomas.

Christenson, S. L., & Cleary, M. (1990). Consultation and the parent-educator partnership: A perspective. *Journal of Educational and Psychological Consultation, 1*(3), 219–241.

Christian, L. A., & Poling, A. (1997). Using self-management procedures to improve the productivity of adults with developmental disabilities in a competitive employment setting. *Journal of Applied Behavior Analysis, 30*(1), 169–172.

Christiansen, J., & Vogel, J. R. (1998). A decision model for grading students with disabilities. *Teaching Exceptional Children, 31*(2), 30–35.

Cipani, E. (1985). The three phases of behavioral consultation: Objectives, intervention, and quality assurance. *Teacher Education and Special Education, 8*(3), 144–152.

Cipani, E. C. (1995). Be aware of negative reinforcement. *Teaching Exceptional Children, 27*(4), 36–40.

Cipani, E. D. (1998). *Classroom management for all teachers: 11 effective plans.* Upper Saddle River, NJ: Merrill.

Clark, G. M. (1994). Is a functional curriculum approach compatible with an inclusive education model? *Teaching Exceptional Children, 26*(2), 36–39.

Clark, G. M., & Kolstoe, O. P. (1995). *Career development and transition education for adolescents with disabilities.* Boston: Allyn & Bacon.

Clark, T. A. (1992). Collaboration to build competence: The urban superintendents' perspective. *The ERIC Review, 21*(2), 2–6.

Cobb, R. B., & Neubert, D. A. (1998). Vocational education: Emerging vocationalism. In F. R. Rusch & J. G. Chadsey (Eds.), *Beyond high school: Transition from school to work* (pp. 101–125). Belmont, CA: Wadsworth.

Cohen, L. G., & Spenciner, L. J. (1996). Research digest: Transition assessment. *Diagnostique, 21*(3), 59–74.

Cohen, M. (1983). Instructional management and social conditions in effective schools. In A. O. Webb & L. D. Webb (Eds.), *School finance and school improvement: Linkages in the 1980's.* Cambridge, MA: Ballinger.

Cohen, P. A., Kulik, J. A., & Kulik, C. C. (1982). Educational outcomes of tutoring. *American Educational Research Journal, 19,* 237–248.

Cohen, S. B., & Lynch, D. K. (1991). An instructional modification process. *Teaching Exceptional Children, 23*(4), 12–18.

Collet-Klingenberg, L. L. (1998). The reality of best practices in transition: A case study. *Exceptional Children, 45*(1), 67–78.

Colvin, G., Ainge, D., & Nelson, R. (1997). How to defuse confrontations. *Teaching Exceptional Children, 29*(6), 47–51.

Colvin, G., Kameenui, E.J., & Sugai, G. (1993). Reconceptualizing behavior management and school-wide discipline in general education. *Education and Treatment of Children, 16*(4), 361–381.

Colvin, G., & Lazar, M. (1997). *The effective elementary classroom: Managing for success.* Longmont, CO: Sopris West.

Colvin, G., Sugai, G., & Patching, B. (1993). Precorrection: An instructional approach for managing predictable problem behaviors. *Intervention in School and Clinic, 28*(3), 143–150.

Conderman, G., & Katsiyannis, A. (1995). Section 504 accommodation plans. *Intervention on School and Clinic, 31*(1), 42–45.

Cone, J. D., DeLawyer, D. D., & Wolfe, V. V. (1985). Assessing parent participation: The parent/family involvement index. *Exceptional Children, 51*(5), 417–424.

Conoley, J. C., & Conoley, C. W. (1982). *School consultation: A guide to practice and training.* New York: Pergamon.

Conroy, M., Fox, J., Crain, L., Jenkins, A., & Belcher, K. (1996). Evaluating the social and ecological validity of analog assessment procedures for challenging behaviors in young children. *Education and Treatment of Children, 19*(3), 233–256.

Cook, B. G., & Semmel, M. I. (1999). Peer acceptance of included students with disabilities as a function of severity of disability and classroom composition. *Journal of Special Education, 33*(1), 50–61.

Cook, L., & Friend, M. (1995). Co-teaching: Guidelines for creating effective practices. *Focus on Exceptional Children, 28*(3), 1–16.

Cooke, N. L., Heron, T. E., & Heward, W. L. (1983). *Peer tutoring: Implementing classwide programs in the primary grades.* Columbus, OH: Special Press.

Cooper, H., & Nye, B. (1994). Homework for students with learning disabilities: The implications for policy and practice. *Journal of Learning Disabilities, 27*(8), 470–479.

Cooper, J. O. (2000). Tutoring Joe: Winning with the precision teaching team. In W. L. Heward (Ed.), *Exceptional Children* (6th ed., pp. 268–270). Upper Saddle River, NJ: Merrill.

Cooper, J. O., & Edge, D. (1981). *Parenting: Strategies and educational methods.* Louisville, KY: Eston.

Cooper, J. O., Heron, T. E., & Heward, W. L. (1987). *Applied behavior analysis.* Columbus, OH: Merrill.

Cooper, L. J., Wacker, D. P., Sasso, G. M., Reimers, T. M., & Donn, L. K. (1990). Using parents as therapists to evaluate appropriate behavior of their children: Application to a tertiary diagnostic clinic. *Journal of Applied Behavior Analysis, 23,* 285–296.

Copa, G. H., & Pease, V. H. (1992). *A new vision for the comprehensive high school: Preparing students for a changing world.* Executive Summary Report from the National Center for Research in Vocational Education. Minneapolis: University of Minnesota, Department of Vocational and Technical Education.

Cordisco, L. K., & Laus, M. K. (1993). Individualized training in behavioral strategies for parents of preschool children with disabilities. *Teaching Exceptional Children, 25*(2), 43–47.

Corno, L. (1996). Home is a complicated thing. *Educational Researcher, 25*(8), 27–30.

Council for Exceptional Children. (1999). *IEP Team Guide.* Reston, VA: Author.

Council for Learning Disabilities. (1993). Concerns about the full inclusion of students with learning disabilities in regular education classrooms. *Learning Disability Quarterly, 16*(2), 126.

Courson, F. H. (1989). *Comparative effects of short- and long-form guided notes on social studies performance by seventh grade learning disabled and at-risk students.* Unpublished doctoral dissertation, The Ohio State University, Columbus.

Cox, J. (1980). Operation divert: A model program for learning disabled juvenile offenders. In R. H. Riegel & J. P. Mathey (Eds.), *Mainstreaming at the secondary level: Seven models that work.* Plymouth, MI: Wayne County Intermediate School District.

Craft, M. A., Alber, S. R., & Heward, W. L. (1998). Teaching elementary students with developmental disabilities to recruit teacher attention in a general education classroom: Effects on teacher praise and academic productivity. *Journal of Applied Behavior Analysis, 31,* 399–415.

Cramer, S., Erzkus, A., Mayweather, K., Pope, K., Roeder, J., & Tone, T. (1997). Connecting with siblings. *Teaching Exceptional Children, 30*(1), 46–51.

Cronin, M. E., & Patton, J. R. (1993). *Life skills instruction for all students with special needs: A practical guide for integrating real life content into the curriculum.* Austin, TX: PRO-ED.

Crooks, T. J. (1988). The impact of classroom evaluation practices on students. *Review of Educational Research, 58*(4), 438–481.

Crowner, T. T. (1985). A taxonomy of special education finance. *Exceptional Children, 51*(6), 503–508.

Cuenin, L. H., & Harris, K. R. (1986). Planning, implementing, and evaluating timeout interventions with exceptional students. *Teaching Exceptional Children, 18*(4), 272–276.

Cummins, J. (1981a). Age on arrival and immigrant second language learning in Canada: A reassessment. *Applied Linguistics, 2*(2), 131–149.

Cummins, J. (1981b). The role of primary language development in promoting educational success for language minority students. In *Schooling and language minority students: A theoretical framework* (pp. 3–49). Los Angeles: Evaluation, Dissemination and Assessment Center, California State University–Los Angeles.

Cummins, J. (1984). *Bilingualism and special education: Issues in assessment and pedagogy.* San Diego, CA: College-Hill Press.

Cummins, J. (1986). Empowering minority students: A framework for intervention. *Harvard Educational Review, 56,* 18–36.

Cummins, J. (1991). The development of bilingual proficiency from home to school: A longitudinal study of Portuguese-speaking children. *Journal of Education, 173*(2), 85–97.

Cummins, J. (1992). Bilingual education and English immersion: The Ramírez report in theoretical perspective. *Bilingual Research Journal, 16*(1–2), 91–104.

Curtis, M. J., & Meyers, J. (1988). Consultation: A foundation for alternative services in schools. In J. L. Graden, J. E. Zins, & M. J. Curtis (Eds.), *Alternative educational delivery systems: Enhancing instructional options for all students* (pp. 35–48). Washington, DC: National Association of School Psychologists.

Czarnecki, E., Rosko, D., & Fine, E. (1998). How to CALL UP noting skills. *Teaching Exceptional Children, 30*(6), 14–19.

Dachman, R. S., Alessi, G. J., Vrazo, G. J., Fuqua, R. W., Kerr, R. H. (1986). Development and evaluation of an infant-care training program with first-time fathers. *Journal of Applied Behavior Analysis, 19,* 221–230.

Dahlquist, L. M., & Gil, K. M. (1986). Using parents to maintain improved dental flossing skills in children. *Journal of Applied Behavior Analysis, 19,* 255–260.

Daly, E. J., III, Martens, B. K., Dool, E. J., & Hintze, J. M. (1998). Using brief functional analysis to select interventions for oral reading. *Journal of Behavioral Education, 8*(2), 203–218.

Daniel, P. T. K. (1997). Educating students with disabilities in the least restrictive environment: A slippery slope for educators. *Journal of Educational Administration, 35*(5), 397–409.

*Daniel R. R. v. State Board of Education.* (1989). *Education of the Handicapped Law Reporter.* U.S. Court of Appeals, Fifth Circuit.

Daniels, T. D., & DeWine, S. (1991). Communication process as target and tool for consultancy intervention: Rethinking a hackneyed theme. *Journal of Educational and Psychological Consultation, 2*(4), 303–322.

Daniels, V. I. (1998). How to manage disruptive behavior in inclusive classrooms. *Teaching Exceptional Children, 30*(4), 26–31.

Darch, C., Carnine, D., & Gersten, R. (1984). Explicit instruction in mathematics problem solving. *Journal of Educational Research, 77,* 350–359.

Darder, A. (1995). *Culture and difference: Critical perspectives on the bicultural experience in the United States.* Westport, CT: Bergin & Garvey.

Darder, A., Torres, R. D., & Gutierrez, H. (Eds.). (1997). *Latinos and education: A critical reader.* New York: Routledge.

Dardig, J. C., & Heward, W. L. (1976). *Sign here: A contracting book for children and their parents.* Kalamazoo, MI: Behaviordelia.

Dardig, J. C., & Heward, W. L. (1981a). *Sign here: A contracting book for children and their parents* (2nd ed.). Bridgewater, NJ: F. Fournies and Associates.

Dardig, J.C., & Heward, W.L. (1981b). *A systematic procedure for prioritizing.* DAS Information Bulletin, No. 64, Washington, DC.

Dardig, J. C., & Heward, W. L. (1981c). A systematic procedure for prioritizing IEP goals. *The Directive Teacher, 3*(2), 8.

*David D. v. Dartmouth School Committee,* 775 F. 2d 411 (1985).

Davitz, J. (1964). *The communication of emotional meaning.* New York: McGraw-Hill.

deBettencourt, L. U. (1999). General educators' attitudes toward students with mild disabilities and their use of instructional strategies. *Remedial and Special Education, 20*(1), 27–35.

DeBoer, A. L. (1986). *The art of consulting.* Chicago: Arcturus Books.

Deering, P. D. (1998). Making comprehensive inclusion of special needs students work in a middle school. *Middle School Journal* (January), 12–19.

Deitz, S. M., & Repp, A. C. (1973). Decreasing classroom misbehavior through the use of DRL schedules of reinforcement. *Journal of Applied Behavior Analysis, 6,* 457–463.

Delgado, L. E., & Lutzker, J. R. (1988). Training young parents to identify and report their children's illnesses. *Journal of Applied Behavior Analysis, 21,* 311–319.

Delquadri, J. C., Greenwood, C. R., Whorton., D., Carta, J. J., & Hall, R. V. (1986). Classwide peer tutoring. *Exceptional Children, 52*(6), 535–542.

de Mesquita, P. B., & Zollman, A. (1995). Teachers' preferences for academic intervention strategies in mathematics: Implications for instructional consultation. *Journal of Educational and Psychological Consultation, 6*(2), 159–174.

Derby, L. M., Wacker, D. P., Berg, W., DeRaad, A., Ulrich, S., Asmus, J., Harding, J., Prouty, A., Laffey, P., & Stoner, E. A. (1997). The long-term effects of functional communication training in home settings. *Journal of Applied Behavior Analysis, 30*(3), 507–531.

Deshler, D. D., Ellis, E. S., & Lenz, B. K. (1996). *Teaching adolescents with learning disabilities: Strategies and methods* (2nd ed.). Denver, CO: Love.

Deshler, D. D., & Schumaker, J. B. (1988). An instructional model for teaching students how to learn. In J. L. Graden, J. E. Zins, & M. J. Curtis (Eds.), *Alternative education delivery systems: Enhancing instructional options for all students* (pp. 391–411). Washington, DC: National Association of School Psychologists.

Deshler, D. D., Schumaker, J. B., Lenz, B. K., & Ellis, E. (1984). Academic and cognitive interventions for LD adolescents: Part II. *Journal of Learning Disabilities, 17*(3), 170–179.

Dettmer, P. A., Dyck, N. T., & Thurston, L. P. (1996). *Consultation, collaboration and team work for students with special needs* (2nd ed.). Boston: Allyn & Bacon.

Developmental Disabilities Services and Facilities Construction Amendments of 1970, P.L. 91–517.

Developmentally Disabled Assistance and Bill of Rights Act of 1974, P.L. 94–103.

*Diana v. State Board of Education of California,* (N.D. Cal., January 7, 1970, and June 18, 1973). Civil No. C-70, 37 RFP.

Dickinson, T. S., & Erb, T. O. (Eds.). (1997). *We gain more than we give: Teaming in middle schools.* Columbus, OH: National Middle School Association.

Dieker, L. A., & Barnett, C. A. (1996). Effective co-teaching. *Teaching Exceptional Children, 29*(1), 5–7.

Dobbert, M. L. (1982). *Ethnographic research: Theory and application for modern schools and societies.* New York: Praeger.

Donley, C. R., & Williams, G. (1997). Parents exhibit children's progress at a poster session. *Teaching Exceptional Children, 29*(4), 46–51.

Dougherty, A. M., Tack, F. E., Fullam, C. B., & Hammer, L. A. (1996). Disengagement: A neglected aspect of the consultation process. *Journal of Educational and Psychological Consultation, 7*(3), 259–274.

Dowds, B. N., Ness, D., & Nickels, P. (1996). Families of children with learning disabilities: A potential teaching resource. *Intervention in School and Clinic. 32*(1), 17–20.

Downing, J., & Bailey, B. (1990). Developing vision use within functional daily activities for students with visual and multiple disabilities. *Review, 21,* 209–221.

Downing, J. A. (1990). Contingency contracts: A step-by-step format. *Intervention in School and Clinic, 26*(2), 111–113.

Doyle, C. (1999). The use of graphic organizers to improve comprehension of learning disabled students in social studies. Kean University M.A. Research Project (ED427313).

Dreikurs, R. (1948). *The challenge of parenthood.* New York: Duell, Sloan, and Pearce.

Dreikurs, R. (1967). *Psychology in the classroom* (2nd ed.). New York: Harper & Row.

Dryfoos, J. (1994). *Full-service schools.* San Francisco: Jossey-Bass.

Ducharme, D. E., & Holborn, S. W. (1997). Programming generalization of social skills in preschool children with hearing impairments. *Journal of Applied Behavior Analysis, 30*(4), 639–651.

Duffy, M. L., Jones, J., & Thomas, S. W. (1999). Using portfolios to foster independent thinking. *Intervention in School and Clinic, 35*(1), 34–37.

Dugan, E., Kamps, D., Leonard, B., Watkins, N., Rheinberger, A., & Stackhaus, J. (1995). Effects of cooperative learning groups during social studies for students with autism and fourth-grade peers. *Journal of Applied Behavior Analysis, 28*(2), 175–188.

Duncan, M., & Biddle, B. (1974). *The study of teaching.* New York: Holt, Rinehart and Winston.

Dunlap, L. K., & Dunlap, G. (1989). A self-monitoring package for teaching subtraction with regrouping to students with learning disabilities. *Journal of Applied Behavior Analysis, 22,* 309–314.

Dunlap, L. K., Dunlap, G., Koegel, L. K., & Koegel, R. L. (1991). Using self-monitoring to increase independence. *Teaching Exceptional Children, 23*(3), 17–22.

Dunst, C. J. (1985). Rethinking early intervention. *Analysis and Intervention in Developmental Disabilities, 5,* 301–313.

Dunst, C. J., Johnson, C., Trivette, C. M., & Hamby, D. (1991). Family-centered early intervention policies and practice: Family-centered or not? *Exceptional Children, 58,* 115–126.

Dunst, C. J., Leet, H. E., & Trivette, C. M. (1988). Family resources, personal well-being, and early intervention. *Journal of Special Education, 22*(1), 108–116.

Dunst, C. J., & Trivette, C. M. (1987). Enabling and empowering families: Conceptual and intervention issues. *School Psychology Review, 16,* 443–456.

Durrant, M. (1995). *Creative strategies for school problems: Solutions for psychologists and teachers.* New York: W.W. Norton.

Duvall, S. F., Ward, D. L., Delquadri, J. C., & Greenwood, C. R. (1997). An exploratory study of home school instructional environments and their effects on the basic skills of students with learning disabilities. *Education and Treatment of Children, 20*(2), 150–172.

Dyke, N., Sundbye, N., & Pemberton, J. (1997). A recipe for efficient co-teaching. *Teaching Exceptional Children* (Nov/Dec), 42–45.

Dyson, L. L. (1996). The experiences of families of children with learning disabilities: Parental stress, family functioning, and sibling self-concept. *Journal of Learning Disabilities, 29*(3), 280–286.

D'Zurilla, T. J., & Goldfried, M. R. (1971). Problem solving and behavior modification. *Journal of Abnormal Psychology, 78,* 107–126.

Echevarria, J., & Graves, A. (1998). *Sheltered content instruction: Teaching English-language learners with diverse abilities.* Boston: Allyn & Bacon.

Economic Opportunity Act Amendments of 1972, P.L. 92-424.

Edens, J. F. (1997). Home visitation programs with ethnic minority families: Cultural issues in parent consultation. *Journal of Educational and Psychological Consultation, 8*(4), 373–383.

Edgar, E. (1987). Secondary programs in special education: Are many of them justifiable? *Exceptional Children, 53,* 555–561.

Edgar, E. (1991). Providing ongoing support and making appropriate placements: An alternative to transition planning for mildly handicapped students. *Preventing School Failure, 38*(2), 7–12.

Education of All Handicapped Children Act of 1975, P.L. 94-142, November, 1975.

Education Amendments of 1972, June 23, 1972, P.L. 92–318.

Education Amendments of 1974, August 21, 1974, P.L. 93–380.

Education of the Handicapped Act of 1970, P.L. 91-230.

Education of the Handicapped Act Amendments of 1986, P.L. 99-457.

Education of the Handicapped Act Amendments of 1990, P.L. 101–476.

Edwards, J., Norton, S., Taylor, S., Weiss, M., & Van Dusseldorp, R. (1975). How effective is CAI? A review of the research. *Educational Leadership, 33,* 147–153.

Ehly, S. W., & Macmann, G. M. (1994). Reinventing consultation. *Journal of Educational and Psychological Consultation, 5*(2), 169–172.

Eiserman, W. D., Weber, C., & McCoun, M. (1995). Parent and professional roles in early intervention: A longitudinal comparison of the effects of two intervention configurations. *Journal of Special Education, 29*(1), 20–44.

Elbaum, B., Vaughn, S., Hughes, M., & Moody, S. W. (1999). Grouping practices and reading outcomes for students with disabilities. *Exceptional Children, 65*(3), 399–415.

Elementary and Secondary Education Act of 1965, P.L. 89–10.

Elksnin, L. K., & Elksnin, N. (1991). Helping parents solve problems at home and school through parent training. *Intervention in School and Clinic, 26*(4), 230–233, 245.

Elliot, D., & McKenney, M. (1998). Four inclusion models that work. *Teaching Exceptional Children, 30*(4), 54–58.

Ellis, D. G., & Fisher, B. A. (1994). *Small group decision making: Communication and the group process* (4th ed.). New York: McGraw-Hill.

Englemann, S., & Carnine, D. (1982). *Theory of instruction: Principles and applications.* New York: Irvington.

English, K., Goldstein, H., Kaczmarek, L., & Shafer, K. (1996). "Buddy skills" for preschoolers. *Teaching Exceptional Children, 28*(3), 62–66.

English, K., Goldstein, H., Shafer, K., & Kaczmarek, L. (1997). Promoting interactions among preschoolers with and without disabilities: Effects of a buddy-skills training program. *Exceptional Children, 63*(2), 229–243.

Ennis, B. J. (1976). Reaction comment to Strauss. Due process in civil commitment and elsewhere. In M. Kindred, J. Cohen, D. Penrod, & T. Shaffer (Eds.), *The mentally retarded citizen and the law* (pp. 474–479). New York: Free Press.

Epstein, M. H., Polloway, E. A., Foley, R. M., & Patton, J. R. (1993). Homework: A comparison of teachers' and parents' perceptions of the problems experienced by students identified as having behavioral disorders, learning disabilities, or no disabilities. *Remedial and Special Education, 14*(5), 40–50.

Epstein, R. (1985). The positive side effects of reinforcement: A commentary on Balsam and Bondy (1983). *Journal of Applied Behavior Analysis, 18,* 73–78.

Erchul, W. P., & Schulte, A. C. (1996). Behavioral consultation as a work in progress: A reply to Witt, Gresham, and Noell. *Journal of Educational and Psychological Consultation, 7*(4), 345–354.

Erickson, F. (1973). What makes school ethnography ethnographic? *Council on Anthropology and Education Newsletter, 4,* 10–19.

Espin, C. A., & Deno, S. L. (1989). The effects of modeling and prompting feedback strategies on sight word reading of students labeled learning disabled. *Education and Treatment of Children, 12*(3), 219–231.

Esquivel, G. B., & Yoshida, R. K. (1985). Special education for language minority students. *Focus on Exceptional Children, 18*(3), 1–8.

Evans, E. D., & Richardson, R. C. (1995). Corporal punishment: What teachers should know. *Teaching Exceptional Children, 27*(2), 33–36.

Evans, I., & Meyer, L. H. (1985). *An educative approach to behavior problems: A practical decision model for interventions with severely handicapped learners.* Baltimore: Paul H. Brookes.

Evans, S. S., Evans, W. H., & Gable, R. A. (1989). An ecological survey of student behavior. *Teaching Exceptional Children, 21*(4), 12–15.

Everington, C., & Stevenson, T. (1994). A giving experience: Using community service to promote community living skills and integration for individuals with severe disabilities. *Teaching Exceptional Children, 26*(3), 56–59.

Ezell, H. K., Kohler, R. W., & Strain, P. (1994). A program description of evaluation of academic peer tutoring for reading skills of children with special needs. *Education and Treatment of Children, 17,* 52–67.

Fad, K. S. (1990). The fast track to success: Social-behavioral skills. *Intervention in School and Clinic, 26*(1), 39–43.

Fad, K. S., Ross, M., & Boston, J. (1995). We're better together: Using cooperative learning to teach social skills to young children. *Teaching Exceptional Children, 27*(4), 28–34.

Fafard, M-B., Hanlon, R. E., & Bryson, E. A. (1986). *Jose P. v. Ambach:* Progress toward compliance. *Exceptional Children, 52*(4), 313–322.

Falik, L. H. (1995). Family patterns of reaction to a child with a learning disability: A mediational perspective. *Journal of Learning Disabilities, 28*(6), 335–341.

Felber, S. A. (1997). Strategies for parent partnerships. *Teaching Exceptional Children, 30*(1), 20–23.

Feldman, M. A., Towns, F., Betel, J., Case, L., Rincover, A., & Rubino, C. A. (1986). Parent education project II. Increasing stimulating interactions of developmentally handicapped children. *Journal of Applied Behavior Analysis, 19,* 23–37.

Fiedler, C. R., & Simpson, R. L. (1987). Modifying the attitudes of nonhandicapped high school students toward handicapped peers. *Exceptional Children, 53*(4), 342–349.

Field, S. L., & Hill, D. S. (1988). Contextual appraisal: A framework for meaningful evaluation of special education programs. *Remedial and Special Education, 9*(4), 22–30.

Fine, M. J. (1990). Facilitating home-school relationships: A family-oriented approach to collaborative consultation. *Journal of Educational and Psychological Consultation, 1*(2), 169–187.

Fine, M. J., & Gardner, A. (1994). Collaborative consultation with families of children with special needs: Why bother? *Journal of Educational and Psychological Consultation, 5*(4), 283–308.

Fischer, T. C. (1970). *Due process in the student-institution relationship.* Washington, DC: American Association of State Colleges and Universities. (ERIC Document Reproduction Service No. ED 041 189).

Fisher, R., Ury, W., & Patton, B. (Eds.). (1998). Getting to yes: Negotiating agreement without giving in (2nd ed.). New York: Viking.

Flannery, K. B., O'Neill, R. E., & Horner, R. H. (1995). Including predictability in functional assessment and individual program development. *Education and Treatment of Children, 18*(4), 499–509.

Flynn, C. C., & Harbin, G. L. (1987). Evaluating interagency coordination efforts using a multidimensional, interactional, developmental paradigm. *Remedial and Special Education, 8*(3), 35–44.

Forman, S. G. (1995). Organizational factors and consultation outcomes. *Journal of Educational and Psychological Consultation, 6*(2), 191–195.

Forness, S. R., Kavale, K. A., Blum, I. M., & Lloyd, J. W. (1997). Mega-analysis of meta-analyses: What works in special education and related services. *Teaching Exceptional Children, 29*(6), 4–9.

Fox, C. L. (1989). Peer acceptance of learning disabled children in the regular classroom. *Exceptional Children, 56*(1), 50–59.

Fox, N. E., & Ysseldyke, J. E. (1997). Implementing inclusion at the middle school level: Lessons from a negative example. *Exceptional Children, 64*(1), 81–98.

Foxx, R. M. (1982). *Decreasing behaviors of severely retarded and autistic persons.* Champaign, IL: Research Press.

Foxx, R. M., & Bechtel, D. R. (1983). Overcorrection: A review and analysis. In S. Axelrod & J. Apsche (Eds.), *The effects of punishment on human behavior* (pp. 133–220). New York: Academic Press.

Fradd, S. H. (1990). Transdisciplinary teaming. In V. I. Correa & S. H. Fradd (Eds.), *Bilingual/ESOL special education collaboration and reform modules.* Gainesville, FL: University of Florida.

Fradd, S. H., & Tikunoff, W. J. (Eds.). (1987). *Bilingual education and bilingual special education: A guide for administrators.* Boston: College Hill Press.

Franklin, M. E. (1992). Culturally sensitive instructional practices for African-American learners with disabilities. *Exceptional Children, 59*(2), 115–122.

Franklin, M. E., James, J. R., & Watson, A. L. (1996). Utilizing a cultural identity developmental model to plan culturally responsive reading and writing instruction. *Reading and Writing Quarterly: Overcoming Learning Difficulties, 12,* 21–58.

Frea, W. D., & Hughes, C. (1997). Functional analysis and treatment of social-communication behavior of adolescents with developmental disabilities. *Journal of Applied Behavior Analysis, 30*(4), 701–704.

Freiberg, K. L. (Ed.). (1999). *Educating exceptional children* (11th ed.). Guilford, CT: Dushkin/McGraw-Hill.

Friedman, R. C. (1994). Upstream helping for low-income families of gifted students: Challenges and opportunities. *Journal of Educational and Psychological Consultation, 5*(4), 321–338.

Friend, M. (1984). Consultation skills for resource teachers. *Learning Disabilities Quarterly, 2,* 70–78.

Friend, M. (1985). Training special educators to be consultants. *Teacher Education and Special Education, 8*(3), 115–120.

Friend, M. (1988). Putting consultation into context: Historical and contemporary perspectives. *Remedial and Special Education, 9*(6), 7–13.

Friend, M., & Bursuck, W. (1999). *Including students with special needs: A guide for classroom teachers.* (2nd ed.). Boston: Allyn & Bacon.

Friend, M., & Cook, L. (1988). Pragmatic issues in school consultation training. In J. F. West (Ed.), *School consultation: Interdisciplinary perspectives on theory, research, training, and practice* (pp. 127–142). Austin, TX: Research and Training Project on School Consultation, University of Texas.

Friend, M., & Cook, L. (1992). *Interactions: Collaboration skills for school professionals.* New York: Longman.

Friend, M., & Cook, L. (1996). *Interactions: Collaboration skills for school professionals* (2nd ed.). White Plains, NY: Longman.

Friend, M., & Cook, L. (1997). Student-centered teams in schools: Still in search of an identity. *Journal of Educational and Psychological Consultation, 8*(1), 3–20.

Friman, P. C. (1990). Nonaversive treatment of high-rate disruption: Child and provider effects. *Exceptional Children, 57*(1), 64–69.

Frith, G. H., & Armstrong, S. W. (1986). Self-monitoring for behavior disordered students. *Teaching Exceptional Children, 18*(2), 144–148.

Fuchs, D., & Fuchs, L. (1994–1995). Sometimes separate is better. *Educational Leadership, 52*(4), 22–26.

Fuchs, D., & Fuchs, L. (1996). Consultation as a technology and the politics of school reform. *Remedial and Special Education, 17*(6), 386–392.

Fuchs, D., & Fuchs, L. (1989). Mainstream assistance teams to accommodate difficult-to-teach students in general education. In J. L. Graden, J. E. Zins, & M. J. Curtis (Eds.), *Alternative educational delivery systems: Enhancing instructional options for all students* (pp. 49–70). Washington, DC: National Association of School Psychologists.

Fuchs, D., Fuchs, L., & Bahr, M. (1990). Mainstream Assistance Teams: A scientific basis for the art of consultation. *Exceptional Children, 57*(2), 128–139.

Fuchs, L. (1986). Monitoring progress among mildly handicapped pupils: Review of current practice and research. *Remedial and Special Education, 7*(5), 5–12.

Fuchs, L. S. (1987). Program development. *Teaching Exceptional children, 20*(1), 42–44.

Fuchs, L. S., & Deno, S. L. (1991). Paradigmatic distinctions between instructionally relevant measurement models. *Exceptional Children, 57*(6), 488–500.

Fuchs, L., Fuchs, D., & Hamlett, C. L. (1990). Curriculum-based measurement: A standardized long-term goal approach to monitoring student progress. *Academic Therapy, 25*(5), 615–632.

Fueyo, V. (1997). Below the tip of the iceberg: Teaching language-minority students. *Teaching Exceptional Children, 30*(1), 61–65.

Fullen, M. (1982). *The meaning of educational change.* New York: Teachers College Press.

Gable, R. A., Hendrickson, J. M., & Sasso, G. M. (1995). Toward a more functional analysis of aggression. *Education and Treatment of Children, 18*(3), 226–242.

Gajar, A., Goodman, L., & McAfee, J. (1993). *Secondary schools and beyond: Transition of individuals with mild disabilities.* New York: Merrill.

Gallagher, J. J., Trohanis, P. L., & Clifford, R. M. (Eds.). (1989) *Policy implementation and PL 99-457: Planning for young children with special needs.* Baltimore: Paul H. Brookes.

Gallagher, P. A., Sulzbacher, S. I., & Shores, R. E. (1976, March). *A group contingency for classroom management of emotionally disturbed children.* Paper presented at the meeting of the Kansas Council for Exceptional Children, Wichita.

Gallessich, J. (1982). *The profession and practice of consultation.* San Francisco: Jossey-Bass.

Gallessich, J. (1985). Toward a meta-analysis of consultation. *The Counseling Psychologist, 13*(3), 336–354.

Garcia, R. (1982). *Teaching in a pluralistic society: Concepts, models, strategies.* New York: Harper & Row.

Gardill, M. C., DuPaul, G. J., & Kyle, K. E. (1996). Classroom strategies for managing students with attention-deficit/hyperactivity disorder. *Intervention in School and Clinic, 32*(2), 89–94.

Gardner, D. P. (1983). *A nation at risk: The imperative for education reform.* Washington, DC: National Commission on Excellence in Education.

Gardner, N. (1974). Action training and research: Something old and something new. *Public Administration Review, 34,* 106–115.

Gardner, R., III. (1981). *The effect of cross-age tutoring on the mealtime behavior of severely disturbed children.* Unpublished master's thesis, The Ohio State University, Columbus.

Gardner, R., III, Heward, W. L., & Grossi, T. A. (1990, November). Helping without hurting: Supporting at-risk students in the regular classroom. 38th Annual Convention, Ohio Federation Council for Exceptional Children, Cleveland.

Gardner, R., III, Heward, W. L., & Grossi, T. A. (1994). Effects of response cards on student participation and academic achievement: A systematic replication with inner-city students during whole-class science instruction. *Journal of Applied Behavior Analysis, 27,* 63–71.

Gardner, R., III, Sainato, D., Cooper, J. O., Heron, T. E., Heward, W. L., Eshleman, J., & Grossi, T. A. (Eds.). (1994). *Behavioral analysis in education: Focus on measurably superior instruction.* Monterey, CA: Brooks-Cole.

Garner, H. G., & Orelove, F. P. (Eds.). (1994). *Teamwork in human services: Models and applications across the lifespan.* Boston: Butterworth-Heinemann.

Garrett, J. N. (1998). Local interagency coordinating council personality: A factor in consultation. *Journal of Educational and Psychological Consultation, 9*(3), 261–266.

Gartland, D. (1993). Elementary teacher-parent partnerships: Effective communication strategies. *LD Forum, 18*(3), 40–42.

Gast, D., & Wolery, M. (1987). Severe maladaptive behaviors. In M. E. Snell (Ed.), *Systematic instruction of people with severe handicaps* (3rd ed., pp. 300–332). Columbus, OH: Merrill.

Gately, F. J., Jr., & Gately, S. E. (1993, April). Developing positive co-teaching environments: Meeting the needs of an increasing diverse student population. Paper presented at the annual meeting of the Council for Exceptional Children, San Antonio, TX.

Gaylord-Ross, R. (1980). A decision model for the treatment of aberrant behavior in applied settings. In W. Sailor, B. Wilcox, & L. Brown (Eds.), *Methods of instruction for severely handicapped students* (pp. 135–158). Baltimore: Paul H. Brookes.

Gerber, M., & Kauffman, J. M. (1981). Peer tutoring in academic settings. In P. S. Strain (Ed.), *The utilization of classroom peers as behavior change agents* (pp. 155–187). New York: Plenum Press.

Gersten, R., Carnine, D., & White, W.A.T. (1984). The pursuit of clarity: Direct instruction and applied behavior analysis. In W. L. Heward, T. E. Heron, D. S. Hill, & J. Trap-Porter (Eds.), *Focus on behavior analysis in education* (pp. 38–57). Columbus, OH: Merrill.

Gersten, R., & Hauser, C. (1984). The case for impact evaluations in special education. *Remedial and Special Education, 5*(2), 16–24.

Gersten, R. M., & Jiménez-Gonzalez, R. T. (1998). *Promoting learning for culturally and linguistically diverse students: Classroom applications from contemporary research.* Belmont, CA: Wadsworth.

Giangreco, M. F., Baumgart, D. M. J., & Doyle, M. B. (1995). How inclusion can facilitate teaching and learning. *Intervention in School and Clinic, 30*(5), 273–278.

Gibbs, J. (1980). The interpersonal orientation in mental health consultation: Toward a model of ethnic variations in consultation. *Journal of Community Psychology, 8,* 195–207.

Gilhool, T. K. (1973). Education: An inalienable right. *Exceptional Children, 39,* 597–609.

Gilliam, J. E. (1993). Crisis management for students with emotional/behavioral problems. *Intervention in School and Clinic, 28*(4), 224–230.

Glass, R. M., Christiansen, J., & Christiansen, J. L. (1982). *Teaching exceptional students in the regular classroom.* Boston: Little, Brown.

Gleason, G. (1981). Microcomputers in education: The state of the art. *Educational Technology, 21*(3), 7–18.

Glickman, C., Gordon, S., & Ross-Gordon, J. (1995). *Supervision of instruction: A developmental approach* (3rd ed.). Needham Heights, MA: Allyn & Bacon.

Gmeinder, K. L., & Kratochwill, T. R. (1998). Short-term, home-based intervention for child noncompliance using behavioral consultation and a self-help manual. *Journal of Educational and Psychological Consultation, 9*(2), 91–117.

Goddard, Y. L. (1998). *Effects of self-monitoring and self-evaluation on the written language performance and on-task behavior of elementary students with learning disabilities.* Unpublished doctoral dissertation, The Ohio State University, Columbus.

Gola, T. J., Holmes, P. A., & Holmes, N. K. (1982). Effectiveness of a group contingency procedure for increasing prevocational behavior of profoundly mentally retarded residents. *Mental Retardation, 20*(1), 26–29.

Goldberg, I. (1995). Implementing the consultant teacher model: Interfacing multiple linking relationships and roles with systemic conditions. *Journal of Educational and Psychological Consultation, 6*(2), 175–190.

Goldberg, S. S. (1986). Reimbursing parents for unilateral placements in private special education schools. *Exceptional Children, 52*(4), 390–394.

Goldenberg, C., & Gallimore, R. (1991). Local knowledge, research knowledge, and educational change: A case study of early Spanish reading improvement. *Educational Researcher, 20*(8), 2–14.

Goldstein, B. C. (1996). *Spanish-speaking families with special needs members.* Unpublished manuscript. Pasadena, CA: Pasadena Unified School District.

Goldstein, B. S. C. (1998). Creating a context for collaborative consultation: Working across bicultural communities. *Journal of Educational and Psychological Consultation, 9*(4), 367–374.

Goldstein, S. (1975). Due process in school disciplinary proceeding: The meaning and implication of *Goss v. Lopez. Educational Horizons, 54,* 4–9.

Goldstein, S., Strickland, B., Turnbull, A. P., & Curry, L. (1980). An observational analysis of the IEP conference. *Exceptional Children, 46*(4), 278–286.

Golightly, C. J. (1987). Transdisciplinary training: A step forward in special education teacher preparation. *Teacher Education and Special Education, 10,* 126–130.

Gollnick, D. M., & Chinn, P. C. (1990). *Multicultural education in a pluralistic society.* Columbus, OH: Merrill.

González, V., Bauerle, P., & Féliz-Holt, M. (June, 1994). Assessment of language-minority students. *NABE News,* 13–15.

González, V., Brusca-Vega, R., & Yawkey, T. (1997). *Assessment and instruction of culturally and linguistically diverse students with or at risk of learning problems: From research to practice.* Needham Heights, MA: Allyn & Bacon.

Goodenough, W. H. (1976). Multiculturalism as the normal human experience. *Anthropology and Education Quarterly, 7,* 4–7.

Goor, M. B., & Schween. J. O. (1993). Accommodating diversity and disability with cooperative learning. *Intervention in School and Clinic, 29,* 6–16.

Graden, J. L., Casey, A., & Bonstrom, O. (1985). Implementing a prereferral intervention system: Part II. The data. *Exceptional Children, 51*(6), 487–496.

Graden, J. L., Casey, A., & Christenson, S. (1985). Implementing a prereferral intervention system: Part I. The model. *Exceptional Children, 51,* 377–384.

Graubard, P. S., Rosenberg, H., & Miller, M. B. (1971). Student applications of behavior modification to teachers and environments or ecological approaches to deviancy. In E. A. Ramp & B. L. Hopkins (Eds.), *A new direction for education: Behavior analysis 1971* (pp. 80–101). Lawrence: University of Kansas.

Green, C. W., Reid, D. H., White, L. K., Halford, R. C., Brittain, D. P., & Gardner, S. M. (1988). Identifying reinforcers for persons with profound handicaps: Staff opinion versus systematic assessment of preferences. *Journal of Applied Behavior Analysis, 21*, 32–43.

Greene, G. (1994). Research into practice: The magic of mnemonics. *LD Forum, 19*(3), 34–37.

Greenwood, C. R. (1991). Longitudinal analysis of time, engagement, and achievement in at-risk versus non-risk students. *Exceptional Children, 57*, 521–535.

Greenwood, C. R., Delquadri, J. C., & Hall, R. V. (1984). Opportunity to respond and student academic achievement. In W. L. Heward, T. E. Heron, D. S. Hill, & J. Trap-Porter (Eds.), *Focus on behavior analysis in education* (pp. 58–88). Columbus, OH: Merrill.

Greenwood, C. R., Hart, B., Walker, H., & Risley, T. (1994). The opportunity to respond and academic performance revisited: A behavioral theory of developmental retardation and its prevention. In R. Gardner, J. O. Cooper, T. E. Heron, W. L. Heward, J. Eshleman, & D. Sainato (Eds.), *Behavioral analysis in education: Focus on measurably superior instruction* (pp. 213–223). Monterey, CA: Brooks-Cole.

*Greer v. Rome City School District,* 762 F. Supp. 936 (N.D. Ga. 1990), aff'd 950 F. 688 (11th Cir. 1991), withdrawn and reinstated in part, 967 F. 2d 470 (11th Cir. 1992).

Gresham, F. M. (1981). Social skills training with handicapped children: A review. *Review of Educational Research, 51*, 139–176.

Gresham, F. M. (1982). Misguided mainstreaming: The case for social skills training with handicapped children. *Exceptional Children, 48*(5), 422–433.

Gresham, F. M. (1983). Use of a home-based dependent group contingency system in controlling destructive behavior: A case study. *School Psychology Review, 12*(2), 195–199.

Gresham, F. M., & Gresham, G. N. (1982). Interdependent, dependent, and independent group contingencies for controlling disruptive behavior. *Journal of Special Education, 16*(1), 101–110.

Griffin, B. W., & Griffin, M. M. (1997). The effects of reciprocal peer tutoring on graduate students' achievement, test anxiety, and academic self-efficacy. *Journal of Experimental Education, 65*(3), 197–209.

Grigal, M., Test, D. W., Beattie, J., & Wood, W. M. (1997). An evaluation of transition components of Individualized Education Programs. *Exceptional Children, 63*(3), 357–372.

Gumpel, T. P., & Frank, R. (1999). An expansion of the peer tutoring paradigm: Cross-age peer tutoring of social skills among socially rejected boys. *Journal of Applied Behavior Analysis, 32*, 115–118.

Gunter, P. L., & Coutinbo, M. J. (1997). Negative reinforcement in classrooms: What we're beginning to learn. *Teacher Education Special Education, 20*(3), 249–264.

Guralnick, M. J. (1981). The social behavior of preschool children at different developmental levels: Effects of group composition. *American Journal of Child Psychology, 31*(1), 115–130.

Guskin, A. E., & Guskin, S. L. (1970). *A social psychology of education.* Reading, MA: Addison-Wesley.

Gutkin, T. B., & Conoley, J. C. (1990). Reconceptualizing school psychology from a service delivery perspective: Implications for practice, training, and research. *Journal of School Psychology, 28*, 203–223.

Gutkin, T. B., & Curtis, M. J. (1999). School-based consultation theory and practice: The art and science of indirect service delivery. In C. R. Reynolds & T. B. Gutkin (Eds.), *The handbook of school psychology* (3rd ed., pp. 598–637). New York: Wiley.

Gutkin, T. B., & Hickman, J. A. (1990). The relationship of consultant, consultee, and organizational characteristics to consultee resistance to school-based consultation: An empirical analysis. *Journal of Educational and Psychological Consultation, 1*(2), 111–122.

Gutmann, D. (1969). Psychological naturalism in cross-cultural studies. In E. P. Willems and H. L. Rausch (Eds.), *Naturalistic viewpoints in psychological research* (pp. 162–176). New York: Holt, Rinehart and Winston.

Habel, J., Bloom, L. A., Ray, M. A., & Bacon, E. (1999). Consumer reports: What students with behavior disorders say about school. *Remedial and Special Education, 20*(2), 93–105.

Hadden, S., & Fowler, S. A. (1997). Preschool: A new beginning for children and parents. *Teaching Exceptional Children, 30*(1), 36–39.

Hagopian, L. P., Fisher, W. W., Thompson, R. H., Owen-DeSchryver, J., Iwata, B. A., & Wacker, D. P. (1997). Toward the development of structured criteria for interpretation of functional analysis data. *Journal of Applied Behavior Analysis, 30*, 313–326.

Hakola, S. R. (1992). Legal rights of students with attention deficit disorder. *School Psychology Quarterly, 5*, 285–295.

Hall, E. T. (1976). *Beyond culture.* Garden City, NY: Anchor Books.

Hall, R. V., Axelrod, S., Foundopoulos, M., Shellman, J., Campbell, R. A., & Cranston, S. (1971). The effective use of punishment to modify behavior in the classroom. *Educational Technology, 11*, 24–26.

Hall, R. V., Cristler, C., Cranston, S. S., & Tucker, B. (1970). Teachers and parents as researchers using multiple baseline designs. *Journal of Applied Behavior Analysis, 3*, 247–255.

Hall, R. V., Lund, D., & Jackson, D. (1968). Effects of teacher attention on study behavior. *Journal of Applied Behavior Analysis, 1*(1), 1–12.

Hallenbeck, M., & Beernick, M. (1989). A support program for parents of students with mild handicaps. *Teaching Exceptional Children, 21*(3), 44–47.

Halpern, A. S. (1994). The transition of youth with disabilities to adult life: A position statement of the Division on Career Development and Transition, The Council for Exceptional Children. *Career Development for Exceptional Individuals (CDEI), 17*(2), 115–124.

Halpern, A. S., & Benz, M. R. (1987). A statewide examination of secondary special education students with mild disabilities: Implications for the high school curriculum. *Exceptional Children, 54*(2), 122–129.

Halpern, A. S., Herr, C. M., Wolf, N. K., Lawson, J. D., Doren, B., & Johnson, M. D. (1997). *NEXT S.T.E.P.: Student transition and educational planning. Teacher's manual.* Austin, TX: PRO-ED.

Hammill, D. D., & Bartel, N. R. (1990). *Teaching students with learning and behavior problems* (5th ed.). Boston: Allyn & Bacon.

Handicapped Children's Protection Act, P.L. 99–352.

Handon, B. L., Feldman, R. S., & Honigman, A. (1987). Comparison of parent and teacher assessments of developmentally delayed children's behavior. *Exceptional Children, 54*(2), 137–144.

Hanft, B. E., & Place, P. A. (1996). *The consulting therapist: A guide for OTs and PTs in schools.* San Antonio, TX: Therapy Skill Builders.

Hanley-Maxwell, C., Pogoloff, S. M., & Whitney-Thomas, J. (1998). Families: The heart of transition. In F. R. Rusch & J. G. Chadsey (Eds.), *Beyond high school: Transition from school to work* (pp. 234–264). Belmont, CA: Wadsworth.

Hanley-Maxwell, C., Whitney-Thomas, J., & Pogoloff, S. (1995). The second shock: Parental perspectives of their child's transition from school to adult life. *Journal of the Association for Persons with Severe Handicaps, 20*(1), 3–16.

Hanline, M. F., & Halvorsen, A. (1989). Parent perceptions of the integration transition process: Overcoming artificial barriers. *Exceptional Children, 55*(6), 487–492.

Hanson, M. J., & Carta, J. J. (1996). Addressing the challenges of families with multiple risks. *Exceptional Children, 62*(3), 201–211.

Harding, J., Wacker, D. P., Cooper, L. J., Millard, T., & Jensen-Kovalan, P. Brief hierarchical assessment of potential treatment components with children in an outpatient clinic. *Journal of Applied Behavior Analysis, 27*(2), 291–300.

Hardman, M. L., Drew, C. J., & Egan, M. W. (1999). *Human exceptionality: Society, school, and family* (6th ed.). Boston: Allyn & Bacon.

Haring, K. A., Lovett, D., & Saren, D. (1991). Parent perceptions of their adult offspring with disabilities. *Teaching Exceptional Children, 23*(2), 6–10.

Harper, G. E., & Maheady, L. (1999). Aligning course objectives, student practice activities, and testing: Effectively using classwide student tutoring teams. *Proven Practices, 1*(2), 55–59.

Harper, G. F., Mallette, B., Maheady, L., Bentley, A. E., & Moore, J. (1995). Retention and treatment failure in classwide peer tutoring: Implications for further research. *Journal of Behavioral Education, 5*(4), 399–414.

Harris, K. C. (1981). *The classroom program of a special education teacher: A case study.* Unpublished doctoral dissertation, Temple University, Philadelphia, PA.

Harris, K. C. (1991). An expanded view on consultation competencies for educators serving culturally and linguistically diverse exceptional students. *Teacher Education and Special Education, 14*(1), 25–29.

Harris, K. C. (1995). School-based bilingual special education teacher assistance teams. *Remedial and Special Education, 16*(6), 337–343.

Harris, K. C. (1996). Collaboration within a multicultural society: Issues for consideration. *Remedial and Special Education, 17*(6), 355–362, 376.

Harris, K. C. (1998a). *Collaborative elementary teaching: A casebook for elementary special and general educators.* Austin, TX: PRO-ED.

Harris, K. C. (1998b). *Collaborative teaching casebooks: Facilitator's guide.* Austin, TX: PRO-ED.

Harris, K. C. (2000). Professional competencies for working with culturally and linguistically diverse students. In *Encyclopedia of Special Education* (2nd ed.).

Harris, K. C., Harvey, P., Garcia, L., Innes, D., Lynn, P., Muñoz, D., Sexton, K., & Stoica, R. (1987). Meeting the needs of special high school students in regular education classrooms. *Teacher Education and Special Education, 10*(4), 143–152.

Harris, K. C., & Little, J. (1982, September). *The emotionally disturbed mentally retarded student in the classroom.* Paper presented at the Matthew J. Guglielmo Endowed Chair in Mental Retardation Special Education Conference, Los Angeles.

Harris, K. C., & Smith, M. (1996, April). *How bilingual teacher assistance teams can help change general educator's views.* Paper presented at the annual conference of the Council for Exceptional Children, Orlando, FL.

Harris, K. C., & Smith, M. (1998). *Collaborative secondary teaching: A casebook for secondary special and general educators.* Austin, TX: PRO-ED.

Harris, K. R. (1986). Self-monitoring of attentional behavior versus self-monitoring of productivity: Effects on on-task behavior and academic response rate among learning disabled children. *Journal of Applied Behavior Analysis, 19,* 417–423.

Harris, K. R., Graham, S., Reid, R., McElroy, K., & Hamby, R. S. (1994). Self-monitoring of attention versus self-monitoring of performance: Replication and cross-task comparison studies. *Learning Disability Quarterly, 17*(2), 121–139.

Harris, T. A., Peterson, S. L., Filliben, T. L., Glassberg, M., & Favell, J. E. (1998). Evaluating a more cost-efficient alternative to providing in-home feedback to parents: The use of spousal feedback. *Journal of Applied Behavior Analysis, 31*(1), 131–134.

Harry, B. (1996). These families, those families: The impact of researcher identities on the research act. *Exceptional Children, 62*(4), 292–300.

Harry, B., Allen, N., & McLaughlin, M. (1995). Communication versus compliance: African-American parents' involvement in special education. *Exceptional Children, 61,* 364–377.

Harry, B., Grenot-Scheyer, M., Smith-Lewis, M., Park, H. S., Xin, F., & Schwarz, I. (1995). Developing culturally inclusive services for individuals with disabilities. *Journal of the Association for Persons with Severe Handicaps, 20*(2), 99–109.

Harvard Medical School & Deaconess Hospital. (1997). *Teacher training materials Mind/Body Medical Institute Education Initiative.* Boston: Author.

Haslett, B., & Ogilvie, J. R. (1992). Feedback process in task groups. In R. Cathcart & L. Samovar (Eds.), *Small group communication* (6th ed., pp. 342–356). Dubuque, IA: Brown.

Hasselbring, T. S., Goin, L. I., & Bransford, J. (1988). Developing math automaticity in learning handicapped children: The role of computerized drill and practice. *Focus on Exceptional Children, 20*(6), 1–7.

Hassett, M. E., Engler, C., Cooke, N. L., Test, D. W., Weiss, A. B., Heward, W. L., & Heron, T. E. (1984). A telephone-managed, home-based summer writing program for LD adolescents. In W. L. Heward, T. E. Heron, D. S. Hill, & J. Trap-Porter (Eds.), *Focus on behavior analysis in education* (pp. 89–103). Columbus, OH: Merrill.

Havighurst, R. J. (1952). *Developmental task and education* (2nd ed.). New York: McKay.

Hawkins, R. P., & Sluyter, D. J. (1970). *Modification of achievement by a simple technique involving parents and teachers.* Paper presented at the American Education Research Association convention, Minneapolis, MN.

Heath, R. W., & Nielson, M. A. (1974). The research basis for performance-based teacher education. *Review of Educational Research, 44,* 463–484.

Heaton, S., & O'Shea, D. J. (1995). Using mnemonics to make mnemonics. *Teaching Exceptional Children, 28*(1), 34–36.

Hepp, E. S. (1991). Reflections on Part H: One state's experience. *Infants and Young Children, 4,* v-viii.

Heron, T. E. (1978a). Maintaining mildly handicapped children in the regular classroom: A decision-making process. *Journal of Learning Disabilities, 11,* 210–216.

Heron, T. E. (1978b). Punishment: A review of the literature with implications for the teacher of mainstreamed children. *Journal of Special Education, 12,* 243–252.

Heron, T. E. (1983). Direct instruction: In search of instructional solutions for educational problems. Comments. In D. Carnine, D. Elkind, A. D. Hendrickson, D. Meichenbaum, R. L. Sieben, & F. Smith (Eds.), *Interdisciplinary voices in learning disabilities and remedial education* (pp. 61–63). Austin, TX: PRO-ED.

Heron, T. E. (1990). Lessons from the classroom: Using a cooperative learning arrangement to facilitate consultation. *Journal of Educational and Psychological Consultation, 1*(4), 359–363.

Heron, T. E., & Axelrod, S. (1976). Effectiveness of feedback to mothers concerning their children's work recognition performance. *Reading Improvement, 13*(2), 74–81.

Heron, T. E., & Catera, R. (1980). Teacher consultation: A functional approach. *School Psychology Review, 9,* 283–289.

Heron, T. E., & Harris, K. C. (1982). *The educational consultant: Helping professionals, parents, and mainstreamed students.* Boston: Allyn & Bacon.

Heron, T. E., & Harris, K. C. (1987). *The educational consultant: Helping professionals, parents, and mainstreamed students* (2nd ed.). Austin, TX: PRO-ED.

Heron, T. E., & Harris, K. C. (1993). *The educational consultant: Helping professionals, parents, and mainstreamed students* (3rd ed.). Austin, TX: PRO-ED.

Heron, T. E., & Heward, W. L. (1982). Ecological assessment: Implications for teachers of LD students. *Learning Disability Quarterly, 5,* 115–125.

Heron, T. E., Heward, W. L., Cooke, N. L., & Hill, D. S. (1983). Evaluation of a classwide peer tutoring system: First graders teach each other sight words. *Education and Treatment of Children, 6,* 137–152.

Heron, T. E., & Kimball, W. (1988). Gaining perspective with the educational consultation research base: Ecological considerations and further recommendations. *Remedial and Special Education, 9* (6), 21–28.

Heron, T. E., Martz, S. A., & Margolis, H. (1996). Ethical and legal issues on consultation. *Remedial and Special Education, 17*(6), 377–385, 392.

Heron, T. E., & Skinner, M. E. (1981). Criteria for defining the regular classroom as the least restrictive environment for LD students. *Learning Disability Quarterly, 4*(2), 115–121.

Heron, T. E., & Swanson, P. (1991). Establishing a consultation assistance team: A 4–step practical procedure. *Journal of Educational and Psychological Consultation, 2*(1), 95–98.

Heron, T. E., & Welsch, R. G. (1999, May 30). Tutoring systems with nontraditional applications: An analysis of skills, methodologies, and results. Presentation address to the 25th annual conference of the Association for Behavior Analysis, Chicago.

Heshusius, L. (1986). Paradigm shifts and special education: A response to Ulman and Rosenberg. *Exceptional Children, 52*(5), 461–465.

Heshusius, L. (1991). Curriculum-based assessment and direct instruction: Critical reflections on fundamental assumptions. *Exceptional Children, 57*(4), 315–328.

Heward, W. L. (1987). Some thoughts on the development and delivery of systematic instruction. *Jornal de Psicologia, 6*(1), 20–24.

Heward, W. L. (1994). Three "low-tech" strategies for increasing the frequency of active student response during group instruction. In R. Gardner, D. M. Sainato, J. O. Cooper, T. E. Heron, W. L. Heward, J. Eshleman, & T. A. Grossi (Eds.), *Behavioral analysis in education: Focus on measurably superior instruction* (pp. 283–320). Monterey, CA: Brooks-Cole.

Heward, W. L. (1996). *Exceptional children: An introduction to special education* (5th ed.). Englewood Cliffs, NJ: Prentice Hall.

Heward, W. L. (2000). *Exceptional children: An introduction to special education* (6th ed.). Upper Saddle River, NJ: Prentice Hall.

Heward, W. L., & Chapman, J. (1981). *Improving parent-teacher communication through recorded telephone messages.* Unpublished master's thesis, The Ohio State University, Columbus.

Heward, W. L., Courson, F. H., & Narayan, J. S. (1989). Using choral responding to increase active student response during group instruction. *Teaching Exceptional Children, 21*(3), 72–75.

Heward, W. L., Dardig, J. C., & Rossett, A. (1979). *Working with parents of handicapped children.* Columbus, OH: Merrill.

Heward, W. L., Gardner, R., III, Cavanaugh, R. A., Courson, F. H., Grossi, T. A., & Barbetta, P. M. (1996). Everyone participates in this class: Using response cards to increase active student response. *Teaching Exceptional Children, 28*, 4–10.

Heward, W. L., Heron, T. E., & Cooke, N. L. (1982). Tutor huddle: Key element in a classwide peer tutoring system. *Elementary School Journal, 83*, 115–123.

Higbee, K. L. (1988). *Your memory: How it works and how to improve it* (2nd ed.). Englewood Cliffs, NJ: Prentice-Hall.

Higgins, E. L., & Raskind, M. H. (1995). Compensatory effectiveness of speech recognition on the written composition performance of postsecondary students with learning disabilities. *Learning Disability Quarterly, 18*(2), 159–174.

Higgins, S. T., & Morris, E. K. (1985). A comment on contemporary definitions of reinforcement as a behavioral process. *Psychological Record, 35*, 81–88.

Higher Education Amendments of 1972, P.L. 92–328.

Hill, J. P. (1980). *Understanding early adolescence: A framework.* Carrboro, NC: Center for Early Adolescence.

Hill, J. W., Seyfarth, J., Banks, P. D., Wehman, P., & Orelove, F. (1987). Parent attitudes about working conditions of their adult mentally retarded sons and daughters. *Exceptional Children, 54*(1), 9–23.

Hoffman, E. (1975). The American public school and the deviant child: The origins of their involvement. *Journal of Special Education, 9*, 415–423.

Hollinger, J. D. (1987). Social skills for behaviorally disordered children as preparation for mainstreaming: Theory, practice, and new directions. *Remedial and Special Education, 8*(4), 17–27.

Holmes, R. M. (1991). A lesson learned: Teacher's aide or child's aide. *Intervention in School and Clinic, 26*(3), 159–162.

Homans, G. C. (1950). *The human group.* New York: Harcourt Brace.

Homme, L., Csanyi, A. P., Gonzales, M. A., & Rechs, J. R. (1969). *How to use contingency contracting in the classroom.* Champaign, IL: Research Press.

*Honig v. Doe,* 108 S. Ct. 592 (1988).

Hoover, J. J. (1993). Helping parents develop a home-based study skills program. *Intervention in School and Clinic, 28*(4), 238–245.

Hoover, J. J., & Collier, C. (1998). Methods and materials for bilingual special education. In L. M. Baca & H. T. Cervantes (Eds.), *The bilingual special education interface* (2nd ed., pp. 264–289). Columbus, OH: Merrill.

Hord, S. M. (1986). A synthesis of research on organizational collaboration. *Educational Leadership, 44*, 22–26.

Hoskins, B. (1996). *Developing inclusive schools: A guide.* Port Chester, NY: National Professional Resources.

Houghton, S., & Bain, A. (1993). Peer tutoring with ESL and below-average readers. *Journal of Behavioral Education, 3*, 125–142.

Hourcade, J. J., Parette, H. P., Jr., & Huer, M. B. (1997). Considerations in assistive technology assessment. *Teaching Exceptional Children, 30*(1), 40–43.

House, E. R. (1990). Trends in evaluation. *Educational Researcher, 19*(3), 24–28.

Howe, K., & Eisenhart, M. (1990). Standards for qualitative (and quantitative) research: A prolegomenon. *Educational Researcher, 19*(4), 2–9.

Howell, K. W., & McCollum-Gahley, J. (1986). Monitoring instruction. *Teaching Exceptional Children, 19*(1), 47–49.

Hudson, P., & Fradd, S. (1990). Cooperative planning for learners with limited English proficiency. *Teaching Exceptional Children, 23*(1), 16–21.

Hudson, P., & Miller, S. P. (1993). Home and school partnerships: Parent as teacher. *LD Forum, 18*(2), 31–33.

Hughes, C. A., & Boyle, J. R. (1991). Effects of self-monitoring for on-task behavior and task productivity on elementary students with moderate mental retardation. *Education and Treatment of Children, 14*(2), 96–111.

Hughes, C. A., & Ruhl, K. L. (1987). The nature and extent of special educator contacts with students' parents. *Teacher Education and Special Education, 10*(4), 180–184.

Hughes, C. A., Ruhl, K. L., & Gorman, J. (1987). Preparation of special educators to work with parents: A survey of teachers and teacher educators. *Teacher Education and Special Education, 10*, 81–87.

Hughes, C., Ruhl, K. L., & Peterson, S. K. (1988). Teaching self-management skills. *Teaching Exceptional Children, 20*(2), 70–72.

Hundert, J. (1982). Some considerations of planning the integration of handicapped children into the mainstream. *Journal of Learning Disabilities, 15*, 73–80.

Hunt, P., & Goetz, L. (1997). Research on inclusive educational programs, practices, and outcomes for students with severe disabilities. *Journal of Special Education, 31*(1), 3–29.

Hyun, J. K., & Fowler, S. A. (1995). Respect, cultural sensitivity, and communication: Promoting participation by Asian families in the individualized family service plan. *Teaching Exceptional Children, 28*(1), 25–28.

Idol, L. (1988). A rationale and guidelines for establishing special education consultation programs. *Remedial and Special Education, 9*(6), 48–58.

Idol, L. (1990). The scientific art of consultation. *Journal of Educational and Psychological Consultation, 1*(1), 3–22.

Idol, L. (1998). Collaboration in the schools: A master plan for staff development. *Journal of Educational and Psychological Consultation, 9*(2), 155–163.

Idol, L., Nevin, A., & Paolucci-Whitcomb, P., (1994). *Collaborative consultation* (2nd ed.). Austin, TX: PRO-ED.

Idol, L., Nevin, A., & Paolucci-Whitcomb, P. (1995). The collaborative consultation model. *Journal of Educational and Psychological Consultation, 6*(4), 347–361.

Idol, L., Paolucci-Whitcomb, P., & Nevin, A. (1986). *Collaborative consultation.* Austin, TX: PRO-ED.

Idol, L., Paolucci-Whitcomb, P., & Nevin, A. (1995). A collaborative consultation model. *Journal of Educational and Psychological Consultation, 6*(4), 329–346.

Idol, L., & West, J. F. (1987). Consultation in special education. Part II: Training and practice. *Journal of Learning Disabilities, 20*(8), 474–494.

Idol-Maestas, L. (1983). *Special educator's consultation handbook.* Rockville, MD: Aspen.

Idol-Maestas, L., Nevin, A., & Paolucci-Whitcomb, P. (1984). *Facilitator's manual for collaborative consultation: Principles and techniques.* Reston, VA: National RETOOL Center, Teacher Education Division, Council for Exceptional Children.

Idol-Maestas, L., & Ritter, S. (1985). A follow-up study of resource/consulting teachers. *Teacher Education Special Education, 8*(3), 121–131.

Illback, R. J., Zins, J. E., & Maher, C. A. (1999). Program planning and evaluation: Principles, procedures, and planned change. In C. R. Reynolds & T. B. Gutkin (Eds.), *The handbook of school psychology* (3rd ed., pp. 907–932). New York: Wiley.

Inclusive Education Program. (1997). Block scheduling and inclusion: A boon to LD students? *Inclusive Education Programs: Advice on Educating Students with Disabilities in Regular Settings, 4*(12), 1, 9–11.

Individuals with Disabilities Education Act of 1997, P.L. 105-17.

*Ingraham v. Wright,* 430 U.S. 651 (1977).

*Irving Independent School District v. Tatro,* 104 S. Ct. 3371 (1984).

Ivory, J. J., & McCollum, J. A. (1999). Effects of social and isolate toys on social play in an inclusive setting. *Journal of Special Education, 32*(4), 238–243.

Iwata, B. (1987). Negative reinforcement in applied behavior analysis: An emerging technology. *Journal of Applied Behavior Analysis, 20,* 361–378.

Iwata, B. A., Dorsey, M. F., Slifer, K. J., Bauman, K. E., & Richman, G. S. (1994). Toward a functional analysis of self-injury. *Journal of Applied Behavior Analysis, 27,* 197–209.

Iwata, B. A., Pace, G. M., Cowdery, G. E., Edwards, G., & Miltenberger, R. G. (1994). What makes extinction work: An analysis of procedural form and function. *Journal of Applied Behavior Analysis, 27*(1), 131–144.

Iwata, B. A., Pace, G. M., Dorsey, M. F., Zarcone, J. R., Vollmer, T. R., Smith, R. G., Rodgers, T. A., Lerman, D. C., Shore, B. A., Mazaleski, J. L., Goh, H., Cowdery, E., Kalsher, M. J., McCosh, K. C., & Willis, K. D. (1994). The functions of self-injurious behavior: An experimental-epidemiological analysis. *Journal of Applied Behavior Analysis, 27*(2), 215–240.

Jackson, P. (1968). *Life in classrooms.* New York: Holt, Rinehart and Winston.

Jayanthi, M., Bursuck, W., Epstein, M. H., & Polloway, E. A. (1997). Strategies for successful homework. *Teaching Exceptional Children, 30*(1), 4–7.

Jayanthi, M., Epstein, M. H., Polloway, E. A., & Bursuck, W. D. (1996). A national survey of general education teachers' perceptions of testing adaptations. *Journal of Special Education, 30*(1), 991–1115.

Jayanthi, M., Nelson, J. S., Sawyer, V., Bursuck, W. D., & Epstein, M. H. (1995). Homework-communication problems among parents, classroom teachers, and special education teachers: An exploratory study. *Remedial and Special Education, 16*(2), 102–116.

Jenkins, J. R., & Heinen, A. (1989). Students' preferences for service delivery: Pull-out, in-class, or integrated models. *Exceptional Children, 55*(6), 516–523.

Jenkins, J. R., & Jenkins, L.M. (1981). *Cross age and peer tutoring: Help for children with learning problems.* Reston, VA: Council for Exceptional Children.

Jenkins, J. R., Odom, S. L., & Speltz, M. L. (1989). Effects of social integration on preschool children with handicaps. *Exceptional Children, 55,* 420–428.

Jenson, W. R., Sheridan, S. M., Olympia, D., & Andrews, D. (1994). Homework and students with learning disabilities and behavior disorders: A practical, parent-based approach. *Journal of Learning Disabilities, 27*(9), 538–548.

Jesness, J. (1999, September). Why Johnny can't fail. *Harper's,* 21–24.

Johnson, D. C. (1988). *Effects of self-monitoring and self-reinforcement on academic performance and goal behaviors of students with severe behavior handicaps.* Unpublished master's thesis, The Ohio State University, Columbus.

Johnson, D. W., & Johnson, F. W. (1994). *Joining together: Group theory and skills* (5th ed.). Englewood Cliffs, NJ: Prentice-Hall.

Johnson, D. W., & Johnson, R. T. (1975). *Learning together and alone: Cooperation, competition, and individualization.* Englewood Cliffs, NJ: Prentice-Hall.

Johnson, D. W., & Johnson, R. T. (1987). *Learning together and alone: Cooperative, competitive, and individualistic learning.* Englewood Cliffs, NJ: Prentice-Hall.

Johnson, D. W., & Johnson, R. T. (1989). Cooperative learning and mainstreaming. In R. Gaylord-Ross (Ed.),

*Integration-strategies for students with handicaps* (pp. 233–248). Baltimore: Paul H. Brookes.

Johnson, D. W., & Johnson, R. T. (1995). *Reducing school violence through conflict resolution.* Alexandria, VA: Association for Supervision and Curriculum Development.

Johnson, D. W., Johnson, R., & Maruyama, G. (1983). Interdependence and interpersonal attraction among heterogeneous and homogeneous individuals: A theoretical formulation and meta-analysis of the research. *Review of Educational Research, 53,* 5–54.

Johnson, H. L. (1993). Stressful family experiences and young children: How the classroom teacher can help. *Intervention in School and Clinic, 28*(3), 165–171.

Johnson, L. J., & Pugach, M. C. (1991). Peer collaboration: Accommodating students with mild learning and behavior problems. *Exceptional Children, 57*(5), 454–461.

Johnson, L. J., Pugach, M. C., & Hammitte, D. J. (1988). Barriers to effective special education consultation. *Remedial and Special Education, 9*(6), 41–47.

*Joint Anti-Fascist Committee v. McGrath.* (1951). 341 U.S. 123.

Jones, C. B. (1986). Grandparents read to special pre-schoolers. *Teaching Exceptional Children, 19*(1), 36–37.

Jones, R. J. (Ed.). (1988). *Psychoeducational assessment of minority group children: A casebook.* Berkeley, CA: Cobb & Henry.

Jordan, L., Reyes-Blanes, M. E., Peel, B. B., Peel, H. A., & Lane, H. B. (1998). Developing teacher-parent partnerships across cultures: Effective parent conferences. *Intervention in School and Clinic, 33* (3), 141–147.

*Jose P. v. Ambach,* 3EHLR 551:245, 27 (E. D. N. Y. 1979).

*Jose P. v. Ambach,* 557 F. Supp. 1230 (E. D. N. Y. 1983).

Joyce, B., & Showers, B. (1980). Improving inservice training: The message of research. *Educational Leadership, 37*(5), 379–385.

Justen, J. E., III., & Howerton, D. L. (1993). Clarifying behavior management terminology. *Intervention in School and Clinic, 29*(1), 36–40.

Kabler, M., & Genshaft, J. (1983). Structuring decision making in multidisciplinary teams. *School Psychology Review, 23*(2), 150–159.

Kahng, S. W., & Iwata, B. A. (1998). Play versus alone conditions as controls during functional analyses of self-injurious escape behavior. *Journal of Applied Behavior Analysis, 31,*(4), 669–672.

Kahng, S. W., & Iwata, B. A. (1999). Correspondence between outcomes of brief and extended functional analyses. *Journal of Applied Behavior Analysis, 32,* 149–159.

Kameenui, E. J., & Darch, C. B. (1995). *Instructional classroom management: A proactive approach to behavior management.* White Plains, NY: Longman.

Kampwirth, T. J. (1999). *Collaborative consultation in the schools: Effective practices for students with learn-ing and behavior problems.* Upper Saddle River, NJ: Merrill.

Katsiyannis, A., & Conderman, G. (1994). Section 504 policies and procedures: An established necessity. *Remedial and Special Education, 15*(5), 311–318.

Katsiyannis, A., & Klare, K. (1991). State practices in due process hearings: Considerations for better practice. *Remedial and Special Education, 12*(2), 54–58.

Katsiyannis, A., & Maag, J. W. (1997). Ensuring appropriate education: Emerging remedies, litigation, compensation, and other legal considerations. *Exceptional Children, 63*(4), 451–462.

Kauffman, J. M., & Hallahan, D. P. (1995). *The illusion of full inclusion.* Austin, TX: PRO-ED.

Kauffman, M. J., Gottlieb, J., Agard, J. A., & Kukic, M. B. (1975). Mainstreaming: Toward an explication of the construct. *Focus on Exceptional Children, 7,* 1–12.

Kavale, K. A., & Forness, S. R. (1987). Substance over style: Assessing the efficacy of modality testing and teaching. *Exceptional Children, 54*(3), 228–239.

Kay, P. J., & Fitzgerald, M. (1997). Parents + teachers + action research = real involvement. *Teaching Exceptional Children, 30*(1), 8–11.

Kay, P. J., Fitzgerald, M., Paradee, C., & Mellencamp, A. (1994). Making homework work at home: The parent's perspective. *Journal of Learning Disabilities, 27*(9), 550–561.

Kazdin, A. E., & Klock, J. (1973). The effect of nonverbal teacher approval on student attentive behavior. *Journal of Applied Behavior Analysis, 6,* 643–654.

Kelley, M. L., & Stokes, T. F. (1982). Contingency contracting with disadvantaged youth: Improving classroom performance. *Journal of Applied Behavior Analysis, 15,*(3), 447–454.

Kennedy, J. H. (1995). Teachers', student teachers', paraprofessionals', and young adults' judgments about the acceptable use of corporal punishment in the rural South. *Education and Treatment of Children, 18*(1), 53–64.

Kerr, M. M., & Nelson, C. M. (1983). *Strategies for managing behavior problems in the classroom.* Columbus, OH: Merrill.

Kerr, M. M., & Nelson, C. M. (1998). *Strategies for managing behavior problems in the classroom* (3rd ed.). Upper Saddle River, NJ: Prentice-Hall.

Kidd, T. A., & Saudargas, R. A. (1988). Positive and negative consequences in contingency contracts: Their relative effectiveness on arithmetic performance. *Education and Treatment of Children, 11*(2), 118–126.

Kimball, W. H., & Heron, T. E. (1988). A behavioral commentary on Poplin's discussion of the reductionistic fallacy and holistic/constructivist principles. *Journal of Learning Disabilities, 21,* 425–428.

Kimball, W. H., Heron, T. E., & Weiss, A. B. (1984a). Federal regulation: One more time. *Remedial and Special Education, 5,* 36–37.

Kimball, W. H., Heron, T. E., & Weiss, A. B. (1984b). New federalism and deregulation: Impact on special education. *Remedial and Special Education, 5,* 25–31.

King-Sears, M. E., Mercer, C. D., & Sindelar, P. T. (1992). Toward independence with keyword mnemonics: A strategy for science vocabulary instruction. *Remedial and Special Education, 13,* 22–33.

Kitano, H. (1973). Highlights of institute on language and culture: Asian component. In L. A. Bransford, L. Baca, & K. Lane (Eds.), *Cultural diversity and the exceptional child* (pp. 14–15). Reston, VA: Council for Exceptional Children.

Kitano, M. D., Steihl, J., & Cole, J. T. (1978). Role taking: Implications for special education. *Journal of Special Education, 12*(1), 59–74.

Klapstein, S. (1994). A collaborative interagency diagnostic classroom. *Intervention in School and Clinic, 29,* 180–183.

Kline, C. (1986). *Effects of guided notes on academic achievement of learning disabled high school students.* Unpublished master's thesis, The Ohio State University, Columbus.

Knight, M. F., Meyers, H. W., Paolucci-Whitcomb, P., Hasazi, S. E., & Nevin, A. (1981). A four-year evaluation of consulting teacher service. *Behavior Disorders, 6,* 92–100.

Knoske, J. L. (1996). *Effects of peer tutoring on the acquisition and maintenance of plant identification with vocational students.* Unpublished master's thesis, The Ohio State University, Columbus.

Knowlton, H. E. (1983). A strategy for rational and responsive program evaluation. *Teacher Education and Special Education, 6*(2), 106–111.

Koegel, R. L., & Rincover, A. (1977). Research on the differences between generalization and maintenance in extra-therapy responding. *Journal of Applied Behavior Analysis, 10,* 1–12.

Kohler, P. D. (1993). Best practices in transition: Substantiated or implied? *Career Development for Exceptional Individuals, 16,* 107–121.

Kohr, M. A., Parrish, J. M., Neef, N. A., Driessen, J. R., & Hallinan, P. C. (1988). Communication skills training for parents: Experimental and social validation. *Journal of Applied Behavior Analysis, 21,* 21–30.

Kopp, H., & Kazis, R., with Churchill, A. (1995). *Promising practices: A study of ten school-to-career programs.* Boston: Jobs for the Future.

Kortering, L. J., & Braziel, P. M. (1999). School dropout from the perspective of former students. *Remedial and Special Education, 20*(2), 78–83.

Kosma, R. B. (1991). Learning with media. *Review of Educational Research, 61*(2), 179–211.

Kramer, J. J. (1985). Best practices in parent training. In A. Thomas & J. Grimes (Eds.), *Best practices in school psychology* (pp. 263–273). Washington, DC: National Association of School Psychologists.

Kramer, J. J. (1990). Best practices in parent training. In A. Thomas & J. Grimes (Eds.), *Best practices in school*

*psychology II* (pp. 519–530). Washington, DC: National Association of School Psychologists.

Krashen, S. D. (1981). Bilingual education and second language acquisition theory. In *Schooling and language minority students: A theoretical framework* (pp. 51–79). Los Angeles: Evaluation, Dissemination, and Assessment Center, California State University.

Krashen, S. D. (1982). *Principles and practices in second language acquisition: Language teaching methodology series.* New York: Pergamon.

Krashen, S. D. (1985). *Inquiries and insights: Second language teaching: Immersion and bilingual education: Literacy.* Hayward, CA: Janus.

Krashen, S. D. (1999). *Condemned without a trial: Bogus arguments against bilingual education.* Westport, CT: Heinemann.

Kratochwill, T. R., & Bergan, J. R. (1978). Evaluating programs in applied settings through behavioral consultation. *Journal of School Psychology, 16,* 375–386.

Kratochwill, T. R., Elliott, S. N., & Rotto, P. (1990). Best practices in behavioral consultation. In A. Thomas & J. Grimes (Eds.), *Best practices in school psychology II* (pp. 147–169). Washington, DC: National Association of School Psychologists.

Kratochwill, T. R., Sheridan, S. M., & Van Someren, K. R. (1988). Research in behavioral consultation: Current status and future directions. In J. F. West (Ed.), *School consultation: Interdisciplinary perspectives on theory, research, training, and practice* (pp. 77–102). Austin, TX: Research and Training Project on School Consultation, University of Texas.

Kratochwill, T. R., Sladeczek, I., & Plunge, M. (1995). The evolution of behavior consultation. *Journal of Educational and Psychological Consultation, 6*(2), 145–157.

Kratochwill, T. R., & Van Someren, K. R. (1995). Barriers to treatment success in behavioral consultation: Current limitations and future directions. *Journal of Educational and Psychological Consultation, 6*(2), 125–143.

Krieg, F. J., Brown, P., & Ballard, J. (1995). *Transition: School to work.* Bethesda, MD: National Association of School Psychologists.

Kronich, D. (1969). *They too can succeed: A practical guide for parents of learning disabled children.* San Rafael, CA: Academic Therapy.

Kroth, R. L. (1980). The mirror model of parental involvement. *The Pointer, 25*(1), 19–22.

Kroth, R. L. (1985). *Communicating with parents of exceptional children: Improving parent-teacher relationships* (2nd ed.). Denver: Love.

Kroth, R. L., & Edge, D. (1997). *Strategies for communicating with parents and families of exceptional children* (3rd ed.). Denver: Love.

Kruger, L. J., & Struzziero, J. (1997). Computer-mediated peer support of consultation: Case description and evaluation. *Journal of Educational and Psychological Consultation, 8*(1), 75–90.

Kruger, L. J., Struzziero, J., Watts, R., & Vacca, D. (1995). The relationship between organizational support and satisfaction with teacher assistance teams. *Remedial and Special Education, 16,* 203–211.

Kubetz, B. J. (1972). Education equality for the mentally retarded. *Syracuse Law Review, 23,* 1141–1165.

Kulik, J., Bangert, R. L., & Williams, G. W. (1983). Effects of computer-based teaching on secondary school students. *Journal of Educational Psychology, 75,* 19–26.

Kurpius, D. (1978). Consultation theory and process: An integrated model. *Personnel and Guidance Journal, 56,* 335–338.

Kurpius, D. J., & Lewis, J. E. (1988). Assumptions and operating principles for preparing professionals to function as consultants. In J. F. West (Ed.), *School consultation: Interdisciplinary perspectives on theory, research, training, and practice* (pp. 143–154). Austin, TX: Association of Educational and Psychological Consultants.

Kurpius, D., & Robinson, S. E. (1978). Overview of consultation. *Personnel and Guidance Journal, 56,* 321–323.

*Lake v. Cameron.* (1966). 364 F. 2d 657.

Lancioni, G. (1982). Normal children as tutors to teach social responses to withdrawn mentally retarded schoolmates: Training, maintenance, and generalization. *Journal of Applied Behavior Analysis, 15,* 17–40.

Landerholm, E. (1990). The transdisciplinary team approach in infant intervention programs. *Teaching Exceptional Children, 22*(2), 66–70.

Lane, G. (1995). Empowerment in transition planning: Guidelines for special educators. *LD Forum, 21*(1), 34–38.

Langdon, H. W. (1983). Assessment and intervention strategies for the bilingual language-disordered student. *Exceptional Children, 50*(1), 37–46.

Lange, C. M., Ysseldyke, J. E., & Lehr, C. A. (1997). Parents' perspectives on school choice. *Teaching Exceptional Children, 30*(1), 14–19.

Larrivee, B., & Cook, L. (1979). Mainstreaming: A study of the variables affecting teacher attitude. *Journal of Special Education, 13,* 313–324.

*Larry P. v. Riles.* (1972). 343 F. Supp. 1306.

Larsen, S. (1995). What is "quality" in the use of technology for children with learning disabilities? *Learning Disability Quarterly, 18*(2), 118–130.

Lasater, M. W., & Brady, M. P. (1995). Effects of video self-modeling and feedback on task fluency: A home-based intervention. *Education and Treatment of Children, 18*(4), 389–407.

Laurie, T. E., Buchwach, L., Silverman, R., & Zigmond, N. (1978). Teaching secondary learning disabled students in the mainstream. *Learning Disability Quarterly, 1*(4), 62–72.

LaVor, M. L. (1976). Federal legislation for exceptional persons: A history. In F. J. Weintraub, A. Abeson, J. Ballard, & M. L. LaVor (Eds.), *Public policy and the education of exceptional children* (pp. 96–111). Reston, VA: The Council for Exceptional Children.

Lawry, J. R., Storey, K., & Danko, C. D. (1993). Analyzing problem behaviors in the classroom: A case study of

functional analysis. *Intervention in School and Clinic, 29*(2), 96–100.

Lawton, E. J. (1989). *A journey through time: A chronology of middle level education resources.* Columbus, OH: National Middle School Association.

Lazarus, B. (1986). *Effects of home-based parent tutoring managed by an automatic telephone answering machine on word recognition of kindergarten children.* Unpublished doctoral dissertation, The Ohio State University, Columbus.

Lazarus, B. (1993). Guided notes: Effects with secondary and post-secondary students with mild disabilities. *Education and Treatment of Children, 16*(3), 272–289.

Learning Disabilities Association. (1993). Position paper on full inclusion of all students with learning disabilities in the regular education classroom. *Journal of Learning Disabilities, 26*(9), 594.

*LeBanks v. Spears.* (1973). 60 F.R.D. 135.

Lebzelter, S., & Nowacek, E. J. (1999). Reading strategies for secondary students with mild disabilities. *Intervention in School and Clinic, 34*(4), 212–219.

Leconte, P. J., Castleberry, M., King, S., & West, L. (1994–95). Critical issues in assessment: Let's take the mystery out of assessment for vocational preparation, career development and transition. *Diagnostique, 20* (1–4), 33–51.

Lee, E., & Smith, J. B. (1994). *Effects of high school restructuring and size on gains in achievement and engagement of early secondary school students.* Madison: University of Wisconsin, Center on Organization and Restructuring of Schools.

Lehman, C. M., & Irvin, L. K. (1996). Support for families with children who have emotional or behavioral disorders. *Education and Treatment of Children, 19*(3), 335–353.

Lehner, R. (1988). *Effects of communication training on the acquisition and generalization of collaborative consultation skills by high school special education tutors.* Unpublished master's thesis, The Ohio State University, Columbus.

Lehr, D., & Haubrich, P. (1986). Legal precedents for students with severe handicaps. *Exceptional Children, 52*(4), 358–365.

Lenz, B. K., & Hughes, C. A. (1990). A word identification strategy for adolescents with learning disabilities. *Journal of Learning Disabilities, 23,* 149–158.

Leonardi, A., Duggan, T., Hoffheins, J., & Axelrod, S. (1972, March). *Use of group contingencies to reduce three types of inappropriate classroom behaviors.* Paper presented at the meeting of the Council for Exceptional Children, Washington, DC.

Lerman, D. C., & Iwata, B. A. (1995). Prevalence of the extinction burst and its attenuation during treatment. *Journal of Applied Behavior Analysis, 28*(1), 93–94.

Leung, E. K. (1990). Early risks: Transition from culturally/linguistically diverse homes to formal schooling. *Journal of Educational Issues of Language Minority Students, 7,* 35–51.

Levinson, E.M. (1993). *Transdisciplinary vocational assessment: Issues in school-based programs.* Brandon, VT: Clinical Psychology Publishing.

Lewin, K. (1951). *Field theory in social science.* New York: Harper.

Lindsley, O. R. (1990). Precision teaching: By teachers for children. *Teaching Exceptional Children, 22*(3), 10–15.

Linnehan, F. (1996). Measuring the effectiveness of a career academy program from an employer's perspective. *Educational Evaluation and Policy Analysis, 18,* 73–89.

Linscheid, T. R., Iwata., B. A., Ricketts, R. W., Williams, D. E., & Griffin, J. C. (1990). Clinical evaluation of the self-injurious behavior inhibiting system (SIBIS). *Journal of Applied Behavior Analysis, 23*(1), 53–78.

Lippitt, G. L. (1969). *Organizational renewal.* New York: Appleton-Century-Crofts.

Litow, L., & Pumroy, D. K. (1975). A brief review of classroom group-oriented contingencies. *Journal of Applied Behavior Analysis, 8,* 341–347.

Little, S. G., & Witek, J. M. (1996). Inclusion: Considerations from social validity and functional outcome analysis. *Journal of Behavioral Education, 6*(3), 283–291.

Lloyd, J. W., Forness, S. R., & Kavale, K. A. (1998). Some methods are more effective than others. *Intervention in School and Clinic, 33*(4), 195–200.

Lloyd, J. W., & Hughes, C. (1993). Introduction to the self-management series. *Journal of Behavioral Education, 3*(4), 403–404.

Lohrmann-O'Rourke, S., & Zirkel, P. A. (1998). The case law on aversive interventions for students with disabilities. *Exceptional Children, 65*(1), 101–123.

Lombard, R. C. (1994). The collaborative transition model: An interdisciplinary approach to meeting transition needs of rural communities. *Rural Special Education Quarterly, 13*(1) 24–28.

Lombard, R. C., Larsen, K. A., & Westphal, S. E. (1993). Validation of vocational assessment services for special populations in tech-prep: A model for translating the Perkins assurances into practice. *Journal for Vocational Special Needs Education, 16*(1), 14–22.

Longo, J., Rotatori, A. F., Kapperman, G., & Heinze, T. (1981). Procedures used to modify self-injurious behaviors in visually impaired, mentally retarded individuals. *Education of the Visually Handicapped, 13*(3), 77–83.

Lopez, E. C., Dalal, S. M., & Yoshida, R. K. (1993). An examination of professional cultures: Implications for the collaborative consultation model. *Journal of Educational and Psychological Consultation, 4*(3), 197–213.

Lounsbury, J. H. (Ed.). (1984). *Perspectives: Middle school education, 1964–1984.* Columbus, OH: National Middle School Association.

Love, L., & Malian, I. (1997). What happens to students leaving secondary special education services in Arizona? Implications for education program improvement and transition services. *Remedial and Special Education, 18*(5), 261–269.

Lovitt, T. C. (1989). *Introduction to learning disabilities.* Boston: Allyn & Bacon.

Lovitt, T. C., Plavins, M., & Cushing, S. (1999). What do pupils with disabilities have to say about their experience in high school? *Remedial and Special Education, 20*(2), 67–76, 83.

Lowenthal, B. (1991). Ecological assessment: Adding a new dimension for preschool children. *Intervention in School and Clinic, 26*(3), 148–151, 162.

Loyd, R. J., & Brolin, D. E. (1997). *Life centered career education: Modified curriculum for individuals with moderate disabilities.* Reston, VA: Council for Exceptional Children.

Lubeck, R. C., & Chandler, L. K. (1990). Organizing the home caregiving environment for infants. *Education and Treatment of Children, 13*(4), 347–363.

Luckasson, R. A. (1986). Attorney's fee reimbursement in special education cases: *Smith v. Robinson. Exceptional Children, 52*(4), 384–389.

Lynch, E. C., & Beare, P. L. (1990). The quality of the IEP objectives and their relevance to instruction for students with mental retardation and behavioral disorders. *Remedial and Special Education, 11*(2), 48–55.

Lynch, E. W., & Hanson, M. J. (Eds.). (1998). *Developing cross-cultural competence* (2nd ed.). Baltimore: Paul H. Brookes.

Lynch, E. W., & Stein, R. C. (1987). Parent participation by ethnicity: A comparison of Hispanic, Black, and Anglo families. *Exceptional Children, 54*(2), 105–111.

Lyon, C. S., & Lagarde, R. (1997). Tokens for success: Using the graduated reinforcement system. *Teaching Exceptional Children, 29*(6), 52–57.

Lyytinen, P., Rasku-Puttonen, H., Poikkeus, A., Laakso, M., & Ahonen, T. (1994). Mother-child teaching strategies and learning disabilities. *Journal of Learning Disabilities, 27*(3), 186–192.

Mace, F. C., McCurdy, B., & Quigley, E. A. (1990). A collateral effect of reward predicated by matching theory. *Journal of Applied Behavior Analysis, 23,* 197–205.

Madden, N. A., & Slavin, R. E. (1983). Mainstreaming students with mild handicaps: Academic and social outcomes. *Review of Educational Research, 53,* 519–569.

Maddox, T. (Ed.). (1997). *A comprehensive reference for assessment in psychology, education, and business.* Austin, TX: PRO-ED.

Maheady, L. (1997). Four classwide peer tutoring models: Commonalities, differences, and implications for research and practice. A symposium presentation at the annual convention of the Association for Behavior Analysis, Chicago.

Maheady, L., Harper, G. F., & Sacca, M. K. (1986). *Classwide student tutoring teams: Teacher's manual.* East Lansing: Michigan State University.

Maher, C. A. (1983). Goal attainment scaling: A method for evaluating special education services. *Exceptional Children, 39,* 141–147.

Maher, C. A., & Barbrack, C. R. (1980). A framework for comprehensive evaluation of the individualized education program (IEP). *Learning Disability Quarterly, 3*(3), 49–55.

Maher, C. A., & Bennett, R. E. (1984). *Planning and evaluating special education services.* Englewood Cliffs, NJ: Prentice-Hall.

Malcolm, C. B., Polatajko, H. J., & Simons, J. (1990). A descriptive study of adults with suspected learning disabilities. *Journal of Learning Disabilities, 23,* 518–520.

Mamlin, N. (1999). Despite best intention: When inclusion fails. *Journal of Special Education, 33*(1), 36–49.

Marable, M. A., & Raimondi, S. L. (1995). Managing surface behaviors. *LD Forum, 20*(2), 45–47.

Margalit, M., Rochberg, Y., & Al-Yagon, M. (1995). Home-computing model and children with learning disabilities: A systemic approach. *Learning Disability Quarterly, 18*(2), 68–75.

Margolis, H. (1991). Understanding, facing resistance to change. *NASSP Bulletin, 75*(537), 1–8.

Margolis, H. (1994). *Monitoring IEPs.* Unpublished paper, Queens College, New York, NY.

Margolis, H. (1998). Avoiding special education due process hearings: Lessons from the field. *Journal of Educational and Psychological Consultation, 9*(3), 233–260.

Margolis, H., & Brannigan, G. G. (1986). Building trust with parents. *Academic Therapy, 22,* 71–74.

Margolis, H., & Fiorelli, J. (1987). Getting past anger in consulting relationships. *Organization Development Journal* (Winter), 44–48.

Margolis, H., Fish, M., & Wepner, S. B. (1990). Overcoming resistance to prereferral classroom interventions. *Special Services in the Schools, 6*(1–2), 167–186.

Margolis, H., & McCabe, P. P. (1988). Overcoming resistance to a new remedial program. *The Clearing House, 62*(3), 131–134.

Margolis, H., & Tewel, K. (1990). Understanding least restrictive environment—A key to avoiding parent-school conflict. *Urban Review, 22*(4), 283–296.

Marinelli, J. J. (1976). Financing the education of exceptional children. In F. J. Weintraub, A. Abeson, J. Ballard, & M. L. LaVor (Eds.), *Public policy and the education of exceptional children* (pp. 151–194). Reston, VA: Council for Exceptional Children.

Markham, P., Green, S. B., & Ross, M. E. (1996). Identification of stressors and coping strategies of ESL/bilingual, special education and regular education teachers. *Modern Language Journal, 80*(2), 141–150.

Marks, E. S. (1995). *Entry strategies for school consultation.* New York: Guilford Press.

Marshall, K. J., Lloyd, J. W., & Hallahan, D. P. (1993). Effects of training to increase self-monitoring accuracy. *Journal of Behavioral Education, 3*(4), 445–459.

Martin, G., & Pear, J. (1996). *Behavior modification: What it is and how to do it* (5th ed.). Upper Saddle River, NJ: Prentice-Hall.

Martin, J. E., & Marshall, L. H. (1996). ChoiceMaker: Infusing self-determination instruction into the IEP and transition process. In D. J. Sands & M. L. Wehmeyer (Eds.), *Self-determination across the life span: Independence and choice for people with disabilities* (pp. 211–232). Baltimore: Paul H. Brookes.

Marwell, G., & Schmidt, D. (1975). *Cooperation.* New York: Academic Press.

*Maryland Association for Retarded Children v. State of Maryland,* (Circuit Court, Baltimore, MD, 1974). Equity No. 100–182–77676.

Mason, S. A., McGee, G. G., Farmer-Dougan, V., & Risley, T. (1989). A practical strategy for ongoing reinforcer assessment. *Journal of Applied Behavior Analysis, 22,* 171–179.

Mastropieri, M. A., Scruggs, T. E., & Whedon, C. (1997). Using mnemonic strategies to teach information about U.S. presidents: A classroom-based investigation. *Learning Disability Quarterly, 20*(1), 13–21.

Mathes, M. Y., & Bender, W. N. (1997). The effects of self-monitoring on children with attention-deficit/hyperactivity disorder who are receiving pharmacological interventions. *Remedial and Special Education, 18*(2), 121–128.

*Mattie T. v. Holladay,* Civ. Act. No. DC 75–31–S (N.D. Miss., file 4/25/75).

Mayer, G. R., Mitchell, L. K., Clementi, T., Clement-Robertson, E., Myatt, R., & Bullara, D. T. (1993). A dropout prevention program for at-risk high school students: Emphasizing consulting to promote positive classroom climates. *Education and Treatment of Children, 16*(2), 135–146.

Mazaleski, J. L., Iwata, B. A., Vollmer, T. R., Zarcone, J. R., & Smith, R. G. (1993). Analysis of the reinforcement and extinction components in DRO contingencies with self-injury. *Journal of Applied Behavior Analysis, 26*(2), 143–156.

McCallon, E., & McCray, E. (1975). *Planning and conducting interviews.* Austin, TX: Learning Concepts.

McCarthy, E. F., & Sage, D. D. (1982). State special education fiscal policy: The quest for equity. *Exceptional Children, 48*(5), 414–419.

McClellan, E., & Wheatley, W. (1985). Project RETOOL: Collaborative consultation training for post-doctoral leadership personnel. *Teacher Education Special Education, 8*(3), 159–163.

McClure, W. P. (1975). Alternative methods of financing special education. *Journal of Education Finance, 1,* 36–51.

McCracken County School District, 18 IDELR 482 (OCR, 1991).

McDaniel, L. (1982). Changing vocational teachers' attitudes toward the handicapped. *Exceptional Children, 48*(4), 377–378.

McDaniels, G. (1980, May 23). Office of Special Education policy paper, Washington, DC.

McDonnell, J., Wilcox, B., & Hardman, M. L. (1991). *Secondary programs for students with developmental disabilities.* Boston: Allyn & Bacon.

McDougall, D., & Brady, M. P. (1998). Initiating and fading self-management interventions to increase math fluency in general education classes. *Exceptional Children, 64*(2), 151–166.

McEvoy, M. A., & Brady, M. P. (1988). Contingent access to play materials as an academic motivator for autistic and behavior disordered children. *Education and Treatment of Children, 11*(1), 5–18.

McGill, N. B., & Robinson, L. (1989). Regular education teacher consultant. *Teaching Exceptional Children, 21*(2), 71–73.

McGimsey, J. F., Greene, B. F., & Lutzker, J. R. (1995). Competence in aspects of behavioral treatment and consultation: Implications for service delivery and graduate training. *Journal of Applied Behavior Analysis, 28*(3), 301–315.

McGonigel, M. J., Woodruff, G., & Roszmann-Millican, M. (1994). The transdisciplinary team: A model for family-centered early intervention. In L. J. Johnson, R. J. Gallagher, M. J. LaMontagne, J. B. Jordan, J. J. Gallagher, P. L. Hutinger, & M. B. Karnes (Eds.), *Meeting early intervention challenges: Issues from birth to three* (pp. 95–131). Baltimore: Paul H. Brookes.

McGuffin, M., Martz, S., & Heron, T. E. (1997). The effects of self-correction versus traditional spelling on the spelling performance and maintenance of third grade students. *Journal of Behavioral Education, 7*(4), 463–476.

McIntosh, R., Vaughn, S., & Zaragoza, N. (1991). A review of social interventions for students with learning disabilities. *Journal of Learning Disabilities, 24*(8), 451–458.

McLean, M., & Hanline, M. F. (1990). Providing early intervention services in integrated environments: Challenges and opportunities for the future. *Topics in Early Childhood Special Education, 10*(2), 62–77.

McLeskey, J., & Henry, D. (1999). Inclusion: What progress is being made across states? *Teaching Exceptional Children, 31*(5), 56–62.

McLeskey, J., Henry, D., & Hodges, D. (1998). Inclusion: Where is it happening? *Teaching Exceptional Children, 31*(1), 4–10.

McLeskey, J., Henry, D., & Hodges, D. (1999). Inclusion: What progress is being made across disability categories? *Teaching Exceptional Children, 31*(3), 60–64.

McLoughlin, J. A. (1978). Roles and practices of parents of children with learning and behavior problems. In D. Edge, B. J. Strenechy, & S. I. Mour (Eds.), *Parenting learning problem children: The professional educator's perspective* (pp. 79–87). Columbus: National Center for Education Media and Materials for the Handicapped, The Ohio State University.

McLoughlin, J. A., & Lewis, R. B. (1994). *Assessing special students* (4th ed.) Upper Saddle River, NJ: Merrill/Prentice Hall.

McLoughlin, J. A., & Lewis, R. B. (1990). *Assessing special students* (3rd ed.). New York: Macmillan.

McLoughlin, J. A., & Senn, C. (1994). Siblings of children with disabilities. In S. K. Alper, P. J. Schloss, & C. N. Schloss (Eds.), *Families of students with disabilities* (pp. 95–122). Needham Heights, MA: Allyn & Bacon.

McMahon, R. J., & Forehand, R. (1981). Self-help behavior therapies and parent training. In B. Lahey & A. Kazdin (Eds.), *Advances in clinical child psychology* (vol. 3). New York: Plenum.

McNamara, J. R., & Diehl, L. A. (1974). Behavioral consultation with a head start program. *Journal of Community Psychology, 2*, 352–357.

Medina, V. (1982). Issues regarding the use of interpreters and translators in a school setting. In *Proceedings of the Conference on Special Education and the Bilingual Child* (pp. 31–37). San Diego, CA: National Origin Desegregation Law Center, San Diego State University.

Medway, F. J. (1982). School consultation research: Past trends and future directions. *Professional Psychology, 13*, 422–430.

Medway, F. J., & Forman, S. G. (1980). Psychologists' and teachers' reactions to mental health and behavioral school consultation. *Journal of School Psychology, 18*(4), 338–348.

Medway, F. J., & Updyke, J. F. (1985). Meta-analysis of consultation outcome studies. *American Journal of Community Psychology, 13*, 489–505.

Meece, R. L. (1997). Student fights: Proactive strategies for preventing and managing student conflicts. *Intervention in School and Clinic, 33*(1), 26–29, 35.

Mehran, M., & White, K. R. (1988). Parent tutoring as a supplement to compensatory education for first-grade children. *Remedial and Special Education, 9*(3), 35–41.

Mercer, J. R., & Rueda, R. (1991, November). *The impact of changing paradigms of disabilities on assessment for special education.* Paper presented at the Council for Exceptional Children Topical Conference on At-Risk Children and Youth, New Orleans, LA.

Merriam, S. (1988). *Case study research in education: A qualitative approach.* San Francisco: Jossey-Bass.

Meyen, E. L. (1978). *Exceptional children and youth: An introduction.* Denver: Love.

Meyen, E. L., & Lehr, D. (1980). Evolving practices in assessment and in intervention: The case for intensive instruction. *Exceptional Education Quarterly, 1*(2), 19–26.

Meyers, B., Valentino, C. T., Meyers, J., Boretti, M., & Brent, D. (1996). Implementing prereferral intervention teams as an approach to school-based consultation in an urban school system. *Journal of Educational and Psychological Consultation, 7*(2), 119–149.

Meyers, C. E., & Blacher, J. (1987). Parents' perception of schooling for severely handicapped children: Home and family variables. *Exceptional Children, 53*(5), 441–449.

Meyers, J. (1995a). A consultation model for school psychological services. *Journal of Educational and Psychological Consultation, 6*(1), 59–71.

Meyers, J. (1995b). A consultation model for school psychological services: Twenty years later. *Journal of Educational and Psychological Consultation, 6*(1), 73–81.

Meyers, J., Parsons, R. D., & Martin, R. (1979). *Mental health consultation in the schools.* San Francisco: Jossey-Bass.

Miles, M. B., & Huberman, A. M. (1984). *Qualitative data analysis: A sourcebook of new methods.* Beverly Hills, CA: Sage.

Miller, A. D., Barbetta, P., Drevno, G. E., Martz, S. A., & Heron, T. E. (1996). Math peer tutoring for students with specific learning disabilities. *Learning Disability Forum, 21*(3), 21–28.

Miller, A. D., Barbetta, P., & Heron, T. E. (1994). START tutoring: Designing, training, implementing, and adapting tutoring programs for school and home settings. In R. Gardner, J. O. Cooper, T. E. Heron, W. L. Heward, J. Eshleman, & D. Sainato (Eds.), *Behavioral analysis in education: Focus on measurably superior instruction* (pp. 265–282). Monterey, CA: Brooks-Cole.

Miller, P. W. (1986). *Nonverbal communication* (2nd ed.). Washington, DC: National Education Association.

Miller, S. P., & Hudson, P. (1994). Using structured parent groups to provide parental support. *Intervention in School and Clinic, 29*(3), 151–155.

*Mills v. Board of Education of the District of Columbia.* (1972). 348 F. Supp. 866.

Mills, P. E., Cole, K. N., Jenkins, J. R., & Dale, P. S. (1998). Effects of differing levels of inclusion on preschoolers with disabilities. *Exceptional Children, 65*(1), 79–90.

Miltenberger, R. G., & Thiesse-Duffy, E. (1988). Evaluation of home-based programs for teaching personal safety skills to children. *Journal of Applied Behavior Analysis, 21,* 81–87.

Miner, C. A., & Bates, P. E. (1997). Person-centered transition planning. *Teaching Exceptional Children, 30*(1), 66–69.

Minner, S., Minner, J., & Lepich, J. (1990). Maintaining pupil performance data: A guide. *Intervention in School and Clinic, 26*(1), 32–37.

Mithaug, D. E., Martin, J. E., & Agran, M. (1987). Adaptability instruction: The goal of transitional programming. *Exceptional Children, 53*(6), 500–505.

Moody, S. W., Vaughn, S., & Schumm, J. S. (1997). Instructional grouping for reading: Teachers' views. *Remedial and Special Education, 18*(6), 347–356.

Moore, K. J., Fifield, M. B., Spira, D. A., & Scarlato, M. (1989). Child study team decision making in special education: Improving the process. *Remedial and Special Education, 10*(4), 50–58.

*Morales v. Turman,* 364 F. Supp. 166 (E.D., Texas, 1973).

Morningstar, M. E., Turnbull, A. P., & Turnbull, H. R. (1996). What do students with disabilities tell us about the importance of family involvement in the transition from school to adult life? *Exceptional Children, 62,* 249–260.

Morse, W. (1976). The helping teacher/crisis teacher concept. *Focus on Exceptional Children, 8*(4), 3–11.

Morse, W. (1994). Mental health professionals and teachers: How do the twain meet? *Beyond Behavior, 3*(2), 12–20.

Mostert, M. P. (1998). *Interpersonal collaboration in schools.* Boston: Allyn & Bacon.

Mount, B., & Zwernick, K. (1988). *It's never too early. It's never too late. A booklet about personal futures planning for persons with developmental disabilities, their families and friends, case managers, service providers and advocates.* St. Paul, MN: Metropolitan Council. (ERIC Document Reproduction Service No. ED 327 997).

Mouton, S. G., Hawkins, J., McPherson, R. H., & Copley, J. (1996). School attachment: Perspectives of low-attached high school students. *Educational Psychology, 16,* 297–304.

Mowder, B. A. (1994). Consultation with families of young, at-risk, and handicapped children. *Journal of Educational and Psychological Consultation, 5*(4), 309–320.

Muir, K. A., & Milan, M. A. (1982). Parent reinforcement for child achievement: The use of a lottery to maximize parent training effects. *Journal of Applied Behavior Analysis, 15*(3), 455–460.

Murdick, N. L., & Petch-Hogan, B. (1996). Inclusive classroom management: Using preintervention strategies. *Intervention in School and Clinic, 31*(3), 172–176.

Murphy, J. J. (1988). Contingency contracting in schools: A review. *Education and Treatment of Children, 11*(3), 257–269.

Muscott, H. S., & Gifford, T. (1994). Virtual reality and social skills training for students with behavioral disorders: Applications, challenges, and promising practices. *Education and Treatment of Children, 17*(3), 417–434.

Myles, B. S., Moran, M. R., Ormslee, C. K., & Downing, J. A. (1992). Guidelines for establishing and maintaining token economies. *Teaching Exceptional Children, 27,* 164–169.

Myles, B. S., & Simpson, R. L. (1989). Regular educators' modification preferences for mainstreaming mildly handicapped children. *Journal of Special Education, 22*(4), 479–491.

Myles, B. S., & Simpson, R. L. (1990). Mainstreaming modification preferences of parents of elementary-age children with learning disabilities. *Journal of Learning Disabilities, 23*(4), 234–239.

Nakano, Y., Kageyama, M., & Tsukuba, S. (1993). Using direct instruction to improve teacher performance, academic achievement, and classroom behavior in a Japanese public junior high school. *Education and Treatment of Children, 16*(3), 326–343.

Narayan, J. S., Heward, W. L., Gardner, R., Courson, F. H., & Omness, C. K. (1990). Using response cards to increase student participation in an elementary classroom. *Journal of Applied Behavior Analysis, 23*(4), 483–490.

National Education Association. (1994). *Toward inclusive classrooms.* Washington, DC: National Education Association Teacher-to-Teacher Books.

National Information Center for Children and Youth with Disabilities. (1997, February). Parenting a child with special needs: A guide to reading and resources. *News Digest* (2nd ed.).

National Joint Committee on Learning Disabilities. (1993a). Providing appropriate education for students with learning disabilities in regular education classrooms. *Journal of Learning Disabilities, 26*(5), 330–332.

National Joint Committee on Learning Disabilities. (1993b). A reaction to full inclusion: A reaffirmation of the right of students with learning disabilities to a continuum of services. *Journal of Learning Disabilities, 26*(9), 596.

National Middle School Association. (1995). *This we believe: Developmentally responsive middle level schools.* Columbus, OH: Author.

National Technical Institute for the Deaf Act of 1965, P.L. 89–36.

Neef, N. (1994). Editor's note. *Journal of Applied Behavior Analysis, 27*(2), 196.

Neel, R. S. (1981). How to put the consultant to work in consulting teaching. *Behavioral Disorders, 6*(2), 86–91.

Nelson, C. M., & Stevens, K. B. (1979). *Mainstreaming behaviorally disordered children through teacher consultation.* Paper presented at the Third Annual Conference on Severe Behavior Disorders of Children and Youth, Tempe, AZ.

Nelson, J. R., Smith, D. J., & Colvin, G. (1995). The effects of a peer-mediated self-evaluation procedure on the recess behavior of students with behavior problems. *Remedial and Special Education, 16*(2), 117–126.

Nevin, A. (1989). Cooperative learning with adults. *Teaching Exceptional Children* (Spring), 66–67.

Nevin, A., & Hood, R. (1998, August). Face to face and cyberspace: Impact on achievement and attitudes towards teaching students with special needs: A systematic evaluation of the Internet as an instructional delivery model. Paper presented at the Annual Conference of the Association for Teacher Education Europe, Limerick, Ireland.

Nevin, A., Thousand, J., Paolucci-Whitcomb, P., & Villa, R. (1990). Collaborative consultation: Empowering public school personnel to provide heterogeneous schooling for all—Or who rang the bell? *Journal of Educational and Psychological Consultation, 1*(1), 41–67.

Nevin, A., Thousand, J. S., & Villa, R. A. (1993). Establishing collaborative ethics and practices. *Journal of Educational and Psychological Consultation, 4*(4), 293–304.

Niemeyer, J. A., & Fox, J. (1990). Reducing aggressive behavior during car riding through parent-implemented DRO and fading procedures. *Education and Treatment of Children, 13*(1), 21–35.

Noel, B., Hess, D., & Nichols, P. (1996). Families of children with learning disabilities: A potential teaching resource. *Intervention in School and Clinic, 32*(1), 17–20.

North Dakota Study Group on Evaluation. (1977). *First California Conference on Educational Evaluation and Public Policy, 1976.* Grand Forks: University of North Dakota, Center for Teaching and Learning.

Nowacek, E. J. (1992). Professionals talk about teaching together: Interviews with five collaborating teachers. *Intervention in School and Clinic, 27*(5), 262–276.

*Oberti v. Board of Education of the Borough of Clementon School District,* 789 F. Supp. 1322, 75 Ed. Law Rep. 258, (D.N.J. 1992).

Obiakor, F. E., & Utley, C. A. (1997). Rethinking preservice preparation for teachers in the learning disabilities field: Workable multicultural strategies. *Learning Disabilities Research & Practice, 12*(2), 100–106.

O'Dell, S. L. (1985). Progress in parent training. In M. Henson, R. M. Eisler, & P. M. Miller (Eds.), *Progress in behavior modification* (vol. 19, pp. 57–108). New York: Academic Press.

Odom, S. L., & Karnes, M. B. (Eds.). (1988). *Early intervention for infants and children with handicaps: An empirical base.* Baltimore: Paul H. Brookes.

Odom, S. L., & McEvoy, M. A. (1990). Mainstreaming at the preschool level: Potential barriers and tasks for the field. *Topics in Early Childhood Special Education, 10*(2), 48–61.

Okyere, B. A., Heron, T. E., & Goddard, Y. (1997). Effects of self-correction on the acquisition, maintenance, and generalization of the written spelling of elementary school children. *Journal of Behavioral Education, 7*(1), 51–69.

O'Leary, E. (1998). *Transition: Terms and concepts.* Des Moines, IA: Mountain Plains Regional Resource Center.

Olmi, D. J., Walker, D. W., & Ruthven, A. J. (1995). Extended school services: Prediction, description, and impact of judicial precedence. *Journal of Special Education, 29*(1), 72–83.

O'Malia, M. C., & Rosenberg, M. (1994). Effects of cooperative homework teams on the acquisition of mathematical skills by secondary students with mild disabilities. *Exceptional Children, 60,* 538–548.

Opper, S. (1977). Piaget's clinical method. *Journal of Children's Mathematical Behavior, 1*(4), 90–107.

O'Reilly, M. F. (1997). Functional analysis of episodic self-injury correlated with recurrent otitis media. *Journal of Applied Behavior Analysis, 30*(1), 165–167.

Orelove, F. P., & Sobsey, D. (1996). *Educating children with multiple disabilities: A transdisciplinary approach* (3rd ed.). Baltimore: Paul H. Brookes.

Ortiz, A. A. (1988). Evaluating educational contexts in which language minority students are served. *Bilingual Special Education Newsletter, 7,* 1, 3–4.

Ortiz, A. A., & Garcia, S. B. (1995). Serving Hispanic students with learning disabilities: Recommended policies and practices. *Urban Education, 29*(4), 471–481.

Ortiz, A. A., & Wilkerson, C. Y. (1989). Adapting IEPs for limited English proficient students. *Academic Therapy, 24*(5), 564–566.

Ortiz, A. A., & Yates, J. R. (1989). Staffing and the development of individualized educational programs for the bilingual exceptional student. In L. M. Baca & H. T. Cervantes (Eds.), *The bilingual special education interface* (2nd ed., pp. 183–203). Columbus, OH: Merrill.

Osborne, A. G., Jr. (1988). The Supreme Court's interpretation of the Education for All Handicapped Children Act. *Remedial and Special Education, 9*(3), 21–25.

Osborne, A. G., Jr., & Dimattia, P. (1994). The IDEA's least restrictive environment mandate: Legal implications. *Exceptional Children, 61*(1), 6–14.

O'Shea, D. J., & O'Shea, L. J. (1998). Learning to include: Lessons learned from a high school without special education services. *Teaching Exceptional Children, 31*(1), 40–48.

O'Shea, D. J., O'Shea, L. J., & Nowocien, D. (1993). Parent-teacher relationships in school renewal and educational reform. *LD Forum, 18*(3), 43–46.

Ovando, C. J., & Collier, V. P. (1985). *Bilingual and ESL classrooms: Teaching in multicultural contexts.* New York: McGraw-Hill.

Paclawskyj, T. R., & Vollmer, T. R. (1995). Reinforcer assessment for children with developmental disabilities and visual impairments. *Journal of Applied Behavior Analysis, 28*(2), 219–224.

Pajares, F. (1997). Current directions in self-efficacy research. In M. L. Maehr & P. R. Pintrich (Eds.), *Advances in motivation and achievement* (pp. 1–49). Greenwich, CT: JAI Press.

Palmer, D. S., Borthwick-Duffy, S. A., & Widaman, K. (1998). Parent perceptions of inclusive practices for their children with significant cognitive disabilities. *Exceptional Children, 64*(2), 271–282.

*Panitch v. Wisconsin* (1974), supra n. 8.

Paolucci-Whitcomb, P., & Nevin, A. (1985). Preparing consulting teachers through a collaborative approach between university faculty and field-based consulting teachers. *Teacher Education and Special Education, 8*(3), 133–143.

Pappas, V. C. (1994). Interagency collaboration: An interdisciplinary application. In H. G. Garner & F. P. Orelove (Eds.), *Teamwork in human services: Models and applications across the lifespan* (pp. 6–85). Boston: Butterworth-Heinemann.

Parette, H. P., Brotherson, M. J., Hourcade, J. J., & Bradley, R. H. (1996). Family-centered assistive technology assessment. *Intervention in School and Clinic, 32*(2), 104–112.

Parson, L. R., & Heward, W. L. (1979). Training peers to tutor: Evaluation of a tutor training package for primary learning disabled students. *Journal of Applied Behavior Analysis, 12,* 309–310.

Parsons, R. D., & Meyers, J. (1984). *Developing consultation skills.* San Francisco: Jossey-Bass.

Pasanella, A. L., & Volkmor, C. B. (1981). *Teaching handicapped students in the mainstream: Coming back or never leaving.* Columbus, OH: Merrill.

Patching, W., Kameenui, E. J., Carnine, D., Gersten, R., & Colvin, G. (1983). Direct instruction in critical reading skills. *Reading Research Quarterly, 18,* 406–418.

Patterson, G. R. (1975). *Families: Application of social learning to family life.* Champaign, IL: Research Press.

Patton, J. (1994). Practical recommendations for using homework with students with learning disabilities. *Journal of Learning Disabilities, 27*(9), 570–578.

Patton, J., Beirne-Smith, M., & Payne, J. (1990). *Mental retardation* (3rd ed.). Columbus, OH: Merrill.

Pearl, R., Donahue, M., & Bryan, T. (1986). Social relationships of learning disabled children. In J. K. Torgesen & B. Y. L. Wong (Eds.), *Psychological and educational perspectives on learning disabilities* (pp. 193–224). Orlando, FL: Academic Press.

Pearl, R., Farmer, T. W., Van Acker, R., Rodkin, P. C., Bost, K. K., Coe, M., & Henley, W. (1999). The social integration of students with mild disabilities in general education classrooms: Peer group membership and peer-assisted social behavior. *Elementary School Journal, 99*(2), 167–185.

Pedron, N. A., & Evans, S. B. (1990). Modifying classroom teachers' acceptance of the consulting teacher model. *Journal of Educational and Psychological Consultation, 1*(2), 189–200.

*Pennsylvania Association for Retarded Children v. Commonwealth of Pennsylvania.* (1972), 343 F. Supp. 279.

Pepper, F. C. (1976). Teaching the American Indian child in mainstream settings. In R. L. Jones (Ed.), *Mainstreaming and the minority child* (pp. 133–158). Reston, VA: Council for Exceptional Children.

Perl, J. (1995). Improving relationship skills for parent conferences. *Teaching Exceptional Children, 28*(1), 29–31.

Perry, M., & Garber, M. (1993). Technology helps parents teach their children with developmental delays. *Teaching Exceptional Children, 25*(2), 8–11.

Peters, M., & Heron, T. E. (1993). When the best is not good enough: An examination of best practice. *Journal of Special Education, 26*(4), 371–385.

Peters-Walters, S. (1998). Accessible Web site design. *Teaching Exceptional Children, 30*(5), 42–47.

Phillips, L., Sapona, R. H., & Lubic, B. L. (1995). Developing partnerships in inclusive education: One school's approach. *Intervention in School and Clinic, 30*(5), 262–272.

Phillips, N. B., Fuchs, L. S., & Fuchs, D. (1994). Effects of classwide curriculum-based measurement and peer tutoring: A collaborative researcher-practitioner interview study. *Journal of Learning Disabilities, 27*(7), 420–434.

Phillips, V., & McCullough, L. (1990). Consultation-based programming: Instituting the collaborative ethic in schools. *Exceptional Children, 56*(4), 291–304.

Piazza, C.C., Fisher, W. W., Hagopian, L.P., Bowman, L. G., & Toole, L. (1996). Using a choice assessment to predict reinforcer effectiveness. *Journal of Applied Behavior Analysis, 29*(1), 1–9.

Picciotto, L. P. (1996). *Student-led parent conferences.* New York: Scholastic Professional Books.

Pickett, A. L., & Gerlach, K. (Eds.). (1997). *Supervising paraeducators in school settings: A team approach.* Austin, TX: PRO-ED.

Pierce, M. M., & Van Houten, R. (1984). Preparing materials for peer tutoring. *The Directive Teacher, 6*(2), 24–25.

Pilewskie, A. A. (1995). *Effects of peer tutoring on the percussion instrument performance of a student with moderate developmental disabilities.* Unpublished master's thesis, The Ohio State University, Columbus.

Plata, M. (1993). Using Spanish-speaking interpreters in special education. *Remedial and Special Education, 14,* 19–24.

*Polk v. Central Susquehanna Intermediate Unit 16.* (1988). *1988–89 Education for the Handicapped Law Report.* Court of Appeals for the Third Circuit.

Polloway, E. A., Bursuck, W. D., Jayanthi, M., Epstein, M. H., & Nelson, J. S. (1996). Treatment acceptability: Determining appropriate interventions within inclusive classrooms. *Intervention in School and Clinic, 31*(3), 133–144.

Polloway, E. A., Cronin, M. E., & Patton, J. R. (1986). The efficacy of group versus one-to-one instruction: A review. *Remedial and Special Education, 7*(1), 22–30.

Polloway, E. A., Epstein, M. H., Bursuck, W. D., Jayanthi, M., & Cumblad, C. (1994). Homework practices of general education teachers. *Journal of Learning Disabilities, 27*(8), 500–509.

Polloway, E. A., Patton, J. R., Payne, J. S., & Payne, R. A. (1989). *Strategies for teaching learners with special needs* (4th ed.). Columbus, OH: Merrill.

Polsgrove, L., & McNeil, M. (1989). The consultation process: Research and practice. *Remedial and Special Education, 10*(1), 6–13, 20.

Pomplun, M. (1997). When students with disabilities participate in cooperative groups. *Exceptional Children, 64*(1), 49–58.

Potter, M. L., & Wamre, H. M. (1990). Curriculum-based measurement and developmental reading models: Opportunities for cross validation. *Exceptional Children, 57*(1), 16–25.

Powell, D. E. (1990). Home-based intervention for preschoolers with serious emotional disturbances and autism. *Preventing School Failure, 34*(4), 41–45.

Powers, L. E. (1996). *TAKE CHARGE transition planning project.* Grant H158U50001, U.S. Department of Education and Oregon Health Sciences. Portland: Oregon Health Sciences University.

Prasse, D. P. (1986). Litigation and special education: An introduction. *Exceptional Children, 52*(4), 311–312.

Prasse, D. P. (1990). Best practices in legal and ethical considerations. In A. Thomas & J. Grimes (Eds.), *Best practices in school psychology II* (pp. 469–489). Washington, DC: National Association of School Psychologists.

Prater, M. A., Bruhl, S., & Serna, L. (1998). Acquiring social skills through cooperative learning and teacher-directed instruction. *Remedial and Special Education, 19*(3), 160–172.

Prater, M. A., Serna, L., & Nakamura, K. K. (1999). Impact of peer teaching on the acquisition of social skills by adolescents with learning disabilities. *Education and Treatment of Children, 22,* 19–35.

Price, M., & Goodman, L. (1980). Individualized Education Programs: A cost study. *Exceptional Children, 46*(6), 446–454.

Project Vision. (1993). *Resistance to change* (videotape). Mocow: University of Idaho, Center on Disabilities and Human Development.

Pryzwansky, W. B., & Noblit, G. W. (1990). Understanding and improving consultation practice: The qualitative case study approach. *Journal of Educational and Psychological Consultation, 1*(4), 293–307.

Pugach, M. C., & Johnson, L. J. (1988). Peer collaboration. *Teaching Exceptional Children, 20*(3), 75–77.

Pugach, M. C., & Johnson, L. J. (1989). Prereferral interventions: Progress, problems, and challenges. *Exceptional Children, 56*(3), 217–226.

Pugach, M. C., & Johnson, L.J. (1995). *Collaborative practitioners, collaborative schools.* Denver: Love.

Purkey, S. C., & Smith, M. S. (1985). School reform: The district policy implications of the effective schools literature. *Elementary School Journal, 85,* 353–389.

Putnam, M. L., Deshler, D. D., & Schumaker, J. B. (1993). The investigation of setting demands: A missing link in learning strategy instruction. In L. J. Meltzer (Ed.), *Strategy assessment for students with learning disabilities.* Austin, TX: PRO-ED.

Quadland, C., Rybacki, S., Kellogg, A., & Hall, S. (1996). *A parent's guide to transition for youth with disabilities.* Madison: Wisconsin's Design for Transition Success, Department of Public Instruction and Division of Vocational Rehabilitation.

Rademacher, J. A., Callahan, K., & Pederson-Seelye, V. A. (1998). How do your classroom rules measure up? Guidelines for developing an effective rule management routine. *Intervention in School and Clinic, 33*(5), 284–289.

Raffaniello, E. M. (1981). Competent consultation: The collaborative approach. In M. J. Curtis & J. E. Zins (Eds.), *The theory and practice of school consultation* (pp. 44–54). Springfield, IL: Charles C. Thomas.

Raimondi, S. L. (1994). Challenging behaviors: Helping the regular educator change misbehaviors of students with learning disabilities. *LD Forum, 19*(3), 38–41.

Rainforth, B., & York-Barr, J. (1997). *Collaborative teams for students with severe disabilities: Integrating therapy and educational services.* (2nd ed.). Baltimore: Paul H. Brookes.

Ramey, C. T., & Ramey, S. L. (1992). Effective early intervention. *Mental Retardation, 30,* 337–345.

Rankin, J. L., & Aksamit, D. L. (1994). Perceptions of elementary, junior high, and high school student assistant team coordinators, team members, and teachers. *Journal of Educational and Psychological Consultation, 5,* 229–256.

Ratnesar, R. (1999). The homework ate the family. *Time, 153*(3), 54–63.

Raywid, M. A. (1993). Finding time for collaboration. *Educational Leadership, 51*(1), 30–34.

Reed, F., & Monda-Amaya, L. E. (1995). Preparing preservice general educators for inclusion: A survey of teacher preparation programs in Illinois. *Teacher Education and Special Education, 18*(4), 262–274.

Reed, H., Thomas, E., Sprague, J. R., & Horner, R. H. (1997). The student guided functional assessment interview: An analysis of student and teacher agreement. *Journal of Behavioral Education, 7*(1), 33–49.

Reeve, P. T., & Hallahan, D. P. (1994). Practical questions about collaboration between general and special educators. *Focus on Exceptional Children, 26*(7), 1–11.

Rehabilitation Act of 1973, July 26, 1973, P.L. 93–112.

Reid, R. (1996). Research in self-monitoring with students with learning disabilities: The present, the prospects, and the pitfalls. *Journal of Learning Disabilities, 29*(3), 317–331.

Reisberg, L. (1988). Developing a consulting model of service delivery in special education. In J. F. West (Ed.), *School consultation: Interdisciplinary perspectives on theory, research, training, and practice* (pp. 201–211). Austin, TX: Association of Educational and Psychological Consultants.

Reisberg, L. (1990). Curriculum evaluation and modification: An effective teaching perspective. *Intervention in School and Clinic, 26*(2), 99–105.

Reisberg, L., Brodigan, D., & Williams, G. J. (1991). Classroom management: Implementing a system for students with BD. *Intervention in School and Clinic, 27*(1), 31–38.

Reisberg, L., & Wolf, R. (1986). Developing a consulting program in special education: Implementation and interventions. *Focus on Exceptional Children, 19*(3), 1–14.

Reisberg, L., & Wolf, R. (1988). Instructional strategies for special education consultants. *Remedial and Special Education, 9*(6), 29–40, 47.

Renehan, E. J., Jr. (1995). *1001 really cool Web sites.* Las Vegas, NV: Jamsa Press.

Repp, A. C., Felce, D., & Barton, L. (1991). The effects of initial interval size on the efficacy of DRO schedules of reinforcement. *Exceptional Children, 57*(5), 417–425.

Reschly, D. J. (1989). Alternative delivery systems: Legal and ethical influences. In J. L. Graden, J. E. Zins, & M. J. Curtis (Eds.), *Alternative educational delivery systems: Enhancing instructional options for all students* (pp. 525–552). Washington, DC: National Association of School Psychologists.

Reynolds, M. C., & Rosen, S. W. (1976). Special education: Past, present, and future. *Educational Forum, 40,* 551–562.

Reynolds, M. C., Wang, M. C., & Walberg, H. J. (1987). The necessary restructuring of special and regular education. *Exceptional Children, 53,* 391–398.

Rhode, G., Jenson, W. R., & Reavis, H. K. (1998). *The tough kid book: Practical classroom management strategies.* Longmont, CO: Sopris West.

Rice, F. P. (1996). *The adolescent: Development, relationships, and culture* (8th ed.). Boston: Allyn & Bacon.

Richman, G. S., Harrison, K. A., & Summers, J. A. (1995). Assessing and modifying parent responses to their children's noncompliance. *Education and Treatment of Children, 18*(2), 105–116.

Rieth, H. J., & Semmel, M. I. (1991). Use of computer-assisted instruction in the regular classroom. In G. Stoner, M. R. Shinn, & H. M. Walker (Eds.), *Interventions for achievement and behavior problems* (pp. 215–239). Washington, DC: National Association of School Psychologists.

Rindfuss, J. B. (1997). *Using guided notes and response cards to improve quiz and exam scores in an eighth grade American history class.* Unpublished master's thesis, The Ohio State University, Columbus.

Risley, T. R., Clark, H. B., & Cataldo, M. F. (1976). Behavior technology for the normal middle-class family. In E. J. Marsh, L. A. Hamerlynick, & L. E. Handy (Eds.), *Behavior modification and families* (pp. 34–60). New York: Brunner/Mazel.

Rivera, B. D., & Rogers-Adkinson, D. (1997). Culturally sensitive interventions: Social skills training with children and parents from culturally and linguistically diverse backgrounds. *Intervention in School and Clinic, 33*(2), 75–80.

Robbins, J. R., & Gutkin, T. B. (1994). Consultee and client remedial and preventive outcomes following consultation: Some mixed empirical results and directions for future researchers. *Journal of Educational and Psychological Consultation, 5*(2), 149–167.

Roberts, C., Pratt, C., & Leach, D. (1991). Classroom and playground interaction of students with and without disabilities. *Exceptional Children, 57*(3), 212–224.

Robinson, P. W., Newby, T. J., & Ganzell, S. L. (1981). A token system for a class of underachieving hyperactive children. *Journal of Applied Behavior Analysis, 14,* 307–315.

Robinson, V. M., Cameron, M. M., & Raethel, A. M. (1985). Negotiation of a consultative role for school psychologists: A case study. *Journal of School Psychology, 23,* 43–49.

Roderique, T. W., Polloway, E. A., Cumblad, C., Epstein, M. H., & Bursuck, W. D. (1994). Homework: A survey of policies in the United States. *Journal of Learning Disabilities, 27*(8), 481–487.

Rogers, C. R. (1942). *Counseling and psychotherapy.* Boston: Houghton Mifflin.

Rogers, C. R. (1951). *Client-centered therapy.* Boston: Houghton Mifflin.

Rogers, C. R. (1959). A theory of therapy, personality and interpersonal relationships, as developed in the client-centered framework. In S. Koch (Ed.), *Psychology: A study of science: Vol. II Formulations of the personal and social concept.* New York: McGraw-Hill.

Rogers, C. R. (1965). *Client-centered therapy.* Boston: Houghton Mifflin.

Rogers, J. (1993, May). The inclusion revolution. *Phi Delta Kappan, 11,* 1–6.

*Roncker v. Walter,* 700 F. 2d 1058 (6th Cir. 1983), cert. denied, 464 U.S. 864 (1983).

Rose, T. L. (1989). Corporal punishment with mildly handicapped students: Five years later. *Remedial and Special Education, 10,* 43–52.

Rosenfield, S. (1987). *Instructional consultation.* Hillsdale, NJ: Erlbaum.

Rossmiller, R. A., Hale, J. A., & Frohreich, L. E. (1970). *Educational programs for exceptional children: Resource configurations and costs.* (National Educational Finance Project Study No. 2). Madison: Department of Educational Administration, University of Wisconsin.

Ruef, M. B., Higgins, C., Glaeser, R. J. C., & Patnode, M. (1998). Positive behavioral support: Strategies for teachers. *Intervention in School and Clinic, 34*(1), 21–32.

Ruiz, N. T. (1995). The social construction of ability and disability: II. Optimal and at-risk lessons in a bilingual special education classroom. *Journal of Learning Disabilities, 28*(8), 491–502.

Ryan, S., & Paterna, L. (1997). Junior high can be inclusive: Using natural supports and cooperative learning. *Teaching Exceptional Children* (Nov/Dec), 36–41.

Sabornie, E. J., & Kauffman, J. M. (1985). Regular classroom sociometric status of emotionally disturbed adolescents. *Behavioral Disorders, 10,* 191–197.

Sabornie, E. J., & Kauffman, J. M. (1986). Social acceptance of learning disabled adolescents. *Learning Disability Quarterly, 9*(1), 55–60.

Safer, N., & Hobbs, B. (1980). Developing, implementing, and evaluating individualized education programs. *School Psychology Review, 9*(3), 212–220.

Safran, S. P., & Safran, J. S. (1996). Intervention assistance programs and prereferral teams. *Remedial and Special Education, 17*(6), 363–369.

Sage, D. (Ed.). (1993). It means more than mainstreaming . . . *Inclusion Times, 1*(1), 2.

Sailor, W. (1991). Special education in the restructured school. *Remedial and Special Education, 12*(6), 8–22.

Sailor, W., Anderson, J., Halvorsen, A. T., Doering, K., Filler, J., & Goetz, L. (1989). *The comprehensive local school: Regular education for all students with disabilities.* Baltimore: Paul H. Brookes.

Sale, P., & Carey, D. M. (1995). The sociometric status of students with disabilities in a full-inclusion school. *Exceptional Children, 62*(1), 6–19.

Salend, S. J. (1984). Factors contributing to the development of successful mainstreaming programs. *Exceptional Children, 50*(5), 409–416.

Salend, S. J. (1987). Group-oriented behavior management strategies. *Teaching Exceptional Children, 20*(1), 53–55.

Salend, S. J. (1998). Using portfolios to assess student performance. *Teaching Exceptional Children, 31*(2), 36–43.

Salend, S. J., Dorney, J. A., & Mazo, M. (1997). The roles of bilingual special educators in creating inclusive classrooms. *Remedial and Special Education, 18*(1), 54–64.

Salend, S. J., & Duhaney, L.M.G. (1999). The impact of inclusion of students with and without disabilities and their educators. *Remedial and Special Education, 20*(2), 114–126.

Salend, S. J., & Gajria, M. (1995). Increasing the homework completion rates of students with mild disabilities. *Remedial and Special Education, 16*(5), 271–278.

Salend, S. J., Johansen, M., Mumper, J., Chase, A. S., Pike, K. M., & Dorner, J. A. (1997). Cooperative teaching: The voices of two teachers. *Remedial and Special Education, 18*(1), 3–11.

Salend, S. J., & Lamb, E. A. (1986). Effectiveness of a group-managed interdependent contingency system. *Journal of Learning Disabilities, 19,* 268–273.

Salend, S. J., & Lutz, J. G. (1984). Mainstreaming or mainlining: A competency-based approach to mainstreaming. *Journal of Learning Disabilities, 17*(1), 27–29.

Salend, S. J., & Taylor, L. (1993). Working with families: A cross-cultural perspective. *Remedial and Special Education, 14*(5), 25–32, 39.

Salisbury, C. L. (1991). Mainstreaming during the early childhood years. *Exceptional Children, 58*(2), 146–155.

Salisbury, C. L., Gallucci, C., Palombaro, M. M., & Peck, C. A. (1995). Strategies that promote social relations among elementary students with and without severe disabilities in inclusive schools. *Exceptional Children, 62*(2), 125–137.

Salvia, J., & Munson, S. (1986). Attitudes of regular education teachers toward mainstreaming mildly handicapped students. In C. J. Meisel (Ed.), *Mainstreaming handicapped children: Outcomes, controversies, and new directions* (pp. 111–128). Hillsdale, NJ: Erlbaum.

Sandoval, J., Lambert, N., & Davis, J. M. (1977). Consultation from the consultee's perspective. *Journal of School Psychology, 15*(4), 334–342.

*San Francisco Unified School District v. State,* 182 Cal. Rptr. 525 (1982).

Santos, K., & Rettig, M. D. (1999). Going on the block: Meeting the needs of students with disabilities in high schools with block scheduling. *Teaching Exceptional Children, 31*(3), 54–59.

Sapon-Shevin, M. (1979). *The ethics of group contingencies.* Paper presented at the Annual Meeting of the Association for Behavior Analysis, Dearborn, MI.

Sapon-Shevin, M. (1990). Student support through cooperative learning. In W. Stainback & S. Stainback (Eds.),

*Support networks for inclusive schooling* (pp. 65–79). Baltimore: Paul H. Brookes.

Sarason, S. B. (1982). *The culture of the school and the problem of change* (2nd ed.). Boston: Allyn & Bacon.

Saski, J., Swicegood, P., & Carter, J. (1983). Notetaking formats for learning disabled adolescents. *Learning Disability Quarterly, 6,* 265–272.

Sasso, G. M., Reimers, T. M., Cooper, L. J., Wacker, D., Berg, W., Steege, M., Kelly, L., & Allaire, A. (1992). Use of descriptive and experimental analyses to identify the functional properties of aberrant behavior in school settings. *Journal of Applied Behavior Analysis, 25*(4), 809–821.

Schaeffler, C. (1988). Making toys accessible for children with cerebral palsy. *Teaching Exceptional Children, 20,* 26–28.

Schein, E. H. (1969). *Process consultation: Its role in organizational development.* Reading, MA: Addison-Wesley.

Schloss, P. J. (1987). Self-management strategies for adolescents entering the work force. *Teaching Exceptional Children, 19*(4), 39–43.

Schloss, P. J., Kobza, S. A., & Alper, S. (1997). The use of peer tutoring for the acquisition of functional math skills among students with moderate retardation. *Education and Treatment of Children, 20,* 189–208.

Schmuck, R. A. (1995). Process consultation and organization development today. *Journal of Educational and Psychological Consultation, 6*(3), 207–215.

Schmuck, R. A., & Runkel, P. J. (1972). Organizational training. In R. A. Schmuck (Ed.), *Handbook of organizational development in schools.* Palo Alto, CA: Mayfield.

Schmuck, R. A., & Runkel, P. J. (1985). *The handbook of organizational development in schools* (3rd ed.). Palo Alto, CA: Mayfield.

Schoor, L. B. (1988). *Within our reach: Breaking the cycle of the disadvantaged.* New York: Anchor Books.

Schrader, B., & Valus, V. (1990). Disabled learners as able teachers: A cross-age tutoring project. *Academic Therapy, 25,* 589–597.

Schulte, A. C., Osborne, S. S., & Kauffman, J. M. (1993). Teacher responses to two types of consultative special education services. *Journal of Educational and Psychological Consultation, 4*(1), 1–27.

Schulze, K. A., Rule, S., & Innocenti, M. S. (1989). Coincidental teaching: Parents promoting social skills at home. *Teaching Exceptional Children, 21*(2), 24–27.

Schumaker, J. B., Deshler, D. D., Alley, G. R., & Warner, M. M. (1983). Toward the development of an intervention model for learning disabled adolescents: The University of Kansas Institute. *Exceptional Education Quarterly, 4*(1), 45–74.

Schumaker, J. B., Deshler, D. D., Nolan, S. M., & Alley, G. R. (1994). *The self-questioning strategy.* Lawrence: University of Kansas.

Schumm, J. S., & Vaughn, S. (1991). Making adaptations for mainstreamed students: General classroom teachers' perspectives. *Remedial and Special Education, 12*(4), 18–27.

Schumm, J. S., Vaughn, S., Gordon, J., & Rothlein, L. (1994). General education teachers' beliefs, skills, and practices in planning for mainstreamed students with learning disabilities. *Teacher Education and Special Education, 17*(1), 22–37.

Schumm, J. S., Vaughn, S., & Harris, J. (1997). Pyramid power for collaborative planning. *Teaching Exceptional Children, 29*(6), 62–66.

Scott, B. J., Vitale, M. R., & Masten, W. G. (1998). Implementing instructional adaptations for students with disabilities in inclusive classrooms. *Remedial and Special Education, 19*(2), 106–119.

Scruggs, T. E., & Mastropieri, M. A. (1996). Teacher perceptions of mainstreaming/inclusion, 1958–1995: A research synthesis. *Exceptional Children, 63*(1), 59–74.

Seabaugh, G. O., & Schumaker, J. B. (1994). The effects of self-regulation training on the academic productivity of secondary students with learning problems. *Journal of Behavioral Education, 4*(1), 109–133.

Searcy, S., Lee-Lawson, C., & Trombino, B. (1995). Mentoring new leadership roles for parents of children with disabilities. *Remedial and Special Education, 16*(5), 307–314.

Shaper Walters, L. (1998, May/June). The bilingual education debate. *Harvard Education Letter, 14*(3), 1–4.

Sharan, S., & Hertz-Lazarowitz, R. (1980). A group-investigation method of cooperative learning in the classroom. In S. Sharan, P. Hare, C. D. Webb, & R. Hertz-Lazarowitz (Eds.), *Cooperation in education* (pp. 14–46). Provo, UT: Brigham Young University Press.

Sharpe, M. N., York, J. L., & Knight, J. (1994). Effects of inclusion on the academic performance of classmates without disabilities: A preliminary study. *Remedial and Special Education, 15*(5), 281–287.

Shea, T. M., & Bauer, A. M. (1985). *Parents and teachers of exceptional students: A handbook for involvement.* Boston: Allyn & Bacon.

Sheridan, S. M., & Colton, D. L. (1994). Conjoint behavioral consultation: A review and case study. *Journal of Educational and Psychological Consultation, 5*(3), 211–228.

Sheridan, S. M., Welch, M., & Orme, S. F. (1996). Is consultation effective? A review of outcome research. *Remedial and Special Education, 17*(6), 341–354.

Shields, J., & Heron, T. E. (1989). Teaching organizational skills to students with learning disabilities. *Teaching Exceptional Children, 21,* 8–13.

Shields, J., Heron, T. E., Rubenstein, C. L., & Katz, E. R. (1995). The eco-triadic model of educational consultation for students with cancer. *Education and Treatment of Children, 18*(2), 184–200.

Short, R. J., Talley, R. C., & Kolbe, L. J. (1999). Special issue: Integrating education, health, and social services for young people. *Journal of Educational and Psychological Consultation, 10*(3), 193–200.

Shriner, J. G., & Yell, M. L. (1996). Legal and policy developments in the education of students with emotional/

behavioral disorders. *Education and Treatment of Children, 19*(3), 351–385.

Siders, J. Z., Riall, A., Bennett, T. C., & Judd, D. (1987). Training leadership personnel in early intervention: A transdisciplinary approach. *Teacher Education and Special Education, 10,* 161–170.

Sileo, T. W., & Prater, M. A. (1998). Creating classroom environments that address the linguistic and cultural backgrounds of students with disabilities. *Remedial and Special Education, 19*(6), 323–337.

Sileo, T. W., Sileo, A. P., & Prater, M. A. (1996). Parent and professional partnerships in special education: Multicultural considerations. *Intervention in School and Clinic, 31*(3), 145–153.

Simpson, R. L. (1990). *Conferencing parents of exceptional children* (2nd ed.). Austin, TX: PRO-ED.

Simpson, R. L. (1996). *Working with parents and families of exceptional children and youth: Techniques for successful conferencing and collaboration.* Austin, TX: PRO-ED.

Simpson, R. L. (1998). Behavior modification for children and youth with exceptionalities: Application of best practice methods. *Intervention in School and Clinic, 33*(4), 219–226.

Singletary, E. E., Collings, G. D., & Dennis, H. F. (1978). *Law briefs on litigation and the rights of exceptional children, youth, and adults.* Washington, DC: University Press of America.

Sitlington, P. L. (1996). Transition to living: The neglected component of transition programming for individuals with learning disabilities. *Journal of Learning Disabilities, 29*(1), 31–39, 52.

Sitlington, P. L., Neubert, D. A., & Leconte, P. J. (1997). Transition assessment: The position of the Division on Career Development and Transition. *CDEI, 20*(1), 69–79.

Skiba, R. J., & Deno, S. L. (1991). Terminology and behavior reduction: The case against "punishment." *Exceptional Children, 57*(4), 298–313.

Skinner, M. E. (1979). *Effects of an in-service program on the attitudes, knowledge, and student-teacher interaction patterns of regular classroom teachers.* Unpublished master's thesis, The Ohio State University, Columbus.

Slavin, R. E. (1983). *Cooperative learning.* New York: Longman.

Slavin, R. E. (1987). *Cooperative learning: Student teams* (2nd ed.). Washington, DC: National Education Association.

Slavin, R. E. (1990). *Cooperative learning: Theory, research, and practice.* Englewood Cliffs, NJ: Prentice-Hall.

Slavin, R. E. (1991). Cooperative learning and group contingencies. *Journal of Behavioral Education, 1*(1), 105–115.

Sloane, H. N. (1988). *The good kid book: How to solve the 16 most common behavior problems.* Champaign, IL: Research Press.

Smith, E. P., Connell, C. M., Wright, G., Sizer, M., Norman, J. M., Hurley, A., & Walker, S. N. (1997). An ecological model of home, school, and community partnerships: Implications for research and practice. *Journal of Educational and Psychological Consultation, 8*(4), 339–360.

Smith, J. K. (1983a). Quantitative versus interpretive: The problem of conducting social inquiry. In E. House (Ed.), *Philosophy of evaluation* (pp. 27–51). San Francisco: Jossey-Bass.

Smith, J. K. (1983b). Quantitative versus qualitative research: An attempt to clarify the issue. *Educational Researcher, 12*(3), 6–13.

Smith, L. M. (1979). An evolving logic of participant observation, educational ethnography, and other case studies. In L. S. Shulman (Ed.), *Review of research in education: No. 6* (pp. 316–377). Itasca, IL: F. E. Peacock.

Smith, M. A., & Misra, A. (1994). Behavior management: Using group contingencies with students with learning disabilities. *LD Forum, 20*(1), 17–20.

Smith, S. J., Martin, K. F., & Lloyd, J. W. (1998). Preparing prospective teachers on the Web. *Teaching Exceptional Children, 30*(5), 60–64.

Smith, S. W. (1990a). Comparison of Individualized Education Programs (IEPs) of students with behavior disorders and learning disabilities. *Journal of Special Education, 24*(1), 85–100.

Smith, S. W. (1990b). Individualized Education Programs (IEPs) in special education—From intent to acquiescence. *Exceptional Children, 57*(1), 6–14.

Smull, M. W., & Harrison, S. (1992, September). *Supporting people with severe reputations in the community.* (Available from National Association of State Mental Retardation Program Directors, Inc., 113 Oronoco Street, Alexandria, VA 22314).

Sontag, J., & Schacht, R. (1994). An ethnic comparison of parent participation and information needs in early intervention. *Exceptional Children, 16*(5), 422–431.

Soodak, L. C., & Erwin, E. J. (1995). Parents, professionals, and inclusive education: A call for collaboration. *Journal of Educational and Psychological Consultation, 6*(3), 257–276.

Soodak, L. C., Podell, D. M., & Lehman, L. R. (1998). Teacher, student, and school attributes as predictors of teachers' responses to inclusion. *Journal of Special Education, 31*(4), 480–497.

Soo-Hoo, T. (1998). Applying frame of reference and reframing techniques to improve school consultation in multicultural settings. *Journal of Educational and Psychological Consultation, 9*(4), 325–345.

Speltz, M. L., Shimamura, J. W., & McReynolds, W. T. (1982). Procedural variations in group contingencies: Effects on children's academic and social behaviors. *Journal of Applied Behavior Analysis, 15*(4), 533–544.

Spindler, G. (Ed.). (1970). *Being an anthropologist: Fieldwork in eleven cultures.* New York: Holt, Rinehart and Winston.

Spock, B. (1976). *Baby and child care*. New York: Pocket Books.

Spradley, J. P. (1979). *The ethnographic interview*. New York: Holt, Rinehart and Winston.

Spradley, J. P. (1980). *Participant observation*. New York: Holt, Rinehart and Winston.

Sprick, R. S., & Howard, L. M. (1997). *The teacher's encyclopedia of behavior management: 100 problems/500 plans*. Longmont, CO: Sopris West.

Stading, M., Williams, R. L., & McLaughlin, T. F. (1996). Effects of a copy, cover, and compare procedure on multiplication facts mastery with a third grade girl with learning disabilities in a home setting. *Education and Treatment of Children, 19*(4), 425–434.

Stainback, S., & Stainback, W. (1988). Changes needed to strengthen regular education. In J. L. Graden, J. E. Zins, & M. J. Curtis (Eds.), *Alternative educational delivery systems: Enhancing instructional options for all students* (pp. 17–32). Washington, DC: National Association of School Psychologists.

Stainback, W., & Stainback, S. (1984). A rationale for the merger of special and regular education. *Exceptional Children, 51*, 102–111.

Stainback, W., Stainback, S., Courtnage, L., & Jaben, T. (1985). Facilitating mainstreaming by modifying the mainstream. *Exceptional Children, 52*(2), 144–152.

Stainback, W., Stainback, S., Etscheidt, S., & Doud, J. (1986). A nonintrusive intervention for acting-out behavior. *Teaching Exceptional Children, 19*(1), 38–41.

Stake, R. E. (1978). The case study method in social inquiry. *Educational Research, 2*, 5–8.

Stanovich, P. J. (1996). Collaboration—The key to successful instruction in today's inclusive schools. *Intervention in School and Clinic, 32*(1), 39–42.

*State ex. rel. Beattie v. Board of Education of City of Antigo (Wis.)*. (1919). 172 NW 153.

Staub, D., & Peck, C. A. (1994). What are the outcomes for nondisabled students? *Educational Leadership, 52*(4), 36–40.

Steege, M., & Northup, J. (1998). Functional analysis of problem behavior: A practical approach for school psychologists. *Proven Practices, 1*(1), 4–11.

Steere, D., Wood, R., Pacnsofar, E. L., & Butterworth, J. (1990). Outcome-based school to work transition planning for students with severe disabilities. *Career Development for Exceptional Individuals, 13*, 57–69.

Stein, M., Carnine, D., & Dixon, R. (1998). Direct instruction: Integrating curriculum design and effective teaching practices. *Intervention in School and Clinic, 33*(4), 227–234.

Stein, M., Silbert, J., & Carnine, D. (1997). *Designing effective mathematics instruction: A direct instruction approach* (3rd ed.). Upper Saddle River, NJ: Merrill.

Steinzor, B. (1950). The spatial factor in face to face discussion groups. *Journal of Abnormal Social Psychology, 45*, 552–555.

Stephens, T. M. (1977). *Teaching skills to children with learning and behavior disorders*. Columbus, OH: Merrill.

Stephens, T. M., Blackhurst, A. E., & Magliocca, L. A. (1982). *Teaching mainstreamed students*. New York: Wiley.

Sterling, R., Barbetta, P. M., Heward, W. L., & Heron, T. E. (1997). A comparison of active student response and on-task instruction on the acquisition and maintenance of health facts by fourth grade special education students. *Journal of Behavioral Education, 7*, 151–165.

Stevenson, C. (1998). *Teaching ten to fourteen year olds* (2nd ed.). New York: Longman.

Stoddard, K., Valcante, G., Roemer, F., & O'Shea, D. J. (1994). Preparing teachers for family support roles. *LD Forum, 19*(2), 33–35.

Stokes, T. F., & Baer, D. M. (1977). An implicit technology of generalization. *Journal of Applied Behavior Analysis, 10*(2), 349–367.

Stokes, T. F., Baer, D. M., & Jackson, R. L. (1974). Programming the generalization of a greeting response in four retarded children. *Journal of Applied Behavior Analysis, 7*, 599–610.

Stone, W., & La Greca, A. (1990). The social status of children with learning disabilities: A reexamination. *Journal of Learning Disabilities, 23*, 32–37.

*Stoner v. Miller*. (1974). 377 F. Supp. 177.

Stormont-Spurgin, M. (1997). I lost my homework: Strategies for improving organization in students with ADHD. *Intervention in School and Clinic, 32*(5), 270–274.

Stotland, J. F., & Mancuso, E. (1981). U.S. Court of Appeals decision regarding *Armstrong v. Kline*: The 180 day rule. *Exceptional Children, 47*(4), 266–270.

Strain, P. S. (1983). Identification of social skills curriculum targets for severely handicapped children in mainstreamed preschools. *Applied Research in Mental Retardation, 4*, 369–382.

Strain, P. S., & Kerr, M. M. (1981). *Mainstreaming of children in schools: Research and programmatic issues*. New York: Academic Press.

Strain, P. S., Odom, S. L., & McConnell, S. (1984). Promoting social reciprocity of exceptional children: Identification, target behavior selection, and intervention. *Remedial and Special Education, 5*(1), 21–28.

Strenecky, B., McLoughlin, J. A., & Edge, D. (1979). Parent involvement: A consumer perspective in the schools. *Education and Training of the Mentally Retarded, 14*(2), 54–56.

Strickland, B. A., & Turnbull, A. (1990). *Developing and implementing individualized education programs*. Columbus, OH: Merrill.

Striefel, S. (1981). *How to teach through modeling and imitation*. Austin, TX: PRO-ED.

Sugai, G. (1985). Case study: Designing instruction from IEPs. *Teaching Exceptional Children, 17*(3), 232–239.

Sugai, G., & Colvin, G. (1997). Debriefing: A transitional step for promoting acceptable behavior. *Education and Treatment of Children, 20*(2), 209–221.

Sugai, G. M., & Tindal, G. A. (1993). *Effective school consultation: An interactive approach.* Pacific Grove, CA: Brooks-Cole.

Sussell, A., Carr, S., & Hartman, A. (1996). Families R us. Building a parent/school partnership. *Teaching Exceptional Children, 28*(4), 53–57.

Swicegood, P. (1994). Portfolio-based assessment practices. *Intervention in School and Clinic, 30*(1), 6–15.

Swick, K. J., Flake-Hobson, C., & Raymond, G. (1980). The first step—Establishing parent-teacher communication in the IEP conference. *Teaching Exceptional Children, 12*(4), 144–145.

Symons, F. J., McDonald, L. M., & Wehby, J. H. (1998). Functional assessment and teacher collected data. *Education and Treatment of Children, 21*(2), 135–159.

TASH. (1990). *The Association for Persons with Severe Disabilities: Position statement on inclusion.* Baltimore: Author.

Tateyama-Sniezek, K. M. (1990). Cooperative learning: Does it improve the academic achievement of students with handicaps? *Exceptional Children, 56,* 426–437.

Tawney, J. W., & Gast, D. L. (1984). *Single subject research in special education.* Columbus, OH: Merrill.

Taylor, B. R. (1994). Inclusion: Time for a change—A response to Carr. *Journal of Learning Disabilities, 27*(9), 579–580.

Taylor, R. (2000). *Assessment of exceptional students: Educational and psychological procedures.* Needham Heights, MA: Allyn & Bacon.

Taylor, R., Richards, S. B., Goldstein, P. A., & Schilit, J. (1997). Teacher perceptions of inclusive settings. *Teaching Exceptional Children, 29*(3), 50–54.

Terrell, T. D. (1981). The natural approach in bilingual education. In *Schooling and language minority students: A theoretical framework* (pp. 117–146). Los Angeles: Evaluation, Dissemination and Assessment Center, California State University.

Test, D. W. (1985). Evaluating educational software for the microcomputer. *Journal of Special Education Technology, 7*(1), 37–46.

Tharp, R. G., & Wetzel, R. J. (1969). *Behavior modification in the natural environment.* New York: Academic Press.

Tharp, R. G. (1975). The triadic model of consultation: Current considerations. In C. A. Parker (Ed.), *Psychological consultation: Helping teachers meet special needs* (pp. 135–151). Minneapolis, MN: Leadership Training Institute/Special Education.

Tharp, R. G. (1994, June). *Cultural compatibility and the multicultural classroom: Oxymoron or opportunity?* Paper presented at the Training and Development Improvement Quarterly Meeting, Albuquerque, NM.

Tharp, R. G., & Wetzel, R. J. (1969). *Behavior modification in the natural environment.* New York: Academic Press.

Tharp, R. G., & Yamauchi, L. A. (1994). *Effective instructional conversation in Native American classrooms* (Educational Practice Report No. 10). Washington, DC: National Center for Research on Cultural Diversity and Second Language Learning.

Thiele, J. E., & Hamilton, J. L. (1991). Implementing the early childhood formula: Programs under PL 99–457. *Journal of Early Intervention, 15,* 5–12.

Thomas, C. C., Correa, V. I., & Morsink, C. V. (1995). *Interactive teaming: Consultation and collaboration in special programs* (2nd ed.). Englewood Cliffs, NJ: Merrill/Prentice-Hall.

Thomas, K. G. F., Gatz, M., & Luczak, S. E. (1997). A tale of two school districts: Lessons to be learned about the impact of relationship building and ecology on consultation. *Journal of Educational and Psychological Consultation, 8*(3), 297–320.

Thomas, S. B., & Rapport, M. J. K. (1998). Least restrictive environment: Understanding the directions of the courts. *Journal of Special Education, 32*(2), 66–78.

Thompson, L., Lobb, C., Elling, R., Herman, S., Jurkiewicz, T., & Hulleza, C. (1997). Pathways to family empowerment: Effects of family-centered delivery of early intervention services. *Exceptional Children, 64*(1), 99–113.

Thorp, E. K. (1997). Increasing opportunities for partnership with culturally and linguistically diverse families. *Intervention in School and Clinic, 32*(5), 261–269.

Thousand, J. S., & Villa, R. A. (1990). Sharing expertise and responsibilities through teaching teams. In W. Stainback & S. Stainback (Eds.), *Support networks for inclusive schooling: Interdependent integrated education* (pp. 151–160). Baltimore: Paul H. Brookes.

Thurlow, M., & Elliott, J. (1998). Student assessment and evaluation. In F. R. Rusch & J. G. Chadsey (Eds.), *Beyond high school: Transition from school to work* (pp. 265–296). Belmont, CA: Wadsworth Publishing.

Thurlow, M. L., & Ysseldyke, J., & Silverstein, B. (1995). Testing accommodations for students with disabilities. *Remedial and Special Education, 16*(5), 260–270.

Thurston, L. P., & Dasta, K. (1990). An analysis of in-home parent tutoring procedures: Effects on children's academic behavior at home and in school and on parents' tutoring behavior. *Remedial and Special Education, 11*(4), 41–51.

Tincani, M. J., Castrogiavanni, A., & Axelrod, S. (1999). A comparison of the effectiveness of brief versus traditional functional analyses. *Research in Developmental Disabilities, 20*(5), 327–338.

Tindal, G. (1987). Graphing performance. *Teaching Exceptional Children, 20*(1), 44–46.

Tindal, G. A., & Taylor-Pendergast, S. J. (1989). A taxonomy for objectively analyzing the consultation process. *Remedial and Special Education, 10*(2), 6–16.

Tollison, P., Palmer, D. J., & Stowe, M. L. (1987). Mothers' expectations, interactions, and achievement attributions for their learning disabled or normally achieving sons. *Journal of Special Education, 21*(3), 83–93.

Tombari, M., & Bergan, J. (1978). Consultant cues and teacher verbalizations, judgments, and expectancies concerning children's adjustment problems. *Journal of School Psychology, 16,* 212–219.

Torgesen, J. K., & Barker, T. A. (1995). Computers as aids in the prevention and remediation of reading disabilities. *Learning Disability Quarterly, 18*(2), 76–87.

Totten, S., Sills-Briegel, T., Barta, K., Digby, A., & Nielsen, W. (1996). *Middle level education: An annotated bibliography.* Westport, CT: Greenwood.

Trivette, C. M., Dunst, C. J., Boyd, K., & Hamby, D. W. (1996). Family-oriented program models, helpgiving practices, and parental control appraisals. *Exceptional Children, 62*(3), 237–248.

Trovato, J., & Bucher, B. (1980). Peer tutoring with or without home-based reinforcement for reading remediation. *Journal of Applied Behavior Analysis, 13,* 129–141.

Turnbull, A. P., & Ruef, M. (1997). Family perspectives on inclusive lifestyle issues for people with problem behavior. *Exceptional Children, 63*(2), 211–227.

Turnbull, A. P., & Schulz, J. B. (1979). *Mainstreaming handicapped students: A guide for the classroom teacher.* Boston: Allyn & Bacon.

Turnbull, A. P., Strickland, B. B., & Brantley, J. C. (1982). *Developing and implementing Individualized Education Programs* (2nd ed.). Columbus, OH: Merrill.

Turnbull, A. P., Strickland, B., & Hammer, S. E. (1978). The IEP-Part 2: Translating law into practice. *Journal of Learning Disabilities, 11*(2), 67–72.

Turnbull, A. P., & Turnbull, H. R. (1990). *Families, professionals and exceptionality: A special partnership* (2nd ed.). Columbus, OH: Merrill.

Turnbull, H. R., III. (1986). Appropriate education and Rowley. *Exceptional Children, 52*(4), 347–352.

Turnbull, H. R., III. (1993). *Free appropriate public education: The law and children with disabilities* (4th ed.). Denver: Love.

Turnbull, H. R., III, & Turnbull, A. P. (1978). *Free appropriate public education: Law and implementation.* Denver: Love.

Turnbull, H. R., III, & Turnbull, A. P. (1998). *Free appropriate public education* (5th ed.). Denver: Love.

Tyler, V. L. (1987). *Intercultural interacting.* Provo, UT: Brigham Young University, David M. Kennedy Center for International Studies.

United States Department of Education, National Center for Educational Statistics. (1993). *The condition of education.* Washington, DC: U.S. Government Printing Office.

University of Kansas Institute for Research in Learning Disabilities. (June, 1987). *Assumptions about the change process.* Handout.

Valencia, S. W., & Pearson, P. D. (1988). Principles for classroom comprehension assessment. *Remedial and Special Education, 9*(1), 26–35.

Valletutti, P. J., Bender, M., & Hoffnung, A. S. (1996). *A functional curriculum for teaching students with disabilities* (vol. 1, 2, & 3, 3rd ed.). Austin, TX: PRO-ED.

Vandercook, T., York, J., & Forest, M. (1989). The McGill Action Planning System (MAPS): A strategy for building the vision. *Journal of the Association for Persons with Severe Handicaps, 14,* 205–215.

Van Houten, R. (1980). *Learning through feedback: A systematic approach for improving academic performance.* New York: Human Sciences Press.

Van Houten, R. (1984). Setting up performance feedback systems in the classroom. In W. L. Heward, T. E. Heron, D. S. Hill, and J. Trap-Porter (Eds.), *Focus on behavior analysis in education* (pp. 114–125). Columbus, OH: Merrill.

Van Houten, R., Axelrod, S., Bailey, J. S., Favell, J. E., Foxx, R. M., Iwata, B. A., & Lovaas, O. I. (1988). The right to effective behavioral treatment. *The Behavior Analyst, 11,* 111–114.

Van Houten, R., & Sullivan, K. (1975). Effects of an audio cueing system on the rate of teacher praise. *Journal of Applied Behavior Analysis, 8*(2), 197–201.

Van Reusen, A. K., & Bos, C. S. (1994). Facilitating student participation in individualized education programs through motivation strategy instruction. *Exceptional Children, 60,* 466–475.

Vargas, J. (1984). What are your exercises teaching? An analysis of stimulus control in instructional material. In W. L. Heward, T. E. Heron, D. S. Hill, & J. Trap-Porter (Eds.), *Focus on behavior analysis in education* (pp. 126–141). Columbus, OH: Merrill.

Vargo, S. (1998). Consulting teacher-to-teacher. *Teaching Exceptional Children, 30*(3), 54–55.

Vaughn, B. J., Clarke, S., & Dunlap, G. (1997). Assessment-based intervention for severe behavior problems in a natural family context. *Journal of Applied Behavior Analysis, 30*(4), 713–716.

Vaughn, S., Bos, C. S., & Lund, K. A. (1986). But they can do it in my room: Strategies for promoting generalization. *Teaching Exceptional Children, 18*(3), 177–178.

Vaughn, S., Erbaum, B. E., & Schumm, J. S. (1996). The effects of inclusion on the social functioning of students with learning disabilities. *Journal of Learning Disabilities, 29*(6), 598–608.

Vaughn, S., & Klingner, J. K. (1998). Students' perceptions of inclusion and resource room settings. *Journal of Special Education, 32*(2), 79–88.

Vaughn, S., & Schumm, J. S. (1995). Responsible inclusion for students with learning disabilities. *Journal of Learning Disabilities, 28*(5), 264–270, 290.

Vaughn, S., Schumm, J. S., & Arguelles, M. E. (1997). The ABCDEs of co-teaching. *Teaching Exceptional Children, 30*(2), 4–10.

*Victoria L. by Carol A. v. District School Board of Lee County, Florida,* 741 F. 2d 369 (1984).

Villa, R. A., Thousand, J. S., Paolucci-Whitcomb, P., & Nevin, A. (1990). In search of new paradigms for collaborative consultation. *Journal of Educational and Psychological Consultation, 1*(4), 279–292.

Villenas, S. (1996). The colonizer/colonized Chicana ethnographer: Identity, marginalization, and co-optation in the field. *Harvard Educational Review, 66*(4), 711–731.

Vitello, S. J. (1986). The Tatro case: Who gets what and why. *Exceptional Children, 52*(4), 353–356.

Vocational Amendments of 1968, P.L. 90–576.

Voltz, D. L. (1994). Developing collaborative parent-teacher relationships with culturally diverse parents. *Intervention in School and Clinic, 29*(5), 288–291.

von Bertalanffy, L. (1950). *The theory of open systems in physics and biology.* Science, 111, 23–28.

Wacker, D. P., Berg, W. K., Cooper, L. J., Derby, K. M., Steege, M. W., Northup, J., & Sasso, G. (1994). The impact of functional analysis methodology on outpatient clinic services. *Journal of Applied Behavior Analysis, 27,* 405–407.

Wadsworth, D. E. D., & Knight, D. (1999). Preparing the inclusion classroom for students with special physical and health needs. *Intervention in School and Clinic, 34*(3), 170–175.

Wagner, M., Newman, L., D'Amico, R., Jay, E. D., Butler-Natlin, P., Marder, C., & Cox, R. (1991). *Youth with disabilities: How are they doing? The first comprehensive report from the National Longitudinal Transition Study of Special Education Students.* Menlo Park, CA: SRI International. (ERIC Document Reproduction Service No. 341228).

Wahler, R. G. (1980). The insular mother: Her problems in parent-child treatment. *Journal of Applied Behavior Analysis, 13,* 207–219.

Walberg, H. J., & Wang, M. C. (1987). Effective educational practices and provisions for individual differences. In M. C. Wang, M. C. Reynolds, & H. J. Walberg (Eds.), *Handbook of special education: Research and practice: Vol. I Learner characteristics and adaptive education* (pp. 113–128). Oxford, England: Pergamon.

Waldron, N. L., & McLeskey, J. (1998). The effects of an inclusive school program on students with mild and severe learning disabilities. *Exceptional Children, 64*(3), 395–405.

Walker, H., & Sylwester, R. (1998). Reducing students' refusal and resistance. *Teaching Exceptional Children, 30*(6), 52–58.

Walker, J. E., & Shea, T. M. (1999). *Behavior management: A practical approach for educators* (7th ed.). Upper Saddle River, NJ: Prentice-Hall.

Wall, M. E., & Dattilo, J. (1995). Creating option-rich learning environments: Facilitating self-determination. *Journal of Special Education, 29*(3), 276–294.

Walther-Thomas, C., & Brownell, M. (1998). An interview with Dr. Mitchell Yell: Changes in IDEA regarding suspension and expulsion. *Intervention in School and Clinic, 34*(1), 33–38.

Walther-Thomas, C., Bryant, M., & Land, S. (1996). Planning for effective co-teaching. *Remedial and Special Education, 17*(4), 255–Cover 3.

Wang, M. C., & Birch, J. W. (1984). Effective special education in regular classes. *Exceptional Children, 50*(5), 391–398.

Wang, M. C., & Lindvall, C. M. (1984). Individual difference and school learning environments. In E. W. Gordon (Ed.), *Review of research in education* (pp. 165–225). Washington, DC: American Educational Research Association.

Wang, M. C., Reynolds, M. C., & Schwartz, L. L. (1988). Adaptive instruction: An alternative educational approach for students with special needs. In J. L. Graden, J. E. Zins, & M. J. Curtis (Eds.), *Alternative educational delivery systems: Enhancing instructional options for all students* (pp. 199–220). Washington, DC: National Association of School Psychologists.

Wang, M. C., & Walberg, H. J. (Eds.). (1985). *Adapting instruction to individual differences.* Berkeley, CA: McCutchan.

Ward, P., & Ward, M.C. (1996). The effects of peer tutoring on correct cardiopulmonary resuscitation performance by physical education majors. *Journal of Behavioral Education, 6,* 331–342.

Warger, C. D., & Pugach, M. C. (1996). Curriculum considerations in an inclusive environment. *Focus on Exceptional Children, 28*(8), 1–12.

*Warren v. Nussbaum,* 64 Wisc. 2d 314, 219 N.W. 2d 577 (1974).

Watson, T. S., & Sterling, H. E. (1998). Brief functional analysis and treatment of a vocal tic. *Journal of Applied Behavior Analysis, 31*(3), 471–474.

Waxman, H. C., Wang, M. C., Anderson, K. A., & Walberg, H. J. (1985). *Adaptive education and student outcomes: A quantitative synthesis.* Pittsburgh, PA: University of Pittsburgh Learning Research and Development Center.

Weaver, C., & Heron, T. E. (1998, October 10). *Growing up with a learning disability: Ways to improve the home-school connection.* Presentation at the second annual regional conference of the Ohio Council for Learning Disabilities, Columbus, OH.

Webber, J., & Scheuermann, B. (1991). Accentuate the positive . . . eliminate the negative. *Teaching Exceptional Children, 24*(1), 13–19.

Wehmeyer, M. L., & Kelchner, K. (1995). *Whose future is it anyway? A student-directed transition planning process.* Arlington, TX: Arc National Headquarters.

Weinbaum, M. L. (1996). *The effect of peer tutoring on inappropriate behavior of a child with multiple disabilities while playing games.* Unpublished master's thesis, The Ohio State University, Columbus.

Weintraub, F. J., & Abeson, A. (1974). New education policies for the handicapped: The quiet revolution. *Phi Delta Kappan, 55*(8), 526–529.

Weisberg, P. (1994). Helping preschoolers from low-income backgrounds make substantial progress in reading through direct instruction. In R. Gardner, J. O. Cooper, T. E. Heron, W. L. Heward, J. Eshleman, & D. Sainato (Eds.), *Behavioral analysis in education:*

*Focus on measurably superior instruction* (pp. 115–129). Monterey, CA: Brooks-Cole.

Weiss, A. B. (1984). *The effects of a telephone managed home-school program using parents as tutors on the academic achievement of learning disabled students.* Unpublished doctoral dissertation, The Ohio State University, Columbus.

Weiss, A. B., Cooke, N. L., Grossman, M. A., Ryno-Vrabel, M., Hassett, M. E., Heward, W. L., & Heron, T. E. (1983). *Home-school communication.* Columbus, OH: Special Press.

Welch, M. (1998). The IDEA of collaboration in special education: An introspective examination of paradigms and promise. *Journal of Educational and Psychological Consultation, 9*(2), 119–142.

Welch, M., Judge, T., Anderson, J., Bray, J., Child, B., & Franke, L. (1990). CO-OP: A tool for implementing prereferral consultation. *Teaching Exceptional Children, 22*(2), 30–31.

Welch, M., & Sheridan, S. M. (1995). *Educational partnerships: Serving students at risk.* Fort Worth, TX: Harcourt Brace.

Welch, M., Sheridan, S. M., Wilson, B., Colton, D., & Mayhew, J. C. (1996). Site-based transdisciplinary educational partnerships: Development, implementation, and outcomes of a collaborative professional preparation program. *Journal of Educational and Psychological Consultation, 7*(3), 223–249.

Welch, S. J., & Holborn, S. W. (1988). Contingency contracts with delinquents: Effects of a brief training manual on staff contract negotiations and writing skills. *Journal of Applied Behavior Analysis, 21*(4), 357–368.

Werle, M. A., Murphy, T. B., & Budd, K. S. (1993). Treating chronic food refusal in young children: Home-based parent training. *Journal of Applied Behavior Analysis, 26*(4), 421–433.

Werts, M. G., Caldwell, N. K., & Wolery, M. (1996). Peer modeling of response chains: Observational learning by students with disabilities. *Journal of Applied Behavior Analysis, 29*(1), 53–66.

West, J. F. (1985). *Regular and special educators' preferences for school-based consultation models: A state-wide study* (Report No. 101). Austin: University of Texas, Research and Training Project on School Consultation.

West, J. F. (Ed.). (1988). *School Consultation: Interdisciplinary perspectives on theory, research, training, and practice.* Austin: University of Texas, Research and Training Project on School Consultation.

West, J. F., & Brown, P. A. (1987). State departments of education policies on consultation in special education: The state of the states. *Remedial and Special Education, 8*(3), 45–51.

West, J. F., & Cannon, G. S. (1988). Essential collaborative consultation competencies for regular and special educators. *Journal of Learning Disabilities, 21*(1), 56–63.

West, J. F., & Idol, L. (1987). School consultation (Part I): An interdisciplinary perspective on theory, models, and research. *Journal of Learning Disabilities, 20*(7), 388–408.

West, J. F., & Idol, L. (1990). Collaborative consultation in the education of mildly handicapped and at-risk students. *Remedial and Special Education, 11*(1), 22–31.

West, J. F., Idol, L., & Cannon, G. (1989). *Collaboration in the schools: An inservice and preservice curriculum for teachers, support staff, and administrators.* Austin, TX: PRO-ED.

West, R. P., Young, K. R., & Spooner, F. (1990). Precision teaching: An introduction. *Teaching Exceptional Children, 22*(3), 4–9.

Whinnery, K. W., Fuchs, L., & Fuchs, D. (1991). General, special, and remedial teachers' acceptance of behavioral and instructional strategies for mainstreaming students with mild handicaps. *Remedial and Special Education, 12*(4), 6–17.

White, R., & Calhoun, M. L. (1987). From referral to placement: Teachers' perceptions of their responsibilities. *Exceptional Children, 53*(5), 460–468.

Whittaker, C. R. (1992). Transitional consultation strategies: Finding the time to collaborate. *Journal of Educational and Psychological Consultation, 3*(1), 85–88.

Whitten, E., & Dieker, L. (1995). Intervention assistance teams: A broader vision. *Preventing School Failure, 40*(1), 41–45.

Wiederholt, J. L., Hammill, D. D., & Brown, V. (1978). *The resource teacher: A guide to effective practices.* Boston: Allyn & Bacon.

Wilcox, B., & Bellamy, G. T. (1987). *A comprehensive guide to the activities catalog: An alternative curriculum for youth and adults with severe disabilities.* Baltimore: Paul H. Brookes.

Willen, W. W. (1987). *Questioning skills for teachers* (2nd ed.). Washington, DC: National Education Association.

Williams, V. L., & Cartledge, G. (1997). Passing notes to parents. *Teaching Exceptional Children, 30*(1), 30–34.

Willig, A. C., & Greenberg, H. F. (Eds.). (1986). *Bilingualism and learning disabilities: Policy and practice for teachers and administrators.* New York: American Library.

Willig, A. C., & Ortiz, A. A. (1991). The nonbiased individualized education program: Linking assessment to instruction. In E. V. Hamayan & J. S. Damico (Eds.), *Limiting bias in the assessment of bilingual students* (pp. 281–302). Austin, TX: PRO-ED.

Willis, J. W., Hobbs, T. R., Kirkpatrick, D. G., & Manley, K. W. (1975). Training counselors as researchers in the natural environment. In E. Ramp & G. Semp (Eds.), *Behavior analysis: Areas of research and application* (pp. 175–186). Englewood Cliffs, NJ: Prentice-Hall.

Wilson, C. L. (1995). Parents and teachers: "Can we talk?" *LD Forum, 20*(2), 31–33.

Wilson, C. L., & Hughes, M. (1994). Involving linguistically diverse parents. *LD Forum, 19*(3), 25–27.

Wilson, R. (1987). Direct observation of academic learning time. *Teaching Exceptional Children, 19*(2), 13–17.

Wilson, R., Majsterek, D., & Simmons, D. (1996). The effects of computer-assisted versus teacher-directed instruction on the multiplication performance of elementary students with learning disabilities. *Journal of Learning Disabilities, 29*(4), 382–390.

Wilson, S. (1977). The use of ethnographic techniques in educational research. *Review of Educational Research, 47,* 245–265.

Winzer, M. A., & Mazurek, K. (1998). *Special education in multicultural contexts.* Upper Saddle River, NJ: Prentice-Hall.

*Wisconsin v. Constantineau.* (1971). 400 U.S. 433.

Witt, J. C. (1990). Collaboration in school-based consultation: Myth in need of data. *Journal of Educational and Psychological Consultation, 1*(3), 367–370.

Witt, J. C., Elliott, S. N., Daly, E. J., Gresham, F. M., & Kramer, J. J. (1998). *Assessment of at-risk and special needs children* (2nd ed.). New York: McGraw-Hill.

Witt, J. C., Gresham, F. M., & Noell, G. H. (1996). What's behavioral about behavioral consultation? *Journal of Educational and Psychological Consultation, 7*(4), 327–344.

Wolery, M. (1991). Instruction in early childhood special education: "Seeing through a glass darkly . . . knowing in part." *Exceptional Children, 58*(2), 127–135.

Wolery, M., & Sainato, D. M. (1996). General curriculum and intervention strategies. In S. L. Odom & M. E. McLean (Eds.), *Early intervention/early childhood special education: Recommended practices* (pp. 125–158). Austin, TX: PRO-ED.

Wolf, D., Bixby, J., Glenn, J., III, & Gardner, H. (1991). To use their minds well: Investigating new forms of student assessment. In G. Grant (Ed.), *Review of research in education 17* (pp. 31–74). Washington, DC: American Educational Research Association.

Wolf, J. S., & Stephens, T. M. (1990). Friends of special education: A parent training model. *Journal of Educational and Psychological Consultation, 1*(4), 343–356.

Wolf, M. M. (1978). Social validity: The case for subjective measurement or how applied behavior analysis is finding its heart. *Journal of Applied Behavior Analysis, 11,* 203–214.

Wolfe, L. (1997). *Effects of self-monitoring on the on-task behavior and written language performance of elementary students with learning disabilities.* Unpublished master's thesis, The Ohio State University, Columbus.

Wolfensberger, W. (1972). *The principle of normalization in human services.* Toronto: National Institute on Mental Retardation.

Wong, B. Y. L., & Wong, R. (1980). Role-taking skills in normal achieving and learning disabled children. *Learning Disability Quarterly, 3*(2), 11–18.

Wong, K. L. H., Kauffman, J. M., & Lloyd, J. W. (1991). Choices for integration: Selecting teachers for mainstreamed students with emotional or behavioral disorders. *Intervention in School and Clinic, 27*(2), 108–115.

Wong Fillmore, L. (1991a). *The NABE no-cost study on families.* Unpublished report, University of California, Berkeley.

Wong Fillmore, L. (1991b). A question for early-childhood programs: English first or families first? *Education Week,* p. 36.

Wood, B. A., Frank, A. R., & Hamre-Nietupski, S. M. (1996). How do you work this lock: Adaptations for teaching combination lock use. *Teaching Exceptional Children, 28*(2), 35–39.

Wood, J. W. (1998). *Adapting instruction to accommodate students in inclusive settings* (3rd ed.). Upper Saddle River, NJ: Merrill.

Wood, J. W., & Miederhoff, J. W. (1989). Bridging the gap. *Teaching Exceptional Children, 21*(2), 66–68.

Woodruff, G., & Sterzin, E. D. (1988). The transagency approach: A model for serving children with HIV infection and their families. *Children Today, 17*(3), 9–14.

Wright, J. E., Cavanaugh, R. A., Sainato, D. M., & Heward, W. L. (1995). Somos todos ayudantes y estudiantes: Evaluation of a classwide peer tutoring program in a modified Spanish class for secondary students identified as learning disabled or academically at-risk. *Education and Treatment of Children, 18,* 33–52.

*Wyatt v. Stickney,* 344 F. Supp. 387 (M.D. Ala. 1972).

Yavorsky, D. K. (1978). *Discrepancy evaluation: A practitioner's guide.* Charlottesville: University of Virginia, Evaluation Research Center.

Yell, M. L. (1991). Reclarifying *Honig v. Doe. Exceptional Children, 57*(4), 364–368.

Yell, M. L. (1994). Timeout and students with behavior disorders: A legal analysis. *Education and Treatment of Children, 17*(3), 293–301.

Yell, M. L. (1995). Least restrictive environment, inclusion, and students with disabilities: A legal analysis. *Journal of Special Education, 28*(4), 389–404.

Yell, M. L., Cline, D., & Bradley, R. (1995). Disciplining students with emotional and behavioral disorders: A legal update. *Education and Treatment of Children, 18*(3), 299–308.

Yell, M. L., Rogers, D., & Rogers, E. L. (1998). The legal history of special education: What a long, strange trip it's been! *Remedial and Special Education, 19*(4), 219–228.

Yocum, D. J., & Cossairt, A. (1996). Consultation courses offered in special education teacher training programs: A national survey. *Journal of Educational and Psychological Consultation, 7*(3), 251–258.

York, J., Rainforth, B., & Giangreco, M. F. (1990). Trandisciplinary teamwork and integrated therapy: Clarifying misconceptions. *Pediatric Physical Therapy, 2*(2), 73–79.

York, J., Vandercook, T., MacDonald, C., Heise-Neff, C., & Caughey, E. (1992). Feedback about integrating middle-school students with severe disabilities in general education classes. *Exceptional Children, 58*(3), 244–258.

Young, K. R., West, R. P., Smith, D. J., & Morgan, D. P. (1997). *Teaching self-management strategies to adolescents.* Longmont, CO: Sopris West.

Ysseldyke, J. E., & Algozzine, B. (1982). *Critical issues in special and remedial education.* Boston: Houghton Mifflin.

Ysseldyke, J. E., & Christenson, S. L. (1987). *The instructional environment scale: A comprehensive methodology for assessing an individual student's instruction.* Austin, TX: PRO-ED.

Yulevich, L., & Axelrod, S. (1983). Punishment: A concept that is no longer necessary. *Progress in Behavior Modification, 14,* 255–382.

Zigmond, N., & Sansone, J. (1986). Designing a program for the learning disabled adolescent. *Remedial and Special Education, 7*(5), 13–17.

Zins, J. E. (1988). Examination of the conceptual foundations of school consultation practice. In J. F. West (Ed.), *School consultation: Interdisciplinary perspectives on theory, research, training, and practice* (pp. 17–34). Austin: University of Texas, Research and Training Project on School Consultation.

Zins, J. E., Graden, J., & Ponti, C. R. (1988). Prereferral intervention to improve special services delivery. *Special Services in the School, 4*(3/4), 109–130.

Zins, J. E., & Heron, T. E. (1996). Improving and expanding the practice of consultation. *Journal of Educational and Psychological Consultation, 15*(6), 332.

Zins, J. E., Heron, T. E., & Goddard, Y. (1999). Secondary prevention: Applications through intervention assistance programs and inclusive education. In C. R. Reynolds & T. B. Gutkin (Eds.), *The handbook of school psychology* (3rd ed., pp. 800–821). New York: Wiley.

Zins, J. E., & Illback, R. J. (1995). Consulting to facilitate planned organizational change in schools. *Journal of Educational and Psychological Consultation, 6*(3), 237–245.

Zins, J. E., & Ponti, C. R. (1990a). Best practices in school-based consultation. In A. Thomas & J. Grimes (Eds.), *Best practices in school psychology II* (pp. 673–693). Washington, DC: National Association of School Psychologists.

Zins, J. E., & Ponti, C. R. (1990b). Strategies to facilitate the implementation, organization, and operation of system-wide consultation programs. *Journal of Educational and Psychological Consultation, 1*(3), 205–218.

Zirpoli, T. J., & Melloy, K. J. (1997). *Behavior management: Applications for teachers and parents* (2nd ed.). Upper Saddle River, NJ: Prentice-Hall.

Zorfass. (1994, June). An electronic conversation on inclusion. *The TAM Newsletter, 9*(2), 4.

Zurkowski, J. K., Kelly, P. S., & Griswold, D. E. (1998). Discipline and IDEA 1997: Instituting a new balance. *Intervention in School and Clinic, 34*(1), 3–9.

**Acculturation.** The degree to which an individual develops his or her own culture based on an integration of dominant and home cultures.

**Active or critical listening.** A process whereby the consultant engages the speaker actively, analyzes what the speaker says, and analyzes his or her own listening behavior.

**Active student response (ASR).** Describes those instructional strategies under which students actually produce observable and measurable behavior.

**Activity reinforcer.** Can be defined as any game, free time, or social event that is used to reinforce a desired behavior.

**Adapted instruction.** An instructional approach that accommodates the unique learning needs of individual students within every classroom.

**Affective conflict.** Focuses on the ineffective interpersonal interactions of group members; it usually results from inappropriate interpersonal skills.

**Annual goal.** A statement of the behavior the student is expected to achieve within a calendar year. It is anticipated that annual goals for each major need identified in the evaluation procedures will be attained through implementation of the IEP or IFSP.

**Appropriate education.** An education in the least restrictive environment from which the student benefits.

**Assimilation.** A process whereby diverse cultures are merged into a homogeneous society with common lifestyles, language, and cultural practices.

**Assistive technology.** Any type of equipment or system that has been developed or modified or is available commercially that can be applied to improve the independent functioning of students with disabilities.

**Balancing Standard.** The four-part standard that courts have applied in determining whether a district has violated the intent of LRE: educational benefit, nonacademic benefit, potential detrimental presence in the general education room, and cost.

**Basic interpersonal communication skills (BICS).** Everyday conversational skills.

**Behavior consultation.** A model in which emphasis is placed on the role of environmental factors (e.g., antecedents and consequences) and on the functional relationships between antecedent events, behaviors, and environmental variables.

**Best practice.** Educational practice that occurs when the following five questions are answered affirmatively: Does the practice have a sound theoretical base? Is the methodological integrity of the research convincing and compelling? Is there consensus with existing literature? Is there evidence that desired outcomes are consistently produced? Is there evidence of social validity?

**Bilingual education.** An educational program in which the teacher uses two languages to provide instruction.

**Bilingual Support Model.** A model in which the teacher is trained in special education but is not trained in bilingual education and is not proficient in the languages of all the children in the class. In this situation, a bilingual special education paraprofessional provides native language support to the instruction that the special education teacher is providing in the self-contained class. Besides limiting the contact CLDE students have with their nondisabled peers, this model does not provide for a teacher trained in bilingual education to deliver bilingual services to students.

**Block scheduling.** In block scheduling, class periods are combined into three or four periods per day of approximately 80 to 120 minutes each.

**Brainstorming.** An idea-generating technique in which all participants are encouraged to propose solutions. All possible solutions are named but not discussed, initially; no one judges the ideas at that point. A recorder lists the ideas, preferably so that they are visible to all participants.

**Career academies.** A form of a school-based learning curriculum for career options.

**Career assessment.** This is conducted as a part of transition assessment and addresses the skills needed for lifelong career development.

**Career pathways.** Broad clusters of occupations that revolve around a theme (e.g., health occupations).

**Case law.** See *litigation*.

**Case study.** A qualitative approach that has also been referred to by educators as educational ethnography, participant observation, qualitative observation, field study, and field observation.

**Change process.** The process undergone by professionals who incorporate consultation into their school role and attempt personal and institutional changes.

**Checklist.** A device or recording system that reflects the presence or absence of a particular characteristic according to some predetermined set of categories.

**Choral responding.** Refers to all students responding together, in unison, to a teacher's questions.

**Class action suit.** Litigative actions filed by individuals on behalf of themselves and others.

**Class-wide peer tutoring (CWPT).** All students working in tutor-tutee pairs simultaneously.

**Class-wide student tutoring teams (CSTT).** Combine CWPT with a teams-games-tournament, and cooperative learning; incorporates study guides, repeated active student practice, student learning activities, and high motivation during daily instructional sessions.

**Coaching.** Helping a teacher analyze the content to be taught, decide on the teaching approach to be taken, and make a specific plan to help students adapt to the teaching approach.

**Cognitive/Academic Linguistic Proficiency (CALP).** Abstract skills characteristic of academic instruction.

**Cognitive behavior modification.** A behavior-change program that assumes that faulty thinking is the cause of emotional and behavioral problems; treatment aims to correct faulty thinking.

**Coincidental teaching.** A method to improve parent skills. Coincidental teaching can be conducted in a 1-hour session during which the consultant helps parents select a behavior of their child's to change, prompting opportunities to occasion the behavior, reinforcing the behavior when it occurs, and scheduling daily routines.

**Collaborative consultation.** An interactive process that enables people with diverse expertise to generate creative solutions to mutually defined problems. It produces solutions that are different from those individual team members would produce independently.

**Collaborative consultation model.** In its most basic form, this model is a linear sequence that portrays the relationships between the consultant, the consultee or mediator, and the client or target.

**Collaborative planning guide.** A matrix of people, tasks, dates, and responsibilities for designing and implementing a school-wide program.

**Collaborative problem solving.** A strategy for dealing with conflict that preserves the goals and relationships of group members faced with solving a problem.

**Collaborative relationship.** An interactive relationship between the consultant and consultee that connotes parity, reciprocity, mutual problem solving, shared resources, responsibility, and accountability.

**Compensatory techniques.** Survival strategies to overcome or circumvent the lack of a specific skill.

**Competency resistance.** Resistance based on an individual's fear of being unable to do what will be required as the result of a proposed change.

**Comprehensible input.** Presenting content in a way that is understood by students and uses a low-anxiety learning environment.

**Computer-assisted instruction.** A computer-based instructional approach that can be divided into broadly defined areas such as drill and practice, tutoring, simulations and problem solving, and writing.

**Conditioned reinforcer.** A stimulus, object, or event that acquires its reinforcing capability when paired repeatedly with an unconditioned reinforcers or previously acquired conditioned reinforcers.

**Conflict management techniques.** A general class of problem-solving strategies that include majority vote, third-party arbitration, and authoritative rule. Collaborative problem-solving is the preferred strategy for conflict management because it preserves goals and relationships.

**Connecting activities.** Activities that link school-based and work-based learning.

**Consensus.** General or unanimous agreement of a group on substantive issues.

**Consent decrees.** A negotiated agreement or compromise between or among parties achieved outside of a court.

**Constructive conflict.** A stage of a group decision-making process that focuses on group members testing ideas.

**Consultation.** Has several definitions, varying in substance and context, depending upon the setting, target, or intervention. In the main, consultation should be voluntary, reciprocal, mutual, and it should lead to the prevention and/or resolution of identified problems.

**Consultation assistance teams (CATs).** They involve a consultant problem-solving with another. They are designed to achieve two main outcomes: (1) to alleviate or reduce invalid special education referrals and placements, and (2) to provide immediate assistance to classroom teachers with respect to solving academic or social problems short of full-scale referral.

**Consultation assistance team structures.** The systems of organization used to deliver consultation assistance team services. The structure of consultation assistance teams should depend on school resources and the needs of students.

**Consultative relationship.** A relationship in which people share expertise and perform activities consistent with the definition of consultation.

**Contingency contracting.** A behavioral approach in which the criteria for task completion and the conditions for reinforcement delivery are specified before the assignment is begun.

**Cooperative learning.** An approach that involves small groups of learners working together as a team to solve a problem, complete a task, or accomplish a common goal.

**Cooperative relationship.** One in which independent agents (e.g., a preschool teacher and a special education teacher) work autonomously to improve their separate instructional methods for the benefit of a commonly shared student.

**Coordinated Services Model.** A model in which a special education teacher and a teacher of CLD students combine their expertise to serve a CLDE student. CLDE students thus benefit from the services of two well-trained individuals.

**Co-teaching.** Two or more teachers planning and instructing the same group of students at the same time and in the same place.

**Co-teaching structures.** The mechanisms by which co-taught instruction is delivered. Co-teaching structures change as the co-teaching partnership matures.

**Critical questioning.** Asking for elaboration, clarification, or justification of information.

**Cross-age tutoring.** Occurs when the student tutor is approximately two or more years older than the tutee.

**Co-planning.** The planning that occurs when two or more teachers determine the who, what, where, and how of co-taught instruction.

**Cross-cultural competence.** The ability to think, feel, and act in ways that acknowledge, respect, and build upon ethnic, sociocultural, and linguistic diversity.

**Cultural identity.** The degree to which one identifies with a cultural group.

**Culturally and linguistically diverse (CLD) students.** Students whose home culture is different from the culture of the school; typically, they are not members of the predominant Euro-American culture. Some differ from their European American peers in physical appearance, language, and culture-based behavior.

**Culturally and linguistically diverse exceptional (CLDE) students.** CLD students who also have a disability such as a learning disability or visual impairment.

**Curriculum-centered problem-solving approach.** Incorporates the essence of the problem-solving process and includes four steps: (1) establish rapport and set boundaries for collaboration, (2) identify the problem, (3) develop an intervention plan, and (4) evaluate the collaboration.

**Daubert Standard.** Requires protocols that are reliable and valid, not just popular and available. Further, if a child's primary language is not English, or if a child does not use expressive language, provisions must be made to test the child through his or her primary language or mode of communication.

**Defensive communication.** Communication characterized by evaluating others, threatening others, or communicating lack of interest.

**Destructive conflict.** Much like affective conflict in that it can result in the group failing to make a decision or, if the group makes a decision, it is done without consensus and commitment.

**Differential reinforcement of incompatible behavior (DRI).** Reinforcement of a behavior that cannot occur simultaneously with another, undesirable, behavior.

**Differential reinforcement of low rates (DRL).** Reinforcement of lesser amounts of an undesirable behavior.

**Differential reinforcement of other behavior (DRO).** A procedure to reduce unwanted behavior by reinforcing any acceptable behavior except the target behavior.

**Direct Instruction.** The careful and systematic arrangement and orchestration of three main variables: organization of instruction, program design, and teacher presentation techniques.

**Direct service.** Service provided by a consultant to a student without a mediator. Instructing a student is the most common example of direct service to a student.

**Doctrine of least restrictive alternative.** Doctrine stating that the most powerful but least intrusive intervention should be attempted before more restrictive or time-consuming approaches are tried.

**Due process.** A vehicle for judicial protection of liberty and property against unreasonable governmental action.

**Early intervention.** A wide variety of infant and preschool educational, nutritional, child-care, and family supports designed to reduce the effects of a child's disabilities or prevent learning and developmental problems later in life for children presumed to be at risk for such problems.

**Ecological assessment.** Assessment or evaluation of a student's behavior in relation to its environmental context, under the belief that changing one environment may produce behavior changes in other environments and that a change in one behavior may affect other behaviors. Ecological assessment is usually conducted to sample a student's behavior beyond the classroom.

**Economic resistance.** Resistance based on the fear of losing one's job.

**Edible reinforcer.** Any food item that is delivered contingent on the occurrence of a particular behavior and that increases the likelihood that that behavior will occur again in the future.

**Eligibility.** A student's ability to perform academic and social competencies deemed necessary for successful functioning in the general education classroom, or to meet conditions based on state or federal standards.

**Emotional resistance.** Resistance based on fear of the situation (e.g., being afraid to touch a child with physical disabilities).

**Empathetic responding.** A type of passive listening that through the listener's physical presence conveys understanding of another's feelings, thoughts, values, or beliefs.

**Empowerment.** The parental perception of having the necessary capability and skill to make a significant difference in one's child's life.

**English as a second language (ESL).** A system of teaching English to people who speak another language first; it is not a bilingual approach per se because it relies exclusively on English as the language of teaching and learning. In schools, ESL instruction can be offered as an independent program, or it can be incorporated as a method of promoting English fluency in bilingual programs. Bilingual education and ESL are compatible, and, if possible, both programs should be used in developing an appropriate educational program for a CLDE student.

**Exchangeable reinforcer.** A token, checkmark, or star earned by a student for appropriate behavior and later traded for another reinforcing object or event. Exchangeable reinforcers serve a dual purpose: First, they reinforce the target behavior immediately; second, they can be exchanged by the student for a stronger reinforcer in the future.

**Extinction.** The discontinuation of reinforcement for a previously reinforced behavior.

**Full inclusion.** The integration of all students with disabilities and a rich mixture of culturally diverse students into the general education classroom.

**Functional curriculum.** A curriculum designed to help students acquire independent-living skills. It is sometimes referred to as life-skills instruction, and it delivers instruction in personal-social, daily living, and occupational adjustment.

**Gaylord-Ross decision model.** A model that provides a least-intrusive method to consider when deciding at what point to introduce punishment.

**Good behavior game.** An example of a "package" group contingency because it combines punishment, differential reinforcement of lower rates of behavior, stimulus control, and reinforcement. Its applicability in a wide variety of classroom situations makes it a desirable alternative for the consultant working with group problems.

**Group contingency.** The relationship between a single student or multiple students' behavior, an event presented immediately subsequent to that behavior, and the future probability of that behavior.

**Group decision-making process.** The decision-making process engaged in by several individuals working together; therefore, it involves the social dimension of effective group interaction as well as the completion of the task or decision.

**Group-oriented contingency.** A contingency applied to the whole class regardless of individual behavior, which allows the teacher to take advantage of peer group influences.

**Guided notes.** Teacher-prepared handouts that "guide" a student through a lecture with standard cues and space in which to write key facts, concepts, and relationships.

**Home-based educators.** Parents who help at home to supplement the instruction their child receives at school.

**Home-based tutoring.** A tutoring arrangement in which parents (or siblings) serve as tutors for their child after receiving skill training from the teacher.

**Home-school communication.** A broad range of oral and written messages between parents and teachers for the purpose of exchanging information and providing training to the parents.

**Impartial hearing process.** In an impartial hearing, three hierarchical steps are available to the dissenting party: First, a hearing may be called at the local level to review all pertinent information (e.g., assessment results, placement, related service needs). If the dissenting party is not satisfied, a state-level review may be called. If the dissenting party is still aggrieved, civil action through a state or federal district court may be taken.

**Inclusion.** Like other terms related to integrating students with disabilities in general education settings (e.g. mainstreaming, least restrictive environment), inclusion has multiple definitions, connotations, and meanings. No single meaning exists in the literature. Inclusion may be full or partial.

**Inclusion Standard.** A standard comprising two main prongs: (1) Can the student be satisfactorily educated in the general education classroom if supplemental learning aids are provided? (2) If education in the general education classroom cannot occur satisfactorily, is the student placed with nondisabled peers to the maximum extent possible?

**Indirect service.** Service provided by a consultant who works with a mediator (e.g., a teacher or parent), who in turn, works to change a student's behavior. Indirect services to students are accomplished by providing direct service to the mediator.

**Individual contingency.** The relationship between a single student's behavior, an event presented immediately subsequent to that behavior, and the future probability of that behavior.

**Individualized Education Program.** All students receiving special education services under IDEA '97 must have an Individualized Education Program (IEP), a written document describing the student's needs and the services to the student.

**Individualized Family Services Plan.** An IFSP must be developed for children who receive special education and related services at preschool or school-age levels, respectively. Like the IEP, the IFSP details the preschool child's needs and services to be rendered.

**Individuals with Disabilities Education Act of 1997 (Public Law 105-17).** Law signed by President Clinton on June 4, 1997, and referred to as IDEA '97, which mandates a number of changes related to the IEP, conflict resolution between the school district and parents, proactive behavioral management plans, and disciplinary procedures for students with disabilities.

**Instructional integration.** Teaching arranged so that children with disabilities engage in the same educational activities as their general education peers but do not share in areas that are too difficult for them.

**Integrated Bilingual Special Education Model.** A model in which the bilingual special education teacher provides all the educational services for the CLDE student in a self-contained special program. To offer this program, the teacher must be fluent in the languages of all the children in the class as well as knowledgeable and sensitive to the children's various cultural and linguistic differences.

**Integration stage.** Stage of staff development at which teachers apply what they've learned to their classrooms or schools. Teachers must develop competence and confidence to make new knowledge and skills part of their standard repertoire of instructional strategies.

**Interagency collaborative teams.** Teams of people across relevant agencies who develop and implement interventions for individuals with multiple needs.

**Interdisciplinary teams.** Teams composed of various professionals and family members who share information, discuss individual assessments jointly, and plan interventions collaboratively.

**Interim alternative educational setting (IAES).** Setting that allows the student to maintain his or her special education program during a period when he or she is not able to be maintained in the general education classroom.

**Intermittent schedule of reinforcement.** An intermittent schedule of reinforcement falls within the dichotomous boundaries of continuous reinforcement (all responses produce reinforcement) and extinction (no response produces reinforcement).

**Interpreters.** People who generally facilitate communication by mediating the message between speaker and listener in a variety of languages, contexts, and situations.

**Intervention assistance teams.** A group composed of general and special educators. Team members generate ideas for solving problems that teachers are having with students.

**Judicial opinion.** See *litigative decision.*

**Language dominance.** Greater proficiency in one language than another.

**Language proficiency.** Level of skill in a language.

**Large-group instruction.** Instruction that occurs when a teacher directs a lesson to a whole class simultaneously, usually 30 or more students.

**Learning strategies curriculum.** Curriculum developed for adolescents with learning disabilities by researchers at the University of Kansas Institute for Research in Learning Disabilities to address limited basic skills, deficiencies in study skills and strategies, and social skills deficits.

**Least restrictive environment.** By federal rule, the environment where the student with disabilities is to receive instruction with his or her general education peers to the maximum extent possible, to be removed only when he or she cannot achieve, even with supplemental learning aids. It may also be that educational setting that maximizes a student's opportunity to respond and achieve, permits proportional interaction with the teacher, and fosters acceptable social relationships between nonhandicapped students and students with learning disabilities.

**Legislation.** The act or process whereby elected representatives embody within a single document the law that becomes applicable to the general public. The intent of a federal or state statute is to serve the common good: the greatest majority of the citizens.

**Lesson plan.** A written document prepared by a teacher on a daily basis that contains four major elements: objectives, materials, method of presentation, and evaluation.

**Level system.** A motivational method for behavioral improvement that employs graduated steps with increasing student responsibility at each step.

**Limited English proficient (LEP).** Refers to the population of students who have limited skills in English reading, writing, speaking, and understanding.

**Litigation.** The act or process of bringing a court suit against another party for the purpose of redressing an alleged injustice.

**Litigative decision.** A judicial ruling that results from a fully tried case.

**Locational study skills.** Skills designed to help students find and understand material that can assist them in mastering specific content.

**Mainstream assistance teams.** Teams generally consisting of two professionals: consultant and consultee. Consultants generally use a behavioral consultation approach that has been shown to produce measurable improvement in student learning.

**Mainstreaming.** The temporal, instructional, and social integration of eligible exceptional children with their general education peers.

**Maintenance.** Continuing to perform a desired behavior after training has terminated.

**Maintenance programs.** Programs that promote English-language proficiency as well as literacy in a student's native language. An example of a maintenance program is one that continues to provide native-language instruction after the student demonstrates English proficiency and is receiving instruction in English.

**Manifestation determination evaluation.** An evaluation to ascertain whether a student's violent, drug-related, or dangerous behavior is part of his or her disability. It is warranted if any of the following three questions is answered affirmatively: (a) Were weapons or guns involved in an infraction? (b) Is the student's conduct dangerous? or (c) Were school rules of conduct violated?

**Mastery.** Refers to the completion of tasks at a rate above 99% correct.

**Measurably superior instruction.** Those instruction practices across early childhood, school-age, and transition levels that produced viable and consistent outcomes for learners and were conceptually and technologically intact.

**Mediator.** A person who has access to the target student and has some influence over him or her, while the consultant serves as a catalyst to activate the mediator.

**Mental health model.** A model that attempts to modify the consultee's behavior by focusing on his or her understanding of client problems and belief systems. There are three types of mental health consultation: system-centered, teacher-centered, and child-centered.

**Middle school.** A school organized to include some combination of Grades 5 through 9. The mission is to address the diverse needs of 10 to 14 year olds.

**Mirror Model of Parental Involvement.** This model is divided into two major areas—professional service and parental service. Within each area there are four levels of participation designated by the terms *all*, *most*, *some*, and *few*. The model can be used to ascertain parent and professional engagement with respect to a child's educational program.

**Mnemonics.** Mnemonics are memory-improving techniques that relate new material to already known materials.

**Modeling.** The presentation of an antecedent stimulus to the learner for the purpose of having him or her imitate it.

**Multidisciplinary teams.** Teams of professionals from several different disciplines (e.g., school psychologists, speech and language therapists, physical therapists, educators) working independently of each other.

**Multimodal data collection.** Data collection that begins with a narrative description of what is happening in a given situation for a period of time, similar to an anecdotal record. Observations are usually conducted over a long enough period of time to ascertain patterns of behavior. The descriptive narrative then provides the basis for other means of data collection.

**Narrative recording.** A qualitative observational and recording approach used to generate questions and to help the consultant learn what additional data will be necessary to answer questions. Since multimodal data come from many sources, they provide the consultant with a wider database and lend objectivity to this method.

**Negative reinforcement.** Occurs when a stimulus is removed contingent upon the performance of a particular behavior. Consequently, the likelihood of the behavior occurring in the future is increased. Negative reinforcement has the effect of increasing the desired behavior, not decreasing it. Negative reinforcement is not synonymous with punishment.

**Negative reinforcer.** The stimulus that is removed in negative reinforcement.

**Nominal group technique.** An idea-generating technique whereby group members work individually and use a process to share their ideas with the group.

**Nondiscriminatory evaluation.** Evaluation by tests that have been normed or standardized for a child's particular age, ethnic, or cultural group, as specified in Section 504 and the Education for All Handicapped Children Act.

**Nontraditional applications of tutoring.** Using a tutoring system with subject or skill areas other than those that are academically oriented.

**Nonverbal communication.** Communication that occurs through facial expressions, body postures, and use of space.

**One-to-one tutoring.** Tutoring arrangement in which only select student dyads participate.

**Opportunity to respond.** The interaction between prompts, questions, or signals to respond and success in establishing the academic responding desired or implied by the prompts.

**Organizational study skills.** Skills taught to students to help them organize the information they are learning.

**Organizational and systems consultation models.** A model in which consultants may work with groups at various levels within an educational system, including classrooms and grade levels or building, district, county, and state levels.

**Orientation stage.** In this stage of staff development teachers become aware of the actions necessary to use the content that is presented.

**Overcorrection.** A behavior reduction approach that consists of one or both of two components: restitutional overcorrection and positive practice overcorrection. In *restitutional overcorrection* the individual restores the damaged environment to a state better than existed prior to the disruption or infraction. *Positive practice overcorrection* means that the individual engages in the appropriate behavior repeatedly.

**Parent conference.** A formal meeting between parents and teachers that can occur in one of three contexts: procedural meetings such as the IEP or IFSP conferences, crisis sessions occasioned by an emergency, or scheduled meetings.

**Parent training program.** A formal behavior-change program that involves teaching parents new skills by (1) using a consistent theoretical instructional model, (2) determining parental skills to be mastered in advance, (3) allowing for varying rates of learning by parents, (4) employing a systematic and functional approach, and (5) providing follow-up.

**Parent tutoring program.** A program in which parents teach their children in the home to supplement instruction received at school.

**Passive listening.** Listening technique in which the listener remains quiet but attends to the speaker and gives encouraging nonverbal feedback to the speaker through the use of head nods, facial expressions, and body postures.

**Path of least resistance.** A reluctance to do anything different from the status quo.

**Pattern interruption.** A technique to address a problem that involves introducing a small change into the sequence of events that surround a problem.

**Peer-mediated approach.** Approach in which the students themselves, after training, assume the primary role of delivering instruction and provide the prompts, cues, reinforcement, and feedback during each learning trial.

**Portability Standard.** The portability standard comprises five major questions: Can the services that made a segregated classroom superior be provided in the general education environment? Can the student with disabilities benefit from a general education environment? Are the benefits of a general education placement outweighed by the benefits gained from services that could not feasibly be provided in a general education placement? Would the student with disabilities significantly disrupt the general education environment? Is the cost so excessive as to deprive students without disabilities of an education?

**Positive behavioral support.** A concept that relates to preemptive tactics that teachers can use to avoid student behavior problems. It rests on the multi-factored evaluation team conducting a functional behavioral assessment for any student with disabilities where there is a high probability that suspension will occur at some point during the academic year for longer than 10 school days.

**Positive climate.** An environment of open discussion is encouraged so that all group members can communicate without negative consequences, one that enhances communication and positive relationships.

**Positive reinforcement.** The occurrence of a stimulus or event that immediately follows a behavior, making that behavior more likely to occur again.

**Positive reinforcer.** A stimulus or event that immediately follows a behavior (its consequence), making that response class of behavior more likely to occur again.

**Preferred reinforcers.** Consequences that students choose more frequently than other reinforcers. Teachers can determine preferred reinforcers in three ways: (1) teacher can ask the students what they like, (2) teachers can watch students to see what they like to do during free time, and (3) teachers can set up a forced-choice situation.

**Premack principle.** Often dubbed "Grandma's law" and, explained in Grandma's own words, states: "When you finish your meat and beans, you will be able to have your ice cream." In our context, the Premack principle means that access to a high-frequency behavior (eating ice cream) is contingent upon the performance of low-frequency behavior (eating meat and beans).

**Principled negotiation.** Often used to describe an approach similar to collaborative problem solving.

**Proactive feedback.** The use of prompts and cues delivered to teachers during an actual lesson as a way of shifting their praise ratio in a direction that is more likely to build positive student repertoires.

**Procedural due process.** Standards that specify how due process is applied. The procedural safeguards delineated in IDEA '97 provide an example of procedural due process.

**Proportional interaction.** A teaching approach in which all students receive the teacher's attention for appropriate behavior on a consistent enough basis to maintain desired levels of performance.

**Punishment by contingent presentation of a stimulus.** Presentation of a stimulus or event immediately subsequent to the occurrence of a behavior, decreasing the future probability of that response class of behavior.

**Qualitative information.** Information that describes and interprets a situation from the perspective of the participants in that situation rather than being predetermined by a data gatherer.

**Quantitative information.** Numerical scores designed to portray the occurrence of specific behaviors.

**Rating scale.** A device or recording system that represents an estimate of the degree to which a particular characteristic is evident along a basic continuum.

**Rational resistance.** Reluctance to accept a proposed change because of a lack of understanding about how that change could occur.

**Reciprocity.** The tendency to behave similarly to others in response to their behavior. This norm is nearly universal among social systems.

**Refinement stage.** This stage of staff development requires synthesis of different types of previous learning into new learning.

**Reinforcer.** A generic term that embraces either a positive or negative reinforcer.

**Remedial curriculum.** A curriculum in which teachers provide basic skills instruction for academic skill deficits.

**Response cards.** Cards, signs, or other items (such as felt boards) that are simultaneously held up by all students in a class to display their responses to questions or problems presented by the teacher. Response cards can be preprinted or write-on.

**Response cost.** The loss of a specific amount of positive reinforcement contingent upon a behavior. The response or behavior "costs" the child a reinforcer.

**Response generality.** The extent to which a learner performs a variety of functional responses in addition to the trained response.

**Right to education.** A principle that states that all children are entitled to receive free appropriate instruction.

**Rules and regulations.** Published statements indicating how a law will be implemented and interpreted. Definitions for key terms in the law are provided as well as regulations for implementing the law.

**School-based consultation.** A means by which psychological and educational services can be provided in a reciprocal and systematic problem-solving way to prevent and solve problems.

**Schools-within-a-school.** Basic learning subcommunities of approximately 400 students each within the greater community of a school.

**School-to-work programs.** Secondary programs that help adolescents make the transition from school to the workforce by involving their families, educators, and members of the community in planning and implementing programs.

**Second-language acquisition.** The acquisition of a language in addition to one's native language.

**Section 504 of the Rehabilitation Act of 1973 (P.L. 93-112).** The first federal civil rights law to specifically protect the rights of the disabled against discrimination on the basis of physical or mental disability.

**Security resistance.** Reluctance to accept a proposed change that includes an understanding of the need for the change but a level of discomfort in implementing it.

**Self-determination skills.** Skills that provide a student with the opportunity to collect information and make choices. Self-determination skills include tracking one's skill development with such tools as self-management charts and progress portfolios; using assertive problem-solving techniques such as self-correction strategies and compensatory strategies; making decisions such as how to schedule activities and when to ask for help; and creating personal incentives such as rewards.

**Self-management.** Management of one's own behavior independent of external controls.

**Self-monitoring.** Recording information about one's own targeted behaviors.

**Semi-independent and independent approaches.** A teaching approach in which a student assumes the primary role of delivering his or her own instruction, after training, providing prompts, cues, reinforcement, and feedback during each learning trial.

**Sharewriting.** An idea-generating technique similar to *brainstorming*, except that team members write down their solutions and exchange them

with other members. In turn, members extend the ideas in writing and initialize them so as to be able to identify the author later in the process. The process continues until all possible ideas are produced.

**Sheltered instruction.** Teaching academic subject matter in English to nonnative English speakers using comprehensible language and context, enabling information to be understood by the learner.

**Short-term objective.** An intermediate step—a benchmark— between a child's current level of performance and his or her annual goal. Such steps are measurable and act as milestones toward the annual goal. Short-term objectives are less detailed than daily instructional objectives, which usually require more specific outcomes or products.

**Small-group instruction.** An arrangement whereby a teacher works with one group of students while other students may be assigned seatwork, boardwork, or independent activities.

**Small-group tutoring.** A tutoring arrangement in which two procedural variations are possible: (1) select small-group tutoring pairs who need additional (or remedial) practice with skills are arranged, or (2) the whole class participates, but on a rotating basis.

**Social integration.** Providing all students with the opportunity to establish relationships with peers and others.

**Social reinforcers.** These are delivered when a verbal comment is delivered immediately subsequent to a behavior, and the future probability of that response class of behavior increases. Praise is the foremost example of a social reinforcer. Other types of social reinforcement include smiles, pats on the back, approving facial expressions, and positive teacher attention.

**Social relationships.** The complex mixture of personal and direct verbal and nonverbal interactions among students and adults.

**Social resistance.** Reluctance to accept a proposed change because of failure to see the need to change.

**Specific level.** Refers to the consultant collecting information during problem identification about the factors contributing to the problem.

**Staff development programs.** Programs conducted in schools for staff members to increase job-related skills.

**Status resistance.** Reluctance to accept proposed change because of fear that the situation might become worse (e.g., one's job might require more skill).

**Stimulus generality.** The extent to which a target behavior is performed in the presence of stimulus conditions other than those in which it was directly trained.

**Structured feedback.** A system of observing teaching behavior and providing an opportunity to reflect on teaching. Structured feedback can be self-administered, provided by observers, or provided by peers or coaches on a regular basis.

**Structured interview.** A process whereby questions are designed to target variables influencing behavior, to target alternative intervention strategies, to define the mission and responsibility of each educator for systematic implementation of the strategies, and to identify strategies and techniques for monitoring and evaluating learner progress.

**Substantive conflict.** An intellectual opposition to the content of certain ideas, the type of conflict one would expect to experience in a group decision-making process. It is focused on the content of the group task, and includes communication around issues that are pertinent to that task.

**Substantive due process.** The judicial and regulatory standard that refers to the threatened or actual denial of life, liberty, or property. It weighs fundamental fairness against arbitrariness or unreasonableness. That is, a court decision cannot be based on whim, but must follow a logical process.

**Supportive communication.** Communication that focuses on issues and solutions, minimizes differences among group members, and communicates openness to others.

**Survey level.** An observational technique that refers to the consultant's attempts to identify the problem. The focus can be an individual, a classroom, or the whole school.

**Symbols of respect.** Nonverbal communications designed to transmit respect for people of different cultures.

**Tangible reinforcer.** Any type of physical object presented immediately subsequent to the occurrence of a behavior that has the effect of increasing the future probability of that behavior.

**Target.** An individual (or group) for whom the consultative service is intended.

**Teacher assistance teams.** Groups composed of general educators. Team members generate ideas for solving problems teachers are having with students.

**Teacher-directed approach.** A teaching approach in which the teacher assumes the primary role of delivering instruction, providing the prompts, cues, reinforcement, and feedback during each learning trial.

**Team roles.** Roles of team members within the team. They vary depending on the team but can include the following: information seeker, coordinator, orienter, encourager, compromiser, and group observer.

**Tech-prep programs.** A program in which vocational education provides a way to increase academic and vocational skills development and bridge the gap between secondary and postsecondary training.

**Temporal integration.** The total amount of time a student with disabilities spends with his or her general education peers, expressed in periods per day or academic subject areas.

**Time-out.** See *time-out from positive reinforcement.*

**Time-out from positive reinforcement.** Withdrawal of the opportunity to earn positive reinforcement or loss of access to positive reinforcers for a specified period of time, contingent upon the occurrence of a specific behavior.

**Token reinforcers.** Any of a variety of responses immediately subsequent to the occurrence of a behavior. A token reinforcer can be a physical object such as a chip or a star, or it can be a written symbol such as a checkmark. It acquires stronger reinforcing capability when exchanged for a back-up reinforcer such as free time or an activity reinforcer.

**Transdisciplinary teams.** Teams that include professionals and parents and/or other family members. Family members play a crucial role in the decisions made by the team for the education of students with disabilities.

**Transition.** A term used in the 1990 reauthorization of the Individuals with Disabilities Education Act (IDEA) to refer to the period between adolescence and adulthood.

**Transition assessment.** An umbrella term that includes career assessment, vocational assessment, and ecological or functional assessment practices. Transition assessment relates to all life roles and to the support needed before, during, and after the transition to adult life.

**Transition coordinator.** A person who helps a student pass from youth to adulthood by providing community-based vocational education experiences, collaborating with vocational educators to interpret assessment data, and developing and implementing transition plans.

**Transition programs.** Programs that use the native language and culture of a student to teach that student the general school curriculum and develop English language proficiency. Typically, students in these programs are exited within 2 to 3 years; hence, these programs are sometimes called "early exit" bilingual programs.

**Transition services.** A coordinated set of services for students with disabilities designed to promote movement from school to postschool activities including, but not limited to, postsecondary education; vocational training; integrated, competitive employment (including supported employment); continuing and adult education; adult services; independent living; and community participation.

**Transition team.** A group of people responsible for planning and implementing transition services, which should include all primary stakeholders including the student and his or her family, educators, and other service providers.

**Treatment acceptability.** The acceptability to a teacher of the instructional interventions applied with a student, including those involving adaptations or modifications.

**Tutorial curriculum.** A curriculum in which the emphasis is on teaching content, such as identifying the factors that led to the Civil War. The goal of this approach is to help students with disabilities receive passing grades in general education classrooms.

**Tutoring system.** Any formal and comprehensive approach to teaching students to prompt, praise, test, and chart the academic, social, or nontraditional skills of their partners on a regular basis.

**Two-way enrichment bilingual education programs.** Programs designed to foster bilingualism and biliteracy in students from different language backgrounds. These programs must be carefully constructed, as the teaching methods are different for native English speakers and nonnative English speakers.

**Unconditioned reinforcer.** A biologically determined stimulus event that satisfies basic human needs. Foods and liquids are unconditioned reinforcers.

**Unstructured feedback.** A strategy of staff development that consists of informal discussions between consultants and staff following observation of staff member by consultant.

**Unstructured interview.** An interview that uses a conversational approach and permits a discussion of those aspects believed to be important by the interviewee.

**Verbal feedback.** The verbal statements made by group members to each other to facilitate the problem-solving process.

**Vocal intonations.** Vocal elements such as inflection or emphasis that influence communication. If vocal intonation contradicts verbal expression, vocal intonation will dominate.

**Vocational assessment.** Conducted as a part of transition assessment and measures skills needed to perform specific jobs.

# About the Authors

**Timothy E. Heron** received his B.A., M.Ed., and Ed.D. from Temple University. He is a professor in the School of Physical Activity and Educational Services at The Ohio State University. Dr. Heron also served as an educational consultant to Children's Hospital Learning Disability Clinic in Columbus, Ohio. Prior to his appointments, he served as a developmental and day-care supervisor for students with brain injury and cerebral palsy, taught students with learning disabilities, and supervised a training program for resource room teachers in an inner-city school. He has published several books and articles, presented numerous papers at regional, national, and international conferences, and served as a consultant to teachers, parents, and administrators on issues related to inclusion, tutoring systems, parent training, and applied behavior analysis.

**Kathleen C. Harris** received her B.A. from Douglass College, her M.Ed. from Rutgers University, and her Ph.D. from Temple University. She is a professor in education at Arizona State University, West. Before her appointment at ASU, West, Dr. Harris served on the faculty in the Division of Special Education at California State University, Los Angeles. She also served as a learning consultant and teacher for students with disabilities in public and private inner-city schools. Dr. Harris has published several books and articles, presented at national and international conferences, and consulted with numerous school districts on issues related to teaming and co-teaching for diverse students, including those with disabilities who are culturally and linguistically diverse, as well as students receiving services in gifted, pre-K, elementary, and secondary programs.